Behavioral Science
Frontiers in Education

Behavioral Science Frontiers in Education

Eli M. Bower

Consultant, Mental Health in Education,
National Institute of Mental Health, Bethesda, Maryland

William G. Hollister

Director, Community Psychiatry Section, Department of Psychiatry,
University of North Carolina School of Medicine,
Chapel Hill, North Carolina

CONTRIBUTORS

Barbara Biber
Urie Bronfenbrenner
John Glidewell
and Lorene Stringer
Nicholas Hobbs
Donald C. Klein
Florence Rockwood Kluckhohn
Lawrence S. Kubie
Nadine M. Lambert
Henry Clay Lindgren

Ronald Lippitt, Robert Fox,
and Richard Schmuck
Elton B. McNeil
M. Robert Newton
and Racine D. Brown
William C. Rhodes
Nevitt Sanford
J. Richard Suchman
Hilda Taba
Herbert A. Thelen

To Fran and Phyllis

Foreword

Many of us have experienced the beauty of riding high in an airliner over the vast stretches of America on a clear, moonless night. Below, the light clusters of a hundred towns unroll in succession much like terrestrial constellations set on a background of velvet.

With keen eyes one can quickly pick out the brighter lights of "main street" and the streams of headlights that trace the highways. On closer look, one can occasionally identify a school with lights ablaze and wonder, "What's going on down there tonight?"

One can envision a PTA meeting, a night school, a faculty meeting, or even a school board session. As town after town unrolls its glittering lights on the carpet below, the traveler may call to mind that each of these towns has a trenchant investment in its schools. Each town has its school board members, its teachers, and its parents asking over and over again, "What is good education for our children?" Every school board and every faculty group below is involved in the search for the ideas that will help education become a meaningful learning experience for every child in the school and community.

This goal of a "meaningful learning experience for every child" sounds like one of those glittering generalities that at first dazzle, then distract us. The implementation of this goal, however, is the prime purpose of this book. We have not been interested in fabricating a shimmering, ephemeral abstraction. Instead, what follows represents our best efforts to reduce fuzziness and generality to specificity and reality; to spell out in concrete terms the most fruitful understandings and the most productive practices that the behavioral sciences and education have to contribute toward the goal of helping each day's school experience make a significant contribution to children's growth and behavior.

In joining the search for crucial ideas, each of the contributors has accepted the responsibility of weeding out and selecting germinal ideas for presentation. Instead of attempting to catalogue the vast array of scholarly ideas and experimental programs, we have chosen to select the concepts and practices that we believe have the greatest potential for enriching education.

In this search, we have been avid explorers of theory and conceptual models. A theory or conceptual model, like a map, allows one to plan direction and envisage goals. A good theoretical schema can help create new relationships, can unify disparate elements, and can suggest new processes and sequences. Often it helps the professional worker make sense out of situations or behavior that once seemed irrational or puzzling. A theory is a platform from which to view phenomena and a system for unifying within a professional self the meaning of a learning. Of all the classes of thought, theory is the most germinal. In this book, you will find much theory—but theory that is seldom far afield from its implementation in educational practice.

The theoretical formulations and programs have been selected on the basis of their ready applicability in every school. Emphasis is not solely on the valid research findings but on the utilization of the research in providing the best education for children and adolescents of all kinds. In presenting such research utilization material, we have attempted to synthesize some rigorous but necessarily atomistic studies into new integrative conceptualizations that might have more direct application to educational processes and products.

We have undertaken what we believe to be a difficult task—the translation of theory, research, and intuitive hunches of the behavioral sciences into pragmatic procedures for teachers and school administrators. In every case, we hope the basis on which such practices are proposed or recommended will be evident.

The principal creative thrust of this book lies in its attempt to mobilize the most viable and potent ideas of the emergent behavioral sciences for utilization and creative refinement in the fields of educational practice. We hope to stimulate our readers to new integrations of their own, and new readiness to explore or experiment. We hope that this book will expand the degrees of intellectual freedom, extend the boundaries of the possible and unleash a new stream of creative effort that will bring to more children the kind of education that will unfold and mature their unique individual potentials. All this has been written for students, behavioral scientists, educators, and interested lay persons. Wherever possible, we have tried to avoid hiding behind professional lingo or esoteric concepts; on the other hand we have not, we think, oversimplified the complexities of the greatest of human dramas—the development of human beings.

We wish to thank John Balbalis for his creative art work and each of the contributors for their courage and stamina in sticking with us from the bitter beginning to the final curtain.

Eli M. Bower
William G. Hollister

January 1967

CREDITS

CHAPTER 1

Hogg Foundation for Mental Health, The Univ. of Texas, Austin (Lough-miller, Campbell. *Wilderness Road*); *Basic Books, Inc.* (Osgood, Charles E. "An Exploration into Semantic Space," in *The Science of Human Communication*, edited by Wilber Schramm); *Princeton Univ. Press* (Machlup, Fritz. *The Production and Distribution of Knowledge in the United States*); *Harpers Magazine* (Drucker, Peter. "American Directions: A Forecast"); *Amer. J. of Orthopsychiatry* (Hobbs, Nicholas. "Mental Health's Third Revolution"); *Harvard Univ. Press* (Langer, Susanne. *Philosophy in a New Key*); *Doubleday and Co., Inc.* (Keller, Helen. *The Story of My Life*); *McGraw-Hill Book Co.* (McLuhan, Marshall. *Understanding Media: The Extensions of Man*), *Amer. Psychological Assn.* (Bruner, Jerome S. "The Course of Cognitive Growth"); *The Macmillan Co.* (Brown, Claude. *Manchild in the Promised Land*); *Pacific Books, Palo Alto, Calif.* (Fry, William F. Jr. *Sweet Madness: A Study of Humor*).

CHAPTER 2

Harcourt, Brace and World, Inc. (Rovere, Richard. *Senator Joe McCarthy*); *Harper and Row, Inc.* (Wright, Richard. *Black Boy*); *The Macmillan Co.* (Koestler, Arthur. *The Act of Creation*).

CHAPTER 4

Robert Leeper and the Association of Supervision and Curriculum Development, NEA (Kubie, Lawrence. *Nurturing Individual Potential*, edited by A. Harry Passow, 1964).

CHAPTER 5

N. Y. Times Magazine (Gross, R. "Two-Year-Olds Are Very Smart"); *Harvard Educational Review* (Friedlander, B. Z. "A Psychologist's Second Thoughts on Concepts, Curiosity, and Discovery in Teaching and Learning"); *Child Study* (Deutsch, K. W. "What do our New Computers Tell Us About the Way Our Children Grow?"); *Basic Books, Inc.* (Mitchell, Lucy S. *Young Geographers*); *Univ. of Pa. Bulletin* (Mitchell, Lucy S. "Research on the Child's Level: Possibilities, Limitations, and Techniques"); *Harvard Educational Review* (Bruner, J. S. "Learning and Thinking"); *Holt, Rinehart and Winston* (Munroe, Ruth L. *Schools of Psychoanalytic Thought*); *Univ. of Pa. Press* (Winsor, Charlotte B. "What Are We Doing in Social Studies?" in Forty-fifth (1957) *Annual School Men's Week Proceedings*); *Nat'l. Council for Social Studies* (Winsor, Charlotte B. "Social Education of Young Children," in Mary Willcockson (ed.) *Social Education of Young Children, Kindergarten-*

Primary Grades. Curriculum series, No. 4); *McGraw-Hill Book Co.* (Torrance, E. P. "Education and Creativity," in C. W. Taylor (ed.) *Creativity: Progress and Potential*); *Harcourt, Brace and World* (Murphy, Gardner. "Non-rational Processes in Learning," in R. Gross and Judith Murphy (eds.) *The Revolution in the Schools*); *Psychological Issues* (Erikson, E. H. *"Identity and the Life Cycle"*); *Bank Street College of Education* (Levinger, Leah. "Dramatic Play—An Intellectual and Creative Process," in Associates of Bank Street College of Education, *Imagination in Education*).

CHAPTER 6

Rand McNally and Co. (Getzels, J. W. and P. W. Jackson. "The Teacher Personality and Characteristics," in *Handbook of Research on Teaching*, N. L. Gage, ed.).

CHAPTER 9

Appleton-Century-Crofts (Itard, Jean-March-Gaspard. *The Wild Boy of Aveyron*); *Bantam Books, Inc.* (Ashton-Warner, Sylvia. *Teacher*).

CHAPTER 10

The Nat'l. Elementary Principal (*Elementary School Organization*).

CHAPTER 12

Harvard Univ. Press (Kluckhohn, Clyde. "Values and Value Orientations in the Theory of Action," in Talcott Parsons, Edward A. Shils, et al., *Toward a General Theory of Action*); *Barnes and Noble* (Calhoun, Arthur W. *The Social History of the American Family*); *Holt, Rinehart and Winston* (Fromm, Erich. *Escape from Freedom*).

CHAPTER 15

Educational Leadership (Combs, Arthur W. *"The Personal Approach to Good Teaching"*); *American Council on Education* (Ryans, David G. *Characteristics of Teachers*).

CHAPTER 17

Teachers College Bureau of Publications, Columbia Univ. (Miles, Matthew. *Learning to Work in Groups: A Program Guide for Educational Leaders*).

CHAPTER 20

The Ronald Press Co. (Hunt, J. McV. *Intelligence and Experience*).

CHAPTER 19

Herman E. Wornom, General Secretary of the Religious Education Association of the United States and Canada. (Urie Bronfenner). July–August 1962 supplement of *Religious Education*, pp. S45–S61).

Part One

Part Two

Behavioral Science
Frontiers in Education

Part One

Introduction

The long courtship and marriage of education and the behavioral sciences have proved to be a most productive and mutually enhancing relationship. Not only has education been enriched and extended by this interaction, but the behavioral sciences have been challenged and energized by the vast needs and problems of education. As in all marriages, the relationship needs to be constantly renewed and redefined if it is to engender individual and mutual growth. Each of the conceptual and program offspring of this union *needs help* in order *to survive* the vicissitudes of birth shock and developmental crises and in order to create clear and vigorous identities of its own. This book is dedicated to the enrichment of the relationship between education and the behavioral sciences and to a healthy and zestful family of rich ideas and effective practices.

As in any undertaking of this kind, there are several philosophical and behavioral assumptions implicit in the approach. Not all of these can be made explicit. Let us, however, in the very beginning note those premises which need visibility and clarification.

The first is that educational success has become for children and adolescents a necessary (but not sufficient) ingredient for adult functioning. The business of going to school is for a child what going to work is for an adult. Each must find ways of being successful in his endeavor.

Second, we support the notion that the goals of schools are educational and that the goals of the behavioral sciences are to assist schools in reaching such goals for all children. We conceive of effective educational processes as resulting in eventual behavioral modification or growth. We see learning as mediations between content and student, as a transaction undergone by an individual child and not as an application of a glossy epidermal shellac.

We support the proposition that behavioral science research and know-how can be applied in "hardnosed" and practical ways to strengthen educational processes and reach educational goals. Let us be clear about this—what we are talking about in the marriage of the behavioral sciences to education is how to teach English, history, social studies, science, mathematics, reading, industrial arts, physical education, home economics, and other content, as well as how to teach interested children, culturally different children, mentally retarded, emotionally disturbed, and gifted children. Our assumption is that the effectiveness of educational processes for all children can be increased and enhanced and that the behavioral sciences have something to offer in this quest.

In a world of exploding population and knowledge, we contend that one of the major aims of education is to help children become more effective information processers and mediators. Such data processing implies the ability to manage affective as well as cognitive stimuli that are always experienced as a cognitive-affective blend. Therefore, the processing of data and its utilization by the learner can best be understood as a cognitive-affective transaction and relationship. We contend that this information processing ability can be significantly nurtured and enriched by the content and experiences inherent in the school curriculum.

This book focuses on the learner and his daily cognitive-affective experiences in the school. It is important to note that the discrete disciplines in the behavioral sciences such as psychiatry, psychology, sociology, and social work attempt to make their contribution to education by strengthening the nature and quality of educational processes rather than through the imposition of their own goals or processes.

Our major concern is with building effectively functioning learners. Although we believe in repair, rehabilitation, and other corrective processes when needed, we think that the major contribution of the behavioral sciences to education lies in the development and strengthening of ego processes. Our hope for this book is that it will denote and demonstrate the conceptual and practical value of utilizing knowledge of the ego processes in planning learning experiences for children. Under this philosophy, school experiences that do not result in more effective ego-development, that is, the expansion, differentiation, and integration of intellectual capacity and personality, are uneconomical and unproductive educational transactions. Through the ego-processes of the organism, knowledge is organized, new ideas created, values formulated, and behavior determined. Such processes stand squarely and unequivocally between stimulus and response. An understanding and pragmatic use of this key concept to build effective learners will, we hope, be a major contribution to readers of this book.

Chapter 1

Three Rivers of Significance to Education

Eli M. Bower

About the Author

How does one bridge the gap between teaching biology and an emerging passion for translating ego processes into curriculum? Eli Michael Bower graduated from New York University College of Arts and Sciences in 1937 and after a Masters from Columbia obtained a job at Hawthorne Cedar Knolls School in Hawthorne, New York, where he attempted to teach biology to emotionally disturbed, delinquent children. After two years of this, he spent four years in the Navy attempting to understand his Hawthorne experience. Getting back on the track again, he studied clinical and educational psychology at Claremont College and U.C.L.A., became a school psychologist in California, and a consultant in mental hygiene and retarded children for the California State Department of Education. During this period, 1950–60, he took leave to finish his doctorate at Stanford. After initiating several studies on the education of emotionally disturbed children, he was named director of a three-year research study of the problem authorized by the California State Legislature. The findings and recommendations of these studies are presently incorporated in the State Education Code of California.

In 1960, Governor Edmund G. Brown appointed him Deputy Director for Liaison and Prevention Services in the California Department of Mental Hygiene. He was enticed to Bethesda in 1962 by the co-editor of this volume and is presently Consultant, Mental Health in Education for the National Institute of Mental Health.

The longer he works in the mental health field, the more vehement and consuming his passion becomes for the preventive possibilities in education through educational institutions. Someday he feels we will begin to be able to monitor each developing child in our society and intervene effectively to help children and their families in a positively oriented setting. His interest at present in addition to two children, tennis, Gilbert and Sullivan, Wagnerian music dramas and outlining possible detective stories, is to set down effective ego processes and the educational programs which will help children acquire these human traits. He is hoping this book will add to this goal.

4

Three Rivers of Significance to Education

In addition to its practical uses for drinking, cleanliness, and transportation, water in all its forms and motions seems to have enjoyed great popularity as one of man's universal symbols. Its symbolic power is used to induct children into a Christian community as well as to wash away the sins of the dead and secure rebirth in the Hindu world. Metaphorically, man is spoken of as rising from the waves, sailing on or being carried by the stream of life and, when exhausted, being ferried across the River Styx.

Whether it be a morose Old Man River, a reminiscing Swanee River or a sprightly Blue Danube, the river has become a metaphorical force akin to a "stream of life." Its tranquility and violence, cleanliness and filth, utility and danger, depth and shallowness, and its life-giving and death-producing qualities make it appropriate for conceptual as well as fishing expeditions. As a *body* of water, the river enjoys a youthful, vigorous early life, begins a slow, sluggish loss of energy during its middle years (helped out immeasurably by increased deposits of silt in the delta), and passes calmly into the vast sea of life and death.

We have no intention of continuing this analogy except to note that the purpose of this and the following chapter is to examine three growing and converging streams of development in our society, to identify the exact location of their confluence and to point out the consequences, both good and bad, of this event. These growing streams have developed throughout man's history, but until now they have been disparate, desultory rivulets of minor or moderate significance. Each is now rapidly expanding in size, in strength, breadth, depth, and power. It appears likely that the combined force of their flood waters is pointed squarely at the processes and institutions of education (see Figure 1.1).

These converging, high velocity rivers are (1) the increasing quantity and changing nature of knowledge in the service of man, (2) the increasing need, development, and utilization of public health

5

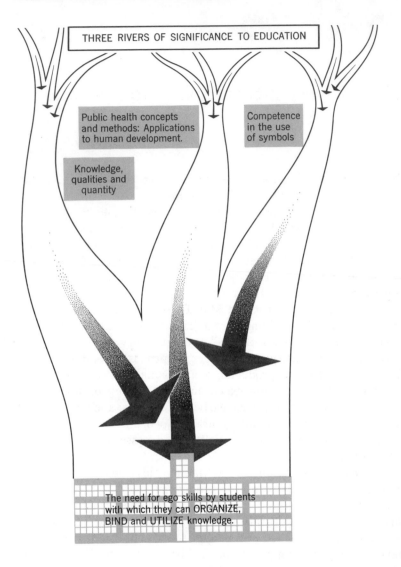

THREE RIVERS OF SIGNIFICANCE TO EDUCATION

Public health concepts
and methods: Applications
to human development.

Competence
in the use
of symbols

Knowledge,
qualities and
quantity

The need for ego skills by students
with which they can ORGANIZE,
BIND and UTILIZE knowledge.

Figure 1.1.

methods and concepts in the management and solution of human problems, and (3) the increasing need for human beings who are competent
in the creative and communicational uses of symbols.

As these combined forces converge and bring their full impact to
bear on the schools, as they already have begun to do in many places,
more than a little Dutch boy with a handy thumb will be needed

to stem the tide. What is needed is a modern day Cecil B. De Mille who can part the muddied waters and permit laymen and professionals to reexamine the basic assumptions, goals and processes in education.

Let us, however, go up and down each of these developmental streams separately before examining the full force of their confluence.

KNOWLEDGE—ITS CHANGING NATURE AND GROWTH

Three Illustrations of Knowing

This stream is composed of two parallel tributaries of equal significance. Let us first examine the qualitative stream of knowledge.

A junior high school student was discussing her English assignment with her father. Her job, as she explained it, was to read several short stories and explain the meaning of each story and its title. She felt she had done this rather successfully except for one story, *Clothe the Naked,* by Dorothy Parker. Here she had had some difficulty and needed to call on her father, the fount of knowledge and funds. After her father read the story, he suggested that perhaps Miss Parker had a different kind of "knowing" in mind when she wrote the story. "Fine," said the daughter, "explain it to me." "Words fail me," said the father, "I suppose one can say the story is better understood than explained." "That's fine," said the student, "but what do I tell my teacher?" "Perhaps," said the father, "you could explain that not all knowing is of the one-plus-one-equals-two variety or that being able to explain actions and events is not the same as understanding them in an experiential sense." The father continued in his erudite manner making vague references to gut level reactions; inner feelings; self concept; Rogers, Freud, and Spinoza. "Oh, well," said the daughter, "I guess you don't know what the story means either."

In November 1957, Samuel Beckett's play *Waiting for Godot* opened in San Francisco at Marines Memorial Auditorium to an eager and interested audience. This was a different kind of play, they had been told, but was it really a play? "I don't mind something different," said one excited playgoer, "but just because it's different doesn't mean it's any good or that I have to like it."

Audiences were puzzled and many who stayed left angry. One could hardly blame them, since Beckett's play has almost no action; it explores a static situation. It places the audience in an uneventful, actionless theatre and asks them to meditate. "Nothing happens, nobody comes, nobody goes, it's awful," as one of the characters says. Alan Schneider, who directed the first production of *Waiting for Godot* asked Beckett about the meaning of the play. "If I knew," replied Beckett, "I would have said so in the play." (17, p. 12)

The San Francisco production was moderately successful as a sort of side show and curiosity piece. Because Beckett's play was acted by an all male cast, the group was invited to give their performance about 20 miles away to a select group of men living in a state residential institution called San Quentin Prison.[1] Herbert Blau, the director of the play, worried about the limited possibilities for this audience to express disapproval or negative feelings (walking out was discouraged even during intermissions), decided to talk to the audience about the play prior to the performance. Blau explained that the meaning of the play might be somewhat obscure but compared it to a piece of jazz music "to which one must listen for whatever one may find in it."

This may or may not have helped. In any case, this captive audience was enthralled and excited. Somehow they "knew" what the play was all about. Prisoners and staff agreed that Beckett somehow "knew" all about waiting—that no matter who or what Godot was, if he finally did show up it would be a disappointment. The *San Quentin News* commented ". . . We're still waiting for Godot and shall continue to wait. When the scenery gets too drab and the action too slow, we'll call each other names and swear to part forever—but then, there's no place to go." (17, p. XVI)

Whatever it was that Beckett had created, it was clearly communicated, understood, and known by this unsophisticated, less well-educated group of theatre goers. How and when had such learning been assimilated within members of the audience at San Quentin?

Let's move to yet another situation—a college junior discussing his decision to drop out of school despite the fact that he is getting good grades, is in good health, and is relatively happy. To the somewhat puzzled parent the boy explains, "Look, Dad, I know what this is costing you and what my graduation would mean to you and Mom. You've always taught me to be honest and involve myself in my work as a human being, but I've suddenly realized I don't believe in what I am doing. I'm a robot being filled up with vast amounts of knowledge but I've got nothing in me to hold on to. Things sort of go in and through the top of my head at high speed, but I can't pull it down into me. Sure, I know history, math, English, literature, philosophy and French, but I have difficulty feeling what I learn has any relationship to me or my growth as a human being."

[1] The following is a summary of some misty memories of articles in the *San Francisco Chronicle* and of Esslin's description of the events.

KNOWLEDGE ABOUT KNOWLEDGE

Knowledge means possessing or being the possessor of information about anything and everything. Strangely enough, one cannot be said to own or have information unless one has some way of communicating it to self or others. Indeed the essence of knowledge is its communicability. In his development as a knowledge-producing and -using animal, man had to strive to find acceptable rules and assumptions with which to establish the factual nature of facts. As the methods of science and understandings of man as a data processer became part of the knowledge of man, the quantity of one kind of knowledge began to rise astronomically. Man became increasingly able to scan the heavens, the earth, the seas, and the unexplored territories within him to bring forth weighty treasures without end. Educational institutions, scholars, and philosophers now had to decide what kinds of information should be communicated and how such knowledge should be organized to facilitate such transmission.

It was quite late in the game before man had any substantial knowledge of his own nature or his information-using capabilities. Yet many of man's institutions for transmitting knowledge, as McNeil points out in Chapter 10, still contain mystic notions about the nature of knowledge and of man. There is still the belief that the organization and meaning of knowledge resides in its bulk, or that man's desire to organize and seek knowledge for meaning is fulfilled by filling him up with all of it. Can knowledge be poured into empty brains without conceptual receptacles? Is meaning a pouring over facts in an effort to coldly, that is, scientifically, explain what is there? Can we learn about the nature of time when it skips by us swiftly and painlessly; do we have any knowledge about "serving time" or understanding the passage of time as part of a "knowing" experience? Can this form of knowledge be learned when the medium of communication fragments, constricts, and distorts the reality of self and life? Have we, as McLuhan (34) states, acquired from our knowledge the power to act without reacting?

Man's development as a knowledge-processing and -using organism is somewhat akin to the production of a successful opera or musical comedy. In both cases the words, the action, and the emotion have to fit together. Beckett concretizes this notion in his plays by having one line of speech completely obliterated by the next or by illustrating how language and action are often in contrapuntal relationship to each other. "Let's go," the characters in *Waiting for Godot* say to each other, but the stage directions indicate they don't move. "The comedy is over" sobs Canio in *I Pagliacci,* as he kills his wife and her lover.

A major onrushing tributary of the stream of knowledge is the need to organize it so that effective learning ties together the intellectual and experiencing processes of man. In the past such trickling streams disappeared in the assumption that such organization was best left to students. There is a difference, however, in learning about history and understanding history, between learning about time and the experiencing of time, between learning about science and being able to think like a scientist. The planned exposures to knowledge by our vast array of information-mongering institutions must now, of necessity, consider content organization, themes, overtones, continuities, discontinuities, priorities, relevance, and meaning to the human condition. There seem to be varieties of knowing and knowledge that the human organism employs in responding to himself and his environment. There are also levels of awareness of such knowledges and a multitude of specific learning processes that reach each level. All are held together by man's need to explore and master himself and his world and to find ways of differentiating between the explanation of human life and its understanding.

Qualities of Knowledge

Educational institutions as information-mongering agencies are aware of the varieties and range of knowledge within its ivy or brick-covered walls and faculty. Yet many educated persons wend their way through these institutions conceptualizing knowledge as a narrow one-dimensional scientific stream of information. Arthur Miller reports an interview by a psychologist from the National Science Foundation on one of his plays. Referring to one of his plays, the psychologist asked Miller how he had figured out the connections between the characters. Miller admitted that he hadn't figured out—he had imagined it. The psychologist then wanted to know on what theory Miller had figured it out—Jungian, Freudian, Behaviorist, or what? Miller reminded the psychologist that Oedipus, before he became a disease, was a character in a play and that he had been best understood by poets who felt; "that the very concept of a unitary mankind, its inner laws and definition, has been held together in the mind of man and in the conscience of man through the symbols which artists have given the world." (35, p. 17)

Knowledge is a coat of many colors. Scientific rational knowledge is one kind. The Miller, Beckett kind is another. The problem that schools and universities face is to build connections by which one kind of knowledge can be related to another.

Most students and institutions search for perceptual and conceptual knowledge by which living experiences and learning experiences can be bridged. Some seem satisfied with small connections between varieties of courses. A few years ago the University of Michigan offered a course on "Growth" in which a number of departments such as biology, economics, psychology, astronomy, political science, mathematics, and chemistry presented the meaning and function of this concept from their respective disciplines. An attempt was then made by students and seminar leaders to tie the strings and bindings together across disciplines into life.

Small but significant advances have been made in broadening our cognizance of knowledge and about the kind of learning processes required to reach some of these levels and varieties of knowing. A few of these learning processes have been used in educational institutions for many years. To some extent they are still perceived as distant relatives to be housed only for a short visit and only under dire circumstances. Some of these new-old learning approaches are (1) the use of educational systems as a learning society or laboratory, (2) the use of opportunities for adventure and challenge in camping, outdoor education, and "Outward Bound" programs, and (3) the planned incorporation of simulations, metaphors, and game experiences for specific learning purposes.

Educational Institutions as Learning Societies and Laboratories

One of the key concepts in the game of football is the notion of impetus. To score, a team must provide the impetus for getting the ball over the goal line. In education, the impetus for learning is often provided by the teacher who may be actively engaged in making meaning clear to himself by attempting to teach it to others. If learning is an active engagement between students and content, the impetus must come from students. Some school systems such as Nova, in Fort Lauderdale, Florida, and the Oakleaf Elementary School in Pittsburgh, Pennsylvania, have arranged their teacher-content-student relationships so that students must provide their own power and push in learning or nothing will happen. Other programs have picked up the notion that good teachers learn more than their students and have provided opportunities for older students to teach younger ones. Such students work as aides with preschool or kindergarten children or with students having learning problems. One student-teacher working in a day care center was helping Judy—a three-year-old—to drink milk. For several days Judy had refused to drink even when the student-teacher poured a little in her glass. One day she drank a little and the next a little more. In discussing his success, the student-teacher felt he had demonstrated that example was more effective than lecturing. "These kids learn more by actions than words," he noted (14, p. 42). Two (5, 31) among several studies of cross age relationships in education present additional examples of preadolescent and adolescent "teachers" working with younger, often disadvantaged underachieving children (5). The pilot projects directed by Peggy Lippitt and John Lohman make several assumptions on which such projects are based. Some of these are as follows: In the process of socialization younger children use older children as models and are less likely to regard the older child as an authority figure. Conversely, the older child recognizes the responsibility placed upon him and is able with help to work through some of his own relationship problems to peers and siblings. There is the additional increment that there is no better way to learn than having to teach it to someone else. In one of the sessions with the student-teachers, they were asked what they would say to a shy child who suddenly said, "I'm a hippopotamus and am going to bite you." One boy answered, "I'm a tiger and I am your friend;" and another, "I am a baby hippopotamus and you can take care of me." (31, p. 117)

The school as an instructional system is moderately open to change. Various jobs are possible in it, some related to specific content areas and some to the whole pattern of human relationships within the system. Work, however, is only a means to learning; there is the additional requirement of a mediator to extract knowledge out of the experience. Nor need it be exciting, highly provocative situations from which one learns—to learn about monotony is as much a lesson as a ride on a roller coaster.

Apparently some knowledge can be gained only as an action-thinking experience. Learning about children in a college classroom is like discussing a Rembrandt without ever seeing one. The education of a teacher begins when he steps into a classroom, subjects himself to the problems therein and is given the opportunity to experience their meaning with the help of a supervisor, principal, or psychologist.

Technology has made such learning experiences more readily and accurately available to learners. Jacques Kaswan of UCLA and Gerald Bloom of the University of Colorado Medical School have explored the use of video tape as a means of providing instant feedback to teachers and consultants on the nature of a teaching-learning experience or looking at how a teacher interacts with a particular child or with a specific area of content.[1] Under such conditions a teacher can react to his own voice, mannerisms, gestures, or selection of words, as well as observe his impact on particular students or the class as a whole. Needless to say, the teacher can find little to learn in such situations if he perceives himself apprehensively or is unable to establish a trustful relationship with a colleague or consultant who can assist in viewing, perceiving, and reacting. Audio and video tapes can also be helpful to students in classes where such activities can be integrated to fit the content and purpose of the experience.

Another type of knowledge and learning experience possible in school is the so-called T group or Sensitivity Training group in which the goal is increased knowledge and sensitivity to ourselves as receivers and senders of messages. We learn something about self as a selective processor of knowledge and also some skills that can increase effectiveness in transcribing the meaning of messages sent to oneself and others. In the process, one discovers how we learn and how groups can enhance or inhibit learning.

Opportunities for Adventure and Challenge

Challenging physical activity can be one of the royal roads to ego growth. A nation of spectators and TV gawkers may find little need for active physical games or exciting challenges with nature. As Blake wrote, "Great things are done when men and mountains meet; this is not done by jostling in the street."

What is the meaning of responsibility as a symbolic abstraction in a classroom compared to the specific meaning of the term in a camp setting? As Loughmiller says about his program,

"We have left with the boys all the responsibility that we feel is commensurate with their years and maturity. Generally speaking, we have not done anything for them that they can do reasonably well for themselves. In this way they are thrown up against objective reality every hour of every day. . . . They feel the consequences of any failure on their part to handle their responsibilities satisfactorily." (32, p. 18)

[1] Several students of Henry Murray at Harvard have experimented with dyadic interactions between self and another person after viewing a motion picture of self; see *Studies in Self Confrontation*, by Gerhard Nielsen, Copenhagen: Munksgaard, 1962.

Other school camping programs held during the regular school year have shown positive effects on self concept and social relationships of children (3).

To most children and most schools, learning takes place within four walls in a sitting position. Where outdoor education is possible, it must be justified on the basis of wildflower and leaf identification, study of rocks, conservation, wildlife identification, and other hardcore subjects. A program begun in Wales in 1941 called "Outward Bound" (25) was developed on the premise that educational systems need increased opportunities for character building and that this could be accomplished through a child's natural love of adventure. Most boys and girls who attend find the experience growth producing—they have been challenged by life itself, at sea or in the mountains. They have carried responsibility, worked with others, depended on themselves for survival, and they have succeeded. The programs are staffed by men who in their own adventurous lives have learned something about the nature of their own experience. At present there are four such programs in the United States—in Colorado, Minnesota, Massachusetts and Maine.

Metaphors, Games, and Learning

One of the connecting bonds between one kind of knowing and another is the metaphor. Metaphors are conceptual matrices in which symbols find their connections. When one conceptual matrix is free to cross another, new ways of perceiving and mediating objects or ideas are possible. The major metaphorical bridge crossed by man in his journey to human stature and functioning was undoubtedly the span connecting his primary or nonlogical thought processes with his secondary or rational thought processes. In a sense this is a child's major metaphorical hurdle—to gradually replace, control, and connect his dreams, fantasies, and impulses to his rational, reality-based thought processes.

The psychotherapist and the educator stand on common ground as each wrestles with this problem. The psychotherapist tries to make the connection by interpreting unconscious metaphors; the educator by helping the child became more competent in the use of rational processes. However, the goals of both disciplines are to help the client or student to perceive and conceive differently, that is, to adopt a new or modified metaphorical mode from which objects, ideas, people, and events can be experienced. When the processes of psychotherapy and/or education are ineffective, the cause is often a lack of or a fragmentation of the metaphorical matrix from which new ideas, new connections, and new facts can be perceived. When we say a person lacks understanding of a subject or a problem, this is probably what we mean. Often such persons can "explain" a subject in detail or know what their problem is intellectually, yet are unable to connect such knowledge to any significant part of self. The example of "knowing" or understanding *Waiting for Godot,* cited earlier, suggests that the metaphor of waiting, of serving time, had been learned by the convicts but was not a conceptual reality in the paying theatre goers of San Francisco.

Most educational experiences are aimed at learning to think through associative processes—connecting symbolic thoughts with other data within the same conceptual or metaphorical boundaries. Occasionally one is injected into formal or informal learning experiences which provide skills in connecting symbols across metaphorical or conceptual boundaries. This kind of bisociative thinking permits the learner to perceive data within more mobile and expanded conceptual boundaries. When new frames of reference can be mobilized from which to view old problems, objects, and events can be seen as they have not been seen before. The essence of discovery lies in this learned skill. As Szent-Gyorgi put it: creative thinking is to see what everyone has seen but to think what no one has thought.

The Hitchcock and Allen stories cited on pp. 37 and 38 illustrate the functional rigidities with which objects are bound in our thinking. A frozen leg of lamb is to eat, a shovel is to dig, a book is to read and a bullet is to kill. Koestler (20) describes the phenomenon of bisociation in its simplest and most revealing form as a "visual pun." He cites the case of Sultan, the chimpanzee who was faced with the problem of a banana lying on the ground outside his reach. Within Sultan's sight and grasp was a tree with long branches. Somewhere in Sultan's mind the conceptual boundaries between branch-tree and branch-tool was crossed. Eureka, a ripe, luscious banana.

It seems equally important for a student to learn the skills and pathways of getting from one metaphor to another as knowing all there is about a single metaphor. The richness and varieties of knowing are often found in transmetaphorical experiences. To apprehend Wagner's *Tristan Und Isolde,* we need to cross a bridge between sound and affect; to conceptualize a benzine molecule, we need to be able to imagine rapidly moving molecules turning into a six-sided snake as did Kekule Von Stradonitz.

To learn how to shift skillfully, comfortably, and appropriately in our thinking from one metaphorical matrix to another and back again is a consummation devoutly to be wished in all educational processes. Although many metaphors seem to occupy symbolic space somewhat unique and different from other content areas, small parts in each have common boundaries. A factor analytic study of metaphors used in music criticism suggests that metaphors preserve (1) correlations laid down in early language experiences and (2) sense qualities inherent in human perception of the environment (10). Osgood points out why this may be true:

"It is because such diverse sensory experiences as a white circle (rather than black), a straight line (rather than crooked), a rising melody (rather than a falling one), a sweet taste (rather than a sour one), a caressing touch (rather than an irritating scratch)—it is because all these diverse experiences can share a common affective meaning that one easily and lawfully translates from one sensory modality into another in synesthesia and metaphor. . . . In other words, the "common market in meaning" seems to be based firmly in the biological systems of emotional and purposive behavior that all humans share." (37, p. 37)

One educator, William J. J. Gordon, has over a period of years developed a system called synectics to develop the conscious use of metaphor in creative problem solving and learning. As he puts it:

"To make the familiar strange is to distort, invert, or transpose the traditional ways of looking at and responding to, the secure and familiar world . . . the child who bends and peers at the world from between his legs is experimenting with the familiar made strange." (22, p. 96)

Gordon has directed some of the teaching efforts at Harvard to produce in students a conscious use of metaphors through (1) personal analogy, (2) direct analogy, and (3) symbolic analogy. In another context but working toward the same goal, Gombrich (21) suggests parlor games where we can regress, aggress, or perhaps even caress metaphors. In such a game a film star, a television celebrity, or a political figure is to be identified through a series of somewhat appropriate symbols or signs but in a different metaphorical context. The question asked is, if so and so could be an insect, a flower, animal, automobile, or piece of music, which would he be? As Gombrich indicates, the values of such games lies not only in the ability to guess correctly but in the post-mortem comparison of one metaphorical reality with another. If students were given a variety of such game experiences, it might be possible to investigate how effective such curricula were in loosening the transition from one metaphorical binding to another.

Indeed, Spolin's (42) practical volume on teaching and directing groups in theatre games moves boldly and inspirationally into this kind of knowing. Here are presented a curriculum for learning and developing metaphorical change techniques as part of a spontaneous, active experience. The objectives of such theatre games are to enhance learning and teaching by experiencing techniques, to increase spontaneity in thinking and behavior, and to learn how to be supportive and helpful to others in the group. In the "Transformation of Relationships" game, members of the group playing the game decide on two hypothetical persons who are involved in a relationship and where they meet. The group begins by selecting (let us say) a Radio City Music Hall Rockette, a male ski instructor, and a specific dive in Greenwich Village where the couple meets. Two players are selected or volunteer to play these roles and leave the room. The group then selects four normal human emotions, two of which are assigned randomly to the Rockette and two to the ski instructor. Let us say that anger, joy, pity, and despair were chosen. These would be written on a blackboard facing the players as follows:

Rockette—anger → joy
Ski instructor—pity → despair

The game is begun with the Rockette and ski instructor taking a moment to look at their assignment on the blackboard and beginning their relationship in the emotional mood designated. To do this they need to learn to support each other's feeling. At the same time they need to begin to think of ways of moving from anger to joy (Rockette) and pity to despair (ski instructor). Each must help the other make their relationship genuine as well as assist each other to reach his or her respective goal. Although this may appear to be difficult, a little practice, a supportive group, and some confidence makes such learning easy. Again, post-mortem discussions by the role players can be educationally helpful to all the participants.

Another type of game is "transformation of object." The first player in the game "creates" an object by doing something with "it" in pantomine, such as bouncing a ball, driving a car, catching a fish, or petting a dog, etc. He passes on this object and activity to the next player, who handles it and transforms it into another object and passes it on to the next, who transforms it into still another object. For example, the object, ball (bouncing a ball by moving hand up and down), can be transformed by the next player into a handkerchief by slowly moving the hand at the wrist toward a distant point. All transformations are done spontaneously and held only long enough for another player to come into the action, take "hold" of the object, and transform it.

Spolin describes over 200 such theatre games where the curriculum is aimed at learning to work with others in a spontaneous and experiential manner to solve a problem. Self-consciousness, the bugaboo of this kind of activity, is diminished as players and nonplayers alike begin to see the game not as a performance but as an active sharing of experience. And as Spolin points out, good theater is good for this very reason—that the performers have succeeded in drawing the audience into the game as active participants, not as viewers. The grip which good theater has on audiences indicates this is one of the few planned social opportunities for an active and highly personal sharing of laughter and tears.

Good "theater," as the sharing or getting inside an experience, can be utilized in a variety of educational curricula. Such opportunities are abundant in history, humanities, literature, home arts, and even dramatics. For example, James Humphrey of the University of Maryland has demonstrated the use of a simple relay game to help children understand the concept of electricity.

The children line up to simulate a wire and conduct electrical charges in the form of volleyballs pushed under their legs. By having one child out of place a short circuit can be played out. Humphrey has developed games to help children understand the concept of grouping in mathematics and a variety of language games. Most of his games require physical activity on the part of learners; he calls them "motorvating" as well as motivating games (24).

Rose Frutchey, an agricultural and science teacher in Laos with the International Voluntary Service, designed a teaching game for the villagers called "The Community Game of Southeast Asia." Frutchey's game requires a large map of a typical southeast Asia community with its rice paddies, local temple, and other observable landmarks. All participants then draw a number of cards on which are pictures of rice, schools, roads, and hospitals. Each player in turn tries to "build" what he thinks the village needs most. He soon finds, however, that he can't build by himself; he must get together with others by moving his pieces to the local temple where they can "talk." A player can block construction of a project if he wishes or players can swap pieces. The object of the game is to win, and playing it has been a real learning experience for the villagers. It is now being used by the Peace Corps and the International Voluntary Service as part of their training program.

Joe Brown, an architect at Princeton, has attempted to design play equipment to combine both stable and mobile elements so that what one child does in the play system affects what every other child does. The child must choose how to manage himself in the equipment which utilizes steel cored rope, spring steel, and fiber glass. In play, "unpredictability—within reasonable limits—is the basis of man's creativity." (9, p. 226)

Games provide opportunities for role playing and simulations in which children can rehearse situations that may be anticipated as being difficult to master in real life. Suchman, in Chapter 20, describes a game process which can help students get involved with and become skillful in problem solving. Boocock and Coleman (6) describe three games a "Career Game," a "Legislative Game," and a "Community Disaster Game" which have been tried out and tested with children and adolescents. They see the use of such games in schools as one means of correcting the structural rigidity of present-day education with its prescribed courses, lecturing teachers, homework, textbooks, and examinations. Games make it possible for many children to see the future in terms of the present. In playing games, students play to win, according to prescribed rules. They learn that nothing can transpire in a game without agreement as to rules and their acceptance by all. They also learn that rules can be changed—not by individual players arbitrarily but by all the game players as a group.

Boocock and Coleman have used the "Life Career Game" as a guidance learning experience in high school. The game is organized into rounds or decision periods representing a year in the life of a student. During this period the player must plan his activities for a typical week and allocate his time. When players have made their decisions for a given year, scores are computed in four areas—education, occupation, family life, and leisure. The game requires a set of tables and spinners and a calculator which compute probabilities of happenings based on U.S. Census and other national data. One girl player evaluated her game experience with the thought "All the possibilities that popped up in the game made me realize how difficult decisions will be when I get older." Another said, "Most students would have had impractical views of their future lives before they played this game, just as I did. After playing the games they would learn that a twenty-four-hour day is not long enough to allow a girl to hold a job, be a wife, raise a family, and get an education. Something must be left out." (6, p. 231)

I once watched a cricket match in London and became concretely aware of the real meaning of the phrase "it isn't cricket." As the teams broke for high tea, I was reminded of Lord Mancroft's observation on the relationship of this game to British character. "My countrymen," said the Lord, "have never been a spiritually minded people so they invented cricket to give them some notion of eternity." There is little doubt that games reflect the character of a people and the style of life of a society. Its potential as a motivating and learning experience has only begun to be tapped. Games may provide a helpful and effective match in the introduction and motivation of all children to early school life. Especially for lower-class children, games can provide immediate consequences for decisions, an ongoing system of reinforcement and present- rather than future-oriented rewards.

The games previously presented are only samples of small beginnings in unlocking school curricula and maximizing the learning modalities of education. Many of these small beginnings were made many years ago and are neither new nor revolutionary. In our rush to fill children up with the symbols and appurtenances of educational status, the kinds of knowledge learned in games are often overlooked. However, educators are aware of the increasing need in students for varieties of information about self and the world and the need to build broad and creative knowledge-processing skills into their personalities. They are also aware that students and parents often perceive educational goals somewhat narrowly yet realistically as "how do I get into college X or Y." Educational innovations as pseudoactions have replaced educational change. A school with a number of "show and tell" educational innovations can keep its basic educational program intact since it is already abreast of everything new and desirable. Such principles and practices described and discussed in this section are intended to be part of the whole fabric of learning and should be developed as such.

The Avalanche of Knowledge

Let us leave the qualitative stream of knowledge for the moment and examine the other fork of this significant development. Man's relationship to the production of knowledge of all kinds has been somewhat like the sorcerer's apprentice who started something that soon overwhelmed him and that once started, he could not stop. So it is that in the next fifteen years man is expected to learn as much about his environment including himself as in all previous history. If we can keep our fingers away from our destructive buttons and bombs, man will be swimming in new and ever expanding seas of knowledge. Machlup notes that (1) the knowledge-producing occupations are continuing to outdistance other occupations of man, (2) since the beginning of the twentieth century knowledge-producing occupations have tripled in the total labor force, and (3) the income of occupations producing new knowledge has increased sharply. As an economist, Machlup concludes that "while the ascendency of knowledge-producing occupations has been an uninterrupted process, there has been a succession of occupations leading this movement, first clerical, then administrative and managerial, and now professional and technical personnel. Thus the changing employment pattern indicates a continuing movement from manual to mental, and from less to more highly trained labor." (33, p. 397)

What does such knowledge about knowledge mean? It would appear that living and making a living will demand reasonable success in educational institutions. Our technology and way of life is gradually pinching off those jobs where sweat and physical labor can be rewarded (with the possible exception of professional baseball, football, and other paying sports) and is making the use of symbols a mandatory skill in the market place. It has rocketed our once lonely and prodigal institutions of public and private education into national defense, national politics, the solution of historical inequities of race relations, and into solving the problems of the amoebic growth of cities.

As the significance and importance of educational skills increases, the cost of acquiring such skills increases. The ritual of getting into a college, which has taken on the quality of waiting for the fall of the guillotine, will take on increasing stress rites in the seventies when 50% more students than there are today will be looking anxiously for a friendly institution. Indeed what Drucker calls the "Knowledge State" is upon us. Enrollment in private and public schools will reach 64 million by 1975; teachers will be our largest single occupational group, and the total school budget may, under peaceful conditions, exceed the defense budget. (15, p. 42)

The most sweeping result of this flood of knowledge production and distribution is a world where human transactions entailing rapid and accurate encoding and decoding of symbols (words and figures) reach a flood level. The knowledge industry is one of those unique monsters that feeds and grows on its own products. Moreover, "a static society can exchange with relatively little effort its small store of knowledge, but a rapidly changing society needs to organize a vast daily flood of communication, most of which is not specifically calculated to advance any productive process. This stream of communication is an essential part of the modern environment; without it civilization would cease to breathe." (12, p. 128)

Man's need to breathe and live in his own environment mandates a re-examination of the processes of education. It is no longer possible, if indeed it ever was, for any human being to "absorb" all knowledge. The old mug-jug processes (that is, teacher as the jug containing the juices of knowledge who is able, when plugged into a lectern, to tip over and fill up the little empty mugs), can no longer be defended even on a traditional basis. Knowledge is too vast and the human body and mind too tiny to think of filling it; knowledge will need to be organized for effective distribution and processing. Learners will need conceptual bindings to hold on to the vast array of labels and concepts. The institutions of education will need to consciously plan and develop learnings that enhance the organizing or mediating processes of the human organism. Such planning and developing must go on in the content fields of knowledge as well as in the transmitting activities through which learners are informed.

Knowledge in a Knowledge State is no longer a commodity of necessity for the few or for the professionally trained citizen. Like food, it has become a necessity for all. Our society's paramount interest in school dropouts is not a result of increasing numbers of such failures but a realization of the significance of the consequences on the defeated child. For such a child there are no other avenues available for learning the significant educational skills. This nation will have no participating possibilities for the uneducated in the work and life of its culture and economy. The uneducated will not only have been priced out of the labor market, but out of life itself.

THE ECOLOGICAL-PUBLIC HEALTH APPROACH TO HUMAN GROWTH AND HUMAN PROBLEMS

This brings us to our second mainstream of human development in today's world—an increasing need for and utilization of the content and processes of public health knowledge and methodology in the solution of human problems. Such knowledge has accumulated slowly in the history of man, but its utilization and translation into the educational scene and its applicability to educational problems is growing.

Dr. John Snow, a shy and studious physician, was asked in the summer of 1854 to look into a cholera plague in London. We should note that in 1854 ideas about the causes of cholera involved "dust colored flies, cholera animalcules carried by the wind from India,

spores thrown off by mouldy growths in damp places," (41, p. 32),
and other wild guesses. In his investigations, Snow found more than
five hundred persons had died in ten days within 250 yards of the
corner of Broad and Cambridge Streets and that at the center of
this circle of death stood the community water pump. Snow made
a house-to-house canvass of the area including a nearby brewery
whose workmen had miraculously escaped the plague and a workhouse
whose occupants drank from a private well and had also survived.
Snow prevailed upon the authorities to take the handle off the pump
and thus ended the plague. Snow, however, continued his investigations. He found a woman who had died in the west end of London
but had moved from the neighborhood of the well just the day before,
a dead relative from Brighton who had visited his brother's house
and had mixed water with his brandy (the lesson is obvious), and
other evidence to confirm the wisdom of his action. As Geddes Smith
points out, "The method here is as significant as the results. Sydenham
had tried to generalize from his own practice; Webster and many
other commentators generalized from masses of historical information
and misinformation uncritically heaped together; Snow generalized
from groups of cases accurately counted and classified." (41, p. 54)

Public health procedures and techniques have helped build a way
of life characterized by sound sewage disposal, effective food preparation and storage, specific disease control, and health practices based
on prevention of illness or disabilities. It has sought pump handles
to prevent human disease, not by attacking specific pathogenic bacteria but by enhancing the conditions of life that prevent such bacteria
from flourishing. Public health methodology is basically a "systems"
approach to human functioning; we study organisms interacting with
other objects, events, or organisms as an ecological unit.

The ecological concept of *man-in-his-society-in-his-physical-world*
is best visualized as a balloon that if pushed in on one side, bulges
on the other. We live in a society held together by visible and invisible
bonds, where consciously and unconsciously felt forces interact in
an orderly and predictable manner. Such bonds have become more
visible and have been drawn taut by population and technological
expansions. Such ecological units or systems can be considered as
isolated enclosures such as a school, community, or earth in which
"all measurements that can be made of what goes on in the system
are in some way correlated." (7, p. 188)

Such correlations, however, must differentiate significant from non-
significant factors or objects since all objects in the universe can
be said to be correlated with all other objects. In estimating high

and low tides a hydrometric engineer is certainly aware of the fact that the planet Pluto is somewhere in the system; its contribution is, however, too small under ordinary circumstances to include its correlative measurement. As Karpus (27) points out, the grouping of objects and factors into an interacting system requires sophistication and learning. For example, in a game of tug-of-war, boys interact with each other via the rope but soon learn that an integral part of the system is the nature of the ground on which they are standing and the kind of shoes they are wearing. To win the game, we must be able to appraise all aspects of the system and know where objects and factors can be modified or introduced to make the system work better for us.

An excellent illustration of changes in the system as a result of the introduction of a new object or factor is the impact of a spindle on the effectiveness of service in a restaurant (39). A restaurant is a system requiring the ordering of food (customer to waiter), communication of order (waiter to cook), preparation of order (cook's memory to plate), and conveying of food to customer (waiter's memory to customer). However, under ordinary circumstances cooks do not like to be the recipient of verbal orders from waiters, restaurants become overloaded during the noon or evening rush hours, and there is a great deal of loud communication by different waiters to different cooks, while the manager tears his hair out. What does a spindle do for the system? It enables the system to pace itself, that is, to reduce the overload stress by queuing up the orders while the waiters are free to go about other duties. It provides the system with a method of processing overloads much like the ego-process described under this heading in the next chapter. The system also becomes more effective since waiters no longer need to communicate verbally or directly with cooks; the spindle acts as a memory and queuing up device, facilitates information flow, provides feedback to cook and waiter, reduces error, makes for happy customers and hairy-headed managers. Porter's description of the conceptual elements in a system (inputs, feedback loops, memory devices, chunking, channeling, and filtering) are somewhat analogous to elements in ego-processes discussed in the next chapter.

To some extent the ecological approach to human problems attempts to identify those elements in a living experience which are significantly related, the strength and character of the relationship, their impact on the functioning of the individual, and his impact on the system. Although the clinical or individual approach to problems of health or functioning ineffectiveness is necessary, like John Snow, we search for specific reasons for specific sources of illnesses or other kinds of effective interventions that prevent epidemics. Humanity demands that alcoholics receive treatment, that bleeding ulcers be controlled, that aspirins be available for headaches. However, individual services to individuals in need will not solve the ecological and human living problems that produced the disequilibrium and disorder in the first place.

Public health thinking and methodologies are now finding conceptual application to the problems of human malfunctioning such as crime, mental illnesses, or deficiencies in human development. In this approach we attempt to identify interacting factors, their level of significance, the source of conflict, dissonance or deficiencies in the system, and specific fulcra for intervention in the system to make it more effective for all. In some cases it may mean identifying difficult transitional points for groups of children in the system and mobilizing resources at these bridges to insure effective passage. Note that the aim of this activity is not to pick up system casualties or rush people to hospitals or clinics at the earliest possible time, necessary as this may be. What is being sought are ways of building strength—a healthy mediation of stress by persons in a system so that one grows more effective in managing increasing or decreasing loads of stress. Each system has its own points of greatest stress and disequilibrium for individuals. Behavioral scientists have identified a variety of such transitional points and suggested how systems can reinforce individual growth at these points. Chapter 21 by Newton and Brown examines a specific preventive program utilizing school entrance as the point of leverage.

The public health approach to human problems is not based on the notion that human institutions are effective when they are characterized by warmth, consideration, friendliness, love, health, kindness, and selfishness, whatever these may mean operationally. A humanizing institution is successful when it has solved the problem of carrying out its goals more effectively for all those in it. For example, the employment of mental health consultants to work with teachers may result in more meaningful referrals, better individual diagnoses, and even better understanding of individual problems; nevertheless, the significant impact of such consultant services, as in the case of the spindle, must be felt somewhere in the bones, joints, and sinews of the system itself. This is made more difficult where personnel in a school view their mental health consultants as caretakers of casualties or disposers of the inadequate. Under these assumptions the discordant expectations of the teacher and the consultant may move them in different directions toward disparate goals. However, with mental health programs finding their way into the community systems from which illness stems, involvement of mental health consultants in schools as a preventive resource becomes mandatory. Indeed, one of the major missions of the Community Mental Health Centers authorized by the 88th and 89th Congresses is to work toward the use of such consultation as a public health, preventive program.

Fit for Change

In a society where educational achievement is rapidly supplanting material acquisition as a value goal, where jobs for the unskilled are disappearing, where the basic anxieties have shifted from the economic to the atomic, where the significant decisions for children are coming earlier, where life is being lengthened and narrowed, where institutions are becoming increasingly large and impersonal—where all these and other factors converge on individuals—we need to plan specific ways of building human strengths and resources. This can be done only through successful and enhancing experiences in the humanizing institutions of our society. As Dubos comments, "There is no reason to doubt the ability of the scientific method to solve each of the specific problems of disease by discovering causes and remedial procedures . . . but solving problems of disease is not the same thing as creating health and happiness." (16, p. 22)

Hobbs identifies the penetration of concepts of public health into the field of education and mental health as mental health's third revolution. In this revolutionary society the mental health specialist will be required to work primarily with and through the humanizing institutions of the community rather than with individual persons.

"I have found instructive a study by Harland Cleveland of the successful foreign service officer who is in a position very much like that of the public health, mental health officer. He is confronted with a tremendous problem, his resources are limited, his staff is inadequate, and he is expected to make a difference in the lives of a substantial number of people. Cleveland found that the highly effective foreign service officer had among other attributes, a strong institutional sense, a sense of the ways in which social groups invent institutions to serve their ends, and a notion of how this process can be furthered." (23, p. 829)

The causes of man's disabilities have traced a long history from miasma, weather, humours, bad air, the presence of devils, air borne corpuscles, invisible insects, invisible animalcules, heat, cold, light, and darkness, to name only a few suspected culprits. Some or all of these factors translated into modern dress can be made scientifically respectable, but the concept of fitness of the individual to function as the basic factor in health and development is perhaps most significant.

Man's equilibrium and disequilibrium with his own bodily system is intricately and significantly tied up with other systems in which he functions. Hippocrates pointed out that it is change which is chiefly responsible for diseases; that changes in living conditions which are too rapid or abrupt do not permit adaptive mechanisms to function effectively. Cassel (13) reinforces this notion and suggests that disproportionate rates of change in any one of the four linked systems of man—the physiological, psychological, social, and cultural—could effect the others in a way that might lead to illness or breakdown. In one study he compared the health of rural mountaineers who were the first of their families to engage in industrial work with that of co-workers drawn from the same stock but who were the children of parents who had worked in this factory before them. In another study, rural residents living in counties with differing degrees of urban growth were studied. He hypothesized that the larger the size of the city, the greater the problems and rates of illness in the ex-rural residents. Cassel and his associates found in both cases that no matter how they measured human difficulties—illness, absence from work, scores on the Cornell Medical Index, coronary heart disease or death—the group undergoing the greatest change had the higher rates.

In another study cited by Cassel, the serum cholesteral levels of two groups of hourly paid male employees doing similar jobs were observed. In one group (A), the employees worked with a constant set of fellow workers. In the other (B), they worked with employees who changed shifts periodically, or they themselves changed shifts periodically. However they worked, Group B had little or no opportunity for close interaction with the same group of workers. The investigators were somewhat startled by their results which showed that after adjusting for age difference, the proportion of Group B men who were hypercholesteremic was twice as great as was the proportion of Group A men.

These and other studies such as the high incidence of crime and illness in immigrant or transitional groups are especially significant in a culture in which change is rapid, getting ahead is an individual responsibility, and mobility a social fact of life. We do not need more formidable evidence in order to implicate rapid change as a villain unless our society can build into institutions experiences by which the mediation and management of change can be learned and integrated within the ego-processes of individuals.

This idea is reinforced by studies of the effect of mobility on emotional disturbances in children. Pedersen and Sullivan, in their studies of the effect of geographical mobility on children of military families, suggest considerable caution in linking geographical mobility as an etiological agent in the development of emotionally disturbed children. They indicate that parental attitudes relevant to mobility do differentiate significantly between the disturbed and normal groups and that the mediation of the stress of change is the critical factor in the family (38).

If this assumption is correct, it reinforces the need to study institutions, their peak transitional points, and how persons can be helped to manage changes in an enchancing manner. The school, as one of our major humanizing institutions, will require greater flexibilities in its programs to help children with greater inflexibilities in their experiential or biological development. The school must find ways to serve all children within the system. The basic needs of living now include adequate health and education in addition to food, shelter, and clothing. As Mark Twain said, "Soap and education are not as sudden as a massacre, but they are more deadly in the long run."

COMPETENCE IN THE USE OF SYMBOLS

Man's social and individual competence as a human being in a Knowledge State rests squarely on his skill and effectiveness as a processor and user of symbols. Knowledge is packaged in symbols created and organized by men. Behind these symbols "lie the boldest, purest, coolest abstractions mankind has ever made." (30, p. 27)

One of these cool abstractions has been the notion that to develop effective human beings in a society requires effective humanizing institutions. Such institutions are man-made arrangements born out of man's experiential, social, and scientific knowledge, focused on the problem of transforming "curly, dimpled lunatics" (according to Emerson) or children (according to parents) into rational, effective, and competent human beings. One of the key kinds of arrangements with the greatest survival value has been that of tying a legal knot between two adults of differing sexes with strong implicit and explicit instructions to provide their children and each other the physical, emotional, and cognitive nutrients necessary for competent participation in society.

This arrangement, often called a family or home, a woman's workhouse, a night hostel for male commuters, a place ever so humble where, "when you really need to go there, they have to take you in"—this institution has been assigned the major executive and co-ordinating job of the child humanizing effort.

A second key arrangement was man's slickest idea with perhaps the least effective implementation—the common school. School, like the family, is a basic institution for children. Whereas the family may make minimal behavioral demands on the child and stick to such areas as toilet habits, cleanliness, showing up for meals on time, and no football in the house, the school expects him to pay attention, to work, and to produce. Children, through their cabalistic antennae, sense the significance of the institution in the absolute lack of choice given them about attending and the tenseness in their parents when the time comes to take the fateful step.

What has happened to make this step even more critical for children is (1) a kind of knowing à la Beckett that the skills and understandings preferred and proferred by the school are absolutely essential for adult life and (2) there are no exits or other institutional alternatives.

How Man Invented Symbols—Probably

In the past, education was an important factor in a man's social and individual functioning. In the latter half of the twentieth century educational skills have become an absolute necessity for the growth and social participation of every single person in the work and life of society. These are skills in the processing of symbols and an understanding of the conceptual paradigms from which such symbols derive their meaning. Such conceptual sets are primarily language and mathematics, followed by science, history, philosophy, psychology, geography, poetry, and including home arts, physical education, and human development, to name but a few.

Symbols have another significance relevant to the goal of social competency. Von Bertalanffy suggested some years ago that if a stranger from another world came down and studied humans and human life without knowing the range of its problems, he would in time need to hypothesize a kind of human malfunctioning which we call mental illnesses. That is, any culture which is heavily invested in the creation and rapid transmission of sets of symbols (knowledge) in a variety of human relationships (family, school, peer groups, or work groups) faces the probability that such symbols will be transmitted with degrees of diffuseness, distortion, fragmentation, and constriction and with inappropriate degrees of emotional overloading or underloading. If the degrees of diffuseness, distortion, fragmentation, constriction, and inappropriate loading of symbols in an individual reach an arbitrary and shifting line of nonacceptability in our culture, mental illness or instability can be called by our professional umpires.

To Sleep, Perhaps to . . .

Where and why in this evolutionary scheme of things did man come to the device of symbolization as his primary tool and skill? The picture we tend to slide into focus is that of some preaustralopithecus man with his new and magnificent opposable thumb, and his additional cerebral convolutions holding up some object to his mate, pointing to it and babbling a sound related to the object's use, its smell, feel, shape, size, or green stamp redemption value. The sound is then repeated a number of times (here we have the origin of the drill and grill method) and is then available for conversation and labeling. From such motivation and learning it is suggested that language and speech evolved.

I'm more inclined, however, to see the picture as Langer does. In her slide our preaustralopithecus man arises one morning puzzled, pained, and burdened. He has experienced a series of inside images while asleep—or was it outside? In any case, the images were connected in strange ways and seemed to tell a story or mean something. Where did these images come from? Could he relate what happened to someone else? Lacking video tape equipment,[1] our preaustralopithecus man found it difficult to communicate the experience to himself or others. He also sensed that these kaleidoscopic images were indeed telling him something.

It would appear to be more in keeping with what is known about the human animal to suspect man's need to express primary processes[2] of thought as in dreams as the culprit that got him into this symbolic world. Somewhere in his evolutionary meanderings man developed this extraordinary ability to flit pictures through his mind during

[1] The danger of such dream equipment is illustrated by a Whitney Darrow, Jr. cartoon in the January 1, 1966, *New Yorker*. Pictured is a club car of a train with a harried passenger telling his companion, "The nightmare I had wasn't enough. Before I woke up, there was a video tape replay!"

[2] The kind of "strange" thinking that goes on in dreams including the telescoping and condensing of time, representation of the whole by a part of the whole, treating words as things, falling off a cliff and flying away—all in technicolor.

his sleeping state. Consequently, to paraphrase Prospero, symbols are such stuff as dreams and man are made on.

Dreams, however, are not images of unrelated objects, events or feelings—the whole, however misty and confused, is an idea, a thought, an expression. Dreaming involves the same psychological and physiological apparatus as conscious, rational thinking; both "sleep" thinking and "wakeful" thinking apparently serve similar human and biological purposes in enabling man to cope with himself and his environment. Dreams may help us to sleep by providing an avenue for discharging emotional overloads; symbols may help us to live by providing a similar avenue for charging and sparking between mind, self, and the external world.

If we are willing to dream just a little more, the structure and function of man's symbols might be seen as a vehicle to provide him with significant and viable metaphors for living. Language, therefore, is not an attempt to represent objects and events and then to think with them. It probably emerged out of man's past and continuing attempt to describe and express an idea.

The essence of man's relationship to his dreams (sleep or waking) is to find ways of expressing the nature and meaning of the images. It is also probable that the action of communication through written words or spoken sounds helps make the ideas or thoughts additionally real since such acts are seen or heard by our own visual and auditory perceptual apparatus. Speech and writing then become economical and available energy outlets for the communication of thoughts. When babbling and scribbling became understandable activities of man, the Knowledge State was born. But let us not forget how this state was born. In the words of Langer,

"Before terms are built into propositions, they assert nothing, preclude nothing; in fact although they may *name* things and convey ideas of such things, they say nothing. . . . Even so obvious a distinction as that between sign-functions and symbol-functions passed unnoticed; so that careless philosophers have been guilty of letting ambitious genetic psychologists argue them from the conditioned reflex to the wisdom of G. Bernard Shaw, all in one skyrocketing generalization." (30, p. 66)

The Magic of Symbols

Symbols are often talked or written about as representations of specific objects, events, or feelings so that we are often led to conceptualize a symbol as interchangeable with whatever "it" is that is being substituted for. One of the important notions inherent in man's use of symbols is that x (the symbol) does not *equal* anything in man's external world. As a symbol it contains *"n"* degrees of individual interpreting, organizing, experiencing, and meaning. Where such degrees of individual interpretation are relatively absent, it would be more accurate to call x a sign. Stop!, as in a stop sign or a policeman's raised hand, has relatively few degrees of freedom as do natural signs such as moss growing on the north side of a tree, the sound of thunder, or vegetation flowering in the desert. Few persons in our culture would have difficulty with the meaning of a policeman's raised hand in traffic, a red light, or a stop sign. Symbols, however, cannot be so easily interchanged. Signs proclaim; symbols conceive. Obviously a child who has "heard" his mother say, for the one-hundredth time, to *stop* what he is doing, is not reacting to the sign function of the term. "Stop" in this instance contains within its symbolic structure the child's knowledge about the parent, his past experience with the word in this situation, and a knowledge of the consequences of his interpretation.

A. human responds to signals and symbols, but his realities and his behaviors are symbol oriented. As Thorndike (43, p. 119) said so succinctly, "An animal can think things, but it cannot think about things." The differences between signal-using and symbol-using animals are not differences in degree. Symbols conceptualize and define externality. Each man defines what is out there with his own symbols. This notion was aptly summarized by Bill Klem, an experienced baseball umpire who happened to be calling balls and strikes behind the plate with a catcher who liked to anticipate Klem's calls. The catcher turned to Klem after a particularly close pitch and said "Strike?" "Young man," said Klem, "it ain't nothing till I calls it!"

What is reality in baseball is no less reality in life; human life is invented and created by the symbolic matrices in which it is defined. Events cannot be transformed into experiences, feelings cannot be differentiated or objects bound into memory without man's ability to use symbols. Without the ability to "call it," life is a misty, diffused, jumbled conglomeration of objects, feelings, and events. Meanings are conceptual processes woven out of symbolic cloth. To be without such symbolic equipment is to be bound by "invisible hands." "The few signs I used," wrote Helen Keller, "became less and less adequate, and my failures to make myself understood were invariably followed by outbursts of passion. I felt as if invisible hands were holding me, and I made frantic efforts to free myself—after awhile the need of some means of communication became so urgent that these outbursts occurrred daily, sometimes hourly." (28, p. 17)

Those who saw Gibson's dramatization of Annie Sullivan's attempt to teach the meaning of language to Helen Keller will remember the passionate moment when Helen learned to use symbols. The drama of the transition of Helen the "animal" to Helen the human brought cheers and tears to dowdy shoppers and a multitude of housewives. Helen in her own words recalled that, "As the cool stream gushed over one hand, she [Miss Sullivan] spelled into the other the word water, first slowly, then rapidly. I stood still, my whole attention fixed upon the motion of her fingers. Suddenly I felt a misty consciousness as if something forgotten—a thrill of returning thought; and somehow the mystery of language was revealed to me. That living word awakened my soul, gave it light, hope, joy, set it free Thus I came out of Egypt and stood before Sinai and a power divine touched my spirit and gave it sight so that I beheld many wonders." (28, pp. 20, 23)

Man's Number is Up

Symbols are man's greatest invention and mathematics his symbolic Hercules. Whereas words need to be tied to real things and experiences, the strength and power of mathematics lies precisely in its pristine avoidance of symbolizing anything real or tangible. McLuhan, writing about man's need for numbers, suggests that it emerged from man's haptic sense—his sense of touch as a necessary part of his *integral* existence. "The ancient world associated number magic with the properties of physical things and with the necessary causes of things, much as science has tended until recent times to reduce all objects to numerical quantities. . . . Take 36-24-36. Numbers cannot become more sensuously tactile than when mumbled as the magic formula for the female figure while the haptic hand sweeps the air." (34, p. 109) The notion of the sense of touch in relation to mathematics is most visible in the expressions "putting the finger on a man" and "so and so's number is up." (Anyone having trouble with these phrases might watch an old Humphrey Bogart or James Cagney movie.)

I recall vividly one of my high school mathematics teachers spending significant time blocks trying to convince us of the practical utility of higher algebra, analytic geometry, and trigonometry. In my case he succeeded in convincing me it wasn't worth it just to measure the height of a tree or the span of a river. We are reminded of Molloy, a crusty character in one of Beckett's novels, who wrapped himself in swathes of newspaper (*The London Times Literary Supplement*, *no less*) during the winter and did not shed them until there were definite signs of spring. Unfortunately, Molloy had a tendency or predilection for abdominal eructations which, considering his armored condition, gave him some concern. However, using applied and creative mathematics, Molloy consoled himself with his calculated facts that at least, in this one characteristic, he seemed to be somewhat average. "Extraordinary," he exclaimed jubilantly, "how mathematics helps you to know yourself." (1, p. 39) Never has mathematics or the *Times Literary Supplement* been in greater service to humanity.

To get back to my mathematics teacher, the exciting notion which we both missed was that what he was teaching and I was attempting to learn had no direct relationship at all to the external world. It was a system of symbols and a conceptual extension of man not specifically related to any objects, events, or feelings.

"What is the secret power of mathematics to win hardheaded empiricists . . . to its purely rational speculations and intangible "facts?". . . . The secret lies in the fact that a mathematician does not profess to say anything about the existence, reality or efficacy of *things* at all. His concern is the possibility of *symbolizing things* and of symbolizing the relations into which they might enter with each other. . . . To the true mathematician, numbers do not "inhere in" denumerable things, nor do circular objects contain degrees. Numbers and degrees and all their ilk only *mean* the real properties of real objects. It is entirely at the discretion of the scientists to say, "Let X mean this, let Y mean that." All that mathematics determines is that then X and Y must be related thus and thus." (30, p. 28)

The overwhelming problem for man in the use of symbols is to differentiate between a conceptual system such as language as we know it, which relates to objects, events, and feelings, and a symbol system such as mathematics, which has meaning within its own assumptions and relationships.

New Skills in the Use of Symbols

The Knowledge State requires its citizens to learn to use symbols in a variety of ways. We need to learn to use words and ideas in a consensually validated[1] manner both as a listener and communicator; we need to learn to use symbols creatively and imaginatively in thinking, writing, music, art, and human relationships; and we

---

[1] Con means *with,* sensual means *state of mind,* and validation stands for *demonstrating truth* (Harry Stack Sullivan).

need to learn how to use and enjoy symbols as objects for play and fun.

To accomplish these things several new (actually old but revigorated) approaches need to find their way into the processes of education. In a world where life is spun out in greater and greater amounts of symbols and increasing levels of abstractions, communication with self and others may become highly diffused or distorted. Often we find it easier or more satisfying to substitute the symbol for its reality without knowing either one well. We are like the proud parent who while wheeling her newborn baby in the park was stopped by an admiring friend. "My, what a pretty baby," said the friend. "That's nothing," said the mother, "you should see his picture."

Indeed at times it seems we have shifted the responsibility for defining the real world from our senses and our sense to the written word. Events and words are too readily interchangeable. The printed or spoken word has in many ways become the authentic world to which we respond.

Symbols and Action

The sum and substance of a child's experience in school must, in large part, result in his ability to process and use symbols. The construction and differentiation of his world, of self and others, rests on the child's experiences with symbols and the events or actions in which the symbol was learned.

Objects or events cannot be raised to the domain of the mind without the tools to do so—*the ability to conceptualize the object or event symbolically.* The insidious outcome of this process for man, however, is that meaning resides not in things and events but primarily in the symbol concept. This peculiarity of symbols highlights its elusiveness in consensual validation, especially in instances where men attempt to communicate significant but highly abstract ideas. What, for example, can the words "democracy," "freedom," "equality," "hope," "future," or "love" mean to one whose knowledge of the concept has been limited to explanations via other words? Or what common meaning would a word such as "hope" have to a well-educated, white American male; a poorly educated, Negro boy of sixteen; a child; a resident of a prison; a blind person or a psychotic individual. The great paradox, as Moffet points out, is man's attempt to separate symbol from symbolized. "We cannot free data from the symbols into which they have been abstracted, the message from the code. . . . Every code or language says something about itself while delivering its message. 'Codification is the substitution of one set of events for another.' (Gregory Bateson)." (36, p. 22) It is important to reemphasize that the meaning of symbols of objects or events contain in their nucleus the individual's action and the consequences of his action; indeed as Shibutani puts it, "meanings are primarily a property of behavior and only secondarily a property of objects (40, p. 81)."

The school as a social system is primarily engaged in mediating symbols to children. The clinical behavioral scientists such as psychiatrists, clinical social workers, and clinical psychologists are primarily involved in unmediating symbols that have somehow gotten misused or distorted by past behavior. Educators are involved in helping the individual use his symbolic lore and equipment to become more effective interactors with their environments. Both groups are concerned with the development of individuals as information processors. The psychiatrist with his patients and the teacher with his students seek to install and improve the information processing equipment of their clients or students so that objects and events can be effectively symbolized, assimilated, differentiated, and integrated into the personality.

Actions and objects cannot literally be raised to the domain of the mind without the ability to represent them symbolically. Without an adequate repertoire of symbols such as a language and the ability to use it effectively, an individual is like a repertory company limited to a single production.

Symbolic Ties—Firmly but Loosely

An effective relationship to others and to the external world could not exist without a system of symbols that have been learned through common actions and experiences. Probably the most significant factor in the differentiation and validation of our symbolic learning is the process of self-representation. Yet paradoxically, such correctness and accuracy about self must allow, indeed encourage, degrees of amplitude and tentativeness about such perception. Action-symbol meaning cannot be conceptualized within a learner as imprints cast in concrete. Such symbols must somehow be learned in a firm but malleable media. However we represent ourselves when alone, we are continually shifting (if we can) our symbols of self to accommodate changing realities. We conceptualize ourselves differently in church, at a party, at home, or at a formal dinner. A study by Block (4) suggests that in general a well-functioning individual is able to hold on to a core self in all transactions and has about 50% flexibility to vary his *persona* as situations and conditions change.

The major task then of our schools of the seventies and eighties and beyond is to help children learn to use symbols as differentiators and validators of externality but with sufficient degree of freedom and conceptual flexibility to develop new or different meanings. In any society where programs of symbolic meanings can be stamped in through mass media, schools must in their instructional programs provide for both the imprinting and deimprinting of meaning. The teaching of symbols as consensual validators of objects and events must therefore avoid the constriction and freezing of the mediated idea or event. The teacher needs to consider such encoding or language development as having two apparently diametrically opposite but similar purposes; to encode correctly the common symbols of our society but to avoid doing so in a flat, binary, absolutistic manner. The stability and flexibility in self, suggested by Block, must find its roots in the educational action and mediational experiences by which such symbols are created in the minds of children. The representation of events and objects as black or white, good or bad, all or none, me or you, they or we, presents such representation with only two conceptual possibilities, like a North and South Pole. Children are limited by such learning in much the same manner as a deaf child is handicapped in trying to learn the word "run." A boy can run fast, slow, or at a trot, but what about a silk stocking, a river, a politician, or the silvery Grunion of the Pacific?

Stereotyped thinking emerges out of obstinate and unalterable conceptualizations of objects and events. Occasionally when such symbolic rigidities are deftly uncovered, the energy is released in a most salubrious and uniquely human manner—laughter. For example, a young man[1] was recounting to his friends his miraculous escape from death that afternoon. It seems that the young man was brought up in the grand tradition of the West and as a small boy had received a silver bullet from his dad. "Son," his father told him at the time, "keep this bullet close to your heart; it will bring you good luck." As a dutiful son, the young man always kept the bullet in a vest pocket over his heart. One day the young man was walking down one of New York City's busy streets when a strong-minded hotel manager, who had previously warned representatives of the Gideon Society he did not wish Bibles placed in his hotel rooms, happened to find one hidden in an outside room. Furious, the irate, atheistic hotel manager hurled the book through the open window. "I saw that book coming at me lickety-split," the young man told his aston-

[1] Woodrow Allen, Esq.

ished audience," and I'm sure it would have gone right through my heart if it hadn't been for Pappy's silver bullet!"

The reversal of the sterotyped symbolism of "Bible" and "bullet" jolts one's validations of those objects and their usual action consequences. This tickles our imagination since the symbols are rarely, if ever, associated with such realities (bullet = shield; Bible = deadly missile). Alfred Hitchcock drolly illustrated this interchanging of symbolic attachments in the story about a wife who slaughters her husband by hitting him on the "noggin" with a frozen leg of lamb. She then casually defrosts and cooks the lamb and serves it to the police officers who have been searching for the murder weapon. Within the several possible realities of "leg of lamb" (frozen), these budding Sherlock Holmeses find none which suggest that the evidence is being destroyed by their own digestive systems.

To what extent does having learned a symbol in one way restrict other modes of interpretation? Does too great a concentration on the consensual validation of symbols in the early school years freeze the symbols and reduce their conceptual and behavioral alternatives? Some behavioral scientists and educators have commented on the loss of creativity and *joie de vivre* in school children. Is loss of flexibility in the use of action-symbol complexes a price we need to pay for validation? If man's symbolic skills go beyond the simple signal possibilities and provide him with a means of letting x equal whatever complex of ideas or events he wishes, there certainly needs to be common agreements on what x equals. But we need, at the same time, to enhance the symbolic world of the child by increasing the possibilities of other meanings for x.

Symbols and the Development of Imagination

In addition to the need to learn to use symbols in order to communicate to ourselves and others, and to be free to take on new conceptual models of knowledge, the child needs to learn how to use symbols to create realities of his own. Symbols are time-binding tools that allow men to move in time and space with relative freedom. With symbols a man can conjure up the future, re-experience the past, and play with the structure and function of the external world as he wishes. The teaching of the skills of utilizing symbols as conceptualizers of events, actions, and ideas beyond what can be seen, heard, touched, tasted, or felt is education's unique contribution to the humanizing of children.

Research on children's skills in conceptualizing time confirm the difficulty of the symbolizing function where time-related action has been limited. If children between eight and ten are asked to invent stories, those created by middle-class children cover greater periods of time than do those of lower-class children (19). As Fraisse points out, for children the conceptual and action reality of time was approximately the perceived distance between the awakening of a desire and its gratification. However, when children are pervasively involved in an activity, they are more surprised than adults by the rapid passage of time.

Time, as a symbolic and meaningful concept, is learned through action consequences. In one of Piaget's experiments children were asked to transfer objects from one box to another using a small pair of tongs. In one case the objects were small pieces of wood; in the other, heavy pieces of lead. It was easier to move the wood, and therefore, more pieces of wood were transferred than of lead in the same time period. When asked which took longer, a minority said "the wood because more pieces were moved"; the others said "the lead because it was more difficult." In any case, what counts in the conceptualization of time by children is the nature of the task and its mediation. The conceptualizations of time and space seem to grow out of and are enhanced by the enjoyment of symbol skills such as reading and speaking.

Clinical observation and descriptive evaluations of delinquent and nondelinquent children of the same socioeconomic status point to the enjoyment of reading as a significant differentiating characteristic. Delinquent and nondelinquent children in the same neighborhood face much the same difficult and unpleasant environment, but the delinquent can deal with the objects and events only with concrete and labeling kinds of symbols. Their symbolic lore does not contain a way of using symbols as a "release from immediacy." With this achievement Bruner suggests "the child can delay gratification by virtue of representing to himself what lies beyond the present, what other possibilities exist beyond the clue that is under his nose. The child may be ready for delay of gratification, but he is no more able to bring it off (without language) than somebody ready to build a house, save that he has not yet heard of tools." (11, p. 14)

Without reading-skill enjoyment, a child is caged by his own senses and vicarious images from mass media. One is struck by an occasional but notable example in which severe deprivation, either sensory or environmental, is overcome by what appears to be the singular skill of reading. Claude Brown's narration in *Manchild in the Promised Land* of his growth and development in the wild, hopeless, and dehumanizing slums of Harlem is a case in point. He could not wait to get to school so he could learn the game all the kids were playing—hookey. When he was later told he was a bad boy for doing so, he tried to explain to his mother that he was really a good boy trying to avoid trouble with the teacher.

Brown as an energetic, unsocialized, and uneducated adolescent spent a revolving-door existence between Harlem and various rehabilitation and treatment institutions. In one, he meets the kindly wife of the Superintendent of Warwick, Mrs. Cohen, whom he finds he can like. One day Mrs. Cohen gives him a book, the autobiography of "some woman," as Claude Brown puts it, named Mary McLeod Bethune. This is followed by books on Jackie Robinson, Sugar Ray Robinson, Einstein, and Schweitzer.

"After reading about a lot of these people, I started getting ideas about life. . . . This Einstein was a cat who really seemed to know how to live. . . . He seemed to be living all by himself; he's found a way to do what he wanted to in life and just make everybody accept it. . . . Then I read a book by Albert Schweitzer. . . . The man knew so much. I really started wanting to know things. I wanted to know things and I wanted to do things. . . .

"I kept reading and I kept enjoying it. I used to just sit around in the cottage reading. I didn't bother with people and nobody bothered me. *This was a way to be in Warwick and not to be there at the same time.*" [Italics mine.] (8, p. 151)

And so Brown found a way out of the constrictive immediacy of his life, new action and ideational resources, and an enjoyable skill to enlarge his time and space concepts. Sanford, in Chapter 3, comments on the same notion illustrated in *Studs Lonigan*.

In the area of research, a comparative study of the incidence of reading disability among boys found the highest, 83%, in a sample of delinquent and predelinquent children as compared to 33% of children in a child guidance clinic sample, and 10 per cent in a normal school group (16). Clinical studies confirm this major deficiency among delinquent children. Another study compared the time orientation of underachieving readers as compared to normal (up to grade level) readers in the New York City Public School System (26). It was hypothesized that children who were behind in reading would tend to be more constricted in their abilities to use time as an abstract concept. As expected, normal readers were able to project themselves into the future to a significantly greater degree than poor readers.

The Weightlessness of Symbols

Having learned to use symbols as binders of ideas, as openers of new knowledge, and as vehicles for imaginative thought, the child is ready to look "under the hood" at the essence of the tool he is using. He must learn the reality arbitrariness, and weightlessness of his symbolically constructed world. He needs to learn not to be over-burdened with words or to wallow, as Bellows' anti-hero Moses Herzog does, in his own ponderous excrescences and weighty overloads in the world of words. How to do this?

In the beginning was the pun, says Samuel Beckett. In his novel *Murphy*, Kelley wonders if Celia or any other human being really exists. "Celia," says Mr. Kelley, to himself, '*S'il ya*." (2, p. 115) We must be free to play with words to learn their true nature. It is only in this context that the Emperor can be seen as God made him—in his bare skin.

Words as symbols often weigh persons down with millstones and lead ballast. Educational processes have a way of wearing down a child's spontaneity and playfulness to funereal solemnity or a Wag-nerian Ring opera. To be able to see and generate humor with words enables the student to begin to differentiate between seriousness and play. "Participation in play and humor provides opportunity for prac-tice with this balancing skill. Becoming skilled in playing or joking (or riddle-telling or slapstick) provides us with a degree of skill in maintaining equilibrium of the two antithetical states spontaneity and thoughtfulness. When the balance is stable, the spontaneity of the ongoing process of life is not paralyzed by the detachment of thoughtfulness or self watchfulness or is not lost in a hysteria of spontaneity." (20, p. 22)

The pun, as Koestler points out, is the untying of an acoustic knot containing two strings of thought. He goes on to illustrate the strong ties between sound and meaning shown in the universal practices of word magic, spells and incantations. "Next to repetition, association by sound affinity—punning—is one of the notorious games of the un-derground, manifested in dreams, in the punning mania of children, and in mental disorders. The rhyme is nothing but a glorified pun—two strings of ideas tied in an acoustic knot. . . . Thus rhythm and assonance, pun and rhyme are not artificially created ornaments of speech; the whole evidence indicates that their origins go back to primitive—and infantile—forms of thought." (29, p. 315)

We have but to glance through *Peanuts* or *101 Elephant Jokes* to recognize the fun children can have playing with words and relieving themselves of the heavy bindings on these cultural vehicles. "How do you stop a herd of elephants from charging?" "By taking away their credit cards," is a form of word play that allows "charging" to change context and meaning abruptly, spontaneously, and pleasurably.

In the same way a pun can raise to a child's level of awareness the capricious nature of meaning and help him understand the arbitrary nature of symbols. If a symbol can be played with, it can be many things. When we shift contexts abruptly to show words up for what they are, we have been tricked and enlightened. Such double dealing is usually responded to by mass groaning and wailing. But no matter—as Boswell noted: "A good pun may be admitted among the smaller excellences of lively conversation."

The Symbolic Destiny of Man

The essence of education's mystique for man lies in his ability to use symbols such as words, numbers, sound symbols—like musical notes—and various art forms. As has been mentioned before, all knowledge and experiencing are packaged and shipped back and forth in the minds of men as symbols.

But wherein lies the vigor and force of man's symbolic development and skills? Its power lies in allowing man to perceive himself (the baldest of all abstractions), to lift himself out of his physical world, to manage Father Time, to bind events, objects, and feelings (that is, to learn), to create ideas, worlds, and values of his own making. It is the power by which man is able to create for himself "n" degrees of freedom despite the limitations of his biological origin and physical environment. Life and death may well be circumscribed boundaries for human functioning; whereas death may destroy him, the concept of death enables him to live.[1]

With his symbols man has learned to produce and distribute some forms of knowledge to some members of its communities; he has learned to use public health approaches to prevent many contagious diseases but not as yet how to build more healthful and growth producing environments for all people; man has learned to enslave symbols with increasing technical skill only to find himself trapped and constricted by his own bonds. Nevertheless, these three currents are at flood level as they approach our educational institutions. Knowledge

[1] Hegel said it this way: "While death may destroy a man, the idea of death saves him."

being the kind of avalanche it is, it will no longer be possible, indeed if it ever was possible, for anyone—student or teacher—to "cover the course." Lack of success by large groups of children in the processes of learning can no longer be regarded as amenable to remedial or treatment processes, necessary as these may be for individual children. The school must find its own swamps, its own vitamin deficiencies, its own Salk and Sabin vaccines to make children more effective and more healthy learners right from the start. Ecologically minded educational administrators will need to anticipate the points in the systems of the community and the school where children are at risk and to strengthen the child-system interaction at these points. (See Chapter 21.)

Finally, it is becoming clear that man has been so seduced by his symbolic tools that his goals have been displaced and short circuited. Symbols are vehicles for increasing the freedom of human behavior. The process by which such symbols are learned significantly affect their utility. For example, symbols have a way of being mediated to children without being grounded in sensory or cerebral experiences; high level abstractions are piled on higher level abstractions until Cloud Nine begins to look like solid earth. Symbols and knowledge become so inextricably and firmly tied together that new knowledge and new concepts have difficulty getting into action. Learning, in other words, can and often does curtail rather than enhance human growth. Symbols, like people, need a firm base but also freedom to grow and change.

Education as a process and the school as a primary humanizing institution stand squarely in the middle of these swirling waters. Although there are small beginnings in some places[1] and in some content-child relationships such as mathematics, physics, and language arts programs, the catch-up distance for educational systems as a whole is vast.

All that has gone before, and man's attempt to make more and better human beings out of his children is now focused on man's one unique resource—the unheralded hero of his learning potential, his ego processes.

REFERENCES

1. Beckett, Samuel. *Molloy*. New York: Grove Press, 1955.
2. Beckett, Samuel. *Murphy*. London: Routledge Press, 1938.

[1] Nova Elementary and High School, Fort Lauderdale and Melbourne, Florida; Oakleaf Elementary School in Pittsburg, Penn., and a few other places, but not many.

3. Beker, Jerome. "The Influence of School Camping on the Self Concepts and Social Relationships of Sixth Grade School Children." *J. Educational Psych.,* **51,** 1960, 352–356.
4. Block, Jack. "Ego Identity, Role Variability and Adjustment." *J. Consulting Psych.,* **25,** May 1961, 392–397.
5. Bloomberg, Claire M., and Carolyn H. Troupe. "Big Brothers to Troubled Children." *NEA Journal,* **53,** No. 1, Jan. 1964, 22–25.
6. Boocock, S. S., and J. S. Coleman. "Games with Simulated Environments in Learning." *Sociology of Education,* **39,** Summer 1966, 215–236.
7. Bridgman, P. W. *The Way Things Are.* Cambridge: Harvard University Press, 1959.
8. Brown, Claude, *Manchild in the Promised Land.* New York: Macmillan Co., 1965.
9. Brown, Joseph. "Unpredictability—Margin for Inspiration." *Architectural Record,* Sept. 1955, 225–228.
10. Brown, Roger W., Raymond A. Leiter, and Donald C. Hildum. "Metaphors from Music Criticism." *J. Abnormal and Social Psychology,* **54,** May 1957, 347–352.
11. Bruner, Jerome, S. "The Course of Cognitive Growth." *Amer. Psychol.,* **19,** January 1964.
12. Burck, Gilbert. "Knowledge: The Biggest Growth Industry of Them All." *Fortune,* November 1964.
13. Cassel, John. "Social Science Theory as a Source of Hypotheses in Epidemiological Research." *Amer. J. Public Health,* **54,** Sept. 1964, 1482–1488.
14. *Community Apprentice Program: Disadvantaged Youth in Human Services,* 1965. Center for Youth and Community Studies, Howard University, Washington, D.C.
15. Drucker, Peter. "American Directions: A Forecast." *Harpers Magazine,* Feb. 1965.
16. Dubos, Rene. *Mirage of Health.* New York: Harper and Row, 1959.
17. Esslin, Martin. *The Theatre of the Absurd.* New York: Anchor Books, 1961.
18. Fabian, A. A. "Reading Disability: An Index of Pathology." *American J. Orthopsychiatry,* **35,** April 1955, 319–328.
19. Fraisse, Paul. *The Psychology of Time.* New York: Harper and Row. 1963.
20. Fry, William F. Jr. *Sweet Madness, A Study of Humor.* Palo Alto, Calif.: Pacific Books, 1963.
21. Gombrich, E. H. "The Use of Art for the Study of Symbols." *Amer. Psychol.,* **20,** Jan. 1965, 34–50.
22. Gordon, William J. "The Metaphorical Way of Knowing," in Gyorgy Kepes (Ed.), *Education of Vision.* New York: George Braziller Inc., 1965.
23. Hobbs, Nicholas. "Mental Health's Third Revolution." *Amer. J. Orthopsychiatry,* **34,** Oct. 1964, 822–833.
24. Humphrey, James H. "Comparison of the Use of Active Games and Language Workbook Exercises as Learning Media in the Development of Language Understandings with Third Grade Children." *Perceptual and Motor Skills,* **21,** 1965, 23–26.
25. James, David (Ed.) *Outward Bound.* London: Routledge and Kegan Paul, 1957.

26. Kahn, Paul. "Time Orientation and Reading Achievement." *Perceptual and Motor Skills,* **21,** 1965, 157–158.

27. Karpus, Robert. "One Physicist Looks at Science Education." Presented at the eighth ASCD Curriculum Research Institute, April 27, 1963.

28. Keller, Helen. *The Story of my Life.* New York: Grosset and Dunlap, 1902.

29. Koestler, Arthur. *The Act of Creation.* New York: Macmillan Co., 1964.

30. Langer, Susanne. *Philosophy in a New Key.* New York: Mentor Books, 1948.

31. Lippitt, P., and J. E. Lohman. "Cross-Age Relationships—An Educational Resource." *Children,* **12,** 1965, 113–117.

32. Loughmiller, Campbell. *Wilderness Road.* Austin, Texas: The Hogg Foundation for Mental Health and the University of Texas, 1965.

33. Machlup, Fritz. *The Production and Distribution of Knowledge in the United States.* Princeton, N.J.: Princeton University Press, 1962.

34. McLuhan, Marshall. *Understanding Media: The Extensions of Man.* New York: McGraw-Hill, 1964.

35. Miller, Arthur. "The Writer as Independent Spirit." *Saturday Review,* June 4, 1966.

36. Moffet, James. "A Structural Curriculum in English." *Harvard Educational Review,* **36,** Winter 1966.

37. Osgood, Charles E. "An Exploration into Semantic Space," in Wilbur Schramm (Ed.), *The Science of Human Communication.* New York: Basic Books, 1963.

38. Pedersen, Frank A., and Eugene J. Sullivan. "Relationships Among Geographical Mobility, Parental Attitudes and Emotional Disturbances in Children." *American J. Orthopsychiatry,* **34,** April 1964, 575–580.

39. Porter, E. H. "Parable of the Spindle." *ETC.,* **20,** 1963, 291–311.

40. Shibutani, Tamatsu. *Society and Personality.* Englewood Cliffs, N.J.: Prentice-Hall, 1961.

41. Smith, Geddes. *Plague On Us.* New York: The Commonwealth Fund, 1941.

42. Spolin, Viola. *Improvisation for the Theater: A Handbook of Teaching and Directing Techniques.* Evanston, Ill.: Northwestern University Press, 1963.

43. Thorndike, E. L. *Animal Intelligence.* New York: Macmillan Co., 1911.

Chapter 2

The Confluence of the Three Rivers— Ego-Processes

Eli M. Bower

The Confluence of the Three
Rivers—Ego Processes

There have been times when man could be said to have lost his mind; but to never have discovered his ego-processes is, as Allport pointed out, one of the oddest events in the history of modern psychology and education (1). For whatever knowing is or knowing does, ego-processes are and do. All of man's symbolic activities—his primary and secondary processes of thinking and conceptualization—are managed by and through ego-processes. The problem which education and the behavioral sciences face is how to organize content and learning processes so that the individual becomes a more effective, freer, and creative ingester and user of knowledge.

EGO PROCESSES AS MEDIATORS OF KNOWLEDGE

The concept of mediation as the major function of ego-processes needs specification and clarification. Mediation means active interpretation or conceptualization of sensory data. To mediate is to find meaning or to connect what is perceived as being out there with what is inside self. Jensen defines mediation as the process of responding to our responses or associations to sensory stimulation. The ability and capacity for verbally mediated responding "frees the learner from having his responses bound to specific stimuli and it makes for a degree of generalization and transfer of experience far beyond the narrow limitations of primary stimulus generalization. (15, p. 101) Jensen goes on to describe several specific kinds of mediational processes such as labeling (ego-differentiation processes), transposition, abilities to shift figure and ground, and syntactical mediation. But where and how does such mediation take place?

Somewhere between the external and internal world of man and his behavior is a dark tunnel in which the symbolically structured learnings travel back and forth. The tunnel seems to have magic

48

qualities by which it can select incoming vehicles, pattern or change them, and have them emerge in stereotyped, somewhat changed, or surprisingly unexpected responses. This dark tunnel is a complex series of personality functions called ego-processes. The mystique of educational competency lies somewhere in the stygian darkness of these functions.

Being able to get a little more light into the dark tunnel would probably help the reader (and the writer). At present all we know are inferences and concepts which seemingly explain the properties of the tunnel by its consequences. Ego[1] is a learned pattern of personal functioning *organized and organizing* to process information from the inner and outer environment. Another way to define "it" is as follows: those aspects of the personality which take in and use data. Or if you wish: those functions of the personality which scan the inner and outer world, select inputs, assign meaning, select meaning, assign inputs, and use such meaning and input in behavior.

Ego-processes are the chief administrator of the human body and personality. They are patterned, forged, and developed as the child learns to cope with himself and his environment. Ego-processes, however, are not synonomous with self-concept—they are the processes that select data from the environment to fashion and refashion a self.

Some of the specific functions of ego-processes will be discussed in the last section. There are, however, three major functions that are generally observable and that may help in understanding the relationship of ego and educational processes. These are the (1) organizing, (2) binding, and (3) testing functions.

THE ORGANIZING FUNCTION

That old venerable war horse of educational practice, the law of effect, postulated learning as a consequence of association—contiguous, Pavlovian conditioned, operantly conditioned and others—between a stimulus or input and a response or a behavior. Under normal conditions responses were learned where associations between stimulus and response could be said to be reinforced, that is, bound together by pleasure, reward, or some positive payoff. However, the administration of the law was complicated by the fact that one child's pleasure turned out to be another's Chinese torture. In addition, what was enjoyable in one context became at times gruesome in another. A

[1] Ego-processes, that is—another example of making things out of functions. We will use "processes" to remind us of this fact.

savory slice of roast beef (medium rare) might be a hedonic delight when hungry but the unkindest cut of all when satiated. Or a child who had mastered a pleasurable skill would seldom continue to pursue these ends, despite his lengthy rewarding experience with the task.

Studies of children with high dependency needs (clinging to mother, doesn't like baby sitter, needs to see mother around at all times) show that when mothers "punish" (negatively reinforce) such behavior by scolding, shouting, placing in a locked room, and so forth, such behavior is increased. We might say then that the child's ego-processes are so organized that what appears to the mother as negative reinforcement is seen by the child as positive reinforcement. So then when clinging, dependent behavior is "rewarded" by words, a soft pat or other signs of spoiling or giving in to the child, clinging behavior may decrease depending on the ego-organization of the child (26).

We are not out of the woods yet, since many parents know that approximately the same stimulus will have different learning consequences at different times. Clinging behavior *can* be reduced, suppressed, or inhibited by punishment and enhanced, encouraged, and developed by reward. Conceptually, the differential behavior responses can best be understood in relation to the organization of ego-processes at the time.

As an organized executive, the ego seeks rational or logical concepts around which to build its strength. As was suggested earlier, man's ego-processes emerged out of a need to understand and explain his own primary processes of thinking. Whether we consider the environment ordered, rational or natural, the ego seeks some conceptual organization from which to look inside and outside self. Unfortunately, not all of the conceptual organization of ego-processes are at levels of awareness where we can say they are visible or known to the individual.

Where an individual's experiential or biological development has been severely harassed and his ego processes function like a student driver on a crowded 70-mile-an-hour freeway, survival may depend on the variety and depth of defensive measures the ego can work into the organism's personality. The greater the degree and extent of such defenses, the greater the rigidity and constriction of the personality. It is also possible for some children to grow up with little or loosely organized ego-development. These persons have difficulty hanging on to experience or internalizing the moral imperatives of society. Such children process data without much chance for integration or expansion of ego-processes. The horror of Capote's recounting of the development of the murderers, Hickock and Smith, from small

children to adult children lies in Smith's statement: "I didn't want
to harm the man. I thought he was a very nice gentleman. Soft-spoken.
I thought so right up to the moment I cut his throat. . . . I wonder
why I did it. . . . I don't know why. . . . I was sore at Dick. The
tough guy. The phony brass boy." (18, p. 67)

There is one characteristic of the organization of ego-processes
which puts it in the forefront in relationship to the external world.
The ego is an active seeker of inputs, a constructor of patterns,
mosaics, and meanings. Objects and events do not enter ego-processes;
they are selected, assigned properties and meaning, and actively
ingested.

Ego-processes are not empirical bits and pieces; they seek stimuli
that are perceived as preserving and enhancing the organism. Effective
ego-processes are organized to seek and find challenging and novel
exchanges with the environment, much as a tennis player seeks bigger
and better opponents to sharpen his game. Buhler (5) contends that
the thrust of the ego's force is toward mastery of the environment
and that a well-paced, exciting stream of stimuli is its goal. Others
like Craik (9) suggest that the nervous system seeks a symbolic model
of the world so that it can help the organism react in a safer, more
competent manner. Koestler (16) feels that humans function not
only by responding to the environment but by asking it questions.
Such ego-processes tend to steer the organism toward experiences
which have possibilities for surprise, conflict, uncertainty, and novelty.
Studies of effectively functioning adolescents seem to bear this out.
Such students were found to be characterized by tendencies to explore,
scan, and reach out for new experiences in a pleasurable and exciting
manner (28).

THE BINDING FUNCTION OF THE EGO

Ego-processes not only organize and reorganize knowledge and
themselves, but can tie or hold on to such knowledge. Symbols are
the tools by which this magic is accomplished. Without the tools of language and numbers, little if any knowledge can be packaged and
stored. To tie knowledge effectively into symbols, the symbols need
meaningful conceptual glue.

Among the primary kinds of knowledge needed to be bound into
ego-processes are data about time, space, and human relationships.
We need to learn about the nature of solids, liquids, and gases, the
laws of gravitation, flight, and thermodynamics, as well as the consequences of colliding with an automobile, an older sister or an outraged

father. Although the reality of clock time may be visible to the child, the abstract conception of time is often difficult to learn. The entire process of education involves binding a positive concept of "future"—a concept of much relevance and some understanding to middle-class children. It may, however, be difficult for lower-class children to conceptualize future time as pleasurable and meaningful when they are fighting for their self-respect and survival. Or it may be difficult to a Mexican-American child whose time-binding experiences are intimately tied to his family's traditions and past history (see Chapter 12 by Kluckhohn).

Knowledge packed into symbols contains a number of things: intellectual content, the learning process itself, the beliefs, feelings, and manner of the teacher as perceived by the learner, the tone, texture, and trivia of the experience. It seems probable that when the knowledge is unpacked or used, all its contents are released. Knowledge is bound as cognitive-affective transactions, and these multidimensional entities find their separateness only in the perceptions of overambitious parents, hostile intellectuals, and overworked mental health workers.

THE REALITY TESTING FUNCTION OF THE EGO

At one time personality theorists drew their conceptual bindings from Freud and modified Freudian theories. Such theories began with a description of personality which, like Gaul, was divided into three inherently contentious factions—the id, ego, and superego. Much early psychoanalytic practice focused on uncovering the newly discovered unconscious psychic life, especially the repressed instincts or drives (id) and the internalized, introjected parents (superego). In this interplay of id, ego, and superego the source of the energy for the fighting came from libidinal or sexually tinged wellsprings in the id. Personality then was seen as an automobile with the id under the hood providing four, six, or eight cylinders of power; the ego at the wheel attempting to keep the car from hitting others, being hit, or running out of gas; and the superego or rules of the road tucked somewhere in the ego's driving cap. Unfortunately, in these early days the driver of the car received less attention than the engine. It was with techniques for the exploration and uncovering of unconscious repressed drives that the psychoanalysts led the early mental health workers into battle. To some extent the ego or mediating processes were seen as blocks or obstructions in getting at the deeper recesses of the person.

In 1911 Freud proposed a new concept of mental functioning which he called the reality principle. (11) In this essay Freud proposed that in addition to their job as mediators of conflict, ego processes grow out of conflict-free experiences. The ego or ego-processes of the personality in this scheme take on the job of searching or scanning the outer world, perceiving, assimilating, testing, and storing data of value and significance to the individual. In the development of the reality principle (expressed by G. B. Shaw as being "able to choose the line of greatest advantage instead of yielding in the direction of least resistance"), ego-progresses are developed to mediate objects, events, and stresses in the real world as well as managing and holding on to the fantasy-making processes of the pleasure principle. Freud suggested that just as a nation preserves certain territory within its boundaries in a wilderness state for play and vacations, so effective ego-processes need to include manageable access to its primitive areas.

There was, unfortunately, little follow-up to Freud's 1911 formulations. Psychoanalysts continued to expand and describe the machinations of the ego as it attempted to fend off onrushing id drives or restrictive superego guilt. Although psychotherapists began to pay more attention to ego-processes as the key to effective treatment, much of the focus was on uncovering defenses so that the war within the person could become less hectic or even be made to disappear.

But absence of war does not make a nation or a person effective in his environment. Skills, knowledge, organization, goals, and rewards may be required. Releasing highly constricted and defended ego-processes may in some persons allow such abilities to emerge. In others the removal of such defenses may reveal lack of social and educational skills, lack of purpose and goals. In recent years it has become clear that ego-processes, which mediate the individual's attempts to be successful in his environments (inner and outer) are developed and molded not only by the resolution of ego-id, ego-superego conflicts but by independent or conflict-free spheres of human challenge and growth.

Like Cinderella in her disheveled rags, these aspects of ego-processes have always been around but without the glamour and visibility of the other sisters. Although some "old-fashioned" social workers and school teachers seemed to be aware of the potential of this aspect of ego-processes, it took a number of princes [Hartmann, (13) Rapaport, (22) R. W. White, (32) and others] to fit the glass slipper to Cinderella's foot and bring her to the attention of the world. Hartman's monograph (13) said directly that ego-processes are concerned with and are born out of the individual's attempts to be competent in his environment. Effectiveness in control of body, in the use of muscles, in sensory experiences, in play and games, becomes significant stuff for ego-adaptation. As White points out (32), when most animal research was being performed on frightened or sexually aroused animals, play, curiosity, learning, and exploration behavior were seldom observed. In his review of animal research up to 1958, Butler concludes that learning does not require recourse to rewards such as food, water, sex, or escape from pain but instead that often perceptual consequences of behavior can and often do serve as the reward. (6)

To increase the social and individual competency of an experientially deprived child, ego skills of differentiation must be learned. How do we help a child who experiences the world in diffused, misty images, and who lacks sufficient concepts and symbols to separate and file a wide variety of objects, events, and feelings? The reality function of ego-processes in the child is different from that of animals—it is primarily one of wrestling with human institutions and societal demands for human behavior. The normal expectations of the ego are for a succession of positive events, a succession anticipated correctly by most children but which does not develop for some.

PROGRAMMING SPECIFIC EGO-PROCESSES INTO EDUCATIONAL EXPERIENCES

What kinds of information-processing equipment is required to enhance a child's growth and development? Often the question is asked in reverse: what ego-deficiencies or inadequacies block learning and development? Although we have learned much from studies of human malfunctioning, there is no reason to believe that the "flip side" of these concepts can be useful in understanding how to build effective humanizing ego-processes.

Past research on ego-processes related to educational activities has been scattered and the results difficult to implement in any humanizing institution. Lois Murphy has enumerated several positive ego-processes or coping mechanisms in young children. She sees mental health as a balance between ego and instinctual strengths observable in such behavior as perceptual clarity, motor tension release, flexible distribution of energy, ability to accept limits, and resilience in mobilizing resources under stress (20, p. 235).

Kroeber differentiates the characteristics of defensive ego-behavior from coping ego-behavior in behavioral dimensions and goes on to identify ten ego-mechanisms and their manifestations. These are (1) discrimination, (2) detachment, (3) means-end symbolization, (4) selective awareness, (5) sensitivity, (6) delayed responses, (7) time reversal, (8) impulse diversion, (9) impulse transformation, (10) impulse restraint. Using specific definitions related to each of these ego processes, Kroeber found that ratings of ego-mechanisms from tapes could be used to predict responses on the Rorschach Test to a significant degree. He emphasizes the need to investigate the relationship of general intelligence to ego processes as well as studies of ego-mechanisms over long periods of time. (17)

In the following section, five specific ego-processes have been polarized into effective and ineffective types. They have been chosen as dimensions for exploration because of the possibilities of programming the positive ones into educational practices. The examples of such programs given in each section are exploratory. We would be hard pressed to cite research on these programs within this conceptual model. Also the separation of each of the dimensions does not in reality untie it from the other four. All are part of the organizing, binding, and reality testing of personality and serve as a unit in processing data from the inner and outer environment of the child.

An attempt has been made to take advantage of the odds that one good picture can equal a thousand words. Each of the ego dimensions described in the text is represented graphically with some of the mediational skills developed in each process listed underneath. To understand the flow and meaning of each figure one should begin with the center photograph which is the same in each of the five figures. The photograph contains an object, in this case a woman or mother. Somewhere in his writings Norbert Wiener comments on the remarkable skill of the human mind to recognize outline drawings. He suggests therefore that our perceptual processes probably see boundaries more clearly and succinctly and other aspects less clearly. In any case, the lower arrows suggest the *organization* of this object by the perceptual-affective-cognitive apparatus of the beholder. Such organization will be based on the mediational or ego skills present in the person at the time. In Figure 2.2, for example, the skills conceptualized as ego differentiation has helped the perceiver to separate mother from other women and give her shape and clarity as a person. On the other side, ego diffusion has resulted in an object difficult to separate from other objects and a hazy, unspecified figure ground relationship.

In each case the individual calls up some symbol with which he can control and bind the perceptual experience. The symbol however conceptualizes the perceived image to include all its clarity and conciseness on the left hand and all its fogginess and nebulousness on the right hand. The symbol then becomes the motor vehicle which moves between the self and the inner and outer world of objects, events, and feelings.

Experiences are continually being deposited by active engagements with the environment and being "banked" by symbols. The unique characteristic, however, of this banking process is that one cannot withdraw deposits and start over with a clean slate. One can alter or recount deposits as a result of new experiences but, unlike our wonderful machines, one cannot wipe the slate clean for a new problem.

The top arrows represent feedback mechanisms with the flow moving swiftly from the differentiated or diffused symbol and the external world to ask and answer such questions as: Is my perception confirmed or rejected, clarified or confused by other perceptions; what other experiences confirm or clarify my interpretation; why is a diffused perception of mother better for me than a differentiated one? Feedback represents the reality testing mechanism in all ego functions and is needed to process data on the basis of the survival, safety, and self-esteem of the organism.

The diagrams are, of course, flat and static representations of ego-processes which are in constant multidimensional motion during our wakeful hours and to some extent during sleep.

THE DIFFERENTIATION-DIFFUSION DIMENSION
(See Figure 2.1)

All ego-processes are sharpened and developed out of the mediation of experiences and symbols which encourage active, exploratory relationships with the environment. Research by Bowlby (4), Goldfarb (12), Spitz (30), Skeels, and Skodak (29) implicates early social deprivation as a prime factor in the development or organismic lethargy and a deficiency of *joie de vivre*. The differentiation-diffusion dimension has to do with the quality, quantity, and content of a child's transactions with persons and things so that images and symbols can be focused and delineated one from another. To some extent ego-differentiation processes are the food and vitamins of the other ego-processes. Children who are fed balanced meals and vitamins have a base from which to grow. Ego-processes developing on diets deficient in basic ingredients will be woefully weak as a result of insufficient mediational energy or a lack of varieties of objects, events, and symbols to bind into effective ego processes.

Deutsch and his staff at the New York University (10) have set their sights at reversing the ego-diffusion processes in lower-class children through planned exposure to transpersonal experiences in differ-

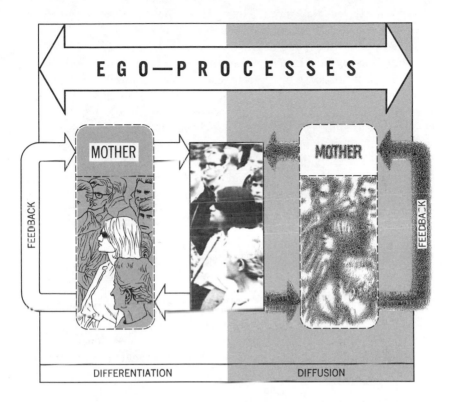

Figure 2.1. Skills in ego differentiation.
1. *Separating* objects, events and feelings.
2. *Discovering* symbols for objects, events, and feelings.
3. *Conceptualizing* objects, events, and feelings.
4. *Relating* to mediational adults.

entiating objects, events, and feelings. For example, in their experimental preschool classes, the teacher, when speaking to the child, will bend down close to him, face him at eye level and speak with full lip movement. The program also includes games in which names are used in different contexts and where label and image are repeatedly linked by concepts.

Toy telephones and tapes have been found helpful in the development of language usage and in the differentiation of words. Toy telephone booths separated by opaque walls make talking mandatory for the nonverbal child. Taping and playback are often helpful to the child in his learning to designate, separate, and communicate about objects, events, and feelings. Here the emphasis is on giving the experientially deprived child competence and confidence in language as a mode of communication.

Many Nursery and Project Head Start programs utilize exercises in the differentiation of figures from their backgrounds, training in the differentiation and identification of sounds, the manipulation of a variety of objects, colors, shapes, textures, and visually symbolic materials. Also included in such programs are self-identification exercises such as self-labeling games before a mirror, photographs, and stories that lend themselves to identification. Time binding is stressed through activities that are routinized and ordered and that move logically from one activity to another.

Hess (14) has approached the problem of ego-differentiation processes from another direction—that of extending and expanding the mother-child learning relationship into specific conceptual areas. In one study the mothers are taught three simple tasks and asked to teach these tasks to the child. The tasks include (1) simple sorting of objects by color and function, (2) complex sorting using blocks with varied shapes and markings, and (3) copying designs on an "Etch-a-Sketch" toy. This is a device on which lines can be drawn through the use of two knobs, one for mother, one for child.

In differentiating the styles of mothers in teaching their children the sorting tasks, here is an example of a middle-class mother outlining the task and explaining the conceptual differentiation required by the child. "All right Susan, this board is the place where we put the little toys; first of all you are supposed to learn how to place them according to color. Can you do that? The things that are all the same color you put in one section; in the second section you put another group of colors, and in the third section you put the last group of colors. Can you do that? Or would you like to see me do it first?" Child: "I want to do it." She does. Contrast this with a mother who introduces the same task thus: "Now I'll take them all off the board; now you put them all back on the board. What are these?"

Child: "A truck."
Mother: "All right, just put them right here; put the other one right here; put the other one right here; all right, put the other one there." A third mother introduces the task thus: "I've got some chairs and cars; do you want to play the game? No response. "O.K., what's this?"
Child: A wagon.

Mother: Hmm?
Child: A wagon.
Mother: This is no wagon; what's this?

There are little or no clues by which the latter two children can master the task and communicate with their mothers about the conceptual rationale to be used in the game. There is also very little differentiation of data processes in this relationship, since the goal of the task is unclear and unfocused for the child. As Hess points out, the latter two mothers lack tags or symbols for encoding the task, and consequently the child lacks decoding experience. As a result, curiosity and interest in differentiating out the objects and perceptions is discouraged. Ego-processes remain diffused, unformed, and unable to focus on particular sights, sounds, and meanings and their vehicles.

The lack of sufficient ego-differentiating experiences in lower-class, deprived children makes this personality defect a major source of individual and social maladjustment. This is especially critical for children in the school, since this institution demands skill and competency in the utilization of this ego-process. Indeed the binding and tying of symbols cannot proceed without emotional support and motivation for processes of differentiation. Similarly, processes of differentiation cannot go far forward without a repertoire of symbols by which things, events, and feelings can be delineated. In essence, the processes of differentiation require both symbols in the form of language and numbers and also a feeling that it is safe to explore the environment to see, touch, hear, smell, and taste all there is.

Finally, differentiation processes require biological and physiological capacities to differentiate objects and use symbols. Severely retarded or neurologically impaired children often find such tasks difficult but not impossible to accomplish. Some of the earliest and best work in creating instructional programs to enhance ego-differentiation processes were developed by professional persons concerned with the education of environmentally or biologically retarded children. In 1799 Itard, a young French medical student, attempted and was partially successful in educating Victor, the Wild Boy of Aveyron, by "preparing his senses to receive keener impressions." Seguin, Froebel, Pestalozzi, and Montessori, among many, have proposed many interesting and provocative ideas for increasing human capabilities for differentiation. Montessori's idea of encouraging movement, discovery, and work in a prepared environment and Froebel's use of play as a learning mode are finding new adherents in the schools of today.

THE FIDELITY-DISTORTION DIMENSION (See Figure 2.2)

Metaphorically there is some sense in conceptualizing fidelity ego-processes as processing sound (or any other sense impression) with high clarity and accuracy. In essence, the binding of symbols in the development of ego-processes is to help the organism to be safe in his environment. His safety depends on his knowing cognitively and affectively where he is, who he is, and what is what.

To "test" reality or more accurately to encounter and learn the nature of the environment, we need ego-processes that do not significantly distort the external world of things, people, and stuff. All ego-processes distort to some extent, since all ego-processes are products

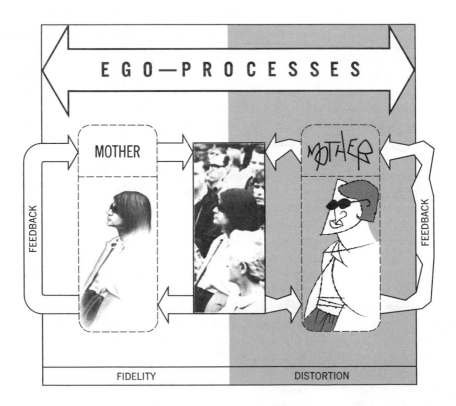

Figure 2.2. Skills in ego fidelity.
1. *Testing* perceptions of objects, events, and feelings.
2. *Tying* symbols to objects, events, and feelings.
3. *Untying* symbols as in play, jokes, games, and creative writing.
4. *Linking* words and action.

of idiosyncratic experiences. Our perceptions are always deviations from or approximations to the external object or event.

One type of distortion of perception takes place by means of defenses or mental mechanisms that carry such tags as projection, rationalization, reaction formation, undoing, and displacement. In projection, the behavior of others may be regarded as threatening or hostile as a result of our ego-processes casting on to others what we are perceiving. In displacement, emotion that has been bound in symbols of earlier experiences can be set off by what appear to be similar experiences with objects, interpersonal relationships, or transactions.

Ego-processes with high fidelity perceive and process inputs in a consensually validated manner. Such processes also permit and encourage use of imagination or creativity in response to environmental input. Since such flights of fancy are not frightening to the ego-processes they can be allowed to proceed in a controlled yet spontaneous manner. Individuals with ego-processes that distort inputs usually have little insight or awareness to the nature and extent of the distortion. The individual perceives "correctly" and acts on this. Yet his deviation or approximation to the object or event may be so wide of the mark that communication with him becomes difficult or in some cases impossible.

One of the basic tasks of the school is to help children use symbols as accurately as possible but with sufficient degrees of freedom to permit change in the meaning of the symbol. The teacher needs to consider the encoding of accurate meaning or experience in symbols a prime task of education. He must help the child take on the common symbols of our society with all their denotative and connotative encumbrances, avoiding the hardened cliché, rigid categorical, or absolutistic notions which often emerges in the process of learning. Moreover, the school must, in some cases, provide the real events, objects and relationships to which symbols can be tied. Democracy and Freedom as words are meaningless and dangerous unless they grow from real experiential roots and action bindings. This need is especially true of symbols with high level abstract meaning. Such symbols, unless tied down by meaningful experiences, are like boats in a storm that can be tossed this way or that depending on the wind or current.

In this connection schools can extend children's awareness of the properties of symbols which can be used to mean anything we wish. A word often can and does cut like a sword, and recovery from such a wound can be just as difficult as that from pierced skin. In a society where words and acts are often interchangeable, words are often substituted for somewhat unrelated realities. To some extent, educational transactions can be like Koko's reply to the Mikado when His Highness learns that an order to behead Nanki-Poo, the Mikado's son, has not been carried out.

"It's like this," says Koko, "when your Majesty says let a thing be done, it's as good as done—practically, it is done—because your Majesty's will is law. Your Majesty says kill a gentleman and a gentleman is told off to be killed. Consequently, that gentleman is as good as dead, practically he is dead—and if he is dead why not say so?" To which the Mikado replies, as any educated person would, "Nothing could possibly be more satisfactory!" (8, p. 399)

Often children are given the symbols of an education with few if any conceptual or action correlates. Rovere, commenting on Senator Joe McCarthy and the McCarthy era, points out that "we will take the symbols of the established fact for the fact itself." "I discovered this weakness in myself," says Rovere,

". . . Examining his (McCarthy's) photostats and his onion skin carbons of official correspondence, I had taken their relevance for granted; relevance had seemed somehow a condition of their existence and the "fact" that they were facts, i.e. they existed, they could be seen with the naked eye, they could be held in the hand had induced me to follow him quite a distance down his garden path. But of course they were no "facts," relevant or otherwise, but only symbols of factuality, and he knew it was characteristic of most Americans to make the mistake I had made. The characteristic is encouraged if it is not developed by our education and its acquisitive approach to data." (23, p. 167)

THE PACING—OVERLOADING DIMENSION

Pacing is the ability of ego-processes to manage the slings and arrows of fortune and misfortune with increasing competence, control, and spontaneity. The constructive and controlled release of emotional energy requires a spindle which can take care of overloads and keep messages in order. The capacity to pace and control inputs from the inner and outer environment is a product of learnings not often taught in formal curriculum. Pacing entails the ability to show joy as well as tears when appropriate. A symbol or concept that is overloaded

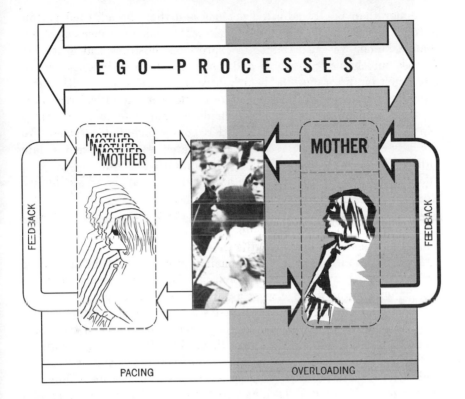

Figure 2.3. Skills in ego pacing.

1. *Regulating* heavy or light environmental inputs.
2. *Adjusting* disproportionate loads on symbols.
3. *Enhancing* and controlling imaginative and spontaneous activities.
4. *Exploring* new and varied unloading techniques and platforms.

with emotion and tightly bound to its action source can weigh down the communication possibilities of the symbol or concept. In some cases the overloading will result in a blandness or sterility of response, as in one too frightened to let go for fear his entire structure will crack.

Some types of experiences seem to be helpful in building more balanced and paced ego-processes. One is the conscious introduction of humor into school curriculum. Humor supplies a way to discharge emotional energy held in check by our rational or secondary processes. O'Connell, in his investigation of the adaptive functions of wit and humor, found that well-adjusted persons have a greater appreciation of humor than poorly adjusted persons and that the adjusted person is freer to use hostile wit under stress (21). Schopenhauer suggested that in humor we get a chance to express our hostility and bitterness against our chains—the words and language which enslave us. Therefore, such bindings must be held lightly if we are to play with them. Laughter requires social appropriateness and a metaphorical readiness to see resemblances in things which differ and differences in things which appear to be similar. Koestler points out that although we are all seriously embarrassed by a stutterer, someone like the late Jimmy Savo could make us laugh by imitating a stutterer. Setting and expectation are crucial. Children will not laugh or see humor where the teacher sees none and expects none.

There is little doubt that the comprehension of humor is related to age, ability to differentiate joke from nonjoke setting, and a psychological openness for rapid shifts in meaning.

Another resource for learning pacing processes can be a puppet or role-playing area in a classroom. In one fourth grade room, a set of puppets and a stage were used by a boy to replay periodically the hectic and disorganized breakfast scene he had just left at home. This was done as a solo while the teacher straightened the room and other children were readying themselves for reading groups.

The use of problem stories as role-playing initiators can be effective and helpful (27,31). Teachers, however, need to become competent in managing this kind of learning within the experience and curriculum content of the class. When so done, it can be supportive for some children and helpful in learning pacing techniques for others. Any class in English, poetry, literature, or drama can become an excellent unloading platform. Literature can represent the drama and crisis of life in a way that arouses a student's identification and empathy with the personal or interpersonal problems in the story or play. Often, student feelings are touched by the writer; and with the help of an insightful teacher, these feelings can be identified, externalized, and expressed.

Pacing processes require effectiveness in dealing with periods of boredom (underloading) as well as with large gulps of activity and personal crisis (overloading).

One final note on the pacing-overloading dimension. Overloading can and does occur as a result of deficient physiological mechanisms as in the case of sensory deprivation or brain injury. The consequence of sudden discharges in a *grand mal* seizure may be as difficult for the ego-processes of a child to manage as severe environmental stress or neglect.

THE EXPANSION—CONSTRICTION DIMENSION

As a system open to the environment, ego-process needs new energies and new inputs in order to develop new adaptive skills, to permit higher levels of symbol development, and to encourage conceptual breadth and depth. Such growth brings with it increasing degrees of freedom for behavior and learning; as a result, the organism actively seeks new and varied inputs. Ego-processes can only expand quantitatively and qualitatively if they are able to successfully manage the challenge of new stresses and new sources of stimuli. Expansion of ego-processes is a dual victory; we have successfully coped with a new problem and we have incorporated a new experience.

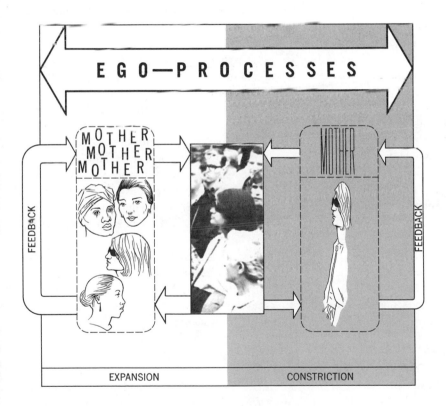

Figure 2.4. Skills in ego expansion.
1. *Seeking* new metaphors for objects, events, and feelings.
2. *Playing* new and exciting matches with objects, events, and feelings.
3. *Binding* old symbols with new knots.
4. *Coping* with ambiguity, complexity and uncertainty.

Education is the business of expanding ego-processes; by its very nature it approaches ego-processes with tasty tidbits of knowledge and meaty ideas, with succulent concepts and provoking mysteries. On the other hand, constriction of ego-processes reduces the interest of the organism in the environment, especially in its new, unfamiliar, or adventurous aspects. The pinching of information inputs which constricted ego-processes produce in the individual limits learning and the possibilities of personality change. Constricted ego-processes hold the individual to a limited number of alternatives or choices and in some cases to only one choice in responding to the stresses of normal living. Symbols are used rigidly and inflexibly; spontaneity and zest are lost. Channels to life have hardened and in doing so have frozen the organism, as it were, in place.

Where expansion is possible (where constriction is only partly a result of unconscious factors), extension of a student's conceptual understanding of subject matter such as history, science, mathematics, economics, English literature, or psychology can be of help in opening up doors and avenues for expansion. Collinson (7) suggests that ego-processes function much like concept formation processes and that the two are perhaps learned in similar ways. Concepts about knowledge interpenetrate ego-concepts in some osmotic way related to perceived meaning and interest. Ego-processes expand as a result of effective learning experiences; as Sanford points out, any educational experience that induces students to exercise their intellects can produce ego expansion. "Insofar as knowledge of facts or understanding of relationships enables the individual to predict events, that is to see things go according to his expectations, the ego is strengthened." (24, p. 279)

As has been mentioned before, reading has helped ego-processes expand where the environment had almost foreclosed human growth. At the end of his autobiography, Richard Wright asks himself how it was possible for him to escape from his depressed and terrorizing early experiences as a child and adolescent:

"What was it that made me conscious of possibilities? From where in this southern darkness had I caught a sense of freedom? Why was it that I was able to act upon vaguely felt notions? . . . How dare I consider my feelings superior to the gross environment that sought to claim me?

"It had been only through books—at best no more than vicarious cultural transfusions—that I had managed to keep myself alive in a negatively vital way. Whenever my environment had failed to support or nourish me I had clutched at books. Consequently my belief in books had risen more out of a sense of desperation than from any abiding conviction of their ultimate value. . . .

"It had been my accidental reading of fiction and literary criticism that had evoked in me vague glimpses of life's possibilities. . . . And it was out of these novels, stories and articles, out of the emotional impact of imaginative constructions of heroic or tragic deeds, that I felt touching my face a tinge of warmth from an unseen light. . . ." (33, pp. 282, 283)

As a child, Richard's grandmother had boarded a school teacher who had aroused the boy's curiosity by her ability to enjoy symbols on a page. Richard implored her to read to him and was read the story of *Bluebeard and His Seven Wives* at an early age. As he listened, Richard "ceased to see the porch, the sunshine, her face, everything . . . my imagination blazed. The sensations the story aroused in me were never to leave me." (28, p 47) Although *Bluebeard and His Seven Wives* would hardly receive curriculum approval in Richard's (or anyone else's) school, its magic did the trick, and once kindled, his interest grew.

It is significant that reading competence or incompetence has emerged as an epidemological index of institutional functioning. Miller reviewed the reading achievement data for an entire school population of 45,000 children, over a two-year period and found that certain school districts were characterized by low reading levels and others high reading levels and that retarded readers, almost without exception, had serious social and academic difficulties (19).

It is not surprising to find reading failure and delinquency interwoven comrades. A child who cannot conceptualize and utilize symbolic possibilities for adventure, hope, and a future life must play out his circumscribed alternatives in a walled environment. His ego-processes and his environmental limitations conspire to straightjacket him leaving only senseless rebellion or withdrawal. In working with delinquents as a young man, it was always puzzling to me that the boys and girls desperately wanted to have fun but seldom knew how. Often fun and fight were confused. Such children wanted to do things well but seldom could, wanted to create but were seldom successful, wanted to learn but were frightened of the consequences. Almost all had been hurt repeatedly in school; another possible encounter was seldom attractive. To help such children learn is a task worthy of a modern miracle worker.

THE INTEGRATION—FRAGMENTATION DIMENSION

The fragmentation of human personality is most evident in the mentally ill. Searle's (25) metaphor of schizophrenic ego-processes as a mind with little islands but no bridges between them is apt. Such ego-processes cannot integrate past into present or present into future; the absence of bridges within self encourages a lack of bridges to the outside. Fragmentation splits the self into many selves, each seeking separate, contradictory or inconsistent goals within the same individual.

Integration is the harmonious orchestration of the separate parts of the person and personality—emotions, skills, knowledge, thoughts,

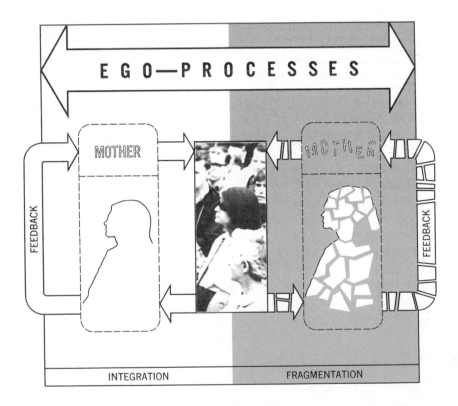

Figure 2.5. Skills in ego integration.

1. *Assimilating* knowledge within appropriate layers of self.
2. *Connecting* a variety of roles into one flexible, stable self.
3. *Interweaving* knowledge with action, action with knowledge.
4. *Identifying* self with the human condition—past, present, and future.

imagination. The significance of new knowledge needs to be perceived and its relationship to other parts of the person bridged. Basic to this process is the integration of learning and living. Education can, in some instances, become a special compartment in the personality so that what we know and what we do are separate and unintegrated.

Effective integrative learnings must take into account the fact that a child's world is activity centered. Objects and things are perceived in the context of what can be done with them. As the child acts, discovers, and changes, it is this experience that gets bound into the mediating symbols. For example, it is not at all uncommon for adults to revisit neighborhoods where they had lived as small children and to be surprised by the reduction in the size of physical objects such as roads, lakes, houses, and distances that were experienced when they were small.

If objects are not bound into symbols by action, they remain unintegrated and fragmented things. Henri Bergson points out that in some men perceiving and acting are separate entities. When such persons look at a thing, said Bergson "they see it for itself, not for themselves. These are people who are born or have developed a detachment from life. This is a reminder of the Swiss gentleman who when given a choice between going to paradise or going to a lecture about paradise, chose the latter." (2)

Intellectual learning can often be compartmentalized and walled off from the rest of an individual's personality. In some ways this danger is inherent in educational processes conceived as a passive receiving of knowledge. The villainous aspect of ego-processes is their ability to take in data, lectures, discussions, TV films, and other instructural media and to encode them as totally separate from behavior. Although it is generally true that education leads to greater capacities for integration of experiences and symbols, it would appear helpful for child and adolescents to maximize the integrative nature of the educational process and content.

Often the growing signs of fragmenting ego-processes are evident before the major crash becomes evident. In a study of high school students who became schizophrenic within five years after graduation, approximately 75% (as compared to 11% of a control group) showed definite signs, as perceived by teachers and counselors, of loss of interest, lethargy, inability to concentrate, and a significant reduction in participation in school activities (3).

Various kinds of emotional experiences can also be undergone without knowledge of them being integrated with other cognitive-affective knowledge. We need to be prepared to learn from all human experience. Intellect *sans* integration can produce the kind of educational human being who, divorced from his own emotion, can seldom find the "tinge of warmth" that Richard Wright felt touching his face.

Another factor required for integration of emotion and intellect is meaning. Ego-processes have not only to help the organism to adapt but to synthesize its interactions with the environment. Without an integrating principle, differentiation, pacing, expansion, and fidelity are empty processes. Integration provides the conceptual base from which the mediation of perceptions can be harmonized and utilized for ego development and growth.

The processes of integration varies as do individuals. Each individual has an unique way of synthesizing experiences and symbols. This individual style has repetitive, recognizable aspects that Rosen suggests may be studied through the individual's characteristic responses to ambiguity, or in situations where definitive answers are not available. Integrative style may also be studied in artistic creations, use of fantasy, the nature of differentiation processes, work, and interpersonal relationships. Styles in personality change as they do in clothing. We need to keep in mind that a variety of integrative styles are within the normal ranges and that differences in the manner of integration are part of the normal deviations of personality and development in a free society.

REFERENCES

1. Allport, G. W. "The Ego in Contemporary Psychology." *Psychol. Rev.,* **50**, Oct. 1943, 451–478.
2. Bergson, Henri. *Creative Evolution.* New York: Modern Library, 1944.
3. Bower, Eli M., Thomas A. Shellhammer, John M. Daily, and Murray Bower. *High School Students Who Later Became Schizophrenic.* Sacramento: California State Dept. of Education, 1960.
4. Bowlby, John. *Maternal Care and Mental Health.* Geneva: World Health Organization, 1951.
5. Buhler, Charlotte. "The Reality Principle." *Amer. J. Psychotherapy,* **8**, Oct. 1954, 626–647.
6. Butler, R. A. "Exploratory and Related Behavior: A New Trend in Animal Research." *J. Individual Psychol.,* **14**, April 1958, 111–120.
7. Collinson, J. B. "The Concept." *Archives of General Psychiatry,* **6**, Feb. 1962, 76–89.
8. *The Complete Plays of Gilbert and Sullivan.* New York: The Modern Library (undated).
9. Craik, K. J. W. *The Nature of Explanation.* Cambridge, England: Cambridge University Press, 1943.
10. Deutsch, Martin, L. Goldstein, M. Whiteman, Estelle Cherry-Peisach, Vera P. John, and B. Brown. *Language and Cognitive Aspects of Social Deprivation.* New York: Blaisdell Publishing Co., 1966 (in preparation).

11. Freud, Sigmund. "Formulations on Two Principles of Mental Functioning," in *Collected Papers,* Vol. 4. New York: Basic Books, 1959, pp. 13–21.
12. Goldfarb, William. "The Effects of Early Institutional Care on Adolescent Personality." *J. Experimental Education,* **12,** April 1943, 106–129.
13. Hartmann, Heinz. *Ego Psychology and the Problem of Adaptation.* New York: International Universities Press, 1958.
14. Hess, Robert. "Educability and Rehabilitation: The Future of the Welfare Class." Paper prepared for the Thirtieth Groves Conference on Marriage and the Family, April 15, 1964, Knoxville, Tenn. (mimeographed).
15. Jensen, A. R. "Verbal Mediation and Educational Potential." *Psychology in the Schools,* **3,** 1966, 99–109.
16. Koestler, Arthur. *The Act of Creation.* New York: Macmillan Co., 1964.
17. Kroeber, Theodore C. "Coping Functions of the Ego Mechanisms," in Robert W. White (Ed.), *The Study of Lives.* New York: Atherton Press, 1963.
18. *Life* Magazine, Jan. 7, 1966.
19. Miller, Alan D. "The Role of the School System in a Mental Health Program," in Morris Krugman (Ed.), *Orthopsychiatry and the School.* New York: American Orthopsychiatric Association, 1958.
20. Murphy, Lois. "Preventive Implications of Development in the Pre-School Years," in Gerald Kaplan (Ed.), *Prevention of Mental Disorders in Children.* New York: Basic Books, 1961.
21. O'Connell, Walter E. "The Adaptive Functions of Wit and Humor." *J. Abnormal and Social Psychology,* **61,** April 1960, 263–270.
22. Rapaport, David (Ed.). *Organization and Pathology of Thought.* New York: Columbia University Press, 1951.
23. Rovere, Richard. *Senator Joe McCarthy.* New York: Harcourt, Brace and World, 1957.
24. Sanford, Nevitt (Ed.). *The American College.* New York: John Wiley and Sons, 1962.
25. Searles, Harold F. "Integration and Differentiation in Schizophrenia: An Overall View." *British J. Medical Psychology,* **32,** Oct. 1959, 261–281.
26. Sears, Robert, Eleanor Maccoby, and Harry Levin. *Patterns of Child Rearing.* New York: Harper and Bros., 1957.
27. Shaftel, George, and R. Fannie. *Role Playing the Problem Story.* New York: The National Conference of Christian and Jews, 1952.
28. Silber, Earle, et al. "Adaptive Behavior in Competent Adolescents." *Archives of General Psychiatry,* **5,** Dec. 1961, 517–527.
29. Skeels, Harold M., and Marie Skodak. "Techniques for a High-Yield Followup Study in the Field." *Public Health Reports,* **80,** March 1965, 249–257.
30. Spitz, Rene. "Hospitalism: An Inquiry into the Genesis of Psychiatric Conditions in Early Childhood," in *The Psychoanalytic Study of the Child,* Vol. 1. New York: International Universities Press, 1945, pp. 53–74.
31. Sugarman, Daniel A., and Rolaine A. Hochstein. *Seven Stories for Growth.* New York: Pitman Publishing Corp., 1965.
32. White, R. W. *Ego and Reality in Psychoanalytic Theory* (monograph 11). New York: International Universities Press, 1963.
33. Wright, Richard. *Black Boy.* New York: Signet Books, 1951.

Chapter 3

The Development of Cognitive-Affective Processes Through Education

Nevitt Sanford

About the Author

Nevitt Sanford, Professor of Psychology and Education and Director of the Institute for the Study of Human Problems at Stanford University, has been in turn a prison psychologist, a practicing psychoanalyst, and director of major studies in child development, personality assessment, political and social attitudes, the social psychology of higher education, alcoholism, and other related problems. Prior to joining the Stanford faculty in 1961 he was associated with the University of California for 20 years as a Professor of Psychology and a member of research organizations at the Institute of Human Development, the Berkeley Public Opinion Study, the Office of Strategic Services in Washington, D.C., the Institute of Personality Assessment and Research, and the Mary Conover Mellon Foundation at Vassar College.

Among Dr. Sanford's many publications are contributions to H. A. Murray's *Explorations in Personality*, S. Koch's *Psychology: A Study of Science*, and B. Wolman's *Handbook of Clinical Psychology*. He has also served as editor and senior author of *Physique, Personality and Scholarship; The Authoritarian Personality; The American College;* and *College and Character*, and has authored an article on "The Field of Personality" for the new Encyclopedia of the Social Sciences.

Past president of the Society for the Psychological Study of Social Issues and of the Division of Personality and Social Psychology, he received his doctorate from Harvard University, and has served as a member of the Board of Directors of both the American Psychological Association and the Social Science Research Council. Previously he was a research affiliate of the Tavistock Institute of Human Relations in London, England, and an instructor at the Salzburg Seminars in American Studies in Salzburg, Austria.

Introduction to the Chapter

It may be helpful to those bewildered or challenged by the last two chapters to find some of the same problems and processes attacked in new ways. Here we have the myth of the disembodied intellect and some delineation and differentiation of our high-level behavioral science and educational abstractions such as health, maturity, development, and learning.

The process of education, Sanford points out, is a matter of transmitting symbols in the service of human development, and that all such development occurs in response to some kind of strain. Effectively managed strain helps to produce a healthy and effective organism. Psychotherapy is no substitute for inadequate personality development, says Sanford; expanding personality and growth must be planned for and acquired through education.

But Sanford saves his spotlight for those processes that free and expand the impulse life and for that simple gift described by Holofernes in *Love's Labour's Lost*. "This is a gift I have, simple, simple; a foolish extravagant spirit, full of forms, figures, shapes, objects, ideas, apprehensions, motions, revolutions: these are begot in the ventricle of memory, nourished in the womb of pia mater and delivered upon the mellowing of occasion. But the gift is good in those in whom it is acute and I am thankful for it." (Act IV, Scene II)

The gift, of course, is imagination—a gift which few children obtain in their educational experiences. As Sanford notes, the individual who has learned to use his imagination is not only in touch with his thoughts and impulses *but has the means of expanding them*. Moreover, imagination can produce the metaphors by which human life is planned and lived out. Nor is it at all contradictory to find that good, that is, academically excellent, students had, in their childhood, more opportunities for imaginative play, for play-acting, and for being read to. Sanford's conclusions reinforce Bruner's notion that "children, like adults, need reassurance that it is all right to entertain and express highly subjective ideas, to treat a task as a problem where you *invent* an answer rather than *finding* one out there in the book or on the blackboard." (*American Psychologist*, 20, December 1965, p. 1014)

Imaginative thoughts may not produce the "right" answer, but they extend the conceptual possibilities for the child when expressed. Can such thoughts be evaluated by self and others without closing down or discouraging further imaginative and creative production? How can schools become increasingly effective in opening up and expanding personality and cognitive development in students? Sanford will tell you in his own way.

The Development of Cognitive-Affective
Processes Through Education

Where did educators get the idea of the desembodied intellect? In their efforts to arrive at general laws, the psychologists have abstracted—and isolated experimentally—such processes as perceiving, learning, and emotion and have demonstrated relationships between variations in these processes and external stimuli.

It is widely believed that knowledge of this kind can somehow be applied in school. But it cannot in fact be directly applied because in any classroom situation a great many variables are operating. The vaunted general laws of psychology—laws of perceiving considered without reference to the perceiver, or laws of learning that do not refer to the learner—are not really very general. If a new variable is introduced, the demonstrated relationship changes, and since in any life situation there are always more variables than could possibly be controlled in a laboratory situation, the generality of the laws is bound to be quite limited.

Lifting learning out of its living context in this way contributes heavily to the dullness of much of the educational psychology now taught to unwary graduate students. It is not always made clear that cognitive changes in the person influence functioning in the rest of him so that cognitive development is all of a piece with emotional and characterological development. Yet undoubtedly development after the age of about two—after the acquisition of language—is very much a cognitive matter.

The activities in the ordinary classroom can serve as a means of promoting psychological health and development in children. Before we go into the importance of learning how to read, to write, and to do other things of this kind, however, let us re-examine some of our terms.

Without a doubt, education, psychological health, and adequately paced development are all desirable goals. These are usually construed as adding up to maturity. However, in the strictest sense of each term, they are highly differentiated concepts, and as goals they are not necessarily achieved together. Instead of considering education alone or lumping education, health, maturity, and high levels of development together in our minds and surrounding them with a vague aura of that which is good, let us examine each goal separately and see how the separate goals sometimes do and sometimes do not go together.

THE MEANING OF EDUCATION

Let us restrict education here to its traditional, and somewhat narrow, meaning: the inculcation in the individual of his cultural heritage. The process of education, when we use the term in this sense, is primarily a matter of transmitting symbols. And this is what happens most characteristically in the classroom.

If we define education in this way, it is clear that a person can be highly educated but at the same time unhealthy—in the sense of being neurotic. He can carry on his neurotic activities in an educated way, perhaps using symbols of high culture. Similarly, a person could be prejudiced or anti-Semitic without being poorly educated; indeed, he might carry on his anti-Semitic activities with the help of much knowledge of writings in history, statistics, or biology. But such a person could not be highly developed, as I shall use this term, because prejudice, if psychologically determined, bespeaks a low level of integration of the personality.

HEALTH

Health can be defined as the capacity for dealing in some more or less adaptive fashion with the problems and strains that life offers. We do not define it in terms of what is most common in the statistical sense, or in terms of freedom from symptoms or freedom from suffering, even though these things might actually favor the development of future capacity for coping. We cannot define it strictly as stability because, as Caplan has shown, much of the instability to be observed in young people can be understood as the beginning of a new and possibly quite healthy adaptation. On the other hand, where there is adequate adaptive capacity, there is probably a fundamental stability, in that the individual can adapt or deal with present strains while somehow remaining fundamentally himself.

MATURITY

People have tended to use the term "maturity" to stand for something that we would all like to have more of—an aggregate of virtues. Since this is rather misleading, let us restrict the word to its biological and statistical meanings. Biologically, we are mature when we have reached a place where we are no longer developing. Psychologically, "maturity" may perhaps be used to stand for the aggregate of traits that appear more often in adults than in children or adolescents. Be it noted, however, that maturity in this sense is not an ethical norm; such desirable traits as spontaneity and honesty are probably to be found more often in children than in adults.

DEVELOPMENT

This leaves then, the concept of development, or optimum development, or high levels of development—all of which may be defined as how close we come to the maximum realization of our human potentials. Even here we could be relatively neutral with respect to value. We might take the view that human beings develop in the same way as all other living things—and even things that are not "living."

A building, for example, in the process of being put together develops through the addition of new parts or the enlargement of existing parts. In living systems, and in other systems that are to be functional, expansion is accompanied by differentiation, and then there is some degree of integration of parts or features which have previously been differentiated. All of this seems to happen regularly and naturally, and it is easy to speak of it as if it were independent of value. This is, however, not quite the case. In underdeveloped societies, highly developed individuals may be maladapted. If, for example, in a simple, preliterate society the family is the essential unit and the individual does not ordinarily differentiate himself from it, psychological differentiation would not be positively valued. Strictly speaking, then, even to say that we are in favor of people developing is to express a value.

But why *not* express a value? Actually, most of the virtues expounded in the great ethical systems of the western world can be understood as expressions of high levels of development in the individual. The individual's freedom depends upon his development. He must develop if he is to be free from the limitations of ignorance and incompetence. He must develop if he is to be free of the pressures of the immediate social group or of authority or tradition; and he especially needs to develop if he is to be free of unrecognized tendencies within himself. All conceptions of developmental goals, however, should remain open-ended, because as yet we do not know the extent or the limits of human potential. Theoretically, every human being can develop a little more, whatever his current stage or status.

According to this general scheme, it is possible to be healthy without being highly developed. A child, for example, because he *is* a child, cannot be highly developed in the absolute sense, yet he may cope with strains in a way that is entirely appropriate for his age. Further, high development does not guarantee good mental health, for development involves the generation of new needs and, hence, increased possibilities of frustration and conflict. Thus we encounter people with effective ego-expansion processes who are complex, interesting, and creative, but who seem not to be doing a good job of coping with the problems of life. One might say of such people that their expansion and differentiation processes have run too far ahead of integration processes. In the main, however, high development is favorable to mental health. The highly developed person is not free of strains, nor is he stable from moment to moment, yet in a truly critical situation he would probably be able to call forth the resources that were needed.

THE CONTRIBUTION OF EDUCATION

How can education in the narrow sense of the inculcation of the cultural heritage actually contribute to the development of personality. We have seen that it does not necessarily do so. In approaching this task, we must go, a little way at least, into the theory of personality and its development.

First, the personality functions as a whole. This is not just a slogan. We must not permit educators categorically to separate the intellectual or the cognitive from the rest of the personality. Conceptually, they may do this. Cognition, feeling, emotion, action, and motivation are easily separated by abstraction, but no single one of these can function independently of the others. This point is of great importance to anyone interested in the psychology of learning because he will be told many times by teachers: "We'll take care of the intellect, and the psychologists can take care of personality development, if they're interested in that sort of thing."

It is not difficult to show that intellectual performances and intellectual development depend on events in the personality as a whole. All we need do is consider some of the familiar emotional barriers to learning in school. The facts that the teacher is eager to have a student learn will *not* be learned unless they are in some way integrated with the fundamental purposes of the individual. Facts, if they are not to remain inert but are to be retained and put to use later on, must be related to the ego-processes of the person as the previous chapter has suggested.

THEORIES OF DEVELOPMENT

There is a fundamental notion that development in general occurs in response to some kind of strain, that a challenge must be present if the individual is to generate a new kind of response or adaptive device. When such a device is generated, we say that development has occurred, for the personality is now expanded: something new has been added.

This view of the matter puts the emphasis upon intervention from outside the individual. Not much that is psychologically interesting can be said to happen as a result of a natural unfolding. After the child has developed a few mechanisms for dealing with his problems, further development is not likely to occur unless the challenges put to him are of such intensity, and of such quality, that his old adaptive mechanisms will not suffice. Yet if the challenge is too severe, there is the likelihood that he will fall back on primitive devices which, though they might serve for the moment, are in the long run maladaptive.

Denial and repression are such devices. They enable the individual to manage strains of the moment, but as modes of adaptation they are both unfavorable to later development and difficult to modify. The child or the older student can learn from a crisis, but not if it is so severe—and the people around so unhelpful—that he is forced to fall back upon primitive devices that have served in the past.

Children, by and large, inevitably have to deal with enough strains so that we need not spend much time thinking of ways to challenge them. But as the child grows and acquires a larger and larger repertory of adaptive devices, and thus finds support for his natural hope that he can deal with any new situation without having to change, we then must begin thinking of situations that will challenge this young person so that he will continue to develop. Yet we need to be careful about our efforts to manage crises. It is possible that the effort may so well prepare the individual for a crisis that the crisis never really occurs, and nothing happens to induce developmental changes.

Implicit in what I have been saying are some assumptions concerning goals of development. Development involves ego-expansion and differentiation processes in all the major areas of the personality, integration within each of these areas, and integration among the areas. With respect to the impulse life of the individual, it seems that one developmental task is to find ways for obtaining emotional satisfaction that are in accord with the requirements of the real world and of society.

As soon as we speak about the requirements of society, we remind ourselves that individuals are social beings and that they become further socialized in the course of their development. They all have some kind of conscience, primitive or otherwise. A further developmental task would be the enlightenment of this conscience—a state of affairs in which the requirements of conscience are in accord with the individual's best thought and judgment, and not simply rigid rules adopted automatically in childhood. With higher development there is greater enlightenment and hence, greater individualization of conscience. It is this, most essentially, that makes the conscience dependable. "Best thought and judgment" refers to the major processes of control, those ego-functions according to which the individual gains mastery of the environment and control over himself.

In all of these kinds of development, cognitive processes have an important and perhaps crucial role. And for this, psychotherapy is no substitute. Expanding the major areas of the person, making the individual capable of responding to more and more aspects of the world, and enabling him to do more and more kinds of things—these are not benefits to be gained directly from psychotherapy or even psychological counseling. These things have to be acquired through education.

EDUCATION AS INTERVENTION

We come, then, to education—an "outside intervention" that expands and frees the impulse life. Here the accent is on the cultivation of the life of the imagination. The individual must be able to deal with his problems in his imagination, if he is not to be restricted always to concrete action or to sensation.

Let us first consider what happens when imagination cannot function. It has been suggested that alcoholics cannot really enjoy movies or television, not because they do not want to be away from the bottle that long, but because they are incapable of participating with satisfaction in collective fantasies. They are too addicted, we might say, to their own version of reality based on sensation. This is a severe handicap. This handicap is also present in the case of delinquency.

Consider James T. Farrell's *Studs Lonigan,* a vivid treatment of young people with no inner resources. Meeting on the street in the evening, these adolescents could think of nothing to do that did not involve overt sexual or aggressive action. The motion picture "Marty" made the point again; young males met each day after work and asked each other, "Now what will we do tonight?"—and there was no answer. This is the kind of impoverishment we constantly find in people who do not know how to read or have not learned to enjoy reading or who cannot deal with problems in the realm of imagination. It is interesting to note the difference between Studs Lonigan and his friend, Danny O'Neill who went on to become a scholar and writer. Danny was at home reading, or being read to, while most of the boys in his neighborhood were out in the streets doing what boys insist on doing. Danny, of course, could do in his imagination all kinds of things that Studs and his friends couldn't even dream of.

On the positive side, there is evidence of the vast importance for the individual of developing early imaginative experiences. Observations conducted at Vassar College, for example, showed clearly that "good" students—those who performed very well academically and showed signs of creativity—differed from other students in what they had to say about their play as children. The "good" students had more often played alone, made up games to play, had engaged in play-acting, and enjoyed imaginary companions, had read and been read to. In other words, for these more creative students, the life of the imagination was allowed to be, or by some accident became, important in childhood; they went on from there to scholarship and an interest in the things of the mind.

Similarly, assessment studies of graduate students in the natural sciences have strongly indicated that the outstanding students are distinguished by their broader interests and greater esthetic sensitivity.

According to one well-recognized theory, the individual who has learned to use his imagination is not merely in touch with his impulse life; his impulse life has itself expanded. The way this happens, in my view, is that the symbols of our culture become available to the individual, enabling him to deal with his basic impulses through fantasy and through his imaginative participation in literature, plays, movies, TV, and various other art forms.

The enormous importance of this can be appraised by noting that knowledge has had two basic functions in human history: the practical function of enabling us to master our "real" environment and the imaginative function of permitting us to extend the real world and enrich it by getting beyond sensation and the immediate situation. The imaginative function may, of course, also favor withdrawal from reality, but this special—ultimately pathological—phenomenon need not detain us at this moment. The point to be accented is that a fantasy starting as a way of expressing a basic impulse becomes a plan, and a plan is necessary for any kind of intelligent action.

THE DEVELOPMENT OF IMAGINATION

Education in the nations of the West, and especially in the United States today, tends to put the accent overwhelmingly on the practical aspects of knowledge, to the neglect of the imaginative aspects. But our concern here is with development; and in order to develop, the individual needs the kind of knowledge that expands and differentiates his impulse life. He can acquire this kind of knowledge as he becomes familiar with the symbols of our culture. From this point of view, then, culture is the friend of impulse rather than its enemy.

The basic theory, of course, comes from Freud—from his notion that in the infant a frustration of a need is followed immediately by an image of something that would be gratifying. This is the *primary process*. Fantasy, dreams, autism thus come naturally to the child; and of this stuff, poetry and art and other creative products are made. The generation of images is in itself gratifying to the child—despite admonitions from his elders against "idle fantasy." The kind of reading that was really gratifying to us as children was usually something that our teachers and parents didn't want us to read. That much gratification of our impulses was considered suspect. But it is to be hoped that this kind of gratification can be available to everyone in the present generation of children through reading what has been judged aesthetically "good"; culture, and particularly "high" culture, is the means, *par excellence,* for the gratification of the human being's most primitive emotional needs, once the necessary symbols have been acquired.

This, then, is how the individual may expand, and release the impulse life. By making the cultural world available to him and teaching him symbols and how to use them, we enable him to perform symbolically all kinds of psychological functions that would be impossible if he were restricted to transactions with "real" things. We might say that this is the only way in which civilized adults can gratify the infantile needs which are still very much with them and which demand to be satisfied in some way.

In the highest forms of intellectual, artistic, and scholarly endeavor, which are rewarding in various concrete and adult ways, there is always some expression of the most primitive emotional needs. The beauty of it is that by doing this kind of work a man can find gratification for some of his most infantile cravings. Not all of us can do something about our oedipus complex by writing a story about it. But we *can* try to deal with our problems imaginatively.

We can go from this to the general issue of taste and the question of what is "good" at various stages of an individual's development. From the present point of view, taste would be just the right balance between impulsive gratification on the one hand and the requirements of convention on the other. In really good literature there is always a strong element of passion and primitiveness. This is why good literature is so often banned; but at the same time, for a piece of writing to be classed as art, it must conform well enough—*just* well enough— with the demands of convention so that a sophisticated person can enjoy it.

THE IMPORTANCE OF READING

These comments on imagination are important in practice. Above all, children must be taught to enjoy reading. It is sad to contemplate how many of them read without enjoyment—because they have been taught, not that reading is a glorious means of satisfying their impulses, but that it is primarily a duty. Teachers must somehow counteract this prevailing notion. The first developmental task, the first educational task, is to teach *every* child to enjoy reading, to enjoy making up stories, and to enjoy imaginative work. If this is not done, there is hardly any use troubling with the many other educational tasks that come later. In personality development, first things must come first.

It is not difficult to teach children to enjoy imaginative work, even though the earlier spontaneous imaginative life that all children know has been dampened by the adults around them. When children are beginning to read, it probably does not matter too much what sort of thing they read. If comic books will induce them to read, let them read comic books. The "act" of reading at an early age can later become the "art" of reading. We can usually count on an improvement in taste as time goes on. As a matter of fact, boys on the edge of delinquency may seek comic books as a means of preventing themselves from becoming delinquent rather than as stimuli and encouragement for later delinquent behavior. Much of what can be done in the imagination doesn't really have to be done in action.

Finally, on this point, the collective fantasies that are expressed even in the most atrocious comic books, TV shows, and the like are probably less antisocial than what any child is capable of cooking up for himself. In a way, there's a kind of socialization already at work in the participation in any kind of collective fantasy, however primitive it might be. Every child can be taught to enjoy the life of the imagination. This may be a matter of knowing where to start. In her book, *Spinster*, Sylvia Ashton Warner describes how she was able to teach the Maori children of New Zealand to read. In the beginning they had no conception of what school was about; they sat day after day, year after year, without learning to read or learning anything. She found, however, that she could get at the fantasy life of these children and then connect a few words-to-be-taught with what she now knew to be a basic interest or fear. And thus a start was made. This kind of thing takes time, but it is undoubtedly worth it.

EGO DEVELOPMENT AND EDUCATION

It goes almost without saying that learning in school is essential to the development of the controlling processes, the ego processes that underlie the child's mastery of reality and control of himself. This is what classroom activity is mainly about. We teach facts about the real world so that the child can make predictions of what will happen, gain a sense of confidence in his ability to judge events, and learn to make decisions about what he is going to do. He builds his sense of independence on the basis of his confidence that he can make judgments for himself and that these will work out well in the end. In order for this kind of development of ego-processes to occur, the child must have the experience of mastering harder and harder tasks. These tasks can be school tasks as well as any other. The essential thing is that there be attention to the grade of the task; it must be hard enough to push him along, to require new adaptations, but not so difficult that it will lead to failure, humiliation, and regression.

The big problem is how we can keep the young child's imaginative life going even after he gets into the second or third grade, where he has to concentrate on learning about reality. Often, it seems, a child leads a wonderful life of the imagination until he is about age five; then he is taken into school and given the necessary discipline. This may lead him to dismiss altogether his earlier life of the imagination. The great task for the teacher is to develop the higher ego-functions without doing so at the expense of the rich emotional life of the child.

To develop conscience and develop capacities for socialization during the primary school years, external authority is necessary and important. Books, literature, and instruction can be used to put before the child models of good social behavior. Here once again, we would be using cognitive function in order to develop personality in its more general aspects. The matter of judgment and enlightenment with respect to conscience seems to belong later in the school years. Possibly the last high school year is time enough for the individual to begin questioning the values according to which he was brought up, for until then he has needed to believe firmly in certain values in order to inhibit the direct expression of the impulses of adolescence. But once adolescence is over, the time for deeper probing of his values is at hand. College, probably, is the time for him to gain the relativity with respect to values that is necessary to the greater enlightenment and hence eventual stability of conscience.

At various times in the life of the individual there are unconscious maladaptive processes which influence what happens consciously. At such times we may feel the necessity of finding out why the child has a problem, but it is by no means always wise to do that. What we can do instead is stimulate those parts of the personality which are not being influenced by the unconscious maladaptive process and thus are still open to wholesome development. It is quite possible for the teacher to accent what can be developed, while ignoring parts of the personality that are foci of problems; indeed, this happens all the time. Teachers do not need to wait for the clinical psychologist to straighten out a particular problem of the child before proceeding by educational means to attack the great developmental tasks.

Theoretically and frequently in practice when the teacher does aim at developing the parts of the personality that are still open to experience—that are not under the influence of unconscious complexes—and when he succeeds, the relationship between the conscious and the unconscious parts of the personality can be changed, and the unconscious complexes may actually recede into relative insignificance. They may even fade, becoming irrelevant as the other parts of the personality expand.

In short, ordinary educational procedures, even the most academic ones, can be vitally important in personality development. But if this transaction is to succeed, or succeed more often than it usually does, the educational work itself must be guided by psychological theory and psychological knowledge. So far, however, educational psychology of this kind has not been highly developed. Much needs to be discovered about the conditions and processes by which personality changes are induced through the use of school materials and classroom activity. Let us hope then that school psychologists, while not neglecting any of the other matters they are called upon to handle, will take some responsibility for developing the kind of theory and producing the kinds of facts that will enable us better to utilize the regular processes of education in the interests of personality development.

REFERENCES

Barron, F. *Creativity and Psychological Health.* Princeton, N.J.: D. Van Nostrand, 1963.

Boulding, K. "A General Theory of Growth," in L. Von Bertalanffy (Ed.), *General Systems Theory.* Los Angeles: Society for General Systems Theory, 1956.

Bower, E. M. *Early Identification of Emotionally Handicapped Children in School.* Springfield, Ill.: Charles C Thomas, 1960.

Buhler, C. "Maturation and Motivation." *Personality: Symposia on Topical Issues* 1, 1951, 184–211.

Caplan, G. *An Approach to Community Mental Health.* New York: Grune and Stratton, 1961.

Erikson, E. H. "Crises of Normal Development," in C. Kluckhohn, H. Murray, and D. M. Schneider (Eds.), *Personality in Nature, Society, and Culture,* Rev. Ed. New York: Alfred A. Knopf, 1955.

Freud, S. *An Outline of Psychoanalysis.* New York: W. W. Norton, 1949.

Goldstein, K. *The Organism.* New York: American Book, 1939.

Gough, H. G. "Techniques for Identifying the Creative Research Scientist," in D. W. MacKinnon (Ed.), *The Creative Person.* Berkeley, Calif.: Institute of Personality Assessment and Research, 1961.

Katz, J., and N. Sanford. "The Curriculum in the Perspective of the Theory of Personality Development," in N. Sanford (Ed.), *The American College.* New York: John Wiley and Sons, 1962.

Klein, G. S. "The Personal World through Perception," in R. R. Blake and G. V. Ramsey (Eds.), *Perception: An Approach to Personality.* New York: Ronald Press, 1951.

Murray, H. A., et al. *Explorations in Personality.* New York: Oxford University Press, 1938.

Sanford, N. "Developmental Status of the Entering Freshmen," in N. Sanford, (Ed.), *The American College.* New York: John Wiley and Sons, 1962.

Sanford, N. "Personality: Its Place in Psychology," in S. Koch (Ed.), *Psychology: A Study of a Science.* Vol. 3. New York: McGraw-Hill, 1963.

Sanford, N. *Self and Society.* New York: Atherton Press, 1966.

White, R. W. *Lives in Progress.* New York: Holt, Rinehart and Winston, 1952.

Chapter 4

The Utilization of
Preconscious Functions
in Education

Lawrence S. Kubie

About the Author

Lawrence S. Kubie has been a clinical Professor of Psychiatry at Yale University and the University of Maryland, a Visiting Professor of Psychiatry in the Jefferson Medical College of Philadelphia, Director of Training at the Sheppard and Enoch Pratt Hospital in Towson, Maryland, on the faculty of the New York Psychoanalytic Institute, and a Lecturer in Psychiatry at the College of Physicians and Surgeons of Columbia University in New York City and in the Johns Hopkins Medical School in Baltimore, Maryland. He is Editor-in-Chief of the *Journal of Nervous and Mental Disease,* and was a practicing neurologist, psychiatrist, and psychoanalyst for more than forty years. He is now retired and lives and writes in Sparks, Maryland.

Author's Prologue

I doubt that there was any one moment when the realization came that it is not enough to be educated, erudite, a scholar, or a master of some field of learning. Instead a gradual understanding came that in the current state of human culture the relationship between erudition and wisdom, erudition and maturity, erudition and mental health is almost accidental (4) (5) (9). I made a tentative formulation of this in studies published in the *American Scientist* in 1953 and 1954 (2) called "Some Unsolved Problems of the Scientific Career" and again in "The Forgotten Man of Education" in the Harvard *Alumni Bulletin* in 1954 (3). The observations on which these studies were based reached back over my years as a medical student and as a student of neurophysiology, neuroanatomy, experimental neuropathology, clinical neurology, psychiatry, and finally psychoanalysis. I had come to know as friends and as patients academic leaders not

90

only in the sciences but also in other fields of learning, as well as many creative artists and writers. It was this that convinced me that no high discipline holds the key to wisdom and maturity; not the arts, humanities, philosophy, or theology; not politics or economics; not engineering, or the mathematical, physical, of biological sciences; not medicine; not the behavioral sciences; not psychiatry, or even psychoanalysis. All that these last can do is to ask more precise questions. Furthermore I had heard many savants from each of these fields argue unhappily that it was one of the others who must hold the key to wisdom.

Still later, during years of psychoanalytic practice the tragic paradox impressed me that scholarly attainments may actually mask processes of neurotic illness under a surface gloss of erudition and success. This was observable from a child's earliest years of schooling, to postgraduate levels, and equally among those who were prodigious scholars or prodigious athletes, and even among those who excelled in both. Ultimately athletic and intellectual prodigies were seen to share other traits. Among these was the disconcerting fact that neither knew how he attained his superlative excellence. The great teacher of tennis was not Don Budge but his relatively unknown brother. The great violin maestro was not one of the great virtuosi, but Leopold Auer. The man who succeeds by virtue of some exceptional inherent talent can rarely if ever help others to excel (16) (17) (18).

The next step in my personal Odyssey brought the realization of the equal failure of policemen, judges, jailors, and clergymen, of believers and nonbelievers, to solve the problems of ethical education (15). This brought the conviction that because of the distorting and hampering effect of the ubiquitous masked neurotic process in all human life, the very processes of learning, of teaching, and of educating are still unsolved problems in human culture, so that with rare exceptions the best we produce are savants who are emotional and moral infants. Of course there are rare and happy exceptions, which must be studied as intensively as the failures. To learn how to educate to wisdom and maturity will require that we also learn to free human development from the influence of hidden residues from the neurotic episodes of childhood, whose persistence distorts the educational process. Once we can resolve each neurotic episode in childhood as it occurs, it will not leave behind these hidden residues which deform the developing personality and the learning process (1) (6) (7) (8) (14).

I have said this many times; but to it I would add here that this would have the incalculable positive advantage of freeing the student to use those inherent preconscious processes without which neither education nor creativity is possible (16). The analytic study of gifted and creative folk and the comparative study of those whose creativity is thwarted and stunted shows: (1) that the freedom to learn and the freedom to use creatively that which we have learned are the two most searching tests of freedom from masked neurotic processes; and (2) that certain traditional educational mores and methods actually reinforce the neurotic process which the child brings to school with him (10) (12) (13).

The psychiatrist, psychoanalyst, psychophysiologist, and experimental psychologist cannot pretend to have ready solutions to these problems. What we have are techniques by which answers can be sought: but this search will not occur unless we acknowledge the existence of the problem, its universality, its importance, and its essential nature.

Introduction to the Chapter

Kubie wrestles with several of the problems which Bower and Sanford consider also; but from the point of view of a psychiatrist's concern with the relationship of educational processes to psychological healthy and illness. Like Sanford, Kubie suggests ways which might be tried in an effort to educate children without stunting their potential creativity and constricting their imagination. Kubie's description of the neurotogenic limitation which the mere acquisition symbolic tools imposes parallels Bower's discussion of how symbols may bind mental processes so tightly they cause difficulties in perceiving new data and in processing these observed data and the concepts which derive from them.

Kubie questions the premise which underlies all conventional techniques of instruction, that is, that we think and learn consciously. His hypothesis is that the continuous preconscious stream which processes all psychological data is the essential instrument of all learning, thinking, and creating; that in order to become fruitful this stream must remain free even as it eventually is ordered and coded, and finally given symbolic representation. This is the sampling process which according to Kubie is the core of what is called "consciousness"; and its vital contribution and purposes are rumination, communication, and reality testing. He also indicates that both this preconscious stream and also its symbolic sampling and representation are vulnerable to neurotogenic distortions which traditional educational processes intensify.

Kubie points to the need for pathologists in education who will have the courage to stand at the autopsy table of our educational failures and who will develop new techniques for finding out what it is that so often kills effective learning even in our most gifted students. As a clinician and scientist, he feels that the need for research on all educational processes is urgent, and he suggests the formation of a National Institute for Basic Research in Educational Processes to parallel the National Institutes of Health.

It is important to recognize that Kubie writes from a background of many years as a neurologist and psychoanalyst, as well as many years of personal and professional interest in education. He is interested in the tremendous potential of our educational institutions for making people more effective processors of information. Along with Bower, Sanford, and Biber, whose contributions follow, he points us toward those educational and humanizing processes which the schools of the future must develop.

The Utilization of Preconscious Functions
in Education

LEARNING AND THINKING AS PRECONSCIOUS
PROCESSING PLUS CONSCIOUS SAMPLING

Traditional conceptions of how human beings think and learn have started from a natural but incorrect and misleading assumption *that we think and learn consciously*. This is not true. Conscious processes are important not for thinking but for sampling, checking, reality testing, correcting, ruminating, and communicating. Even the intake of bits of information, whether from the soma or from the outer world, is predominantly preconscious. It consists largely of an incessant subliminal bombardment which goes on unceasingly whether we are awake or asleep. All afferent modalities take part in this; but the relative roles which each modality plays vary between the waking and the sleeping phases. In the waking state the dominant input is exteroceptive (from the distance deceptors of sight and hearing) and proprioceptive (from muscles, joints, tendons, and deeper layers of skin). In sleep and also in experiments on relative afferent isolation (which has been misleadingly miscalled "sensory deprivation") (11), the dominant input is enteroceptive (from the body's interior), with a relative reduction of proprioceptive input and with a near elimination of exteroceptive input. But whether the input is largely from distance and surface receptors (as in the normal waking state) or predominantly from within the body (as in sleep), the major input is always subliminal. The conscious component is never more than a fragment of the total input. This neglected but basic psychophysiological fact is of major significance and is relevant to all educational processes.

Once they have registered in us, all bits of information, whether subliminal or conscious, are "processed" by mechanisms which in turn are also largely subliminal the "imageless thought" of the Wurzburger School (19)]. This is just another way of restating the thesis

94

that thinking is preconscious rather than conscious and that the conscious component is only a weighted sample of the continuous stream of preconscious processing of data: a sample which is given conscious symbolic representation.[1]

Of this continuous preconscious stream we take conscious samples and then represent these samples by combinations of symbolic units. Both the sampling process itself and its symbolic representation consist of projections that utilize the data from distance receptors, which consist primarily of visual and to a much lesser extent auditory modalities. In its more primitive form (as in dreams) the process of sampling consists primarily of fragmentary, condensed visual after-images. These condensed hieroglyphics always represent not merely one thing but many things simultaneously. Because the symbols are predominantly visual, this involves their externalization or projection as though we were seeing them on a screen. We can observe and study such fragmentary, condensed after-images not only in dreams but also in other states: under drugs, in hypnoidal and hynagogic states, and in delirium.

The fragmentary samples are then regrouped into larger generalizations (or abstractions), which in turn are represented by large symbolic units, that is, words, which then are grouped into phrases as numbers are grouped into equations; phrases into sentences and paragraphs, as equations evolve into mathematical models. Yet all of this complex thought work is carried out preconsciously. These elaborations from the elementary building blocks of the sampling process provide us with magnificent new and exciting tools; but the conscious component is a constantly recurring process of sampling the stream of preconscious processing but conscious component is not itself the *thinking or learning process.*

We have already seen that the conscious component in any afferent input is not the total input from the environment, but only a meager fragment of the whole. Were it otherwise, the supply to our thinking apparatus would be impoverished, and our thinking processes would become pedestrian and hamstrung. Furthermore, the sampling process is always both fragmentary and by its very nature slanted by emotional processes, many of which are themselves subliminal (that is,

[1] This has been demonstrated experimentally and clinically, and also in the testimony of creative writers, artists, mathematicians, and scientists. In them it is clear that their learning and their creative thinking consist of just such a continuous preconscious processing of experiences, in which the major input has been subliminal, and the output as well, until it reaches its ultimate symbolic forms.

preconscious) and also unconscious. The final step occurs when the sample of the input which we have represented symbolically is projected again in the processes of recall, reproduction, and communication.

THE IMPACT OF CONCEALED NEUROTOGENIC PROCESSES

The child buries pain every day; and the accumulation of buried pain gradually isolates him from his elders and his age peers, and makes him afraid to allow his mental processes to flow freely. He becomes in varying degrees constricted. This destructive process could be held in check and reversed if that which the child buries were to be exhumed day by day as he is burying it. Thus the early introduction into the educational process of techniques borrowed from group psychotherapy but not identical with it could unlock the doors which imprison us in our masked neuroses. If we are to do this we will have to abandon the conspiracy of silence in which schools and parents alike shroud the painfully charged experiences which are important in human development. We process all experience preconsciously without words; but that of which we *cannot* speak we finally lose words for; and that for which we have no words we finally cannot correct. Thus the conspiracy of silence is one primary source of the tendency to dissociation and repression which is one of the roots of the neurotic process. To limit and reverse as it occurs this splintering of experience into unrelated, dissociated, inaccessible, and repressed fragments would be far more economical than is any much later attempt to reunite those parts of psychic life that have already been set apart and buried. Some fission is inescapable, but prompt refusion can prevent its becoming permanent, especially if the fusing were done not once but repeatedly in each school year, and in every year throughout the successive stages of child development, and on into the years of higher education. Any such program will require the conjoint efforts of educators, experimental and clinical psychologists, plus psychiatrists and psychoanalysts who are trained and experienced in working with children, adolescents, and adults. This is an awesome prospect, yet nothing less will even have a chance to create an educational process which will no longer intensify neurotogenic dissociative processes, but will lessen and limit and reverse them instead. Many previous studies have pointed out the subtle ways in which traditional educational procedures, with their emphasis on repetitive drill and repetitive grill, become interwoven with the automatic, uncontrollable, obligatory repetitions which are at the heart of the neurotic process. Other studies have pointed out how the rivalries of classroom and playground or for academic honors and status recapitulate and therefore prolong the residues from nursery rivalries. Therefore these points do not require further elaboration here. It will be sufficient to refer to the source studies (13) (5).

All who deal with other human beings are confronted by this problem. Whether as educators or parents, we must ask ourselves if we know how to educate without destroying. "How can I bring up my child or educate the child of another without doing him harm by interfering with his healthy growth?" "How can I use psychotherapeutic processes without at the same time becoming psychonoxious?" Since this restatement of the question may be surprising to some, I would point out that any process that has the power to help must also have the power to harm, whether it be education, psychiatry, religion, or a pill. The therapeutic can never be wholly dissociated from the noxious. Therefore I push the challenge further: "Can we find methods by which we can educate without limiting and distorting both the learning processes and the processes of emotional maturation?" Or to phrase the question even more specifically, "How can we equip our children, our students, our patients with the tools that they will need in life without destroying that free play of preconscious processing and of the derived creative imagination which they will need if they are ever to be able to use the tools which they acquire?" We have learned that input-overload and the excessive use of drill and grill can tumble the learner into a paralyzing rigidity that ends in ignorance. Out of this rigidity emerges either the neurotically inhibited ignoramus, or that special form of the idiot-savant who is a scholar in one field, frozen into labored uncreativity, and deficient in every other aspect of human wisdom as well. At the opposite end of the spectrum, excessive permissiveness can do similar harm. We are familiar with the uncluttered mind, master of nothing, free of any burden of facts, yet equally under the domination of neurotic processes. Between the neurotic ignoramus and the neurotic scholar there is not very much to choose, except that the neurotic ignoramus is almost always more fun, or at least less objectionable because he is less pretentious.

As educators, we have shut our eyes to this. We have no right to be complacent about our educational processes. On the other hand, no one should assume that some other educational system has solved these problems. Educators cannot permit themselves the luxury of this type of oversimplification. (I will return to this issue later.)

THE CRITICAL PERIODS OF GROWTH

There are three phases of growth in which the educational process is especially vulnerable. These were discussed recently at a conference of engineering educators in Boulder, Colorado, sponsored by the National Science Foundation (12) (17) (18). This statement does not imply that crises of vulnerability cause trouble three times in the life of a student, but only that some students manifest this is one, some in another, and some repeatedly in two or in all three. Educators and psychiatrists alike have paid too little attention to this clinical fact.

The first of these phases of vulnerability occurs between the ages of three and six. At this time, except for rare and still accidental exceptions, children tend to lose their capacity to use their native imaginations freely and creatively. Before this the child manifests a magnificient facility in learning new things painlessly and spontaneously. Children learn symbolic speech, bodily mimicry, spontaneous dance, tunes, facial expressions, and presently the uses of color and form just by living out their preconscious identifications with others. Furthermore, at this early age the child is able to take his daily experiences apart and put them together into new combinations with an imaginative and poetic use of gestures, sounds, and words, much as he plays with his early toys.

Yet as the child however spontaneously acquires the capacity to represent his experiences in the formal symbols of speech, a more pedestrian process takes over, because the process of symbolic representation itself, necessary though it is, is also a hampering and delaying process which ties the analogic and metaphorical preconscious processes down to pedestrian realities (8). In this process his natural capacity to learn preconsciously is seriously impaired. At the same time the child is struggling in the toils of early loves, lusts, hates, and rivalries. In his struggle to resolve these inner conflicts, his freedom to be creative is often overwhelmed by the struggle to conform, be good, do right, and thus win acceptance. Consequently two vital freedoms are endangered in the same phase of growth: the freedom to be creative and the freedom to learn preconsciously. Instead of learning confidently and joyously by preconscious identifications, he parrots consciously and painfully. Thus any pedantic teaching of the three R's tends to lock the jail door which imprisons the child's capacity to learn and create.

I hope that this point will not be misunderstood. There can be no objection to teaching a child how to relate his fantasies to reality, how to correct his unruly imagination, how to distinguish between reality and dream, and ultimately how to represent his internal experiences by externalizing them in drawings and words and numbers as he learns how to read, write, and count. All of this is essential. The challenge is to reconsider which sequence of learning experiences is optimal, which sequence has the best chance of reaching goals without exacting the toll that in the past has been accepted and inevitable. Should affective or naturational learning precede the three R's or follow them or be acquired concurrently? and when should each step begin? This issue has practical consequences. No doubt whipping up a child by various systems of rewards and punishments can teach some children to read, spell, write, and count. But not all. Many misconceptions exist about this, examples of which can be found in our newspapers and periodicals. Many demagogues maintain that we can go forward by going backwards, that if we imitate everything which is wrong in German, French, British, or Russian education, we will compete with them more effectively. No one has asked what percentage of French, German, British, and Russian children is effectively taught by drill and grill, rewards and punishments, or what percentage of them is merely dropped by the wayside. It is easy for an educational system to create the illusion that it achieves a high percentage of successes merely by using the simple device of dropping out its failures. Any method of teaching can produce spurious scores by quietly discarding those who cannot learn by that particular method, turning its back on the question of how many of the discards might have learned by some other method. If we apply this to the American scene, we should be proud of our effort to try to teach *all* children; but we must not underestimate the difficulties which this goal creates. Nor should these difficulties lead us to inflate the apparent successes of other countries who try to teach only those students who can successfully use traditional methods, shunting the rest off to some second-class type of trade-school.

A second crisis occurs during the years of transition from puberty into adolescence. It is well known that this is a time of high emotional complexity. What is not always realized is that its inner storms are projected onto every object in the outer world, including inanimate objects or even words or "nonsense" syllables. The pubescent child may giggle at an innocuous word, giving it a forbidden connotation. The dictionary becomes an erotically exciting adventure. He will find something surreptitiously bawdy in the definition of words like "friction." A Boy Scout rubbing two sticks together will find tabooed overtones in this. We might wonder whether it is wise to attempt to teach during this phase at all, a phase which is miscalled by some educators "the adolescent slump" because during it so many previously bright young school children are caught up in fear, guilt, and depression which destroys for a time their ability to do well in school. It is at least possible that we could salvage many a child's capacity for learning and for creative thinking by plucking him out of school for an undetermined interval during this critical period of physiological and psychological change. It would be equally rigid to pluck every child out of school at some predetermined age, since some go ahead without apparent trouble and since the appropriate age for such an interruption and its optimal duration will vary from child to child. Obviously any general recommendation would be unwarranted; yet we should have the courage to search for alternatives which would free us from the traditional sequences of the past.

We must also acknowledge that the behavioral sciences do not as yet have instruments which can determine whether and when for any particular child the educational process should be interrupted, and also when it can safely be resumed. This lack is due at least partly to the fact that the behavioral sciences have not asked themselves these questions and in consequence have not sought to develop the appropriate techniques.

The third crisis in education comes several variable years later. The student is on the way to becoming a "scholar," that is, an advanced graduate student, or beyond. He has reached the period when he should be flowering into his greatest creativity. Instead, all too often it is here that cramming to pass advanced competitive examinations and to fulfill formal requirements for graduation or for doctoral or higher academic status delivers the *coupe de grace* to creative learning. Engineering educators and indeed all other teachers of postgraduate disciplines know this well.

It is a surprising fact that any students survive these three destructive crises with intact capacities to learn and create freely. We know so little about this, that today such survivals are happy accidents which ought to be studied as closely as the failures. For the majority, however, mere survival in the postgraduate race is not enough. We learn to our dismay that graduation, the passing of exams, the winning of advanced degrees and even honors and initial positions on the rungs of the academic ladder are no indices that the creative potential has survived and can be used effectively. Too often survival has been at the cost of all later creativity (17) (18).

THE DANGERS OF PRECOSITY

Let us bring our attention back to the critical issue with which we began. This is the danger inherent in a premature emphasis on articulate, conscious formulations of what one is learning, a premature demand on the student to convert the new data which he is processing preconsciously into articulate forms, a premature demand that he test what he is learning *as he is learning it* by reviewing it consciously, that he examine through conscious symbols that which he has perceived largely at a subliminal level, and that he reproduce it and project it prematurely through conscious symbols. This premature introduction of conscious sampling through the repetitive emphasis on drill and grill increases the imprisoning and restricting effect of the processes of conscious sampling and conscious symbolic representation. Conscious processes thereby become inhibiting and paralyzing forces which restrict the free play of preconscious function. One goal of basic research in education must be to find better substitutes, to find other ways of tapping what is going on, of finding out what is being taken in subliminally and what is being processed preconsciously. We must find out how to dip a tin cup into the rushing preconscious stream without damming it up or diverting it. This conscious sampling process is not itself education; but it can become an important adjunct to education, a guide and a corrective, provided that it is not allowed to become a paralyzing, hamstringing, or distorting implement.

THE NEED FOR BASIC RESEARCH IN EDUCATION

Insofar as this chapter is at all critical, its criticisms are directed not against educators and teachers any more than psychiatrists and experimental and clinical psychologists. Its real target is the complacency of any of us over entrenched traditions. The only true pessimist is Pollyanna, who secretly feels that things are so bad that the badness does not exist or else sugar-coats them. On the contrary, the optimist whose hopefulness is a creative force is not afraid to face just how bad and how inadequate the past has been, because he harbors a sturdy hope that with hard thinking and research better ways can be found. In this spirit, we can say that the greatest optimist in medicine is the tough-minded pathologist who spends his life at the autopsy table studying medicine's mistakes and failures (15). It is my thesis that similarly any forward movement in education waits for education to develop its own corps of pathologists with courage to study its failures, perhaps with special emphasis on those which are due to a tendency to follow tradition blindly and rigidly.

The educator must ask such general questions as these: "What do we do to creativity as we teach?" "How as we educate do we contribute to the destruction of the creative potential which is so universal, spontaneous, and free at the start of the life of every uneducated child who is not defective, and even in some defectives?" This destruction is the measure of failure in a vital element in human culture; and it applies equally to all of us—parents, teachers, and psychiatrists. At the same time the educator must ask how it sometimes happens that "accidentally" the creative potential in a few survives the onslaught of the educational process.

If as educators we pretend that things are good or even "not so bad," if we refuse to face that fact that we fail and that much intellectual and creative potential is actively destroyed in the process that we call "education," we will invest little money, personnel, time, space, or even thought in the exploration and solution of the problem. It has been the courage to face their failures openly at the autopsy table in the presence both of their colleagues and of their students which has moved medical men to search for causes, cures, and preventives. Just as the pathologist in medicine studies the failures of medicine by studying individual cases, so the educational pathologist will have to study individual examples of educational failure; and he will have to do this in spite of his realization that the home, society at large, and every form of economic and human deprivation contribute to such failures. But the clearest gains in knowledge will come from the study of educational failure "in pure culture," that is, where they are free of the complications which are due to extrinsic separation and deprivation. Only research on the failure of our educational processes where they operate under optimal circumstances will discover new processes by which to impart the free and spontaneous use of knowledge without crippling and imprisoning creative potential.

Let us consider as an example the so-called "natural" athlete who can imitate with his body anything he sees anyone else do even once. He may see someone swing a tennis racket or a baseball bat, catch and throw a ball, skip rope, or skate. He then picks up the bat and ball or the tennis racket or the lacrosse stick or he puts on skates and uses them with natural precision and grace, sometimes even better than the model whom he has been watching. He has a freedom to move with confidence and to put movements together into new combinations with bodily imagination and without anxiety. He is like the naturally gifted artist who looks at something casually, hardly glancing at it, merely scanning it, and then can reproduce it freely, swiftly, automatically, and faithfully. Subsequently, he can go further. He can take the whole apart and play with the parts, putting them together into new combinations, elaborating with free creative fantasy the initial representational image into a new synthesis.

There is other evidence that the best learning is effortless, as can be demonstrated under hypnosis. The need to depend on drill and grill seems to be a consequence of a loss of the freedom to learn. We have always known that we learn to swim in winter and to skate in summer. If we will merely stop to think, we will know that by grinding in error practice makes imperfect far more often than it makes perfect. Otherwise we would all be virtuosi. Clearly the behavioral sciences must aid education to search for other paths to the same goals, paths which are suitable for the work of education at every level and stage, paths which teach without imprisoning and destroying.

I have already pointed out that in the educational field the first threat to a comparable freedom occurs as a result merely of the acquisition of such symbolic tools as words and numbers. Repetition causes a further loss, not a gain. Thus learning and creativity are destroyed by that drill and grill on which our educational systems depend so blindly. In fact, the amount of drill and grill used may be a measure of the inefficiency of the learning process and of the extent to which neurotic mechanisms have impeded it. Here are the first targets for basic research.

TECHNIQUES OF RESEARCH

The search for new methods always begins as an effort to increase the precision of primary observations. But the wonder of all psychologies, including psychiatry and analysis, starts here. How have they been able to make any progress at all when their raw data have consisted of brief impressions of fleeting moments of behavior which can never recur in exactly the same way? In the moment of action the actors change. They may try to reproduce what they had just thought or felt or done, but the reproduction can never be exact. Yet it is this fleeting internal event or this brief interaction which is to be studied. If such a study is to meet scientific standards it has to be perceived, recorded, recalled, and reported without distortions. Yet we know that during any such experience, the subject, the observer, the recorder, and the reporter are all involved emotionally. This makes it even more difficult to perceive without distortion, record accurately, recall and report without bias. Similarly, considerations warp our judgment of our roles as parent, teacher, preacher, psychologist, or psychiatrist. In each of these relationships our emotions are inextricably involved in swiftly moving sequences of events. When we have wanted to study these we have been dependent for our basic data upon our imperfect and fallible memories of visual and auditory perceptions that were themselves subject to distortion. Relevant to this is Abraham Kaplan's magnificent comment that science begins to come of age only as it abandons the doctrine of "immaculate perception." In states of high emotional involvement, we make maculate perceptions of moments that pass swifly and cannot be recaptured. Then we have to redistill this material through fallible processes of memory and reproduce them with equally fallible techniques of reporting and communicating. Furthermore, we ourselves can never go back to reexamine the primary data or compare our observations with those made by others using the same data. Fallible reports on fallible recollections of fallible perceptions have hardly been a firm basis on which to build a science.

All of this violates not only basic scientific principles, but elementary common sense. We can call in a colleague to look through our microscope and compare what he sees with our own observations. And we can go back to the microscope ourselves as many times as we want. Up to the recent past no such cross-checking of primary observations has been possible in psychological affairs, not in the clinic, the school, or the home. We have had to try to make accurate observations the first time, to remember them accurately, and to report them correctly. Because this is humanly impossible, our slavery to tradition is not surprising. It is amazing rather that we have made any progress at all.

This is why gadgetry has been forced upon us, and this is why gadgetry if used wisely will make a new scientific stature inevitable in our respective fields. Techniques are now at hand whereby we can record with precision, both for individuals and for groups, the behavior of child and parent in the home, of child and teacher in the school, of a patient or patients and therapist, and of the subjects of experiments. We can record the behavior of child, student, and patient together with parents, therapists, experimenters, and teachers, and of the interplay among all of them. We can then sit down to study these recordings and films not merely once but a hundred times; and not just one observer alone but a dozen can discuss and compare what each sees. This has long been true for other scientific disciplines:

it has only recently begun to be true for any of the psychological disciplines, including education.

Any individual moment of human behavior is itself a many-ringed circus. Therefore it is only by repeated observation by many observers that we can take it all in, and then take it apart and put it together again. As educators we must study those we attempt to educate; but at the same time we must have the humility to study ourselves in our respective roles. Now, for the first time in history, the behavioral sciences (among which education should become one of the most important) can begin to meet this basic requirement of scientific methods. In this way the introduction of "gadgetry" brings the study of the learning process into line with other areas of science. Of course, any gadget, be it a microscope or a sound-camera, introduces its own errors. But science progresses by learning first to recognize the artifacts which are due to the new instruments, and then to limit and control them, to make them uniform, and to allow for them. In educational research, we will have to learn how to do this with these new gadgets.

BUILDING A NEW PROFESSIONAL
IMAGE FOR THE TEACHER

Another important aspect of educational research involves its potential contribution to the professional selves of teachers. The young psychiatrist learns not merely to observe the patient, but even more to observe himself in relation to the patient. This he can do only in one way, by seeing himself in action on brief rushes of films and by hearing himself on tape. A young man shows that he has started on the long road to becoming a psychiatrist when in the presence of a group of his peers he has the courage to say publicly and without defensiveness or shame: "What I said was not so bad; but why did I have to say it that way?" Or even: "What I said was not so bad. The way I said it was not so bad. But why did I have to *look* like that?" Something like this must happen to every teacher in the process of learning more about how to teach. And the same thing must someday become part of a future training for parenthood. Let us imagine for a moment what it might do for our children and for our vision of family life if before undertaking the role of parenthood, would-be parents were able to study films *of their own behavior* in relation to infants and children during work with them in day nurseries, nursery schools, kindergartens, primary classes, and playgrounds. Such studies of their own images are beginning to make a difference among psychiatrists. It could make similar differences in future parents. It must become a repeated part of the training experience of teachers throughout the whole span of their professional lives.

There may be a further lesson for education in the fact that in psychiatry the child psychiatrist receives special training. The small child is acutely responsive to cues to which the older child has usually lost his original sensitivity. One of the manifestations of the influence of universal concealed neurotic mechanisms is the way in which as we grow older we wall ourselves off from innumerable subliminal cues. The little child has not yet had as much time to be damaged by his elders. He can still respond to these subtle cues. If we expect to develop free children we will first have to develop free teachers. The teacher of the small child has to be, if anything, healthier, freer, and more adaptable and therefore more subtle than the teacher of the graduate student. Therefore the younger the child, the more important it is for his teacher to have won his way to freedom through unsparing self-study and self-awareness.

THE SCHOOL AS A RESEARCH INSTITUTION

Any school from which we are to learn new ways of educating must be both a school and a laboratory. Just as there are units for research and self-study in every first-rate hospital, so every public and private school system must set up budgets, facilities, and personnel for research. Only a few special hospitals are dedicated solely to research; but all first-rate hospitals integrate research into their care of patients. Medicine would not have made its magnificent progress had not many hospitals been built quite literally around their laboratories and their autopsy rooms. Furthermore, the hospitals which are the leaders have staffs of medical scientists several times as numerous as their patient capacity (20). In such a hospital each patient is fully aware that he is the focus of research by a multidisciplinary team. He is proud of it and grateful for it, because it is in these hospitals that patients receive the best treatment. Thus there is no conflict between research and treatment. There need be none between research in education and education itself.

There will be schools where teachers can sit down with consultants from the fields of child neurology, clinical psychology, cultural anthropology, child psychiatry, and child analysis to study together the films of children alone, in the classroom, and in the playground. These films will show fragmentary samples of episodes in the life of the class as a whole, in the daily life of the group, in the daily lives of individuals in the group. They will follow the same individual children through their years of growth. It will take time to review and study what goes on over time. This is why in addition to the permanent research staffs these schools will require teaching staffs larger even than the best staffed schools of today. Long-term appointments and tenure are essential for long-run longitudinal observations.

Such studies of recorded data will in the end be far more important for each child than are the hours that the teacher of today spends marking papers. Among other reasons this is because long, patient seminars for the study of such material will not isolate the teacher from the child but will bring him into closer touch with the living spirit of the child than does the classroom itself, where the teacher has too many individuals to watch at one time. Therefore such research will also bring to the teacher a steady expansion of spirit and a deepening of insight. It is along these lines that studies can be made which can salvage our future education from enslavement to the past, achieving step-by-step that emancipation from entrenched tradition which has been the greatest cultural achievement of medicine as a whole, and towards which psychiatry is struggling.

This is precisely what we need in education: research schools to parallel research hospitals. The best schools of tomorrow will be the schools that carry on daily basic research on every detail of the educational process, schools fully equipped with observing chambers, one-way mirrors, closed circuit TV, and recording devices; schools with as many professionals as students and with mature research staffs. They must have their own "pathologists" to study their failures, paralleling the pathologists of medical science. There must be research scientists in education working beside the general practitioners of education, just as there are research scientists in medicine working beside the practitioners of medicine, each learning from the other. The practitioner is an applied scientist, and one of his functions is to remind the "pure" scientist (that is, the research man) of the full complexity of problems as they arise in the classroom and in real life. The investigator or pure scientist in turn reminds the practitioner of the need for more precise methods of observing, or recording, documenting, and reporting his observations. Thus each is the critical conscience of the other; and since no one really loves his conscience, the individuals from these two groups do not always get along together too well. Occasionally they may even fight. Nevertheless the alliance between them is indissoluble.

Clearly there are no ready answers, no quick panaceas. We can offer only organizational changes and techniques by which to accumulate precise primary observations, not only of the child in relation to us, but of ourselves in relation to the child. With an honest acknowledgment of the impact on learning of the neurotogenic process, with research and experimentation toward freeing the child from the neurotic processes which he brings into school, and with research designed to change those educational patterns which reinforce these neurotogenic patterns, we may build an educational process that will blend the values of high erudition with wisdom, maturity, creativity, and above all the freedom to keep on changing and growing throughout life.

A NATIONAL INSTITUTE FOR BASIC RESEARCH ON THE EDUCATIONAL PROCESS

Educators need an opportunity to carry on basic research if they are to discover answers to these challenging questions. Congress must be persuaded that we need to parallel the National Institutes of Health with a National Institute for basic research in the educational process, with experimental schools and laboratories, and funds for research (20).

It would bring such an institute into harmony with the federal structure of our country if there were also state institues of education that would be centers for applied research, where practical field-tests of the basic findings of the national institute could be carried on under varying local conditions. This would parallel the organization of medicine and psychiatry. For instance, for many years New York State has had the New York State Psychiatric Institute. This is not merely another hospital to take care of people who are ill. It is a center for training and for research for those who man the entire system of psychiatric state hospitals. Ideally the department of education of each state would have a department for research on the educational process which would be able to call upon not only the National Institute personnel, methods, and funds, but also on the resources of all local school and university facilities, through their departments of education, psychiatry, psychology, sociology, and cultural anthropology.

Such a development would inaugurate a new period of growth in our understanding of the educational process and in its struggle with the ubiquitous neurotic process in all cultures known to man.

REFERENCES

1. "The Concept of Normality and Neurosis," Ch. 1, pp. 3–14, in *Psychoanalysis and Social Work,* Heiman, J. (ed.); International Universities Press, N.Y., 1953, 346 pp.

2. "Some Unsolved Problems of the Scientific Career." *American Scientist,* **4,** No. 4, Oct. 1953, 596–613, and **42,** No. 1, Jan. 1954, 104–112.

3. "The Forgotten Man of Education." *Harvard Alumni Bulletin,* **56,** No. 8, Feb. 1954, 349–353.

4. "The Search for Maturity in Pre-Professional Education." *Clinical Research,* **VII,** No. 2, April 1959, 177–183.

5. "Education and the Process of Maturation," in *Today's Children are Tomorrow's World.* New York: Associates of Bank Street College of Education, Fifth Annual Conference, Feb. 1957, pp. 7–18.

6. Freud's Legacy to Human Freedom." *Perspectives in Biology and Medicine,* **1,** No. 1, Autumn 1957, 105–118.

7. "The Neurotic Process as the Focus of Physiological and Psychoanalytic Research." Read in part before the Royal Soc. of Med., London, on Sept. 10, 1957; *J. of Mental Science,* London, **104,** No. 435, Apr. 1958, 518–536.

8. *Neurotic Distortion of the Creative Process:* Porter Lectures, Series **22,** University of Kansas Press, Lawrence, Kansas, 1958, p. 151. Paperback edition, Noonday Press, New York, 1961, 152 pp.

9. "Are We Educating for Maturity?" *NEA Journal,* **48,** No. 1, Jan. 1959, pp. 58–63; digested in *Panorama,* Spring 1959, 14–16.

10. "The Relation of the Conditioned Reflex to the Preconscious Functions." Transactions of the 84th Annual Meeting of the American Neurological Association, Atlantic City, June 15–17, 1959, 187 188.

11. "Hypnotism: A Focus for Psychophysiological and Psychoanalytic Investigations." *Archives of General Psychiatry,* **4,** January 1961, 40–54.

12. "The Fostering of Creative Scientific Productivity." *Daedalus,* **91,** No. 2, Spring 1962, 294–309.

13. "The Unsolved Problem in Education." Maryland Conference on Elementary Education, Baltimore, April 11, 1962; pp. 36–44 from Pamphlet published by The Maryland State Dept. of Education, Baltimore, Md., 1962, 77 pp.

14. "Neurosis and Normality." *The Encyclopedia of Mental Health,* Deutsch, Albert, Editor-in-Chief, Vol. IV, Franklin Watts, New York, 1963, pp. 1346–1353.

15. "The Spiritual Challenge of Medicine and Psychiatry to Human Culture"; published under the shortened title of "Medicine As A Spiritual Challenge" in *Journal of Religion and Health,* **3,** No. I, October 1963, 39–55, by The Academy of Religion and Mental Health.

16. "Research in Protecting Preconscious Functions in Education." Papers and Reports from the ASDC Seventh Curriculum Research Institute, held in Washington, D.C., on December 2, 1961. Transactions published by the Association in April, 1964, pp. 28–42.

17. "Blocks to Creativity." *International Science and Technology,* June 1965, pp. 69–78.

18. "Unsolved Problems of Scientific Education." *Daedalus,* **94,** No. 3, Summer 1965, 564–587.

19. "A Reconsideration of Thinking, The Dream Process, and "The Dream.'" *The Psychoanalytic Quarterly,* **XXXV,** 1966, 191–198.

20. "The Need for a National Institute for Basic Research on the Educational Process." Presented at the Hickory Hill Seminar, Washington, D.C., October, 1963 *(unpublished).*

Chapter 5

A Learning-Teaching Paradigm Integrating Intellectual and Affective Processes

Barbara Biber

About the Author

For many a young person whose adolescence coincided with the end of World War I, visions of a better world, not yet named The Great Society, determined the course of personal careers. From Barnard College, Barbara Biber moved into workers' education, a deeply educative experience but not the right personal "fit." During several years at the University of Chicago as a graduate student in psychology and with an apprenticeship under Dr. Herman Adler, pioneer child psychiatrist, new and lasting directions began to take shape. Interest, excitement, dedication, even faith, grew spontaneously wherever the psychology of human behavior was put to the service of childhood.

A crucial point was a meeting, in 1928, with Lucy Sprague Mitchell and an invitation to join the staff of the Bureau of Educational Experiments (the forerunner of Bank Street College of Education) as a research assistant. From then on, for the almost four decades which followed, the process of learning and the meaning of school experience for the developing personality has been the core of professional interest. In the thirties, as a psychologist for the Bank Street Nursery School, and as teacher of child psychology to the newly organized graduate teacher-education program, there was opportunity to systematize knowledge and to lay the foundation for a style of research that was to become integral to this experimental venture in education. There were, at the same time, the pleasures of a young family and the sorrows of the Depression.

The decade of the forties was a busy one for a psychologist who had chosen education as her field and Bank Street College as her locale. There were training programs for the teachers who would man the day care centers as part of a war effort. Out of preference for the use of the schoolroom as a proper field for the study of the psycho-social aspects of learning came a comprehensive analysis of a group of seven-year-old children in their school milieu. In teacher education a method of psycho-educational counseling was developed and instituted as a central aspect of the training program. The establishment of the Bank Street Public School Workshops built a bridge between the small experimental milieu that was Bank Street and the complex public school system of a great city. A method of school consultation combining curriculum revision with the study of child development was accompanied by a comparative research study, in different types of schools, on what children expect of teachers. Outside of Bank Street, short-term, part-time teaching assignments at New York University and the Vassar Summer Institutes were fitted in with the completion of a Ph.D. at Columbia.

By the 1950's, Barbara Biber, in the position of Director of Research at Bank Street College, concentrated on developing a research program focused on the role of the school in relation to healthy personality and built around the basic concept of cognitive-affective interaction in learning and development of ego-strength. All this was made possible by foundation and federal support. An assessment study of teacher personality utilized a projective test developed within this program. The assumptions of the earlier years were put to test under her directorship in a systematic comparative study of nine-year-olds attending four schools which varied along a dimension of modern-traditional ideology in education. A multi-faceted program concerned with mental health at the level of primary prevention further extended the scope of previous work to include contrasting child populations, home-school interaction, and sociological studies of the school and its relations to parents and community. In addition to the team work of psychologist and educator that had been well-established, the viewpoints and skills of anthropologist and sociologist were brought to bear on complex problems of the educational structure from the classroom to the school board.

In 1963, Barbara Biber resigned from her position as Director of Research at Bank Street College of Education in order to assure completion and publication of the research studies which had been undertaken under her aegis as principal investigator over the previous decade. Her present appointment as Distinguished Research Scholar enables her to write and edit on the one hand and, on the other, to take part in the national upsurge of interest in revision and innovation in education.

Introduction to the Chapter

Biber argues that education is a complex, epigenetic process involving many aspects of the teaching-learning interaction; yet she is specific enough to make sense to educators seeking both the rationale and the specific route to educational effectiveness of our schools.

Biber suggests that the present concentration on intellectual excellence has its assets and liabilities. She commends our moving ahead in upgrading the nature and variety of cognitive experiences for children, but she frowns on our blindness to some of the aspects of education discussed by Bower, Sanford, and Kubie. The standards of educational excellence must, according to Biber, include an operational and instructional awareness of the associated emotional processes in learning.

She is tough minded about her goals, methods, and rationale. She wants the school to increase the child's openness to knowledge, to help the child become an intellectual and cognitive powerhouse. Beyond that, she encourages the admission of nonrational processes of dealing with knowledge as a significant dimension of educational power and wants the schools to utilize this power.

In her schema, Biber presents what she sees as the goal of educational instruction, then the method by which the goal might be achieved, the rationale for doing it this way, and the associated processes of learning and development in the instructional method.

A Learning-Teaching Paradigm Integrating Intellectual And Affective Processes[1]

THE STATE OF AFFAIRS IN EDUCATION

The present state of affairs in education in the United States has one heartening aspect. At long last, the potency of the school as a social institution is being recognized. Yet there is an almost frightening quality in the degree to which our effectiveness as a society, our progress as a nation, and the maintenance of our power position in the world scene are currently perceived as dependent upon the relative excellence of our system of schooling. The strong impetus for improving education in recent years can easily be traced to the urgent needs associated with social crises: training more scientists and engineers in order to sustain a position of leadership in an atomic age; eliminating or substantially decreasing the illiteracy rate as a means of counteracting the psychological damage and job handicap of minority groups, and the impoverished; producing techniques for accelerating learning and elevating intellectual levels in order to assure an employable population for an increasingly automated production system; using mechanized and mass media as teaching tools to meet the manpower drain in the teaching professions as more and more children are enrolled for more and more education.

The atmosphere engendered by what is rightly called *The Revolution in the Schools* (Gross and Murphy, 1964) is mixed; compounded of attack and innovation, anxiety and excitement, social conscience and personal aggrandizement, professional controversy and lay bandwagonism, it is not exactly what might be envisioned as the ideal *Zeitgeist* with which to get American education out of its rut. But such a reaction is to be expected when public moneys, in amounts inconceivable a very short time ago, are suddenly made available, when directives for the spending of such money are established in

[1] I wish to thank Doris Wallace for her valuable editorial assistance in the preparation of this chapter.

haste and when, to be executed, they have to filter down through unprepared administrative levels.

It may well be that only a crisis, or a series of them, could engender such a white heat of concern for our educational system and, with it, so much investment of talent, energy, and public moneys, confidently dedicated to making the process of schooling a panacea for our social ills. Certainly, educators and members of related professions working for decades within the normal processes of change did not succeed in making education into front page news or in elevating it to a position of importance in political strategy. The argument that a democratic society depends on maximizing the potential of the individual did not have the impact that Sputnik had. The further argument that the national level of adaptive, creative functioning could reach new heights if known principles of psychological functioning could be integrated with educational practice and theory, did not prove as convincing as has the current assumption that a major breakthrough in the battle against delinquency can come through an attack on illiteracy.

Education has gained immediately and ultimately the attention which its processes and problems have received from professionals and lay citizenry alike. The fact that this breathless concern and expanded expectation is crisis-born, however, is cause for anxiety. Reasoning based on plausibility rather than experimental evidence, simplicity of implementation rather than profundity of concept, disparate dealing with parts rather than masterful comprehension of organized complexities has become the accepted, even attractive, rule; it· has become modish to base program planning on these criteria in the interest of accomplishing a great deal in a short time. Yet, the dialectic of critique has already asserted itself, since there are thoughtful people for whom newness or the appearance of newness is not a foregone virtue or an assurance of true progress. A quick look at a few of the important innovations currently to the fore and at the equally important questions sprouting up around them seems worthwhile.

INNOVATIONS AND CRITIQUE

We can turn, to begin with, to the impact that the teaching machine and, more generally, the technique of programmed learning have made upon our schools. This innovation can be defended, as it has been, as a clear case of progress, of updating antediluvian teaching practices. It represents the application of the experimental findings and convictions of B. F. Skinner (1954), an eminent and experienced psychologist; it brings another piece of machinery into the classroom which, by itself, adds an apparent assurance that whatever is taking place is being carried on more efficiently; it claims to release the teacher from rote tasks, thus freeing her for the subtler, nonmechanized aspects of her role.

But the learning theory basic to the Skinnerian teaching machine is a matter of controversy, not certitude. Some eminent psychologists have questioned Skinner's basic postulate that operant conditioning constitutes the basic form of human learning; they dispute the assumption that there is a qualitative sameness in learning situations ranging from the establishment of simple responses to the development of complex cognitive organization.

Wohlwill (1962) makes the point that, at the level of reasoning and concept formation, reliance upon continuous variation of the context of the stimulus is no substitute for a theory of concept formation from which to develop rules for the variation.

Wohlwill's critique brings into this controversial field not only the shifting sands of theory but also the indeterminate vista of goals: what kind of learner, of thinker do we aim to develop? He takes a position as protagonist of an old, now newly accented goal—to stimulate the kind of questioning that leads to the discovery of principles and keeps viable the inclination of children to wonder, to be curious, to engage in energetic intellectual pursuit. The students' natural tendency to question cannot survive when the available modes of acquiring information are in conflict with these tendencies. Wohlwill believes that teaching machine methodology creates such a conflict.

The relation between programmed learning and learning theory, or theories, has been dealt with incisively by Hilgard (1964). What the learning process is, essentially, is differently perceived and explained by learning theorists of varying persuasions. As Hilgard has pointed out, there are those among Skinner's fellow behaviorists, such as Lumsdaine (1960), who question the operant conditioning model and suggest that a contiguous association model may be more appropriate. Furthermore, those who identify themselves as cognitive theorists question the whole idea that the learning process can be adequately conceived in terms of linkage of stimuli and responses through contiguous association or reinforcement. They object strenuously to the atomistic emphasis in the learning paradigm in which teaching machines have been constructed.

"In summary, then," Hilgard says, "I believe that the advances made in programmed learning have been based very little upon a

strict application of learning theory. . . ." From this position he does
not dismiss the potential values and uses of programmed learning but
asks for a balanced view of what its place should be in the total
educational enterprise and he spells out its limitations. A teacher,
a skillful teacher to be sure, is essential if schooling is to achieve
certain basic aims: helping the student learn to "initiate inquiry on
his own," providing the student an opportunity "to take satisfaction
in small evidences of his own creativity" and to emerge in "idiosyncratic specialization," enabling him to move toward "greater diversi-
fication of talent" rather than toward "greater uniformity," and helping him to gain "the skills of effective participation with others"
in solving problems or in taking civic responsibility. These educational
functions cannot be replaced by the machine or programmed learning.
This does not gainsay a place in the classroom for programmed learning appropriate to other aspects of schooling. However, it does constitute a serious warning that overenthusiasm for programmed learning
could lead to an unfortunate skewness of the total educational
enterprise.

The active entrance of scholars into the field of education is another
innovation. Beginning with the task of bringing high school curricula
in physics and mathematics in line with contemporary knowledge
in these fields, this program has been extended to other subject matter
and is having the powerful impact that often accompanies high-
powered jurisdiction and generous funding from government and
foundation sources. The goals are ambitious and represent advanced
thinking with respect to optimal structuring of knowledge and the
cognitive potential of children. An underlying principle in this work
has been that curriculum should be based on the logic and relationships intrinsic to the particular field; what constitutes these inherent
structures is not easily agreed upon, even for the more exact fields.
In the social sciences agreement is even more difficult, since there
are so many differing, though valid, perspectives of those fields. Another principle holds that the materials prepared for classroom use
should be real and important and relevant to the contemporary world
and the lives children live in it; but again, views as to what elements
of the contemporary world are "real and important" to the healthy
maturing of first grade children differ widely. For example, a new
economics program in Elkhart, Indiana, aims for a mastery of basic
concepts in economics in the early grades—scarcity, division of labor,
specialization, investment, and unemployment. An exercise for first
graders in this program is described as follows (Gross, 1964):

"In one class, two teams produce gingerbread men. Each child on Team A makes his own gingerbread man, starting from scratch—with visible waste of material, duplication of equipment, slowness of execution, and low production. On Team B, the youngsters form an assembly line, with one child rolling dough, another cutting forms, a third pressing in the eyes, and the last child putting the cookies in the oven. The hypothesis that division of labor increases production is dramatically confirmed."

The very thing that pleases Dr. Senesh (1963), who devised this program, namely, the derivation of an abstract idea through a device, actually fractionizes the child's direct personal experience with his work and therefore with its meaning. Such procedures give cause for dismay when one considers them in the light of contemporary principles of child development or the psychology of personality. Where is the recognition that for the six-year-old the transformation of the shapeless, meaningless piece of dough into the final recognizable gingerbread man, and the going through of all the intermediate steps is a way of gaining mastery over the complexity of all the "making" processes? The gingerbread man, made on one's own from beginning to end, is a beloved gingerbread man, self-invested and a source of pride in work completed. The final array of singly made gingerbread men, each sure to show the mark of individual craftsmanship, is symbolic evidence of how subtly different the same things can be. Those who feel that children should be given opportunities to experience work as a gratifying self-investment, to gain mastery over complexity, and to value variation more than uniformity would consider more to have been lost than gained in the assembly line production of gingerbread men. Is the assembly line mode of production in our economy the "real and important" material for first graders? Is efficiency of production, which it represents, a goal around which work experiences for children should be organized? The fact that by such devices young children can grasp this and many other abstract concepts is insufficient criterion for judging whether these experiences are suitable, optimal rather, for a given stage of development.

The movement for curriculum revision, as is to be expected, encompasses far more than subject matter change. Its goals are equally concerned with how children learn, and, therefore, how they should best be taught. The position taken is that classrooms can come closer to a model of the search for understanding that we associate with the scientist. By the use of an inductive approach and curriculum designs in which specificity and differentiation alternate with increasingly complex general and global concepts, children can become skilled in intellectual search and more adept at reasoning, generalizing, and hypothesizing. This proposition carries with it the provision that teachers be found and trained, or retrained, to carry a radically new role of guide rather than expert, to take responsibility for strengthening the learning process rather than merely conveying information, and to be more invested in the process of thinking than in the end product.

To meet this requirement, far more than a program of retraining institutes, no matter how far-flung, is necessary. The teaching role envisaged here constitutes much more than an intellectual shift. It requires the capacity to empathize with the mental processes of young children, to deal without anxiety with the ambiguity necessarily associated with exploration-search patterns rather than right-wrong paradigms, to deal with variations not only in rate of mastery but in cognitive style, and thus to carry a multiple series of evaluative criteria by which to judge when learning or teaching is being productive for different children.

Recently, Professor Max Beberman of the University of Illinois made a public statement pointedly criticizing the rapid curriculum change in the field of mathematics. Professor Beberman favors the new approach, indeed he was one of its initiators, but he decries the damage done when new curricula are introduced "without proper attention to essential pedagogical principles or the need for relating mathematics to the real world, as well as relating it to the logical principles now receiving great emphasis." He reports unsatisfactory results in many cases and also "frightened teachers. . . . Elementary school teachers have become so frightened by the prospect of using esoteric mathematics, they have lost all common sense." His attack is sharpest against those "charlatans who get a grant from the Government or publisher and then slap together a program they insist should be used everywhere so they can maximize the amount of money received."

In a thoughtful, comprehensive commentary on contemporary trends, Friedlander (1965) points to the errors implicit in neglecting the role of fact as raw material in children's thinking and in assuming that basic curiosity and spontaneous desire to learn are strong enough in all children to generate the effort necessary for mastery. He argues that the discovery method for those in the beginning stages of learning is not always a productive route to making "true" discoveries. Although he is identified with the basic purposes of the newer trends, he is at the same time concerned that:

". . . important ideas about teaching and learning might lose their potency due to oversimplification, misunderstanding, empty ritualistic application, and the frustrated disappointment among both teachers and students that would be sure to follow. . . . My true conclusion is that the factor of judgment is crucial. When we recognize the complications of the teaching and learning process, with all its delicate balances between freedom and discipline, between imagination and critique, between fact and concept, and between memory and forgetting, it hardly seems likely that any one method or formula can fit all cases. Only the wise intervention of the teacher's judgment can hold these shifting stresses in equilibrium."

Some of the problems associated with curriculum revisions are intrinsic—perceived as such by the scholars themselves—having to do with the uncertain state of knowledge in many fields. Such uncertainty makes sequential organization from global to differentiated concepts more an ambition than a realizable goal. Nevertheless, the creation of a learning atmosphere in which children will become independent, imaginative explorers in the realm of knowledge depends upon developing an altogether new kind of raw material for classroom use. In the past, there have been teachers with high intellectual goals and understanding of the mental processes of young children who themselves were sufficiently informed and creative to devise appropriate materials. But education cannot afford to depend upon this occasional order of creative teaching. There are too few great teachers, and too vast a body of knowledge to be encompassed. It is therefore education's gain that the scholars of the country are taking active interest and decision in the selection and organization of knowledge to be mastered at various stages in the course of schooling.

Fortunately, the scholars who have done this are aligned with the cognitive psychologists in their concepts of the learning process and their goals for educating children. They are welcomed particularly by those educators, and they are considerable in number, who for many years have advocated and enacted almost identical concepts and goals, insofar as the school community was receptive. These educators are convinced that children can be motivated to learn through their basic drive to explore; they feel that conventional methods of schooling do not approach the limits of the learning potential of children and that fulfillment of any child's intellectual development is a function, within wide limits, of the nature of his life environment—an environment in which the school plays a salient role. It is their belief that children have more capacity for perceiving relationship among facts, for generalizing, for reasoning, and for inferring than they have a chance to exercise or develop in the average classroom. The promulgation, by many scholars of these concepts of learning and motivation in childhood as new to the American scene, or the frequent, and often exclusive, reference to historically remote figures such as Montessori or Rousseau as the sole authorities for these educational goals, is an astonishing aspect on the edge of this scene.

A major problem to be recognized in the work of the curriculum revision movement is its intellectualistic concentration, which has both merit and deficit. The merit lies in its potential contribution to the much needed up-grading of the cognitive experience offered children at all levels in school. The deficit lies in its seeming disinterest—or blindness—to the interdependence of cognitive and affective experience and growth; between the growth of the mind as a powerful tool and the building of the person as a self. Such an image of the self comprises a social being who has an internalized model for interchange among people and a confident expectation that skill and competence will become the means for effective participation in the work of the world.

A wider span of interacting variables is involved in the learning process than is taken into consideration by programs focused on altering cognitive experience in the classroom. These variables have to do with processes ordinarily subsumed under the rubric of personality development: the sense of autonomy and participation in one's own growth; equilibria to be attained between dependence and independence, originality and communication, exploration and resolution, impulse and control. These processes do not, certainly, enact their ferment in vacuo. They are as much dynamically part of the cognitive processes and of the quality of cognitive interchange among people—child to child or teacher to pupil—as they are related to the interpersonal relations or the socialization of impulses associated with maturing.

Knowledge of changing conflicts, drives, and energies at different stages of development and understanding of how the self develops a style of relationship to the world of people, things, and ideas are all contributions of psychodynamic psychology needed as a foundation for changes in educational materials and teaching methods. If this knowledge of the developing individual is not taken into account, guiding principles for what should be changed are inadequate because they are incomplete. The application of such partial principles, no matter how sound they be in the restricted area with which they deal, leads to distortion and misapplication.

A widened concept of the role of the school to include, but also go beyond the present day call upon education to produce greater intellectual excellence demands the construction of a suitable learning-teaching paradigm. Innovating thrusts, no matter how sound or imaginative each in its own way, are parts to be fitted into a conceptual whole, not for the sake of elegance of idea but because a classroom is a complex, human field of interacting forces and no part can have an insulated existence, theoretical or practical. Most significant for this task is the knowledge of human behavior available through advances made by developmental theorists in the analysis of cognitive processes, the growing interest in ego-development among psychoanalysts, the wealth of studies of the creative process and the recognition of the self as a psychic dynamism. These constitute basic sources for what we need to know in order to educate the growing child.

A revised concept of what schooling can and should be actually emerged several decades ago from the field of education itself and not from progress in these other fields. This concept developed independently, under the auspices of private institutions or in experimental centers in universities; its impact has been important but limited, usually affecting only the preschool and elementary levels. The educators who developed this revised concept of education—which did not conform with established practice—described the role of the school in theoretical and practical terms. They saw the School[1] that most closely practiced the principles they postulated as one which:

brings about maximum use of the child's potential in effective interaction with his environment,

works in the awareness that each child's ultimate competence is a resultant of many levels of psychological functioning, among them mastery, self-understanding, resolution of basic conflict, motivated pursuit,

provides such varied encounters with people and with the phenomena, events and ideas of society, that diversity and change become an intrinsic part of the child's eventual *Weltanschauung*,

[1] In the pages that follow, the use of the capital S denotes, collectively, the schools whose purposes and practices have been aligned with this concept.

builds the experience of learning in childhood so that it assumes an integrating function through which personal meaning can be universalized and take socialized forms and non-personal reality becomes part of personal commitment.

The connection between the advances in knowledge of human behavior and the educational philosophy and practice developed at the frontier can be perceived in different ways. In one sense, the advances represent a concurrent influence in the sphere of educational change; in another, knowledge from these behavioral science sources represents a validation of principles that were derived empirically by educators who observed and analyzed while they taught. But what is most important is the recognition of these sources as seminal, requiring further refinement of educational method.

The School is already practiced in searching for new knowledge in the field of human behavior to stimulate educational change and test trends that have developed empirically in the field. But it is at this time, when the ferment in education is at a high pitch, when changes being made on a national scale are likely to affect education for many years to come, that it is important to base these changes on the broadest possible knowledge of the developmental processes and motivational forces that are such a profound influence on learning.

Broad concepts of the School's role must be, and have been, reduced to the methods, processes, and transactions of daily life in the classroom (although it is well to keep in mind that translation of an educational goal into the actual operations of classroom life takes as much inventiveness and ingenuity, and has as much chance of missing the mark as have research measures devised to study a complex psychological variable). In the pages that follow I shall consider a series of goals[1]—sensitivity, discovery, mastery, and synthesis—and then discuss relevant teaching methods and related psychological processes.

The educator, at all levels in this context, is being asked to exercise a kind of binocular perception of the learning child, so that awareness of associated emotional processes is as naturally and knowledgeably considered as is intellectual gain. This, and no less, is the standard of excellence to be held as an ideal for education in our times.

[1] The inclusion of a further three goals would complete this concept of a learning-teaching paradigm. They are: to facilitate communication and interaction, to establish social order in the school essential to the learning goals, and to advance self-understanding.

SENSITIVITY

Goal

Much of the practice of the School is related to a broad, inclusive goal, which is *to increase the range and depth of children's sensitivity to the world around them.* There are alternative psychological worlds in which people live. There is a restricted world in which potential for sensory-perceptual responsiveness is meager and color, form, and sound are monotonous. In such a world, the experiences offered for intellectual mastery limit thinking to acquisitive, repetitive, precoded activity. Interaction with people in this world has an established pattern that blunts perception of the intricacies and nuances of human interchange and behavior. The alternative, at the opposite extreme, is a world that is open and varied and invites penetration. In such a world, there is active, varied sensory-perceptual responsiveness; sensory experience is probed, discriminated, unraveled; and the human interchange is experienced across a full range of emotions. The School's goal is to construct and continuously reconstruct this latter kind of world as a milieu for learning, one that brings the child into lively contact with a vital flow of experience and stimulates sensitive, discriminating perception as the basis for action and interaction, on many levels, in varying circumstances.

This particular concept of one of the functions of the School is in no sense the private concern of professional educators. It emerges repeatedly in other contexts. Karl Deutsch [1959] calls it "openness" and provides a definition built on his knowledge of computer models and communication systems.

"Openness—the ability to increase the sensitivity in the range of our channels of intake, the ability to interact and to receive, to learn more about the universe around us and from the human beings around us—is perhaps one of the most critical and most precious qualities of any system of communication . . ."

Deutsch goes on to an interesting, though arguable, elaboration in saying that learning capacity, in the image of the computer model, is proportionate to the availability of internal resources or facilities which are uncommitted, available for free "dissociation and re-combination" in response to "messages" to the computer. These resources are equivalent to what we think of as environmental stimuli for the child. This provides a conceptual scheme for a principle that has been vague in formulation but firm in commitment by the School: that a rich fund of direct experience built up in the early years or in the early stages of learning endeavor assures that, at later stages, while attaining standard's of effectiveness, the child can, at the same time maintain the flexibility necessary for change and new learning. Deutsch himself relates these concepts to alternative models of education, making the point that "progressive education" in contrast to the traditional authoritarian approach, is conducive to sustaining "openness" in intellectual functioning and provides the kind of "free activity . . . which is so essential for dissociation and recombination."

Method and Rationale

The School, then, plans for variety and abundance of encounters, possibilities and alternatives. Refinement of sensory response grows from the wealth of sense experience offered: the vivid color on the walls or in the illustrations in the books, the low bong of the drums or the whisper of the triangles, the feel of wet in the clay, the softness of the rabbit's fur, and the straightness of the ridges on the turtle's shell. When the content is intellectual, the same principle governs: there are different ways of solving a problem or expressing an idea, many sources to be probed for a full assembly of facts, contrasting opinions to be deduced from a common body of information. Most vital for the intended outcome is the teacher's own impressionability and the subtlety of the communication system she has established with the children.

Stimulating to greater sensitivity is achieved through the technique of actively guiding the child to a more differentiated perception and through increasing the proportion of direct contacts he has with the phenomena about which he is learning. The world outside the school walls, the larger environment, is therefore important material for study. For example, a group of seven-year-olds is going to observe how the foundation of a nearby building is proceeding. The children may have memories of the old building that once occupied this spot or even of the big skull cracker rhythmically demolishing the old brick wall and of the man in the cabin of the truck who made it all happen. Before them they see the teeth of the steam shovel scooping up the earth and the swinging crane that lifts it high and steers it to just the right spot for dumping into the truck.

From such experiences in guided observation, several kinds of learning are expected. The first is amorphous and therefore often neglected when education follows a too highly structured pattern from the beginning to end of the learning process. It has to do with the arousal of wonder, the absorption of sights and sounds and thoughts, and the freedom and pleasure to sustain a relaxed flow of association without compulsion to channel, select, and organize the early response. It might be called lowering the threshold of impressionability or, returning to Deutsch, "preserving and protecting . . . the capacity for that sense of wonder which the Greeks held as the beginning of philosophy." But there is also the kind of learning that is organized and consolidated, that is the fruit of an ability to use discriminating observation to acquire knowledge; it may be knowledge of how work gets done, what the machines do, what people do, how the control levers work, what makes buildings stand firmly in all their height, which kind of foundation is built on rock and which on sandy earth, and what walls unsuspectingly contain in their insides.

There is a third kind of yield from a varied exposure on all levels of functioning that has to do with potential for further learning. It is useful here to consider new insights derived from the theoretical positions of investigators such as Hebb (1949) and Piaget (1936, 1945) and the analysis and implications of their work as pursued by Hunt (1961). Some physiologists, and psychologists such as Hebb, have emphasized that the development of central nervous system functioning is contingent on the history of sensory stimulation. Hebb and other psychologists have given considerable emphasis to the idea that the quality and quantity of early experience, considered in both physiological and psychological terms, determines the subsequent course of the organism's development. In this connection, a general principle, derived from Piaget's work, is summarized by Hunt:

". . . the greater the variety of situations to which the child must accommodate his behavioral structures, the more differentiated and mobile they become, the more rapid is his rate of intellectual development and the greater is his range of interests in the novel and the new."

To sum up briefly, the methods adopted, represented here by guided observation, to fulfill the goal of increasing the scope and depth of sensitivity can be expected to have three general effects: first, the general effect of activating responsiveness; second, the more specific effect of gaining concrete knowledge, and third, the establishing of strategies for information processing that will serve later intellectual functions such as accommodation or problem-solving.

Associated Processes

Everything that has been said so far about this goal and principle is primarily relevant to the perceptual-cognitive aspects of the child in relation to his world. No human functioning is, of course, either entirely intellectual, or mediated through perceptual-cognitive structures alone. Any learning-teaching paradigm, therefore, is incomplete unless it consciously deals with the processes of personality formation that are inevitably associated with the particular methods for accomplishing its goals. This constitutes an additional criterion for judging the suitability of any method: it is necessary to know why a particular method may be expected, to enhance learning but, further, the method itself needs evaluation in order to explain how it is likely to affect formation of attitudes toward work, self and others. Thus, the method, through its effects on attitude, and therefore on motivation, becomes a secondary determinant of how far the original learning goal will be realized.

What is involved in awareness of this somewhat complex process? At one level we are confronted with questions subsumed under the broad rubric of positive mental health. It seems justifiable to assume that the experience of becoming a discriminating observer, of looking and seeing, and, in a sense, submitting oneself to being impressed, is one way of establishing connectedness between the self and the nonself aspects of experience. Connectedness, thought of as a psychological dimension, is readily seen as a kind of involvement. Such involvement is surely a primary form of investment in living, one of Jahoda's (1958) original criteria for positive mental health that seems to survive successive reconceptualizations. So here we see an extension of the goal line of the School: to increase sensitivity, using methods that are assumed to enhance learning, but also, by means of the method selected—guided observation—to strengthen the attachment of the growing child to the world.

In the realm of emotion, the content, structure, and quality of learning experience, though directed to activating intellectual processes, also contain a dynamic potential as resonators of feelings which can stir the inner life, the "private" world, in Frank's terms (1946), that each child brings to the learning situation. Being witness to controlled destruction by the skull cracker or the steam shovel, for example, can resound in many different ways. It may arouse anxiety, stir up hard-to-control aggressive impulses, echo danger from without or within. Or it may be reassuring that so much destruction can be so smoothly controlled, and a word with the man who controls the lever may be emotionally strengthening to boys who are at the stage of struggling uncertainly toward adult masculinity. Certainly, it cannot be assumed that these alternative emotional responses will be uniform in any group of children or that a teacher could with certainty predict the probable impact of any given experience for any one child. What seems essential is the realization that these emotional processes are universally active and that the dominance of one response over another differs, not only from child to child "privately," but also from developmental stage to stage. This emotional resonance is not to be avoided. Far from it. The fact that it interacts with gains in intellectual mastery and that the environmental context is removed from the urgency and intimacy of family relations may well argue for the expectation that this emotional resonance will help to resolve conflicts and reduce anxiety.

DISCOVERY

Goal

In a paper discussing research on the child's level in education, Mitchell (1944) states:

". . . If we think of research as an 'essay in discovery' . . . we can say that children can conduct research. Moreover, we can say that research is a natural pursuit of children though recognized by schools only in recent years. It is in this . . . sense, as an essay in discovery, that I wish to consider research on a child's level . . . . The evidence is overwhelming that the essay in discovery is a native drive of children . . . . The traditional attitude toward learning . . . made little use of the fact that children are filled with all sorts of curiosities, intellectual and social, and that they naturally attempt to get answers to their incessant questioning through active investigations. . . . The traditional school . . . assumed that children would learn faster if information were handed out to them with all the relationships neatly worked out by some adult. This is still the typical method of the class room where resources for gathering information are largely confined to a textbook! . . . A textbook is not meant to be thought-provoking. It is meant to be an orderly, accurate, condensed statement of facts . . . they are to be accepted and remembered. There is no essay in discovery intended or expected."

Embedded in this statement is a second major goal of the School—*to develop techniques and attitudes for learning by discovery*, relying on the assumption that information and understanding gained through independent pursuit would be functional and that the experience of learning by discovery would stimulate a lasting love of learning. Much that has happened in schools during the twenty years since Mitchell's statement has involved the complex problems of achieving this goal— searching for suitable methods, changing classroom climate and radically changing teacher attitudes.

Recently, the theme of learning by discovery has become virtually a battle cry for contemporary educational change. In the progress report of the Panel on Educational Research and Development (1964), we read:

". . . the Panel can be said to favor a particular approach to teaching, an approach called 'inductive teaching' or 'the discovery method.' The plan is to get students to discover things for themselves. . . . The idea of inductive teaching is not new, either. Only recently, however, has it been widely recognized that the extra burden of this approach falls not on the child but on the adults concerned with his education."

Bruner (1961a) puts the case generally:

"Whether one speaks to mathematicians or physicists or historians, one encounters repeatedly an expression of faith in the powerful effects that come from permitting the student to put things together for himself, to be his own discoverer."

He then proceeds to analyze the "benefits derived from the experience of learning through discoveries that one makes oneself" in terms of greater intellectual power, an intrinsic reward system, learning the usefulness of heuristic inquiry, and as an aid to preserving memory. From the programs launched around this theme, there has been an impressive product representing the combined efforts of scholars and schoolmen in the form of revised curricula in subject matter areas (Heath, 1964), the development of specific techniques to match this goal (Suchman, 1961), and a variety of plans for reorganizing the classroom and the school (Shaplin, 1961; Brown, 1963; King, 1964).

Method and Rationale

In the days when the School launched the method of making each child a discoverer in counteraction to the passive role of the child in traditional education, there were two underlying convictions that were based primarily on observation of childhood and on John Dewey's theories of learning and thinking. The first was the importance of being actively involved; the second was that curiosity, the desire to learn, was a fundamental human quality.

Obviously, the traditional classroom was not well suited to active learning, independent discovery, or the expression and pursuit of curiosity. The changes brought about by the School, then as now, involved changes in curriculum and organization of school life; but in a more comprehensive way, every effort was made to create a pervasive intellectual climate suited in all its aspects to these new goals and concepts of the learning process. Classrooms became workrooms with new criteria for noise, mobility, concentration, productivity. Emphasis was placed on guiding the children toward basic materials from first hand sources at the beginning stages of inquiry by using observation, interview, maps, artifacts, and government bulletins in connection, for example, with a problem in social studies:

"Anything which gives a relevant fact or a relevant image . . . a chance to collect a diversity of facts . . . an opportunity to continue the essay in discovery in distant or past situations . . . to work with raw sources and not always with pre-digested materials" (Mitchell, 1944).

Above all this, the milieu was ripe for the discovery approach only when the teacher valued exploration as a preparatory stage for arriving at insights and could accommodate and absorb the relatively indirect path to the goal which exploratory search involves. At this point, it may be well to consider the underlying convictions of the discovery approach in the context of recent theoretical formulations.

The redirection of psychoanalytic thinking toward study of ego-functioning, represented in the contribution of Hartmann (1939) and developed by Rapaport (1958), has close bearing on motivational sources for learning and on the functional value of what is learned, as well as on the patterns established in the course of learning. The educator's contention that all children are basically curious and impelled to make an impact on their environment is intrinsically similar to the theoretical bias of psychoanalytic ego-psychology: that there are basic capacities for interacting with the environment which are autonomous ego-functions, not drive-derived; the exercise and development of these functions is a direct source of satisfaction and pleasure. The quality of adaptation to reality, which an individual makes is related to the course of differentiation and elaboration of these autonomous ego-functions.

The "enlargement of the conflict-free sphere"—the ability of the organism to perceive, learn, remember, think, move, and act—is not predetermined; it is a response to the nature of the individual's encounter with his world, particularly to the ways in which he has been reared and educated. Modes of adaptation are also influenced by the interaction of ego-functions and instinctual drives as the ego becomes increasingly important in regulating these drives. The adaptive patterns, established in the course of this process, become generalized as ways of dealing with reality. Ego-strength can be said to be developing to the extent that these ego-functions can channel drive energies toward constructive action (Holt, 1960).

In White's formulation (1963), ego-functions attain a position of even greater autonomy, and the dependence of adaptation on learning through action becomes the central concept. The learning process, in early stages, and also later when verbal and conceptual aids become the mediators of experience, is fundamentally active; knowledge is gained, reality tested, and adaptive patterns established through exploration, manipulation, and investigation. The main pleasure in these responses is associated with a given tendency to be active, to produce an effect on the environment; the energies for this tendency are regarded by White as independent and unrelated to conflict-induced tensions. The core of ego-strength is competence and, subjectively, the sense of competence, and this is the fruit of action: what is learned by action and the effect of action on the physical and human universe. Knowledge gained through the exercise of instinctual energies is recognized by White as also contributing to competence, but its "contribution is necessarily narrower than that of neutral energies which stand ever ready to promote exploration for its own sake." White's position, based on an analysis of animal studies, work in the field of psychoanalysis, and research on the development of cognitive processes in children, constitutes an invaluable formulation in support of the discovery approach to learning. The work of Lois Murphy (1962) on coping patterns of a group of Midwestern children further corroborates this position with respect to learning and mechanisms for adaptation.

Teaching that enacts this line of thinking is expected to produce in children special cognitive skills assumed to be more flexible and successful as tools for intellectual activity than the kind of thinking styles learned by children who are made the passive recipients of didactic teaching. Further, the pleasure derived from fulfilling curiosity through a style of learning that encourages children to try out their capacities becomes its own reward and generates the motivation to keep on learning. Nor should we neglect the special dimension of self-feeling associated with these learning activities, the awareness of being the discoverer, the explorer of the unknown.

Children have their own ways, outside of school, when life is not too restricted, of testing this pleasure in living: the venture into the street three turns beyond one's own familiar block to get a good look at the fire engine while it is standing still or into the thicket down the road where the light is dim and a quick squirrel can be seen stowing his nuts into the hollow of the tree. The School is dedicated to bringing this quality of pleasure into the learning life of children in school.

The relation between the discovery method and the development of autonomy as part of the life style should be pursued to another level. All the materials of a school program are not equally suitable to the techniques of exploration and discovery. Some subject matter is intrinsically right-wrong structured, and here an extended exploratory phase may be not only wasteful but illusory. Even where the content is suitable to an open approach, there is a point where the teacher has to exercise a delicate judgment as to when the child requires new cues, leads, and direction. In the progress report of the Panel on Educational Research and Development, a hint appears of the need to balance independent learning experience with other ways of learning, requiring acceptance of prestructured information and previously established rules of the game. To quote the report:

"This interest in learning through the experience of discovery is not meant to imply that each child must relive the entire experience of the human race. In the learning process there is a certain balance between discovery and presentation, and it may be that, as the learner advances in a given field, smaller amounts of discovery will balance greater amounts of presentation."

Appreciation of the pleasures and benefits of the discovery approach should not, need not, exclude awareness of the satisfactions to be gained from fitting in with established structure and putting the products of other people's discoveries to good use. There is a danger of overlearning the discovery approach, especially when to child and teacher it becomes something of a status symbol.

Associated Processes

The emphasis on exploration and independent pursuit in approach-ing the unknowns of the world of knowledge has wider relevance than its effect on cognitive style and motivation. It is easily recog-nizable as an important support of the maturing of fundamental autonomous processes or, the opposite, reliance on the safety of docil-ity and submission (Henry, 1963). But the School cannot afford to shut off its vision of the learning experience at the point where it affects intellectual output or cognitive style only; it is inevitably involved also in the associated effects on broader modes of dealing with life experience.

The maturing of the autonomous processes is not, optimally, unilat-eral. It involves attaining equilibrium between dependence and inde-pendence; it includes the capacity to think and act independently while being able to accept a position of dependence (to take help) where insufficient knowledge, experience, or strength dictates the need. In a condition of equilibrium, dependence is not experienced as sub-mission; independence does not become a defense against excessive fear of submission or of being dominated. A balanced curriculum, in terms of ways of learning, can thus be seen as a flexible medium contributing toward attaining this kind of autonomy, giving the child the personally felt experience of his independent powers of pursuit and initiative at the same time that he accepts and uses established fact and method without feeling the acceptance as weakness or sub-mission. In other words, overdoing the discovery method or rather investment in its exclusive pre-eminence could contribute to a pitched battle with authority.

MASTERY

Goal

There is nothing novel in the idea that the major job of education is to teach people to think. It is voiced by every critic of what schools do; by those who look back on what appear in retrospect as wasted hours and days and years and by those who feel professionally frus-trated by the dominance of archaic concepts and a too narrow vision of what is required, in this day and age, for social survival and regeneration.

The School rejected the acquisition of facts as an ultimate criterion of intellectual success. It reconceived intellectual mastery not only as a way of learning (see section on Discovery), but also as a condition, a quality of knowledge, in which items of experience are in a continuous state of organization and reorganization with reference to their connective meanings. The modes in which relevance between and among the items of experience is perceived vary with content, developmental cognitive level, and the complex of purposes constituting the motivational substratum. But the cognitive search is increasingly directed toward establishing the nature of the relationship among discrete items, and thereby toward reaching increasingly general principles and generic meanings. This can be thought of as a patterning of conceptual mastery of experiential elements or, more functionally, as a tool for more effective thinking. A third goal of the School then, is *to promote cognitive power and intellectual mastery*.

In the early days of the School, Mitchell (1934) pleaded the case:

". . . the old schools tended to postpone the opportunities for active creative thinking. . . . It was assumed . . . that children are not mature enough to 'think' and must accumulate a certain amount of erudition by a more or less passive absorption as a preliminary to and as a basis for their thinking. . . . The modern school, in contrast, asserts that children grow in mental maturity from the very beginning by the active process of discovering relationships and regards the school essentially as a laboratory where such discoveries may be made. . . . Keep feeding children with source material and provide them with tools for discovering relations and for making their images active, and thinking and playing will continue to any height—up to Einstein or Conrad or Eugene O'Neill or James Trusloe Adams or any other scientist or artist who thinks in relationships and makes his images active."

"Relationship thinking" was the password for her students and colleagues.

The case for relationship thinking is still being argued; the great majority of our schools were affected only minimally by these concepts or the practices that were developed to enact them in the classroom. The contemporary "revolution" in our schools may be more successful in contributing to their ascendency partly because advocacy and evidence of their worth is now coming from other sources with high prestige. In particular, the field of cognitive psychology, both through theoretical analysis and experimental work, is substantiating and extending earlier insights. Furthermore, many psychologists have become interested and unembarrassed to be involved in traveling the bridge from their discipline to that of education. "The child must get the full benefit of what he learns . . . (this) is a way of honoring the connectedness of knowledge. Two facts and a relation joining them is and should be an invitation to generalize, to extrapolate, to make a tentative intuitive leap, even to build a tentative theory . . . ," Bruner says (1961b) and, at another time (Bruner, 1959), "A homely example is provided by the relationship in arithmetic between addition and multiplication. If the principle of addition has been grasped in its deepest sense, in its generic sense, then it is unnecessary to learn multiplication. For, in principle, multiplication is only repeated addition. . . . Learning something generically is like leaping over a barrier. On the other side of the barrier is thinking." Although they emerge independently from different sources, there is a common quality in these views of intellectual mastery, a means-ends quality. It is this kind of cognitive power that is regarded as the optimal means of achieving competence in the logos of Western society and in sustaining effectiveness in adapting to accelerating social and technological change.

Method and Rationale

The School, then, developed methods designed to encourage understanding of relationships and principles of a general nature. The nature of the relationship that the teacher accented or elicited differed according to the cognitive level of the children. To one level, she may point out similarities and differences based on sensory-perceptual experience and to another the organization of objects by function or of events in a time sequence. To a more advanced level she may introduce abstract complexities such as the kinds of evidence that institute proof, the interplay between behavior and motivation or that between fact and opinion.

Variety of method was part of a major teaching aim, "to enrich the experience that intervenes between question and answer or, in other words, to give the question a life of its own" (Biber, 1959). An example of this teaching mode was the substitution of the discussion method for the recitation period. In a successful discussion period, a free movement of thought around the question posited courses back and forth among the children and between teacher and children, adding facts, injecting criticism, analyzing vague concepts, melding evidence from personal and impersonal sources—all in contrast to the teaching style in which the teacher owns the questions and the answers exist ready-made and encapsulated in a verbal formula. In this connection, it is interesting to note that Thelen's (1963) criticism of orthodox programmed learning is based on what he regards as an essential step following the period of discovery, namely the "dialogue," the interactive experience (with peers and teachers) which takes place when the "testimony of . . . different individuals . . . can be analyzed, compared and brought into dynamic interplay . . . teacher-guided discussion can provide the core structure for dialogue."

The most highly developed method with a conscious rationale for this concept of intellectual mastery is a series of techniques devised by Mitchell (1934) for the study of the environment (which she categorized as human geography) and which, in common school jargon, represents a curriculum for social studies. Disputing the logic of beginning with the simplest and, therefore primitive cultures, Mitchell maintained that "the dominating logic (of sequence) should be of the children's experiences . . . and that their environment furnishes a field for explorations and discoveries." The complex modern world can be simplified so that encounters of the people and phenomena of the functioning environment could be planned even for young children. In this way, they could explore and come to understand relationships such as, for example, the dependence of city people on distant workers for food or how an island locale affects every aspect of daily living. Excerpts from a description of Mitchell's of a lesson with a group of twelve-year-old children illustrates the priority of providing children, differently at different stages, with experiences and tools to think through and unfold the salient relationships in a sequence of conceptual maneuvers.

"A group of twelve year olds were to study the relationship between the natural geographic boundaries and the political boundaries of Europe. They were given a graphic relief tool map, about five by six feet, painted in oils on oilcloth to look like water, mountains, valleys and plains, told to regard the map as an unknown section of land and water and to consider the problem of placing many nations on this land in such a way that they could live alongside of one another with least friction . . . the children decided that rivers were not good boundaries . . . that mountains were good boundaries and that the natural dividing line was the line of the watershed . . . then followed a discussion of natural resources, access to the sea, easy routes for railroads, etc. . . . these resources were marked off . . . the children consulting many atlases and monographs to get their data . . . then they marked off the areas which seemed to them might be reasonably isolated . . . England . . . Spain and Italy cut off by mountain ranges, etc. The problems that troubled them (most) were:

that the Volga led to a salt sea with no outlet and suggested as a solution the digging of a canal exactly where the USSR had cut one; how to divide the area we call roughly the Balkans saying: 'Any boundaries are likely to make messes!' When they (later) drew the political boundaries directly over the (tool map) they were shocked at several things: 'How can Russia get out to the sea? Don't France, Belgium, the Netherlands and Germany need to guard their boundaries every minute? There's no sense to their boundaries!' "

Because the history of ideas is so directly intriguing and incidentally affords such good material for sustaining the humility we aspire to as people and scientists, I should also like to quote here from an experiment conducted by the Center for Cognitive Studies at Harvard (Bruner, 1959), which describes an experimental and control group of fifth-grade children studying the geography of the North Central States.

"A set of unknowns was presented (to the control group) . . . blank maps, containing only tracings of rivers and lakes of the area as well as the natural resources. They were asked as a first exercise to indicate where the principal cities would be located, where the railroads, and where the main highways. Books and maps were not permitted and 'looking up the facts' was cast in a sinful light. Upon completing this exercise, a class discussion was begun in which the children attempted to justify why the major city would be here, a large city there, a railroad on this line, etc. The discussion was a hot one . . . permission was given to consult the rolled up wall map. I will never forget one young student, as he pointed his finger at the foot of Lake Michigan, shouting, 'Yippee, Chicago is at the end of the pointing-down lake.' And another replying, 'Well, but Chicago's no good for the rivers and it should be here where there is a big city (St. Louis).' These children were thinking, and learning was an instrument for checking and improving the process . . . learned geography as a set of rational acts of induction—that cities spring up where there is water . . . etc."

This account, so close in concept and substance to that of Mitchell, was written exactly twenty-five years later. There is, however, one important difference between them: in the latter, the idea and the method are being put to systematic test in a way that should break ground for new levels of insight.

The principle of learning inductively is being tried out in new forms—in subject matter fields such as mathematics and physics or as exercises in thinking, such as Suchman's technique for Inquiry Training. These developments are raising questions requiring a closer look at the formulations and findings of developmental psychologists, notably Werner (1957) and Piaget (1936). Is there not a basic developmental sequence in the elaboration of the thinking processes, or more generally, in the organization of all experience, that is as relevant to a learning-teaching paradigm as is the intrinsic structure of any field of knowledge?

The concept of development as a succession in stages, characterized by qualitatively different capacities and interests as well as motivations, was a governing principle of the teaching methods evolved by the School. Salient developmental concepts, identifiable as the themes of developmental psychology, were derived from observing and interacting with children. These concepts influenced the selection of content, activities, and teaching methods for different levels of maturity. I refer to developmental progressions such as the sequence from global to differentiated perception; from concrete, action-dominated to abstract mental operations; and from affect-ruled to logical meanings. The growing acceptance and systematic refinement of this direction in psychological thinking is reinforcing and refreshing; as developmental knowledge is discriminated and tested, essential material, as well as the stimulation, will be provided to review and revise existing educational procedures.

Using again the method of study of the environment to illustrate the School's way of working toward its goal for intellectual mastery, the basic congruence can be seen between this educational approach and contemporary developmental psychology. To quote again from Mitchell (1934):

"A child will understand the fundamental relationship contained in our word 'island' if he thinks of himself as a boat and goes tooting around a ring of other children on a piece of blue oilcloth until he finds himself where he started. He thereby gets a muscle image of an island. After that he may understand a visual image—an airplane picture of an island where, like as not, he will go through the same process of being a circumnavigating boat though this time he may accomplish his voyage with his finger or his eyes—a more mature tool than legs! After this, a circle, with, perhaps, surrounding blue may bring up the image of an island and he is well launched on symbols which will lead to understanding two-dimensional maps. . ."

Covering a longer developmental span, Mitchell sees ability to deal with the geographic abstractions, such as map projection, sphere, and equator, as having "experiential roots" in the six-year-old's groping with space concepts while painting on a two-dimensional surface and the five-year-old's use of blocks for creating "embryonic map forms." This view of geographic thinking fits the general formulation of epigenetic progress in learning as recently stated by Hunt (1964).

Matching the teaching procedures to the stage of cognitive maturity, that is, introducing the child to new ideas which he can assimilate according to his available schemata but which still require from him a degree of accommodation and new thinking, is the psychologist's way of stating a principle familiar to educators: start where the child is but lead him on. What is involved, however, is not merely the fancy restatement of an old idea. It represents rather a resource—a promise for a whole new body of knowledge through research—with which to mold a general idea into an exquisite instrument for education. All the more pity that, for some subjects curriculum revision seems to proceed with only a limited awareness of the premises and findings of developmental psychology and returns to chronology of subject matter as the basis of reform in curriculum sequence. Thus Turner (1964) reports work on a new curriculum for social studies which "would introduce children in the early grades to the concept of evolution and to the modes of life practiced by hunting and gathering societies" with complete awareness that this is a reversal of the principle of proceeding from the known to the unknown, for young children. He finds justification in the postulate that children can absorb abstract ideas much earlier than has been thought. He means to take into account another postulate, that children learn first by action, by giving them replicas of the materials unearthed in archaeological digs to manipulate! The extent of the psychological mis-match exemplified here is obvious when we consider how much the child already knows about his society and what a fund of impressions and information he has absorbed upon which he can built an understanding "of the regularities in the world of man and his institutions. . ." His intellectual processes are centrifugal, their path is outward from the self, but the self is the prime reality, and self experience is the basis from which other people, or other peoples and societies, become comprehensible. Replicas of rocks do not seem to be the ideal tool.

Associated Processes

Personality, like cognition, evolves epigenetically through a series of stages, the product of the impact of child-rearing practices and other socializing forces on the basic instinctual drives. This classical Freudian view was extended and somewhat altered when Erikson (1959) showed how alternative ways of dealing with the successive phases of "zonal primacy" influence which, of possible modes of behavior patterning, become generalized or dominant in personality functioning. Analogously, it is of the greatest importance, especially for educators, to know how alternative educational methods for developing autonomous ego-processes (central to the subject of intellectual mastery) also determine which alternative modes of behavior become dominant in the interaction between individual and environment.

Munroe's (1955) analysis of trends in psychoanalytic thinking leads her to the same position, stated theoretically:

"This chapter has described the Freudian view of the course of development in the erogenous zones, and the more general modes of behavior patterned upon them, in relationship to the actual handling of the child. I believe this view is essentially correct and important— except in its exclusiveness. The neuromuscular and other systems which I have called 'nonsexual' seem, in the classical Freudian view, to develop merely as a matter of biological maturation. Implications of character formation are not stressed, except as they relate to personality trends arising from the 'sexual' modes. My suggestion is that these ego functions and apparatuses have implication for character formation in their own right; that the ways in which the 'nonsexual' systems of the child are handled must be more carefully studied . . . I have tried to suggest that in fact the non-sexual systems do tend to coalesce into a personal-social unit by virtue of the fact that they are the major media of interchange with the milieu, especially in a reality-oriented culture such as our own."

The methods selected for promoting intellectual mastery, in this view, also influence general modes of behaving in given directions. The inductive method establishes a relatively prolonged period of not knowing, a kind of groping, in the belief that there will be a "clearing in the forest"; it involves acceptance and willingness to take many steps to achieve a given goal in the knowledge that there is no prior assurance of the relative potency of any one step in the final achievement. In terms of attitudes and generalized patterns of behavior, we see in the qualities of this way of learning the possibility of a long term influence—toward a general tolerance for ambiguity in life situations, a general attitude that does not see uncertainty as stupidity, and a general expectation that clarity can come at the end of a process as an emergent of experience. These attitudes are all components of what is likely to be regarded as a flexible style of life, in contrast to a fixed and rigid one. It would probably not be difficult to get agreement on the desirability of these behavioral patterns from a mental health point of view. But even so, we cannot assume that the life experience of all children makes it possible for them to sustain the psychological state of mind that the method requires. Excessive rigidity in previous periods of development may make this method anxiety-inducing. This is an instance where epigenetic sequence in the intellectual processes crosses over with epigenetic sequence in generalized behavior modes, sometimes condensed into terms such as "affective," since emotional experience figures so largely in behavioral modes.

Another method, such as the discussion period, which allows children to draw on their entire reservoir of experience, merges knowledge gained through personal as well as impersonal channels. There are two possible gains in this. One is that the objective world gathers a charge for the child because he has encountered it as a personal experience which in turn protects him against viewing the world with indifference or dismissing it as an inactive externality. The second possible gain is that the child who encounters the world as a personal experience is more likely to escape the dangers of solipsistic preoccupation because the experience extends his capacity for objective evaluation. In later years, other things are in process while the discussion follows its intellectual pursuit. For example, agreement and disagreement are carriers of support and destruction, and intellectual agility can be used in the service of either. The discussion becomes an arena for coming to terms with the conflict between the wish to conquer and the pain of inflicting defeat. Whether the discussion contributes to a constructive resolution of this kind of conflict depends upon the teacher's understanding and skill in guiding what are often deep currents of feeling embedded in the expression that the intellectual activity takes.

Basically a social studies program has been conceived of as a series of organizing principles relevant to children in their direct encounter with their functioning life environments. The associated psychological processes to be considered, like intellectual capacity, change qualitatively from stage to stage: The maturing of autonomous processes, the shifting relationship of child to adult, the changing direction and urgency of the desire to master, the place of fantasy in the search for explanation and then for meaning, and the identity of the self in an ever-widening world. At its most imaginative, curriculum planning takes into account what appear to be the dominant themes of these processes at given stages of development and allows them, together with other considerations, to influence the choice of content. For the preschool child, origin is a highly suitable theme for extending and integrating knowledge. It has "basic meaning on a psychodynamic level in terms of the child's highly motivated interest in his own origin. To study 'Where did the carrots come from?' is not a cold intellectual inquiry; it interacts with the deeper question: 'Where did I come from?' " (Biber, 1961).

In the middle years of childhood the urge to master is not limited to conceptual elaboration and insight. Skill in making and doing are a source of deep gratification, related to a dominant trend at this stage to respect accuracy, precision, and the specific "how" of a task or a rule for a game. The relation between the meaning of work at this stage and how the activities of a social studies program interlocks with it is described by Winsor (1958):

"There is a glow that comes to an eight or nine-year-old as he discovers how ingeniously primitive man fashioned a tool to serve his purposes, how he made his home warm and comfortable with nothing but his hands and his good brain. Exclamations of surprise as well as wonder are heard from children as they try to reproduce the good work of primitive man and find it devilishly hard to do as well. Have you ever watched an eight-year-old fashioning a clay bowl? or a ten-year-old attempting to fire an arrow from a home-made bow? I have such a clear memory of an eight-year-old who struggled manfully to fashion a dugout canoe out of a small piece of balsawood. There was pride in his achievement, disappointment when a visitor to the class was unimpressed. What he said was, 'Do you know how long it took me to make this? Three weeks! Just think how long it took the Indians to make their great big dugout canoes.' "

In another paper, Winsor (1952) deals with the motivation of children to extend their skill in communication to include competence with written symbols—one of the paths for fulfilling the urgent wish to gain competence in the ways of the adult world. "The roots of our culture pattern—language . . . become appropriate material for study" in a program where ten- and eleven-year-old children have taken on a job of school printing. From the children come the questions: " 'Why do we make an "A" like this? What is an alphabet? What good is it? Who invented it anyway? What kind of people were these and how did they live?' " For the social studies program a precept crystallized (Winsor, 1956):

". . . man does more than live in his physical environment and structure his society. He makes possible the ongoing of his society because he records his efforts, functions and knowledge. This wonderful invention of recording is available for young children to explore with delight, especially as they struggle to become adept in using these records or symbols."

These are only sparse instances of endless possibilities to synchronize content with the drives, conflicts, and sources of gratification that characterize successive periods of development, and in so doing, to put the learning experience, in the fullest sense, to the service of ego-strength.

SYNTHESIS

Goal

Anxiety about the deficiencies of education is not limited to those who have taken the initiative in revising method and subject matter in the interest of advancing the intellectual level of children. Psychologists and educators who have a special interest in creativity, both as a deepening personal process and as a requisite for a healthy society, have been working with equal energy and commitment on needed reorientation in educational practice and thinking.

In 1959, Guilford wrote "the preservation of our way of life and our future security depend upon our most important natural resources: our intellectual abilities and, more particularly, our creative abilities." Torrance [1964] begins to close in on the image of the creative person:

"It takes little imagination to recognize that the future of our civilization—our very survival—depends upon the quality of the creative imagination of our next generation. . . . Democracies collapse only when they fail to use intelligent, imaginative methods for solving problems. The kind of citizen here called for is a far cry from the model of a quiz-program champion of a few years ago, and he is also more than a 'well-rounded individual' . . ."

Out of the prodigious amount of work and complex findings on creativity in recent years, certain themes appear concerning the relation between creativity and intellectual, motivational, and personality factors. Intellectual functioning is known to be infinitely complicated, multi-faceted, having at least "three faces." Certain intellectual factors are considered to contribute directly to creative power, others less directly. The kind of thinking in which variety of response is produced, for example, and in which the thinker allows himself to go off in different directions, sometimes called "divergent thinking," appears to be important to creativity; this is also true for the kind of intellectual activity represented in "transformation," that is, changes of arrangement, organization, or meaning (Guilford, 1959). A long list of other intellectual manifestations—the tendency to toy with ideas, to see patterns in data, the capacity to be puzzled, to sense ambiguities, or to discriminate—have been associated with creative functioning through studies of "creative" individuals. On two points there seems to be general agreement. First, it is these aspects of intellectual functioning that have traditionally been neglected in education and, second, conventional measures, especially the I.Q., are inadequate and incomplete measures of intelligence when its full complexity is taken into account. These studies have frequently led to suggestions for changes in education that would foster creativity. Actually, these suggested changes overlap greatly with the recommendations made by those concerned with raising the level of cognitive mastery (see section on Mastery). Their recommendations are to value self-initiated learning, to revise readiness concepts, to develop self-concept, to remove the constraints against questioning and exploration, and to shift away from an assumed dichotomy of work and play.

Still the question of creativity appears more complex than can be seen when its relation to intellectual functioning is mainly considered. From his studies of creativity in mature professional life, MacKinnon (1962) concludes ". . . we may have overestimated in our educational system the role of intelligence in creative achievement." He advocates closer attention to nonintellectual factors "intimately associated with creative talent," such as "openness to experience and especially to experience of one's inner life," "disposition to admit complexity and even disorder into their perceptions without being made anxious by the resulting chaos," and thus a preference for the "richness of the disordered to the stark barrenness of the simple." Barron (1958) places his experimental work in a framework of psychoanalytic theory. Like MacKinnon, he sees the creative person as having a stronger impulse to render experience intelligible, to find order where none may be apparent. By his more dynamic view, he sees this disposition of the creative person to integrate diverse stimuli as supported in part by concomitant respect and contact with irrational elements in the person himself; he sees a general intimacy with nonrational processes leading up to a commitment and ability to effect complex personal synthesis.

At this point concepts of creativity and ego-strength seem to share common ground. The idea that optimal psychological functioning is synonymous with a synthesis of processes—personal and impersonal, subjective and objective, rational and nonrational—has gained in general importance, especially in recent years, as criteria of positive mental health, of maturity, of ego-strength have been conceptualized as processes rather than as traits or behavior patterns. The application of this postulate to education and the learning process has had, however, very few articulate spokesmen; and unfortunately, this view of learning, in its full complexity, seems largely absent from the most prominent revisions of curriculum and teaching method. Gardner Murphy (1964) has argued against the contemporary trend to extrapolate thought processes from the impulsive and motivational life of the child, making specific reference to the role of the teacher:

". . . the nurture of rationality may perhaps lie in other efforts than the sheer encouragement of rational thought . . . the learner must not be deprived of the riches of his impulse life, and the teacher must be a quickener of that impulse life through which thought can grow, indeed a shaper and molder of impulse into the rationality which comes from a healthy craving for contact with reality . . . there is, moreover, within us a world of inner stimulation and challenge, an inner world of physiological response, of memories, of images, and of fantasies . . . the teacher who responds to this inner world can convey it just as she or he can respond to the outer world . . . these two forms of motivation—the impulse to know and the impulse to gratify the inner needs—are two aspects of one reality. The cognitive need is as commanding and constraining, and at the same time as fulfilling, as any realization of the more primitive organic needs."

It is the concept of synthesis of inner and outer worlds, of rational and nonrational processes, elaborated in studies of creative functioning, that is closely related to the fourth goal of the School, namely, *to support the synthesis of learning experience through opportunity for symbolic expression.* This goal is really part of a general view that learning as experience is incomplete unless it is carried through to a synthesizing phase in which new material is absorbed by being processed through the child's individual, prior store of ideas, images, feelings, and strivings. Piaget's analysis of assimilation and accommodation provides us with a theoretical foundation of the processes whereby known and unknown, in the cognitive realm, are joined (1936). A solution to a problem or a new concept uniting previously disparate facts represents one kind of synthesis. The use of newly learned arithmetic manipulations in some practical operation of measurement is a more functional example of synthesis. But synthesis of another kind, cutting across the cognitive and affective domains, occurs when the outcome of the learning experience takes symbolic form and results in a transformation of some part of the child's encounter with the outer world that reflects and utilizes the forces—the cumulated meanings, feelings, wishes, conflicts—of his inner life of impulse and affect.

There is an assumption behind the School's interest and emphasis on providing materials, techniques, and a climate of values that support symbolic re-expression as a basic part of learning. The assumption is that the admission of nonrational processes into the learning life of children adds an additional dimension of power to potential mastery of objective material. This appears to be borne out by Torrance (1964), who found that a group of "high creative" children matched the academic performance of a comparative group of "low creative" children who had a significantly higher I.Q. rating; the "high creative" group attained this with less obvious strain or pressure. Torrance attributes this difference to the incidental learning that can take place when learning is enjoyed in the relaxed spirit of "playing around." Might it not be that the success of the creative group was also related to the qualities of "openness to experience of one's inner life" and the freedom from rigidity associated with access to and utilization of the nonrational processes identified with creativity? The goal, stated in more general terms elsewhere (Biber and Minuchin, 1965), is "to develop people whose deep feelings remain generative in connection with their intellectual functioning and channel and qualify the nature of their performance."

Method and Rationale

Not only equipment and program design, but also the content and quality of the free-floating interchange from person to person in the classroom, bear the imprint of this goal. Intuitive processes, feeling, emotion, the "reflective" kind of thinking, and fantasy modes of reorganizing experience—all these are admitted and highly valued as balance and enrichment of the more systematic, analytic attitudes, the emotional controls and reality-dominated ordering of information, that are essential to adaptation and competence in society.

More particularly, in terms of curriculum, the presence of a variety

of materials—paint, clay, blocks, or musical forms—and the opportunity to choose and use them freely without the constraints of models
or established evaluative criteria, is one way of fulfilling this goal.
It is also a testament to the School's recognition that children differ
in the modes they find most suitable for re-expression. In such settings
the children engage in the process of "play." In the use of the materials, the child's projected meanings, that is, the way his inner self
has elected to choose, embellish, exaggerate, reorganize, or distort
the encounter with reality, are hidden rather than apparent. This
is a familiar problem to those people who have attempted to objectify
and validate techniques for projective analysis.

The mechanism of free dramatic play, the "pretending" and "make
believe" that young children use to make their lives more encom-
passable and endurable, has been developed by the School as a major
teaching technique, up to the second or third grade. A variation, which
might be called free-form dramatizing, is part of the social studies
program in the later elementary years. Time, space and materials
for macrocosmic and microcosmic reproduction of experience—blocks,
figures, animals, trains, planes, dolls, houseplay objects, dress-up
clothes—are there in abundance in raw and representative form. For
the children, the play activates multiple modalities—verbalization,
manipulation, construction, plot invention and role portrayal. For
younger children, dramatic play is remarkably fluid; it makes rapid
shifts, without embarrassment, of projected object meanings and role
identities, and moves back and forth between reality and distortion
of reality.

Still, thinking is very active, and growing mastery of reality is
expressed in play through the increasing detail and differentiation
of the activities reproduced, through the widening scope of experience
selected for representation in the play world, and through the progress
from short, simple, almost momentary play schemes, to involved, prolonged, connected series of imagined events. In dramatic play the
extrapolation of thinking from the realm of feeling, which Murphy
fears and deplores, cannot happen. Transactions in play contain the
same interweaving of thought and emotion that characterizes molar
life experience. Whether the figures of the play are people, animals,
or anthropomorphized objects, their interactions, as agents or subjects,
carry the charge of love, hate, destruction, rescue, loss, recovery, wish,
defeat, pain, conquest—emotion that is relived and externalized from
the inner personal life history, sometimes directly, more often indirectly, through symbolic forms, displacements, or distortive mechanisms that grant the safety of distance from that part of the subjective
life that is inevitably conflict-laden.

The younger the child, the less does the product of his dramatic play have to adhere to the logic of reality; for older children, who no longer permit themselves open distortion of reality to meet their inner needs or wishes, the projective channels are narrowed; but free-form dramatizing[1] still affords an opportunity to re-express idea content, in a matrix derived less from identification and more from empathy of what it feels like to be this or that person in this or that situation.

Thus dramatic play, as developed and refined by the School, is a special kind of tool for learning, suited to the idiom of childhood, which fuses the wondering, problem-solving, and conceptualizing of the groping child mind with the symbolic expression of the wishes and fears, longings for strength, pleasures, and pains of the forming inner self. The fact that this fusion takes place actively in dramatic play is further reason to recognize it as a form of learning contributing to mastery and ego-strength. Thus, Erikson (1950): ". . . to hallucinate ego-mastery is the purpose of play . . ." and ". . . the child's play is the infantile form of the human ability to deal with experience by creating model situations and to master reality by experiment and planning . . . ," and in Omwake (1963) ". . . play of this nature provides a proving ground for the development and gradual refinement of the full range of emerging ego functions. These include language, motor skills, memory, concept formation, reality testing, control of impulse, and secondary process thinking . . ."

Furthermore, if the importance placed by investigators in the field of creativity, MacKinnon and Barron particularly, upon "openness to one's feeling life" and "valuing nonrational components of experience" is valid, then the use of dramatic play and free-form dramatizing represents a kind of teaching method that should encourage creativity, originality, and invention because of the externalization and active fusion of subjective and objective meanings which these forms of play facilitate.

Associated Processes

What has been said here about synthesis as an educational goal and symbolic expression through dramatic play as a method has, in fact, already involved considerations that are readily subsumed under the rubric of "personality processes." At any stage of development, the value of such learning experience lies in calling into activity the

[1] This term refers to play making in the upper elementary years when children dramatize freely around a given theme, using factual information that they have gathered. The properties and dramatic business of their production is original.

repertoire of ego-functions in the children's representational, symbolic search for coherence and mastery of perplexities of thought and impact of emotion. But both the process and the product are substantially different as the child moves from stage to stage in his development. It is interesting at this point to consider what is constant in the play experience when it is included sequentially, albeit in progressively changing form, as part of curriculum design, and what may be the relevance of such constant elements to certain epigenetic concepts of personality development.

At any developmental level, the dramatic play form of reorganizing experience involves the fusion of personal and impersonal meanings and utilizes, even depends on, the more elemental aspects of human response in order to achieve its essential function. This is in contrast to the modes of reorganization of experience where excellence is synonymous with attaining the highest degree of abstraction and where personal, particular, individual meanings are stripped away for the sake of arriving at universals. Genetically, the latter mode is an advance over the former, but complete integration and adaptability of the individual would suffer if the earlier, more immature forms were altogether displaced by the later ones or allowed to atrophy. This view is expressed by Werner (1957) in his concept of developmental heterogeneity. By this concept, an individual's creativity and flexibility, his capacity to operate on different levels in accord with the requirements of the situation, are functions of how wide a range of operations are available to him, or, in other words, how great his capacity is to utilize primitive as well as advanced operations.

The theoretical formulation of ego-identity by Erikson (1959) as an evolving, cumulative process has closest bearing on the meaning of dramatic play in relation to personality development. By this theory, ego-identity, when it is established toward the end of the adolescent period, is a resynthesis of the multiple, varied identifications of all the years of childhood.

"It arises from the selective repudiation and mutual assimilation of childhood identifications, and their absorption in a new configuration . . . it is a lifelong development . . . children at different stages of their development identify with those part-aspects of people by which they themselves are most immediately affected, whether in reality or in fantasy . . ."

In dramatic play, we see a synchronized outcome of the rethinking of the facts and relations of the objective world—partly real, partly transformed to give fantasy needs a full measure of prerogative—and of an endless experimenting with people, animals or even things *to be*—baby, dog, tiger, engineer, mother, farmer, captain, doctor, cyclone. In these roles the children identify, at times, with the functional aspects of these figures, with what they are understood to do typically, in their roles in the real world. At other times (or at the same time), the roles become vehicles for reifying the children's deepest feelings—wishes and conflicts, real or fantasied—which are the residue, conscious and unconscious, of their relations with the important people in their lives. It would be as true to say that in these roles they are victim, aggressor, punisher, protector, outsmarter, adored one, and helpless one.

In the early years, play roles are defined as much or more by emotional content and the child's feelings and image of his place, as a child, in the world of adults, as they are by the real functions of the characters in their occupational and social roles. Since reality does not govern the process, distortions and exaggerations are common. Levinger (1956) compares these distortions to dream processes, which similarly utilise grotesque, unrealistic symbolization but truthfully depict inmost feelings. She goes on to cite how shifts in identification figures become the means for solving inner problems and thus contribute to the long, complex evolution of identity:

"As we work with the school age pre-adolescent children, it is well to keep this growth process in mind. We must not expect the school age child to develop neat, final solutions in dramatic play—or anything else. He is striving and groping through a series of roles, to find out who he can be some day, to hold on to what he was before, and in his dramatic play, to deal with such experiences as anger, shame, thwarted tenderness, imagination too vast to settle in the confines of daily routines, and unresolved questions of the nature of the world, himself and others. The grotesque part-aspects of his identifications must be accepted by the adult, as the child is on his way to developing his unique sense of identity."

In the course of maturing, fantasy becomes increasingly less satisfactory as a way of dealing with the problematic aspects of knowledge and emotion. When the child moves into the middle years of childhood, when his positive identifications turn toward those who are accomplished according to the criteria of effectiveness in the real world, identification figures in his play reflect this change in his interest. The three-year-old's "engineer" sits strong and tall, turning a prop wheel and making appropriate sounds, whereas the six-year-old's "engineer" has responsibilities. Decisions must be made, perhaps with others, about where the train is going, what freight it carries along with the passengers, who collects the tickets, where the signal towers are, and whether the express stops at the next station. The feeling of borrowed power is still strong, but now what it means to be an engineer who does his particular job in the world is being tried on.

Where free-form dramatizing is used as a technique in the social studies program, the identification process is more complex. It extends beyond the feeling and function aspects of separate characters to the meanings of the transactions among them and their dilemmas. Now the engineer may be the man who, unemployed and desperate, betrays his ethical contract with his union; the "players" are trying on those perplexing part-aspects of life experience from which values are crystallized. Thus, although differently at different stages, dramatic play serves ego-identity by the extended opportunity it offers for experimenting with multiple identifications, all part of the complex growth of continuity within the self and resynthesis of "all childhood identifications in some unique way, and yet in concordance with the roles offered by some wider sections of society." The once-useful phrase, "learning by doing," has come into disrepute; still it is tempting to describe the process here discussed in similar verbal shorthand, as "learning by being."

SUMMARY

I dare not attempt a summary of the content that has been reviewed in this presentation but I find it easier to say, looking back, what I have tried to do, than it was to express my intentions in the beginning. I have tried to discuss a learning-teaching paradigm, made explicit in a series of goals for education, which represents the *Anschauung* of Schools that have been at the frontier in education for several decades. It has been possible to take only four from a more complete series of seven salient goals. In each case I have selected one or more methods developed and adapted by the School as holding promise for fulfilling these goals; I have tried to show how the underlying conceptualization of childhood and the learning process partly predated, but was simultaneously influenced and is now being reinforced and refined by advancing knowledge in the fields of developmental and psychoanalytic ego-psychology. I have tried to deal with the methods from two vantage points—their rationale for a particular educational goal and their simultaneous selective influence on the course of personality development. I have argued that, since development is a complex epigenetic process involving cognitive elaboration, motivational systems, styles of behavioral interaction, conflict-resolution, and attitudinal structures, new thrusts in revision of curriculm are faulty when they fail to build on available knowledge of all these factors and processes.

REFERENCES

Barron, F. "The Needs for Order and for Disorder as Motives in Creative Activity." In C. W. Taylor (Ed.), *The Second (1957) Conference on the Identification of Creative Scientific Talent.* Salt Lake City: University of Utah Press, 1958, pp. 119-128.

Biber, Barbara. "Premature Structuring as a Deterrent to Creativity." *American J. Orthopsychiatry,* 24, No. 2, April 1959.

Biber, Barbara. "Integration of Mental Health Principles in the School Setting." In G. Caplan (Ed.), *Prevention of Mental Disorders in Children,* New York: Basic Books, 1961.

Biber, Barbara, and Patricia Minuchin. "The Role of the School in the Socialization of Competence." Working paper for Conference on Socialization for Competence, Social Science Research Council, Puerto Rico, April 1965, Bank Street College of Education (mineo). Also (abbreviated version) in B. Rosen, et al. (Eds.), *Achievement in American Society,* Cambridge, Mass.: Schenkman Publishing Co., in press; with Minuchin, Patricia.

Bruner, J. S. "Learning and Thinking." *Harvard Educational Review,* 29, No. 3, Summer 1959, 187-188.

Bruner, J. S. "The Act of Discovery." *Harvard Educational Review,* 31, 1961, 21-32. (a)

Bruner, J. S. "After John Dewey, What?" Associates of Bank Street College of Education Conference: Roots of Excellence, March 1961. (b)

Brown, B. F. *The Non-graded High School.* Englewood Cliffs, N. J.: Prentice-Hall, 1963.

Deutsch, K. W. "What Do Our New Computers Tell Us About the Way Our Children Grow?" *Child Study,* 36, No. 3, Summer 1959, 25.

Erikson, E. H. *Childhood and Society.* New York: W. W. Norton and Co., 1950.

Erikson, E. H. "Identity and the Life Cycle." *Psychol. Issues,* I, No. 1, 1959, 112-113.

Frank, L. K. "Creativity: An Inquiry." *Western Arts Bulletin,* 40, No. 4, 1946, 5-17.

Friedlander, B. Z. "A Psychologist's Second Thoughts on Concepts, Curiosity, and Discovery in Teaching and Learning." *Harvard Educational Review,* 35, No. 1, Winter 1965, 36.

Gross, R., and Judith Murphy (Eds.). *The Revolution in the Schools.* New York: Harcourt, Brace and World, 1964.

Gross, R. "Two-Year-Olds Are Very Smart." *New York Times Magazine,* September 6, 1964, 39.

Guilford, J. P. "Three Faces of Intellect." *American Psychologist*, **14**, No. 8, 1959, 469–480.

Hartmann, H. *Ego Psychology and the Problem of Adaptation*. (Originally published in 1939.) New York: International Universities Press, 1959.

Heath, R. W. (Ed.). *New Curricula*. New York: Harper & Row, 1964.

Hebb, D. O. *The Organization of Behavior*. New York: John Wiley and Sons, 1949.

Henry, J. *Culture Against Man*. New York: Random House, 1963.

Hilgard, E. R. "Issues Within Learning Theory and Programmed Learning." *Psychology in the Schools*, **1**, No. 2, April 1964, 129–139.

Holt, R. "Recent Developments in Psychoanalytic Ego Psychology and their Implications for Diagnostic Testing." *J. proj. Tech.*, **24**, No. 3, 1960, 254–266.

Hunt, J. McV. *Intelligence and Experience*. New York: The Ronald Press Co., 1961.

Hunt, J. McV. "The Psychological Basis for Using Pre-school Enrichment as an Antidote for Cultural Deprivation." *Merrill-Palmer Quart.*, **10**, No. 3, July, 1964.

Jahoda, Marie. *Current Concepts of Positive Mental Health*. New York: Basic Books, 1958.

King, J. "The New Schoolhouse." In R. Gross and Judith Murphy (Eds.), *The Revolution in the Schools*. New York: Harcourt, Brace & World, 1964.

Levinger, Leah. "Dramatic Play—An Intellectual and Creative Process." In Associates of Bank Street College of Education, *Imagination in Education*. New York: Bank Street College of Education, 1956, 29–30.

Lumsdaine, A. A., and R. Glaser (Eds.) *Teaching Machines and Programmed Learning*. Washington D.C.: Nat. Educ. Assoc., 1960.

MacKinnon, D. W. "The Nature and Nurture of Creative Talent." *American Psychologist*, **17**, No. 7, 1962, 484–495.

Mitchell, Lucy S. *Young Geographers*. New York: Basic Books, 1934, 11, 30, 31, 33–34.

Mitchell, Lucy S. "Research on the Child's Level: Possibilities, Limitations, and Techniques." *University of Pennsylvania Bulletin*, 1944, 112–113.

Munroe, Ruth L. *Schools of Psychoanalytic Thought*. New York: Holt, Rinehart, and Winston, 1955, 230–234.

Murphy, G. "Non-rational Processes in Learning." In R. Gross and Judith Murphy (Eds.), *The Revolution in the Schools*. New York: Harcourt, Brace & World, 1964, 158, 162, 163.

Murphy, Lois B. *The Widening World of Childhood*. New York: Basic Books, 1962.

Omwake, Eveline B. "The Child's Estate." In A. J. Solnit and Sally A. Provence (Eds.), *Modern Perspectives in Child Development*. New York: International Universities Press, 1963.

Piaget, J. *The Origins of Intelligence in Children*. (Originally published in 1936.) New York: International Universities Press, 1952.

Piaget, J. *Play, Dreams and Imitation in Childhood*. (Originally published in 1945.) New York: W. W. Norton, 1951.

Panel on Educational Research and Development. "Innovation and Experiment in Education: A Progress Report to the U.S. Commissioner of Education, the Director of the National Science Foundation, and the Special Assistant to the President for Science and Technology." Washington, D.C.: U. S. Government Printing Office, March 1964.

Rapaport, D. "The Theory of Ego Autonomy: A Generalization." *Bulletin Menninger Clinic,* **22,** 1958, 13–35.

Senesh, L. *Our Working World, Families at Work.* Chicago, Ill.: Science Research Associates, 1963.

Shaplin, J. T. "Team Teaching." *Saturday Rev. Educ. Suppl.,* May 20, 1961.

Skinner, B. F. "The Science of Learning and the Art of Teaching." *Harvard Educational Review,* **25,** 1954, 86–97.

Suchman, R. "Inquiry Training: Building Skills for Autonomous Discovery." *Merrill-Palmer Quart.,* July, 1961.

Thelen, H. A. "The Concept, Characteristics, and Use of Discovery Materials in Teaching." 1963 (mimeo).

Torrance, E. P. "Education and Creativity." In C. W. Taylor (Ed.), *Creativity: Progress and Potential.* New York: McGraw-Hill, 1964, 55.

Turner, G. B. "The American Council of Learned Societies and Curriculum Revision." In R. W. Heath (Ed.), *New Curricula.* New York: Harper & Row, 1964.

Werner, H. "The Concept of Development from a Comparative and Organismic Point of View." In D. B. Harris (Ed.), *The Concept of Development.* Minneapolis: University of Minn. Press, 1957.

White, R. W. "Ego and Reality in Psychoanalytic Theory." *Psychol. Issues,* **III,** No. 3, 1963.

Winsor, Charlotte B. "The Bank Street program. child growth and learning in social studies experiences." In Loretta E. Klee (Ed.), *Social studies for older children: programs for grades four, five, and six.* National Council for Social Studies, Washington, D.C.: 1952, 78.

Winsor, Charlotte B. "Social Education of Young children." In Mary Willcockson (Ed.), *Social Education of Young Children, Kindergarten-Primary Grades.* National Council for Social Studies, Curriculum Series, No. 4, 2d rev. ed. Washington, D.C.: 1956, 119.

Winsor, Charlotte B. "What Are We Doing in Social Studies?" In Forty-Fifth (1957) Annual School Men's Week Proceedings. Philadelphia, Pa.: University of Pennsylvania Press, 1958, 396.

Wohlwill, J. F. "The Teaching Machine: Psychology's New Hobbyhorse." *Teach. Coll. Rec.,* **64,** No. 2, November 1962, 139–150.

Chapter 6

Teaching Strategies for Cognitive Growth

Hilda Taba

About the Author

Hilda Taba began her career as a student of economics and business in order to avoid becoming a teacher. When the prospects of being an economist began to smell of packing cases, she shifted to pure philosophy at the University of Tartu, Estonia. Just before the doctoral thesis faced her, an obscure notice about a scholarship to Bryn Mawr College in the United States eventually brought her to graduate study in educational philosophy. She had the good fortune to participate in the last seminar of John Dewey at Teachers College, Columbia University.

From there on she became interested in bridging the gap between curriculum planning and theoretical foundations. This search became a lifetime for a person who had the additional encumbrance of being both a woman and a foreigner. The doctorate in Philsophy of Education was no guarantee of a professorship at the University of Tartu, even though she was the sole doctorate in that field in that country. According to the University Senate at that time, women were just not considered as professorial material.

Returning to the United States and the joblessness of the 1930's, she finally connected with the Eight Year Study via curriculum directorship in the Dalton Schools, a member of the thirty schools. This directorship involved a complete reshaping of the senior high school curriculum into an integrated study of the United States: its technology, roots and relationships, obliterating the isolating barriers between the subjects, perhaps the first attempt of this kind on this level. Apprenticeship in test evaluation and development in the areas of social values and attitudes and thinking as a member of the Eight Year Study Evaluation Staff, under the tutelage of Ralph Tyler followed. This job, also the first challenge to systematize the thinking about curriculum, was begun in a doctoral dissertation entitled *Dynamics of Education.*

After six years at Ohio State University and the University of Chicago, she attempted to study normal development of adolescents under the auspices of the Committee on Human Development. This

158

eventuated in a report with Robert J. Havighurst of the study, *Adolescent Character and Personality*. This was a useful interlude and initiation—an introduction to the methods of analyzing contemporary culture, to the role of the social-class structure, and its impact on education. It constituted a splendid preparation for the next venture—experimentation with the curriculum development in intergroup relations. An opportunity to direct a national program in Intergroup Relations under the auspices of the American Council on Education came as a by-product of her substituting for the director of a workshop in Intergroup Relations at Harvard University.

For six years the staff of that project, including its director, roamed around the eighteen school systems that were members of the project, inventing teaching techniques for groups that are now called culturally deprived, wrestling with racial and religious segregation in the communities, introducing teachers from minority backgrounds into white schools and in the process refining the methods of curriculum development, inventing new teaching strategies and experimenting with group processes. In a sense all this was a predevelopment, for obviously this was ahead of the times. The eleven publications that emanated from the project had a relatively meager distribution except for the famous *Reading Ladders* that are still being reissued and the pamphlet on the use of sociometric techniques in studying and managing human relations in the classroom.

Somewhere in the dim past, Miss Taba, being a confirmed urbanite, had decided that when she stopped being a traveling woman, she would settle down in some nice metropolitan center like New York, Paris, or San Francisco. When teaching summer school at San Francisco State in 1951, it occurred to her that she *was* in one of those spots. When she inquired whether there was anything in that up-and-coming institution, the then President Paul Leonard not only invited her to join the staff, but even asked her to "write her own ticket." She has been at San Francisco State since then: teaching, researching, consulting in schools and pursuing the frail trail of theory of curriculum development.

Introduction to the Chapter

From Biber to Taba is a short and continuing pathway into more specific instructional strategies and concepts. Taba suggests that there is as yet no coherent theory of instruction or of learning. She questions the assumption that a knowledge of content on the part of a teacher bears any direct relationship to teaching effectiveness or that the chief function of teaching is to impart information. Not surprisingly, Taba feels that the business of education is to teach students to think.

But what is thinking and how do you recognize it when you see it? Taba says it has something to do with concept formation including the ability to differentiate objects and events, the ability to group or classify objects and events, and finally, the ability to categorize or symbolize the whole business. Thinking with abstract symbols is developed during the elementary school years as the child moves from the operational and concrete to the more abstract. Therefore, our author states that we should pay attention to how we can enhance thinking in students during these years.

Taba points out the primacy of learned and experienced concepts such as units of measurement in managing problems requiring such concepts. For example, the processes of gauging larger distances is for many men based on the one hundred yards they experienced as high school football players. Since football is not played on water, they may have difficulty applying this learning in estimating distances over water. It is also interesting to note as mentioned in Chapter 1 that distances conceptualized when one is little seem much smaller when one grows up and revisits old haunts.

Taba emphasizes the need for degrees of concrete thinking before conceptual thought can emerge. One of the problems may be that few fields of knowledge are organized by their scholars or teachers so that there is a progression from the concrete into the conceptualizing processes of knowledge. Students taking history courses usually do their utmost to keep the content all chronologically and factually tied together while searching for some theme around which they can organize it all. In the end some decide that their best pneumatic binding was chronological time.

All knowledge is an organized way of thinking; to match these organizations with the information-processing organizations in the child is the goal of all educators.

Teaching Strategies for Cognitive Growth[1]

Perhaps the most deceivingly simple definition of teaching is that it is teaching something to somebody by some process. Complications appear, however, as we try to clarify the elements of this definition. This definition makes it possible to construct a variety of models for teaching depending on how we view the objectives of curriculum, what conception we have of the content and its role in learning, how we perceive the learning process and the conceptions regarding individual differences and the potentialities of the learners. For example, the "something" may be limited to an aspect of subject matter, such as mastering the definition of gravity or the classification of mollusks. Such content may be presented as descriptive information or with the intent of introducing students to the "structure" of the respective discipline: its basic principles and thought system.

Many educational theorists and practitioners include in the "something" also such behavioral objectives as the development of thinking, attitudes, and skills. It is reasonable to assume that the addition of these objectives also involves modification of teaching strategies, because each of these objectives involves unique ways of learning, and, therefore, also different teaching strategies. For example, assigning reading in a text may be the most appropriate way of teaching if the sole aim is to transfer to the students as much information as possible. However, this method of teaching is probably quite inappropriate if the purpose is to generate independent methods of inquiry, creative uses of knowledge, or the ability to draw inferences from data. Giving information may be a necessary function at some points of the learning sequence, whereas asking questions and seeking answers from students may be required at other points and in connection with other learning tasks.

Similar variations in the criteria for effective teaching emerge from the analysis of the types of learners and of their motivational patterns and potentialities.

[1] This material is part of a forthcoming book on thought processes and teaching strategies to be published by Rand McNally.

It appears, then, that this simple definition projects a concept of teaching vastly more complex than is usually thought. The implementation of a concept of teaching requires, furthermore, an intensive and extensive use of a variety of behavioral sciences, such as social and individual psychology, anthropology, and sociology.

This chapter will deal largely with the problem of sharpening the idea of teaching strategies for cognitive development. This does not imply that other objectives, such as the affective domain and the domain of skills, do not merit a similar analysis.

The chief proposition explored in this chapter is that in order to develop a theory of instruction we must both sharpen the analysis of the objectives or targets of teaching and delineate the strategies of teaching appropriate to these objectives. Only as this is done with reference to all important areas of educational objectives can we hope to arrive at a sound instructional theory.

CONCEPTIONS OF TEACHING

Instruction or teaching is one aspect of the educational process that has been neglected by both theorists and practitioners of education. There is no coherent theory of instruction and perhaps not even sufficient basic data for constructing one. In curriculum planning reasonable care is exercised in selecting and organizing the content. Whatever weaknesses exist are caused by deficiencies in the theory and methodology of planning, not by lack of attention or effort. In contrast, the selection and organization of learning activities and the formation of the corresponding instructional strategy are left to the judgment of individual teachers. Curriculum guides tend to offer only general injunctions regarding an over-all approach to teaching. Occasionally a list of suggested learning activities is provided—a smorgasbord from which the teacher is invited to select whatever pleases his or her fancy.

In addition, a series of oversimplified assumptions seem to have governed the models of teaching. The simplest and the most stubborn is the idea that the chief, if not the only, function of teaching is to impart information. This concept of teaching assumes that learning is passive and that the mastering of content is all that is needed to cultivate literate and active minds. A correlate of this idea is the assumption that the teacher's knowledge of subject matter bears a direct relationship to teaching effectiveness (Sarason and Blatt, 1962). This concept of teaching is currently in vogue, as is evidenced in the writings of the critics of education and in the essentially sympathetic suggestions for the improvement of education, such as the recent Conant report on teacher education (Conant, 1963).

Another widely accepted concept of teaching is that it consists of particular procedures to be employed in teaching specific subjects: that there is *a* or even *the* method of teaching history, mathematics, or reading. A large portion of the methods courses of teacher training is predicated on this assumption. This model is based on the assumption that the requirements of the logical structure of the subject matter are the sole source of criteria for adequate teaching strategies and that a method so formulated would be equally effective in the hands of all teachers, for all kinds of students, and under all varieties of learning conditions (Medley and Mitzel, 1963).

A third assumption is that good teachers are born, not made. By this definition teaching is a sort of mystique, an art, the secrets of which a few "good" teachers grasp intuitively or stumble on accidentally. Such a conception practically bars an objective analysis of the processes of teaching and denies the possibility of imparting that "art" to prospective teachers.

Such oversimplifications are extended to the relationships involved in teaching. Usually teaching is represented as a didactic relationship: the proverbial Mark Hopkins at one end of the log and the student at the other. This view is held in spite of the fact that teaching usually occurs in group situations, that models of learning are influenced by peers as well as by teachers, and that a whole science of group dynamics is available to draw upon in order to make possible the use of group processes to facilitate learning.

According to recent analysis, research in teacher education has fared no better, having suffered from an inadequate theoretical framework and from the testing of unproductive hypotheses (Gage, 1963). Essentially, concepts of method have been inferred from studies of learning carried on in laboratory situations that have little relevance to learning in classrooms. Page (1962) suggests, in addition, that such inferences have usually been based on a gross misapplication of the behavioral sciences, especially that of psychology, and that both psychologists and educators engage in verbal "magic." Both have indulged in applying findings generated in very limited situations, such as reactions of rats to electric shock in a laboratory, first to behavior in general and then to learning in a classroom.

Partly because of this verbal "magic" and partly because of inadequate analysis of the teaching process, the models of teaching tend to be stated in global terms that make difficult the establishment of a consistent relationship between a given method of teaching and a particular learning theory that supports it. This global concept of "good teaching" inevitably leads to concentration on content *per se* and fails to make direct provision for behavioral objectives, both in the cognitive and the affective domains. Almost inevitably, such outcomes as thinking and attitudes toward society or self are treated as by-products or "concomitants" of the main business of mastering the content.

Other studies of teaching effectiveness have focused on the characteristics of teachers as persons, possibly on the assumption that teaching style is a product of the personality of the teacher rather than a rational enterprise requiring professional skills. Getzels and Jackson (1962, pp. 83–84) point out, further, that

"despite the critical importance of the problem and half a century of prodigious effort, little is known about either the nature and measurement of teacher personality or about the relationship between teacher personality and teaching effectiveness. The regrettable fact is that many of the studies so far have not produced significant results. Many others have produced only pedestrian findings."

However, recent developments hold promise for a more adequate approach to the study of teaching. Under the dual impact of continued criticism of education and the increased flow of money into educational research and experimentation, a new interest has been kindled in the analysis of the teaching process and in the building of a theory of instruction. Conviction is growing that to understand either we must study teaching as it occurs in the classroom, rather than inferring teaching effectiveness from teacher personality or from *a priori* judgments of what constitutes good teaching.

Smith (1950) maintains that in order to develop an adequate theory of didactics, a description of the actions of teachers is needed first—a description can then be translated into tactics of teaching.

Some descriptive studies of teaching acts in the classroom are now in progress. Recent studies of teaching have shifted the locus of study into the classroom and concentrate on the description and classification of teacher acts that have certain predictable effects on learning.

Marie Hughes (1959, pp. 62–69), for example, examined such categories of teaching acts as controlling children, that is, telling them what to do; facilitating learning, that is, checking, demonstrating, and clarifying; and developing content, that is, elaborating on the structure of the problem and building up data for generalizing.

Flanders (1962, pp. 62–89) has focused on the types of classroom interaction and their effect on the goals and the climate for learning. He sorts the observed behavior of teachers and students into the following categories: accepting feelings, praising, encouraging, using ideas of students, asking questions, lecturing, giving directions, and criticizing or justifying authority. He calls the first five indirect influences and the last three the direct influences. Presumably, the indirect influences extend the freedom of action of students and reduce the dependency on the teacher; the direct influences reduce this freedom and increase the dependency.

Bellak and Davitz (1963) describe the teacher behavior in terms of pedagogical moves, such as structuring, focusing, or eliciting reactions; conveying substantive meaning of the subject matter; conveying logical meaning, such as defining, interpreting, explaining, and evaluating.

Studies such as these have provided a new perspective on the analysis of teaching and laid the groundwork for a new methodology. But they also fall short in several respects. For example, except by inference, it is difficult to determine the effectiveness of the frequent use of certain types of teaching acts without first obtaining data on the products of these acts, namely, on changes in specified aspects of student behavior. Also, the impact on learning may be determined not so much by the frequency of the types of teaching acts as by the way in which they are combined and patterned. Further studies are needed to investigate these aspects of teaching.

THINKING AS AN EDUCATIONAL OBJECTIVE

The proper business of the schools, it has long been urged, is to teach students to think. For a number of reasons the implementation of this objective in curriculum and teaching has been sporadic and ineffective.

First, thinking has been treated as a global process. Thinking has been variously defined as anything that goes on in the head, from daydreaming to creating the concept of relativity. Consequently, the need to define thinking and to identify its specific elements remains, particularly as these elements apply to planning effective teaching strategies. Knowledge of the development of thinking has been inadequate. Also, the study of the development of thinking has largely been carried on by Piaget [1950] and his followers, and the implications of this work have, until recently, received scant attention in the United States.

There is also a questionable assumption, which has wide acceptance, that thinking cannot take place until a sufficient body of factual information is accumulated. Teaching based on this assumption stresses factual coverage and burdens the memory of learners with unorganized and rather perishable information.

An equally unproductive assumption is that thought is an automatic by-product of studying certain subjects and of assimilating the end-products of someone else's thought. Some subjects are assumed to have the power of producing thought independently of how they are taught or learned. Inherently, memorizing mathematical formulae or the steps in mathematical processes is assumed to be better training than memorizing cake recipes, even though both may be learned in the same manner and call for the same mental process—rote memory.

These factors have prevented the focusing of attention on the development of teaching strategies designed to stimulate active, productive, and creative thought. A common criticism of current teaching is that it cultivates passive mastery instead of an active discovery of ideas and a tendency to follow "recipes" in solving problems instead of analyzing them and searching for generalizations with which to organize facts necessary to plan an attack on them (Bartlett, 1958; Buswell and Hersch, 1956).

The Studies of Thinking

Only recently have we acquired both the conceptual and the methodological tools necessary to extend our knowledge of the thinking process and to permit investigation of how teaching procedures may affect its development.

A canvas of recent research projects on thinking reveals several approaches to studying cognition in general and thinking in particular. A number of studies are concerned with individual differences in styles of thinking. Individuals presumably have a predilection or "style" in the manner in which they select, respond to, and organize aspects of their environment.

For example, individuals employ distinct ways of grouping and categorizing phenomena. Kagan, Moss and Sigel (1960) distinguish three types of labeling behavior: (1) *descriptive labeling,* which follows the manifest physical attributes of objects, such as identifying groups of people in uniforms as "soldiers"; (2) *relational-contextual labeling,* in which events and objects are grouped according to their interdependence, such as grouping a man with a cane who is wearing glasses and a boy by saying, "the boy is helping the blind man across the street"; (3) *categorical-inferential* or *class labeling,* in which an object or event is subsumed under a label which represents a class of objects, such as grouping together all objects which are tools or subsuming availability of land and medical care under standards of living.

Peel (1960, pp. 16–18) describes four styles of thinking: (1) *thematic,* such as a pattern employed in creative writing. This style is relatively free, except that the theme controls, directs, and unifies the associations and presents a unified whole. (2) *explanatory thinking,* usually employed in describing and explaining events, in which the practical criterion controls the associations. (3) *productive thinking,* employed when an individual is called upon to apply his knowledge to understand or to explain new phenomena. (4) *integrative thinking,* exhibited in inventing new theories and systems of thought and usually embracing a wide range of apparently dissimilar cognitive operations.

Bartlett (1958) and Rokeach (1960) speak of closed and open systems of thought. A closed system of thought is characterized by a high degree of uniformity of the process and order by which thought processes are performed. An open system of thought breaks out of this mold. Guilford (1960) distinguishes between convergent and divergent modes of thought. Convergent thought is directed toward finding the "correct" answer by a predetermined method. The divergent thinker seeks the novel and unusual and uses spontaneous flexibility as a method of searching.

Suggestive as these studies are, they share one difficulty. The concept of style refers to a global overarching quality of thinking rather than to a process which could be learned and taught consciously. The findings about general styles of thought fail to shed light on the processes by which these styles are acquired and the skills on which they are founded. Consequently, it is difficult to translate the findings from such studies into guidelines for more effective teaching.

THE CONCEPT OF COGNITIVE TASKS

One study of the thinking of elementary school children set out to examine the processes of thought in terms that can shed some light on the learning and teaching of certain specific identifiable cognitive skills (Taba, Levine, Elzey, 1964). The fundamental assumption of this study is that thought consists of specific describable processes or operations that are subject to training. These researchers set out to create categories for analyzing thinking each of which describes learnable, and therefore, also teachable, processes and skills.

Three cognitive tasks were identified: (1) concept formation, (2) the development of generalizations and inferences from interpretation of raw data, and (3) the explanation and prediction of new phenomena by applying known principles and facts. The skills that are necessary for mastering these tasks were specified also.

Concept Formation

In its simplest form concept development may be described as consisting of three processes or operations. One is the differentiation of the properties or characteristics of objects and events, such as differentiating the materials of which houses are built from other characteristics of houses. This differentiation involves analysis in the sense of breaking down global wholes into specific properties and elements.

The second process is that of grouping. This process calls for abstracting certain common characteristics in an array of dissimilar objects or events and grouping these on the basis of this similar property, such as grouping together hospitals, doctors, and medicine as something to do with health care or according to their availability as an index of the standard of living. Naturally, the same objects and events can be grouped in several different ways. For example, hospitals, x-rays, and surgical equipment could be grouped together as health facilities, as types of services, or as indices of standard of living, depending on the purpose of the grouping.

The third process is that of categorizing and labeling. This process calls for the invention or the discovery of categories or labels that encompass diverse objects and events, such as developing the concept of a unit of measurement from measuring with a cup, a yardstick, a plain stick, and a rubber band. It also involves the process of super- and subordination, namely, deciding which sets of items can be subsumed under which category. In classrooms this cognitive task can be performed by first enumerating objects and events, identifying a series of specific items noted in a film or reported by a research committee, then grouping these items according to their similarities, and finally, labeling these groups and indicating which items belong to which labels.

Interpretation of Data and Inference

Essentially, this cognitive task is that of evolving generalizations and principles from an analysis of concrete data. Several subprocesses are involved. The first and the simplest is that of identifying specific points in the data. This process is somewhat analogous to the listing or enumeration preceding grouping. Explaining specific items or events, such as why ocean currents affect temperature, why Mexico employs the "each one teach one" system in eradicating illiteracy, or why the way of life in California changed when its harbors were opened for free trade, is the second sub-process. This process involves relating points of information to each other in order to enlarge their meaning. The third operation is that of forming inferences which go beyond that which is directly given, such as inferring from comparison of data on population composition and standards of living in certain Latin American countries that countries with predominantly white populations tend to have a higher standard of living.

Interpretation of data and the formulation of inferences take place in the classroom whenever students are faced with raw data in one form or another, such as viewing a film, comparing and contrasting research data on the imports and exports of several countries, or trying to identify and to synthesize the factors that determine the level of technological development in a given culture by examining the tools and techniques used in the production of goods.

Application of Principles

A third cognitive task is that of applying known principles and facts to explain new phenomena or to predict consequences from known conditions. For example, if we know what a desert is like, the kind of life conditions it permits, and how water affects the productivity of the soil, we could predict what might happen to the desert way of life if more water became available.

This cognitive task involves essentially two different operations. One is that of predicting and hypothesizing. Predicting and hypothesizing require an analysis of the problem and of the conditions in order to determine which facts or logical relationships are relevant and which are not. It is also necessary to relate what one knows to a new problem, to make possible a rational prediction or explanation.

The second operation is that of developing informational or logical parameters which constitute the causal links between the conditions and the prediction or explanation. For example, if we predict that the presence of water in the desert will cause cities to be built, we must be aware of the chain of causal links that leads from the availability of water to the building of cities. These chains may consist of logical conditions, such as that the soil in the desert requires only water to be productive, or they may consist of factual data, such as whether the desert soil is salty or not.

These predictions and explanations are of different orders of gen-

erality and complexity: for example, the prediction that as a consequence of the availability of water, cities will be built involves a
greater leap than does the prediction that grass will grow.

This last cognitive task permits a greater degree of divergence than
do either of the first two. However, the logical constraints of the
predictions and explanations are greater than those imposed by tests
and exercises that permit sheer unconstrained exercise of ingenuity
and imagination.

NATURE OF THOUGHT

The description of the cognitive tasks and of the operations and
skills they require is insufficient for the development of effective teaching strategies. A theoretical construct of the nature of thought and
of its development is needed also. Space permits the description
of only a few of the principles that make up this theoretical structure.

First, most of the studies of the development of thought indicate
that the learning of thinking is essentially an active transaction between the individual and his environment. This transaction is neither
fully controlled by the environmental stimulation or entirely dependent on mediating intervention, such as training or availability of
models. Environment and training become available to the individual
only to the extent that he attends to or performs certain cognitive
operations upon the material. An individual must work out these operations for himself. They cannot be "given" by the teacher or anyone
else, though it is possible to create conditions that aid and stimulate
the invention and the practice of these operations. These cognitive
operations result in conceptual schemes, which the individual uses to
reduce and to organize the kaleidoscope of environmental stimulation
(Piaget, 1950; Flavell, 1963, pp. 366–68).

The evolution of thought also follows a sequential pattern, in which
the simpler and the more concrete operations precede and prepare
for the more complex and abstract ones. For example, before a child
can grasp the abstract idea of seriation, he can perform seriation concretely in such a form as stringing beads according to their size.

If Piaget's observations can be trusted, this transition from the
concrete and operational to abstract thought takes place during the
elementary school years. The findings of Taba, Levine, and Elzey
(1964) indicate that this transformation of concrete thought or thinking with objects into abstract thought or thinking with symbols begins
in the second grade and goes on at an accelerating rate until in the

fifth and sixth grades one-sixth of the thought expressed in classroom discussions involving this task is on the abstract and formal level.

But the concept of a sequence also applies to the mastery of the cognitive tasks described above. Each of these tasks can be seen as consisting of sequential and, in a sense, hierarchical steps of in which each preceding operation is more concrete than each succeeding one and in which the mastery of each preceding step is a necessary prerequisite to the succeeding one. Thus, in interpreting data the differentiation of specific points is a prerequisite for comparing and contrasting, and the inter-relating of these points is a prerequisite for explaining and inferring. While the general development sequence determines what is fruitful to emphasize at particular age levels, the specific sequence of steps in a given cognitive task determines which strategies of learning and teaching are appropriate at each step.

The chief point about the sequences in the development of thinking is that a deficiency in mastering the first step, such as the analysis of the concrete instances, leads to incapacity to function on the level of the final step, such as the formulation of generalizations.

Finally, the conceptual schemes as well as the cognitive operations undergo a constant reorganization. It is useful to visualize the dynamics of this process as a rotation of two types of activity. One is that of taking in the information and organizing it according to whatever conceptual scheme exists. At each point of his experience the individual fits the information he receives into the conceptual scheme he already possesses. Whether this conceptual scheme is adequate or not, new phenomena have meaning only to the extent that they can assimilate into the patterns of concepts and relationships that already exist in the learner's mind. For example, if a child's concept of a unit of measurement is that of measuring with a yardstick, he will attempt to fit all problems of measuring into this concept.

However, when the requirements of the situation do not fit the current scheme or when the individual faces a problem or task that introduces a dissonance, the second type of activity is generated. An individual is forced to alter or to extend his conceptual scheme to accommodate new information. Piaget (1950) calls this fitting process "assimilation," and the process of alteration "accommodation."

For example, the introduction of the task of measuring the volume of water in a jar will stimulate the child to extend his concept of a unit of measurement to include the measures of volume, such as a cup or a beaker.

The rotation of these two processes is the psychological mechanism for developing increasingly mature conceptual schemes and an increasingly mobile and autonomous use of them. Hunt (1961) points out further that the rotation of these two types of mental operations requires a proper match between the existing conceptual schemes and those which are required by new experience. When the requirements of accommodation are too far beyond the current level, it is impossible for the child to make the leap. When the requirements of accommodation are too close to the existing schemes, there is no stimulus for altering them.

It is important to note also that these reorganizations represent not only quantitative increments, such as greater precision of analysis, but also qualitative transformations.

TEACHING STRATEGIES FOR COGNITIVE PERFORMANCE

The preceding discussion suggests a new perspective for the analysis of teaching and for the role of the teacher. First, it seems that before it is possible to develop a science of teaching or even a good paradigm of teaching, it might be necessary, at least for the time being, to discard the global attack on improvement of teaching and to concentrate instead on creating and analyzing the teaching strategies for specific targets, such as the teaching of thinking. Empirical experimentation with these differentiated teaching strategies might open up new possibilities for articulating generic concepts of productive teaching.

The idea that thinking is essentially an active transaction to be performed by the individual underscores the importance of addressing the pedagogical functions to the development of autonomy in mastering and using the various cognitive skills. If students are to develop cognitive structures by their own efforts and to master the methodology of doing so, the usual role of the teacher needs to be reversed. Instead of being exclusively a source of information, he needs to become an adroit guide of the heuristic process.

In such teaching, the role of questions assumes a crucial importance, and the way of asking questions becomes by far the most influential single teaching act. The focus set by the questions asked by the teacher determines which points students can or cannot explore and influences the kinds of mental operations they acquire. All learning experiences teach "sets to learn." Children may acquire a disposition to search for relationships or to look for single "right" answers. They may learn to organize information and to make inferences or to depend on ready-made generalizations.

Too often the questions teachers ask control and limit the cognitive functioning of the students and actually inhibit productive mental activity. For example, asking students to name the important cities in the Balkans without revealing the criterion for importance or without developing such a criterion with the class leaves them no alternative but to guess what the teacher wants or to recollect what the book said about the matter. Repeated experiences of this sort cause students to adopt irrational, unproductive, and arbitrary models of thinking and to cultivate dependence on memory and authority rather than on judgment or inference.

An adequate programming of active cognitive development requires also a sharper identification of the pedagogical functions of teaching acts. In the study referred to above (Taba, Levine, and Elzey, 1964) three different functions of teaching acts were identified:

1. *Focusing thought,* or determining what the content of the task is to be and which cognitive operations are to be performed. A question such as, "What differences would you expect to see among the countries in Latin America?" directs the attention to differences and asks for listing of the perceived differences.

2. *Extending thought,* or seeking for contributions on the same level, such as asking, "Does anyone have anything different to add to this?"

3. *Lifting thought* to a different and higher level. A question such as, "Is the standard of living in Argentina higher than in Bolivia?" calls for an explanation and identification of the causal factors. This operation is of a higher order than simply describing the standard of living in each country.

The idea of developmental sequence in the various cognitive skills implies that one of the major functions of teaching is to create learning experiences which follow these sequences. For example, if a sequence of steps in formulating inferences starts with the identification of the points of information, proceeds next to comparing and contrasting these points, and ends with the formulation of inferences which go beyond what is given, the strategy of conducting such a discussion should follow this sequence. Such a sequence represents a cycle of learning in which the simple and concrete cognitive operations precede the more complex and abstract ones. Such a cycle of learning may have to be repeated on each successive level of concepts and ideas. Each increment in the abstractness and the complexity of content ideas requires a corresponding upward spiralling of the demand regarding the level of cognitive functioning: a greater degree of precision, a higher level of abstraction, a more refined analysis, as well as appropriate qualitative transformations such as the transformation of the descriptive into the explanatory mode. This leads to an obvious conclusion that the modification of thought is not in the class of instantaneous learning. Shifts in the patterns of thought occur only as a result of continuous and cumulative practice.

The idea of assimilation and accommodation as a psychological mechanism for advancing thought suggests a teaching strategy that includes a systematic rotation of the learning tasks calling for assimilation of new information in the existing conceptual scheme with those requiring an extension and reorganization of the scheme. A prolonged assimilation of facts without the corresponding reshaping of the conceptual schemes with which to organize them is bound to retard the maturation of thought. On the other hand, a premature leap into a more complex or higher level of thought is likely to immobilize mental activity and cause reversion to rote learning or, at any rate, to a lower level of thought. Students need a sufficient amount of assimilation to have the "stuff" to think with. But they need equally a challenge to stretch their modes of thinking and their conceptual schemes.

An appropriate transition from the one to the other requires a proper match between the current level and that which is required. Determining this proper match is perhaps one of the most difficult tasks in teaching and constitutes, in effect, a new concept of readiness and pacing. An effective diagnosis of such a match comes close to what is referred to as an "art of teaching." This task is complicated by the fact that the mastery of abstract communications such as language and number often masks the actual level of thinking. Verbalization may deceive the teacher and lead him to assume that thinking is more advanced than it is and hence to pushing the child's verbal habits of learning beyond his level of thinking (Peel, 1960).

To manage these transitions, teachers need to adapt the size of the steps as well as the timing of them to the level of performance in the group. They need to decide when to shift from the description ("what") to explanation ("why"), or when to make a transition from assimilation of new information into the existing conceptual scheme of introducing experiences requiring modification of that scheme.

These decisions regarding timing and the size of the successive steps to be taken by the students and regarding the pacing of the transformation of cognitive operations naturally require continuous diagnosis of the level of performance. Depending upon both the ability of the students and their previously formed habits of thought, some groups of students require a longer period for assimilating descriptive information before they can successfully cope with explanations. Some students will readily grasp the idea that grouping must be done according to some basis, whereas others need to "mess around" for some time before they "discover" this idea. To perform such diagnosis and to convert it instantly into action according to feedback from the students' performance is an aspect of teaching strategy approximating what is usually described as "the art of teaching"—chiefly because neither the means nor the materials have been available to give teachers adequate clinical experience with the process.

Given an adequate analysis of the learning processes involved in the important cognitive tasks and given teaching strategies that effectively implement the principles of sequence, of active mental organization, and of adequate rotation of assimilation and accommodation, all students should be able to achieve higher levels of cognitive operation than seems possible under current teaching. Furthermore, it is not beyond possibility that by far the most important individual differences may be found in the amount of concrete thinking an individual needs to do before formal thought can emerge. This difference may distinguish the slow but capable learner from one who is incapable of abstract thought. The data from the study of thinking in elementary school children referred to above (Taba, et al. 1964) suggest that many a slow learner can achieve a high level of abstract thought provided that he has an opportunity to linger longer on the level of assimilation of concrete instances than is ordinarily possible in classrooms held to covering content.

REFERENCES

Bartlett, F. E. *Thinking: An Experimental and Social Study*. New York: Basic Books, 1958.

Bellak, A., J. R. Davitz, H. M. Kliebard, and R. T. Hyman. *The Language of the Classroom*. Institute of Psychological Research. New York: Teachers College, Columbia University, 1963.

Buswell, G. T. and Hersch, B. Y. *Patterns of Thinking in Solving Problems*. Berkeley, California: University of California Press, 1956.

Conant, J. B. *The Education of American Teachers*. New York: McGraw-Hill, 1963.

Flanders, N. A. *Teacher Inflence, Pupil Attitudes, and Achievement*. Prepublication manuscript of a proposed Office of Education on monograph. Ann Arbor, Michigan: University of Michigan, 1962.

Gage, N. L. (ed.), *Handbook of Research on Teaching*. American Educational Research Association. Chicago: Rand McNally, 1963.

Getzels, J. W. and P. W. Jackson. "The Teacher Personality and Characteristics," in *Handbook of Research on Teaching*. Chicago: N. L. Gage (ed.), Rand McNally, 1963.

Guilford, P. P. "Basic Conceptual Problems in the Psychology of Thinking," in *Fundamentals of Psychology: The Psychology of Thinking,* annals of the New York Academy of Sciences, **91,** 1960, pp. 9–19.

Hughes, Marie, et al. *Development of the Means for the Assessment of the Quality of Teaching in the Elementary School.* Salt Lake City: University of Utah, 1959. Mimeo.

Hunt, J. McV. *Intelligence and Experience.* New York: The Ronald Press, 1961.

Kagan, J., H. A. Moss, and I. E. Sigel. "Conceptual Style and the Use of Affect Labels." *Merrill-Palmer Quarterly of Behavior and Development,* **6,** July 1960, 261–278.

Medley, D. M. and H. E. Mitzel, "The Scientific Study of Teacher Behavior," in Arno Bellac, ed., *Theory and Research in Teaching,* New York: Teachers College Bureau of Publications, Columbia University, 1963, pp. 85–88.

Flavell, J. H., *The Developmental Psychology of Jean Piaget.* Princeton, New Jersey: D. Van Nostrand Co., 1963.

Page, E. B. "Behavioral Theory, Verbal Magic, and Education." *Educational Theory,* **12,** No. 2, April 1962, 74–75.

Peel, E. A. *The Pupil's Thinking.* London: Oldbourne, 1960.

Piaget, J. *The Psychology of Intelligence.* New York: Harcourt, Brace and World, 1950.

Rokeach, M. *The Open and Closed Mind.* New York: Basic Books, 1960.

Sarason, K. D. and B. Blatt *The Preparation of Teachers: An Unstudied Problem in Education.* New York: John Wiley, 1962.

Smith, B. O. "A Concept of Teaching," *Teachers College Record,* **61,** February, 1950, pp. 229–241.

Suchman, J. R. "Inquiry Training: Building Skills for Autonomous Discovery." *Merrill-Palmer Quarterly,* July 1961.

Taba, Hilda, S. Levine, and F. F. Elzey. *Thinking in Elementary School Children.* Office of Education, Cooperative Research Branch. Project No. 1574. Final Report, 1964.

Chapter 7

Theories of Human Learning Revisited

Henry Clay Lindgren

About the Author

Henry Clay Lindgren, often called "Hank," began his formal education in the public schools of Hilo, Hawaii, where he learned not only the 3 R's, but pidgin English as well. From Hilo High School, he went on to Sacramento J.C. and Stanford, where he got his A.B. in 1934 and his M.A. a year later. He taught for a few years in Hawaii and California and went back to Stanford in time to get a Ph.D. on the eve of entering the Navy, where he was assigned to instructor training and educational services. His last naval billet, assistant rehabilitation officer at the Naval Hospital, Mare Island, led naturally into the counseling of veterans, first for the San Francisco City Schools and later for the Veterans Administration, where he became Assistant Chief of Advisement and Guidance for the Pacific Southwest.

From the Veterans Administration, Hank entered student personnel work at the college level, and in 1947 he became Director of the Counseling Center at San Francisco State College. Two years later he joined the psychology department, where he has been ever since, except for occasional periods abroad. These sojourns have included assignments as Fulbright lecturer at the University of Rome, UNESCO consultant in educational psychology in Brazil, and visiting professor at the American University of Beirut.

Lindgren's early cross-cultural experiences in Hawaii served as the basis of a broad and deep interest in social psychology, particularly as applied to problems of education, mental hygiene, and interpersonal relationships. This interest also led to research on such diverse topics as hostility, attitudes toward tendermindedness in teachers, emotional problems of over- and underachievers, and empathy. He has completed a couple of research studies with the aid of his wife, Fredi, on brainstorming and orneriness as facilitators of creativity, and has written or been involved in a number of textbooks, including *Educational Psychology in the Classroom* (Wiley), *Psychology: An Introduction to a Behavioral Science* (Wiley), and *Psychology of Personal Development* (American Book).

178

His underlying central concern as a psychologist, teacher, and writer is the problem of personal freedom, the freedom to become one's best, most competent, most creative self. For example, Lindgren is disturbed by the ways in which teachers and administrators so often build rigidity and unnecessary restrictions into the educational programs and thus keep students from developing the strengths and the insights that would make them free. Because of this concern you may find in his writing a note of rebelliousness, coupled with a theme of sympathetic concern for the plight of the perennial underdog—the student.

Introduction to the Chapter

When moving from theories of thinking to theories of learning, we should not have to cross a bridge of any great length. There seems to be more than a little conceptual overlap between the two, as suggested by Lindgren's review and resynthesis of our knowledge about human learning.

He speaks the unspeakable horror of research in learning—that it is *possible to find out a great deal about learning without at the same time discovering anything that might be of any help to the teacher.* Human learning takes place in a vast matrix of symbols and concepts all encased in and mediated by unique individuals undergoing idiosyncratic experiences. Where in this unmonitored melee can we find some general laws or guidelines for helping teachers teach and children learn? Most researchers prefer the precision measurements of laboratory exercises and the swift completion of tasks by nonsymbol-using animals. Researchers in human learning have the same avidity for precision and controlled conditions; no one, however, has worked out ways of encapsulating children or teachers into neat experimental learning situations.

Lindgren points out that principles of conditioning can be used to reinforce some appropriate responses but that teachers don't normally ask questions that can be answered by conditional procedures. Teachers ask such things as, "How can I use discussion methods, a workbook, and a laboratory demonstration to teach about the Solar System?" Or, "How do I teach historical concepts in history or an understanding of human behavior in *Hamlet?*"

Field theorists like Lewin, Snygg, Combs, Beatty, Clark, and Rogers have begun to get closer to the crux of the teacher's problem but seem to lack the instructional carryover. Few teachers, notes Lindgren, looking for a revolution. Most would, however, be grateful for a few instructional alternatives and some rationale for their differentiated use.

Theories of Human Learning Revisited

A learning theory, according to English and English's dictionary [1958], is "an attempt to state the general nature of learning." Psychologists, and particularly those psychologists who work in laboratories, have through the years evolved a number of statements or concepts that are loosely termed "learning theory." Although the list of such concepts will vary somewhat from one textbook to another, most lists include the various varieties and subvarieties of conditioning or reinforcement, including classical conditioning, trial-and-error, and operant learning; and the various varieties and subvarieties of Gestalt, self-concept, or field theory. Most of the research that psychologists have done has stemmed from the conditioning-reinforcement group of theories, largely because such theories lend themselves to precise definition, the posing of specific questions, and rigorous controls—conditions that are necessary for scientific exactitude. The Gestalt, field, and self-concept theories of learning, being more comprehensive in character, do not lend themselves so readily to the formulation of specific questions and precise answers and have produced a much smaller quantity of research. Consequently, when psychologists interested in laboratory experimentation speak of "learning theory," they are likely to have in mind concepts drawn from the conditioning-reinforcement group of theories, and often include Gestalt, field, and self-concept theories almost as an afterthought.

Basically, there are two reasons why psychologists, educators, or anyone else, would be interested in theories of learning: (1) curiosity about the nature of learning; (2) a desire to find out how to stimulate, direct, and control learning—in other words, how to teach effectively.

RESEARCH PRECISION AND TEACHING EXPECTATIONS

Unfortunately, it is quite possible to work toward one of these objectives without making any progress toward the other. It is possible to find out a great deal about learning without discovering anything of value to the teacher, and this has been true of most of the work of experimental psychologists. It is also possible to become preoccupied with the perfection of the teaching process, without discovering anything about the nature of how and why students learn (or do *not* learn), and this has been true of a great deal, if not most, of the work in educational methodology. Although experimental psychologists and educators give the outward appearance of sharing common interests in understanding the nature and control of the learning process, even a casual examination of the product of their labors will show that they have been working in distinctly different fields.[1]

This state of affairs has come about partly because of differences in the interests, values, and perhaps in the personalities of psychological researchers and teachers. By the very nature of their work, researchers are interested in concepts that enable them to ask questions that are answerable. It is axiomatic that the more precise the question, the more precise the answer; hence precision can be achieved only by narrowing the area of the field to be researched. Therefore, the kind of person who enjoys asking questions and finding answers, and who admires precision and specificity, is the kind of person who is attracted to or is developed by research activities.

The interests of teachers are by nature more complex than those of researchers. A researcher can congratulate himself on having done a good job if he satisfies his own curiosity and maintains the standards prescribed by his scientific discipline, but before a teacher can consider himself satisfied with his work, he must consider whether he has satisfied the expectations of those on whose behalf he has been employed— that is, society and the learner—as well as the standards of the school, his professional specialty, and his colleagues. In reality, of course, neither the researcher nor the teacher is ever satisfied: the researcher, because each answer poses new questions to be answered, and the teacher, because expectations are based on hopes and potentialities, rather than on realities.

But the essential difference remains: the researcher concerns himself with satisfying his curiosity and his need for precision, and the teacher concerns himself with satisfying quite a collection of individuals and groups, each of whom have different and sometimes conflicting expectations about the outcomes of the teaching-learning process. It is hardly surprising that successful researchers tend to be or to become fact-and-technique oriented, and successful teachers tend to be or

[1] The work of B. F. Skinner, his associates, and his followers in applying principles of operant learning to programmed instruction is a recent, but limited, exception to this.

to become concerned about the thoughts, feelings, and attitudes of people—themselves, as well as others.

Incidentally, when I make this distinction between teachers and researchers in this way, I do not mean to imply that researchers cannot be teachers or that teachers cannot be researchers. The two behavior patterns, with their attendant personality characteristics, may be thought of as two different roles. Everyday observation will show that there are some people who are involved with one kind of professional role, like that of the researcher or the teacher, whereas others are able to develop quite a repertory of roles. Although the person who specializes in one role can be a very useful person, in the social sense, most professional educators and psychologists would agree that the person who has developed some skill at playing a variety of roles is generally speaking a more valuable staff member.

In actuality, most researchers functioning in the academic context play roles as teachers, advisers, committee members, and even administrators, with a greater or lesser degree of facility. Teachers also play a variety of roles, although teachers in elementary and secondary schools are less likely to include research, particularly formal research, among their activities.

Even though a give individual may play the role of both the researcher and the teacher and may be fairly effective in both, one or the other tends to dominate, and the individual tends to think of himself primarily as a researcher or primarily a teacher. And the demands and expectations of the roles are so different that they can often be handled by one person only through a process of compartmentalization, whereby activities, behavior patterns, and attitudes associated with research roles become isolated and even insulated from those pertaining to teaching roles.

In summary, then, the researcher and the teacher have different motives and different interests and live in somewhat different worlds. Even both roles are filled by the same person, the teacher-researcher must find some way to isolate his "researching self" from his "teaching self"—that is, if he is going to be equally successful in both activities.

LEARNING THEORY AND THE TEACHER

Because of this gap between the two specialities, it is hardly surprising that research-oriented learning theory has so little to say to the teacher. Not only are the goals of researchers and teachers different, but there is considerable question as to whether they are referring to the same process when they use the term "learning."

Researchers who want to help the teacher in his quest for greater effectiveness must develop concepts of learning that are different from those usually used as a basis for laboratory research. What the teacher needs are theories of learning more obviously related to what he is doing or trying to do than are the theories devised to satisfy the exigencies of the psychological laboratory. The question thus arises: what standards must a theory meet in order to be useful to a teacher? The following are some suggested criteria:

1. The theory must provide the basis for our understanding of *all* processes of human learning.

2. The theory must provide the basis for our understanding of the significant conditions, forces, or factors that stimulate, inhibit, or affect human learning in any way.

3. The theory must enable us to make reasonably good predictions about the outcomes of learning activity.

4. The theory must be a potential source of hypotheses that can be tested in the classroom, as well as in the laboratory, in order that our understanding of the teaching-learning process may continue to develop and grow.

Let us take a look at the implications of each of these criteria.

The theory must provide the basis for our understanding of all processes of human learning.

We have already taken the psychologist to task for limiting his concepts of learning to those processes that can be studied under rigorous controls. However, the teacher, too, is at fault when he thinks of learning only in terms of classroom learning, or, even worse, when he thinks of learning solely as something that results from his teaching. In order for a learning theory to be an effective tool, it must take into account the full range of human behavior identifiable as learning. It must take cognizance of the fact that students have been learning all their lives, not merely since they entered school, and that most of the behavior they display is learned—feelings, attitudes, emotional states, attitudes, and beliefs. If the teacher thinks of learning as confined to the subject matter encompassed by the curriculum, he will be unable to understand the relationship between what the student has learned and is now learning and what the teacher wants him to learn.

The theory must provide the basis for our understanding of the significant conditions, forces, or factors that stimulate, inhibit, or affect human learning in any way.

A concept of learning that is narrowly specific, whether it be learning related to a laboratory experiment or learning related to the mastery of a unit of subject matter, can too easily serve as a basis for excluding or ignoring learning phenomena relevant to the objectives the teacher is trying to achieve. For example, the teacher who is trying to transmit an understanding of chemistry or physics should be aware of the existence of attitudes or beliefs that would interfere with the students' gaining an adequate comprehension of the subject he is teaching. He should recognize that such attitudes and beliefs were *learned* by the students and that part of his task is to help the students unlearn them, or rather to learn new and more compatible attitudes. He should also be aware of student attitudes that might aid learning in scientific fields. In addition, he should recognize that students learn a great deal more than what is consciously and deliberately taught them. It does little good for a teacher to extoll the virtues of the open, scientific mind and then behave in ways that are rigid, narrow, intolerant, and even arrogant, when it comes to suggestions and ideas contributed by students. What students may learn under such conditions is that the so-called scientific approach is a façade and that science teachers are insincere and cannot be trusted.

The theory must enable us to make reasonably good predictions about the outcomes of learning activity.

If a theory is any good, it should help us to set up test situations that will enable us to judge its validity. Reward-and-punishment theory, which is a layman's version of conditioning-reinforcement theory, tells us that rewarding or punishing children will result in learning. Actual experience shows that rewards and punishments work at some times, but not at others. Evidently the theory does not tell us enough about learning to enable us to use it in making very good predictions. A better theory of learning, however, would enable us to make predictions about learning that would be better than the almost chance results we get with reward and punishment. Another implication of this principle is the need to develop ways of evaluating learning that will enable us to determine whether or not we are succeeding. One of the reasons why reward-and-punishment concepts dominate most teaching today is that our methods of evaluation conceal our failures from us, leaving us confident that we are doing all the right things and that the blame for failure lies at the doorstep of the student, who is inept or lazy or both.

The difficulty with learning theories that have grown out of laboratory research is that they provide teachers with little if any basis for making predictions about learning, at least not the kind of learning most teachers are interested in. Principles of operant learning tell us, for example, that behavior can be shaped by reinforcing appropriate responses and not reinforcing inappropriate ones, but what teachers want to know are answers to questions like these: "What will happen if I use discussion methods in teaching my American history classes, instead of the combination of lecture, textbook, and workbook I have used for the past three years?" Oh, "What will happen if we change textbooks in French this year?" Nor is classical conditioning of much help here either.

The importance of theory as a basis for prediction is much more important than we are ordinarily aware. As Donald Snygg (1963) has pointed out, we need some kind of a theoretical guide for making choices about what to do in an educational situation. "Without theory," he says, "the effect of the slightest difference in two situations is unpredictable."

The theory must be a potential source of hypotheses that can be tested in the classroom, as well as in the laboratory, in order that our understanding of the teaching-learning process may continue to develop and grow.

We have now come to the criterion that interests most teachers. If a learning theory has any value for education, it should be productive of methods and concepts that will enable teaching to be done more effectively. As far as most educators are concerned, this is where learning theory has fallen down: it provides no clues for the improvement of instruction. In defense of learning theory and learning theorists, let it be said that neither has reward-and-punishment theory, the teacher's standby since the beginning of time, been of much help. Indeed, it has led to a preoccupation with the search for more ingenious rewards and punishments, rather than to a critical examination of those conditions in the classroom, at home, and in the community which stimulate or inhibit the learning we are trying to inspire.

WHERE TO LOOK

What is needed, then, is something other than a reworking of laboratory-oriented learning theory or reward-and-punishment formulations of learning. The question is: "Where should we begin?" It might appear that there is a certain temporal sequence to the four criteria we have listed: first we examine all the behavioral phenomena that might be identified as learning, second, we study the conditions that might affect these phenomena, and so forth.

In actuality, however, a truly functional theory of learning, when it does emerge, will be developed more or less simultaneously at all the levels suggested by the criteria. The proper development of such a theory will require that classroom teachers and psychologists maintain close communication and pool their skills and resources.

Classroom methods and approaches that appear to stimulate the kind of learning we are trying to accomplish will provide clues and hypotheses that can be tested further in a broad range of classroom and laboratory situations and will thus provide data suggestive of the nature of learning. These findings will suggest other methodological approaches that can be tested to provide more data. It is only through such communication, feedback, and counterfeedback that a sufficient number of revolutionary ideas can be generated to serve as a sound basis for developing the new theory and at the same time to test the implications of the theory for classroom practice.

The question now arises as to whether any present learning theory fits any of the criteria listed above. If such theories are available, perhaps we are further along than we had supposed in our search for some concept that will provide the means to satisfy our curiosity about the nature of learning and also provide the means whereby teaching may be made more effective.

FIELD THEORIES

There are, in fact, a number of theories more or less loosely affiliated to Gestalt theory, field theory, and self-concept theory, which we dismissed earlier with the statement that they had stimulated relatively little research. It may be well at this point to examine a couple of theories from this group, in order to see whether they could be developed into the kind of theory that would meet the specifications outlined above.

The best known of the field theories is the one proposed by Snygg and Combs (1949,1959), a theory that conceives of learning as a process of differentiation in perception. The individual who is faced with a task is conceived of as surveying or exploring the field available to him and differentiating those aspects of the field that provide clues as to what he should do. The way the learner goes about differentiating between relevant and irrelevant aspects of the field is, of course, determined partly by the kinds of differentiations he has learned to make in previous learning situations, as well as by the way in which he perceives his present situation, including himself. This is obviously an oversimplified statement of the theory proposed by Snygg and Combs, but space does not permit its elaboration here.

Another theory in this group is one suggested by Beatty and Clark (1963), who have developed a "self-concept" theory of learning. Their thinking has been influenced by the work of Carl Rogers (1951) and Prescott Lecky (1945), as well as by Snygg and Combs (1949). According to Beatty and Clark, learning is "the changing of relations between a self and its perceived-world as the self is expressed in striving to become adequate." Two dimensions of behavior that fit into this definition are called "intrinsic" and "instrumental." Intrinsic learning is related to the "why" of behavior—its purpose and direction, instrumental learning is related to the "how" of behavior—its content and procedure.

"Both intrinsic and instrumental learning are going on continuously in the school. As the student finds ways of becoming more adequate, he adds new instrumental learnings. As he changes his picture of his self or his conception of what an adequate person is like, there are intrinsic learnings."

When these theories are examined in the light of the first of the criteria suggested above, they appear to explain a great deal more of what we recognize as learning than do theories of the conditioning-reinforcement type. The latter appear to be formulations of very specific types of behavior, particularly behavior that has some physiological or kinesthetic component, as is indicated by the nature of the research that they have produced. Field theory and self-concept appear to embrace a much larger range of learning, particularly the learning involved in problem solving.

As these theories are presently formulated, however, they are used principally to explain "positive" learning—learning that is for the most part concerned with such dimensions of behavior as personal growth, increase in effectiveness, self-actualization, and the like. Although Snygg and Combs (1949) and, more recently, Combs and Snygg (1959), give some attention to neuroses and anxiety, they tend to regard these forms of behavior as reactions to threat and do not show how they are involved or are related to learning. Man's basic need, as they state in their 1959 edition, is "a need for adequacy," and learning is evidently the process whereby man becomes adequate. However, man also learns to become inadequate.

Although Beatty and Clark have not elaborated their theory to the extent that Snygg and Combs have, what they have said makes it clear that they too think of learning primarily in the positive sense.

Learning, conceived positively, is of course the main concern of teachers, parents, community leaders, and anyone else who is concerned with teaching and learning, although there might be some differences of opinion as to what positive learning is or should be. Some teachers may think of it as learning to be obedient; others would deplore a stress on obedience because it might interfere with the kind of positive learning *they* want to encourage: creativity. Indeed, this lack of consensus on what kind of learning we should try to encourage argues for an even broader and all-encompassing definition of learning, a definition that would include social learning—norms, attitudes, roles, and the like—as well as the various kinds of anxiety-oriented behavior: guilt, concern, cautiousness, behavior mechanisms, and anxiety itself. Since these forms of behavior are the results of attempts on the part of the human organism to adapt its behavior to the environment, they must be considered as forms of learning. Actually, of course, such learning is theoretically within the scope of both of the concepts we have presented. The point is that the proponents of the theories have not made this clear.

In recent years, there has been a steadily increasing number of publications, written from the field theory or self-concept theory point of view, that have explored various aspects of the conditions affecting learning. Some of these publications have been in the nature of discussions of theory and practice, like the writings of Snygg and Combs referred to previously. Some have been texts in educational psychology, whose presentations have been based, at least in part, on theories of this type, books by Mouly (1960) and Lindgren (1967) being examples. Although the theories seem promising as potential sources of information regarding the conditions affecting learning, there is obviously need for a great deal more theoretical and speculative writing here, particularly in the area of social learning and anxiety-oriented learning. This need has been met to some extent by Carl Rogers, whose books on psychotherapy (1951) and self-understanding (1961) contain some provocative and revolutionary ideas on both formal and informal learning.

A great deal of research must be done with hypotheses stemming from the learning theories in this group before we can appraise their ability to predict outcomes of learning. It may be that, like the Gestalt theories, they are better at explaining learning after the fact than predicting it. Our ability to undertake such research will of course depend on whether the theories can meet the fourth criterion: the ability to produce the kinds of hypotheses that can be tested in the laboratory and the classroom. Donald Snygg is optimistic with respect to this last criterion. He ended his 1963 presidential address to the

Division of Educational Psychology of the American Psychological Association with these words:

"In spite of the fact that I have been working with this conceptual framework for some time, the number of new hypotheses and concepts about education and teaching that it is capable of generating still astonishes me."

The research studies conducted for the purpose of testing propositions growing out of these theories have been far fewer than those deriving from conditioning-reinforcement theories, but they have not been lacking entirely. In fact, the amount of research whose findings are supportive of field theory or self-concept theory may be greater than is commonly supposed. Some of these studies, like that of B. Y. Kersh (1958) on independent discovery, have their locus in the classroom, while others, like those of Donald Snygg (1935a,1935b,1936) have their locus in the laboratory. What is obviously needed is a thorough-going review of research that is relevant to field and self-concept theories of learning. Such a review should also be suggestive of hypotheses that can be tested through further research in the classroom and the laboratory.

One further comment should be made with respect to these theories. As Donald Snygg pointed out in his Presidential Address (1963), concepts of learning based on field theories have a long way to go before they gain much acceptance on the part of teachers. Most teachers are relatively satisfied with theories of the reward-and-punishment type that can easily be used to rationalize educational methods currently in use. Self-concept and field theories of the type being proposed are quite rightfully perceived by teachers as threats to the status quo, because if such ideas eventually come to enjoy some measure of acceptance, they will bring about a revolution in educational methods. Few teachers are out shopping for a revolution. As a consequence, it may be difficult to get teachers to cooperate in the kind of classroom research that will be necessary to put theories to the test, and even when sufficient research findings have been accumulated to demonstrate the validity of this type of theory, the problem will still remain: how can the theory be incorporated into educational practice? Indeed, the task of getting teachers to modify their methods in ways that are consistent with research findings will in the end be infinitely greater than the problems to be encountered planning and conducting the research.

REFERENCES

Beatty, W. and R. Clark A Self Concept Theory of Learning, Unpublished Paper, 1960, cited in F. Wilhelms (ed.), *Teacher Education and Mental Health,* Report of the Teacher Education Project, San Francisco State College, 1963.

Combs, A. W. and D. Snygg. *Individual Behavior* (rev. ed.). New York: Harper, 1959.

Kersh, B. Y. "The Adequacy of 'Meaning' as an Explanation for the Superiority of Learning by Independent Discovery." *J. Educ. Psychology,* 1958, **49,** 282–292.

Lecky, P. *Self-consistency: A Theory of Personality.* New York: Island Press, 1945.

Lindgren, H. C., *Educational Psychology in the Classroom* (3rd ed.). New York: John Wiley and Sons, 1907.

Mouly, G. J. *Psychology for Effective Teaching* New York: Holt Dryden, 1900.

Rogers, C. R. *Client-centered Therapy.* Boston: Houghton Mifflin, 1951.

Rogers, C. R. *On Becoming a Person.* Boston: Houghton Mifflin, 1961.

Snygg, D. The Relative Difficulty of Mechanically Equivalent Tasks: I. Human Learning *J. Genet. Psychology,* 1935a, **47,** 299–320.

Snygg, D. The relative difficulty of mechanically equivalent tasks: II. Animal learning, *J. Genet. Psychol.,* 1935b, **47,** 321–326.

Snygg, D., "Another Look at Learning Theory." *Educational Psychologist,* Newsletter of Division 15, American Psychological Association, Vol. I, No. 1, October 1963.

Snygg, D. and A. W. Combs. *Individual Behavior.* New York: Harper, 1949.

Chapter 8

The Concept of Strens in Education: A Challenge to Curriculum Development

William G. Hollister

About the Author

Bill Hollister first started to search for pre-Wisconsin man in the Pleistocene beds of Nebraska, but soon dropped "the glorified ditch-digging called archaeology" to delve into more current "living problems." The social psychologist, James Reinhardt, fanned his smoldering interest in cultural anthropology into a burning interest in human motivation and group behavior.

The road to understanding led beyond an A.B. in Sociology to a B.S. in Psychology, then onward into medicine, psychiatric specialization and eventually to psychoanalytic training. The interruption of World War II provided a serendipitous sensitization to human needs and public health when Hollister was assigned to work with the Mississippi State Board of Health under Dr. Felix Underwood. In 1946, when Dr. Robert Felix was assembling his original staff for the now National Institute of Mental Health, he invited to Washington this young psychiatrist who had started a mental health education program for parents that had spread to several southern states. After additional preparation with a Masters in Public Health from John Hopkins and Specialty Boards in both Public Health and Psychiatry, Hollister spent seven years in the southeastern states as a mental health program development consultant for the National Institute of Mental Health.

The urgent need to create greater public leadership and understanding of mental health as well as the need to re-educate mental health clinicians in community mental health techniques sparked in William Hollister the creative surge that produced the "sociodrama workshop technique" and several types of "experiential" in-service training programs. These experiences aroused a keen interest in group processes, educational methodologies, and the preventive potential of school mental health programs that eventually led him back to Washington to become the first National Consultant on Mental Health in Education. For five years he ranged the country stimulating the development of classroom behavior management training for teachers, behavioral science training of school administrators, more effective health and pupil personnel services and special education for emotionally disturbed children.

Hollister has spent most of his career building bridges between psychiatry and public health, behavioral sciences, and education as well as "bridges of feelings" in human relationships. Five years ago he came alive with the potential of building a bridge between the emerging conceptualizations of ego-analysis of educators' need to create patterns of curriculum development and nurture and strengthen specific capacities of the mind. Although exciting tours of duty as chief of the Research Utilization Branch and the Community Services Branch of NIMH as well as his current professorship in Community Psychiatry at the University of North Carolina have intervened, he has joined with Dr. Bower and others to further the infusion of ego-psychology into school mental health with this book.

Introduction to the Chapter

Sometime ago at a PTA meeting that was unique in one respect— the fathers were all present—the principal speaker separated the men and women, gave them each a card, and asked them to write down as quickly as possible three (and only three) problems they were having with their children. The writing was completed almost before the speaker had finished giving the assignment.

Next, the speaker said, "Turn over your card and write down three things you get a kick out of or enjoy about your children." One half hour later some of the parents were still struggling with the question. Many complained that they did indeed enjoy their children but they just couldn't put it in words. Some even seemed stunned by the question or the allegation that somewhere in this experience there was something to enjoy.

Among the many metaphors with which we conceptualize the process of living, few, if any, cast the experience in a positive framework. Hollister, as any ex-public health officer would, searched for the antonym of trauma and has finally invented the term *stren* to connote the experiences in life which build and strengthen personality. Surprising, isn't it, that we have to invent a term for the positive growth experiences of man?

Read on and you'll find out what he does with it.

The Concept of Strens in Education:
A Challenge to Curriculum Development

The flow of productive work emerging from the field of ego-psychology is creating a reservoir of important ideas awaiting fuller testing, evaluation, and application in education. Education's mission of "developing the mind" stands to be especially enriched by the current studies of the steps in cognitive-affective development and of the developing ego processes by which an individual's mind gains mastery over self and environment. Two of the more intriguing components of this flow of ideas are the identification of "ego strengths" and attempts to measure them. Those of us who are interested in wider utilization of behavioral science concepts in teaching are asking, "How are these mental strengths developed? How can classroom methods contribute to building additional strength into the executive mediating capabilities of the mind?"

During the period dominated mainly by Freudian thought, much attention was focused on the discharge and vicissitudes of the sexual and aggressive impulses as well as on the pathologies, deviations, and defenses of the personality. Fortunately, increased interest in the mechanisms of defense by Anna Freud and others helped to usher in the current psychological era of ego-analysis and ego-psychology with its added interest in the autonomous self-actualizing forces of the mind. Hartmann (3), Kris, Lowenstein and a host of others have carried forward this growing interest in the adaptive mechanisms and the positive approaches to personality development, producing findings and hypotheses of potential value to education.

The literature that describes the executive mediating functions of the mind, collectively called the ego, now abounds with lists of ego-strengths and ego functions.[1] The basic assumptions underlying such listings is that the minds of individuals can become relatively inde-

[1] For an impressive list of ego-strengths see Chapter 1 of *"Personality in Nature, Society and Culture,* edited by Kluckhohn, Murray, and Schnieder. Alfred Knoff, 1953.

pendent, autonomous, self-directing entities, not passive pawns of external or primitive internal forces. Another basic assumption is that growth is possible and that there is a personality or a combination of affective and cognitive capacities that will be stronger or more competent for a given situation. Significantly these premises underlying the work of ego-psychology have long been and still are operational assumptions for the field of education.

THE EMERGENCE OF THE STRENS CONCEPT

Back in 1947, anthropologist Margaret Mead called to my attention a strange deficiency in the English language. She stated, "We have the word 'trauma' to designate an unfortunate blow that injures the personality, but as yet we have no word that describes an experience that is fortunate, that strengthens the personality. The closest we come to this is to say, 'It's a blessing.' Counting our blessings does not really meet our need for a collective noun directly opposite in meaning to 'trauma.' "

Appreciating how productive the words "trauma" and "traumatic" have been in enriching the language and study of psychopathology, I felt that an antonym might have a comparable effect on the field of positive mental health. A collective term to denote the experiences and interactions that produce personality strength might stimulate the search and conceptualization of such positive experiences. Later that night, inspired by Dr. Mead's observation and aided by a dictionary, I dared to hatch a new term. It has been nurtured ever since, refined and extended in workshop discussions, and fed with numerous examples. Because it has appeared to be stimulating and helpful to others, it has been introduced into the literature (6). The antonym is simply the word "stren," an abbreviated and anglicized portion of the German root word "strancan."

What is a stren? In general, it is an experience in an individual's life that builds strength into his personality, or more specifically, extends and strengthens cognitive-affective ego-functions. Discussion of this general definition soon reveals the need to differentiate strens from (1) all stimuli and (2) "everything good that happens" and to reserve the term for more or less discrete experiences that can be either objectively or subjectively identified as having contributed to psychological growth and the emergence of new capacities. With our current, limited ability to measure and thus prove growth along most psychological dimensions, it is probable that, for the present, most strens will be identified subjectively and in retrospect. Clinical studies occasionally refer to such important experiences.

Any theoretical exploration and development of this concept also soon brings the necessity to recognize that an "experience" is only one factor in the complex equation of forces affecting personality change. The presence of what was a growth potentiating experience for one person does not always lead to the strengthening of another person. What counts is the extent to which the experience is used and how it is used. Thus, it is not possible to compile a list of 100% effective strens, since the impact of any one given experience depends on such other factors as the stren being present at the right time and in the right dosage for an individual ready and capable of using the experience. Because of this, it seems wise to differentiate between the "stren event" and the "stren interaction," the latter being the process by which the experience is used by the individual for his psychological growth. Recognition that any stren experience is relative and only one factor in the interaction that produces psychological strength should in no way vitiate its importance as an essential factor in that growth process.

STRENS AND THE EGO-PROCESSES

The concept of strens, that there are defineable interventions or experiences that can and do build personality strengths, is of course not new; only the coining of a collective term is new. Why is such a neologism needed? Mainly because it may help to unite parallel streams of research and help to focus more attention on the specific nature of growth potentiating experiences. Such unification and focus would certainly provide an important behavioral science contribution to education.

From the analyst's search for "mutative interpretations" or "high point experiences" (Maslow) to the child development specialist's search for important "assimilations," "accommodations" (Piaget), or "decisive encounters" (Erikson) on through to the curriculum specialist's daily search to construct a meaningful "learning experience," many disciplines are groping to define these discrete strens. Unfortunately, these several professions recognize too little of the commonality of their mission and make too little use of each other's discoveries. In addition, as a review of the literature will reveal, the preponderance of these works focus on the unfolding maturation or concentrate on the product of the interaction and not enough on describing the specific environmental factors required. Piaget's (5) "ailments," Havighurst's

(4) and Erikson's "phase specific developmental tasks" as well as the work of Hartmann (3) and all those who list "ego strengths," reflect their fascination with defining the growth product. Relatively little effort has been devoted so far to breaking down the generalities of the term, "the environment," into the specifics of just what it is in the environment that needs to be provided and is used in this growth interaction. What is needed is a concerted interdisciplinary attempt to collect, to identify, and to classify stren experiences so we will come to be able to know which experiences can be potentiating to which kinds of personalities, at what stage, at what time and with what dosage. Let us hope coining of this collective term "strens" will help to give name and eventually definition to this common task and to stimulate more collaborative work in this area of "experiential pharmacology." In addition, let us hope that it will focus more attention on the challenge of building strength into growing personalities rather than continuing to devote our major behavioral science energies to the repair of the ravages of "traumas."

A STRATEGY FOR CLASSIFYING STRENS

In trying to work out a schema for classifying the stren experiences that enter into the stren interactions that produce increased psychological capability, several approaches seem feasible. We might try to identify and classify strens by the phase-specific or age-specific time of their usability. For instance, a search could be instituted for the strens related to each step of Freud's psychosexual phases, Erikson's or Havighurst's "developmental tasks," or each of the "key learnings" in a school curriculum. In trial, this approach has proved to be quite difficult.

Another approach might be to link a stren experience with a given strength and to classify them by the strength they produce. This approach immediately encounters the difficulties of proving a certain stren produced a given strength. It also runs headlong into the discovery that many strens might be nonspecific in the strengths they produce. Just as the proteins and fats in the egg you eat go to nurture and strengthen many different sets of muscles and organs, it is possible that some experiences are used to effect multiple kinds of growth.

After considerable discussion, the schema for classifying strens that appears to be most feasible has been derived from one of the basic contributions of Hartmann (3). Adapting the classification he uses in defining the basic "ego-processes," it is possible to classify strens, not by the time of application or the product, but by the ego-functions they catalyze. For instance, "What experiences contribute to growth of the ego-processes of assimilation, differentiation, and integration as defined by Hartmann?"

Use of a taxonomy based on process avoids some of the difficulties of the specificity-nonspecificity problem mentioned above, for example, the problems of linking only one factor with the product of a complex interaction, and the objection that what is ego-strength in one culture will not be so in another culture. Instead it ties the classification process to the synthetic organizing (and perhaps the defensive) ego-functioning psychological processes presumably present at all ages and in all cultures.

EDUCATIONAL ENHANCEMENT OF EGO-PROCESSES

Education has long sought to define the "learning experiences" in which the mental processes are strengthened. For years, the teaching of Latin and algebra were felt to have value in training and disciplining the mind. Educators have devised ways to stimulate deductive, inductive, and analytical thinking. The Russians are now embarked on a style of "moral education" (see Bronfenbrenner, Chapter 19) that nurtures evaluative thinking. Now it becomes possible for curriculum developers to ask, "What stren experiences and what stren interactions that can be fostered in the classroom would extend and elaborate the ego's assimilation process?", "What strens support and further the differentiation process?", and "What educational strens nurture and promote the ego process of integration?" Let us hope that answering these three questions will take us another step along the road away from teaching subjects in the vague belief that they somehow will train the mind toward specific goals or more specific educational interventions more precisely linked to developing mental capacities. In Chapter 6, Taba reflects her formulation of specific teaching strategies to effect greater cognitive capacities.

Assimilation

Obviously the task of identifying the experiences that catalyze the process of assimilation has been going on in education for a long time. It has been long recognized that the mediating, problem solving, impulse controlling, executive, and adaptive mental functions, collectively called the ego, are in part actualized and extended by the acquisition of knowledge and experience. We have learned that the capacities to perceive, assimilate, and retain input not only matures but can be positively augmented by rightly timed and paced stimulation. We have some evidence that the so-called primary ego-functions of perception, memory, intelligence, and motility are not only latent potentials that unfold but are functions that can be extended by appropriate experiences. Erikson's and Havighurst's developmental tasks represent key learnings of a cognitive, affective, and social nature that lead on to further growth and capacities. The task of identifying the environmental conditions and stimuli that enhance the learning process has already been a major focus of research in educational and experimental psychology. Much remains to be done to extend our knowledge about diagnosing and matching the maturing "schema" of Piaget with the appropriate stren experience. We need to do "ego-demiological" (positive counterpart of epidemiological) studies to delineate the role of differences in dosage, pacing, continuity, and other factors in effecting an interaction as well as variations in the impact of an educational stren on differing ages, sexes, psychological types, and cultural groups. Such studies might help us to balance our educational diet and to provide experiential nurturance more suited to the particular learner and his idiosyncratic learning style.

Differentiation

Although we have developed considerable knowledge about catalyzing the assimilation process, the enhancement of the differentiation processes of the ego is relatively new ground. Clinical experiences with the emotionally ill have taught us the importance of some critical differentiations in the psychological effectiveness of individuals. We have found that certain differentiations are prerequisite to freeing an individual from previous stages of development so that he can develop new capacities. For example, at a very primitive level, fostering a child's growing differentiation between self and mother, self and others, as well as between reality and phantasy, helps to free energies for the development of important affective and relationship capacities. Later on, the ability to discriminate feelings from thoughts, emotions from body sensations, and subjective from objective undergirds important affective and intellectual growth.

Just as the maturing human arm differentiates gross movements into finer discrete muscle actions, so the process of psychological differentiation extends the range and appropriateness of responses that are possible. Sensitive interpersonal relating and self-understanding eventually call for the capacities to discriminate between past feeling memories and current reactions to reality, between the possible and the probable, as well as between one's ideal self, social self and inner self. Correspondingly, intellectual growth entails such differentiations as ends and means, causes and effects, as well as discriminating the concrete from the symbolic and the semantic. Therefore, we are faced in education and the behavioral sciences with the task of cataloguing the key differentiations that are related to opening up new cognitive, affective, and social capacities. Then we must follow up by identifying and implementing the "learning experience" strens that have a potential for effecting these differentiations in a high percentage of students.

To give a concrete illustration of how new behavioral science understandings can be used to build and enrich a curriculum that fosters mental differentiations, the work of Dr. J. P. Guilford (1,2) in factoring out intellectual abilities merits attention. By study of the intellectual abilities of men, Guilford has conceptualized a model of some 120 potential intellectual functions, of which some sixty or so are already identified. A glance at this model quickly communicates the challenge to curriculum development specialists to develop learning opportunities that will help to differentiate and nurture the growth of many different capacities: capacities for cognitive, semantic, symbolic, and behavioral terms that can be used to conceive and manipulate units, classes, relationships, systems, changes, and predictions. Here at least there are clusters of capacities to ferret out and nurture with the appropriate stren experiences.

Our task as behavioral scientists and educators is to identify the key differentiations and to construct and test for experiences that will inculcate and strengthen them. In short, the most exciting days of curriculum development are ahead of us. Each of us can anticipate the day when educators and behavioral scientists will sit down to the long and important task of creating a curriculum that not only informs substantively but more precisely whets and sharpens specific differentiation abilities and thus extends the range of intellectual, affective, and social behaviors on the individual.

Integration

The identification and planned utilization of stren experiences that foster the ego-process of integration is also a relatively untouched field of curriculum development. Just as the differentiation of the finger muscles and the independent movement of the thumb permitted man to integrate the new function of grasping an object, so psychological differentiation sets the stage for the recombination of intellectual and affective capacities into new behaviors.

Psychological integration makes possible the synthesis of such constructs as a body image, a sense of self as well as appropriate linkages of thought, feeling, and action. It can also make man capable of thinking in terms of time sequences, successions, processes, and changes. By integration of his differentiated abilities into new combinations, he can create new coping mechanisms to solve his problems. Integration processes are also fundamental to creativity: to the creation of new relationships, new goals, and new values for which to love or die.

Here again we are faced with the challenge of nurturing and catalyzing an important ego-process. Sanford (7) has noted that we often encounter people who are broadly expanded, complex, and informed but who are not coping well with life. He comments, "One might say that such persons' expansion (assimilation and differentiation) has moved too far ahead of their integration." Obviously the nurturance of this ego capability deserves attention.

Much of our current research on creativity and the teaching of gifted children bears directly on promoting a part of the integration process. We have become more aware of both cultural and scholastic pressures that discourage children's spontaneous creativity. We have learned something about styles of teaching (Taba, Chapter 6) and codes of social interaction (Lippett, Chapter 13) that inhibit the development of new approaches. Currently we attempt to encourage ego-integration activities through such subjects as the arts, logic, and English composition. It is interesting to note how careful art instruction in the discrimination of colors, medias, and relationships often serves as the foundation of a student's leaping forward from imitation into original creation.

As Bower states in Chapter 1, one of the major underemphasized areas of education is behavior education, particularly the study of our own development and the range of behavior choices before us. Not only do we need to help students understand the range of behaviors and learn to discriminate the range of feelings, thoughts, and goals possible, but we also need to provide them opportunities to practice new styles of behaving and new roles in relation to others. Much of this proceeds naturally in play and in extracurriculum school activities, but more could be done on a planned learning basis. By use of the processes of imitation and identification, through role playing of basic roles, the student's repertoire of behaviors could be extended. Leadership, fellowship, and relationship building could be taught. By encouraging students to synthesize their own interpretations of the "doctor, lawyer, merchant, chief" they can attain more of that role flexibility than modern living demands. Incidentally, role flexibility has been established as one of the hallmarks of the mentally healthy individual.

Not only can we do more personality-development education to strengthen the integration of wider psycho-social skills and abilities, but we can also nurture much integrative process in the field of intellectual growth. More training in the inductive process of generalizing rules for behavior and the analysis of consequences of behavior would help youth to rediscover for itself the values behind the rules we have codified into law and morals. Perhaps by building such integrative and analytic skills, we could lay the foundation for the next generation's having a higher number of individuals capable of integrating and abiding by a less warlike code of human relations.

It is encouraging to note that the modern teaching of mathematics is moving away from the memorization and application of certain problem solving models toward inculcating the autonomous capacity to analyze the mathematical relationships and to synthesize the principle anew with each problem solving. Perhaps this fresh start in mathematics will not only extend student integrative functioning but also encourage English literature and composition to move beyond appropriate concern with models, form, and communicative process to the exploration of a rich opportunity that writing provides to integrate new meanings. Here again, the reciprocal enhancement relationship between the differentiation and integration processes is evident. Time devoted to discriminating shades of meaning and differentiating feelings and behaviors would set the stage for students' leaping forward beyond imitation into original creation. It will be a significant move in education when behavioral scientists and curriculum development specialists can collaborate to identify and field test the stren "learning experiences" that promote the growth of the integrative processes of the ego. Let us hope the product would be a more completely actualized informed and capable person.

SUMMARY

As the behavioral sciences have moved beyond intensive focus on repairing pathologies to increased interest in psychological development, there are emerging new knowledges about the potentiating forces and experiences; knowledge urgently needed by the educator to fulfill his mission and responsibility.

In a career spent on the borderland between behavioral science and education, I found both groups increasingly interested in the potentiating experience. Because of different languages and often poor communication, these two fields have not often benefitted by each other's interest and findings. As one of the steps toward unifying disparate streams of research and work with children, the suggestion has been made that specific strengthening and potentiating experiences be called "strens" so that both fields will have a positive antonym for trauma and a collective term to unify their common search for such positive key experiences.

A stren experience is only one factor in the interaction that potentiates a new strength, but it is an essential factor. A challenging task, with the possibility of great pragmatic value in curriculum development, lies ahead in collecting, identifying, classifying, field testing, and evaluating strens and matching them to varying receptivities and maturation stages and differing personality structures and learning styles. Let us hope that the emergence of strens with established relationships to strengthening the assimilation, differentiation, and integration functions of the ego would help us realize the vision of a curriculum that, as well as imparting the knowledge of our culture, truly potentiates the capacities of mind.

REFERENCES

1. Guilford, J. P. "Frontiers in Thinking That Teachers Should Know About." *The Reading Teacher*, Feb. 1960, 176–182.
2. Guilford, J. P. *Personality*. New York: McGraw Hill, 1959.
3. Hartmann, Heinz. *Ego Psychology and the Problem of Adaptation*. New York: International Universities Press, 1958.
4. Havighurst, Robert James. *Developmental Tasks and Education*. Chicago: University of Chicago Press, 1948.
5. Piaget, J. from *The Developmental Psychology of Jean Piaget* by John Flavell. Princeton, New Jersey: Van Nostrand, 1963.
6. Mental Health Monograph No. 5. "The Protection and Promotion of Mental Health in Schools." Washington, D.C.: U.S. Dept. of Health, Education and Welfare, Public Health Service.
7. Sanford, Nevitt (ed.). *The American College*. New York: John Wiley and Sons, 1962.

Chapter 9

Psychosocial Learning

William C. Rhodes

About the Author

My professional life began after several years as an army officer. When I started college in 1947 my goal was a Ph.D. in Psychology.

After obtaining my A.B. and my M.A. at Emory University in 1948, I began working as a Georgia Public Health employee and became quite committed to the idea of social service.

Through a fellowship from the Public Health program I was able to obtain a Ph.D. in Clinical Psychology from Ohio State. Beginning in the spring of 1953, I had responsibility for directing the building of a State mental health program within the framework of the Public Health Department. This was a turbulent experience for me in which I had to orient myself to the program realities of power structures, administrative routines, jurisdictional practices and the inevitable inadequacy of social structures in solving human problems.

In the fall of 1956, I moved to Peabody College in Nashville where I directed the Peabody Child Study Center and was a member of the Psychology Department faculty. In 1961 I became Co-principal Investigator and Coordinator of the Project ReED at Peabody and a professor in the Psychology Department.

During a summer quarter leave from Peabody in 1960, I worked with the National Institute of Mental Health. My interest in social process and social change was strongly reinforced by this experience. In 1964, I joined the staff of NIMH in the Child Mental Health Section to pursue both my interests in children and in social process.

Introduction to the Chapter

Our next three contributors are concerned with learning in relation to the society in which the school functions (Rhodes); the school as an organization of administrators, teachers, and children (McNeil);

and finally, the classroom, the microsociety of the child in the school (Thelen).

Rhodes examines changes in our thinking about economic institutions, economic upheavals, and depressions, suggesting not too timidly that we might now be ready to look at upheavals and depressions in institutions having to do with personal-social development of people. Need we continue our laissez-faire policy about human development when human maldevelopment poses such a critical problem to society? Should personal-social development be a matter of incidental learnings through unregulated social processes and unguided social intercourse? What is our public policy on these matters and how did we come by it?

Do programs such as Project Head Start and other preschool attempts to enhance the health and development of children who lack adequate environmental experiences represent meaningful and significant changes in our public attitude toward education? Do we really want to face the problem posed by the chinks in our armadillo-like society, asks Rhodes?

If we do, he suggests needed revisions in the organizational rules and goals of some of our institutions and in the application of our human sciences to the problem of human development. Why is education almost always conceptualized as happening within a building containing separated classrooms? How about an Educational Park or Educational Community?

Rhodes suggests that such organizational arrangements for learning would be more effective in enlisting behavioral scientists and their knowledge as allies and workers in the system and not as so often happens as interested spectators. However arranged, society must find ways of providing children with personal satisfaction in exchange for socially contributive behavior. Both Rhodes and Thelen point out specific *quid pro quo* growth possibilities in which society fails the child or, to put it another way, fails to hold down its end of the learning log.

Citing some of Sylvia Ashton-Warner's reflections on her experiences in educating Maori children, Rhodes wonders how learning can be effective in the compartmentalized, sterile, and noninvolved way it is served up to children. His challenges are bold and inventive. Can we make the most of them?

Psychosocial Learning

Our society seems to be critically lacking in adequate facilitating and regulatory processes and machinery for the realization of human potential and for arresting human erosion. Human resources can easily be wasted or left uncultivated by social default in our current systems and practices.

In the realm of economic resources, modern, developed countries have moved rather far away from the laissez-faire principles of Jeramy Bentham and Adam Smith. What may have been applicable in eighteenth century economic affairs is no longer acceptable in twentieth century economic practices of our society. Economic knowledge has been translated into organizations, processes, and practices that assure economic growth and arrest economic disorder in the nation for the ultimate good of its people.

The deliberate and systematic regulation of economic resources has brought about a more orderly economy than existed under the unregulated principle of enlightened self-interest. There are fewer economic upheavals and disorders, and a more controlled development of the economy.

In the area of human resources, however, our nation is still, to a large extent, operating under the same type of laissez-faire principle as that prescribed for economic affairs by Adam Smith. Consequently, there appears to be greater disorder and more periodic upheaval in human affairs than in economic affairs. As one looks at the current social scene it might be described as a situation of human disarray.

Human resources surveys like the Midtown Manhattan Studies [1962] seem to claim that disorder in human mental health affairs is almost the standard state for individuals in the modern urban society. Juvenile delinquency seems to be out of the control of the social order. Human deviation of all kinds is either mounting, as evidenced by our proliferation of deviation-control programs, or the Nation's fear of such deviations is increasing in such proportions that we are in a constant state of emergency and alarm over one type

210

of behavior or another. For instance, either the categories of exceptional children are increasing very rapidly, or our programs and concepts of exceptionality have themselves gotten out of hand and escalated to a point where we have abandoned all baselines of normality.

Whatever the reason for this apparent acceleration of human problems, we can say that disarray is much greater in human affairs than in economic affairs. There is a more carefully designed and calculated development of our economic resources than of our human resources.

It might be wise, therefore, to re-examine our current public assumptions about the conditions under which human development can best occur and under which human resources are more likely to thrive and flourish. Perhaps we should follow the path taken by the society in the economic sphere and critically examine our present laissez-faire philosophy in the human sphere. This examination might result in a movement away from laissez-faire principles toward systematic design of conditions, circumstances, and machinery to nurture greater psychosocial competence in increased numbers of our society. It might involve the creation of new adaptation facilitators through which greater social-personal development is most likely to flourish.

By national consensus we are very wary of organizing and regulating the social-personal learning of individuals in our society. Social-personal learning is assumed to be the responsibility of the family, supplemented only by the unregulated social processes and unguided social intercourse. We seem to assume that social-personal learning should remain incidental learning and that the least deliberate attention given to it the better for the social good. We have delegated this very crucial and scientifically complex task to families and to social chance, even under those conditions where evidence clearly points to the cultural context of family and environment as a destructive instrument for the social-personal learning of the young, such as in the multiproblem family.

We have gained enough understanding of the conditions and circumstances under which human growth and development is likely to follow an orderly or a disorderly course to know that assuring the full and wholesome realization of an individual's capacities and his personal-social organization is no simple task. We know that certain organized environmental supports are necessary for the individual to flourish, and that the lack of these environmental supports can lead either to distortions or deficits in his personal and social growth.

And yet, this increased knowledge of human affairs, our stabilizing understandings of social and personal development, have not yet found organized avenues for their application. Certainly we cannot expect to develop ways of providing every parent with the full knowledge, resources, and circumstances necessary for the full social and personal education of their young for today's world.

The increasing complexity of the society and the rising standards of human performance required to maintain this complex society, now put increasing emphasis upon the educative process. It becomes more and more necessary that we move toward achieving the goals and potentials of an educative society.

PUBLIC POLICY

And yet, our social policy with respect to public education's formal responsibility for personal-social learning is, at. the best, very ambivalent. At the worst, it is deliberately contradictory. For instance, although we are very critical of education's failure in the case of the culturally deprived, disfranchised, or environmentally handicapped populations, we have furnished limited operating public funds to provide for the crucial educative years. Our human sciences are in agreement that the early preschool years are crucial learning years in which the foundation is built for the complex social and personal learning required in later years. And yet, we have not yet provided even the most vulnerable populations with public educative instruments for these years.

The extension of the educative institutions downward to the crêche or nursery care programs, day care programs, nursery schools and even kindergartens is essential if the learning process is to be built upon a sound foundation. However, we make only token efforts toward such provisions. If we expect an orderly educative process to counteract the disorderly experiences and the deficits in social learning, such as are apparent, for instance, in the environmentally handicapped child, systematic education must begin shortly after the child is born.

Furthermore, if society cannot provide jobs and other necessary social functions for the teen-age population and if it is necessary to extend the educative process beyond the teen years, then we will have to provide organized educative experiences for the youth who does not go on to college.

Our current national criticism of public education implies that it could make a difference in the lives of "disfranchised" population. It seems also to imply that society is willing for educative functions, other than subject-matter instruction, to be applied to these children for the purpose of social-personal learning. However, this is only an implication. It has never been made explicit by public policy.

We have not, as a nation, faced the dilemma that we have imposed on education by asking it to assume a function that we have never granted it or that we have covertly denied it.

A BROADENED ASSIGNMENT

The limitation of education to content-oriented instruction is much more by public design than by educational philosophy. The philosophical position of education has always assumed responsibility for total organismic development. This position was expressed by Pestalozzi [1827] when he said that all sides of our nature should be educated on common lines, and in equal measure.

Educational philosophy has also made explicit the importance of training for social competence. Pestalozzi [1827] said that the ultimate end of education was not perfection in school accomplishments, but fitness for life. Nunn [1920] said that school was not a place where certain knowledge was learned, but where the young were disciplined in certain forms of activity of great and permanent significance to the wide world. William James [1939] said that, in the last analysis, education consisted in organizing the resources and powers of conduct of a human being in a way that shall fit him to his social and physical world.

It seems, therefore, that education is not reluctant to develop individuals in equal measures, and on all sides. What is required is explicit public policy establishing social and personal education as a prerogative and responsibility of the educative enterprise.

If education's task should be broadened in this way, such a task would be quite dependent upon our accumulating body of knowledge in the human sciences. In the present state of such knowledge, it seems apparent that not only would the educative process have to contribute explicitly to the total socialization of the child, but also it would have to assess the forces for dissocialization acting upon any group of children and deliberately design counteracting educative forces. In addition, the educative process would also have to include provisions for effective remediation or restoration of that special part of the population which succumbs organismically to onslaughts from the environment or to disorders caused by environmental disruptions of a physical, economic, social, criminal, or psychological nature.

In order to encompass these added functions, the educative process would have to undergo revision (1) in its organizational forms and (2) in its human technology.

The organizational and the technological changes could be made operational through incorporation of current advances in the behavioral sciences, social sciences, and mental health sciences.

ORGANIZATIONAL MODIFICATIONS

A new synthesis between education and the human sciences might be accomplished within the operational pattern of "school." However, the synthesis could not take the present form of token operational grafts of these sciences upon the corporate body of school. It would require a true operational melding of education with these sciences.

The present peripheral inclusion of special applications of the human sciences, such as counseling programs, school psychology programs, school social work programs, and special education programs, as nonessential extras attached to the school structure is not enough. These programs would have to move from the role of supporters of the instructional task to becoming forms of education in their own right. They would have to become central units devoted to social-personal education, on a par with the present exclusive concentration upon classroom instruction.

Organizationally, this would require a systematic merger of (1) the philosophy, assumptions, and bodies of knowledge of education and human sciences, (2) the professionals of both, and (3) the operational practices and procedures of both.

The present organizational form of education has crystallized into the operational pattern of school and the operational unit of classroom. This organizational crystallization, based solely upon earlier concepts and methods of education, may account for part of the current inability of education to demonstrate how it might make new contributions and meet new social challenges.

School and classroom are not the most flexible of organizational forms. Structurally, schools are intended as a housing for instructional programs. It has been very difficult, therefore, to adapt them to broader influences upon the lives of individuals. The structural and organizational components of the modern school exert tremendous environmental control over teaching and learning behavior. This environmental control guides the teaching-learning transaction toward the channels of subject-matter instruction and away from social learning. As a consequence, life-chance learnings, other than instructional programs, are relegated to the status of somewhat superfluous appendages. The social learning function is never integrated into the daily curriculum as a major contributor to life preparation.

Modern organizational concepts teach us that design should follow function. When functions are modified or extended, the organizational and operational patterns must be redesigned to fit the new version of functions.

The modified or extended educative functions demanded by our society are: socializing the individual for mastery of modern metropolitan life; prevention of social disaffection or extreme social deviance; and renovation or remediation of children or youth whose behavior or living patterns are dissonant within the existing culture. Each of these delineated new social functions is by nature educative. Each would be quite appropriately served through the teaching-learning transaction. However, they would have to be captured in new organizational forms designed to carry out the specified functions.

A number of existing models might serve as the base of such organizational redesign. Two of these will be suggested here.

In one model, the social and personal learning functions specified above could be incorporated into the present organizational form of "school." This model, on the planning boards of several large cities, is called an educational park. The other model creates a new social institution, midway between family and school, with responsibility for the social and personal development of the child. This new social institution does not supplant the family or the school but creates a third developmental force to supplement and augment their functions. This model is the children's institutions in a modern Danish residential collective.

As the educational park model now stands, it does not specifically incorporate the social- and personal-learning functions of social training to enhance competence in coping with the refined social systems of the metropolitan complex; or to prevent disaffection and deviation from these social systems; or to accomplish resocialization in cases of significant personal-social disorders. However, these functions could be much more easily integrated into the educational park than the typical school.

The educational park, essentially, would be an educative complex as an alternative to the neighborhood school. It would be a campus-like complex, drawing students from several socio-economic neighborhoods and offering a range and variety of educational opportunities and services very much like that of a miniature university campus.

Within this single complex could be packaged the social learning functions of training for social competence, prevention of disaffection, and remediation of social-personal disorders. There could, then, be two large divisions within the educational complex. They would be organizational units of equal size, importance, and direct service in the individual programs of each child. The schedule of each child would reflect individual needs for amount of each type of learning. One division would be for instruction, the other for social learning. The director would have equal training in the human sciences and in education. His supervisory staff would consist of educational specialists in the division of instruction and behavioral science specialists in the division of social-personal education.

The social-personal learning division could be subdivided into functional units for training in social-personal competence; prevention of dissocialization; and resocialization or remediation of personal-social disorders. This division could incorporate the current programs of guidance and counseling, clinical services, special education, remedial education, and school social-work services. It could include additions, such as a behavioral training service modeled after current experiments in operant and other psychological learning procedures or a sensitivity training service modeled after the National Training Laboratories.

This redesign of the existing operational pattern requires only slight modifications in the educative apparatus. It demands a change in public policy, a consensus that social-personal education is a prerogative of the public schools, and a reorganization of existing components and emphases.

The second model is much more of a social innovation. It calls for forging and institutionalizing a third educative force in the lives of children and youth in our society. Its major task would be providing facilities and resources for social-personal learning. It would constitute a new social installation, linked to home and school, which would participate in organizing the resources and powers of conduct of the individual toward fitness for, and mastery of, the modern physical and social world.

An existing model can be found in the residential collective town of Carlsro, just outside Copenhagen, Denmark. This is a self-contained town designed both architecturally and social-psychologically for human living. This small planned community was built for 800 families and 2600 inhabitants. The town itself is a product of psychosocial engineering. The children's institutions are only one part of this planned community. These institutions serve children from birth through the age of twenty-one. They are staffed by specially trained educators and provide a practicum training facility for college students preparing for this educative profession. The institutions include a crèche for infants, a nursery school, a kindergarten, a "spare time home" for children of school age, a special teen program, and a youth program for the eighteen-to-twenty-one age group.

Each of these units has a program and an educative regime. Each provides for orderly and systematic social learnings appropriate to specific crucial developmental and chronological age groups. The institutions provide a basic educative philosophy, a group of methods and procedures, a group of specialists trained in the educative tradition, and specific organizational forms or operational patterns that make the delivery of the resources and forces of the environment an organized and orderly process leading to socially competent adulthood.

Having considered the ingredients of public issue, public policy, and organizational design, let us turn now to the educative process and its methods and procedures.

METHODS AND PROCEDURES

General

In the beginning of this century, Boutreaux [1913] said that the process of education was a strange one, ". . . to act on mind and conscience in such a way as to render them capable of thinking and judging of themselves, to determine initiative, arouse spontaneity, and fashion human beings into freedom." This is indeed a delicate and complex process, demanding ever increasing knowledge and precision in its accomplishment. It requires a sensitive balance between deliberate intrusion in the relationship between nature and nurture and careful restraint of intrusion into the internal timetable of the evolving organism.

The good teacher manages to achieve this balance. A good psychotherapist must necessarily achieve this balance. Although the teaching process and the psychotherapeutic process are final common pathways for two different human influence systems, they both lead to these same human ends.

It seems crucial, therefore, that in addition to an organizational merger of human sciences and education, there would have to be a process merger between the two before guided social-personal learning could become operational.

It is quite conceivable, for instance, that those general self-understanding processes of group psychotherapy; sensitivity-training and guided group discussions, could become a basic part of education for all youth. In a fragmented and unsystematic fashion, schools have already drifted toward the melding of psychological and educational processes to contend with the perplexing learning problems confronting them in one special group of "exceptional" children after another. It is quite possible that normal evolution might gradually modify education toward the combined educative-therapeutic resocialization patterns such as found in the "educateur" institutions in Montreal, Canada. However, this direction of development could be hastened by deliberately spelling out some of the characteristics of social-personal learning. Such a statement would have to blend principles of psychological learning with principles of education.

Characteristics of Contrived Experiences

Whatever other characteristics distinguish education, it is a process of contrived occasions for experience.

In discussing the Pestalozzian method, Herbart (1903) said,

"Its peculiar merit consists in having laid hold more zealously than any former method of the duty of building up the child's mind, of constructing in it a definite experience in the light of clear sense-perception, not acting as if the child had already an experience but taking care that he gets one."

There is actually no way to assure an experience for another person. The contribution which the teacher can make is to provide the occasion for an experience.

Out of the total array of possible unselected experiences in social competence that could occur by chance, for instance, the probability of the individual's undergoing a series of successive relevant experiences is quite remote. Therefore, it is the job of the educator to select out the relevant social experiences and contrive the occasions for their occurrence.

For instance, the individual can develop group skills only by experience in groups. For successful functioning in specific roles in particular kinds of groups, the individual must have experiences that at least approximate the role and the type of groups supporting the role. This type of learning could, conceivably, happen by chance, but it is much more likely to happen if the occasion for it is deliberately prepared. It is in this deliberate design of experience that education improves upon nature.

In many cases in our society, the neglect of social and personal education may not be crippling. Those individuals who are lucky enough to be born into the approved classes, into the norm-defining groups, are born into a total habitat that provides many opportunities for the range and continuity of experiences that produce varying degrees of social competence and social mastery. Individuals born into nonacceptable or socially-rejected groups, have little chance for successful social survival. Their chance of falling into one of the negative social statistics, such as the delinquent, criminal, addict, alcoholic, schizophrenic, or unemployable, is much greater than for the latter groups.

By not providing a social instrument through which all citizens have equal opportunities to learn social mastery, a decision has been made, by default, that some of our population will, in all probability, be relegated to socially deviant statistics.

A large proportion of our disadvantaged youth never have the occasion for the type of experiences that leads toward the particular patterns of conduct expected and sanctioned by our society. Many slum boys have never participated in competitive sports. They have seldom, if ever, eaten in a restaurant. They have never dressed up to attend a social function. They have not experienced the routine and "respectability" of a regular job. They have never experienced participation in approved and socially-acceptable clubs.

All of these important learnings occur "naturally" within the lives of middle-class youth. Frequently, they do not occur for the environmentally handicapped youth. The world of work and leisure time, as it is experienced by the middle class, is relatively strange and unknown to the culturally-determined delinquent, who in later life, has a good chance of being an alcoholic, a drug addict, or a state mental hospital patient.

To return now to the characteristics of contrived experiences, educators have long advocated the use of sensory avenues in the students as a means of guaranteeing an experience. It was part of the method of Pestalozzi. It was much more pivotal in the progression of educative methods handed from Itard to Seguin to Montessori. Sense-training was made very explicit as a keystone in the Seguin and Montessori methods.

Another characteristic of contrived experiences is the opportunity for the learner to be active, to vigorously interact with the environment, the situation, or the materials provided for an experience. He must act within the context, impress himself upon the environment so that it gives back a response to him, struggle with the manipulanda involved, and do something with the conditions and surroundings. Passive-receptive relationships with the educator may lead to learning in other realms and with other age groups, but personal-social learning in children demands activity that is directed toward a meaningful environmental experience.

Characteristics of Goals in Social Learning

In social learning, more than any other type of learning, there must be a careful analysis of the social competencies to be attained and the social deficits existing in the individual learner. The goals, in order to lead toward mastery of social circumstances, cannot be too narrow or limited; but they must be clearly conceptualized.

An example of clear goals in social-personal education is contained in Itard's (1962) specifications for the *Wild Boy of Aveyron*. All of his efforts and interactions in the educative endeavors with the wild boy were governed and systematized by these goals. He spelled out five educative aims for the boy: (1) "To interest him in social life by rendering it more pleasant to him than the one he was then leading and above all more like the life he had just left." (2) "To awaken his nervous sensibility by the most energetic stimulation, and sometimes by intense emotion." (3) "To extend the range of his ideas by giving him new needs and by increasing his social contacts." (4) "To lead him to the use of speech by inducing the exercise of imitation through the imperious law of necessity." (5) "To induce him to employ the simplest mental operations over a period of time upon the objects of his physical needs, afterwards inducing the applications of these mental processes to the objects of instruction."

Itard's slim volume which reports his efforts toward these ends is an excellent record of a planned socialization sequence and its successes and failures.

I used a similar procedure of goal-setting in the reeducation of an autistic child. The only difference was that the procedure allowed for successive stages of goal setting as the child progressed. For instance, the first major aim was "to invade the child's private world until he attended to and interacted with the prepared environment presented by the teacher." The second aim, established at the beginning, was "to involve him in a Montessori-type preschool program." Both of these aims were concerned with getting him ready for a regular nursery school program.

After attaining the first aims of invading his private world and engaging him in a Montessori program, it became evident that socialization for a nursery school regime required the development of spoken language. At this point in his program he was making primitive or infantile efforts to communicate verbally. A speech therapist was called upon to help us teach the child to speak. A special speech training program was inaugurated to try to develop his language to the minimum nursery-school level.

After accomplishing this objective, the next hurdle was the fact that nursery school programs were group programs. The child had learned to enter into a learning relationship with the teacher and with other adults; however, he had to learn this in the context of a peer group. Therefore, the next series of contrived experiences were developed toward this end.

Characteristics of the Context of Social Learning

In social learning, the context of the contrived experience is very important. The gradient of similarity and dissimilarity of the learning context to the real, live setting for socially relevant conduct is one of the determinants of ultimate performance. The context not only serves to cue learned behavior, but it also exerts control and organization upon that behavior.

In order to transfer learned expressions or socially relevant performance from the learning context to the natural context, it is necessary that there be a high degree of correspondence between the two.

This characteristic is important both in social learning theory and in practical applications of human learning. For instance, in vocational education or home arts education in institutions, the children are taught in the context replicating that in which ultimate social performance will be expected. Home arts is taught in a modern kitchen, in replicas of the laundry room in the average middle-class home, in bedrooms and living rooms that simulate natural home surroundings. The homemaking skills acquired in this home-simulated setting are more likely to be socially appropriate when transferred to a real home context outside the institution than they might be if the skills were taught in the quite dissimilar institutional context.

In the use of the context for learning purposes, we can anchor our education to two standards. On one side is the standard context that the individual has always known, but from which we wish to wean his behavior. The other standard is the socially relevant, or socially acceptable context toward which we wish to encourage his behavior.

The educator's concept of step-by-step learning, with each step built upon the last one, can be related to this learning context in two ways.

1. In the learning process, the functional context for the behavior can be standard to start with—a context very close to that in which

the individual is accustomed to performing—and then step-by-step it can be gently modified toward the more socially sanctioned context.

In the learning situation, the context that has been the scene for an individual's frustration, trauma, or disjunction with society should be changed enough so that the circumstances, conditions, and cues *appear* to be different, but are actually on a gradient of similarity to them.

An example of the first instance of step-by-step weaning through gradually changing the context of learning from the familiar but socially unacceptable, to the unfamiliar, but socially acceptable, is given in *Teacher*, by Sylvia Ashton-Warner. She talks about the necessity for bridging the gap between the New Zealand Maori culture and the European culture. She writes:

"This transition made by Maori children is often unsuccessful. At a tender age a wrench occurs from one culture to another, from which, either manifestly or subconsciously, not all recover. And I think that this circumstance has some little bearing on the number of Maori who, although well educated, seem neurotic, and on the number who retreat to the mat."

She believes that this transition should be conducted in stages. As a practical application, for instance, she refused to start her Maori children with the American *Dick and Jane* reading series. Instead, she developed transitional books or "pa" (Maori living quarters) books. In the transitional Maori readers, she attempted to capture life in the pa rather than the European context of life reflected in the American reader series. She says: "The Maori transitional books are used not as a substitute for the American books but as a lead up to them." She believes that transitional reading could help to forestall the situation which arises near the end of the average Maori's school years. At fourteen and fifteen, they are too old to go on to the New Zealand high school and too young and untrained to do a skilled job. They hold a grudge against European education and are ripe for delinquency. She says:

"A five, meeting words for the first time and finding that they have intense meaning for him, at once loves reading—When I have observed my Maori fives stalling on the opening of "Janet and John," I have seen in my mind simultaneously the lifetime of comic-book reading to follow and the delinquency beyond. However good a book is it can't supply the transitional needs unless it is in sympathy with the Maori children, has incidents which they understand and temperament which they sense. Only in the familiar atmosphere can reading be evolutionary—Since their purpose is to bridge a gap (a gap of two thousand years between the races) rather than to teach English, I use the pa vernacular as an overlap."

Not only does this kind of attention to the context of learning attempt to analyze and specify the conditions under which learning is most likely to occur, but it also suggests the necessity of an increased consideration for the integrity of the human organism. Sylvia Ashton-Warner is horrified at the violation of the personal-cultural integrations of the young Maori child by the insensitive imposition of the *Dick and June* series. She says that an individual cannot be wrenched, harshly and suddenly, from a cathected context without a lasting personal-social disruption.

The second type of moderation of the context to fit the needs of both the learner and the society also requires step-by-step presentation. However, in this case we take an individual who has learned within a particular context, but the context itself has become a cue to pain, anger, avoidance, and aversion. In this case, it is necessary to reduce the appearance of similarity between the learning context and the standard social context until the learner can tolerate it, and only gradually approach the standard.

We can take reading as an example again. I developed a procedure for teaching remedial reading to children with severe learning disabilities. This procedure, later developed and extended by Peter Hainsworth and Marjorie Snyder into two dissertation studies, was based upon the early work of Mary Cover Jones (1924) in overcoming fear.

In this particular reading procedure, the context of reading was analyzed into component parts: the visual symbol dimension, the auditory dimension, and the stimulus complex of teacher and classroom. An attempt was made to manipulate these components along their separate dimensions, so they would not arouse the aversive response to reading.

To begin with the children were placed in a room that had none of the trappings or arrangement of a classroom. They were presented with visual configurations quite unlike the letter and word symbols which they knew, and yet these visual shapes could be coded just as letters and words are coded. The auditory stimuli were simple sounds and sound patterns for which the children had to guess the meaning.

Gradually, over a period of a few weeks, all of these contexts of reading were altered in the direction of the avoided contexts. The room began to be changed in the direction of a class, with desks in a row, teacher behind a desk, and a blackboard. The symbols gradually moved toward letter symbols, and the sounds moved in the direction of phonics.

In the dissertations by Peter Hainsworth (1962) and Marjorie Snyder (1962), the children with the greatest reading disorders showed greater improvement by this technique than through the traditional remedial teaching technique.

This designed reconciliation of the child and the context gradually altered the negative value of the reading complex toward a more positive or satisfying experience. It gently coaxed the child toward the context that he had formerly shied away from.

As in the case of Sylvia Ashton-Warner's Maori children, there was an attempt to modify the context to provide the bridge or transition into the crucial socially-relevant context in which the child is required to live out his life.

Characteristics of Consequences

The consequences of an individual's performance or conduct appear to be a powerful determinant of the learning of socially relevant behavior. An analysis of the connection between a social performance and its consequence has indicated in many recent psychological studies that reasonable attention to the consequences of an individual's behavior has a significant effect upon its eventual form and stability.

Within limits, socially relevant and personally fulfilling behavior can be developed and maintained when the environment reciprocates with an enhancement of the individual's own personal and tropic urges, needs, and directions. A positive reinforcement from the environment (one which fulfills the individual's desires), in reciprocity with his acts, can shape these acts towards patterns of conduct which are socially relevant and socially desirable. Such *quid-pro-quo* from the environment can obtain behavioral cooperation from the individual.

It seems that as long as the environment continues to provide the individual such personal satisfactions, he will cooperate by reciprocating with behaviors that are considered socially desirable.

The educative task, therefore, is to manipulate the environment during the learning phase so that it provides satisfactions to the individual in return for modifications of his behavior toward social ends. However, unless environmental control in the learning situation bears some similarity to comparable satisfactions attainable in the natural environment of the social world, such learned behavior will probably not be maintained.

This may explain some of the educative failures with many Negro learners prior to our current social and cultural revision. Even though the social learning phase may have succeeded in helping the individual develop socially relevant behavior, these behaviors were not maintained in subsequent exchanges with society. Society did not live up to its end of the bargain by providing continuing personal satisfaction in exchange for socially contributive behavior once the learning phase had ended.

In order to maintain reciprocity between individuals and collective systems, a fair exchange must exist between them. Unless this occurs, the contract is likely to be broken.

It remains to be seen whether society lives up to its part of the contract with submerged populations of the future. If it does, relearning or resocialization attempts will have greater success in maintaining standards of conduct which society deems appropriate.

Society is frequently more unreasonable than individual human beings. It often demands certain behaviors on its own terms, without at the same time demonstrating its own good faith by providing a reasonable standard of exchange.

In the learning phase of social-personal development, one cardinal factor that must be taken into consideration is the probable consequence of any given act. Not only must the connection between acts and consequences be very clear and plain to the learner, but he must have immediate feedback from the environment. The closer in time the return from the environment, the more influential the consequences. Immediate feedback stamps in the connection. If the return message from the environment is immediately favorable and positive, the learner is much more likely to repeat the behavior that elicited the immediate positive response.

Sometimes, however, these immediate connections can stand in the way of the student's learning that immediately satisfying behaviors can have long-term punishing consequences. One of the explanations given by the behavioral scientist for the persistence of delinquent behavior even in the face of punishment is that short-term rewarding consequences maintain the behavior, even though it is punished in the long run. The connection which has relevance for the delinquent is that which takes place between the immediate gains and the behavior.

In such cases, under a regime of relearning, the context has to be structured in such a way that the sequence of consequences is telescoped to bring the punishment into juxtaposition with the behavior. Conceptual representations do not seem to be sufficient. It seems necessary for the learner to have an actual experience of the consequences in order for behavioral modification to occur.

The best conditions for learning exist when the learner becomes aware that his past patterns of response, reaction, or ways of expressing himself are inadequate to achieve the consequences he desires. Therefore, new learnings are accelerated by making available to him a clear conception of the consequences he is seeking.

In the teacher-learner transaction, these consequences can be sorted out, and contexts can then be established to provide direct experience of the connection between the behavior and consequences.

A very simple prototype of this sequence is given in an article in the September–October, 1964 issue of *Transaction,* reporting on the work of Ayllon and associates in changing behavior on a psychiatric ward. Two women in a hospital had refused to eat unless fed by nurses. One had to be taken to the dining room forcefully. Both, however, were proud of their neat and clean clothing. The consultant psychologist, then, had determined that the women wanted to be fed by someone else and also wanted to be neat and clean.

The nurse was instructed to allow a little food to spill during feeding. Within this context a direct experience created conflict between two consequences connected with a particular behavioral pattern.

By letting some of the food spill, the nurse made clear to the patients that it was difficult to feed someone else without spilling food and that the only certain way of keeping clean was for each to feed herself. In time, with some setbacks, both women learned to feed themselves.

Characteristics of the Emotional Content

The emotional content of social-personal learning must resonate to the child's internal dynamics. Social-personal learning cannot be anchored solely in the culture or in the environing context. It should reach inside the child, find what is there, and build upon it.

Sylvia Ashton-Warner used this approach even in teaching basic school skills. In describing her method of teaching writing, she says:

"Back to these first words. To these first books. They must be made out of the stuff of the child itself. I reach a hand into the mind of the child, bring out a handful of the stuff I find there, and use that as our first working material. Whether it is good, or bad stuff, violent or placid stuff, coloured or dun."

What is learned, in order to be learned and become an organic part of the person, must have intense meaning to the child. The teacher can reject nothing of what is inside the child. In working with the child, the teacher must free himself or herself of the culture, must try to gain distance from his or her own internal dynamics, biases, prejudices, and attitudes and must use the child's own dynamics as a bridge between the child and society.

We need to work delicately and sensitively. The use of contexts, the use of consequences, the contriving of occasions for experiences must be accomplished with a sensitive hand. The final ingredient that makes all else meaningful for the child is the content of his own inner dynamics. Without this substance, the learning is only a thin reflection, only a faint portrait of reality.

It is difficult to imagine how learning, divorced from the seething, intense, personal, internal life of the individual, can ever add to what he is, can ever give depth and breadth and wholeness to what he is. The imposition of the content of culture upon the child, without relating the culture to his inner substance, is forcing a foreign body into his being. He will only mobilize defenses against the culture in an attempt to neutralize its harsh, abrasive denials of what he is.

Again, we will use Sylvia Ashton-Warner's example. In talking about the transitional books developed with the Maori children as their first readers, she says:

"It was the temperament of the pa that had to be got into these books. The instinctive living, the drama, the communal living and the violence. Life in the pa is often a sequence of tears, tenderness, brawls, love and song."

She saw a vast contrast between this life and the lifeless books imported from the United States to teach reading.

If we can translate this into the context of slums in the United States, we find the same great gulf between the teeming life of the slums and the aseptic content of the slum schools. The slum schools are models of middle-class aspirations, controls, renunciations, and denials. They attempt to elevate learning above the irrational, violent, intense, and chaotic internal life of the students. Such a divorce from the internal dynamics of the learner makes the culture presented to him a meaningless foreign language that can never be learned without giving up completely the content of the self, and the already-learned excitement of slum life.

In the middle class, where children have learned from infancy to accommodate themselves to the symbolic level of culture and still maintain their own internal personal life, attending school and learning is partly the price we pay for other gratifications and satisfactions. Furthermore, the difference between the school atmosphere and their everyday public life is not so great as it is in the slum sections.

However, with the present inflow of middle-class children and youth into state hospitals, special classes for the emotionally disturbed, clinics, and offices of private psychiatrists, perhaps we might conjecture that even for middle-class children, the price may be too great.

It could be argued that the school or some other institution has to find a more satisfactory and effective mediator role between the internal dynamics of the individual and the external dynamics of the society. What seems to be in question is the right relationship between the internal dynamics of persons and the external characteristics of social systems.

REFERENCES

Ashton-Warner, Sylvia. *Teacher*. New York: Bantam Books, 1964.

Boutreaux, E. *Education and Ethics*. English Translation by F. Rothwell. London: Williams and Morgate, 1913.

Hainsworth, P. K. *Shaping Approach Responses to Reading by Desensitization*. Peabody Contributions to Education, No. 605, Thesis. Nashville: George Peabody College, 1962.

Herbart, J. F. *ABC of Sense Perception and Minor Pedagogical Works*. Translated by W. J. Eckoff. New York: D. Appleton and Co., 1903.

Itard, Jean-March-Gaspard. *The Wild Boy of Aveyron*. Translated by George S. Muriel Humphrey with an Introduction by George Humphrey. Copyright © 1962 by Meredith Publishing Company.

James, William. *Talks to Teachers on Psychology*. New York: Holt, Rhinehart, and Winston, 1939.

Jones, M. C. "A Laboratory Study of Fear. The Case of Peter." *Pedagogical Seminary J. Genetic Psychology*, 31, 1924, 308–315.

Montessori, Maria. *Doctor Montessori's Own Handbook*. New York: Schocken Books, Inc., 1965.

Nunn, J. P. *Education: Its Data and First Principles*. London: Edw. Arnold and Co., 1920.

Pestalozzi, J. H. *Letters on Early Education*. Addressed to J. P. Greaves, Esq. London: Sherwood, Gilbert and Piper, 1827.

Sequin, E. *Idiocy and its Treatment*. New York: Columbia University, Teachers College Foundational Reprint, 1907.

Snyder, Marjorie Sims. *An Experiment in the Effectiveness of Desensitization in the Teaching of Remedial Reading.* Peabody Contributions to Education: Second Series, No. 199, Thesis. Nashville: George Peabody College, 1962.

Srole, L., T. E. Langner, S. T. Michael, M. K. Opler, and T. A. C. Rennie. *Mental Health in the Metropolis. The Midtown Manhattan Study. Vol. I.* New York: McGraw-Hill, 1962.

Staff Report. "Changing Behavior in the Psychiatric Ward." *Transaction,* **VI,** Issue 6, 1964, 18–20.

Chapter 10

Analysis of An Ailing Monster: School Organization

Elton B. McNeil

About the Author

I know what took place but I'm not sure how it happened. After a bachelor's degree from Harvard and a Ph.D. in clinical psychology from The University of Michigan, I had accumulated all the trappings and hallmarks of the traditional clinical psychologist interested only in getting rich via the private practice of psychotherapy. I agreed to stay at The University of Michigan for one year to conclude a research project; that was fifteen years ago, and now I can't even remember where I was going to go.

I looked and acted like a model, traditional clinical psychologist until, by sheer accident, I worked one summer in an interdisciplinary training center serving a population of emotionally disturbed and delinquent boys. Working with teachers, social workers, and psychiatric nurses in a group setting and living twenty-four hours a day with disturbed children forced me to abandon my identification with one-to-one psychotherapy as a way of life. That was twelve years ago, and now I direct the training center that changed me from a repairer of illness to a preventer.

The rest of this tale is predictable. The next thing I knew I had an honorary appointment in education as well as psychology, was deeply immersed in research with my new educator colleagues, and seemed to be spending the bulk of my professional life organizing action programs for mental health in the schools. I got so carried away that I was elected president of the Michigan Society of School Psychologists, even though I had never held such a job. I now have dedicated myself to luring as many clinical psychologists as possible away from their traditional clinical image and into the schools where the children are and where the real mental health action is. Since the last fifteen years of professional work happened as a pleasing accident, I am in no position to predict the character of the next fifteen years.

Introduction to the Chapter

McNeil traces his "ailing monster"—school organization—from the first school, that is, home, to the one-teacher-per-grade arrangement first tried out in Boston about 1848—118 years ago. Despite a few ungraded, nongraded or experimental approaches here and there, this is still the pattern for the United States in 1966. It is indeed startling to consider how many of our twentieth century organizational patterns were nineteenth century innovations. When pushed to the wall, educators would be hard pressed to name a single, meaningful crucial systemwide change in educational organization in the last 25 years. McNeil is forced to conclude that although we believe in continuous and steady progress in sciences, government, and technology, progress in education may be our grand illusion.

What children do in school they do because that's the way things are done in school. Rarely do we find persons who are well-educated, that is, persons who have successfully undergone the rigors, rituals, and ratiocinations of educational content and process and who can describe the way it happened. The school is potentially a first-rate humanizing institution, but it often overlooks the fact that children speed through the processes of education without any attention to their journey or how they came to the land of knowledge. One thinks of the lady who was telling her friend of the wonderful vacation they had on the island of Majorca. "Where is Majorca?" asked the friend. "I don't really know," was the reply, "you see, we flew."

In this chapter we rediscover a lost Indian tribe called parents. Schools unfortunately like to deal with parents in formal tea-drinking rituals—P.T.A. groups, back-to-school night, or scheduled parent-teacher conferences. What happens, McNeil asks, when a parent shows up *un bel vendremo* and wants to just look around? Many schools find such behavior alien to its functioning. But why? Perhaps the smooth, unruffled running of an organization is the real goal of the institution and education a magic hoped-for byproduct.

There is a savage short story by the late Shirley Jackson called *The Lottery* in which villagers gather around each year for fun and games, eat and chatter in friendly groups, and finally culminate the day with a lottery. The lucky winner gets stoned to death by his fine, friendly neighbors.

Perhaps each society needs an occasional person or so upon whom to cast their ills and thus release pent up hostilities. If so, our society has found the school superintendent fairly adequate for such purposes. Does our society seriously believe that any mortal soul, with the exception of a triploid Freud-Schweitzer-Hercules, can do more than survive in this magic role as mediator of all of society's problems and ills? The essential question, as McNeil sees it, has to do with the degree to which educational leadership is developed on a rational, problem-solving, professional-competency basis or on a hit or miss basis. If we prefer the first basis to the second, we need to begin to understand the actual school organization as McNeil does.

Analysis of an Ailing Monster:
School Organization

It has been said that the best place for a person to hide is in a crowd. In much the same fashion, an analysis of how schools are organized is difficult to achieve because what is apparent is rarely what is real. In order to detect this state of affairs, it is probably necessary that the observer of education have a characterological distrust of the obvious, an inability to accept as fact what "everybody" knows, and an awareness that appearances are frequently calculated to deceive.

What analysts of education seem regularly to overlook is that the American Public School System is a daring social experiment which may well be recorded either as a monumental failure or as the most magnificent of achievements in functional democracy. No other society has had the courage to regard education as the individual responsibility of its fifty states and, further, to accept relegation of this authority to the citizen members of more than 40,000 local school boards. We as a nation are committed to a vast social and educational experiment with our children. Reflection and perpetuation of the status quo are inadequate goals because they are static phenomena and make no vital contribution to the dynamic, living organism called a society. Thus education must be a force for change or its bones will bleach alongside those of other institutions that once served a purpose and now are ponderous anachronisms soon to be discarded by an evolving social structure.

The highlights of the history of our society's attempts to organize its educational efforts to match its social needs are fascinating ones that give us the necessary perspective to look forward to what is in store in the next several hundred years. The citizen of the future tomorrows will live in a society that may only slightly resemble the era in which our public school system was formed and the problems of tomorrow will demand social and educational inventions that are probably beyond the limits of our imagination.

235

In the colonial period of our history, the home was school. Teaching the child to read, write, and spell was no more than a means to qualify him for admission to the few secondary schools that funneled selected children to a college where they could prepare for law or the ministry. The teaching methods of those times are uniformly abhored by modern education, since early schools leaned heavily on "read-recite" techniques and were without the professional teachers, special buildings, and other facilities that seem so vital to current educational design.

Expansion of the pupil population was the necessity that became the mother of invention. "Monitors" were one such invention—a system in which pupil assistants who had learned the lessons taught by the masters in turn taught other youngsters. As the subject matter to be taught increased in complexity, this educational device lost much of its usefulness.

In about 1848, what has been described as a development "greater than any other in school organization" occurred with the formation of the Quincy Grammar School in Boston. This was the origin of the one-teacher-per-grade, or graded, school. For a century plus this has remained the basic means of organizing schools and has proved to be bed rock for the notion of the self-contained classroom. The administrative neatness and orderliness of such a system had about it a compelling quality that proved to be irresistible.

The weaknesses of this elegant solution to the educational needs of society could not long remain hidden. Much of the educational innovation of the nineteenth century had as its target the revision, modification, and adaptation of this device to make it a closer fit to the shifting times. Thus, for example, as early as 1862 the St. Louis Plan was devised to break the lock-step imposed by annual grading of all pupils. Attempts to individualize instruction (1888), to set up separate tracks for brighter students (1893), to promote brighter pupils when ready (1895), and to "enrich" talented individuals (1898) were all efforts to fit the educational organism to the new society. It is startling to realize how ancient are the devices which we regularly applaud as new and splendid approaches to modern problems!

When our social needs progressed from education for the elite to universal education, the society was not able to modify the educational system with sufficient speed or accuracy. The nineteenth century was a time of attempts to patch a leaky vessel. Sociologically, it is difficult to account for the inability of education to abandon an obviously sinking ship in favor of a vessel more suitably designed for modern waters, yet, our modern age was witness to a similar institutional lag when we tried, and failed, to make an adequate response to the heavenly course of Sputnik. Too frequently, in history, the observer of education is confronted with the spectre of a single solution to all problems—massive, panic-ridden surgery that is focused on the malignancy with little regard for the patient.

The twentieth century had to concern itself with educational experimentation on a monstrous scale and a host of new alterations were promulgated to keep the educational ship afloat. "Work-study-play" programs (1900), the Platoon Schools (1908), the Burk's Plan of individualized instruction (1913), the Detroit x-y-z plan of ability grouping (1919), and team teaching (1930) were all patches placed atop patches. Three decades later, we have yet to construct a new craft. In 1964, an educator asked an assembled group of experts to name a single, meaningful, and truly crucial innovation that had taken place in education in the last quarter century. After making a rapid inventory, I was forced to conclude that the popular notion of continuous and steady progress toward some ultimate goal in education may be a greater illusion than we choose to believe.

As Havighurst and Neugarten (1957) have emphasized, in training youth for health, morality, and full participation in the culture, the functions of the school have increased in direct proportion to the loss of functions sustained by the family. Today, they note, trades are learned in school rather than from the father, religious training has shifted to the church and sunday school, and recreation is organized in youth groups and movements (Boy and Girl Scouts, YMCA, 4-H, etc.) separated physically and psychologically from the home. This, coupled with the increase in education parents expect and require for their children has made the school an increasingly important social institution. Schools have chosen a course that little resembles the relaxed, unscheduled flow of life in the home and, as is no other element of society, schools are organized fiercely and formally by age and grade. Time is made the master of people, and even student responsibility and extracurricular participation are organized rigidly by age. No other aspect of normal social life is divided into such rigid periods of time as is the school day yet, astonishingly, this slavery to clockwork can claim only a remote kinship to the facts of child development. Rigid age-grading is a function of tradition and administrative convenience; its cost to education has yet to be calculated, and probably the price will be very dear.

The most deceptive facet of any attempt to view the educational system through eyes not clouded by the cataracts of "what everyone knows" is the theoretical neatness of the existing clear-cut, formal organizational structure of schools. This formal, hierarchical, clearly visible structure is a snare and delusion that regularly enmeshes new recruits to the educational system; yet it is much like a Hollywood set—all façade with nothing behind it. If you live for long in the subculture of the schoolroom, you learn that the latent organizational structure is a regularly overlooked and grossly under-estimated facet of the meaning of school. Latent or informal organization encompasses not only cliques and close friendships but reaches to include the "informal patterns of hatred and mutual animosity which may be even more important as a source of undercutting the formal organizational structure." (4)

Education, thus, is a phenomenon whose dimensions are more apparent than real. It is deceptive in the extreme and does not dissolve easily when mixed with any simple collection of intellectual chemicals. What is to follow is an attempt at an appraisal of this system on which our society is so firmly based—an appraisal that is viewed through a deliberately jaundiced eye.

THE CHILD IN THE CLASSROOM

Not until later in life will the child comprehend the degree to which teachers fret about the nature, kind, quality, and sequence of educational experiences to which he is exposed. To the child, what *is* is what's proper, and school becomes just one more of a succession of events that happen as they do because "that's just the way things are." The child may rarely analyze and describe the process he is undergoing, but he reacts to it emotionally and responds to it psychologically in ways that are crucial to his self-image and his view of life. As the child matures and broadens the range of his experience, his perception of the educational process and his evaluation of various aspects of it shifts accordingly. The growing child's perception of education varies along at least two dimensions: (1) the state of his need system at various times during his development; and (2) the cultural and value "starting point" his environment has decreed will be his fate. Thus, the Negro child who is a member of the lower socioeconomic class will experience "education" through a perceptual filter that is immeasurably alien from the point of view of the white child of the town's doctor or bank president. It is this distinction that makes the impression of school organization a highly subjective and individual one—one almost entirely dependent upon the unique and particular history of the individual. In this sense, the response to education is always an individual reaction that cannot be comfortably fitted by broad generalizations. Even if a "typical" child simply does not exist, we can examine school organization for those of its aspects which all children must confront.

It is clear that along certain dimensions, education today bears only a faint resemblance to that of the past. In 1680 students were forbidden to keep firearms or swords in their rooms and the carrying of sticks, stakes, and other offensive weapons *in the classroom* was equally prohibited. We have progressed some distance from the day in the seventeenth century when tavernkeepers, gambling-den proprietors, and hotelkeepers were forbidden to put students up or to take them in as lodgers. These actions strike us as unseemly for students and incompatible with current ideas of childhood and early adolescence, but in the sixteenth and seventeenth centuries, people classified school boys in the same picaresque world as soldiers, valets, and beggars. The concept of the well-bred schoolboy is a modern view that has only recently emerged from the unruliness, roughness, and immorality of the medieval school child.

Modern schools expose the child for the first time to an organized, planned, systematic, and formalized experience with success and failure (1). The child, of course, knew from other life experiences of winning and losing, of having and going without, and of achieving and failing to achieve, but he never devoted his entire day to activities that were flavored so heavily with the bittersweet taste of winning and losing.

As the child begins in earnest to play the game of educational winning and losing, he discovers, to his surprise, this success and failure may have little to do with his actual accomplishment. He finds that these words refer not to "things" but to a psychological distance that exists between accomplishments and a set of goals, expectations, and aspirations. He must face the startling truth that his own goals, expectations, and aspirations seem never to reach a stable state but rather twist and turn as he develops and comes into contact with new persons. Also, in general, the significant peers, parents, teachers, and other adults in his life hold quite discrepant views of what his aspirations and goals ought to be. In this respect the child finds himself in a kind of psychological cafeteria in which he must choose from an array of aspirational dishes in order to select those he will enjoy most and be most capable of consuming without suffering acute or chronic indigestion. In this cafeteria-of-success-and-failure he is forced to sample a great many dishes, and then he is urged to experience a variety of others.

Success and failure become vital components in the mental health of the child, for they begin to characterize an issue to which he may devote an important part of his life's energy. Incorrectly managed it may produce a life in which the child seems subjectively to experience continuous failure, a life in which easy achievements produce little in the way of a sense of accomplishment, or a life devoted exclusively to the never ending pursuit of an ever increasing set of higher and higher aspirations. The core of the self-image of the individual can be molded from experiences with success and failure, and the child may come to organize his perceptions of himself and others exclusively in terms of being ambitious or lazy, productive or unproductive, and successful or unsuccessful.

In a strange fashion, the child's perception of what constitutes success and what indicates failure may, in great part, be an incidental and accidental aspect of his life history. The nature of the era in which he is born and the particular culture, country, school, parents, teachers, and peers with whom he comes in contact all contribute subtly to the view he will have of himself as an adult. Given the context in which he will learn the lessons of success and failure and given the lack of experience and perspective he brings to these first lessons, it is perhaps unfortunate that schools are organized as they are. Schools measure success and failure in terms much more precise than those the child has experienced in the past and in ways he may never again experience in life outside of school. Measurement of success and failure in school is frequent, public final, and an important influence on the nature of our membership in a peer group from which there is no escape. If adults were subjected in daily life to a similar set of measurement pressures, they would find them intolerably anxiety provoking. Yet this is the quality of educational life the school system has designed as a means of learning. If the child is a middle-class pupil, he must adapt to the school's pressures and demands, because school is the single institution, and academic work the single measure, designed to test his acceptability to his parents and important others in middle-class society. Despite other positive characteristics the child may possess, he will be considered a failure if he does not achieve on the academic stage. In adult society we can balance failure in one region of life against successes achieved in others and escape being held accountable for a single standard of performance along a single, rigid, dimension. For children in school, life is not so generous or forgiving.

With the widespread age-graded system of the elementary school, pupil-teacher antagonism early in their relationship is highly likely to disintegrate into a nine-month-long negative discourse. Since the manner in which a teacher relates to the child has a measurable impact on his educational output, this is a matter of some import. The consistent but inequitable distribution of reward and punishment in the classroom, for example, may be a fact of life which may influence the whole tenor of the class yet remain an invisible force in education. The pupil who is subject to high praise and low blame for his educational efforts will experience quite a different "classroom" within the same four walls than a student made the victim of high blame and low praise experiences.

It is fair to say that the teacher and the classroom are social inventions that, potentially, have the utmost meaning in the life of the developing child. Because of the manner in which school organization has evolved, much of the potential has never borne fruit. Too often, the individual needs of the child go unmet as the needs of the system are fulfilled. Much of the nature of school organization amounts to the inheritance of past epochs in which the flaws of the then present system were remedied by inventions dictated more by necessity than a vision of the future and its educational needs.

THE PARENT AND THE SCHOOL

The child's "parent" also has a stake in the nature of public education. Parent-singular, not parent-plural, since the relationship of the father to the public school system is distant at best and begrudgingly intimate at worst. Traditionally, parent-school roles have been defined sharply along lines of sex with school board membership assigned to the male and room motherhood obviously the inheritance of women.

One educational role is reserved for the father—that of aggressive protector of the family integrity when it is threatened by adverse educational judgments regarding the behavior or intellectual production of his child. At few other junctures in family life is the protective-aggressive-virile function of the male so unremittingly demanded and so severely tested. He is asked to "get tough" with the school and "straighten them out" and make them "stop picking on" the child. Thus, as in psychotherapy with the child, the mother becomes the central representative of family life. Success or failure in communication with her becomes a prime determinant of cordial parent-teacher relations and is vital to the child's academic career. The massive growth of school systems has stimulated the professionalization of education and has produced a distinct and uneasy alienation of the parent from the process of education. This unnerving sense of being a stranger to the educational decision-making process may spawn consequences that might range from the failure of bond and millage issues to the steady erosion of national respect for the role of the teacher. This supposition on my part can be validated, experimentally, in the simplest of fashions. All a parent need do is to walk boldly (unannounced) into his or her local school and seek out an impromptu conference with a teacher. While the level of consternation may be disguised, an astute parent would immediately be made conscious of the anxiety occasioned by a sudden visit that makes "rehearsal" and "preparation" impossible. For the parent himself, confusing contact with secretaries, assistant principals, and endless corridors tend to dampen his ardor long before he reaches the person most conversant with the nature of his child. The size of the physical plant and the masses of students are not adequate to account for the degree to which parents are cowed by contact with the educational organization. It is, in part, that the parent must now deal with schools populated by "professionals," where once she met with teachers. The educator's elevation to professional status may have been at the expense of the ultimate consumer of education—the parent who represents the unquestioning child.

At first glance it would seem that parents who are members of the lower socioeconomic or minority classes have been the greatest victims of this educational disenfranchisement. I am convinced middleclass participation in the important decisions in education has suffered a vast, but less visible, erosion. Parents are experiencing these alien feelings in part because they can little comprehend the seeming complexity of modern education or feel comfortable with its size. When school systems increasingly (especially in large cities) find it necessary to meet social pressures by distributing pupils to schools distant from their homes, the emotional distance between parent and school becomes even greater. The community or neighborhood school concept collided head-on with the larger national problem of de facto segregation by social class and race. School organization by geography proved to be inadequate to the needs of the total society and had to be abandoned for newer concepts. Local control of school boards and parental participation in educational decision-making proved, again, to be too little, too late, and too unaware of the nature and direction of societal shifts in emphasis. The active and sometimes violent reaction of parents to this sudden alteration of the status quo stands as mute testimony to the degree to which local parental control of education is inadequate to meet the requirements of social movements that reach beyond the confines of the neighborhood.

Parents have always had the P.T.A. as a mechanism for influencing educational decisions and, in theory, a twelve-million member Parent-Teacher Association ought to be a powerful "force-to-be-reckoned-with" on the American educational scene. In actual fact, since its inception in 1897 as the National Congress of Mothers, it has been variously described as a waste of time, dull, irrelevant, and an inexhaustible source of trite thinking and tiresome meetings. As a powerful voice expressing itself on the vital educational issues of the day, it is notably silent. In its lengthy evolution the P.T.A. has managed to exclude the male half of the parental arrangement. This unrelieved matriarchical structure may, in part, account for the timidity and educational impotence of the group.

If alteration of our educational structure is to occur, it is unlikely to issue from this sterile source. The parent-teacher associations have become the victim of the rigidities of their organizational structure—a rigidity that is now called tradition. Parent-Teacher Associations are a permanent fixture in school organization, but they seldom make important contributions to the shape of education.

EDUCATIONAL ADMINISTRATION

If we look to Socrates as the basic model of a teacher, we find that a number of the vital characteristics of this role have survived, unchanged, for centuries. By contrast, the educational administrator in a mutant spawned by the increasing complexity of human society and the stupendous growth of the educational enterprise (8).

The one-teacher-one-room schoolhouse has been abandoned in favor of school "systems" containing teaching staffs numbering in the tens of thousands and departments designed for each content area. Many relatively new educational roles have been invented for the administration of these systems: the "principal-teacher," the school superintendent, the assistant principal, and a host of related roles. Although necessity mothered the invention of the principal, it was always hoped that the role would more closely resemble that of the spiritual and educational leader of his fellow teachers than that of business administrator and public relations agent. This hope, unfortunately, was not to be realized.

Whatever the original intention, the principal became the natural recipient of all the ills the educational flesh was heir to. The principal became the dumping ground for each educational innovation or experiment without regard for the relevance to education of the task assigned. Many of the obligations of the principal could only be classified as trivia of the worst kind—trivia that shortly began to command the majority of the principal's time.

The modern principal has several important characteristics. He is most often a "he," and "he" comes late to the decision to be an administrator of education. Fewer than one in ten has decided on principalship as a career before completing undergraduate studies, and only one in three has made the choice before completing the master's degree. This means that becoming a principal requires on-the-job training. Learning-by-doing has a variety of hazards. As Jordan (6) has pointed out, "Making a school a smoothly running organization can become so absorbing that one forgets that organization is a means and that educating children is its end. . . ." It is evident that running a tight ship can become a substitute for educational purpose. In the principal's drive to do well he may lose sight of his goal of doing good.

It is apparent that the principal's freedom of action is a gross illusion and that, actually, he is the school system's greatest slave. Not only is he a slave to a multitude of demands and role obligations from which there seems to be no escape, but he must also suffer a growing guilt about his alienation from the most vital transaction of education, the classroom. The superintendent of schools escapes this "neither-fish-nor-fowl" fate because his role has become increasingly clearly defined as that of the public relations-business-personnel-policy administrator. The superintendent's role is a natural extension of the position of principal, and it is a role to which ambitious principals aspire with great energy. As in any executive establishment, the scope and complexity of our previous experience is a prime sign of readiness to assume greater responsibility. Thus, a system of relative prestige has arisen in which the principal of a large high school sits astride the heap and is suborned by his assistants, the principals of junior high schools, and, finally, the elementary principal. This path to the superintendency is somewhat complicated by the continued addition of specialists alongside the educational path, that is, the curriculum specialist, the personnel manager, or the business manager.

Although the elementary principal (the most numerous of the species) may have his eye on the "main chance," his own job requires great managerial acumen in a complicated situation. Not only must he succeed in managing the business aspects of his school, he must also clearly demonstrate his capacity to do well in professional interpersonal relations with his teachers. In this respect he must come to grips with the ever elusive concept of "leadership." In our society, leadership is a near equivalent to "democracy." What the inquiring principal learns (usually through bitter experience) is that "democracy" is an abstraction of such a high order that its definition in action is subject to extreme variety; he discovers that although "democracy" pleases the teacher, it irritates the administrator to whom the principal is responsible. A delicate balance indeed is needed to please both sides of the educational fence, and principals who fail to rise in the educational hierarchy may do so because they have "traded-off" acceptance by one faction at too high a price for the administrative faction to afford.

Krech and Crutchfield (7) point out that a leader can serve his group in a number of ways: as an executive, a planner, a policy maker, an expert, an external representative, a controller of internal relationships, a purveyor of rewards and punishments, an arbitrator and mediator, a model of behavior, a symbol of the group, a surrogate for individual responsibility, an ideologist, a father figure, or a scapegoat. We would have to be incredibly optimistic to state that a good principal should combine all or even a substantial portion of these qualities or roles. If these constitute the raw materials from which each leader must construct his personal pattern of leadership, it is obvious that the astronomical number of possible combinations and degrees of each is staggering. To be sure, there is more than one way to fulfill the role of leadership, and probably success is achievable through the combination of any of a number of the elements listed. The essential question for democratic (or any other kind of leadership) has to do with the degree to which it is developed on a rational, problem-solving basis rather than by accident.

Perhaps the role of principal has deviated grossly from its original purpose and perhaps school organization has thereby lost an important native resource. Two possible solutions exist: a redefinition of the role of principal to make it more relevant to the process of education or the invention of a school position—separate from administration—devoted exclusively to bringing about change in education.

For all its shortcomings and forced limitation, the role of principal is vital to school organization and must be understood by anyone trying to comprehend the organization as a whole. The principal is the "gatekeeper" of the educational process. Without his sanction, stimulation, and support, no educational innovation blossoms, and schools become sterile imitations of the past. It has been said that the American educational system has undergone no significant change in the last quarter century. If this is an accurate appraisal, it may in no small measure be attributed to the principal who has not accepted the educational challenge that is addressed rightfully to him. The principal has become a neutral or negative (limiting) force in education. Principalship has become a means of defining masculinity for the male who occupies the role and has become a means of upward mobility within educational organization. Principalship cannot, unfortunately, serve a multitude of masters, and in its choice of which master it will serve, it has vitiated its strength as a force for revitalization of the educational system.

THE TEACHER

If we love children there are a multitude of ways, other than being a teacher, to enjoy childhood vicariously. Teachers may teach because they love children, or they may choose the occupation because they regard it as a highly respectable task that will enhance their prestige in a community, as a nonreligious life of service, as a highly secure professional effort, or as a job better than clerking-in-the-local-variety-store. Teaching offers certain other rewards. It can fulfill a need to wield power over others, it can express an intense attachment to particular subject matter, or it can reflect a need for an expressive outlet for middle-classness.

As Havighurst and Neugarten (5) indicate being a teacher was, in the early days, one of the few occupations available to the educated and respectable woman. Since modern culture has increased the number of occupational alternatives for females, teachers have begun to be selected from other than the middle class and have been swayed by motives other than occupational desperation. Where once it was a badge of gentility and a visible indication of middle-class status, teaching has now become a means of mobility within the social system. Education remains a particularly middle-class enterprise, but times are changing and upwardly mobile lower-class persons are using the field as a means of advancement. Members of the lower class who were, in their youth, alienated from their own lower-class culture may use education as a path to social status. We are moving slowly but steadily away from the stereotype of the teacher who neither drinks, smokes, enjoys the company of the opposite sex, dresses stylishly, or, in the common parlance, "swings with life."

Yet, the social status of teachers remains less than admirable. They rate about average for all occupations, and they occupy the unique position of a "professional" who is almost totally subject to the dictates of public opinion. The teacher participates regularly in community affairs but seldom as a leader, and he or she is seen primarily as one who understands children but little else in the real world.

The image of do-gooder and child-servicer hangs on tenaciously. The image of the teacher of bygone days was clear and consistent even if not particularly rewarding.

Teaching as a "profession" has certain oddities which distinguish it from other professions. This profession is unique in that full-time professional responsibility is assumed immediately after training, yet the training itself provides little or no supervised practice in the professional task to be performed. Female teachers are taught to see their professional lives as starting and finishing in the classroom with little prospect of advancement. Professional progress, if it occurs, is from smaller to larger schools, from lower to higher grades, or from worse to better schools in the same district.

Members of this profession, when compared with students who elect to pursue other occupational objectives, are selected, typically, from the ranks of just average students. Universities that train students for a variety of professions are aware that most if not all of the usual measures of ability place students training to be teachers at the bottom of the academic scale. This is a continuing social problem, since the quality of teachers we select for our children is a clear reflection of the culturewide ambivalence we feel about education.

We value education in the abstract sense of the word, but we set a great many limits on the form with which it is executed. The degree of financial and moral support for the school system is tied closely to the community consensus about the suitability and usefulness of the education the members perceive their children are receiving. It is equally clear that Western Democracy is getting exactly the kind and caliber of teacher it wants and deserves. A nationwide school system staffed by the best trained and most brilliant academic specimens our society is capable of producing, a school system free to innovate and experiment until it finds the correct path, or a school system capable of building for the future are ideals to be pursued but are realities that our society cannot cope with without excessive anxiety. Any institution that deviates too far from an approximate cultural norm constitutes an immediate threat to the society, since it promises to alienate the young from the familiar and comfortable experiences of those of other generations. At best, then, educational progress seems necessarily limited to small and conservative steps taken one at a time. Perhaps this is one explanation for the fact that so little meaningful innovation has taken place in the last quarter century. Teachers sense the social climate with an almost sixth sense and react accordingly in a manner calculated to assuage the anxieties of the public and assure the continuation of close social connection with the parents who invest most heavily in education by entrusting their children to it. If we ask for the source of significant educational change, we find ourselves saddled with a question for which there is no readily available answer.

As long as the teacher is seen as a paid, professional agent for cultural diffusion of those values the society holds in high esteem, little deviation is permitted. In this position, teachers are expected to be a bit more moral and better models of deportment than the average citizen. Despite the blurring of the image of the teacher, she is expected to be more virtuous than the parents whose children she takes in hand.

Teachers, of course, must solve the same problems of institutional allegiance and peer-relations as do all workers. The basic identification and sympathy she bears is with her fellow teachers and against the administration of the schools, but even in this task she must exercise care not to jeopardize her peer status by achieving too much "popularity" among her students or by the use of teaching techniques or methods that would smack of a nontraditional approach to teaching. It has been pointed out that the child has certain expectations of teachers—expectations that may not be fulfilled by the actual appearance and deportment of the real-life teacher. As the child matures and gains in experience, he needs a teacher image that evolves accordingly and suitably to fit his changing needs. In the midst of the frequently contradictory roles that the teacher must fulfill, she is likely to falter and fail to deliver that which is most needed at the time its presence is most required. The teacher treads a very slender and delicate psychological tightrope indeed.

When, in addition, the teacher is called upon to play the roles of mentor, policeman, judge, jury, and eventual executioner with respect to all things social and academic, the level of complexity may prove much too great. Failure to achieve these ends, from the parents' point of view, is most often attributed to teacher weakness or inability, and parents regularly fail to comprehend the mental-hygiene point of view the teacher may hold. The essential contradiction is to be found in the discrepancy between the current orientation of schools of education to the mental-hygiene and in-class therapy philosophy and the "school-as-I-remember-it" conviction of the parent. With some trepidation parents and teachers approach and circle warily about one another.

Schools have their own peculiar social organization which effects the conduct of the teacher. Most often, the informal, not the formal, structure is most vital to the sense of satisfaction a teacher achieves.

Unfortunately, the teacher is a prisoner of a classroom in which the formal constraints on time and space restrict social contact to after school hours or to the superfice of ritual social contact. Under these circumstances, clique formation tends to violate the formal structure, but this is small in scope and local in form.

EDUCATION—TODAY AND TOMORROW

Suppose society *doesn't* destroy itself. What then will we do about the manner in which our schools are organized? It should be evident that the organization of our schools ought to be designed along several vital dimensions. School organization should, first, eliminate the increasing cultural lag developed during the last several generations. When technology was in its infancy and yesterdays differed little from tomorrows, this issue was not an urgent one. In this era of sudden change and dramatic breakthrough along all social, political, and scientific fronts, delay in adapting to meet the needs of the times can easily render any institution hopelessly obsolete a dinosaur squatting helpless and exposed to attack in the twentieth century.

Educational organization must, with dispatch, abandon its rigid, long standing refusal to replace the old with the new. Throughout the history of education, leaky curriculum and organizational vessels have been patched and patched again to withstand the heavy weather of social change, and it has only been in the face of imminent disaster that fundamental new designs have appeared.

It seems apparent that education sorely needs a built-in organizational device that will keep it more closely attuned to the shifting needs, aspirations, and problems of the society it serves. Having knowledge in advance of the directions society is most likely to pursue can reduce the element of surprise in change and can prompt the educational organism to alter its functions in smaller and less stressful-sized steps. It is my feeling that the growth in size and complexity of the educational process has alienated it from the well spring of the culture which supports it and has introduced a potentially fatal discontinuity in the system. In this respect, a smaller but equally serious cultural lag exists between the pressing needs of society and the character of the teacher-training institutions we have designed. One suggestion for circumventing this educational drag has been to certificate (education-administrative jargon) educated adults to occupy teaching positions without the dubious benefits of the educational clergy.

Further, our educational system needs to achieve something resembling a statement of educational goals to serve as a beacon for educational methods. Even though the absence of a national educational system reduces educational purpose to a local or provincial level, a footing or base of national cohesion exists that will serve as a design for local activity. Although previous efforts to delineate national goals in other areas of our cultural life have met with confusion, contradiction, and, finally, a retreat into the lair of the glittering generality, the attempt itself can be an important factor in delineating some issues, clarifying others, and providing for a clear demarcation of areas of doubt and confusion. As an annual task it might at least serve to outline the form of current and painful social issues that might otherwise be ignored by accident or avoided by calculation. Goals established as an empty exercise in semantics will not, of course, improve our current educational situation. Implementation must be the handmaiden of goal setting if it is to be meaningful. The translation to day-by-day objectives will be most difficult.

No clearer exposition of the problem we face can be found than in this statement: "It is a discredit to us and a disservice to children to say that we believe in each child's working at the level of his own potential—and at the same time subject him to a common course of study, a comparative marking system, a predetermined structure within which to work, and general goals that may or may not be applicable to him." and in the notation, "School organization, per se, is void of life. We cannot accomplish, through organization, what can be accomplished only through good programs, an adequate number of competent teachers and materials and conditions conducive to effective work." (p. 17)

AN ORGANIZATIONAL MODEL FOR EDUCATION

It seems apparent that when a dispassionate observer views educational organization as a whole, he is hard-pressed to make crystal-clear sense of the conglomeration of bits and pieces and odds and ends of which it is composed. So many adults and children spend so many of their waking hours enmeshed in the organizational structure of education that it is paradoxical that so little thought has been devoted to the nature of the organization itself.

Education is compellingly obvious to the casual viewer. So many observers are convinced that the educational process is what it seems to be that few have sought long for new and different visions of it. Educators might well profit from the exercise involved in abandoning the classical conception of education in favor of a brief excursion into the realm of the industrial psychologist's conception of organizational theory. At first glance, it would seem to be an attempt to join two quite alien worlds. When examined more closely, the organization of education and the organization of industry are more similar than dissimilar. For, except for housewives and preschool children, the rest of humanity is intimately associated with organization in one form or another. Educational and industrial organization are congruent if we conceive of education as a product-producing process that is structured in a vein highly similar to that of industry.

Organizational theory in business and industry is a means of applying the findings of the behavioral and social sciences to the working situation of human beings. Unlike education, industrial organizational theory has long been aware that the human being at work presents a highly complex portrait fashioned of a great multitude of facets, aspects, and interlocking dimensions. In one attempt to represent the human at work in diagrammatic form, Sutermeister [9] indicates that employee productivity occupies the center of a series of concentric rings-of-variables that bear directly on it. Expanding throughout the radius of these rings are dimensions such as the individual's ability, skill, and knowledge; his physiological, social, and egoistic needs; his personal motivation, and the degree to which this motivation is a function of the physical and social conditions in which he or she works. Beyond these rings are more rings that place in proper perspective the influence of formal and informal organization and leadership. At the periphery are items that include the specific environment in which the individual works, and these items include personnel policies (for example, job content, selection, placement, standards, incentives, training, and performance ratings); the size, cohesiveness, and goals of the organization; and related variables.

The relevance of this diagrammatic representation for education is to be found in the complexity of the interrelatedness that Sutermeister sees as essential for a theoretical view of the person at work in a complicated work situation. Somehow, education has come to deal with the totality of the person-at-work in too piecemeal a fashion. Somehow, educators have failed to realize that the "workers" in their organization are both the pupil *and* the school employee. Pupils who do or do not produce are the raw material with which we must be most vitally concerned. Pupil "labor unrest" is rarely recognized for what it is. It most often is attributed to social forces external to the educational system and has, consequently, been viewed as the responsibility of no particular member of the educational system. Delinquency, teenage riots, and college student rebellions have too long been treated as symptoms of spring fever, exam pressure, and similar phenomena. It is time we realized that, as educators, we need a closer grasp of the evolution of society as it gets reflected in the behavior of the young.

Theories about industrial organization will not prove to be the ultimate answer to the needs of education. However their use might temporarily help to propel educators along alien and untrodden paths in their search for a new vantage point from which to view education. If such theories accomplish this alone they will have served a purpose. Education has been tied hand-and-foot by tradition for so long a period of time that new departures in thinking are vital to the necessary vigor that will be the future motive source of educational survival.

What is education's product? Ideally, the well-educated, well-rounded student; in actuality, the educational product is measured most often in fragmentary and partial terms—the daily quiz, the regular classroom performance, and completion of the appropriate textbook. In industry the product is easily definable—an automobile, a gear, a TV set; in education, the product is frequently ambiguous and often considered undefinable. Yet, if viewed without emotion, education—grade-by-grade—produces child laborers who are capable of turning out answers to questions and solutions to problems. Inability to produce this product on demand (throughout the semester) results in social-educational sanction in the form of failure and retention in grade. In addition, if the teacher and peer group are not sympathetic, the pupil-worker is subjected to an extreme form of social censure. While the ultimate product is vaguely defined as "education" the immediate production schedule requires intellectual "piece work" in the extreme.

Typically, the principal of any school occupies the neither-fish-nor-fowl position of the foreman of a factory. The foreman is usually promoted from the ranks of workers and finds himself with divided loyalties. As the midwife to executive decision-making he must balance acceptance by the workers against approval by higher management, and this in-between position demands the most delicate footwork imaginable. Like the ancient God, Janus, he must show two faces—each face looking in a different direction. To be successful, every foreman must learn to respond quickly, easily, and properly to each of these two worlds. He must, simultaneously, achieve loyalty from his workers and garner respect from his administrative superiors. So, too, with the principal.

An interesting symptom of the degree to which teachers have come to resemble industrial workers is to be found in the recent trend to unionization of teachers and the device of the teachers' strike. Teachers have always sought to achieve status as a profession, but historically professionals have been independent, have never needed the strength of union participation, and have rarely resorted to strikes as a means of implementing their grievances. Teachers, finding themselves socially compromised in their quest for status, have found it necessary to resort to the familiar industrial pattern of the strike. Although this extreme mechanism has succeeded in producing local progress, it has alienated the populace in immeasurable ways. If teachers must resort to such devices to achieve their ends, the time has come to apply industrial psychology to their working situation. Unionization, and pupil, parent, and teacher strikes spell out an inescapable pattern of distress in our educational system. A new conceptualization of education is needed—one that more closely approximates the facts of life.

The developments in education seem clearly to be symptoms of a disease that needs remedy if education is to move beyond its current conception of its responsibility to the growth of America. The organization of education is due for renovation to adjust the elements of the needs of the individual, the informal group organization, and the formal structure of education. In industrial organizational theory, the nearest approximation to a remedy for education is to be found in an idealized version of the position of industrial research and development.

"Ideally" a corporation hires a specialist in research and development and invests his role with authority and responsibility for all aspects and phases of the operation of the company. This may range from product design, packaging, time study, human relations practices, executive decision making, and employee morale, to consumer marketing and sales promotion. The research and development specialist in such a setting need not become entangled in the multitude of divisions or units of the formal organizational structure. Instead, he is able to command a view of the whole organization as a series of interrelated and, hopefully, integrated efforts all aimed at the successful completion of the final product.

As the educational system in America mushroomed to unbelievable proportions, little thought was devoted to making a choice of the "best" formal organizational design to achieve an ideal educational product. As rapidly as necessity forced the construction of a new fragment of formal organization, the traditionally conservative educator endowed it with the mystical qualities of tradition, and it became a fixed and immutable part of the system. The evolution of teaching and administrative roles in the organization failed to provide any position devoted exclusively to the research and development of the educational process itself. Particular problems were "solved" by employing a variety of specialists, but it has become apparent that the meaning, purpose, and direction of education cannot be discovered simply by adding together each of these narrow, specialized, or departmentalized viewpoints.

Thus, for example, it has long been axiomatic in industry that the formal distribution of power and influence along organizational lines is regularly violated and distorted by the inevitable growth of informal organizational structures within the company. Although the formal group structure may hold the reins of ultimate power, it must be prepared to accomodate human resistance expressed through personality and the informal group. Education has too long ignored or at best given lip service to this state of affairs rather than studying its nature and realigning its formal structure to fit more closely the facts of organizational life. If pupils are viewed as employees in education, it becomes evident that the formal organization of education has taken little account of individual personality or the structure of informal groups. Devices such as textbooks, age-grade compartmentalization, and rigid curricula, as well as the patchwork attempts at repair represented by enrichment, acceleration, multi-track programs, and ability grouping, all reflect attempts to compensate for flaws in the formal organizational structure.

Much of the formal structure of educational organization interferes with the educational product principally by creating restrictive and inhibitory working conditions—of these, the worst offender is the organization of the curriculum. One of the clearest spokesmen regarding the need for systematic research and development of curriculum is William H. Bristow (2). He notes that research is, essentially, ". . . the orderly and systematic treatment of data to answer questions" and that, ". . . many curriculum problems have been inadequately, improperly and ineffectively researched [p. 142]." Often the basic imperatives of curriculum research are overlooked, for instance, those who use the findings in the classroom should participate in the research from its inception; curriculum research should be a practical rather than theoretical nature; and the school climate should be favorable to changing the status quo. Parenthetically, effective research is always a threat to "things-as-they-are" and should never be initiated without adequate preparation of the consuming community. Employee participation in decision making, of course, cuts against the grain of the typical pretended-democratic-actually auto-cratic organization of education.

As Bristow sees it, the prime requisites for effective educational research and development are

". . . willingness to admit limitations, readiness to question prac-tices and conditions no matter who or what is affected, opportunity and encouragement to question and try new motives and ways of doing things, and time for those who are doing research." (p. 144)

Anyone familiar with the American school system is aware that these conditions rarely exist. Still, under ideal conditions, no research or development will succeed if it continues to retreat from Bristow's fundamental observation that "some pupils mature more slowly than do others and therefore must have a differently paced learning pro-gram if they are to master what is being presented." (p. 144)

The single example of curriculum as a fertile ground for research and development is instructive if we are aware that it is only one of a myriad of educational areas to be explored and that it is, in itself, an unbelievably complex and tangled problem. A recital of the host of other educational challenges to be met would be burden-some as well as obvious to anyone familiar with the American school system. The only objection to the views of Bristow and those of like mind is that they have failed to carry their ideas far enough. While they advocate research and development as an integral part of educa-tional progress, they apply it primarily to curriculum, and they house their suggestions in the unfortunately Victorian, gingerbread, structure of educational organization that currently exists. The best of planning in *any* aspect of education would be painfully shackled if restricted only to the current, archaic view of the nature of the educational process.

A new research and development role is called for: one that occupies a position free of the usual demands of department and discipline and one that is fulfilled by an individual who is able to focus on the broad view of the past, present, and future of education. The initial academic training of our model research and development ex-pert is probably less relevant than the breadth of vision that he or she possesses. Professional supply of such persons will clearly require a program of education and training that must depart radically from most of our present conceptions of how best to indoctrinate future educators into education. Furthermore, our educational system will need assistance in understanding that educational research and development specialists are a *necessity* for the survival of education, not a *luxury* occasioned by modern affluence and a generous tax base.

At this moment every school system contains a person capable of meeting the challenge presented here—a person ready, willing, and able to try if some educational administrator is prepared to break with tradition to make the required great leap forward. For too long in the history of American education, innovation and progress has been the responsibility of outsiders to education—outsiders whose grasp of the process is based more in theory than on practical experience. A new conception of the educational process is desperately needed if we are to give the lie to the statement that nothing fundamentally new in education had occurred in the last quarter century and nothing new can be expected until after 1984.

REFERENCES

1. Barker, Roger G. "Success and Failure in the Classroom." *Progressive Education,* **19,** 1942, 221–224.
2. Bristow, W. H. "Problems in Curriculum and Action Research," pp. 141–159, in M. C. Gottsegen and G. B. Gottsegen, (Eds.), *Professional School Psychology.* New York: Grune and Stratton, New York, 1963.
3. "Elementary School Organization," *The National Elementary Principal,* **XLI,** 1961, 3–157.
4. Gouldner, A. "Organizational Analysis," in R. K. Merton, L. Brown, and L. S. Cottrell, (Eds.), *Sociology Today,* New York: Basic Books, 1959, pp. 400–428.
5. Havighurst, R. J. and Bernice C. Neugarten. *Society and Education.* Boston: Allyn and Bacon, 1957.
6. Jordan, W. C. *Elementary School Leadership.* New York: McGraw-Hill, 1959.
7. Krech, D. and R. S. Crutchfield. *Theory and Problems of Social Psychology.* New York: McGraw-Hill, 1948.
8. McNeil, E. B. "The Principal—An Educational Dinosaur?" *National Elementary Principal,* **41,** 1961, 59–64.
9. Sutermeister, R. A. *People and Productivity.* New York: McGraw-Hill, 1963.

Chapter 11

Group Interactional Factors in Learning

Herbert A. Thelen

About the Author

What would happen to teaching and to education in general if we were to take serious account of what we know of behavioral science? Herb Thelen, onetime chemist and high school teacher, has his BS and MS (Chemistry) from the University of California (Berkeley) and his PhD (Education) from the University of Chicago. He is currently Professor of Educational Psychology at Chicago.

Thelen's pursuit of instructional theory began in 1947 with a three month's swing around the country, being handed on from one expert in group dynamics to another. There followed a long and productive summer association with the National Training Laboratories—nine summers in seventeen years. Having given up hope of ever getting out of Chicago, Thelen gave six years to the application of group dynamics in the development of the citizen action program of the Hyde Park-Kenwood Community Conference [1949–1955]. In the meanwhile, a major research was underway, eventuating in *Methods for the Study of Work and Emotionality in Group Operation* (1952), and, with Dorothy Stock (now Whitaker), *Emotional Dynamics and Group Culture* (1958). Between these two works was a thought piece, *Dynamics of Groups at Work* (1954).

In 1954, Thelen and two colleagues, Jacob Getzels and Kenneth Rehage, put their concepts together and launched an experimental "intensive" program for preparing teachers for elementary schools. In 1956 Europe beckoned, and the European Productivity Agency Project 339 team put on human relations training workshops in seven countries. The old T-group and inquiry principles were found to have plenty of pizzazz, but to work out differently in different cultures.

An experiment on team teaching at the Laboratory School led into the effort to uncover classroom-relevant types of students and to discover how best to teach each "type". Types could not be established (fortunately) so the research team settled for an experiment involving the selection of students to "fit" teachers. The results were impressive, and will be found in *Classroom Grouping for Teachability* (Wiley, January 1967).

258

The experience of trying to use behavioral science concepts in the classroom cried out for ideas to be fitted together; hence *Education and the Human Quest* [1960]. Further fitting was attempted at the Center for Advanced Study in the Behavioral Sciences (1960–1961).

Thelen's present projects are: a five year NIMH study of ten to twelve year olds in peer groups, inquiring into their own behavior as a means to help the "maladapted" among them; and an interuniversity project, shared with colleagues Vern Cunningham and Fred Lighthall, to study the "theory" and technology of change in schools and other social systems. For the future, living through these projects may be sufficient, but Thelen admits that his fantasies gravitate to the possibility of cooperation with other researchers and philosophers in a head-first attack on educational theory.

Introduction to the Chapter

The normal reaction of the average teacher to the topic of group interactional factors in learning is not usually one of wild enthusiasm. Social psychologists and group dynamics people who espouse looking at groups as they function in educational processes get short shrift from many educators of the hardnosed or tell'em and teach'em schools. It's one thing to go to Bethel, Idlewild, or some other pleasant place and be part of a Sensitivity Training Group or know in a general way about democratic, autocratic, or *laissez-faire* groups; it's another to face a class of thirty children, some of whom are ill prepared to function with curriculum content or with each other. Although most teachers recognize that classrooms are indeed microsocieties, as Thelen calls them, this knowledge often seems useless in the classroom.

Thelen suggests that we had better come to grips with existing practical knowledge about groups and learning. For example, educators seem unwilling to face the growing homogeneous-heterogeneous grouping problem squarely. When subjected to research, the expected advantages of homogeneous groupings fail to materialize. What does seem to account for the effectiveness of any learning situation is of course how the teacher manages her group and her material. A teacher who likes to power right down the middle with hardnosed work gets results from a good homogeneous, bright class; an emotionally supportive and warm teacher may get similar results with a different kind of group using a different approach. Thelen asks to what extent teachers are aware of how they help their students and their classes pursue learning. If the major organizing principle of the classroom society is the personality of teacher, how can teachers and classes be more effectively matched?

Thelen suggests a few ways beyond this short horizon. He believes that teachers can be helped to differentiate between labor and work. How then do teachers help their microsocieties become competent educational groups? In his no nonsense, here-it-is-if-you-want-to-know fashion, Thelen spells it out—if I might mix a metaphor—by the numbers.

Group Interactional Factors in Learning

.

If we consider a classroom group as a microsociety, the group dynamics that render society as a whole productive of goods and services may give up insight into how its miniature edition, the classroom group can be rendered productive of education.

In this chapter we shall examine the nature of a classroom group and attempt to show what, within its nature, makes it educable under what sort of policies of teaching.

Because this is a fairly complex matter, I had better anticipate my strategy. I shall start dialectically by asserting that classrooms are microsocieties which have salient and distinctive tendencies of the "larger society." I shall then present some researches on classroom grouping and will show that they become highly interpretable if we assume that classroom groups may be regarded as miniature editions of the "larger society."

The grouping studies will help us recognize explicitly three basic activities of the classroom society: psyche-group activity, socio-group activity and task activity. We shall spell out for each some properties which seem most suggestive for education. Having logistically torn the classroom entity apart, it will behoove us to show how it can be put back together again, and this will lead us into the matter of how to teach. Obviously we have been assuming that practically all teaching violates at least some aspects of the nature of the classroom society. I shall suggest that the gamut of violations tends to form a pattern, and that the basis of this pattern is the image of classroom activity as *labor*. I will then say a few kind words about *work* and finally, will try to show how the concept of work can be used to deal integratively and educatively with the psyche, socio, and task facets of the classroom.

SOCIETY[1]

Born into an existential world in which he must find food, shelter, and other necessities of life, man has had to learn the properties of this world and how to interfere in its workings to get what he needs. Here, then, is the reason for knowledge and know-how, collected over milleniums, organized, codified, symbolized, and passed on from generation to generation—with revisions. In addition to pooling ideas, men also learned to pool their individual efforts: faced with a difficult or even hostile environment, they tend to band together in the common cause of overcoming the enemy whether it be starvation, illness, act of God, or alien ideology.

For concerted effort to be possible, man requires language, expectations, authority, and legitimization of the common purposes; all these necessities for group action are developed through agreements, both implicit and explicit. Society's major purpose is to produce the things its members need. Especially when the relationships between production and consumption (of food, ideas, or art) can no longer be clearly seen, maintenance of the society tends to become an end in itself: the "good" society fits a traditional image whose reason and justification may have long ago been forgotten. The society then becomes in some respects a part of the existential world whose properties must be studied and interfered with, along with the rest of the environment.

Within the action context of tasks and the relationship context of organizations, the individual reserves for himself, autonomously, a small bit of psychological space. Here he cultivates his private wisdom, his secret apprehensions, his unspoken hopes; and these become known to him through his reactions to groups, to established knowledge, and to demands for his activity. He selects other persons to assist him, and these preferences generate informal groupings oriented to the individual's mostly private concerns about himself.

All parts of this picture are *necessary*. To get jobs done you need organization; to have organization you need members; to be members persons need know who they are, what they value, and what the *quid pro quo* is. On the other hand, a person cannot develop a "self" except as he tries to participate with others in a variety of enterprises; in order for him to participate with others, organization is necessary; and for organization to exist some purpose is necessary.

Hence we see in society three major and necessary components, each with its own function, organization, body of knowledge, and legitimizing authority: the task force, engaged in transactions with the environment; the socio organization, engaged in maintaining a social order and organization; and the psyche group, comprised of voluntary groupings or "informal" associations through which each individual comes to terms with his private problems and anxieties.

In the classroom, the approximate equivalents of the three major components are: the students working on lessons (task force); the teacher giving instructions and enforcing his rules (organization and social order); children whispering to friends or playing with them outside of class (psyche groups). Just how genuine these "equivalents" really are remains to be seen.

WHAT GROUPING STUDIES SHOW ABOUT THE CLASSROOM SOCIETY

The classroom group, students and teacher, may be considered as a microsociety. No doubt some features of the society or group will be affected by who the members of the group are—their interests, emotional defenses, values, and capabilities[2] (to name a few). In other words, what the persons are like (what they bring into the group) affects how the group operates (management problems) and at least some outcomes of its operation (achievement).

Educators have made many attempts to select students into classes with certain characteristics of process or outcome: greater manage ability, greater achievement, greater ego support for individuals, greater security and less anxiety in the teacher. Homogeneous grouping by "ability" is the most common form of grouping now in use. In so far as "ability" correlates with race, sex, or moral character, grouping by ability is also a form of segregation of these other sorts. Insofar as ability correlates with prestige, ability grouping can satisfy what appears to be a condition that exists (according to Washburne)[3] in all societies: that there be an in-group and an out-group. This would also be in line with Bettelheim's[4] suggestion that the principle of social stratification, threatened by ending of racial discrimination, can be preserved by ability segregation. Apart from these dirty reasons, however, the notion that it would be advantageous to narrow the range of brightness, aptitude, speed, and prior knowledge of the class is a popular and plausible idea. It assumes that the teacher would have fewer "individual differences" to contend with and would therefore teach more effectively.

At any rate, whatever the explanation (or excuse) the results of comparisons of achievement in homogeneous groups with achievement in heterogeneous groups are perfectly clear: the two organizations are superior to each other in about the same number of instances. Three carefully controlled, properly designed studies by Passow,[5] Drews,[6] and Borg[7] show the homogeneous groups to be superior on some scores (achievement, attitude, interest) and the heterogeneous groups on others. However, the patterns differed from one comparison to the next, and the patterns are mostly uninterpretable. Thus, a fourth-grade homogeneous class may show higher scores in spelling than did the heterogeneous class; but the same classes in the fifth grade may reverse their standings.

The failure of homogeneous ability grouping certainly means that the "plausible" reasons for this form of grouping must now appear a little less plausible. Technically, what the findings suggest is that IQ plus achievement is a much less influential factor than some other factor that was not controlled and that *really* accounts for the differences. The popular hunch about narrowing the range of brightness to make the teacher more effective would make sense if verbal fluency, speed, and extensive memory for an assortment of information—which is what group IQ tests tend to measure—have much to do with successful participation, but these are simply *not* the traits demanded in most classroom activities. The notion that academic ability indirectly *indexes* other things like self-directiveness, interest in school work, and creativity is assumed when the course is changed to fit the bright or dull student. Unfortunately, most of these assumptions are wrong: there is no evidence to show that bright students like to work harder or are less dependent than dull students when confronted with equally difficult situations.

On the basis of these studies, we may say that ability is not significant in the classroom society; or that whatever we measure and call ability is not significant; or that task-lessons really are not tasks that require ability as much as they require something else; or that the alleged teaching problems created by differences in ability among students do not exist; or that these alleged problems are easily centralized, contained, or made irrelevant to the business of the classroom; or that the teacher causes ability to be useful for some learnings but not for others.

We do not have to look very far to see what factor *does* account for the differences in the grouping experiments. Ekstrom,[8] in her survey of all published accounts of ability grouping, points this factor out: the teacher. She gives her view that a dull class which has an emotionally warm and supportive teacher may achieve better than the same students distributed throughout regular classes, (Drew also supports this view); and that a strongly work-oriented no-nonsense teacher may get good results with a homogeneous "bright" class. Both of them leave open the extent to which the teachers have any awareness of these qualities, the extent to which they are due to teacher personality or to teacher strategy and procedure.

Shane[9] studied 32 ways of grouping students into elementary school classes. He concluded that the most important factor governing the success of any method of grouping is the extent to which the teacher believes in it and is committed to making it work. This seems to suggest that the teacher has a will of iron; that he has very great power or potency. This is indeed the case, as shown, for example in the works of Withall, Flanders, Anderson, Hughes, Perkins,[10] and now, of Kounin[11]—all of which show that one can predict the morale and achievement of a *class* simply from knowledge of the *teacher's* behavior. Or consider the Lewin, Lippitt, and White studies which demonstrate how deliberate shifts in the role performance of the teacher led to vast differences in the behaviors of pupils. Finally, let us throw in the hopper one further generalization, from Ben Bloom:[12] that the method of teaching seems to have little or no influence on learning of *information;* when the same teacher teaches similar classes by different procedures (telling vs audio-visual, for example) there are no significant differences in amount learned—even though there are differences from one teacher to the next. (Procedures make more difference with respect to learning of "higher mental processes" because demonstration of a rationale is required.)

These studies suggest that the teacher has great power and that this power is exerted in relationships and also through those aspects of transactions which lie below consciousness. In short, teacher "personality," not method, materials, or procedure, is the most important factor. What does this suggest about the classroom society? The psyche structure will be called on to help the child preserve his integrity in the face of the normal threats presented by the teacher's power; the social order and organization will develop the norms the teacher is committed to—or will be torn up in conflict over them; the jobs to be done will be the jobs the teacher approves of, and they will be done the way the teacher wants them to be done. Furthermore, this state of affairs is not necessarily consciously sought by the teacher; in fact, many teachers deny their power, believing its existence to be "undemocratic." And, for the most part, teachers have little or no control over their most significant influences on the child.

We are forced to see that *the organizing principle of the classroom society is the personality of the teacher* and, therefore, the way to improve the classroom society through grouping is to fit students to the teacher in such a way that the educative tendencies within his personality will be most reinforced. Short of intensive clinical study of teachers and students, educational theory at present would offer no suggestions as to how to effect such matching. However, we can make a beginning: we can give the teacher a classful of students he can teach. In such a class the teacher should most effectively achieve his goals, whatever they may be. The reasons for my reluctance to equate the teacher's goals to education will be apparent before long.

One study[13] made such matching for thirteen teachers ranging across five academic subjects and four high school grades in eight suburban schools. The matching was accomplished by having each teacher name students whom he considered were "getting a lot out of his class" and students having the opposite experience. The two lists of nominees were extensively tested on a 405-item battery of classroom-related attitudes, preferences, and associations; then items that empirically discriminated between the two lists were incorporated in a scoring key. Next the students from whom the teacher's next year's classes were to be chosen were tested on the same battery and scored by the special key. The top thirty students, most like the ones earlier nominated as "getting a lot out of class," were selected into the experimental, "compatible" group for the teacher. The teacher was also given a control class, composed by the usual methods in his school.

There were many findings, but a quick summary may suffice for our purposes. The teachable students from one teacher had little in common with those for another, and for no teacher was IQ a desideratum for the "teachable" students. Eleven of the thirteen teachers gave higher marks to their teachable classes, (and one gave the same marks). Nine of the thirteen teachers preferred the students in the teachable class to work with or chat with; the students in eleven of the thirteen teachable classes preferred each other more than did the students in the control classes. There were fewer observed problems in the teachable classes, and the teachers were observed to talk somewhat more of the time, express more affect, and be seen by the students as more interested in the class.

It is obvious that the teachers achieved their purposes better in the experimental classes. This is shown directly by the higher marks and indirectly by the greater liking for the students. It is also mentioned in testimony from five teachers who were followed most intensively—each got what he wanted: more vigorous, personally involving interactions with students; deeper penetration into the principles of algebra; faster coverage of the "content"; a pleasanter, friendlier, less work-oriented class that he could feel more adequate with; more counselling combined with teaching.

But this is not all of the picture. Eight of the *control* classes got higher gain scores on achievement tests given at the beginning and end of the year; and nine of the control classes liked the teacher better than did the corresponding experimental classes. This suggests two things: (1) for at least seven of the thirteen teachers, whatever the achievement test measures is less important to them than are other objectives; and (2) judging by the pupil's liking of the teacher, some of these more important objectives may well have been a bit exploitative psychologically. What we helped the teachers get appears in some instances to have been at the expense of the students' well-being. For example, certain teachers seemed to want mostly to be comfortable; others to have a quiet, orderly, punctual and respectful class; and others to get responses that would reassure them of their expertness, love, or rapport with the kids. The kids were selected to give them these things, but the kids did not necessarily have to like it, nor are these things necessarily educative.

The major job of the classroom society is to accommodate to the teacher's way of life. By picking students like those who have demonstrated *this* ability (IQ indeed!), we get a classroom whose culture is more coherent, whose societal solidarity is greater, and whose accomplishment of common (that is, teacher's) purposes is greater.

From these experiments, what kind of microsociety is the classroom group? It is a microsociety in which the teacher's influence is fantastically great. Much of this influence is exerted in ways of which the teacher is not aware, that is, through interpersonal transactions; and these transactions, reflecting a variety of compatibility factors, develop the classroom society. The nature of this society is only slightly determined by the "jobs to be done;" by the demands inhering in problems, inquiries, lessons, and subject matters; it is much more determined by the teacher's unique personality as actualized in the particular circumstances of the classroom.

The teacher might well ask what power and authority, other than that exuding almost unconsciously from his personality and office, is available to guide the educative process. There are two answers to this question. One answer is that of the behavioral scientist: the children are energy systems, and that they *have to* cope with problems of being a person, a member of the group, and a producer of something. In other words, they also have quests. The problems for the teacher is to see how the encouragement of these legitimate quests of the student can also be the encouragement of educative experience. The second answer is that of the philosopher and epistemologist; knowledge has certain characteristics and, when "learned" in certain ways, knowledge is useful; but learned in other ways it is useless. It is these scientific and epistemological insights, internalized within the teacher, that legitimatize and justify his power and authority.

THE PSYCHE GROUP:[13] THE INTERPERSONAL NETWORK

There are times when a person is anxious, fearful, high, or just feels sociable, and he is likely to seek out someone, a friend, to talk to. Their conversation may be about anything, but its content will be private. After the conversation one or both the persons will probably feel more at peace than before.

This is the operation of the psyche group. It is voluntary, initiated by stress, carried on between people who choose and trust each other, having no particular agenda, and tending to have a quality of privacy, intimacy, or confidentiality.

We see psyche-operations in the backstairs gossip when there is a new principal; in coffee breaks at meetings; in over-the-fence gossip sessions; in the endless phone conversations of our kids. We also see it in the eyebrow raising of cronies at a business meeting, in the occasional "deterioration" of a meeting into side conversations; in those rare moments of truth when the whole meeting is momentarily sharing a common emotion.

The psyche group is a natural group, coming together voluntarily and spontaneously. It forms because the individuals "need" one another, and its function is to reduce a person's anxiety and ambivalence and "strengthen" his ego. Suppose you and I are teachers in a school that has homogeneous ability grouping and in which the teacher whose prestige is highest teaches the brightest kids. I have just been told by the principal—in a nice way, of course—that I am to be stuck with the dumbies for another year. You are my friend. I come to you in haste, without thinking it over. I am in an "emotional state." You talk with me, friend to friend, and, after thirty minutes I am calm, ready to go on teaching, possibly even resigned to the dumbies for another year. What happened? A great many things. First, of course, is my disappointment, and I express this by saying I will cut the so-and-so's gizzard out—(a confidence I could hardly broadcast). Your reply to this is that you don't blame me, you's feel the same way. And you may even add the thought that I really am being unfairly treated. These comments penetrate to deeper levels and are genuinely helpful. I may not realize anything more than that I feel much better, but "underneath," the presumption is that my pain in this situation is due to a sense of guilt, that the guilt comes from the suspicion I am not a decent person, and the suspicion in turn is aroused by my having been punished, that in some way the punishment means that I have been found out (no matter how hard I have tried to conceal it—whatever it is—from myself and others). . . . Well, you see it gets complicated.

The psyche-structure of the class or microsociety is most often measured sociometrically as a network of interpersonal likes and dislikes. In the classroom, students may be invited to form psyche groups (self-selected) to talk over anything that has them emotionally aroused. They can reduce anxiety, try out their ideas on friends, be stimulated with more ideas, rehearse how they are going to report their ideas to the teacher, and develop a greater sense of adequacy and confidence in their participation when the class meets next as a whole.

The "content" of discussion might be called *self-knowledge*. You will find a lot of such stuff in novels: it is the medium of personal interaction. Self-knowledge has a special kind of validity: a statement feels exactly right or it doesn't; each individual is the authority in this matter, and conversations between friends usually keep going until the right words have been found or until the parties *decide* to let it go for now. All the parts of educative activity requiring commitment or motivation from individuals could well be "cleared" through open discussion in self-chosen small groups, for this is the sort of conversation by which one normally reduces his ambivalences preparatory to great undertakings.

The teacher may sometimes overtly be a member of a psyche group for some child; he is very likely to be a covert member with whom the child carries on active, imaginary conversations. For the teacher's power is, as we have seen, exerted somehow in the deeper unaware ways of the psyche group. Much of this power probably comes from the student's *identification* with the teacher. The development of the class as a cohesive group during those first few weeks of the new school year is probably quite dependent on the development of identifications of students with the teacher and on their own awareness that they have this identification in common. The psyche groups, meeting outside of school, or illicitly during class time, or under the guise of working committees are the major mechanism of adjustment and adaptation for most students. The events of psyche groups are to be understood in much the same way as events in therapeutic groups through the use of personality theory and psychotherapeutic models.[14]

THE SOCIO GROUP: THE LEGISLATIVE NETWORK

There is a whole realm of knowledge that has to be legislated, a domain of things that are true simply because people agree that they are true. This is the realm of manners and morals. It includes just about everything that cannot be proved by logical deduction or by empirical test. What fork to use, what to do in order to be bad, how to address the teacher, what will happen to me if I don't keep my promises, how late I can be and still be excusable, what language I can use to cuss with, how openly I may display my autocratic leanings. What do we expect of each other by way of what sorts of participation, leadership, and conformity? What do you have to do to "belong?" What things can the individual freely decide by himself and what things must be discussed with others? When the group makes a decision, what recourse is open for the individual who cannot go along with the decision? What are acceptable ways to dissent, attack, express affection, and run away from hard jobs? These questions can be discussed.[15]

The rules, boundaries, and opportunities for interaction within the classroom social order are legislated by teacher fiat, by conscious group agreement, and by subconscious sharing and concensus. Implicit and explicit rules and expectations "define" the social situation, and the two most important aspects to be clear about are the nature of the authority governing activity and the location of the boundary between that which is public, that is, of legitimate concern to the group, and that which is private, that is, its communication to others is at the discretion solely of the individual. If the authority hierarchy is not clear, then class and individuals have no way to legitimize their decisions, because they do not know what criteria their decisions must satisfy. If the public-private boundary is unclear, individuals cannot tell what part of their experience (or, more precisely, of their reactions to their experiences) are relevant for the organization; hence they are at sea as to what ideas and feelings of their own can or should be expressed and thus "tested" and learned from.

The imperative that sets the socio group into operation is lack of predictability or lack of confidence. These are serious conditions, for without predictability I cannot behave intelligently, and without confidence I may not be able to behave at all. Under conditions of the "rule of law," a person knows what to expect others to do in response to his behavior, and he therefore can use knowledge of probable consequences as an aid in making decisions about what to do. All groups "legislate" the expectations needed for predictability; that is a major function of the initial shake-down period. The person who has the greatest power in the group, being most able to influence legislation and opinion, also can predict best the consequences of action. He is therefore "freest," taking least actual risk when he sticks his neck out.

Note that freedom is relative to a society: because I can very well predict probable responses to a wide range of behaviors in my own department, I am free to consider all sorts of alternatives and select among them with confidence. But were I to move to some other shop, I not only would not know their specific procedures (so that I would be highly dependent on a secretary), I might also make entirely wrong assumptions about what they value and seek to maximize in experiences together (for example, scholarship vs sociability vs harmony) or as to what standards they hold (for example, how thorough, rigorous, or long a Ph.D. dissertation must be to be accepted) or as to what they expect from the dean (for example, he will make all the decisions, vs he will consult with others on certain problems). When we travel to a strange country and find we have lessened confidence about how to behave, we realize what a very large per cent of what we "know" was put in our heads without awareness, without alternatives, without reasons.

There is, of course, a *quid pro quo* involved. If I want maximum freedom, I must belong to the socio group, for only those who belong can fully "know" the rules. And I must not only follow the rules myself (including rules about how to change the rules) but also help enforce them on others. In other words, I must share in making the self-fulfilling hypotheses come true. And I will find myself tending to oppose other members who try to change their own roles, for such changes mean I no longer can predict their behavior and therefore my freedom is diminished just a little (even though theirs is increased until the others get them pegged again).

When a child is described as good or bad, it is the quality of his membership that is ordinarily being evaluated, for good and bad behavior are socially defined. The good child "helps" the organization, fits in, abides by the organization's rules, supports its norms, and influences the group to adopt "better" norms; the bad child makes problems and difficulties for the organization: he violates the norms, lives at loggerheads with the organization, does not belong. The approved pattern of behavior is the member role. Differences in the quality and extent of membership (in the way the member role is actualized) are always found. Some members are more influential, or "central"; they are accorded more prestige; they have more worth than others. The various aspects of membership can be rank ordered; members can be arranged hierarchially, and the organization has a social structure.

The child who does not "fit in" to the social order or organization has not been socialized; he is asocial within *that* organization. And he is punished, ostracized, made to feel bad. For the most part, the social order is maintained through habit, and the habits we need to "fit in" may, as with the family, be instilled long before the child has the equipment to think about them. When the classroom social order is organized around values, language, and thought patterns similar to those of our family, we will normally "fit in" with the classroom organization. But when our socialization in the family is along quite different lines, we will, as members of the classroom group, be located at the bottom of the various membership hierarchies; and we will be "out-group." We will be deprived of what other members expect as a matter of "right"; from our point of view, the "in-group" members are "privileged."

Classroom "groups" are seldom entirely homogeneous with respect to the values, language, and thought of the various members. But if the community from which the members come is more or less homogeneous in its economic and social values and ways of life, the differences among members are likely to be reconcilable. Just how reconcilable and with what expenditure of energy depends on the teacher and especially on his tendency to understand and respect other ways of life than his own. On the other hand, if the community is heterogeneous or divided (as in the case of racial segregation) with respect to some criteria of value, then the reconciliation of different ways of life is much more difficult and the classroom "group" may not become enough of a social order for communication (let alone cooperation) to occur.

TASK, ACTION, AND KNOWLEDGE

In task activity we are concerned with the student as do-er, problem-solver, creator, producer, investigator. These are functional roles carried on vis-à-vis the environment rather than vis-à-vis the self or other persons. The nonpersonal environment contains ideas of the then-and-there, not merely of the here-and-now; it contains objects, natural phenomena, records of past events, technologies, arts and artifacts; it embraces agriculture, manufacturing, transportation. It is the "larger society" and "culture" and all its works—the objective world for which the student is being readied. Much of this environment the student does not know at first hand; it is represented by words, by books, films, relics, myths, encyclopedias. This representation is continually altered, filled out, and reorganized: this is the established knowledge which men have accumulated, the "funded capital of human experience." The environment thus has two manifestations: as "real" things and events, and as knowledge-symbols. The common characteristic of these two things is their *externalization:* they exist "outside" of personality and outside of membership. They have an inherent nature of their own quite apart from the student's needs of capabilities, and, in dealing with the environment, the student must change his information, his ideas, his skills. He must accommodate himself in some way to this objective external world.

We have to experience the objective external world in order to influence it or be influenced by it: contact must be made. The medium of contact, the interface between the person and the environment, is activity. The activity may be primarily a transaction between the student and the objects and situations of the environment or between the student and the organized set of symbols which represent the environment. Performing a chemistry experiment is first hand direct experience with the objects and situations of chemistry. Reading a book is direct first hand experience with an organized set of symbols. When a student is doing an experiment, he is doing his business with the environment, and the extent to which the data of his senses—what he sees, smells, hears, feels—become translated into verbal symbols may be minimal. When the same student is reading a chemistry textbook, he is doing his business with the world of verbal, symbolic representation presumably of the world of objects and situations. But the verbal world is an abstract world, devoid of sight, smell, and touch but replete with assertions and conclusions. The presumption that activity in the verbal world has inevitable correspondence with activity in the existential world is certainly dubious. By itself, activity in the verbal world prepares one to carry on conversations and to answer word questions, such as those in most achievement tests of the present day. By itself, activity in the existential world is unique to each situation and what a student learns through each particular activity may not increase his power in coping with later activities. Both types of activity are necessary if knowledge is to make a difference in a person's life. The experienced existential world provides the sensory data to interpret and utilize; the experienced symbolic world provides the tools of thought for relating one experience to another and for coping with the widest range of situations in the future.

The activities of the student depend upon the school "subject" under whose auspices the activity is conducted. Some school subjects, such as physics, chemistry, and biology, purport to help the student cope directly with the world of objects and situations; other subjects, such as mathematics and foreign language purport to help the student cope with the world of symbols; still other subjects, such as social studies and literature, seem for the most part quite unsure of where their interests lie. Considerations of this sort are at the heart of the true business of curriculum, but the curriculum field has become stagnant because for the most part it concerns itself only with one world, the world of organized symbols.

When it comes to a subject matter field, the "discipline" of the subject comprises the range of occurrences the subject includes; the basic questions found useful in approaching new occurrences; the key concepts and principles that are found to be exemplified over and over again in phenomena; and the basic methods of investigation, demonstration, and proof through which assertions can be granted the status (temporarily and provisionally) of truth. Thus "truth" here depends neither on intuition nor on concensus of participants, but rather on demonstration that assertions satisfy canons of predictability and reliability agreed to by experts in the field.

After this excursion into the mysteries of "curriculum," we are confronted with the nature of the activity the student will undertake in order to learn the knowledge he needs so that he can cope wisely with the world. There has always been great controversy in educational circles, not about the objective just stated, but about how this objective is to be attained. Because the nature of the learning activity is probably no longer a matter of legitimate controversy, we shall not get into the various classical ideas of Herbart, Dewey, or even Skinner. Let us now put our three classroom components back together again, using the contrast between labor and work to lead to a conception of integrative teaching.

LABOR VERSUS WORK

Controversies about education tend to "involve" practically everybody because the educational microsociety closely reflects the larger society and is much easier to fathom. The issue of individual versus society has been around a long time and takes different forms at different times and places: activity versus passivity, subject-centered versus child-centered curriculum, inner versus other direction, traditional versus emergent values—these are not equivalent issues but they provide vocabularies for discussing the same set of perceptions.

For our purposes, Hannah Arendt's[16] brilliant exegesis of the distinction between work and labor enables us to see how the three components of the classroom society can be kept working together for educative purposes. And, as a sort of bonus, Bion's[17] work fits well with Arendt's, and Bion's flight and dependency emotionalities are close to Arendt's labor.

Work, then, is effort that makes a difference. It changes the situation—solves a problem, produces some useful object, develops a new insight. Work is guided or directed by one's understanding of the demand-structure of the situation one is trying to cope with. (You put the load close to the wheelbarrow's wheel because that gives you the best leverage, not because that's the way Joe likes it or because that's the way we always do it.) In other words, work is reality-seeking effort. Work is also "molar" and "significant" to the worker: it is no mean thing to "make a difference" through one's efforts. (Recall the disgruntled shoe makers in the factory: when they made the whole shoe they were working, but when they shifted to assembly line methods with each person doing just a small part of the work, they were laboring.) Work is also creative, involving reorganization of ideas and making of judgments: one is truly coping. During work one has a gamut of feelings, dependent on how things are going; he feels involved; he senses the dramatic quality of existence. He participates in work as a "whole" person. Work is the highest lot of man and is necessary for self-realization.

Labor is pretty much the opposite of that just described. Labor may make a difference, but not in its own right and not to the laborer. To somebody else it may be just dandy to have a ditch; to the ditch-digger, the ditch is just a grave with both ends knocked out or a trough out of which his daily bread can be extracted. Labor, unlike work, has no consummatory value. Labor is directed by someone else, for his reasons, and according to his procedures; and their basis in insight or tradition may not even interest the laborer. Labor is uncreative, partly because the involvement of the laborer in the task is not great enough to generate much by way of discovery; and partly because it is not intended to be creative: it is the application of a formula or technique over and over; it is practice which may perfect the efficiency of a technique (like learning to run covariance analyses on the calculator), but it does not improve the technique. Labor is easy to direct because the tasks are cut and dried. This is the genius of mass production. The laborer is not psychologically involved enough to ask any genuine questions about the task (only about the conditions of employment).

When the activity of the classroom is labor, the corresponding method of teaching is "shaping" or conditioning or training in the narrow sense of training of specific skills.[18] The teacher sets up the activity and makes clear the procedures to be followed. He then gets the students started and tries to keep them delivering the required behaviors. He uses a combination of interventions: warning against "wrong" behaviors, punishing wrong behaviors, encouraging right behaviors, rewarding right behaviors. These interventions occur as the students are laboring. The product of the labor is a test or exercise completed, and the student may be rewarded or punished additionally for the quality of the product. It is simply assumed that engagement in labor is educative and that the educator must therefore keep the students laboring.

In the labor-oriented classroom, the verbal is emphasized to the virtual exclusion of the existential. For the verbal is neat, finite, and tidy; and it requires neither purpose nor rationale. An "assignment" is what you come up with by dividing the number of pages in the textbook by the number of school days in the year.

Under these conditions—of laboring rather than working—interaction between students must be either suppressed or simply tolerated as an unavoidable source of inefficiency.[19] Having set up a face-to-face group, the teacher has to contend with the *inevitable* psyche and socio processes of this group. But this method and concept of teaching regards these processes as irrelevant rather than as a tremendously potent dynamic that can be capitalized on to drive learning. There is a curious bifurcation in the teacher's thinking. He says "Let me manage the class and then I will be able to teach them." He has, in effect, two different theories, one having to do with "management" and the other with "teaching." Trying to serve two masters at once calls for pretty fancy footwork, or it calls for assigning the masters unequal power, so that in case of conflicting demands, he knows which to obey. Generally speaking, the management master dominates the teaching master: the teacher may know very well that if he will listen to the kids they will, possibly, learn more; but kids talking may turn out to be noisy so he tells them to be quiet.

In any classroom, consciously or unconsciously, three kinds of knowledge are utilized: knowledge of self, knowledge of the society in which one participates (the classroom group), the knowledge pertaining to externalized events, processes, and artifacts. Schools which are labor-oriented concentrate only on the third kind of knowledge, considering the other two irrelevant, distracting, soft, or somebody else's business. Any behavioral scientist worth his salt must vigorously disagree with this approach. Since the self and group processes largely determine the educative outcome (not necessarily what the achievement test shows) of the student's transactions with the external world, the teacher (at least) ought to know what is going on at the other two "levels." (Hence the course in Educational Psychology required in teacher preparation programs.)

I think it is fair to say that when instructional activities are largely confined to practice exercises, lecturing, programmed learning,[20] and any other sort of prestructured activities, not only is there no justification for having students organized into classes, but indeed such classes may well foster seriously maladaptive understandings of social and organizational processes.

WORK

Work has many forms and guises. Assessment of situations, making decisions, and carrying out action is the work prototype in business. Having a feeling to express and doing so through painting or music would be work in the world of creative art. In a society, sensing a discrepancy between expectation and behavior, diagnosing the cause, and taking action either to revise the expectation or enforce it—would be work. Two individuals both of whom are upset about the latest edict from on high may help each other become aware of what they feel and think—this, too, is work. Work is reality-seeking, trying to understand in one's own terms and with reference to his own perceptions and needs, what the world is like and how to operate in that world.

Given a class of children who are required to meet every day for forty minutes, there are certain things they can do easily and naturally; and other things that they cannot do so well. What they can do easily and naturally is *work;* what they can do only at a fearful and miseducative cost is *labor.* The method of teaching that makes most sense to a behavioral scientist is that method which keeps the child *working,* not laboring. The elements of this method are: the child purposively contributes skills and ideas to common goals by coordinating his contributions with those of others; the child helps maintain the group as a viable decision-making and communicative medium through which individual goals and contributions can be monitored, assimilated, and legitimized by the larger classroom organization; the child finds support, anxiety-reduction, and awareness of his own thoughts and feelings through interaction with selected other children in small groups. Activity is purposive and genuinely meaningful, which means that old ideas, attitudes, and skills are inadequate and one is under some stress. The stress is different for each person. One person is annoyed at the unexpected difficulty of the task; another is reminded of certain painful experiences from the past and temporarily confuses them with the present activity; another child is extremely sensitive to feelings of being imposed upon. Whatever principles one has to live by may be called into question. The student must be able to deal with unique personal stress in such a way that he can keep on functioning as a member and as a doer. And this is the *raison d'etre* of psyche groups within the class.

When the method of learning is through work, spontaneously arising interpersonal and group processes are objects of interest and attention. For these processes (for example, expressions of emotion, confused actions, acting out, conspiracy, intimacy seeking) provide the evidence that work is going forward, is being resisted or perverted, or is becoming snagged in frustration and pointlessness. During classroom activities, the situation is continually changing as the result of each bit of public overt behavior; and, as the situation changes, so also do the personal, group, and task demands that govern the activity.[21] Since work (by definition) attempts to maintain contact with reality, work activity is continuously responsive to changed demands, and therefore, the work curriculum is emergent, flexible, and natural and the human processes of the classroom are sacred.

Teacher-pupil planning, for example, is a process not only of deciding what action to take in an investigation or project, but of legislating purposes for the society, defining roles, setting up communication channels, and reducing ambiguities in expectations for performance. Teacher-pupil planning also involves the self. During subsequent conversations among friends or during breaks in the official planning, individuals will blow off feelings, check their trepidations with friends and reduce their anxiety over them, possibly diagnose and identify tentative decisions that seem uncomfortable or somehow "wrong."

Work-oriented teaching will make room for self, socio, and externalized knowledge, and will organize the class in whatever way is appropriate to get the kind of knowledge needed at each moment. When individual reaction, awareness, commitment, and anxiety-reduction are imperative, the class will be in small self-selected groups. When a wide range of "bright ideas" is needed as a basis for creating interesting hypotheses, the whole society will be put under highly permissive leadership long enough to get out the ideas. When many individuals have many different ideas as to purposes to be adopted, the entire society will undertake an analysis of the different ideas, seeking for common threads or underlying themes that can be converted into an agenda. Once a variety of topics or questions has been set up for investigation and once each individual has committed him-

self to start on one or another question, the work will be done individually, with the students working on the existential and symbolic
worlds, not on each other. Thus work-teaching continually attends
to the patterning of organizational arrangements, varieties of knowledge, and self, group, and task purposes.

The psyche, socio, and work structures of the classroom continually
shift in their prominence relative to each other. The teacher picks
up cues from the children that enable her to decide which kind of
organization should be strengthened and when it is time to shift.
When the class has seen a dramatic movie, the children are likely
to attempt to express the feelings it aroused, and the teacher seeing
this, may allow the class to divide into small self-selected psyche
groups to give each individual the opportunity to express and "get
hold" of his feelings. When the class is divided into project groups
all working in the same room, the teacher may invite them to meet
together as a socio group to legislate "ground rules" for the activity.
When a period of working is found to be unproductive, the class
attempts to analyze what went wrong, and consciously to anticipate
and circumvent similar difficulties in the future. When discussion begins to be repetitious and dull, the teacher may realize that it is
time to plan another challenging work task so that the students will
have some real first-hand experiences to come to terms with through
another discussion.

If we want students to work, we shall have to redefine social norms
and we shall have to encourage supportive informal or psyche-operations. A major revision of social norms, for example, has to do with
failure. In the labor view of education, one fails because he may
remember or apply information incorrectly as judged by the teacher
or other authority. In the work view of education, wrong answers
simply show him that he is on the wrong track; and they are therefore
quite helpful. The only failure is the inability to learn anything from
wrong or unproductive trys. It is clear that changing the student's
role vis-à-vis the environment requires also changes in the bases for
membership, reward, and leadership in the classroom group; and, possibly for a reconstruction of psyche relations as different sorts of
stresses develop and are handled through new associates with different
temperaments and bases of personal security.

INTEGRATIVE TEACHING

Teaching is the supervision of learning activities. We have suggested
that to the behavioral scientist there are a number of "givens" that

seriously influence the child's experience and therefore the presumed educativeness of learning activities. The psychologist tells the teacher to avoid antitherapeutic interventions, to be sensitive to anxiety states and confusions of individuals, to find ways to support the child's ego and to build on his strengths rather than his weaknesses, to operate the class as a psyche group. The sociologist or group dynamicist tells the teacher that students will perform better if they participate in making the decisions that govern performance; that problems of accepting "membership" and leadership may produce hidden agendas; that group norms are all important and that the teacher's influence on norms is very great. If you know these principles and others, you too can have a "good" group. And the establishment—the prominent leaders—bring home to the teacher that we are fighting a Cold War, that it will be won or lost on the manpower front, and that achievement—standardized, automated, regularized, and efficient—is the aim of education. Finally, our consciences tell us as teachers that the child is precious, and that it is up to us to decide through our actions whether he will live a rich, challenging, and vital life; a scared, thin, anxious life; or a permanently dependent, alien life as a ward of the state.

The question of how to teach is, however, not as "open" as the arguments among "experts" would lead you to believe. Let us see how the ideas so far presented help us to close in on the matter of teaching method.[22]

1. In every classroom there is a psyche group structure of interpersonal attractions and repulsions. These feelings will generate a good deal of behavior, and this behavior is gratifying because it serves the useful purpose of helping individuals discover and maintain their identity. The inevitable occurrence of these psyche phenomena presents us with the problem of how to utilize or channel these interpersonal interactions into education-relevant activity.

2. However the classroom is composed, it is still an involuntary enterprise. That is, the students have to come, they have to be together some of the time, and they have to accept the teacher. They have quite a lot to make the best of! The psyche activity helps them to some extent, but if that were the only kind of activity, the group would divide into anarchic, power-driven subgroups or gangs. A further kind of activity is needed, and the most appropriate further activity is working on a task to accomplish some purpose all the members feel is important. This is the raison d'etre for nonfriends coming together: to take some kind of action no one of them can

quite manage by himself. (This is also the only dynamic through which racial prejudice is reduced.) But in order to coordinate their efforts on the task, they need a body of legislation—expectations and agreements about who will do what, through what sorts of behaviors and expressions a member may channel his contributions, etc.

3. It is quite clear that the psyche-group and the socio-group processes and problems will be determined pretty much by the particular composition of the group, students plus teacher.

4. The demands of the psyche structure and of the socio structure may be partly reinforcing, and partly in conflict. Just as an individual is usually prey to some ambivalence, wanting to work and face reality and at the same time wanting to evade the pain and trouble—so the group has to come to terms with its two natures. In short, it must operate in such a way that each person retains his integrity as a person and can meet some of his private needs, and yet at the same time the group must be a social order and working organization with a well developed body of "rules" that everyone can count on.

5. Given the probable tensions between psyche and socio operations, some higher authority is required to adjudicate the conflict—to decide (when occasion warrants) between tendencies to cooperate and tendencies to seek personal gratification, to dig in versus to flight, to be self-directing versus to be dependent, to operate in a formal way versus to proceed informally.

6. The teacher clearly does have the power and authority necessary to adjudicate all such conflicts—without even giving reasons, without any recourse by the students, without any required reality-testing. Practically the only control over all but the grossest overt behavior of the teacher is his own sense of responsibility and commitment to something over and above his own personal desires.

7. Because the teacher has this power, and because he actually wields it every time he opens his mouth, any child who cannot identify with the teacher's way of life (his professional as well as his hidden commitments) is going to have a tough time. In any direct conflict with the teacher, the child cannot win. The most he can do is make the teacher anxious, and this reduces the teacher's competence, not only to teach this child but also to teach the class. Therefore, children should be fitted to the teacher, since the teacher is not going to yield; and if this makes it too easy for the teacher to do bad or stupid things, the teacher should be fired or re-trained.

8. The teacher's way of life and authority may exalt an amazingly wide variety of purposes and values. Yet, whatever the psychological pattern, by and large the way the teacher actually deals with the

class and supervises its activities can be pretty well understood as exemplifying labor and work orientations.

9. The work orientation (but not the labor orientation) provides criteria and processes by which to adjudicate all the disputes in the classroom: over role, expectations, or evaluation; this is true because work is a transaction with externalized realities, and these realities in effect give the student feedback as to whether he is on the track. Thus there is a higher, unarguable authority than the personality or position of any person; and the "enemy" is a set of conditions or problems to be solved, not another person's unfairness or caprice.

10. To be able to set up activities as work rather than labor, the teacher has to know the discipline of his subject rather more thoroughly than is typically the case in schools today. He has to be able to understand the study of his subject as a "dialectic of inquiry" rather than as the communication of a "rhetoric of conclusions," to borrow two of Joe Schwab's felicitous phrases.

11. The teacher needs to understand consciously some model or strategy or sequence of steps or other guide that enables him to interpret what is going on in front of his nose and thus to make changes in the activity in order to keep it viable. He will need help from the students, and therefore, they must be taught to give this help, which means that they too have to understand the strategy.

12. This increased role of the students, requiring them to take initiative when work is pointless, to help formulate alternative plans, to take many more responsibilities for the work, for themselves and for the classroom society all of these learnings, even though not only ignored but scoffed at in high places, are truly important to the inhabitant of the modern world. In other words, the teacher and students can use their own experiences to exemplify in some respects other societies; and the classroom can (and should) be basically a continuing laboratory for the study of social and societal processes— and for the development of the skills required to participate in these processes.

Of these twelve points the eleventh needs extensive explanation: it is a model of work-teaching. This is a very big subject, and I shall try to illustrate the method by imagining that we are going to "walk through" an educative sequence of classroom activities.

The beginning of an educative sequence is a situation in which individuals can make discoveries freely: a field trip, a silent demonstration, a document from which they are to reconstruct a society. The situation invites speculation; the child is not directed how to respond but is directed to respond in any way he can. Useful confronting situations require selection from a rich supply of stimuli or else a good deal of projection to fill in a pattern when the stimuli are sparse.

Confrontation and initial discovery is followed by *emergence of awareness*. A person who has been stimulated to new feelings, apprehensions, and thoughts usually tends to seek out a friend and talk it over with him. Psyche groups may be utilized in the classroom as a means for the emergence of awareness arising from accumulated stresses and discoveries. Several purposes are served by psyche groups: the children legitimize their thoughts by finding out that the words for them do not sound crazy; they rehearse their opinions and thus process their official version of the confronting events; and they stimulate each other to create and be aware of additional hypotheses. Children tend to engage in these processes among themselves, between themselves and imaginary playmates, and between themselves and their imitations of parents. Scholars "talk it over" with other scholars internalized within their heads. It is not unusual for the most important events within a course to occur outside the classroom.

Having thus done what he can to cause the students to have course-relevant ideas of their own in mind, the teacher now reassembles the class and enters into the first sort of dialogue. He begins by *inviting* a wide range of *testimony*. He says (in effect) "What are the different meanings this (the confronting) situation had for you?" And he puts the testimony on the board. He then invites and guides examination by the students of their own testimony. The sort of examination he directs depends on the nature of the subject discipline. The possibilities include: seeking for differences and similarities of perception and purpose; identifying the categories of sensitivities (political, economic, social), implied by the comments; diagnosing the issues around which the comments revolve (justice, conservation, optimism, rationality, truth). In order to conduct such a discussion, the teacher must himself understand and know the sorts of categories and issues that are the instruments of understanding in his subject field, and he must be able to recognize the students' testimony as naive, blundering, and primitive expressions of these key concepts.

The outcome toward which the discussion is guided is a *sense of problem*, expressed in the formulation of large questions which further experience is to illuminate. A "large question" can be investigated in many different specific instances and in each instance it poses its own specific problem. The range of relevant problems or problematic situations is so great that it seems reasonable to have each student work on one which is especially meaningful to him. The appropriate problem would present the large question in a context that is familiar to the student and important to his needs and present understandings.

Once each student has selected or formulated his problem, *individual work* begins again. This work is called problem-solving, but discovery is its central component. This discovery differs from the initial discovery in the confronting situation in that the problem situation is far more completely defined. It is bounded by agreements and expectations developed during the preceding discussion. The student's task is to find a pathway from the givens, the defined questions and the observed facts, to the "conclusion," a set of more warranted ideas about the large question as exemplified in his problem situation. Materials used for problem-solving must allow for many alternative pathways, so that thought is continually challenged by the need to make decisions. (This is the chief objection to most present "programs": there is very little possibility for the student, through his own decisions, to construct or create a pathway; he is on a guided tour, not a quest.)

Once the students have completed and discovered a pathway (and solution), they now have the task of *organizing* their awareness into communicable testimony for the class. *Report-writing* and review by ad hoc study committees are possible activities for this purpose.

With testimony organized and in mind, the students are now ready for the second kind of dialogue. In contrast to the first dialogue which attended to the various ways in which persons can and do relate themselves to open situations, the second dialogue attends to the various relationships that can be found among parts of problematic situations. The teacher begins by eliciting testimony about the discoveries made during the experience of grappling with the problems. As before, he invites and guides examination of this testimony, using the methods appropriate to the field of knowledge. Generally speaking, two kinds of ideas are to be examined: ideas about the "substance" of the question itself, and ideas about pathways through problems. For example, one student will have worked through trial and error; another, primarily through syllogisms; another, by stating the conclusion first and working backward; another by analyzing the elements and seeing how they combine. According to Professor R. P. McKeon, there are four fundamental methods of inquiry: logistic, dialectical, problematic, and operational. It is time that the profession internalized such categories. The examination of testimony about pathways centers around identifying different sorts of paths and then considering the conditions under which each would be most appropriate.

As can be seen, the dialogue is conducted to cast the students' discoveries in the problem-solving experience up against the established discipline and methods of working. During this discussion, the teacher is also trying to assess what sort of confronting situation will be most appropriate to initiate a new cycle of inquiry.

LAST WORD

Teaching is the educative facilitation of certain natural processes and the inhibition of others. We should not (although we frequently do) expect to create processes that by virtue of human nature cannot exist; and we should attempt to maximize the possibility that educative kinds of natural processes will become central, significant, and leading. In this quest, the task of theory is to identify some set of processes that constitute for us the essence of educational transactions. This essential ingredient is work. In addition, we will anticipate many necessary but not sufficient processes that are facilitative and supportive of the main processes. We cannot ignore these because, regardless of the scope of our theories and our ends, we are in fact dealing with something as broad as human nature and as complex as life. Organizations, with their psyche, socio, and task functions and are the ingredients through which the larger society and the classroom microsociety both achieve their purposes—including education.

NOTES

1. So far as I am concerned, you may insert in place of this section the whole of Weston La Barre's classic, *The Human Animal,* University of Chicago Press, 1954.
2. Five years of experiments with emotionality in groups, including comparisons of groups with different compositions, are described in Stock, Dorothy, and H. A. Thelen. *Emotional Dynamics and Group Culture,* New York University Press, 1958.
3. And this is just about the *only* property characteristic of all societies, according to Sherwood Washburne (Seminar discussion, 1954).
4. Bettelheim, Bruno, "Segregation: New Style," *School Review,* 66, No. 3, 1958, 251–272.
5. Passow and associates report an excellent study, including survey and preceding studies, in Goldberg, M. L., J. Justman, A. N. Passow, and G. Hage. *The Effects of Ability Grouping,* Teachers College Publications, 1962.
6. Drews, Elizabeth, *Student Abilities Grouping Patterns, and Classroom Interrelation,* Office of Research and Publication, Michigan State University, East Lansing, Michigan, 1963.

7. My information comes from a manuscript report by Walter Borg (University of Utah). Both researches were sponsored by the Cooperative Research Branch, U.S. Office of Education.

8. Ekstrom, Ruth B., "Experimental studies of homogeneous grouping: a critical review," *School Review*, **69**, No. 2, 1961, 216–226.

9. Shane, H. G., "Grouping in the Elementary School," *Phi Delta Kappan*, **41**, No. 7, 1960, 313–319.

10. These researchers constructed and used observation instrument to categorize and pattern the teacher's behavior. The behavior of the students was remarkably predictable from that of the teacher! See resumé, Chapter 6, "Measuring Classroom Behavior by Systematic Observation," by Donald Medley and Harold Mitzel in N. L. Gage (ed.) *Handbook of Research on Teaching*, Rand McNally, 1963, pp. 247–328.

11. Of greatest possible interest is Jack Kounin's finding, reported in conversation, that the rate of misbehavior in the classroom depends more on the teacher's "thrust" or straightforwardness and confidence of movement than on his techniques for dealing with the misbehavior! (Work vs. Labor?)

12. The preliminary analysis of what would be involved in a study of grouping was "Classroom Grouping of Students," *School Review*, **67**, No. 1, 1959, 60–78. The final planographed report of the research, Cooperative Research Branch, U.S. Office of Education, Project 428, was prepared in 1961 and is being turned into a book, *Classroom Grouping for Teachability*, John Wiley and Sons, 1967.

13. The terms Psychegroup and Sociogroup were, so far as I know, coined by Helen Jennings and were first presented in her excellent article "Sociometric Differentiation of the Psychegroup and Sociogroup," *Sociometry*, **10**, 1947, 71–79.

14. I devised a model for student inquiry oriented to self-knowledge. "Personal inquiry" is an educative variety of situational therapy. Chapter 6, *Education and the Human Quest*, Harper, 1960.

15. A potent kind of training in "human relations" (T-Groups) centers around the study of what agreements the group must have in order to survive, how the agreements can be reached, what roles different individuals present to the group, etc. The authoritative work in this field is Bradford, L. P., J. R. Gibb, and K. D. Benne. (Eds.) *T-Group Theory and Laboratory Method*, John Wiley and Sons, 1964.

16. Arendt, Hannah, *The Human Condition*, University of Chicago Press, 1958.

17. Work, according to Bion, is learned and is reality oriented, whereas emotionality attempts to evade work. Bion, W. R., *Experiences in Groups*, Basic Books, 1961.

18. Skinner, B. F., "The Science of Learning and the Art of Teaching," *Harvard Educational Review*, **25**, 1954, 86–97.

19. In "The Triumph of Achievement Over Inquiry in Education," *Elementary School Journal*, 1960, 190–197, I present the thesis that the teachers would like to get work done but supervise it as if it were labor. Very sad.

20. John Ginther and I found that teachers who follow the programmer's instructions to the letter have a terrible time with the class because there is no common purpose which justifies their trying to meet as a class. See Thelen, H. A. and John Ginther's chapter on Chicago in *Four Case Studies of Programmed Instruction*, Fund for the Advancement of Education, 1964, 41–64.

21. Steering the group on the basis of feedback from its processes is both intellectually challenging and fun. Two case studies are: "Training for Group Participation: the Laboratory Method," Chapter 5 in *Dynamics of Groups at Work*, University of Chicago Press, 1954; and "Teacher Preparation for the Future," in *Improving Instruction in Professional Education*, Association for Student Teaching, 1958, pp. 83–117.
22. The development of a "behavioral science rationale for education" is my continuing interest. In *Dynamics of Groups at Work*, University of Chicago Press, 1954, I discuss the group "realities" and in *Education and the Human Quest*, Harper, 1960, I speculatively create four educational models that seem to me to fit the facts.
23. In 1963 I tightened up the model and presented it in "Insights for Teaching from Interaction Theory, a chapter in *The Nature of Teaching*, University of Wisconsin, Milwaukee, 1963, pp. 19–32, a portion of which account is quoted here.

Chapter 12

Variations in Value Orientations as a Factor in Educational Planning

Florence Rockwood Kluckhohn

About the Author

Dr. Kluckhohn first encountered the Spanish Americans of the Southwest and the several Indian populations in Arizona and New Mexico in 1932, the year of her marriage to Clyde Kluckhohn.

It was mainly because of the great interest engendered in her by the Spanish Americans that she made the decision to become a social scientist. She posed for herself the question as to why it was, why it could be, that two peoples—quite different in many ways to be sure—could have lived juxtaposed for virtually one hundred years yet still be speaking, culturally that is, "past one another."

Upon making application to the graduate school of Radcliffe College and more specifically to the departments of sociology and anthropology at Harvard University, she made it clear that her intent was to make a study of New Mexico Spanish Americans the basis of her doctoral dissertation.

This research, which was begun in 1936 and has continued to some extent into the present, provided the initial basis for the development of Dr. Kluckhohn's theory of *Variations in Value Orientations* and the research instruments used in the cross-cultural testing of the theoretically postulated variations in value orientations.

The first systematic cross-cultural testing was not done until the years 1951–1952. At that time there had been inaugurated in the Social Relations Department of Harvard University a fairly large-scale project that came to be known as the "Values Project." Clyde Kluckhohn, with funds from a grant of the Rockefeller Foundation, developed the project program. Later it was directed by John M. Roberts and Evon Z. Vogt. The area of research was in New Mexico where five groups of people, most of them culturally distinct from each other, all lived within a forty-mile radius. Two of the groups in this area were the particular community of Spanish Americans Florence Kluckhohn had studied over time. Another was the group of Navaho Indians who had long been one of Clyde Kluckhohn's special research interests. The research on the value orientation theory was incorporated into the "Values Project," but was, as were

290

most of the project programs, an independent study. The results achieved by Florence Kluckhohn and her colleagues appear in the volume entitled *Variations in Value Orientations*.

Varied indeed have been the subsequent applications of the variations theory and testing method by both Dr. Kluckhohn and others in many areas of the world. A long-range study which has absorbed much of Dr. Kluckhohn's own time in recent years is a comparative study of "well and sick" families (meaning *emotionally* "well" and "sick"). In this study a primary aim has been the interrelating of the value orientations theory with sociological theories of social structure and psychological development theories.

The study of family systems has long been an interest of Dr. Kluckhohn's. So also has been the study of aspects of the American educational system. This interest is well illustrated in the chapter presented here that was a paper first formulated and shared with public school educators at the University of New Mexico.

As one might expect the knowledge of and interest in many cultures is reflected in the totality of Florence Kluckhohn's own personal way of life. One of her creations is a small but lovely Japanese garden. And all who know her take great delight in her ability to use her magnificently equipped kitchen to create a truly international cuisine.

Introduction to the Chapter

It may appear a little late in the conceptual material presented in Part I to get into some of the broader questions posed by Kluckhohn. However, an examination of the "givens of biological human nature and the universalities of social interaction" is perhaps an appropriate ending for the first part of the book.

Sanford pointed out that to say we are in favor of people developing as people is to express a value. Scientists always get a little edgy when some of their more philosophical brethren begin delving into the mists of value. Yet Kluckhohn points out that all societies face a limited number of common human problems and that, although the solutions to these problems may vary from society to society, some are preferred more than others. Preferred on what basis, asks Kluckhohn? She goes on to examine how societies have developed value assumptions related to man's innate nature, his relationship to nature, how time is managed, how space is managed, and how he relates to other men.

It is fairly obvious that each society has made decisions on preferences in each of these common human problems *but it is rare indeed for educational processes to encompass within students' learning experiences an awareness of these decisions.* Value or preference is the north star of living; without an orientation to one's own values and its relation to the values of one's culture, education becomes a meaningless crisscrossing of bits and pieces of knowledge.

Educational processes and the knowledge it hopes to transmit are value-laden operations in a society that regards values as absolute or nonexistent. Can we, as Kluckhohn suggests, develop a value guideline for educational curricula with greater degrees of awareness by educators and students? If so, here is a good place to start.

Variations in Value Orientations as a Factor in Educational Planning

Cultures and the values expressed in cultural traditions are in some ways the same the world over. In other ways cultures are also distinctly different—relatively speaking—in their basic values and in their ways of living. These conclusions are in no sense original or startling. The critical problem which emerges from these two conclusions is how to reconcile, understand, and use these differences in an institution such as a school, where curriculum practices and programs tend to reflect one value orientation system—one basic tradition. As Clyde Kluckhohn noted:

"There is a philosophy behind the way of life of each individual and of every relatively homogeneous group at any given point in their histories. This gives, with varying degrees of explicitness or implicitness, some sense of coherence or unity both in cognitive and affective dimensions. . . . The underlying principles arise out of, or are limited by, the givens of biological human nature and the universalities of social interaction. The specific formulation is ordinarily a cultural product (1)."

What Kluckhohn and others have come to regard as "cultural themes," "unconscious systems of meanings," "cultural configurations," or "core culture" (2) are the distinctive ways which groups of people have of viewing (1) the forces of nature, (2) the ordering of human relations, (3) the nature of the historical process and man's place in it, (4) the character of human nature. However, for one interested in reconciling the facts of universality and variability in human behavior, two failings exist in the earlier studies of this problem. First, no theoretical or methodological way is set forth that allows for a systematic comparison of one culture with another. Second, the theories do not adequately cope with variations within cultures and thereby have little impact on understanding social change or planning educational programs to fit such variability.

293

The theories and means of analysis that follow are directed toward finding possibilities for social change through educational programming within the school as an institution and within the society from which the values of the school receives its sanction and support.

The purpose of this discussion is to demonstrate the tremendous significance an understanding of the variations in cultural tradition has for programming in the field of education. It was a felt need to reconcile the facts of universality and relativity in cultures that led to the development of the theory of variations in value orientations. Let us examine in schematic form the classification of the value orientations and briefly explore of the ranges of variations for each.

THE CLASSIFICATION OF VALUE ORIENTATIONS

The theory of variations rests upon these major assumptions. First, it is assumed that *there are a limited number of common human problems for which all peoples at all times must find some solution.* This is one of the universal aspects of cultures, because the common human problems to be treated arise inevitably out of the human situation. The second assumption is: *Although there is variability in solutions of all the problems, it is neither limitless nor random but is variability within a range of possible solutions.* The third assumption, the one which provides the main key to the analysis of the variation in value orientations within cultures, is: *The alternatives of all solutions are present in all societies at all times but are differentially preferred.* In other words, every society has in addition to its dominant profile of value orientations, numerous *variant profiles,* some actually required, others permitted. Moreover, in both the dominant and the variant orientations, a *rank ordering* of the preferences of the value-orientation alternatives almost always exists. In societies undergoing change, the ordering of preferences will not be clear cut for some or even all the value orientations. In other words, great variation exists within cultures and is as important to the understanding of social process as is the fact of the differences between cultures.

Now the common human problems: from a study of culture history, philosophy, and the writings of social scientists, let us single out five such problems common to all human groups. These problems will serve as the beginning phase of the development of a theory of variability. They are stated here as questions: In each case there is a parenthetical designation of the name which hereafter will be used to designate the range of orientations relating to the question.

1. What is the character of innate human nature? (*human nature* orientation)
2. What is the relation of man to nature (and supernature)? (*man-nature* orientation)
3. What is the temporal focus of human life? (*time* orientation)
4. What is the modality of human activity? (*activity* orientation)
5. What is the modality of man's relationship to other men? (*relational* orientation)

A sixth common human problem necessary to the value orientation schema is that of man's conception of *space* and his place in it. Unfor-

Table 12.1 The Five Value Orientations and the Range of Variations
Postulated for Each*

Orientation	Postulated Range of Variation					
Human Nature	Evil		Neutral	Mixture of Good and Evil	Good	
	Mutable	Im-mutable	Mutable	Im-mutable	Mutable	Im-mutable
Man-nature	Subjugation-to-nature		Harmony-with-nature		Mastery-over-nature	
Time	Past		Present		Future	
Activity	Being		Being-in-becoming		Doing	
Relational	Lineality		Collaterality		Individualism	

* The arrangement in columns of sets of orientations is only the accidental result of this particular chart. Although statistically it may prove to be the case that some combinations of orientations will be found more often than others, the assumption is that all combinations are possible ones. For example, it may be found that the combination of *first-order* choices is that of Individualism, Future-*time*, Doing, and Mastery-over-Nature, as in the case of the dominant middle-class culture of the United States, or that it is, as in the case of the Navaho Indians, a combination of the first-order preferences of Collaterality, Present-*time*, Doing, and Harmony-with-Nature.

tunately, this problem and the range of variability in it have not been sufficiently worked out to be included at the present time.

The ranges of variability suggested as a testable conceptualization of the variation in the value orientations are given in Table 12.1.

Human Nature Orientation

To the question of what the innate goodness or badness of human nature is, there are the three quite logical divisions of evil, good and evil, and good. Yet some may argue that the category of good and evil is not one but two categories. There certainly is a significant difference between the view that human nature is simply neutral and the view of it as a mixture of the good and bad. Moreover, the subprinciples of mutability and immutability noted in the chart increase the basic three-fold classification to six possibilities. Human nature can, for example, be conceived to be evil and unalterable or evil and perfectible, as good and unalterable or good and corruptible, as an invariant mixture of good and evil or as a mixture subject to influence. Thus, one may rightly question the validity and usefulness of the three-way classification suggested for the range of this orientation. However, the three categories of evil, good, and good and evil do seem adequate as a first approximation for the analysis of major variations.

Let us illustrate some of these major variations from dominant middle-class American culture itself, around whose values so much of our educational planning has control. Few will disagree that the orientation Americans inherited from Puritan ancestors, which is still strong among many, is that of a basically evil-but-perfectible *human nature*. According to this view, constant control and discipline of the self are required if any real goodness is to be achieved, and the danger of regression is always present. This is portrayed in the words of a Pilgrim preacher, John Robinson:

"Surely there is in all children (tho not alike) a stubbernes and stoutnes of minde arising from naturall pride which must in the first place be broken and beaten down that so the foundation of their education being layd in humilitie and tractableness other virtues may in their time be built thereon. It is commendable in a horse that he be stout and stomackfull being never left to his own government, but always to have his rider on his back and his bit in his mouth, but who would have his child like his horse in his brutishness?" (3)

And it was another of America's Puritan forefathers who proclaimed that children are but limbs of Satan who must be beat into shape.

Some in the United States today, perhaps a growing number, incline to the view that *human nature* is a mixture of good and evil. These would say that although control and effort are certainly needed, lapses can be understood and need not always be severely condemned. Modern educational policies and child guidance programs have contributed greatly in mitigating the harshness of the Puritan orientation. But when we consider some of the attitudes expressed about the measures of controlling juvenile delinquents and criminals, we wonder how much change there really has been. A glaring beacon light of punitiveness so often shines through so many of them.

The definition of basic *human nature* being a mixture of good and evil would actually appear to be more common among the peoples of the world, both literate and nonliterate, than the one held to in the historical past of this country. Whether there are any total societies committed to the definition of *human nature* as immutably good is not as yet known and may even be doubted. Yet the position is a logically possible one, and it certainly is found as a variant position *within* societies.

Man-Nature (-Supernature) Orientation

The three point range of variation in the *man-nature* orientation—subjugation-to-nature, harmony-with-nature, and mastery-over-nature—is too well-known from the words of philosophers and culture historians to need very much explanation. A few illustrations will adequately demonstrate the differences between these conceptions.

The typical Spanish-American sheep herder, and sheep owner as well, in so short a past time period as fifteen years ago, believed firmly that there was nothing man could do to save or protect either land or flocks when damaging storms descended. They simply accepted storms, drought, and all other manifestations of natural forces as inevitable and unalterable. In many of these persons, as well as in many hosts of other cultures throughout the world, we find the same fatalistic attitude toward illness and death. "If it is the Lord's will that I die I die," is an expression so often heard.

Physicians, nurses, and other personnel in clinics and hospitals geared to American middle-class ideas of medicine become frustrated to an extreme when confronted with this fatalistic view. This is as true in areas of our own country, as it is in the so-called underdeveloped countries.

Quite another view of the *man-nature-supernature* relationship is that of harmony-with-nature. In areas where this conception is dominant, the belief is in a wholeness, a oneness, of man, nature, and supernature. The task of man, as conceived by peoples who stress this orientation, is that of striving ever to maintain the harmony. This orientation alternative is not strong in the United States generally, hence it is often little understood. We do find it in areas of the Orient, and it also prevails—or did prevail—in some groups in New Mexico. Traditionally, it was the first-order preference of the Navaho people. Navaho poetry and rituals alike richly express it.

The mastery-over-nature position is the dominant orientation of most middle-class Americans. Natural forces of all kinds are to be overcome and put to the use of human beings. Rivers everywhere are spanned with bridges; mountains have roads put through and around them; new lakes are built, sometimes in the heart of deserts; old lakes get partially filled in when additional land is needed for building sites, roads, or airports; the beliefs in man-made medical care for the control of illness and the lengthening of life is strong to an extreme; and all are told early in life that "the Lord helps those who help themselves." The view in general is that it is a part of man's duty to overcome obstacles; hence there is the great emphasis upon technology.

Time Orientation

The possible cultural interpretations of the temporal focus of human life break easily into the three-point range of past, present, and future. Far too little attention has been given to the full range of major variatons in the *time* orientation. Meaningful cultural differences have been lost sight of in the too generalized view that folk peoples have no time sense and no need of one, whereas urbanized and industrial peoples must have one. Whether days are regarded as sunrise-to-sundown wholes or as time units to be split into hours and minutes and whether or not a clock is deemed a useful culture object are not the critically important criteria for a consideration of the orientation to *time*.

Spengler had quite another order of fact in mind when, in his discussion of "time" in *The Decline of the West*, he made this emphatic statement: "It is by the meaning that it intuitively attaches to time that one culture is differentiated from another (4)." The relationship of Destiny to meanings of *time* is the core of Spengler's conception.

Obviously, every society must deal with all three *time* problems; all have their conceptions of the past, the present, and the future. Where they differ is in the preferential ordering of the alternative (rank-order emphasis), and a very great deal can be told about the particular society or part of a society being studied, and much can be predicted about the direction of change within it, if we know what the rank-order emphasis is.

Illustrations of the variations in temporal focus are also easily found. Anyone who has gone south of the border knows well what the first order *time* preference of many Mexicans is—present *time*. A majority of Mexicans pay little attention to what has gone on in the past and regard the future as both vague and unpredictable. One is often asked by Mexican friends, when making engagements with them; "Do you wish the meeting to be by Mexican or United States time?" If it is agreed that Mexican time is satisfactory the usual comment, made with a merry twinkle in the eyes is: "You know what that means, it could be two o'clock as stated, perhaps later, and quite probably not at all."

This strongly held present-time attitude is troublesome to those United States citizens who live by calendars and date books, ever pressing themselves into minute-by-minute time molds. But there are many in the world, both at home and abroad, who do not wish life to be such a wild rush and do not consider such a way of life to be sensible.

Historic China was a society that gave first-order value preferences to the past-*time* orientation. Ancestor worship and a strong family tradition were both expressions of this preference. So also was the Chinese attitude that nothing now ever happened in the present or would happen in the future; it had all happened before in the far distant past. The proud American who once thought he was showing some Chinese a steamboat for the first time was quickly put in his place by the remark, "Our ancestors had such a boat two thousand years ago."

Many modern European countries also have strong leanings to a past-*time* orientation. Even England—insofar as it has been dominated by an aristocracy and traditionalism—has shown this preference. Indeed, some of the chief differences between the peoples of the United States and England derive from their somewhat varying attitudes toward time. Americans have difficulty in understanding the respect the English have for tradition; the English do not appreciate the typical American's disregard for it.

Anglo-Americans, more strongly than most peoples of the world, place an emphasis upon the future—a future which is anticipated to be "bigger and better." This does not mean they have no regard for the past or no thought of the present. But it certainly is true that no current generation of Americans ever wants to be called "old-fashioned." The ways of the past are not considered good just because they are past, and truly dominant (that is, typical middle-class) Americans are seldom content with the present. This view results in a high evaluation of *change* providing the change does not threaten the existing value order—the American way of life. In speaking of change, we must always distinguish between change that is more of the same thing—that is, pattern elaboration—and basic change. Of this distinction more will be said later.

Activity Orientation

The modality of human *activity* is the fourth of the common human problems giving rise to a value-orientation system. The range of variation in solutions suggested for it is the threefold one of being, being-in-becoming, and doing.

In very large part this range of variation has been derived from the distinctions made long ago by philosophers between being and becoming. Also, the three-way distinction is to some degree similar to the classification of personality components that Charles Morris has developed in his book *Paths of Life* (5).

However, the accordances of the concepts here being suggested with those of the philosophers are far from complete. In the conceptual scheme of value orientations, the terms being and becoming, expanded to a three-point range of being, being-in-becoming, and doing, are much more narrowly defined than being and becoming are in philosophical treatises. Also, I hold to the view that the range of alternatives of the *activity* orientation varies independently from those of *man-nature*, *time*, and *human nature* orientations. The tendency of most philosophers has been to treat these several types of orientations as relatively undifferentiated clusters.

The *activity* orientation centers solely on the problem of the nature of man's mode of self-expression in activity. In the being alternative of the orientation the preferred kind of activity provides a spontaneous expression of what is conceived to be "given" in the human personality. As compared with either the being-in-becoming or the doing orientation, it is a nondevelopmental conception of *activity*. It might even be phrased as a spontaneous expression in *activity* of impulses and desires, yet care must be taken not to make this interpretation a too literal one. In no society, as Clyde Kluckhohn has commented, do we ever find a one-to-one relationship between the desired and the desirable. The *concrete behavior of individuals in complex situations and the moral codes governing that behavior usually reflect all the orientations simultaneously.* A stressing of the "isness" of the personality and a spontaneous expression of that "isness" are not pure license, as we can easily see by turning to a society or segments of a society in which the being orientation is the first order preference. Mexican culture illustrates well this preference in its widely ramified patterning of *fiesta* activities. Yet never in the *fiesta*, with its emphasis on spontaneity, is there pure impulse gratification. The value demands of other orientations make for codes that restrain the activities of individuals in very definite ways.

The being-in-becoming orientation shares with the being one a great concern with what the human being is rather than what he can accomplish, but here the similarity ends. The idea of development, so little stressed in the being orientation, is paramount in the being-in-becoming one. Erich Fromm's conception of "the spontaneous activity of the total integrated personality" is close to the being-in-becoming mode. He states: "By activity we do not mean doing something but rather the quality of the creative activity which can operate in one's emotional, intellectual and sensuous experiences and in one's will as well. One premise of this spontaneity is the acceptance of the total personality and the elimination of the split between reason and nature." (6) A less personally favorable view of this orientation and a more accurately limited statement for the theory being presented is: the being-in-becoming orientation emphasizes that kind of *activity* which has as its goal the development of all aspects of the self as an integrated whole. When the being-in-becoming alternative is heavily stressed, we often find an extensive development of intellectual and aesthetic activities.

The doing orientation is so characteristically the dominant one in American society that there is little need for a detailed discussion of it. Its most distinctive feature is a demand for the kind of activity which results in accomplishments that are measurable by standards conceived to be external to the acting individual. That aspect of self-judgment or judgment of others which relates to the nature of activity is based mainly upon a measurable accomplishment achieved by acting upon persons, things, or situations. What does the individual do, what can he or will he accomplish, are almost always the primary questions in the typical American's scale of appraisal of persons. "Getting things done" and "Let's *do* something about it" are stock American phrases.

Meeting standards of accomplishment and the desire to be judged as "normal" in the meeting of them are two important bases of both the marked anxiety found in many Americans and that compulsion toward rigid conformity that writers such as Riesman, Fromm, and Whyte decry. We all see evidences of this every day. For example, there is the case of the young Cambridge, Massachusetts, mother who was trying her valiant best to be a "good mother" in accord with the latest of the books on proper child rearing practices—the latest in this case being in the direction of "rigid permissiveness" as opposed to "rigid scheduling." She had read in one of the currently accepted books on child-rearing that it was "normal" for a child two to three years old to take crayons or pencils and write on the house walls. Imagine her dismay when she realized her own child of this age was not writing on the walls. What other conclusion could there be but that he was abnormal; so, to take care of this discrepancy in "proper" socialization, she taught him to write on the walls!

Relational Orientation

The last of the common human problems to be treated is the definition of man's relation to other men. This orientation has three subdivisions: The lineal, the collateral, and the individualistic.

Sociologists have long used various types of dichotomies to differentiate homogeneous folk societies from the more complex urban societies. The rural-urban distinction is the most familiar of these. Anthropologists, who have for the most part studied nonliterate or folk peoples, have frequently made much of the difference between lineage and a lateral extension of relationships in their analyses of kinship structure or social organization.

The distinctions made in the value orientation theory obviously owe much to the concepts used in both these fields but are not to be identified with those of either. The lineal, collateral, and individualistic *relational* alternatives are analytical concepts for the purpose of making fine distinctions both *within* and *between* systems rather than generalizing concepts for the specification of the gross differences between systems. All societies and all subgroups within societies utilize all three of the *relational* principles.

Individual autonomy is always found even in the most extreme types of folk societies. The like-mindedness and behavioral similarities of individuals in "homogeneous" groups have been overstressed. It is usually, if not always, the case that considerable leeway is permitted for "individuality" within the confines of the definitely fixed customs which folk cultures require for the ordering of human relationships. Individuality and individualism are both results of attention being given to the autonomy of the individual, but they are vastly different concepts, and significant nuances of meaning are lost when, as is so often the case, they are either confused or equated.

Collaterality also is found in all societies. The individual is not a human being except as he is a part of a social order, and one type of inevitable social grouping is that which results from laterally extended relationships. These are the more immediate relationships in time and space. Biologically, sibling relationships are the prototype of the collateral relationship.

In addition, all societies must take into account the fact that individuals are biologically and culturally related to each other through time. There is, in other words, always a lineal principle in relationships which is derived both from the biological givens of age and generational differences and from the fact of cultural continuity.

When the individualistic principle is dominant, individual goals have primacy over the goals of specific collateral or lineal groups. This in no sense means that there is license for the individual to pursue selfishly his own interests and in so doing disregard the interests of others. It means simply that each individual's responsibility to the total society and his place in it are defined in terms of goals (and roles) that are structured as *autonomous,* in the sense of being independent of particular lineal or collateral groupings. For example, the man who joins a business firm in the United States is expected, in pursuing his own goals of money-making and prestige, to be cooperative with other similarly oriented fellow workers and, in addition, is expected also to have a positive attitude toward the over-all goals (purposes) of the organization. Yet it is *not* expected that this man will remain in cooperation with particular workers or dedicated to the goals of the particular firm if he receives an offer from another firm which will increase his salary or prestige.

A dominant collateral orientation calls for a primacy of the goals and welfare of the laterally extended group. The group in this case is always moderately independent of other similar groups, and the problem of a well-regulated continuity of group relationships through time is not highly critical. The Navaho extended families and the loosely articulated combinations of these, which Clyde Kluckhohn called "outfits," are illustrations of such groups. Although the individual Navaho always has some autonomous roles and goals and also always has some roles and goals which relate to a wider system viewed as continuous in time, the roles and goals which have primacy for him are these which are *representative* of his extended household group or "outfit."

Another illustration of a dominant—a first-order collateral—emphasis is found in the Italian-American groups who settled in this country in the early part of this century.

When the lineal principle is dominant, group goals have primacy, but there is the additional factor that one of the most important of these group goals is continuity through time. Continuity of the group through time and *ordered positional succession* within the group are both crucial issues when lineality dominates the relational system. Although other patterns are possible, the most successful means of maintaining a lineal emphasis appear to be either those based squarely upon hereditary factors such as primogeniture or those assimilated into a kinship structure. For example, in England, where there has been a definite lineality in the aristocracy, there has also been an established pattern of moving successful members of the individualistically-oriented middle class into the peerage. By means of this and other related patterns, a fairly dominant lineality has been maintained in the whole society until fairly recently. In the Spanish-American villages of New Mexico, there also was a definite emphasis upon the lineal principle. The authority of a *patrón*, the dominance of the father figure, and the special role of eldest brothers (*hermanos mayores*) were all indications of the lineal emphasis.

A fact always to be held in mind in analyzing the effects of the variations in the *relational* orientation is that of the differences in training for independent as opposed to dependent behavior. And well may we ask—as many psychologists have—is there an optimum achievable in the independence-dependence scale?

In brief this is the classification scheme basic to the theory of variations in value orientations. Before discussing either testing methods or developments in the theory for the analysis of cultural change, two general points should again be stressed. First: *The theory assumes that in all societies some degree of preference exists for all the alternative positions of each orientation.* Where societies differ is in the rank ordering of preferences and not in an absolute preference for one alternative as opposed to others. Second: *Most patterns of concrete behavior are expressions of all the orientation rankings, not those of single orientations.* No ordering of a single value orientation has determinative effects upon any single area of social behavior such as family life, economic institutions, the religious beliefs and rituals, educational programs, or political life. Behavior in all these areas is to some degree a reflection of all the orientations that are considered a total system. To be sure, some orientations often loom larger than others in these various areas of behavior.

TESTING METHODS AND RESULTS ACHIEVED

Only brief mention can be made of the testing methods utilized to demonstrate the variations *between* cultures and also *within* cultures between groups such as schools or school districts. Even without rigorous testing and statistical techniques, it is possible to discover the value orientations of peoples by a study of their literature, history, ethnology, and by interview material. Indeed, in some ways the novelist and the dramatist are often better interpreters of human behavior than some social scientists. But there are virtues in the more rigorous and systematic techniques. Not the least of these is the matter of time consumed (and as has been noted, time is a precious commodity in American culture).

Testing instruments have been developed, and a main aim in developing them was to make them sufficiently applicable to societies or groups of all kinds so that quite intelligible and accurate translations could be made from one language to another. It has long been maintained that cross-cultural testing in the medium of language is seldom if ever successful. However, for the testing of value orientation preferences, this need not be the case. Thus far the results of using these instruments, still imperfect to be sure, in a fairly large number of cultures, both literate and nonliterate, would seem to substantiate this view (7).

An illustration of what can be done exists in the results of the testing of samples of five populations—three of these are in the State of New Mexico—a Navaho group, a Spanish-American village community, and an Anglo-American farming community. The others are samples from two sub-cultural groups in the Boston, Massachusetts, metropolitan area—Italian-Americans and Irish-Americans. Let us examine the charts giving the results for just one of the several kinds of analysis made. The signs utilized in presenting the data are explained before the charts. Then the presentation begins with a chart showing the postulated orientation orderings of middle-class American culture—the dominant culture of the United States. In each of the charts for the different cultures there appears, first, the orderings that the study of history, literature, and ethnological monographs led us to assume quite confidently were the orderings that each group held to *before* meeting the impact of dominant American culture; and second, the orderings yielded by our testing.

CHARTS ON SHIFTS IN VALUE ORIENTATION ORDERINGS FOR FIVE SUB-CULTURAL GROUPS

These charts are the result of a standard binomial analysis. Other techniques were used but are not here reported. (For these see *Variations in Value Orientations.*) The following two legends explain the symbols utilized in the charts to be presented.

Legend 1

The sign ">" means more than. A rank ordering found as coll > lin > ind means that collaterality is significantly preferred over both lineality and individualism, and that lineality is also significantly preferred over individualism. The sign "≥" means nonsignificantly more than. A rank ordering found as coll > lin ≥ ind means that collaterality is significantly preferred over both lineality and individualism, and lineality is nonsignificantly preferred over individualism.

The sign "=" means equally preferred. A rank ordering found as pres > fut = past means that present is significantly preferred over future, but that the ordering of future and past is equally preferred.

Where an asterisk occurs, as in ind ≥ lin ≥ coll,* the reading is that it is only individualism over collaterality that is significantly preferred.

Legend 2

"Lin"   —Lineality
"Coll"   —Collaterality
"Ind"   —Individualism
"Pres"   —Present
"Fut"   —Future
"Past"   —Past
"Over"   —Mastery-over-nature
"Subj"   —Subjugation-to-nature
"With"   —Harmony-with-nature
"BIB"   —Being-in-becoming
"Being"—Being
"Doing"—Doing

Chart I. Predicated Typical American Middle-Class Bank Orderings

Orientation	Rank Orderings
Relational	Ind > coll > lin
Time	Fut > pres > past
Man-nature	Over > subj > with
Activity	Doing > being > BIB

Cultural Variations in Three New Mexico Communities

Postulated original
rank orderings (before meeting
  dominant American culture)

Rank orderings
revealed by testing

Chart II

Navaho Indian Group		Navaho Indian Group	
Orientation	Rank Ordering	Orientation	Rank Ordering
Relational	Coll > lin > ind	Relational	Coll > lin ≥ ind
Time	Pres > past > fut	Time	Pres > past ≥ fut
Man nature	With > subj > over	Man-nature	With ≥ over ≥ subj*
Activity	Doing > being	Activity	Doing > being

Postulated original
rank orderings

Rank orderings
revealed by testing

Chart III

Spanish-American Village		Spanish-American Village	
Orientation	Rank ordering	Orientation	Rank Ordering
Relational	Lin > coll > ind	Relational	Ind ≥ lin ≥ coll*
Time	Pres > past > fut	Time	Pres > fut > past
Man-nature	Subj > with > over	Man-nature	Subj > over > with
Activity	Being > doing	Activity	Being > doing

Chart IV

Anglo-American		Anglo-American	
Farming community		Farming community	
Orientation	Rank Ordering	Orientation	Rank Ordering
Relational	Ind > coll > lin	Relational	Ind > coll > lin
Time	Fut > pres > past	Time	Fut ≥ pres > past
Man-nature	Over > subj > with	Man-nature	Over > with ≥ subj
Activity	Doing > being	Activity	Doing > being

Note: The Navaho, Spanish-American, and Anglo-American groups in the Southwest were tested on only two alternatives in the activity orientation— "being" and "doing," due to limitations of time.

Cultural Variations in Two Metropolitan Boston Massachusetts Communities

Postulated original
rank orderings

Rank orderings
revealed by testing

Chart V

Irish-Americans			Irish-Americans		
Orientation	Rank Ordering		Orientation	Rank Ordering	
Relational	Lin > coll > ind		Relational	Ind > coll > lin	
Time	Pres > past > fut		Time	Pres $\geq$ fut > past	
Man-nature	Sub- with > over		Man-nature	Over $\geq$ subj > with	
Activity	Being > BIB > doing		Activity	BIB > doing > being	

Chart VI

Italian-American			Italian-American		
Orientation	Rank Ordering		Orientation	Rank Ordering	
Relational	Coll > lin > ind		Relational	Coll $\geq$ lin $\geq$ ind*	
Time	Pres > past > fut		Time	Pres > fut > past	
Man-nature	Subj > with > over		Man-nature	Subj $\geq$ over $\geq$ with	
Activity	Being > BIB > doing		Activity	BIB > doing > being	

Even a cursory glance at the charts reveals four facts important in educational planning. First, not in any one of the four groups that, for want of a better term, we may call the non-Anglo ones, has there been any very marked change in overall orientation preferences from those originally held before they encountered the dominant conventions in middle class cultures. Second, the shifts and changes revealed are unevenly distributed among the orientations. Third, often a shift between a second and third order preference, not first order, is the most noticable. Fourth, a transition state, resulting from failure to make a clear-cut choice, is not infrequent.

Some people regard assimilation as a possible goal for education. Do the facts revealed by this analysis suggest that assimilation is necessarily a good goal or one that can be attained? The analysis makes clear that over long periods of time most groups hold to basic values, deeply imbedded in the unconscious. Assimilation involves changes in all areas of social life: in family patterns, religious observance, political behavior, economic orientation, and educational aspirations. Most of the people in the groups tested had had consistent contact with the dominant American culture over several generations.

In the face of these facts how valid is the melting pot ideology of the United States? If this ideology were one of a fine olio of variations with respect and admiration given to all ingredients as deserved, it might not be affected. However, by and large such has *not* been the case. In the main, the ideology has been one which demands a rapid adjustment to the so-called American "way of life" and one which also contains this refrain: Woe be unto those who are laggards in the process!

The analysis suggests the following hypotheses about the nature of change: first, the rate and degree of the assimilation of any group will depend in large part upon how well its original orientations fit in with those of the dominant culture; and second, shifts in second and third order preferences, as a beginning of the process, will be far less disruptive of both social and personality organization than will either attempted or forced shifts from a first to a third order preference. Differential shifts between orientations were also predicted.

APPLICATION TO EDUCATION

The theories of cultural balance and change of variations and the hypotheses generated from them have now been used by a number of persons in a number of contexts. For, as has been repeatedly stated, the understanding of this kind of variation is not confined to the area of education alone. In recent years the theory has been used for a study of the etiology of mental illness and emotional disturbance in variable family systems. Recently interest has turned more and more to the question of the meaning such variation has for American economic and political relations in foreign areas.

But how can any of these other interests be divorced from the field of education? They cannot, and knowing that the concern of this book is primarily with educational theory and practice, let us first turn to that field. It is a broad one indeed if one considers the programs it encompasses to be both national and international in scope.

Permit me to go back far in my own attempt to assess the problems involved in American efforts—extremely well meaning, even highly altruistic efforts when abstractly considered—to mold many different kinds of persons to fit the standard American model of a future time and achievement oriented individual. I did not really question the efficacy or even the rightness of such programs until I started to evaluate the effects of some of the programs developed in the Southwest for a variety of populations very different in basic values from Anglo-Americans of either the East or Middle West. But come to question the programs I certainly did. I questioned them for the Indian populations of New Mexico and Arizona. I questioned them also for the very large group of Spanish-Americans, most of whom until so very short a time ago were living in compact villages and living in accord with basic values very different from Anglo-American ones.

The great boon the United States offers—and offers in all good faith—is an education for the majority. In the Spanish and Mexican periods of New Mexico history none except a favored few ever expected such an opportunity. But did the programs as planned really offer an education that had much meaning to those receiving it? A curriculum of courses well adapted to communities of the East or Middle West was introduced, the only language to be used in that program was the English language. What my own experience of observation taught me was that rote learners were being produced—both customs and language were being learned by rote but were not being understood. In their own language they were left—for the most part—illiterate. The same kind of program has long been followed in many places all over the United States.

Let us focus on the scene in the eastern seaboard. Some years ago two colleagues of mine and I set out upon a study of the factors involved in the educational achievement and occupational aspirations (both clearly middle-class American goals) of a quite large sample of high school boys in ten quite diverse areas of the total area.

The usual variables—the ones so often cited—were taken into account by our methods. These were the social-class level; the occupational status of parents, fathers especially; the past educational achievements of both fathers and mothers; and some other considerations such as residence areas. And certainly the IQ scores were carefully considered. Much of the variance between the subjects in their academic performance and aspirations was seemingly attributable to a combination of these particular variables. But considerable unexplained variance still remained. Moreover, the question can be raised as to what lies behind the two most telling variables—father's occupational level and the boy's IQ. Is it variation in basic values? Interview material of a carefully selected sample of cases did reveal great differences. Subsequently tests for such variations were developed and administered to two of the large populations, the Italian-American and the Irish-American. The test results are shown in the charts presented earlier.

One case from the interview sample is particularly thought provoking. A young Italian-American lad, to whom we have given the name Bobby Rosselini, was a youngster of great charm who was never a problem pupil in any way, except that by typical American standards his levels of performance and aspiration in no way matched the potential of his fairly high IQ rating.

Why was he in the general high school course; why had he small thought of occupational achievement? Interviews with both Bobby and members of his family gave the picture quite clearly. The family was a large, happy, and well-knit one. But no one in the family had occupational aspirations beyond the holding of jobs that would provide what was deemed necessary from day to day. Moreover, staying together as a total family seemed the important issue. Two older brothers had married and moved as far as three miles away. They had borne this deprivation for only a short period. Both now live in apartments just around the corner from the family home.

The interview material is interesting indeed in showing the difference between the American middle-class values of the interviewer, and of the total project, and those of this family. Consistently the interviewer tried to keep the conversation on the subjects of school performance and occupational aspiration. Always the answers were polite but perfunctory, and then back the discussion went to ball games, music, and family life. When the eldest sister was asked how Bobby had progressed in grade school her reply was: "Oh, well enough I suppose, all the children did all right. The school seemed to like them all and always expected another Rosselini each year. It was not that the boys got especially good grades, for they never did. I think the teachers simply liked their big brown eyes." How do we discuss occupational achievement in typical American middle-class terms when confronted with this view of life?

This interview material was presented for examination to members of a committee in the Group for the Advancement of Psychiatry who had challenged Dr. Spiegel and me to produce evidence that there was such a thing as a "well" family. After two days the several psychiatrists sighed and said: "Yes, it is an emotionally well adjusted family, and would it not be wonderful if more were like it?" But not too long thereafter Dr. Spiegel related this same case to quite another group that included a high-achievement oriented scientist. This man became impatient to an extreme and finally exclaimed: "It is a dreadful case; such families should not be allowed. They are parasites on the body politic."

The only moral to this story is that persons reared in one cultural tradition almost always have negative evaluations of the behavior of those reared in other traditions. Cases like Bobby even greatly disturbed one of my colleagues engaged in the project. It was difficult for him to understand why any child with a high intelligence rating should not be preparing for college and looking ahead to success in the occupational world. I think I had some influence upon his attitudes (perhaps not too much) when I asked whether he really wished to cut the nation down the middle by IQ ratings. Were we not as a whole people to be allowed some choice? Equality of opportunity with which today we are all so gravely concerned is one thing; variations in choice of ways to live is quite another!

But let there be no mistaken impression that all Italian-American boys in our study were of the Bobby Rosselini type. Although the Italian-American group as a whole was low on the scale on all variables, there were Italian-American students in it who shone like stars. As a matter of fact, they out-distanced the group called old Yankee when all background variables were controlled—most especially that of father's occupation.

What all of this tells us is that great variation exists within groups as well as between groups. It also raises a question as to what may happen if value orientations are changed too rapidly. Willing change is one thing; enforced change, either witting or unwitting, is quite another.

In a paper entitled *The Role of Anthropology in Educational Planning* (8). Dr. Walter Taylor, an archaeologist who is chairman of the Department of Anthropology of the University of Southern Illinois, has made the following statement:

"It is an accepted adage that 'to compel change without understanding is nothing more than arrogance.' To insist on changing another person's way of life, merely because of an insular, unread belief in one's own viewpoint, is an act of tyranny. Therefore, since most educational planning tacitly, if not openly, assumes that changes ('for the better') will be made, to do so without first ascertaining the present state of education, as it relates to the total culture pattern, is to perpetrate an arrogant injustice and possibly to do great harm. Once again, what is obviously needed is an understanding of culture values and a studied assessment of the degree to which the present culture helps people to express those values and attain the goals which are inherent in them. Once these matters are understood, then a realistic judgment can be made as to whether or not the values, the educational system, or any other part of the culture needs modification or change."

The question raised in this most succinct statement was one of those raised in the project devoted to a comparative study of "well" and "disturbed" families. Although we never suggested that conflicts in value orientations—both those contained within cultural systems and those created by an assimilation process—would answer all the questions, we considered them to be of paramount importance. We stressed them the more because they have so often been omitted in studies concerned primarily with sociological and psychological processes.

Evidence gleaned after many years of work supports our assumptions. Many of the problems in disturbed families as well as in the disturbed personalities of children in such families are in some large part traceable to value orientation conflicts. The evidence from foreign areas, now mounting as the industrialization process becomes ever more rapid, also lends support to the assumptions.

Are there answers, especially for educators, to all these suggested questions? John Dewey long ago wisely commented that it is a vice of Americans that they assume that because simple questions can be asked simple answers can be found.

The problems raised in this analysis are highly complex. For them there are no simple answers. Instead they must be considered as a challenge! It may be possible, eventually, to so increase the understanding of value orientations variations that educational programs geared necessarily to a curriculum standardization can be expanded and elaborated to include at least some appreciation of both the need and worth of these value variations. However, the task is not and will not be an easy one. It is not only our educators who must themselves understand the significance for all of the variations. Many already do. The greater task is that of providing a milieu of understanding so that dominantly oriented *students* in a school do not heavily penalize their variantly oriented fellow students.

We as a people can so often be most adaptive and inventive because, basically, our good will toward, and concern for all, is very great. But we are now at a crossroad and must question whether good will and concern are enough and whether we should persist in using an unquestioned acceptance of the superiority of the American middle-class way of life as the measure of deserved reward and the value guide line for educational curricula.

The American middle-class way of life is not so nearly perfect that it cannot be improved. Moreover, it would not itself long survive were there not in the total American scene considerable variation from it. Even many educators—as compared to persons who engage themselves in business, industry or the practice of law—are in some ways variant in their basic values.

Nationally the issue is a critical one; internationally it is a crucial one. The United States today faces serious problems of many kinds in its relations with hundreds of groups of highly variable cultural traditions. Thus in conclusion I ask this question: Would not the nation be in a far stronger position had greater advantage been taken of the understanding of variation that its own great heritage of diversity so richly offers?

REFERENCES

1. Kluckhohn, Clyde. "Values and Value Orientations in the Theory of Action," in Talcott Parsons, Edward A. Shils, et al., *Toward A General Theory of Action*. Cambridge, Mass.: Harvard University Press, 1951, pp. 409–10.
2. See the works of Alfred L. Kroeber, Edward Sapir, Robert Redfield, Ruth Benedict, Margaret Mead, Clyde Kluckhohn, Ralph Linton, Gregory Bateson, Morris Opler, A. Irving Hallowell, and Laura Thompson.
3. Arthur W. Calhoun. *The Social History of the American Family*. New York: Barnes & Noble, 1945, Vol. 1, p. 112.
4. Spengler, Oswald. *The Decline of the West,* tr. by Charles F. Atkinson. New York: Alfred A. Knopf, 1926–1928, vol. 1, p. 130.
5. Morris, Charles. *Paths of Life,* New York: Harper and Row, 1942. See especially Chapter II.
6. Fromm, Erich. *Escape from Freedom,* New York: Rinehart and Co., 1941, pp. 258–259.
7. For those interested in both the testing method and the statistical techniques thus far utilized (others are now being developed) for the analysis of the data obtained, expositions can be found in the books and papers already cited by Florence R. Kluckhohn and collaborators.
8. From: *Developing Institutional Resources to Assist with Educational Planning* with particular focus upon *The Interdisciplinary Team Approach to Educational Planning*. An Interdisciplinary Team Study reported by Robert Jacobs, G. Carl Wiegand, and F. G. Macomber. Southern Illinois University, Carbondale, Illinois, October, 1963.)

Part Two

Introduction

In Part One each author seeks not only to stretch conceptual horizons
but also to herald a parade of new program possibilities, new ways
to reintegrate and reinvigorate the "old marriage" of education and
the behavioral sciences. "By their fruits ye shall know them" applies
to theories and research findings as well as deeds.

If Part One, with its focus on potentially productive conceptualizations, in some way "rang the changes" of possibility, it is our hope
that Part Two with its focus on the utilization and application of
research and experience will integrate "themes" worthy of public performance. In integrating feasible programs, the artistic and creative
sides of the scientist comes into play, especially in knowing what
to select from the realms of theory and research in order to blend
a meaningful, purposeful, and replicable program. The program devel-
oper must not only know and understand his resource ideas, he must
also have diagnosed a need, assessed an operational setting, and then
conceptualized a workable solution. Hardest of all, he must trim his
program ideas with "reality scissors" so it will fit a situation, a staff,
and a budget. Feasibility is one of his key watchwords.

The program ideas in Part Two not only stand in sequence and
as an application of Part One, but they also generate their own heuristic, creative contributions to education. The very act of designing
and utilizing an educational intervention often uncovers further unknowns that need research exploration and often also reveals technological gaps requiring methodological inventions and validation. Thus,
application not only generates new needs for research, it also unveils
new data and new phenomena that call for restretching or reshaping
of conceptualizations to match widening experience. In every sense,
the conceptualization and utilization processes that we have artificially dichotomized in this book are in continuous interaction with
each other.

Chapter 13

Innovating Classroom Practices to Support Achievement Motivation and Ego-Development

Ronald Lippitt, Robert Fox,
and Richard Schmuck

About the Authors

Ronald Lippitt spent the formative years of his growth striving to live up to the expectations created by his role as son of a school superintendent and competitor of a brilliant younger sib. One path of escape from the struggle with peer cultures and pressures of elders seemed to be to work with children. A B.S. in Group Work and Youth Guidance at Springfield College in 1936 was interrupted by an exciting year of adventure and stimulation in Geneva with Jean Piaget.

The guidance of mentor Harold Seashore at Springfield led to George Stoddard and Kurt Lewin at The University of Iowa Child Welfare Research Station. The four years of graduate work at Iowa included testing in baby clinics and mental institutions, teaching in a nursery school, judging baby contests, writing a syndicated column on raising children, and helping Kurt Lewin initiate the experimental study of "group dynamics" with a study of autocratic, democratic laissez-faire social climates in childrens' groups. An extracurricular sideline was a series of animal learning experiments on latent learning with Kenneth Spence and Gustav Bergman. Lippitt's next growth gradient was stimulated by a professorship in educational psychology and child development at Southern Illinois University in 1940 where he and his former wife Rosemary conducted a child guidance clinic, trained teachers for one-room rural schools, experimented with parent education and psychodramas, and helped found a consumers co-op and a chapter of the American Federation of Teachers.

Lippitt then went to the New York headquarters of the Boy Scouts of America where he was asked to develop a program of research on leadership and the educational process in scout troops. This extension of Lewinian research into the challenging arena of character education and merit badges was interrupted by World War II and an appointment in the Commissioned Corps of the U.S. Public Health Service where he became involved in two new fields—group therapy with bed-wetters in the Navy and operating a training program for OSS psychological warfare agents with the collaboration of such exciting colleagues as Ruth Benedict, Margaret Mead, Bingham Dai, Bob Chin, and the flashing knife of Colonel Fairbairn.

But temporary peace arrived, and after a tour of conducting staff training in Public Health installations, Ron joined Kurt Lewin and co-workers Cartwright, French, Festinger, and Radke in founding the Research Center for Group Dynamics at M.I.T. in 1945, and in launching the National Training Laboratory program at Bethel, Maine with Lee Bradford, Kenneth Benne, and Kurt Lewin in 1947.

In 1948, after Lewin's death, the band of M.I.T. Lewinians moved to the University of Michigan to join the Likertians of Survey Research Center in founding the Institute for Social Research where Lippitt's work focused on the socialization process in the community arena (delinquency studies), the classroom setting (peer culture influences on learning), and the family unit (interaction patterns and child development).

The final episode in this chronology starts in 1964 when Lippitt co-founded, with Floyd Mann, the Center for Research on Utilization of Scientific Knowledge as a third center in the Institute at Michigan. He is now immersed in a series of studies of the process of research retrieval, dissemination, and utilization aimed at improving family life, the functioning of school systems, and the youth development programs of the community. With his educator wife, Peggy, he is experimenting with "cross-age socialization," training older children to take a skilled role in rearing the younger ones. He rides his bicycle to work all four seasons in Ann Arbor, fly fishes when he can, and flexes a bow at a passing deer when crisp fall air activates childhood memories of such models as Robin Hood and Will Scarlett.

Robert S. Fox occupies an exciting and somewhat unique role in the field of education—his job includes responsibility for dealing with educational problems ranging from those of the three-year-old through elementary and secondary education, undergraduate teacher training, graduate preparation in curriculum and educational administration, and postdoctoral research. As Director of the University School, on the University of Michigan campus, Dr. Fox and his staff enjoy the opportunity to explore creative solutions to problems of curriculum and methods in the teaching of children and youth. As Professor of Education, he teaches courses in Curriculum Theory and Practice and the Elementary School Curriculum, and works with graduate students preparing to be school administrators and curriculum leaders. As Research Associate in the Center for Research on Utilization of Scientific Knowledge, a recently established unit within the University of Michigan's Institute for Social Research, Dr. Fox has been involved in a variety of studies having to do with the social climate of the classroom, exploring social power, relationship between social variables and learning, teacher-pupil interaction, and cross-age interaction in the school. A second major research interest has been in the process of innovation and change in education. The identification and diffusion of new teaching practices and factors involved in developing a school climate supportive of change have been specific foci. A third research involvement is in the development of curriculum materials for teaching behavioral sciences in elementary and secondary schools.

Starting as an elementary school teacher in California, Dr. Fox moved on to a position as Elementary Curriculum Coordinator and Curriculum Laboratory Services Coordinator in the San Diego County Schools. He has been at the University of Michigan since 1950.

Dick Schmuck majored in English literature with special interests in the reasons for human behavior and teaching the relationships between literature and psychology. After completing his B.A. and some practice teaching in high school English, he decided to delve more deeply into the motives of people and the teaching process, itself, by studying psychology. In 1959 he received an M.A. in Psychology from the University of Michigan.

Psychology seemed limited in its omission of group processes and social structure and so, for a time, Dick turned to sociology, anthropology, and social psychology and received his Ph.D. in 1962 in social psychology from the University of Michigan. He was fortunate to have Ronald Lippitt and Robert Fox as his primary tutors.

Since 1962 Dick has directed action research projects on the classroom group relations and learning at the Institute for Social Research of the University of Michigan. He has also served as an Assistant Professor of Psychology at the University of Michigan, teaching courses in group processes and socialization of the child. Most recently, Dick is Associate Professor of Educational Psychology at Temple University. Currently, at Temple University, Dick is teaching social psychology as it applies to group processes in the classroom and school. He is also developing action research in inner city schools in the city of Philadelphia.

Introduction to the Chapter

A major bridge of research utilization, between the conceptual side and the applied side of education is portrayed in this chapter through contribution from authors who are members of the nation's first University Center for Research on the Utilization of Scientific Knowledge. Lippitt, Fox, and Schmuck have demonstrated their processes in the utilization of some of the concepts discussed repeatedly in Part One. Out of a welter of many possibilities, they have selected the tasks of (1) enhancing the affective integration in the pupil of a positive feeling about himself and others and of (2) increasing the cognitive skills and coping mechanisms of the pupil.

The fascinating way that Lippitt and his colleagues sensitize and potentiate a teacher into a self-directed process of innovation and change by creating a "constructive interpersonal spiral" of teacher and pupil interaction becomes doubly exciting when considered in light of the conceptualizations advanced by Sanford, Taba, Tholen, Biber, and others in Part One. In the processes proposed by Lippitt, Biber's proposals of educational processes that create ego-strength are now applied throughout a peer group. A Taba-like analysis of learning sequences and of the dissonances that motivate would help us attain insights into this particular process of fostering achievement and ego-development. Certainly the groupwide study of feelings, impulses, reactions, and group codes as proposed would further the differentiations and symbolizations that Sanford suggests might help to guide and develop the imaginative powers of the child. As teacher satisfaction and creativity are nurtured, these teachers are being actualized on the job in much the same way that Wilhelms proposed for preservice training.

Innovating Classroom Practices to Support Achievement Motivation and Ego-Development

Utilizing the resources of the behavioral sciences to improve classroom teaching practices is an exciting challenge. At least four types of resources are available as are a variety of ways of using them: relevant research knowledge; concepts and conceptual frameworks; diagnostic tools and methods; and scientists themselves as consultants and collaborators.

These four types of resource can be mobilized to stimulate and support an improvement process in several ways. Such patterns of improvement can be roughly classified into two types. In one the needed resources of new knowledge and practice are "imported" into the classroom and the school system from outside. In the second type of pattern the needed knowledge and resources are developed and mobilized within the classroom itself and utilized to make desired improvements. Let us look briefly at examples of these two patterns.

"IMPORTING" THE NEEDED RESOURCES

Through reading or a course or a consultant, the teacher learns about research findings and theory. In order for the materials to be useful, the teacher must perceive the information as relevant to the teaching problems with which she is coping and must be able to derive from it realistic ideas about possible action. The process of making research findings meaningful to the person who teaches has been very poorly developed in the field of education, as contrasted to such more advanced fields of research utilization as agricultural practice, medical practice, and industrial practice. In another "importing" process new educational practices developed in one setting become visible, accessible, and are adopted or adapted by another teacher. This progress requires that innovations be identified by some scanning procedure, be evaluated to eliminate those not worthy of dissemination, and then be communicated in an appropriate way which makes it possible for other teachers to understand and to adapt a new practice in their own teaching situation. One of the tragedies of American education is that so many creative teaching practice inventions consistent with the best behavioral science knowledge remain invisible and unevaluated.

INTERNAL RESOURCE DEVELOPMENT

In the second pattern of improvement the teacher is helped to collect data about her own classroom situation, to interpret the findings as a diagnosis of needs and potentialities for change, and to derive designs for improvement from the diagnosis of her own classroom situation. In other words, instead of importing knowledge from outside, she is involved in creating knowledge and utilizing it for designing improvement in her practice. Typically, in this pattern, resources from outside are required to help in the process. These resources are either diagnostic tools, or a consulting scientist, or both.

The sections which follow contain the results of our experiences in using both of these patterns to help a group of elementary and secondary classroom teachers to stimulate achievement motivation and enhance the ego-development of pupils.

DIAGNOSING THE ACHIEVEMENT AND EGO-DEVELOPMENT NEEDS AND OPPORTUNITIES IN THE CLASSROOM

A pupil with high ego-strength can be characterized in two general ways. First, he has developed cognitive skills and intellectual coping mechanisms through successful classroom learning experiences. Such a pupil has mastered, without an overload of anxiety, most of the academic challenges presented to him. He is able to utilize effectively his intellectual capacities. When a child is not utilizing his academic potential in classroom performance, it is a poor situation for ego-development. In many such cases, energy is being drained off by excessive anxiety, worry, and hostile feelings, so that the pupil is not free to utilize his abilities. He is blocked or distracted or focusing on solving other types of problems.

A second characteristic of ego-strength is affective integration. Such a pupil has positive feelings about himself and others, emanating from personal feelings of strength and worthwhileness. He feels only moderate tension when relating with peers and teachers in the school

setting and perceives the significant people in his life as being supportive and encouraging of his school performance and conduct.

These two aspects of ego-strength, the cognitive and the affective,
are interrelated. For instance, if a pupil experiences anxiety in his
relations with peers and teachers, we find that much of his attention
and energy will be directed toward coping with fears and reducing
tension. Such pupils often have negative feelings about themselves
and perform more poorly in their school work than their intelligence
levels indicate they are capable of. On the other hand, pupils who
experience acceptance and support from peers and teachers often
approach academic tasks with the same mobilization of energy, effort,
and expectations of adequacy and success they have experienced in
these relationships. Such pupils' positive views of themselves facilitate
their academic learning and the development of cognitive skills.

Considerable classroom research indicates that a pupil's interpersonal relationships condition the development of these two facets of
ego-strength. Specifically, the research indicates that pupils who relate
successfully to their peers and who feel relaxed and comfortable in
the presence of teachers, are more likely to utilize their intellectual
and emotional resources in building a strong ego. Furthermore, our
research suggests that we can identify, explain, and create classroom
groups with atmospheres conducive to ego-building. Teachers will be
able neither to influence their pupils constructively nor to teach them
academic subject matter without considering the classroom processes
that offer opportunity for ego-development and enhancement. Since
such problems and issues of interpersonal relations in the classroom
are basic to ego-development, a teacher needs to master a style of
approaching and solving these problems. One purpose of this chapter
is to illustrate ways of approaching such a challenge.

First, the teacher must work toward understanding the network
of interpersonal relationships in her classroom. Children attribute to
each of their classmates levels of social power or ability to influence
others which vary from very high to very low. Moreover, being able
to do things well at school and being liked often constitute important
sources of social power. Pupils assess the status of their classmates
on these variables quickly at the beginning of the school year, and
they maintain their judgments with relatively little variation throughout the school year.

However, even though pupils show considerable agreement when
rating their peers on liking, influence, and expertness, classroom groups
do differ considerably one from the other on how much consensus
there is about these dimensions. In some classrooms, for instance,

interpersonal acceptance and rejection are narrowly focused. Such classrooms are characterized by a large number of pupils who agree in giving high status and acceptance to only a small cluster of their classmates on a sociometric test. Along with this narrow focus on a small number of pupils, many other pupils are neglected entirely. On the other hand, some classrooms are characterized by a wide range of positive and negative choices, that is, little or no focus of interpersonal acceptance and rejection upon a few members. Such groups are distinguished by a more equal distribution of sociometric choices, by no district subgroups whose members receive the large proportion of preferences, and by few entirely neglected pupils.

Our research shows that classroom peer groups characterized by a wide spread of liking relations among members have positive emotional climates and that both peer group liking structure and pupil involvement in the classroom group help to fashion a pupil's perception of himself in the group. Furthermore, the research shows that this pupil evaluation of self in relation to others is associated with his attitudes toward self and school in general and that a pupil's perception of his place in the peer group, high status or low, is related also to his utilization of his ability in academic learning.

Therefore, the teacher who hopes to enhance both the cognitive skills and the affective integration of his pupils will want to learn more about the interpersonal relationships in his classroom. He will ask such questions as: Can a rejected pupil be helped to develop skills of relating to his classmates so that he will be more accepted; so that he will be listened to when he has an idea to contribute; so that he will be given support rather than negative feedback? Can the intellectual capabilities of a bright child with low social power be channeled in such a way as to be seen by his peers as resources for the group?

Besides being interested in the problems of individual pupils, the teacher who is attempting to enhance the ego-strength of his pupils looks for ways in which the general atmosphere of the classroom can become more supportive of wholesome group interaction and learning. Can pupils be taught to seek out the resources of their classmates, to be sensitive to the needs of others who may be less well-endowed than they, and to understand the effects of their own behavior on others. If the classroom atmosphere takes on some of these characteristics, it becomes a supportive setting for ego-development of all pupils.

The teacher's first step in trying to enhance pupil ego-strength through improving interpersonal relations in the classroom involves sensitivity to the dynamics of pupil behavior. The sensitive teacher learns to become objective and analytic in observing pupil behavior in the classroom and on the playground. He perceives clues of pupil aggression, underlying hostility, and negative attitudes toward academic work. He is aware of the friendship patterns in the classroom, the cliques that are influencing pupil activity, and the feelings of ostracized pupils. Perhaps he perceives that although his pupils are controlled and orderly in his presence, they are uncontrolled and disorganized in the gym and on the playground. In any case, the astute teacher is diagnostic, always attending, as best he can, to the dynamics of pupil behavior and classroom interaction. He knows that careful observations of pupil behavior are necessary for the planning of constructive classroom change.

A teacher often finds simple diagnostic tools helpful in getting an accurate picture of a pupil's level of ego-strength, his feelings, attitudes, interpersonal relations, and academic performance. In other words, she seeks to assess the state of affairs in her classroom by having the pupils answer questions, write down their ideas, and express their feelings. Thus, she supplements the general research knowledge gathered in the study of other classrooms. Teachers have found it helpful to use such objective diagnostic inventories as, sociometric tests, attitude questionnaires, self-ratings, and achievement tests. During this diagnosis, the teacher asks: "What is it I wish to know?" Considering the answer to this question, the teacher may employ diagnostic tools similar to the following examples.

Affective Ego-strength

Questionnaires are used often to give the teacher information concerning a pupil's emotional or affective valuations of himself. There are several types of inventories for assessing self-feelings, including the attitude survey, the sentence completion test, and the so-called "pie technique."

An example of an attitude survey item regarding personal work habits is:

How hard would you say that you are working on school work. (Circle one)
A. Very hard
B. Pretty hard
C. Not very hard
D. Not hard at all
A sentence completion item of the same general character is:
When I am doing school work, I feel _____.
Or, in measuring different aspects of feelings about self:

I like myself sometimes because _____.

When I think about other boys and girls and then think about myself, I feel _____.

The "pie technique" has been used as follows:

The plus stands for aspects about yourself that you like, the minuses for things you don't like. Place a check under the circle that stands for how you are usually.

Cognitive Ego-strength

The teacher can assess the relationship between a child's classroom performance and his intelligence and in so doing, get one indication of his cognitive ego-strength. One procedure for doing this is as follows: the teacher first ranks all students according to their academic performance in her class. Then, she independently ranks them in order of their I.Q. score or some other measure of intelligence. The difference between positions on these rankings gives some indication of the child's utilization of intellectual potential. If a pupil ranks higher on intelligence than on achievement, he may be said to be underutilizing. If a pupil ranks higher on achievement than on intelligence, he is said to be more fully utilizing. If the class is made up of many underutilizers, the teacher should focus on improving the interpersonal atmosphere—at least as far as these underutilizers are concerned.

CLASSROOM SOCIAL RELATIONS

Sociometric questions are designed to give the teacher some indication of the social relationship among pupils in the class. He may ask pupils to select what peers they (1) like best, (2) like to work with, (3) like to play with, (4) think are smartest, (5) think like them about school, (6) like least, and so forth. In this manner, the teacher can see which pupils are friendly with one another and which are likely to make compatible work partners. In addition to getting information for grouping, she can sum and rank individual choices to find out who the peer leaders are, whether or not there are cliques, and what the general evaluation patterns are.

The major purpose of collecting such diagnostic information is to gain "leverage for thinking" creatively about the needs and potentialities of the unique teaching-learning situation of this particular classroom group.

MOVING FROM DIAGNOSIS TO ACTION

Using diagnostic information and interpretations to design a program of teaching action is a matter of disciplined professional skill. Actually the process of adopting or developing innovation in teaching practice is quite different from that in such professional fields as industry, medicine, and agriculture. A major difference is that the development or adopting of a new practice in teaching activity usually requires some re-orientation of values and attitudes as well as of behavioral skills. Such consideration of values and attitudes is not necessary in fields where the adoption of a new machine or a new fertilizer or new drug exerts no new requirements of value confrontation and skill development. Let us consider some illustrations of how a teacher can move from diagnosis to action in the classroom.

COPING WITH A COLLUSION OF IGNORANCE

A junior high teacher discovered from an analysis of his questionnaire data that the majority of the students in the classroom perceived that most of their fellow students looked down on enthusiastic participation in classroom discussion and the energetic accomplishment of homework assignments. The same questionnaire data indicated that a majority of the students would like to be more actively involved in classroom discussion and interaction with the teacher but perceived that their fellow students would be negative about this. As he reviewed these data, the teacher decided to share the information with the classroom group as a basis for discussion and mutual enlightenment as long as confidentiality was respected in the presentation of the data. He recognized, however, that their might be some embarrassment and resistance in getting into discussion. Therefore, he decided to consult with three or four of the class leaders about presenting the information and getting their collaboration in helping lead the discussion. He found them very interested in the data, ready to accept it as valid, and ready to help lead a discussion which would move the group toward a norm of enlightened participation rather than collusive withholding. With the leadership of the influential peers, the class discussion was interested, active, and enlightening. As a consequence, there were significant shifts in the pattern of group participation.

PASSIVE YOUNG LEARNERS

A second-grade teacher found that test data confirmed her observations that a significant portion of young learners who had a different racial and economic background from the majority of the class were uninterested in their work on the skills of reading. They were not openly rebellious but passive, distractable, and inattentive in the necessary drill work. The teacher and a consulting scientist discussed the data and decided that slightly older peers of the same race and background might be successful supporters and motivators of school work and might also impress upon the second grades the significance of putting energy into learning activity. With the help of the consultant, a program was designed utilizing volunteer sixth graders as teaching aides in the second grade. The sixth graders had a short seminar period each week on the techniques of being helpful. The response of the young learners was remarkable. They began to have fun working with the older peers, accepted their values about the importance of improving their achievement in reading, and began to relate more effectively to their teacher in other activities. The older peers also showed a significant upsurge in achievement motivation and in openness of collaboration with adults.

ANTI-LEARNING LEADERSHIP

From her diagnostic data collection, a fifth-grade teacher discovered that several of her high status figures in the classroom social structure were anti-schoolwork and anti-teacher in their orientation. It was clear that other members of the group were strongly influenced by this orientation. The teacher rejected several immediate derivations, such as the idea that she should try to downgrade such leadership status by direct confrontation which would have led her into a competitive struggle for leadership. After exploring a number of alternatives, she developed the plan of a classroom steering committee. She initiated the procedure by inviting four top status pupils, two of them pro-school and two anti-school, to meet with her for lunch to discuss the steering committee idea and to plan how it might work. This resulted in a classroom discussion led by the steering committee in which the question for discussion was "If a visitor came from Mars and knew nothing about classrooms and how they work, what might he see that would indicate whether we were or were not having a good day in this classroom?" Two large sheets of paper were put up in the front of the room and the steering committee recorded positive items on one and negative items on the other. Then each day one of the steering committee members served as observer and had the last few minutes of the day to state his observations on the positive and the negative list presented that day. At the end of the week, the steering committee led a discussion evaluating their week, making any revisions in the two lists, and projecting objectives for the next week. Every two weeks the steering committee rotated. Two types of things happened. Several of the negative high status figures changed their attitudes as it became clear to them what was sanctioned as desirable behavior by the classroom group. One or two of the negative high status leaders persisted in their original orientation and lost status with their peers as public group norms emerged providing a basis for peers supporting and sanctioning each other's participation in classroom activities.

In all three of these problem-solving activities, the teacher went through several steps in the problem solving process. First of all she "brainstormed" by herself or with the help of others the possible implications of her findings and some of the alternative possibilities for action. Then there was a period of thinking out the consequences and potential "side effects" of the various courses of action. This was followed by the tentative decision to develop a particular line of action. Then she planned the line of action in detail and rehearsed her new pattern of performance. In all cases, the teacher also secured feedback from the pupils or students of response to the new classroom activity and attempted to guide and improve teaching performance in terms of an analysis of these responses.

It is time now to review some of the elements and conditions necessary for successful improvement of professional practice in the classroom. A desire to experiment is certainly important, but much creativity and enthusiasm has been lost because the professional discipline involved in the improvement of teaching practice has been ignored or neglected.

CONDITIONS FOR SUCCESSFUL CLASSROOM IMPROVEMENT ACTIONS

The creative efforts of classroom teachers to devise ways of building ego-strength in their pupils can become a major channel for improving classroom practice. However, although teachers have been exhorted to rise to their responsibilities as the key figures in effecting change in the learning environment, they are thwarted by rigid schedules, imposed curricula, lack of administrative support for changes that threaten the status quo, peer standards that discourage the seeking of advice from colleagues, lack of consultation resources, and the personal insecurity that effort to change accustomed procedures brings to the innovator. What are some of the conditions necessary to enable the teacher who has developed a plan of action such as those described in the preceding paragraphs to be successful in carrying it through the stages of initial trial, revision, further development, and evaluation? What contribution can the behavioral sciences make to the facilitation of the teacher's efforts?

Let us first look at the teacher, himself. Change in the classroom is most likely to occur if the teacher (1) is sensitive to the dynamics of the teacher-learning situation, (2) is concerned about this particular problem of building ego-strength in his pupils, (3) has some understanding of the forces which affect the development of ego-strength in children, (4) has access to resources and ideas that could be useful in bringing about change, (5) possesses the skills and tools for diagnosing the actual state of affairs within his classroom, (6) develops a strategy for altering the situation, (7) is supported by the principal and by colleagues in trying out the change plan, and (8) has professional consultation and training help available as needed, (9) has some means for evaluating the effectiveness of the change.

In exploring ways of providing for some of these conditions the University of Michigan projects have utilized a variety of techniques and procedures. For one thing, teachers have been given opportunity to experience and to examine some of the forces operating in group life and to become thoughtful about some of their own strengths and shortcomings. A technique used for this sensitivity training was the training group or "T-Group." Over a period of six weeks, within a summer workshop program, the teacher-participants came together for a series of two-hour sessions in which no agenda was provided and no leadership or rules of operation imposed. A staff member designated as "trainer" assisted the participants in focusing from time to time upon the interpersonal processes that occurred while the group engaged in interaction. It was possible to examine such aspects of group behavior as the development of group norms, friendships and influencing relationships, patterns of communication, relationships to authority and leadership, and giving and receiving feedback about the effects of our own behavior. The relevance and contribution of emotionality in group relations was also explored. These and other learnings, brought about through the opportunity to watch their own group behavior and then interpret it with the help of a skilled trainer, caused the participants to value the T-group highly among the workshop activities. They also found many occasions to explore the relevance of these new insights to pupil interaction in the classroom or to staff relationships within the school building.

Another in-service education technique was to assist teachers in learning and applying some of the concepts involving improvement of pupils' ego-strength that were described in the initial sections of this chapter.

A promising way to assist teachers in deciding upon appropriate targets for change in the classroom situation has been to help the teacher gain more information about the state of affairs in his classroom. We have seen how the teacher can learn through the use of diagnostic tools about the current peer standards toward academic work or toward the appropriateness of helping classmates. The teacher can discover the kind of sociometric structure that exists, and can find out something of the forces from the pupil's life space or about his own self-concept. These data may give specificity to "hunches" the teacher has already had, or they may come as something of a shock. Whichever it is, the greater knowledge the teacher has about the conditions in his classroom, the better position he is in to develop an effective plan for change.

The involvement of others in the teacher's plan of action also appears to be of great significance. In some situations it was found that change efforts of teachers were best supported by teacher-administrator "change-agent" teams. In these cases, teachers who had been particularly innovative in improving their classroom practices and who were seen by other teachers as influential in the faculty power structure served with the building principal in planning ways for encouraging other teachers to consider some of the newer practices and for providing support for those who were attempting changes in their own classrooms.

Cross-building or cross-school system clinics of teachers engaged in similar types of change efforts have also proved effective. In many cases where the faculty peer standard within the school building has hampered free communication about classroom practices, teachers welcomed the opportunity to discuss plans for change and to get help on some of the obstacles faced by meeting with teachers from a distance.

Teachers have drawn upon another resource to help them bring about change—the pupils themselves. Pupil collaboration during a "try-out" phase can serve not only to build support and understanding of the change among those affected, but can also provide the teacher with useful feedback. Often the best information about the success of a plan, or about its shortcomings, can come from the pupils. Specific scales have been developed to help teachers get reaction from pupils.

It seems clear that creating the conditions for the continuous improvement of the quality of education and the development of social inventions in teaching practice is a mutual responsibility of school administrators, colleagues, the teacher herself, and also the students and their parents. The individual teacher, by herself, cannot be expected to utilize behavioral science resources creatively in an optimal way as she carries out her mission of high quality educational experience for children.

But we are very optimistic about the potentialities for the improvement of the educational experience because we have found administrators, teachers, and children usually open and eager to collaborate when they are helped to perceive new images of potentiality. Colleagues are hungry to achieve a deeper meaning from and a broader perspective on their teaching function and are ready to provide emotional support to each other. Moreover, children are ready to be invited to share in the responsibility for the adventure of learning if they are authentically and skillfully invited to do so.

The greatest stimulus to ego-development and the support of the motivation to achieve a high quality of learning activity derives from the sense of being invited into a meaningful classroom partnership. The gap between the generations must be coped with creatively in the classroom. To the degree that the adult teacher is ready to invite, listen to, and respond sensitively to the needs and influence attempts of her pupils, to that degree the child learners will be open and ready to receive and utilize the teaching efforts (that is, influence attempts) of the teacher. This respect and acceptance from the teacher is a basic ingredient of ego-development and motivation to learn. And motivating the pupils to learn is basic in the teacher's motivation to improve her teaching performance. The response of the learners is the greatest support for innovative teaching. The sharing by the teacher of power and responsibility for classroom management and learning activity is the greatest support for ego-development and motivation to learn. The growing resources of the behavioral sciences can now provide a school system, building faculty, classroom teacher, or classroom group with significant help in guiding and designing efficient group-learning experiences and effective personal growth opportunities. The challenge is to learn how to use these resources to achieve the big goal—helping children learn and grow.

REFERENCES

Barakat, Halim K. *Alienation from the School System: Its Dynamics and Structure*. Ph.D. Thesis. Ann Arbor: University of Michigan, 1966.

Chesler, Mark, Richard A. Schmuck, and Ronald O. Lippitt. "The Principal's Role in Facilitating Innovation." *Theory into Practice*, 2, No. 5, Dec. 1963, 269–277.

Chesler, Mark, Robert S. Fox, Ronald O. Lippitt, et al. (Eds.) *The Innovation and Sharing of Teaching Practices: A Study of Professional Roles and Social Structures in Schools*. Final Report to the Office of Education, #OE 5-10-241. Ann Arbor: The Institute for Social Research (in preparation).

Dennerll, Donald, and Mark Chesler. "Where Do New Teaching Practices Come From? . . . and Where Do They Go?" *Michigan Elementary Principal*, 39, No. 2, Nov.–Dec. 1964.

Fox, Robert S., Margaret B. Luszki, and Richard A. Schmuck. *Diagnosing Classroom Learning Environments*. Chicago: Science Research Associates, Inc., 1966. (Teacher Resource Booklets on Classroom Social Relations and Learning)

Fox, Robert S. "In-Service Education for Innovation and Change." Paper presented to the Conference on Educational Change, Sponsored by the Illinois Demonstration Project for Gifted Youth, University of Illinois, Urbana. Feb. 28—March 2, 1966.

Fox, Robert S., Ronald O. Lippitt, and Richard A. Schmuck. *Pupil-Teacher Adjustment and Mutual Adaptation in Creating Classroom Learning Environments*. (mimeo)

Fox, Robert, Ronald O. Lippitt, and associates, eds. *Developing Methods to Support the Creation and Spread of Innovative Teaching Practices*. Final Report to the Office of Education, #OE 4-10-197. Ann Arbor: The Institute for Social Research (in preparation).

Jung, Charles, and Ronald O. Lippitt. "The Study of Change as a Concept—in Research Utilization." *Theory into Practice*, 1, No. 1, Feb. 1966, 25–29.

Lippitt, Ronald O. "Processes of Curriculum Change." Robert R. Leeper, ed. *Curriculum Change: Direction and Process*. Washington, D.C.: Association for Supervision and Curriculum Development, NEA, 1966, 43–59.

Lippitt, Ronald O. "The Use of Social Research to Improve Social Practice." *American Journal of Orthopsychiatry*, 35, No. 4, July 1965.

Schmuck, Richard A., Mark Chesler, and Ronald O. Lippitt. *Problem Solving to Improve Classroom Learning*. Chicago: Science Research Associates, Inc., 1966. (Teacher Resource Booklets on Classroom Social Relations and Learning)

Chapter 14

The Re-education of Emotionally Disturbed Children

Nicholas Hobbs

About the Author

Nicholas Hobbs has been chairman of the Division of Human Development at Peabody College in Nashville, Tennessee, since 1951. He received an A.B. from the Citadel in 1936 and an M.A. in 1938. Completion of his Ph.D. at Ohio State was interrupted by five years' service in the Air Force during World War II. Hobbs received his doctorate in 1946 and went to Columbia University Teachers College to teach clinical psychology. From 1950 to 1951, he was chairman of the Psychology Department at Louisiana State University.

Nicholas Hobbs has chosen to work in the South, with children, at a teachers college, with amiable, competent, and concerned colleagues, in a setting where psychologists and educators can work together to invent new institutional forms for furthering research, training, and service. One outcome of this shared purpose and endeavor is Project Re-ED, here reported. Another is the John F. Kennedy Center for Research on Education and Human Development, which Hobbs directs.

Dr. Hobbs has served on the 1955 Joint Commission on Mental Illness & Health, the executive board of the Joint Commission on Mental Health of Children, The NIMH Special Mental Health Review Committee, the National Institute of Child Health & Human Development Advisory Council and has served as President of the American Psychological Association. When he returns from the Center for the Advanced Study in the Behavioral Sciences in Stanford, California in June, 1967, he will become Provost of Vanderbilt University and will continue as Director of the Kennedy Center at Peabody.

Introduction to the Chapter

Our relationship to the mentally ill and socially incompetent has, according to Hobbs, gone through two major revolutions and is now in its third. The first, associated with Pinel in France, Tuke in England, and Rush and Dorothea Lynde Dix in America, brought the insane into the human family and suggested that they should be treated as such. The second followed Freud's discoveries about the nature of personality, the unconscious, and the potential wars between id, ego, and superego. The third revolution, a deep running change, is the second significant river discussed by Bower in Chapter 1. As Hobbs sees it, the "concepts of public health *have finally penetrated the field of mental health.*"[1]

What does this revolution mean? Some of this is discussed in Chapter 1. We will need to know more about man's humanizing institutions and how professional persons can help such institutions be more effective rather than concentrate on helping individuals after we find they cannot function in these institutions. It will require a greater focus on prevention, on the early problems of children, on ways of enhancing the growth and development of all children, and on training of manpower in education and behavioral sciences in public health methodology and thinking.

Hobbs discusses all this in relation to his Project Re-ED, a significant bridge and innovation between concept and practice. It tests Hartmann's theories about independent ego-energies being available for growth and learning, despite conflict and problems, in a practical and research demonstration framework. The project hopes to train a special kind of teacher-counselor who can work with young disturbed children in a boarding school and provide a full day of living experience for each child. The program employs learning as a mental health goal and attempts to teach children the skills, knowledge, and attitudes needed for individual and social competency directly. The program is developed and planned to take advantage of the strength building possibilities in the school and to enhance the system of care and learning so that staff and students can experience a succession of enjoyable and productive days.

One of the high roads to the frontiers of educational practice is to question the basic assumptions of the "status quo," to trade them in for new premises, and to start afresh at solving a problem. Hobbs and his colleagues at the George Peabody College For Teachers have followed this high road in their search for new ways to help children with difficult learning and living problems. They have questioned some of the traditional assumptions of child treatment practices, not in

---

[1] Hobbs, Nicholas, Mental Health's Third Revolution. *American J. Ortho.*, **34**, Oct. 1964, 823.

an iconoclastic manner, but as a springboard to new discovery. They make no claim to have supplanted the old but are searching to supplement our armamentarium of child psychiatric practice with "an experiential approach" that can meet the test of being replicable, economical, and effective.

Hobbs' program departs from the usual psychiatric goals of insight development, regression as a therapeutic tactic, and the interpretation of transference. He intentionally eschews the processes of reorganizing the personality and restructuring the character for more pragmatic goals. He chooses to treat symptoms and to reinforce whatever positive behaviors he can find in children whose orientation is primarily negative.

This particular span of our mythical bridge between concept and practice is a significant combination of new materials from ego-psychology, education, and child development synthesized into a new program conception. It utilizes such conceptualizations as Hartmann's theory of the conflict-free spheres of the ego as discussed by Bower and Biber in Part One. It uses direct, positive learning experiences to teach the skills, knowledge, and attitudes needed for individual and social competency. It blends many of the ideas presented in previous sections of the book into a significant new program for difficult children. It may well prove to be a turning point in meeting the needs of our nation's growing load of children and youth with learning and emotional problems.

The Re-education of Emotionally
Disturbed Children

THE PROBLEM OF DISTURBED CHILDREN

Our nationwide lack of services for emotionally disturbed children is a puzzling phenomenon. We have widespread acceptance of the idea that early intervention can prevent development of intractable disorders; yet we do not intervene early. We have widespread concern about the disturbed child; yet provisions for disturbed children are conspicuously lacking in current programs and in plans for future programs. Why?

Part of the problem is people. There are very few psychologists and psychiatrists prepared to work with children. Most know best how to talk with an adult across a desk, but what to do with a furious child on a playground is not in their training. Another part of the problem is money. It is believed that disturbed children should be put in hospitals, an obviously required solution if they are thought of as being "ill." But hospitals are costly, about sixty dollars per day, and more than families or states can afford. Also the hospital may provide less than an optimum environment for most disturbed children, confirming their fears about themselves, and fixing their deviant behavior. Probably the problem cannot be solved in the way we are trying to solve it. New conceptions seem required, conceptions that are economically feasible, that draw on available sources of manpower, and that manifest an appreciation of the nature of children whom we call emotionally disturbed.

Project Re-ED is one such effort at reconceptualization. It is proving to be a viable solution but is surely not the only one. Perhaps its greatest value will be in suggesting that multiple solutions are available, that sanctioned models need not be adhered to, that invention is possible.

ONE SOLUTION

Project Re-ED, which means "a project for the re-education of emotionally disturbed children," is an effort to apply an educational model to the problem of helping emotionally disturbed children. It is a cooperative undertaking of Peabody College, the State of Tennessee, and the State of North Carolina, made possible by a grant from the National Institute of Mental Health along with matching funds from the two states. Two residential schools have been in operation for about three years, Cumberland House in Nashville and Wright School in Durham. At capacity each will serve forty children of elementary school age in five groups of eight children each, both boys and girls. The schools are staffed for the most part by teacher-counselors, carefully selected young people with experience in working with children, who have completed a special nine-months training program at Peabody. The teacher-counselors are backed by consultants from education, social work, psychiatry, and psychology. A staff social worker develops community resources in the interest of the child and his family, and a liaison teacher maintains close communication with the child's school. Both schools have summer camping programs. Children are in residence for a briefer period of time than follows from hospitalization, about six months usually, the effort being to return the child to his home just as soon as child, family, and school can sustain each other sufficiently for the child to be where he belongs. A research program is evaluating outcomes and doing basic work on the process of re-education; the results thus far indicate a better-than-hoped for success rate.

The Re-ED concept has been developed over a period of years and by a number of people. But these people have provided only the general framework; the substance has been supplied by teacher-counselors on the job. To emphasize the fact that Re-ED today is the product of many minds, the first person plural—"we"—will be employed in the remainder of this description.

SOME GOVERNING ASSUMPTIONS AND BIASES

Re-ED grew not out of a theory but out of an acute social need. Theory had to be developed out of practice and practice out of the pooled skills and concepts brought to the task by the people involved. At times observers have said they could not tell whether we were Rogerians or Skinnerians; whether we were for permissiveness or pellets, love or limits; whether we considered ourselves to be mental health workers or educators; whether indeed, the most skeptical querried, we had any conception at all of what we were doing. Gradually out of our admittedly limited experience and much thinking and talking some core ideas are emerging. We have increasing confidence in these ideas but they must be put to continuing test, be revised, and extended as experience shows the way.

The choice of the title Project Re-ED was clearly no casual business. Presuppositions, biases, the professional histories of the people responsible for designing the project, even some explicit operations, some conceptions of how behavior comes to be modified, are all intimated in the title. We are moving to the point now, in the history of the project, of trying to make explicit just what these assumptions are. We shall define them as assumptions and biases and then try to specify what operations, what kinds of interventions, follow from them. In using the word bias, we want to describe the situation accurately as involving a leaning, a preference, and not a prejudgment of outcome. We are speaking of inclinations and not of prejudices. Although we favor certain kinds of operations and interventions, we have an overriding commitment to experimentation, to putting the whole idea of Re-ED to quantitative and controlled test. But the Re-ED idea must be cast into operational terms in order to communicate just what the terms mean to us, and then to make possible an evaluation of its effectiveness.

A Learning Bias

First of all we have a strong learning bias. In the current controversy between advocates of biological and social determinants of mental and emotional disorders, we clearly line up with those who lay greater emphasis on the learning component. We avoid using the word "mental disease" because of its connotation that the individual is suffering from genetic or biochemical disturbances that have been visited upon him. We prefer to look to his social history for the origins of his difficulties. We assume that he is not ill but that he has acquired bad habits. We assume that he has learned to construe the world in such a way that his world must reject him and that he has acquired specific ways of coping that are immediately rewarding but ultimately defeating. The task of re-education is to help the child learn new and more effective ways of construing himself and his world and to learn habits that lead to more effective functioning. We thus explicitly reject the concept of cure as inapplicable in the Re-ED setting. Cure not only suggests what kinds of interventions are appropriate but also a goal of complete alleviation of "symptoms" or, in our terminology, of a complete restructuring of habit systems. The goal of re-education is more limited than this. The effort is to initiate a learning process that will come to fruition in the weeks and months and years after the child's experience in a Re-ED school. Re-education is a problem in learning to learn.

A Time Bias

In studies of the effectiveness of therapeutic interventions, the patient must improve during the passage of time if the intervention is to be regarded as effective. Thus a control or no therapy group is used to provide a basis for comparisons. When this is done, it is not uncommon to find that the control group has made impressive gains simply as a result of the passage of time. This is another way of saying that in life things tend to get better rather than worse. A child is most likely to get referred to a mental health facility at a time of crisis in his own development or of breakdown in the functioning of his home or school. A decision to refer is usually made at a low point; improvement thereafter may often be expected. The child gets a better hold on himself; things at school settle down; the family gets a bit better organized. To provide nothing more than a benign sanctuary for a child at a time of crisis is a worthy endeavor. The re-education process thus claims time as an ally, not just as an effect to be bettered.

A Growth Bias

The re-education process, as we see it, counts heavily on the normal thrust of growth to help move a child toward more effective functioning. In the years from six to twelve the child grows steadily in stature, in intellectual capacity, in physical skill, in knowledge, in sensitivity. These years may prove to be optimum for providing corrective experiences for people who have been given a poor psychological start in life. We do not assume some mystical growth force as an explanatory principle but simply note descriptively that children in these years are still open to experience and change, with surplus energy to support the operation. A broken bone knits more rapidly at six than at sixty; we assume a comparable viability in the psychological domain.

A Social System Bias

We have a further bias toward seeing the problem of the disturbed child in a broad social context. We have come to call this the "systems concept," a notion that has great influence in selecting strategies for program development. We are trying to get away from the medical concept of cure and from a preoccupation with intrapsychic processes. We are instead concerning ourselves with the functional adequacy of the total ecological system of which the child is a part. We are trying to move beyond concepts of individual adjustment, beyond concern for family-child relationships, beyond role theory and crisis theory of social psychiatry to a program of intervention that constantly assesses and tries to change in appropriate ways the child, the mother, the father, siblings, the child's teachers, the principal of his school, his friends, his minister of his church, the neighborhood playground director, the athletic coach, and miscellaneous special people of importance or potential importance in the ecology of a particular child's world; the director of the children's museum, a philatelist in the neighborhood, the policeman on the block, a music teacher. We assume that life is more healing that we are, that our intervention is an emergency measure, and that our goal is not the complete remaking of a child. What we try to do is to get the child, the family, the school, and the community just enough above threshold of the requirements of each from the other, so that the whole system has a just significant margin of probable success over probable failure. It will be apparent that it is possible for a system to work without the necessity of any intrapsychic change in the child at all. We believe that the systems concept has wide applicability in the field of mental health.

A Bias Away from "Dynamic" Psychology

We have a bias that leans us away from concepts and techniques familiar in child treatment programs. We are not opposed to these ideas, but we accept an obligation to make clear why we do not use them. Treatment programs for children based on psychoanalytic theory give a central place to the concepts of transference, regression, interpretation, and insight. These terms do not appear in the vocabulary of re-education. This of course does not mean that the phenomena do not occur in our work with children but rather that they are not deliberately used, as they are in psychoanalytic treatment, to effect a reorganization of personality or restructuring of character.

That transference will occur in the process of re-education is certainly to be expected. The parent-like role of the teacher-counselor, the temporary separation of the child from his parents, the competition of other children in a group for the attention of the staff member will all evoke transference responses on the part of children. The teacher-counselor needs to be sensitive to what is going on in order to maintain an appropriate level of concern and detachment.

Fenichel's prescription "interpret the transference" is not followed. Transference behavior is handled just like any other affect laden expression. It is recognized and accepted or not according to an agreed upon strategy and sometimes examined not for its psychodynamic significance but as a basis for discussions of how conflicts can be handled more effectively in the immediate future, using manifest material only.

Counter-transference is a problem too. The teacher-counselor's role is a demanding one, heavy with responsibility as well as with rewards. Fatigue, the exposure to sustained hostility from some children, the necessity of coping with adroit manipulation, these and other special circumstances such as the absence of a supporting (if personally limiting) hierarchical structure in Re-ED schools, mean that the teacher-counselor is especially susceptible to counter-transference. As a protection against the prospect of loss of control of a situation the teacher-counselor may sometimes distort the behavior of a child and deal not with the actual behavior of the child but with his own projection of what is occurring. There are several sources of assistance for the teacher-counselor to reduce the frequency or intensity of counter-transference attitudes.

Awareness of the nature of the phenomenon is crucial. Talking with other staff members and with consultants about feelings toward children can be a substantial help. Finally, rest, recreation, and a satisfying personal life are of immense importance.

Regression is not used as a tactic in re-education for several reasons. One is that dealing with regressed behavior calls for more sophistication than can be developed in the brief period of training given the teacher-counselor. The consultant's time and the teacher-counselor's competence are quite sufficiently stretched by the regression that occurs without encouragement. Re-education is a reality oriented process. Finally, a therapeutic program based on deep regression followed by a working through of the psychosexual stages of development simply takes too much time. The process may be essential for some children but surely not for all.

Nor is the development of insight on the part of the child regarded as essential in the process of re-education. The effort is to provide the child with a large number of learning experiences that can lead immediately to more effective functioning. There is no evidence in the literature that insight-based therapies are more effective than those that treat insight as an epiphenomenon. With no clear advantage to be gained from use of a therapeutic strategy that again calls for a high level of psychological sophistication, we have chosen the simpler course: We are impressed enough by the complexity of the simplest seeming solutions to helping the disturbed child.

An Adiagnostic Bias

Similarly we lean away from overconcern with diagnosis. The formal psychiatric diagnosis is of little value in the process of re-education, although it has some utility in communicating with referral agencies and may be instructive for research purposes. We have not been able to specify differentiated intervention procedures for differential diagnoses, nor have we observed thus far any relationship between diagnosis and responsiveness to the school programs.

Actually in defining the process of re-education, we should prefer not to be neutral with respect to the role of diagnosis but to call for a rejection of the diagnostic stance insofar as the teacher-counselor and child are concerned. The act of diagnosis requires the observer to stand outside the system and to assume that the act of observing has no influence on the behavior observed or the observer himself on the child. These assumptions get in the way of the kind of adult-child relationship that we believe will provide the best foundation for the re-education effort. We would suggest that the teacher-counselor abandon the notion that child study is possible. The child must always be studied in relationship to one or more other persons, and the observer is always one of these people. He should appear in any account of events relating to a child. In observation for the purposes of re-education, the least common denominator is two.

PROCESS IN RE-EDUCATION

We can now identify eight components in the process of re-education. Several others, bearing on the ethical character of the adult-child relationships and on the significance of metaphor in bringing order and satisfaction to the life of a child, are being discussed and may emerge as tested ideas in the future. These components, these sub-processes in the process of re-education, are described below.

The Development of Trust

That decent adults are good for children is a notion easy to accept. It has high face validity. It suffers though from overgenerality. To be useful, as for example in the establishment of criteria for the selection of teacher-counselors or in trying to talk meaningfully about the process of re-education, it must be made explicit. What is it about the adult-child relationship that can be counted on to help a child become less fearful, less belligerent, more comfortable with himself and his world?

We think the place to start is this: Adults are the mediators of learning of the child, both of personality and culture. The child must be able to learn from adults; he must be able to use them to grow up. The ability to use adults as a source of instruction is one of the most important learnings in the life of a child, a central component in the process of learning to learn.

The disturbed child is conspicuously impaired in his ability to learn from adults. The mediation process is blocked or distorted by the child's experience-based hypothesis that adults are deceptive, that they are an unpredictable source of hurt and help. He faces each adult with a predominant anticipation of punishment, rejection, derision, or withdrawal of love. It is not only that the parents of a disturbed child have provided him with inadequate models to pattern a life on, they have also impaired the very process by which more mature ways of learning may be acquired.

The normal child grows up with the set: "Most adults are usually willing to be helpful." The disturbed child makes the opposite assumption: "Most adults cannot be trusted." The first step in the re-education process is to help the child make a new distinction, that some adults indeed cannot be trusted, although other adults can be counted on as predictable sources of support, understanding, and affection.

There is nothing to be gained by trying to persuade a child that this difference exists before he has experienced both kinds of relationships. Even then, talking about the general idea will probably be of little help. The core experience is that of being genuinely close to an adult without getting hurt. Intimacy with safety is the cardinal requirement. Perhaps human intimacy is a biologically based requirement, a derivative, in the species, of natural selection; but even if genetic factors are not involved, experience in infancy is sufficient to create a learned requirement for human closeness.

The first step, then, in the re-education process is the development of trust. Trust, coupled with understanding, is the beginning point of a new learning experience, an experience that helps a child know that he can use an adult to learn many things: how to read, how to be affectionate, how to be himself without fear or guilt.

We are intrigued by the possibility, indeed we are almost sure the thesis is true, that no amount of professional training can make an adult worthy of the trust of a child or capable of generating it. This ability is prior to technique, to theory, to technical knowledge. Perhaps it can be acquired by an adult through therapy or through some transforming, self-changing experience such as a satisfying marriage, but a far surer road is through the thousands of learnings in infancy, childhood, and adolescence in relationships to mother and father, and perhaps a few other important life persons, that are the happy lot of the healthy adult, the natural worker with children.

After seeing the difference that teacher-counselors in our two schools have made in the lives of children, we are confident of the soundness of the idea that some adults know, without knowing how they know, the way to inspire trust in children and to teach them to begin to use adults as mediators of new learning.

The Gaining of Competence

The ability to do something well gives a child confidence and self-respect and gains for him acceptance by other children, by teachers, and unnecessary as it might seem, even by his parents. In a society as achievement-minded as ours, a person's worth is established in substantial measure by his ability to produce or perform. There are cultural pockets where a person's value is determined by family membership, but these enclaves are fast disappearing. The idea of acceptance of a person for his own sake independently of what he can do is realized most consistently in the never-never land of textbooks and most preciously in a few rare relationships in life. Acceptance without productivity is a beginning point in the process of re-education, but an early goal and a continuing challenge is to help the child get good at something.

At the Peabody Child Study Center, for example, we have frequently observed over the years that a child who overcomes a handicap in reading often gains dramatically in general adjustment. The common assumption that emotional disturbance causes reading difficulties leads to the conclusion that the emotional difficulty must be cleared up before progress can be made in the improvement of reading. This is a too-simple conception of the relationship between symptom and cause. All evidence calls at least for an interaction hypothesis to account for the improvement in adjustment following improvement in reading skill.

What, then, in the process of re-education, does the acquisition of competence mean? It means first and foremost the gaining of competence in school skills, in reading and arithmetic most frequently, and occasionally in other subjects as well. School is of great importance in the life of a child. If a child feels that he is inadequate in school, inadequacy can become a pervasive theme in his life, leading to a consistent pattern of failure to work up to his level of ability.

Underachievement in school is the single most common characteristic of the children referred to Re-ED. We regard it as sound strategy to attack directly the problem of adequacy in school for its intrinsic value in an achieving society as well as for its indirect effect on the child's perception of his worth and his acceptance by people who are important in his world.

A direct attack on the problem of school skills does not mean a gross assault in some area of deficiency. On the contrary, it requires utmost skill and finesse on the part of the teacher-counselor to help a disturbed child move into an area where he has so often known defeat, where failure is a well-rooted expectancy, where a printed page can evoke flight or protest or crippling anxiety. The teacher-counselor need make no apologies to the psychotherapist with reference to the level of skill required to effect a healing intervention. Indeed it would be interesting to compare experimentally the relative value for a child of: (1) acquiring insight into the origins and nature of his difficulty at school, or (2) achieving an increase in competence in basic school skills, without any increase in awareness, except a greater sense of immediate competence. Knowing that such an Augean experiment is not liable to be undertaken, acquisition of competence seems more important than acquisition of insight as an effective source of general gain for a disturbed child.

The residential character of the Re-ED school means that the acquisition of competence does not have to be limited to increased skill in school subjects. It may mean learning to swim, to draw, to sing; it may mean learning to cook on a Dakota Hole, to lash together a table, to handle a canoe, to build a shelter in the woods; it may mean learning to talk at council ring, to assert one's rights, to give of one's possessions, to risk friendship, to see parents as people and teachers as friends.

One of the minor strategies in the process of re-education should be to help each child acquire some unique competence, some skill that will help him assert himself as a person.

The Control of Symptoms

It is standard doctrine in psychotherapeutic practice that symptoms should not be treated, that when one symptom is removed it will simply be replaced by another, and that the task of the therapist is to uncover underlying conflicts against which the symptom is a defense thus eliminating the need for any symptom at all. In Re-ED we contend, on the other hand, that symptoms are important in their own right and deserve direct attention, usually through reconceptualization or reconditioning. We are impressed that some symptoms are better to have than other symptoms. The bad symptoms are those that alienate the child from other children or from the adults he needs as a source of security or a source of learning. There is much to be gained then from identifying symptoms that are standing in the way of normal development and working out specific plans for removing or altering the symptoms if possible.

A deeply disturbed, nine-year-old boy, confused in sexual identification, had a habit of kissing men. We were able to teach him that men express affection and respect by shaking hands. He switched to shaking hands, perhaps more frequently and enthusiastically than is normal in our culture. Nothing had been done about his sexual disturbance, but he had given up a habit that would increase the possibility of his getting into serious trouble.

Betty goes in and out of a phantasy world with some ease. When her thinking is bizarre and fanciful, adults tend to humor her and to enter at least tentatively into her system for construing the world at the moment. We think we would do better to be quite literal with Betty, responding to her idiosyncratic language with language that is commonplace. If we can increase even in small measure the extent to which Betty's language habits overlap with those of other people, we may in even greater measure increase the possibility of her remaining in the community.

Symptomatic treatment of enuresis is another example of a tactic that would make sense in the process of re-education. Since bed wetting may well be a means of expressing aggression against parents, it is particularly useful to change this habit because such change interrupts the circular pattern of rejection, aggression through bed-wetting, and then more rejection.

The assumption is that children get rejected in large part because of identifiable behaviors that are regarded as unacceptable to family friends, school, or community. Regardless of the child's level of maturity, adjustment, ego-intactness or strength, or other index of psychological health, there are some symptoms that are more obnoxious than others. For example, the kinds of symptoms that maladjusted boys develop are much more unacceptable to schools than are the symptoms developed by maladjusted girls. For the moment we do not concern ourselves with the adequacy of the family, friendship group, school, or community but instead accept some accommodation to them as a *de facto* requirement in the child's life. Indeed for all their inadequacies, we see families, friends, schools, and neighborhoods as a more substantial source of psychological nourishment, of the stuff of adequacy and contentment, than a re-education center could ever be. The problem is to help the child make effective contact with normal sources of affection, support, instruction, and discipline. A first step in this process is to help him unlearn particular habits that keep high the probability that he will be rejected by people whose support he must have if he is to grow.

Learning Middle-Class Values

The well-adjusted and finely functioning child in an understanding family can afford to be unconventional, to follow a somewhat idiosyncratic value system. For the child of marginal adjustment, however, it is just another drain on his limited resources to have to support divergent patterns of behavior. With some mild dismay at the prospect of de-emphasizing the importance of individuality, a long standing commitment, we find ourselves advocating the acquisition of middle-class values and ways of behaving by disturbed children whose behavior does not fall into these accustomed patterns. The issue is largely one of improving the child's social stimulus value to adults on whom he must depend for support and instruction. Among the values that are approved in middle-class groups are good manners, cleanliness, good language, bookishness, work, and the need to achieve. We have taught one child to use a handkerchief or tissue when blowing his nose and to make less frequent use of his rather remarkably well-developed vocabulary of profanities and obscenities. Although this process has done little for his inner psyche, he is now much more likely to be accepted by teachers than when he was told that he could not return to school.

Gaining Cognitive Control for Today and Tomorrow

Clearly, the process of re-education places little emphasis on the acquisition of insight as a source of therapeutic gain or of reorganization of personality. The teacher-counselor relies primarily on immediate experience, or the day-by-day, hour-by-hour, moment-by-moment relationship between himself and the child; he relies on specific events that can be arrayed to provide the child an opportunity to grow in trust, in competence, and in joy. Most of Re-ED is concerned with the living of each day on terms as favorable as possible for the child. In the mastery of each hour the child grows in ability to master all hours.

The ability to use language, to represent experience symbolically, and to store it and pass it on to others over space and time is probably more important than sheer brain power in establishing the marked superiority of man over other species of animal life. This ability is man's most distinctively human attribute and a major source of his susceptibility to neurosis as well as of his control over himself and his world. In Re-ED the problem is how to make effective use of language in self-initiated control of behavior, without getting involved in the intricacies of an uncovering type therapy.

Although the development of insight is not a primary goal and although emphasis in program planning is on immediate experiencing as a major source of growth, the process of re-education does not neglect to help the child gain in cognitive control over his behavior. True, the emotionally disturbed child has a lesser degree of freedom in behavior, or a more limited response repertory than the normal child, yet he is not without the ability to shape his own behavior by self-administered verbal cues. He can signal to himself if he can learn what the useful signals are. The teacher-counselors work constantly to help a child gain cognitive control over his behavior, formally through the night council ring or pow wow and informally as occasions present themselves naturally in the course of a day.

The focus of this effort is on today and tomorrow, not on the past or the future, and on ways of signaling to ourselves to make each day a source of instruction for the living of the next. At the council ring at night, at a place set apart from the business of living, children in a group are helped to consider what was good about the day just past, what went wrong that might be handled better tomorrow, and what was learned, especially in successes and failures in relationships among themselves. Possibly more important than the solving of particular problems is the acquisition of the habit of talking things over for the purpose of getting better control over events, a habit that can frequently be carried over into the child's home and become a new source of strength for his family.

The Development of Community Ties

The systems concept in Re-ED leads to an examination of the relationship of the child to his home community. Most children who are referred to our schools come from families that are alienated or detached from community life or that are not sufficiently well-organized or purposeful to help the child develop a sense of identity with his neighborhood, town, or city. He has little opportunity to discover that communities exist for people and, although the relationship between the two may often leave much to be desired, an important part of a child's education is to learn that community agencies and institutions exist for his welfare and that he has an obligation as a citizen to contribute to their effective functioning. This is especially true for many of the boys referred to Re-ED whose energy, aggressiveness, lack of control, and resentment of authority will predispose them to delinquent behavior when they are a few years older and gain in independence and mobility.

This idea has a number of implications for program planning. Field trips to the fire, police, and health departments are useful. Membership in the YMCA, a children's museum, a playground group, or a settlement house may be worked out for a child. Church attendance may be encouraged and clergymen persuaded to take special interest in a family. A library card can be a proud possession and a tangible community tie. We once thought it would be nice to have a swimming pool at Cumberland House, but we see advantages now to having the children use pools in the city. It is pleasant to have theory take the place of lack of funds as a reason for not building a swimming pool!

Physical Experience as a Basis for Greater Awareness of Self

We are intrigued by an idea that has already been incorporated in our school and camping programs although there is no evidence of its validity. It is one of those ideas that ought to be good and might be used regardless of its contribution to the more effective functioning of a child. The notion is that the physical self is the armature around which the psychological self is constructed and that a clearer experiencing of the potential and the boundaries of the body should lead to a clearer definition of the self, and thus to greater psychological fitness and more effective functioning. The Outward Bound schools in England, developed as an experience for young men to overcome the anomie that is the product of an industrial civilization, are built around the concept. The Peace Corps training program in Puerto Rico involves experience in rock climbing, drown proofing, and survival hiking, not because the volunteers will engage in these activities, but because of their putative effects on the volunteers' self-concepts. Austin Des Laurier's ideas about treatment of schizophrenia in children emphasize differentiating the body from the rest of the world. Thus there are several other programs, all concerned with re-education of some sort, that make use of the notion. Programatically, in Re-ED, the idea has been realized in such activities as swimming, climbing, dancing, tumbling, clay modeling, canoeing, building a tree house and walking a monkey bridge. We hope that in the future we can put even greater emphasis on this aspect of our program, both for children and staff.

The Knowing of Joy

We have speculated about our lack of a psychology of well-being. There is an extensive literature on anxiety, guilt, and dread, but little, actually none that we know of that is well developed, on joy. Most psychological experiments rely for motivation on avoidance of pain or hunger or some other aversive stimuli; positive motivations are limited to the pleasure that comes from hearing an M & M rattle down a slot on an operant conditioning apparatus. This poverty with respect to the most richly human of motivations leads to anaemic psychology. We must thus go beyond contemporary psychology if the re-education process is to touch one of the most vital areas of human experiencing. We must develop skill in developing joy in children.

How do you go about doing this? We are not sure, nor do we have any data to go on that would establish the validity of our thesis. We simply assert that it is immensely important, that it is immediately therapeutic if further justification is required, for a child to know some joy in each day and to look forward with eagerness to at least some joy for tomorrow. We suspect that the events will be pretty simple, that they need not cost much nor require elaborate preparation. They probably require most of all to have them come to pass a sensitivity on the part of the teacher-counselor to what it is that means a lot to a particular child, a belief in the importance of the experience for the child, and some ingenuity in arranging for things to happen.

Billy looked forward with as much joy as he could let himself risk to his father's coming to a Bobcat cookout for parents. To his immense satisfaction, his father made it. The father was there because a teacher-counselor, believing in the importance of this simple joy to Billy, went out of his way to be sure that the father got an extra invitation and a job to do that would make it important for him to come.

Joyous experiences can probably be made to cluster around a sequence of events, to unfold themselves as some enterprise develops. For example, an Indian project at Cumberland House generated a hundred moments of satisfaction as children worked hard to make its realization possible. However, we could not have anticipated all the satisfying experiences it brought to the children as each day was lived and as each day was anticipated. Many subjects, some of them noxious to the children in other contexts, such as reading and arithmetic, geography and history, were swept forward on the current of well-being that flowed from a core idea.

* * * * *

One day a perceptive visitor to a Re-ED school said, "You know, what you are doing here is nothing more than giving these youngsters a good education. Except for your night program, you are just doing what any good school should do." He seemed to expect us to be disappointed by his analysis. We were delighted.

REFERENCES

Hobbs, N. Mental health's third revolution. *American Journal of Orthopsychiatry*, **34**, 1964, 822–833.

Hobbs, N. Helping disturbed children; psychological and ecological strategies. *American Psychologist*, 1966.

Lewis, W. W. Continuity and intervention in emotional disturbance: a review. *Exceptional Children*, **31**, No. 9, 1965, 465–475.

Lafon, R. *Psychopédagogie, Médico-Sociale*. Paris, Presses Universitaires de France, 1950.

Laughmiller, C. *Wilderness Road*. Austin: The Hogg Foundation for Mental Health, 1965.

Rhodes, W. C. "Curriculum and Disordered Behavior." In Nicholas Long, William C. Morse, and Ruth Newman, eds., *Conflict in the Classroom*. Belmont, Calif.: Wadsworth Publishing Co., 1965, pp. 405–410.

Weinstein, L. Social schemata of emotionally disturbed boys. *Journal of Abnormal Psychology*, **70**, 1965, 457–461.

Chapter 15

Actualizing the Effective Professional Worker in Education

Fred T. Wilhelms

About the Author

When Fred Wilhelms completed his undergraduate stint at the University of Nebraska, he was steeped in the classics—Roman, Greek, and English—with overtones of philosophy, and all his interest was in liberal education. But when he became a Latin teacher he found it somehow unsatisfying. He shifted to the teaching of English, but this proved unsatisfying, too. Eventually, the social studies served him best.

Little by little he came to feel that the *whole* secondary curriculum was unsatisfying, because it didn't get to what really matters in human life. He tired of tinkering with "method" and decided to become a "curriculum man." He helped develop a program of supervised correspondence study to enrich the curricula of small schools. He spent some years as a specialist in consumer education because that offered promise of going directly to the conditions of life.

In 1948 he went to San Francisco State College to teach secondary curriculum. Two years later he became head of the teacher education program there. With that excellent faculty he had many opportunities to shift the emphasis away from technique and over to the understanding of human beings through psychology and the social foundations of education.

The pivotal experience in his career began in 1958 when he took charge of an NIMH-sponsored project in teacher education and mental health. In the next five years he and a small crew worked out ideas about how education can be managed so that *the process itself will be healthful.* They developed a radical program of professional education to implement their ideas as well as they could—but, of course, they were thinking of the process of education itself, regardless of field.

Out of all this, in a curious way, Wilhelms has come back full circle to his initial passion for liberal education. Only, he defines it differently now: not as a body of subjects called the "liberal arts," but as any education which uses organized subject matter drawn from high in the culture and *uses it deliberately* to assist a young person in his full personal becoming.

356

As the evidence has accumulated, he has become more and more excited about the real possibility of lifting students to new levels of intellectual functioning and new levels of ego-strength, each contributing to the other—and doing it in the normal course of school life through the subject matter which needs to be taught anyway. He believes it is technically possible to effect a wedding of *learning and becoming*. To him this foreshadows a "new liberal education," capturing both intellectual and personal gains. He knows that to achieve the new liberal education will take an enormous engineering effort in the schools, but he thinks it can be swung. At present he is Associate Secretary of the National Association of Secondary-School Principals, which gives him an excellent leverage to pry at the problem.

Introduction to the Chapter

The long search for a reliable pattern of good teaching, like man's search for the fountain of youth, has suffered from the disillusioning assumption that such an entity exists. The hope that a pattern of competencies and practices could be found that would eventually define good teaching and could be used to train the teachers has lured many educators and behavioral scientists into the swamps of unproductive research and scientific frustration.

Once again, willingness to challenge the established assumptions has led to new premises and a refreshing new rendezvous between behavioral knowledge and educational practice. Utilizing research findings from Dr. Arthur Combs, Dr. Marie Hughes, and many others, Fred Wilhelms has not only looked at teacher training with "fresh eyes" but also explored their "new look" in a living experiment.

By turning to the assumption that the critical factor in good teaching is not a constellation of teaching skills, but a function of the nature of the teacher as a professional person and "how he uses himself," Wilhelms' group launched themselves into formulating a new and different kind of professional education. They found themselves reaching out and utilizing certain personality-building and enriching knowledges and skills from the behavioral disciplines, ideas heretofore rarely used in teacher training. Fortunately, they wisely avoided the

seductive trap of "therapizing" their students or attempting to reorganize their personalities. Recognizing that they were dealing with "able,
dynamic college students at the height of their power," they set out
to explore how changes in the social system and experiential resources
of their school of education could be used to expand and integrate
the ego-processes of their teacher trainees. They sought a way of
professional preparation that would unravel the subtle binds that
the traditional conformity-building, model-imitating, content-memo-
rizing teacher-education approaches use as they try to direct and mold
a teacher trainee into role playing the "good teacher." They recognized
and reconfirmed an old psychiatric discovery, applicable to normal
people, that "people can act a prescribed role for a short period of
time, but in the long run—and particularly in spontaneous interactions—the determiner of behavior is what the person basically is."
They moved on into systematic focusing on the teacher trainee as
a person, helping each one find his own unique capacity to be a teacher
and to discover a new pattern of perceiving himself and his role in
a way "congenial to his personal motivations." Instead of using practice teaching to reinforce an armamentarium of competencies, a wide
range of experiences were afforded each trainee to discover for himself
as his first essential "a deep, unshakeable commitment to teaching
as a satisfying and meaningful way of life."

Self-direction, freedom to explore, freedom to fail, freedom to learn
by doing and thinking, sensitivity building, use of self as instrument,
individual curricular exploratory experiences, feedback, self-trust development, and a dozen other such mutative psychological and social
concepts are the carefully selected ingredients of this creative experiment in teacher training. It was indeed, as Wilhelms admits, "a radical
reformulation." He has written this chapter with modest words, but
it should be known this program has met the acid test of replication
by another group and is continuing on at San Francisco State College.

Actualizing the Effective Professional Worker in Education

"We don't really know what good teaching is," is a sentence with a rare ability to plague the progress of an educational discussion or to stymie the design of an experiment. Often it is said by a speaker naive enough about the disappointing data from scholarly investigations to be merely uttering a cliché that he does not really expect—or want—to be believed. Sometimes the person who says it is simply reacting with wonder to the sudden realization that some of the best teachers he has ever known "used all the wrong methods." His listeners may also be relatively amateurish. Then, if they are administrators who regularly "rate" teachers, they are likely to react defensively and insist that they do too know how to tell the good from the bad. Or if they are investigators trying to compare the results of one teacher-education or supervision program to another, they may react with angry frustration to the argument that they will have no final criterion to judge their results by.

But if the person who says we don't really know what good teaching is and the listeners who hear him are both genuine professionals who have studied the hard data, they will know that he is stating a considered, scholarly generalization. For the evidence of our not-knowing has piled up over the years. After many seasons spent in attempts to analyze teaching effectiveness, Professor A. S. Barr wrote in a wry letter that his main contribution had been to find so many things that did not work! Within the past dozen years two careful surveys of the evidence to date have failed to find anything really substantive: Morsh and Wilder (1954), reporting to the U.S. Air Force on a complete review of the quantitative studies of teaching effectiveness, came up with almost nothing positive. Similarly, after another thorough search of the evidence, the American Association of School Administrators [1961] wrote:

359

"The notion of the 'good teacher' so basic to the study of teacher effectiveness turns out to be almost as vague and diffuse as the range of human experience relative to teaching."

Behind these dry summaries lie dozens upon dozens of searches for a reliable index of the goodness of teaching. Demonstrated over and over again was the failure to find an essential relationship between the effectiveness of teachers and any one total pattern of teaching conduct.

Yet, despite all the failures, there has remained in the air a wistful assumption that, as Plato might have put it, "In Heaven there is laid up for us a perfect pattern"—if only the studies were sensitive enough to discover it! Now at long last it is time to recognize the possibility that the fault never did lie with the studies—that they failed because there simply is no such universal pattern. In a general way some teaching behaviors are no doubt superior to others; but that does not mean there is any one set of behaviors which any teacher can adopt and thereby surely become a good teacher.

Working hypotheses are subject to judgment not merely in terms of their ultimate truth but also in terms of the fruitfulness of the investigations they generate. The old half-conscious assumption that "good" teaching could be identified with some set of competencies and practices has proved its sterility by leading us into a great deal of relatively unproductive work—at the same time that it has frozen teacher education into a competencies-practices orientation. It looks as if it will be far more fruitful to hypothesize deliberately in the opposite direction, to work on the assumption that *there is no set of competencies and practices which equals the difference between good and poor teaching.*

Simply working on that assumption will rid us of a lot of old preoccupations and free us to see once more with fresh eyes. Yet the assumption is not by itself the new concept which fresh investigation needs.

A NEW PREMISE EMERGES

Such a concept has been taking form. It has found perhaps its most definite formulation to date in a statement by Combs [1964] in which he explicitly turns his back on the "competencies approach" and argues for a "self-as-instrument" concept.

"We may define the effective teacher *as a unique human being who has learned to use his self effectively and efficiently for carrying out his own and society's purposes.*"

"The production of this kind of person is not a question of teaching him what to do. Modern perceptual psychology tells us that a person's behavior is the direct result of his perceptions, how things seem to him at the moment of his behaving. To change a person's behavior, it is necessary to help him see himself and his world differently."

From this beginning Combs sketches forty hypotheses regarding the perceptual organization of teachers who are effective. Some of these hypotheses have already been corroborated in research on good and poor counselors; some are now under exploration.

Looking back, we can see that the concept has been foreshadowed for some years. Three studies may be taken as indicators.

1. The large-scale Teacher Characteristics Study [Ryans, 1960], although it began with detailed observations of teaching procedures, finished with emphasis on highly personal characteristics. Consider, for example, its three now-familiar major dimensions of teacher behavior:

Pattern X_0 (Friendly, understanding, sympathetic versus aloof, egocentric, restricted teacher behavior)

Pattern Y_0 (Responsible, systematic, businesslike versus unplanned, slipshod teacher behavior)

Pattern Z_0 (Stimulating, imaginative, surgent versus dull, routine teacher behavior)

By any reasonable interpretation these are something much more than generalized categories of teaching practices. They go back to the person employing the practices.

Even more dramatically, some of the characteristics of outstanding teachers, listed in Chapter 8 of the same report, reveal perceptual organization rather than practices; For example: "[They] manifest extreme generosity in appraisals of the behavior and motives of other persons. [They] believe very few (less than 1 per cent) high school students intentionally try to tax the patience of the teacher."

2. Somewhat similarly, in her monumental study, Hughes (1959) proceeded almost totally through a near-microscopic analysis of teaching acts. Yet, at the end, it seems a reasonable interpretation of her data that the better teaching she found was chiefly the outgrowth of a certain openness of personality, buoyancy, positive outlook on

life, and supportive warmth. (Mrs. Hughes may or may not agree with these inferences.)

3. After a year of preliminary study, the San Francisco State College Project on Mental Health in Teacher Education (Wilhelms et al. 1963), based its work squarely on the assumption that it is—so to speak—*the person within the teacher* that counts for most, that "what a teacher *is* may be more important to the full development of his pupils than anything he *does*."

"The growing of a young person from college student into professional teacher—a leader of children and youth—is a deeply personal becoming. It cannot be thought of or accomplished *en masse*. The objective of teacher education must be to help each aspirant make himself into not only the most competent practitioner but also the most fully developed person he is capable of becoming."

It certainly cannot be said that the assumption was proved by this project. But on the evidence accumulated during four years of evaluated exploratory experience, the secondary education team of the project staff had simply grown firmer in its backing of the proposition, and eager to spell out such ideas as:

The behavior of a teacher is a function of his personality. People can act a prescribed role or follow unassimilated rules of behavior for short periods of time, but in the long run and particularly in spontaneous interactions, the determiner of behavior is what the person basically is.

Teacher education must be concerned with personality and with methods which will change personality.

The whole period of *teacher education is, in essence, a period of personal ferment and development*. Just as adolescence is a period of reorganization and change, so too is becoming a teacher. . . . The role of education itself in personality is one of fostering autonomy, sensitivity to communication, openness to experience, and the freedom to be one's self. These are the traits of a mature person functioning effectively.

To be sure, the hunches and creative insights of a few persons or groups cannot immediately be taken as established truth, but they can promise a fruitful line of inquiry and testing. One thing is certain: It makes an enormous difference whether, on the one hand, the difference between low- and high-quality teaching lies essentially in a body of knowledge and competencies to be mastered and a body of practices to be employed; or whether, on the other hand, the difference is essentially a *personal* one, resting on the developed ability of a unique, mature person to use his self effectively. It is worth emphasizing that if the difference is an important one in terms of the cognitive learning which a teacher can promote in his pupils, it must inevitably be doubly important in terms of the wholesome impact he can have upon their mental health and full personal development.

THE PREMISE HAS IMPLICATIONS FOR PROFESSIONAL EDUCATION

If we accept the person-as-instrument viewpoint, we shall be driven to radical reformulations of our programs of teacher preparation. Not that we shall discard the knowledge and skills; teachers, *let it be said most emphatically,* will still need their tools. But the basic orientation—the focus of attention—will have to be vastly different.

To see why this is true, let us project against this new backdrop of concept and hypothesis two images of teacher-preparation programs as they typically exist. As we do so, we had better leave generous room in our thinking for some notable exceptions; but most programs can be divided roughly into two types—the "traditional" and the "internship."

The traditional professional sequence took its basic set some decades ago, although the details have since been modified. It often begins about midway in the collegiate program, or somewhat later, on the assumption that the student should acquire at least a fair proportion of subject-matter competence first. The professional program generally moves in by way of some sort of theoretical "foundations" program— originally through philosophy and history of education, for quite a long time through educational psychology, and more recently through some combination of the psychological and social foundations of education. The program generally moves next to a focus on methodology, strongly enriched recently by considerations of curriculum development. It generally climaxes in student teaching. The details vary infinitely; for example, there is often provision for observation of teaching or even for some mild participation with young people before the student-teaching period. But the general flow is fairly predictable: from basic theory, to "practical" problems of methodology, to application in practice.

As a complex reaction against this system of "learning all the theory first and getting all the practice last," there have sprung up a great variety of so-called internship programs ("so-called" because very few even approximate the medical prototype of antecedent training and close supervision). In most cases some theoretical preparation precedes, accompanies, or follows the active internship assignment. Sometimes this preparation is thorough and extensive. But because much of the impetus toward internship programs has come from groups skeptical of pedagogical theory, there is often a severe cutback on the theoretical side. In these cases the main thing is *practice*— learning by doing—under an experienced practitioner; not infrequently the intern carries a full teaching load and earns a considerable salary.

Now if we merely compare these two styles of programs in a surface way, they appear greatly different. But if we view them both against the conceptual framework of the person-as-instrument approach, it instantly becomes obvious that they are more alike than different.

1. Both take essentially the "competencies approach."

2. Both conceptualize experience with children—whether in student teaching or internship—chiefly as "practice," with a fundamental commitment to skill-building.

3. Both tend to put the student into a situation where he is supposed to imitate some model. In the theoretical forepart of the traditional program the model may be some vaguely pervasive ideal-teacher type. But in student teaching as well as in the internship, the implication is clear that the student had better learn to do what his master teacher already knows how to do.

4. Student teaching and internship alike constitute a period of great personal stress. The student's very career may be at stake—or seem to be, which can be equally important. He cannot afford to deviate and risk mistakes. Rarely is he in position to explore varied possibilities. Even more rarely is his situation conducive to his taking an honest look at himself. Under the high emotional pressures, perceptual need-distortion is the usual occurrence.

Even more important may be the similarities in what the two programs *fail* to do. Neither opens up much opportunity for long, slow self-exploration, for the discovery of strengths and weaknesses in a setting free enough from tension to permit a relaxed self-appraisal. The theoretical professional courses are about as academic as anything else in college; hence, they give the young professional little chance to see himself in relation to his chosen lifework. The teaching experience is too tension-ridden to encourage openness. Neither does much to encourage self-acceptance or individuality, or the courage to find one's own unique qualities and use them. Neither gives much encouragement to autonomy in the very period when growth in autonomy is almost the greatest need.

All too commonly the system is rigid and restrictive. It is anything but encouraging to spontaneity, to the open-ended exploration of oneself, or to experimentation with growing and changing models of human living and interaction. In the foundations courses—at least as the typical student perceives the situation—a favorable grade may depend on remembering the "right" answer; in the methods courses the instructor may launch virtually a propaganda campaign on behalf of certain "right" practices; and in student teaching, no matter what latitude the student may have in other matters, there is generally a well-enforced consensus on how he must "handle" children, with a high premium on orderliness and "discipline." Far from being a situation dedicated to each student's *finding* himself, it is essentially a system for *moulding and directing* him.

If we accept the conception of good teaching as a body-of-practices, this system is not altogether without logic. If, on the other hand, we accept the self-as-instrument thesis, the inference is unmistakable: We need a whole new approach to the education of a teacher; one capable, in Combs' phrase, of helping him to "see himself and his world differently." Any program attempting so fundamental a task must inevitably be very difficult to fashion, especially in view of the rigidities of college scheduling and the drastic limitations of time permitted for professional education. It will demand an expansion of time for the professional sector of teacher education or, perhaps better, some creative alliance with the liberal arts sector—or both.

Yet the task need not be seen as impossible. Perhaps the most optimistic fact is that we are not dealing here with rigid, fearful psychiatric patients, capable of only narrow change even under long-drawn-out intensive therapy. (The fact that systematic attempts to help people change their perceptual systems are largely associated with such persons may have exaggerated our notion of its difficulty.) We are dealing with able, dynamic college students at the height of their powers. If they have their share of free-floating anxieties, they have also a tremendous resource of free-floating energies. They need to learn a new way of perceiving themselves, their role, and the world of education. It is no small learning assignment, but it is one which will be congenial to their motivations, and they have vast learning resources.

THE TEACHER EDUCATION PROJECT PROVIDES
ONE PRELIMINARY MODEL

To explore the programmatic implications of what has been said so far, let us look at the rationale of the San Francisco State College Teacher Education Project. It is not introduced here as any model of perfection. We who served on it recognize that it was a groping effort, that it *proved* little beyond the administrative feasibility of working in a radically different mode, that some of the most important ideas in it only began to take really clear form about the time the project was over, and that the whole effort was in many respects inadequate. Yet we are confident that its way of analyzing the problem and reasoning through to possible solutions has real value.

Our reasoning ran something like this: The most fundamentally important thing about a teacher (assuming an adequate level of education) is that he be a mature, healthy person who knows his own resources and uses them vigorously with true respect for himself. If he is to throw himself into this without reservation, the first essential is a deep, unshakable *commitment* to teaching as a satisfying and meaningful life for himself. We assumed that such a commitment does not come ready-made, but must be learned. To personally discover and evolve such a commitment takes time and a richness of opportunity. For one thing, it involves developing a true vision of what teaching really is and can be. Our faculty defined teaching simply as the "facilitation of learning." We wanted our students to learn to see themselves and other learners as dynamic, surgent organisms, always learning, always striving to make themselves more adequate, and limited primarily by inadequate perceptions of themselves and of what would truly lead to greater adequacy. We meant to use every means at our command to help students understand learners and the forces of the *milieu* in which they live, to become sensitive to their needs, their perceptions, and their often-inchoate aspirations. We wanted them to grow in seeing how teaching and the schools can help.

In the second place, we reasoned, a genuine commitment is probably impossible unless the individual really comes to see that he has something of value to offer; that, with all his imperfections, he is right for the role. We wanted our students growingly to see themselves with a clear eye; we hoped they would develop the nerve to look at their weaknesses and do something about them; but we were infinitely more interested in their seeing and appreciating their unique strengths and developing the courage to use them with complete respect for their own individuality—without any assumption that there is only one way to be a good teacher.

As any behavioral scientist knows, this is a matter that *really* takes time and opportunity. It is the most fundamental learning human beings engage in, and takes the best of men all their lives. We reasoned that at least three major ingredients must go into it:

1. A wealth of opportunities for revealing, exciting, perhaps baffling experiences must be laid open.

2. The opportunities must occur in an atmosphere of such freedom and autonomy that each student, under guidance, could largely follow his own nose as his initially half-sensed intuitions of his own aspirations and needs grew into clearer and clearer perceptions of himself. Furthermore, the whole system must operate so unflinchingly in a climate of positive regard and personal acceptance that daring would be possible because failure would be all right.

3. Feedback must be facilitated so that each student could learn about himself from consideration of his experiences. This was not a matter of the faculty's telling the student "how he was doing." It involved all the complexities of any genuine learning environment.

As time went on we elaborated these basic themes. "Exploratory experiences" became a common term. We wanted such experiences to be greatly varied, fitted to each student at the stage he was in. We developed a great faith that he could find them better for himself than we could find them for him, although we could set the stage and help him perceive his needs. Our goal, especially in the earlier stages, was not primarily the development of polished professional skills; we thought that could come speedily at a later time, when the groundwork had been laid and motivation from an imminent full-time job was high. Rather, when a student had an experience with adolescents, we were primarily interested in what it revealed to him about himself, how it shaped his drives toward the next step and his perception as to what that next step ought to be.

At each stage we wanted the psychological loading of an experience to be light enough so that the student could afford to look at himself calmly and comfortably—and with growing self-trust. At first thought it might seem that such "lightness" or freedom from pressure would have to be achieved by keeping the experiences themselves "easy" or even trivial. But the truth is, the psychological load on a student is not so much a function of the difficulty of the experience itself as it is a function of expectations. Thus, early in a student's professional program, when he is not yet expected to be expert, he can relax—even be amused—in the face of a "failure" that might make him very tense if it came later. Fundamentally, if a student knows that exploratory experimentation is genuinely desired—and that the faculty is sophisticated enough to expect some failures through new ventures—this student can be reasonably comfortable. It remained one of our major premises that if a student is to find himself, he has to have the courage to look for himself—and that for this purpose a reasonable safety and self-assurance are essential.

We placed great emphasis on full and free opportunity to intellectualize the meaning of such experiences—to think them through and talk them out. To this end, we facilitated long, private talks with faculty members whenever students wanted them; we provided—in the wings, so to speak—a specialized counselor, not a part of the teaching team, to whom students could go with deeper problems—even purely personal ones—when they chose, in full assurance of confidentiality and freedom from any "official" overtones. But we depended much more on group discussions of common problems, and devoted some hours per week to a kind of professional sensitivity training in small, congenial, self-selected groups. (Incidentally, we now feel that when a group of students has time enough together to know one another well and form real friendships, the mutual support and cross-counseling which they provide may be more important than anything the faculty can do.)

Of course, the discussions were not simply group-sharing. Psychology and the other behavioral sciences, as well as the accumulated experience and scholarship in the field of education, have a great deal of insight to offer, and the faculty never intended to let that insight go to waste. As educational problems were identified, the instructors helped to organize systematic, scholarly study. Individuals and student groups carried on study projects, sometimes in considerable depth. Professional reading was encouraged, though kept free and individual. Faculty experts lectured and led thoughtful seminars. The basic effort here was to bring the supporting disciplines to bear in a *synthesized, problem-solving* mode; thus, although there was no separate course in educational psychology or sociology, the content of these and other disciplines was used to help solve problems as they were perceived. (Incidentally, terminal tests of professional knowledge and understanding showed that there was no loss in this respect from the fact that there was less systematic "coverage" of the professional subjects. The students learned about the same things as usual, in about the same degree.)

Through all this—through the experiences in the field, the private talks, and the group seminars—ran a strand of *personal support*. We did everything in our power to help each student learn that he was a free, autonomous young professional in charge of his own life space; that the problem of becoming a good teacher was *his* problem; that we would always back him, even in his failures, and help him to understand; but that the responsibility for making decisions was his own. Again, we hoped to make the climate so accepting and comfortable that each student could see himself and what was going on around him with clear vision, uninhibited by the distortions that accompany fear and high emotional pressure. (It may be said in passing that some students took to the whole thing with delight from the start, accepting the freedom and the responsibility and glorying in the adultness of it all; most came across the line slowly and in their own time; a few probably never got over a yearning for the traditional student role with its freedom from responsibility.)

Operational Features of the Teacher Education Project

It is not at all our intention to argue that other institutions should adopt the format of the Teacher Education Project. Situations vary, some offering advantages we did not have, others undoubtedly facing obstacles that were not important to us. If we had been in some ideal situation, we would have pushed further than we did. Given our working situation, we first thought through our goals and priorities, then tried to figure out what kind of program would harmonize best with them, and then came as close as we could to building such a program. Nevertheless, it may be helpful to others to see how the mechanics of the program were handled.

1. Our emphasis on the personal element led us to reason that a closeness of acquaintance, even a certain intimacy, between and among faculty and students would be desirable. It is hard to open up much of a personal nature when a class of students—most of them relative strangers to one another—stay with an instructor for one term and then disperse to other instructors. We wanted *continuity* in which mutual understanding could grow over time without any hurried pushing or prying. Therefore:

(a) We formed a three-man faculty team, to stay together with the students for the duration of their professional program. The team represented psychology, the social foundations of education, and curriculum and instruction; it was responsible for both on-campus instruction and field supervision, so that everyone would be at least roughly familiar with the total situation. On occasion, this staff was supplemented by others when some specific expertise was needed, but the added staff members did not carry the same responsibility for the students as persons.

(b) Likewise, we formed a student group destined to remain together for their whole professional program, which meant roughly half-time for three semesters. (One element of the professional program, the special methods courses in the students' major and minor fields, was somewhat apart from our program, though some steps were taken toward integrating it into the whole.)

2. We had some very strong feelings about the role of experience in professional education. Traditionally, it has been conceptualized chiefly as *practice*, with goals such as applying theory and acquiring competencies—and, therefore, it has generally been placed late in the sequence. We felt it ought to have much more to do with such functions as arousing motivation, building an apperceptive reality base, and helping students identify problems. We especially wished to use it for guidance purposes, to help students see themselves and their professional identity more clearly. Therefore, we reasoned that it needed a different timing and spacing. As a consequence, in place of the conventional final semester of student teaching supplemented by some prior observation, we made arrangements with a few neighboring schools for a three-semester developmental program of varied and individualized experiences, on a rather free, informal basis. There was much mutual planning between the school and college staffs, and inevitably there must be some orderliness in such a program. But our main purpose was to organize freedom for individuals to get the experiences they needed when they needed them, and the school staffs put remarkable effort into making this possible.

3. We placed a very high value upon the background of knowledge, principles, and theory available through professional education and the behavioral sciences. But we felt that the courses offering this background usually suffered in effectiveness, partly because they were held discrete from one another, partly because they were presented before the students had much chance to sense—and identify with—the problems to which the courses sought to supply solutions. We thought it desirable that this body of content should be synthesized and integrated into an organic whole and that it should be so timed and handled as to become a continuing problem-solving enterprise (not the least of our purposes being to teach a lifelong problem-solving set and process). Therefore, back on campus, we dispensed with the usual series of discrete professional courses. In its place we put a single seminar, continuing over the semesters with varying schedules and arrangements.

The seminar was taught by the faculty team (all three of whom generally found it necessary to be at all general sessions, although they often worked individually with subgroups). In one sense it was very carefully planned, for the students and faculty thought together very carefully, from time to time, about what was needed most. In another sense it was virtually free from preplanning, for there was no commitment to a body of subject matter to be covered. In the final analysis the content consisted of the problems the students identi-fied and the concerns they developed, although on occasion the faculty might build more of an intellectual superstructure upon the basis of a problem than the students had anticipated. As it worked out the curriculum developed a "spiral" characteristic, returning to certain basic problems more than once at greater depth. Students in education commonly complain of repetition; but when these students were free to determine their own needs they called for even more than the usual amount of repetition because a level of analysis which satisfied them at one stage seemed too shallow to them later on.

Actually, the seminar became a mixture of many elements. It met as a whole for two or more hours per week for lectures and group reports as well as for planning and discussion. It broke into a variety of small groups for particular projects. Some of its work was done through purely individual investigations. And some time was spent each week for sensitivity training. (Incidentally, once it had been begun, this last element was the one which the students never per-mitted to be omitted, though almost everything else shifted from time to time.)

4. To help free the situation from unnecessary and artificial ten-sions, grades were dispensed with. Students were simply told that upon successful completion of the whole program they would receive all the necessary credits for a teaching credential, with a grade of "pass." From the beginning, we added two provisos to this: (a) We guaranteed that if any student was "heading for trouble"—of which low grades would normally be the alerting signal—we would get the information to him quite openly in personal conference; (b) we as-sured them that if anyone *needed* conventional grades (for instance, to support a scholarship application or because he was forced by circumstance to move to another college), we would take care of the need in whatever way seemed most effective. In other words, we took no inflexible doctrinaire position against grades. In the main, student reaction was highly favorable.

5. It was a high-priority goal that each student should have maxi-mal opportunity to gain in self-insight and the building of a realistic but positive self-concept. As one means to this end, we strove to

open up opportunities for full and free discussion of personal-profes-
sional problems. In some ways the faculty members were the natural
persons to turn to. And we encouraged students to go to whatever
team member they considered most helpful, without fear of hurting
the feelings of the other two. However, the instructors' time was too
limited to permit them always to follow through on intensive counseling. Furthermore, even in the absence of grades, they did have an
"official" relationship to the students—would finally pass on them
and write recommendations—a factor which we feared might inhibit
full and open discussion. Therefore, we added a highly sophisticated
psychologist-counselor on a part-time basis. We made appropriate
opportunities for the students to get acquainted with him in a rather
casual way. Then we simply announced that he was available, to
be used as they saw fit—with no pressure to use him. We assured
them honestly that he had no "official" relation to them, that whatever
dealings they had with him would be in confidence—that, in fact,
we probably would not even know whether they used his services
or not. In actual fact, a few students used his help in considerable

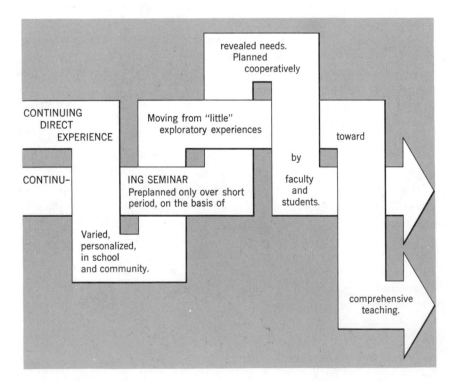

depth, some more used him more casually, and most never went to him at all.

In its simplest abstraction, then, the professional curriculum could be thought of as two major, continuing strands, one of experience, the other of "theory," interwoven at every point, with each supporting and each drawing upon the other, in an "open" atmosphere of support for exploration and experimentation.

The Process in Action

Almost the first thing that happened was that the students were sent into the schools for a couple of weeks with only a general charge to "see what they could see." The principals gave them a general overview, and they were encouraged to "get around" in the whole school. They were also encouraged to spend time in the teachers' lounge and in other ways to get acquainted with the school's faculty. Predictably enough, this acquaintance yielded many invitations not only to come in and observe but also to take some hand in working with the pupils.

There followed, in the seminars, an intensive period of reflecting upon what they had seen and beginning to figure out what they needed to learn. It was a period of great—and sometimes angry—frustration, partly because many students were deeply offended by some things they had seen in the schools and really would have preferred simply to criticize; partly because the problem of developing a study program is intrinsically difficult; but especially because, after some sixteen years of highly directed schooling, these students (most of them, anyway) were simply not ready to take responsibility for themselves and lacked effective skills of group decision-making. They ached to have the faculty take over and tell them what to do, but the faculty simply refused.

Eventually some sort of order emerged. The students chose a steering committee to plan with the faculty. (This device never worked out in a wholly satisfactory way.) Because there were no textbooks, they collected from themselves roughly the usual cost of textbooks and, with faculty guidance, formed a small project library to be built up from semester to semester, which they themselves administered. More important, they began to identify centers of concern and, dividing into interest groups, laid out lines of investigation. The investigations included field study (sociological study of a school neighborhood, intimate study of a small teen-age gang, and so forth) as well as library work. Faculty members were closely involved as consultants, occasionally as lecturers; at first their consultant services were required at least as much with respect to process as on subject matter, for these unskilled groups frequently got stuck on problems of decision-making.

Many persons, hearing a description of the project's *modus operandi,* apparently felt that the faculty was being "too nice" to the students in giving them so much freedom. Our own fears were on the other side—whether we were being "too rough." Teaching a student conditioned by years of closely directed schooling to accept autonomy and responsibility, even to believe that the autonomy exists, is a long, arduous process. A few sturdy souls take to it easily enough, even joyously. But, for many, such responsibility can be seriously threatening. Going out into school and community without neatly prearranged assignments of time, place, and contacts was a rough-and-tumble thing. Add the strains of learning to use democratic group processes for serious decision-making, and you have quite a situation! Evaluations at the end of the program showed that some students credited the painful "sweating out" of this period with major growth in their maturity, but some students were still resentful of the time wasted in fumbling, uncertainty, and indecision.

Fortunately, skill in group process came along fairly rapidly. By the end of a year, groups handled complex problems speedily and generally without strain. This was not altogether the result of sheer practice. The faculty *taught* the theory of group dynamics and continually aided the thoughtful use of democratic processes. Many of the two-hour seminar sessions ended with discussion keyed to some such question as, "What do you think has been going on here today?" Many students became astute observers of process and of the dynamics underlying specific events.

A very great aid in this was the weekly two-hour "sensitivity session." By maneuvering team assignments it was generally possible for this to be held with a group of about twelve students. The students noticeably selected their particular group keeping in mind the other students who would be in it and the instructor who would lead it. There was no set content for these sessions. They consisted of a free-flowing interchange, with techniques akin to T-group (sensitivity) training as well as to group therapy. Although, naturally, there were moments of discomfort and pain, most students developed a firm commitment to these sessions.

After the first month or two, the field experiences of the students became so varied that it is hard to describe them in any generic way. They all did include, generally toward the end of the professional program, concentrated periods resembling conventional student teaching, but students came to this point by many routes. With only the rarest exceptions, the faculty never assigned students to particular "master teachers." What generally happened was that as students and school faculty members got acquainted, affinities developed, and by some subtle process of negotiation they got together in little mutual-assistance pacts. The college faculty consulted a great deal on these arrangements; they encouraged students to work with a variety of persons—to get themselves many models rather than to fixate on one—and they helped each student think through what he needed next. In a general way, they encouraged students to use first the sorts of experience that would help them learn to relate easily and perceptively with adolescents, reserving the added role of directing learning (that is, teaching) till later. But in actual fact a few students did some teaching almost from the start, whereas others were "arrested" for overlong periods in observing some one teacher or in some other rather sterile occupation. Altogether, the variety of experiences that students found for themselves was amazingly rich, although some individuals lacked the security or the energy it took to get themselves into many corners of a school's life.

The faculty's view of the role of experience was, of course, a peculiar one. We were not always so terribly concerned with how well a student did a piece of work; often we were more interested in what it did to him. We valued those experiences—and there were many of them—which turned out to be *self-revealing* and evocative: the kind of experience that led a youngster to get excited and think and talk about himself in relation to his professional role. Experiences having to do with discipline—sometimes even merely *seeing* disciplinary action carried on by someone else—often had such a quality, because it brought into question the whole matter of how a teacher relates to people and feels about them. Toward the end of the professional program, we had to be more concerned with the development of professional skill. Yet, even at that point, we continued to ascribe considerable importance to the part experience played in bringing educational problems into the open, arousing motivation for the study of their possible solutions, and deepening a student's commitment to working with youth.

And so the program rolled on through three semesters, with experience and academic study sometimes alternating, sometimes side-by-side in an intricate relationship. As time went on, it became easier for most students to take charge of their own affairs. As the group acquired skill in group decision-making, it grew easier to plan next stages of the program. As acquaintances became established, more and more students came out in the open (either in the group context or in individual conferences), and it grew easier to talk about what really matters.

In Retrospect

Even if space were unlimited it would be difficult to specify just what this first tentative project *proved*. On the internal things that mattered most, evaluation was, of course, terribly difficult. The more external things could be judged with more confidence. We know, for instance, that such a "loose," highly individualized program can be managed. We know that the various disciplines contributing to professional preparation can be integrated with fair ease and that, when interrelated with experience, they can achieve the role of problem-solving resources. We know, too, that our students learned as much as students usually do from these disciplines, even though the instruction was less systematic. We also know that the dropout rate was abnormally low and although our students had plenty of specific criticisms, they tended to feel that they were engaged in valid, significant work, relevant to their real professional role. (We suspect that this last is highly important. It seems reasonable to suppose that it is hard for a student to form a deep commitment to teaching during his preparatory period if he feels that much of his preparation is irrelevant and will only have to be forgotten—and not a few students in traditional programs do feel this. Conversely, a program which stimulates them to throw themselves into the work with vigor and self-respect may have many positive side effects.)

Beyond these points we feel comfortably sure of some more fundamental things. A substantial proportion of the students appear to have grown significantly in autonomy. (The evidence for this lies more in their subsequent actions than in quantified test data.) Many appear to have developed a strong enough commitment to certain styles of human relations so that they persist in struggling to live up to their ideals under the vicissitudes of busy school life. We believe many have grown so comfortable with "loose," relatively unstructured group process that they turn to it intuitively in their own classes. On the whole we believe they have grown in sensitivity toward others as well as in insight into themselves.

Perhaps it is an error to generalize too much. So far as we can tell, some students went through these three semesters—as they might through any series of courses—too little involved to be much affected one way or another. On the other hand, we are perfectly aware that for at least a few individuals these same three semesters will stand as a watershed line marking deep and fundamental changes.

Finally, it may be added that when students experience a rich variety of experiences with children and youth early in a teacher education program, a process of rather valid self-selection goes on among the candidates. Those who are not well-adapted to the relationships tend to withdraw, if they can find it out before they have too great an investment, and they can do with their self-respect unimpaired.

However modest we may need to be as to the proof we can offer, we do feel that we have moved toward our basic ideal. Without loss of the usual professional knowledge or proficiencies, we came closer than usual to an organization of instruction which was in itself health and strength potentiating; one in which the learning of content was at the same time an affective medium of personal learning.

LOOKING FORWARD

But what this particular project may or may not have demonstrated in its first, inevitably crude try-outs is far less material than some general ideas. With more experience, performance could be improved. Other patterns of organization might be more successful. With more time for professional preparation, much more ambitious things could be attempted; for instance, it may well be that students should be taught much more directly about matters pertaining to mental health.

What seems growingly clear is that *some way* of achieving certain tasks must be found, and that this will require radical reorientations in teacher education programs. To be sure, teachers must know subject matter well and they must develop a wide range of proficiencies. No teacher education program can ignore these needs. But if, when all is said and done, the effective teacher is a mature person who has learned to use his self well as a teacher, then means must be found to get him deeply acquainted with that self. More than that, ways must be found to strengthen him to strike out boldly to use his own distinctive powers in his own unique way. If teaching is, at bottom, a matter of effective human relationships, then ways must be found to increase the teacher's sensitivity to human beings, his ability to accept a wide variety of persons, and his ability to understand and empathize.

Just what those ways and means should be remains an open question. But it seems safe to say that mere intellectual knowledge of psychological principles will not be enough—and, therefore, the traditional type of course will not be enough. The thing must get into the teacher's bones, into his whole perceptual framework, and this means a long and direct involvement. If a teacher is to help youngsters set themselves free and take increasing charge of their own life space, then he had better have worked his own way through that struggle. If he is to help groups learn to make responsible decisions, live with uncertainty, and work through conflict, he had better know what the growing pains feel like. Certainly the study of behavioral science ought to be able to sensitize him greatly, to accelerate and deepen his understanding and acceptance of those he teaches. But he can never understand and accept them if he does not first work at the problem of understanding and accepting himself. And for that something far beyond mere didactic instruction is essential.

Teachers are not psychiatrists; neither are schools psychiatric institutions. Both are and must be primarily preoccupied with the teaching of organized subject matter. Most of what they can accomplish toward vigorous mental health they must accomplish while teaching the subjects they are employed to teach. This probably means they must achieve it largely through a pervasively wholesome, even therapeutic *climate*. And what that climate becomes will be less a matter of what all the school's personnel know than of what, deep down inside themselves, they genuinely *are*.

REFERENCES

1. American Association of School Administrators, *Who's a Good Teacher?* The Association, 1201-16th St., N.W., Washington, D.C., 1961, 54 pp.
2. Combs, Arthur W. "The Personal Approach to Good Teaching," *Educational Leadership* **21**, March 1964, 369–377.
3. Hughes, Marie M. What Is Teaching? One Viewpoint, *Educational Leadership* **19**, January 1962, 251–259.
4. Morsh, J. E., and E. W. Wilder, *Identifying the Effective Instructor: A Review of Quantitative Studies, 1900–1952*. Research Bulletin No. AFPTRC-TR-54-44. San Antonio, Tex., USAF Personnel and Training Center, 1954. 151 pp.
5. Ryans, David G. *Characteristics of Teachers*. American Council on Education, Washington, D.C., 1960.
6. Wilhelms, Fred T., et al. *Report of the Teacher Education Project, Secondary Section*. San Francisco State College, San Francisco, Calif., 1963.

Chapter 16

The Educational Institution and the Health Institution

The Role of the Local Health Department in an Educational Setting

John C. Glidewell and
Lorene A. Stringer

About the Authors

Dr. Glidewell received his Ph.D. in 1953 from the University of Chicago in psychology. Since graduating, he has conducted research, in a variety of settings, on the relationship between social organization and individual behavior. His research career started under the supervision of Herbert A. Thelen in the Human Dynamics Laboratory at the University of Chicago. During the Korean War, while on active duty in the United States Air Force, he conducted similar research with special emphasis on the instructional process in small group settings, at the Air University at Maxwell Air Force Base, Alabama. Since 1953, his research has been conducted in public school settings in St. Louis, Missouri, in the St. Louis County Health Department, and in several communities in the St. Louis area.

He served as Director of Research and Development at the St. Louis County Health Department from 1953–1963. He initiated research programs not only in community mental health but also in chronic disease control, public health education, and tuberculosis control. The development of research at the St. Louis County Health Department represented a successful integration of research functions in a local health department. Dr. Glidewell has published several case studies and analyses of the course of this unusual development of research in a local health department.

During his tour in St. Louis, he held joint appointments at Washington University in medical psychology, in psychology, and in sociology. In 1958, he and his colleagues initiated a program of training in community mental health research for social science students seeking the Ph.D. The program has continued as an interdisciplinary program involving psychologists, sociologists, anthropologists, economists, political scientists, and educational psychologists, conducted within the interdepartmental Social Science Institute.

In 1963, he joined Washington University as a full-time faculty member. He now holds his primary appointment in the Graduate Institute of Education with supplemental appointments in psychology, sociology-anthropology, and medical psychology.

380

Since 1950, he has been one of the group of social scientists associated with the National Training Laboratories of the National Education Association. He served on the National Board, on numerous committees and was among the first Fellows of the National Training Laboratories.

His research reflects his interest in a wide range of studies of the relationship between social organization and individual behavior in elementary schools, in adult education, in community mental health, in school mental health, and in general public health practice. He edited the book, *Parental Attitudes and Child Behavior*, and has contributed to the scientific journals of psychology, sociology, education, psychiatry, and public health.

He is a Fellow of the APA, ASA, APHA, National Training Laboratories Association, and SPSSI.

He married Frances Reed in 1941 and he has two charming daughters, Pamela, born in 1946 and Janis, born in 1953.

Lorene A. Stringer received her professional training (specializing in psychiatric casework) at the George Warren Brown School of Social Work, of Washington University in St. Louis. She worked for some years at St. Louis Children's Hospital and in the psychiatric clinics associated with Washington University Medical School; but the longer she worked with the seriously ill, the more concerned she became about prevention of illness. When she was invited to join the staff of the St. Louis County Health Dept. in 1952, as its school mental health program was just getting under way, she accepted eagerly.

She remained with that school service program, first as one of only two staff workers, then as supervisor of its enlarging staff, and later as program director, until 1959. Early in these years (and under goading from Dr. Glidewell's beginning research evaluation of the service) she became convinced that effective prevention of emotional illnesses could not be achieved on any case-by-case basis. Effective prevention would depend heavily on the development and consistent across-the-board application of school policies so formulated as to promote growth in healthy children while at the same time screening for the sick.

Given opportunity in one district to experiment along these lines, she focused on the schools' promotion policy, recommending that children functioning below grade level repeat that grade, instead of receiving "social promotions." To evaluate what happened to both repeaters and social promotions she used a tool that she called an Academic Progress Chart. The new policy won community support; academic achievement of the total grade school population improved by 25% over a five-year period; and the APC showed promise of being a good tool for the early detection of emotional disturbance in school children, so that the National Institute of Mental Health awarded a grant for further study of its uses. Therefore, she left the service program in 1959 to become Research Project Director of that investigation.

By 1965 that study had clearly indicated that preventive programs in schools should begin as children entered schools, and that mothers were highly receptive to working with mental health consultants at the time of school entry. With Dr. Glidewell she planned a new project, called "Mothers as Colleagues in School Mental Health Work," and combining what they fondly hope is a service in primary prevention with a research evaluation of the service, and investigation of patterns of healthy child development. She is currently Principal Investigator of that project, which began in September 1965.

Since her research has intensified rather than lessened her interest in program development and in-service training of mental health consultants, educators, and parents, since 1963 she has been Community Mental Health Coordinator for the Health Department, and casework consultant to its School Mental Health Service staff. Her writings reflect a steadily sharpening focus on mental health, as opposed to mental illness, and she is at present deeply involved in attempting to develop mental health guidelines that will serve both to encourage better research in this field and to communicate clearly and usefully to people who are not mental health professionals but can become collaborators in promoting mental health.

She is a charter member of the National Association of Social Workers, a member of the Academy of Certified Social Workers and a Fellow of the American Orthopsychiatric Association, and a Fellow of the American Public Health Association, and she seems to have become completely involved in working in the St. Louis County Health Department.

Introduction to the Chapter

The power of a logical idea can often move two social systems into closer contact with each other; however, proximity is no guarantee that a mutually enhancing relationship will develop. There is little doubt that a local health department with a community mental health program should blend its resources with the local school system for the benefit of all children, especially those with emotional problems. As obvious and logical as this may seem, the execution of such a relationship-building endeavor requires a social psychological finesse, a knowledge of each agency, and a knowledge of the community in which they function. Just as two solar systems moving closer together will inevitably create new gravitational pulls and alter individual orbits, the blending of two social systems, like a school and a health department, will inevitably create new performance expectations and individual roles for both staffs.

Glidewell and Stringer, through sensitive use of conceptual tools adapted from the behavioral sciences, have documented the inside story of an important school mental-health relationship. With connubial bliss and naiveté, with high hopes and much good will, a "marriage" was contracted between a health department and some school systems with little anticipation of the problems hidden away in the differing assumptions, mandates, community responsibilities, methods, and value sets of these two agencies. Like the slow unpeeling of an onion, the subtle binds between the group-centered and community-oriented school staff and a patient-and-disease-oriented health staff began to emerge. The concept of "social immunology" appeared as health workers were encapsulated, walled off, or even phagocytized by the body politic of the school system.

Just as in any marriage, the relationship received continual testing, single binds became double binds, and both partners went through defensive episodes, frustrations, and insightful confrontations over the unrealistic expectations they had of each other. Thanks to a mutual sensitivity to the children's needs, to good friendships that had developed, and to an impelling focused idea, the partners did mature and did find new roles and values worth pursuing together.

Make no mistake—this is no "can this marriage be saved?" article. This is a descriptive and experimental example of how to utilize some of the hard-earned skills and knowledges of social psychology to bring about a more meaningful and more mature relationship between mental health trained people and educators. Since both education and mental health, as social systems, are fast becoming parts of a more holistic integration of human services, discussions of the mechanics and dynamics of interagency relationships becomes a highly relevant and practical topic.

The Educational Institution and the
Health Institution

This chapter is a case history and is subject to all the limitations of case histories. Its generalizability is questionable, its post hoc interpretations may be only fortuitous. If it is at least possible, however, that the case is typical, that the forces influencing the development of this case also influence the development of other cases, the abstract concepts used to integrate these empirical observations may be used again to predict future empirical observations. Accordingly, this document begins with a series of abstract assertions, to set this particular case in its place within a broader conceptual perspective.

IN PERSPECTIVE: SOME INITIAL ASSERTIONS

About Community Institutions in General

People in communities create widely differing institutions for themselves. They create institutions to cope with some of the fundamental, consistent, and insistent urges that they feel. Some of their urges are forces toward change and growth; some of their urges are forces toward stability and predictability of gratifications.

The people in each community seek to make available to themselves far more resources than could be mobilized or managed by any one institution. Accordingly, they have developed highly specialized institutions, among which are those dealing with education and health. The educational institution is often concerned with the balance between individual urges toward intellectual achievement and community responsibility to transfer to each new generation both its heritage of knowledge and its responsibility for the wise use of the knowledge. The health institution is often concerned with the balance between individual urges toward relief from pain and community responsibility for the protection of the patient in pain against exploitation of his dependency on what (for the patient) are esoteric cures, available only from the physician, the healer.

Along with specialization goes the problem of organization. There must be some working consensus about the terms and conditions under which the resources of an institution will be made available to the people for whom the institution was created. The establishment of such terms involves the establishment of a method of allocating community resources among the people of the community. Such allocation involves some implicit or explicit weighing of values.

About the Educational Institution and the Health Institution

Specialization of community institutions means also, specialization of values. In the educational institution, the prime criterion has been the value placed on the development and the dissemination of knowledge. In the health institution, the prime criterion has been the value placed, first on the relief of, and then on the prevention of, the pain and distress of illness.

We have said that the educational institution and the health institution were created by people in communities to cope with different human urges and different social responsibilities and that their activities are based on different values. We may also say that both are interested in inducing change in individuals—change in drives toward their conversion to social motivation, change in feelings toward their conversion to work inducing tensions, change in ideas toward their conversion to more valid representations of reality, change in skills toward their conversion to productivity under pressure, change in stamina toward its conversion to stability under stress, change in self-consistency toward its conversion to flexibility in the face of unexpected consequences. It seems likely that the two institutions, educational and health, hold some differing basic assumptions about the process of change induction.

ONE HISTORY: ARRANGEMENTS AND DISARRANGEMENTS

The Initiation

There were no evidences of disharmony, let alone of basic incompatibility and latent conflict between the two institutions, when the St. Louis County Health Department initiated its School Mental Health Program in the fall of 1951. The plan appeared to be simple and well conceived. The arrangements appeared to be ingeniously simple, too. Buchmueller and Gildea (1949) had just completed a pilot project in a few St. Louis schools, using the method of group therapy with mothers of behavior-problem children, and the results, although not record-breaking, were considered good enough to justify extension of the method into a community mental health program. The St. Louis County Council had, shortly before that, empowered their Health Commissioner to enter into a contractual arrangement with county school districts, whereby the districts might obtain the services of public health nurses at near cost level. The same sort of contractual arrangements could as easily supply the schools with part-time services of the staff of the Health Department's Child Guidance Clinic (Buchmueller and Domke, 1956). A special linkage between the community educational institution and the community health institution was to be established. There were many implications; only few were clearly seen.

Contractual Arrangements and Community Responsibility

Three county school districts contracted for the service in its first year, and a clinical psychologist and a psychiatric social worker were assigned to spend half of their time in the schools of those districts. Thus the interaction of the two institutions began.

The community mental health program in St. Louis County had four components, because a different approach had been developed for each of four degrees of disturbance in children. (The program has been described in detail by Margaret Gildea, 1959.) The four components of the program and the degree of disturbance with which they deal were: (1) the Lay Education Service, designed to deal with the usual developmental problems of children; (2) the School-Centered Services, designed to deal with the more moderate degrees of disturbance which do not disrupt school attendance or family organization; (3) the services of the Child Guidance Clinic, designed to deal with disturbances of clinical severity which cannot be handled in the school setting; and (4) the services of residential treatment centers, designed to deal with problems so severe that a complete change of environment is required.

The first component was the Lay Education Services. This approach was intended to focus the attention of normal parents on the emotional problems they are likely to meet as their children grow up (Brashear, et al., 1954). The approach is called "Lay Education," because it is conducted by lay discussion leaders for groups of parents. This service was (and still is) carried out by the Mental Health Association of St. Louis, the organization responsible for its origin and development. The corps of lay discussion leaders are all volunteers. They are trained in discussion leadership techniques and theory in a series of workshops. The discussions center upon a film or a play, using these aids as springboards for group discussions. The programs are offered to parent groups in PTA's, schools, churches, and elsewhere.

As indicated before, the Lay Education Services were aimed toward the parents of children with minimal troubles. This "grade one" disturbance level includes children who develop symptoms in response to discernible environmental stresses, incidental to the developmental tasks of childhood. The symptoms are short-lived, and they do not disrupt school attendance or family relationships for any significant length of time. The demands on the family are not such that the parents seek psychiatric help. These problems, then, are such that they can be approached through the learning experiences to be found in free group discussions among parents.

The second component of the program—the School-Centered Services provided by the County Health Department for the schools of the county—entailed the provision of the services of a mental health counselor, assigned by the Health Department to the school. The counselor was to be a trained professional—either a psychiatric social worker or a clinical psychologist with special training in group therapy. The counselor was to assist the school personnel in case finding, screening of referrals, in-service training, and maintaining liaison with service agencies and clinics. A special and central function of the counselor was to conduct therapy groups for mothers (Buchmueller and Gildon, 1949; Kahn et al., 1951). The groups were to meet once a week in the school. They were to be composed of mothers identified in the screening process as those who must deal with problems in their children at the "grade two" level of severity.

This "grade two" severity level includes children whose disturbances are not so specifically related to precipitating factors as are those in "grade one." The disturbances are of longer duration and not so clearly episodic. Neither school attendance nor family life is seriously disrupted, but the behavior deviations usually cause concern on the part of the teacher and the mother. These, then, are problems amenable to resolution outside the clinic, and the technique of group therapy for mothers in the school had been developed to meet the need for the resolution of such problems (Buchmueller et al., 1954).

The third component of the program was the familiar Child Guidance Clinic, which needs no elaboration. These teamwork services of the clinic were provided by the County Health Department for children with "grade three" disturbances—those whose symptoms are of long duration, disabling enough to threaten to disrupt the family, and actually disrupting school attendance. These children were to be identified and referred as a part of the School-Centered Service, but they could not be adequately dealt with within the school. They required the teamwork facilities of the Child Guidance Clinic.

The fourth component of the program included the residential treatment centers, especially equipped for the care of severely disturbed children on a twenty-four-hour basis. In St. Louis County such centers were operated by several agencies. These centers treated children with "grade four" disturbances. Such children show illnesses severe enough to disrupt their school attendance, and they come from homes so disturbed as to block effective treatment while the child remains at home.

Two Institutions in Linkage

As a tax-supported public agency, the Health Department was expected to be concerned about the whole community, but as a health institution, it was essentially patient-oriented. A prime focus of its concern was to find the patients and prevent the spread of disease in the community.

The educational institution, on the other hand, was essentially group-oriented. Groups of students constituted classrooms, groups of classrooms constituted schools, groups of schools constituted a district, not to mention groups of teachers constituting a faculty, and groups of parents—parents constituting the voting public that could give or could withhold support from the school. Within the educational institution there was a stereotype of "the individual child" and a formulated philosophy that schools must foster development of "the whole child" in carrying out their educative function; but, by and large, schools became concerned about individual children only when—by their deviant behavior—they threatened the integrity and functioning of their group.

Let us put this in another way. St. Louis County (population at that time over 400,000 and mushrooming) is governed by a small county council and an elected supervisor. If the Health Department was theoretically responsible for the public health of the entire county, it was directly responsible only to the County Council and Supervisor. Very few people in the county knew anything about the Department's functions, staff, and methods of operation, nor could most people see any good reason for learning more.

The more than thirty autonomous school districts in the county were each directly responsible to their own boards of education elected by their parent communities. School district superintendents were naturally and necessarily far more sensitive to prevailing attitudes and pressures in their communities than Health Department staff could realize. Thus, even in the contractual arrangements there was a large and unnoticed difference in the kind of community responsibility felt by the two parties to the contracts. This difference remained invisible for a considerable length of time.

Consensual Need and Consensual Validity

There was no organized protest in the school communities against the School Mental Health Program. There seemed to be, in fact, a real consensus that mental health problems existed and, therefore, that mental health services were needed. Whether there was a consensus about the validity of the service was not apparent. Robin Williams (1951) had clearly explicated the cogent distinction among the developmental phases of community service organizations. He had explained how a consensus about the existence of community problems would provide the necessary conditions for the establishment of a community service organization. He had also explained that maintenance and stability of the organization depended upon the emergence of consensus about the validity of the organization—about its competence to deal with the perceived problems. In St. Louis County, neither the practitioners nor their consulting social scientists saw the pointed applicability of Williams' distinction.

There developed very quickly good reason to question the validity of the service. Very quickly the teachers referred their most troublesome and disruptive children. In retrospect, and based on data from more nearly authentic communication from teachers and administrators, it seems very likely that the educators could, by such referrals, do several important things. They could act to maintain the stability of the various groups they dealt with. They could take appropriate action to help the individual child who was causing the disturbance. They could, also, test the competence of this new branch of the health institution—competence to give relief from severe stress, felt by teachers and students to be emergency distress, until then, long unrelieved.

The mental health workers in the schools, therefore, soon found themselves immobilized under case loads of the most severely disturbed children in the schools—children whose parents either resisted any contact whatsoever with the mental health professional, or who proved to be themselves seriously disturbed and unamenable to influence by any treatment that could be offered in the schools. The original plan for a community mental health program of prevention, by group therapy for the parents of disturbed children, was thus shown to be useless and irrelevant here. Following is a statement of one of the workers as published by Stringer (1962):

"A ghastly discrepancy soon appeared between what had been planned and what actually occurred, ghastly at least to those of us who worked in the schools. We found it almost impossible to start the therapy groups that were to have been our major method of operation, and quite impossible to keep them going when we did manage to start them. The mothers whose children were referred to us were not interested in therapy groups. As a matter of fact, they objected strenuously to having any contact with us at all. And the schools, being highly—and by and large, appropriately—concerned about community reactions, became very anxious about us. We were foreign bodies in the system of every school we worked in. Not only were there no pre-established positions in the schools for us to move into, but—as employees of the Health Department—we were not directly subject to control by the schools. To some schools this was so threatening that they found indirect (but quite effective) means to control us. One way was simply to encapsulate us and hold us safely inactive, cooling our heels for the stipulated amount of service time per week. Another was to give us only irremediable cases to work with. Still another was to find no place for us to work in: we interviewed referrals in open school hallways, on stair landings, in lunch rooms while lunch was being prepared or dishes being washed, in unheated attic storerooms, in unventilated boiler rooms, at least once in a broom closet. At the end of our third year we had nothing that we could call a going program anywhere. In two of the three contract districts we were clearly regarded rather as troublemakers than as troubleshooters; in the third, more favorably disposed district, we had roughly sixty referrals that seemed to be immovable."

The Clinician and the Educator

Another kind of conflict was visible from the beginning. Life in the clinic and life in the classroom are very different ways of life. The clinicians went into the schools fully prepared to find teachers and principals abysmally ignorant of mental health theory and practice and—in their ignorance—probably ready to fight the clinicians at every step along the way. The educators, on their part, accepted the coming of the clinicians with a wait-and-see attitude, tinged here and there with hopefulness, but essentially guarded, skeptical, and quite ready for defense, if attacked. Out of their different orientations, the clinicians were strongly committed, by an honorable tradition, to working in behalf of the individual child referred. The teachers were equally committed, by an equally honorable tradition, to working in behalf of the total classroom. Conflicts were bound to arise, and they did. They had varying outcomes, depending on the relative strength and conviction of the clinician versus the teacher; but initially only the educators experienced role conflicts. If the teacher accepted the clinician's recommendation for special—usually at least quasi-clinical—treatment of an individual child, she ministered to the health of the individual child to the cost of the education of all the other children in her class. If she rejected the clinician's recommendations, she left herself open to charges of being callous and inhumane toward the very vulnerable, emotionally upset child—and, by human but invalid generalization, to all such vulnerable children.

Not until the second and third years of the service did the clinicians begin to experience similar role conflicts. In the course of time they were confronted with the manifest results of having their recommendations accepted and carried out by teachers, or rejected and not carried out. Those manifest results were quite clearly mixed, confoundingly so. In some cases, where the recommendations had been most conscientiously carried out, everybody seemed the worse for it—the disturbed child and all of his classmates and the teacher. In other cases, what appeared to be an equally conscientious following of recommendations had resulted in evident improvement in the disturbed child and relief from tension in his classmates and his teacher. Similarly, with respect to recommendations that had been rejected by the classroom teacher or the principal, the results were confusing: sometimes the disturbed child only grew more disturbed; sometimes he made excellent improvement—even from the clinician's point of view. There were still a few cases, in the third year of the program, that yielded an even more disconcerting combination of results. Some disturbed children grew worse with teachers who had faithfully followed the mental health recommendations. The same children, in the next year, moved on to teachers who dealt with them in the opposite way, and clearcut improvement emerged under the "noncooperative" teacher.

Eventually the clinicians began to question whether the attitudes and techniques that were cherished requisites in the clinic were always appropriate and effective in the schools (Stringer, 1963). In fact, a child, when he was in the social system of the clinic, appeared to be somehow critically different from that same child as a part of a social system at school. Earlier intimations of impending need for change began to be no longer intimations, but clear demands. Perhaps, if clinical skills were to be effective in a nonclinical setting, they would have to undergo adaptations for that setting. The schools, however, were not merely nonclinical. They had their own structure and their own repeatedly confirmed traditions. Most children really did learn in school, and without clinical recommendations.

There were two positives in the situation. In spite of the difficulties related to their professional roles, there had been enough good will available to allow for the development of a number of friendships between the clinicians and the educators, friendships that showed promise of becoming productive working relationships. And there had been, and there still was, clear evidence in the schools of the need for effective mental health services. The problem was merely to learn how to give effective mental health services. In one of the three contract districts, the superintendent, his principals, and his special services staff, including the School Mental Health worker, set about learning how to do this.

Research, Resources, and Planning

Meanwhile, for three years our administrators had been busy planning. The power of a credible idea and the impetus of initiative, it seems, can maintain a momentum without regard to life as it is lived outside the institution—be the institution clinical, educational, or administrative. The National Institute of Mental Health awarded a five-year research grant to the Health Department to evaluate the effectiveness of a school program that sought to modify behavior problems in children through modifying the parental attitudes (Glidewell, et al., 1957). A social psychologist came in to direct this research and to recruit a staff that was the beginning of our present Division of Research and Development.

The following is taken from Stringer's account (1962):

"I protested loudly and vehemently that no one could do research on what was not there, but no one paid any attention to me. While the service program withered, the research design went on growing toward completeness and full detail. The final plan called for three consecutive years of work in a larger number of schools than our three contract-districts could provide; so obviously more contract-districts were needed. At the same time, since under County ordinance the service was required to be financially self-sustaining, the contract charge had to be increased. And all reason to the contrary notwithstanding, at the start of the 1954–55 school year, five additional districts signed three-year contracts, and the original three districts renewed their contracts for three more years."

The research program took a year for the planning and the pilot studies; then, it took a year from its first to its second wave of data collection. At the beginning of the third year, the data on the program activities and the first estimates of change became available. The data showed clearly that there were no mothers' therapy groups in progress—none at all.

The administrators were shocked, but now they listened to the field staff. Multi-level conferences were now not only permitted, they were made mandatory. Field workers finally had an open line to the administration. Since the increased programming required an enlarged staff, a new order was proposed and accepted. A full-time field-staff member would spend three days a week in the schools and two days in the Health Department—on school work: conferences, consultation, planning, evaluation. A special psychiatric consultant was assigned to the school services.

This was the first of the varied changes suggested by the research activities. The impact was partly from the data, but the data then were mostly in-process, tentative, and preliminary (Glidewell et al., 1957). It was not really the data that induced the main changes; it was the process of conducting the research.

"To us who were working in the schools, this growth, this proliferation of program, was at first simply unbelievable; and then it was infuriating. We felt compromised and threatened, knowing that we could not deliver the service that the Health Department was selling and the schools were buying. There was only one way in which we could escape defeat and disgrace, and that was to ignore all that went on in the higher echelons, and to seize the opportunity—eighteen schools wide and three years long- to make something good out of the school program." (Stringer, 1962)

Basic Assumptions about Change Induction

To all concerned, it was clearly the aim of both the health institution and the educational institution to induce change in children. They moved toward their aims, however, by widely separated approaches, based upon quite different fundamental assumptions.

In general, the schools seek to induce such change by appealing to the intellect. They try intellectually to clarify their goals for change, clarify the rewards to be gained by changing, and clarify the penalties to be suffered by refusing to change. The child who learns, accepts, and adheres to the value systems held and taught by the school is rewarded by (1) being promoted from grade to next higher grade, year after year, (2) a comfortable feeling of belonging to his group or groups, and (3) the strengthening conviction not only that his own particular set of beliefs are the right beliefs, but that his beliefs are also the beliefs held by right-thinking people everywhere.

Allowance is made, within the schools, for a certain amount of emotional valence attached to the intellectual approach. The behavior of educators toward children is often sympathetic, supportive, affectionate, concerned. Sometimes educators feel frustrated, exasperated, and even hostile toward children. Learning is thought to be facilitated by the positive feelings—but in moderation. Learning is thought to be inhibited by the negative feelings, especially when they are intense. But these emotional conditions are only conditions—the process of learning itself is intellectual. The approach works. The appeal to the intellect has been reinforced in the long and honorable tradition of education. Over the years, the vast majority of children have responded well to this appeal to the intellect. It is only the small minority who do not respond.

Clinicians, in mental health services, attempt to induce change in children by focusing on their feelings. Optimally, this involves a high level of cognitive functioning for the therapist and—at least in a good deal of therapy—for the patient as well; but to be clinically respectable, such cognitive functioning must remain focused upon feelings. No value system, in the usual sense of the term, are involved. The avowed prime aim of the method is not to inculcate dogma or doctrine, or even to transfer knowledge, but to search out cause-and-effect relationships among emotions and behaviors. The clinicians' approach works well, also. The vast majority of children in clinics do not respond to a simple appeal to intellect; they do respond—with improvement or without—to appeals to emotions. As experienced by clinicians, the approach has been regularly reinforced and confirmed over many years.

Associated with these differences of method are differences in subjects and number of subjects. The school's appeal to the intellect not only works much more often than it fails to work, but often works with thirty to thirty-five children all at the same time. Few clinicians would be so bold as to claim that their approach, applied one-to-one, is more often effective than not. Fewer still would attempt to do group therapy with groups anything like the size of the average public school classroom. Nevertheless, when the school's approach fails, as it does with many emotionally disturbed children, it does not often happen that continued use or reinforcement of any appeal to intellect (without any other kind of intervention) produces very much change. With such children the clinical approach is necessary. On the other hand, twelve years of psychotherapy is not likely (without any other kind of intervening aid) to produce adequate socialization in the child or adequate academic achievement to equip him either to enter college or to earn his living in the adult world.

Clinical Relationships and Social Responsibility

It should not be assumed that the institutional differences discussed in the foregoing sections were either clearly seen or formulated by any of the people most immediately involved in our School Mental Health Services. As a matter of record, it was the conflict arising around yet another difference that brought the beginning of a clarification of responsibility. That other difference was privileged communication. The mental health workers were quite unaware that privileged communication had no place in the educational institution. It occurred to none of them, in discussing the service with the school adminstrators, even to mention that they would work with referred children and parents with the promise —implicit or explicit—of customary clinical confidentiality. Similarly, it did not occur to anyone in the schools that they would not be told everything that transpired between the referred person and the mental health worker. The astonishing thing is that there was no real explosion over this issue for more than five years. As the service expanded to cover five additional contract districts, the staff was increased to seven people. Here and there minor discords arose when a disgruntled worker made it clear to a principal that he was going to withhold certain kinds of information from the school. These conflicts remained minor, either because the worker then successfully rationalized the matter, or because the principal was uncertain about how to deal with this new kind of professional practitioner in the schools. Eventually, however, one such case became an emergency, precipitating a head-on clash between the school administration and the Health Department administration over the matter of privileged communication.

The clinicians won that particular battle, but its major consequence was a change within the Health Department—a separation of the School Mental Health Services from the Child Guidance Clinic. A nontraditional, quasi-clinical role was emerging, out of the effort to reduce the tensions and the role conflicts.

Autonomy, Dependency, and Emergency

This separation, although it did not yet define the role of the School Mental Health Services staff, at least allowed staff to see more clearly the distinguishing features of the clinic, on the one hand, and of the educational institution, on the other. Privileged communication was considered to be essential in the clinic. It was considered inappropriate, if not actually disruptive, in the schools. The clinic, following medical tradition, claimed the right to function autonomously, even at times autocratically, on the implied basis that all psychiatric treatment is an emergency corrective. There is a long and honorable tradition, in medicine and in law, especially in war and in disaster, that, in an emergency, dependency on legitimate authority is appropriate and necessary to the discipline required for immediate concerted action. The emergency may be an illness or an injury, a riot or a rebellion, a tornado or a flood. The tradition is the same. The person in distress follows wherever properly constituted authority leads. If properly constituted authority figures are not available, then authority is quickly conferred upon whomever the distressed group perceives as nearest to being a credible authority. The credibility may arise from no more than a strong voice and a confident air, but it arises. Similarly, authority can be quickly revoked by a group or a person in emergency distress. If the authoritarian actions do not release, control, or effect escape from the distress, desperate people can quickly transfer the mantle.

Health authorities have received full social sanction for their authoritarian acts as long as the acts have effectively relieved or controlled the emergency. Any failure to relieve the emergency, however, has evoked discredit and resentment. The schools, primarily concerned with developmental cycles in children, were not prepared to deal with emotionalized emergencies. Most of the teachers involved wanted only to be relieved of them, but they were dependent upon the health institution for such relief. The schools were well aware of their dependency on the clinic for emergency correctives, but they also saw— what the clinicians appeared not to see—that not all the children referred to the clinic were emergencies, that not all clinic treatment was effective, that the clinics were dependent upon the schools for classroom management of disturbed children in the schools, and that, under these nonemergency conditions, autocratic behavior on the part of the clinicians was not justified.

The Emergence of New Roles and New Institutional Linkage

The School Mental Health Services staff now found themselves no longer clinicians in the traditional sense of the term. They stood somewhere in the field between the educational institution and the health institution, feeling rather more like clinicians when they were working in the schools, and rather more like school workers when they were dealing with the clinic, and thus gradually—over time— clarifying further the responsibilities, the interdependencies, and the complementarity of these several roles.

Adopting as policy, the idea that their primary responsibility was to the whole school and not just to the sick children within it, the school mental health workers dispensed with privileged communication in their work. They found their work no less productive without it, while, at the same time, the schools' confidence in them was significantly increased. In the marked reduction of tension that ensued, the school mental health workers developed clearer perceptions, not only of the schools' functions, but also of the value of those functions; not only of the schools' methods, but also of the effectiveness of those methods; and—eventually—not only of the schools' needs, but also of the ways in which mental health workers might meet some of these needs.

Out of these interactions came changes in both school personnel and mental health personnel. Collaboration in direct services to children and parents led to consultation and indirect services. Role modi- fications evolved as teachers and principals proved themselves able to learn educative—not clinical—innovations. They learned not by transfer from clinicians, but from their own creativity, stimulated by interactions with their mental health consultants.

The first step in this new interdisciplinary role complementarity was the mental health worker's acceptance of responsibility for the child whom the teacher could not teach or could not manage in the classroom. The second step was the gradual emergence into clearer light of the teacher's responsibility for the classroom management and effective learning of all the children who are not seriously disturbed.

The third step has been a growing conviction that somehow the educators and the mental health workers can learn how to promote mental health, in addition to learning how (if they move in soon enough) they may alleviate mental illness. In this effort the front-line people will not be the mental health workers or the principals and superintendents, but rather the classroom teachers and the parents. The task of the mental health workers will be to learn and to en- able—to learn what it is in the attitudes and interactions of parents and teachers that promotes mental health in children, and to enable by their own attitudes and interactions with parents and teachers, a fuller use of their old resources and their new ones and of their old and their new ideas and skills and feelings.

One History in Retrospect

Looking back now over the twelve years of the service, a particularly interesting series of changes appears with respect to decision-making. At the inception of the service, the workers' attitudes were essentially autocratic. When they made recommendations about a given child, they expected the schools to follow these recommendations unquestioningly, and they experienced a real sense of outrage when the schools failed to do this. As they began to perceive the power of the schools to hold them impotent, they withdrew from that particular battle line, formulated a new policy, and adopted a new posture. They were, they decided, responsible only for making recommendations. It was the school's right to accept or reject those recommendations, but the school must accept the responsibility for whatever consequences were attendant upon their acceptance or rejection. This was no longer the autocratic attitude, but it still managed to retain at least a modicum of arrogance.

With lengthening experience, however, they have moved toward fuller understanding of the roles of the health department and of the school in the community; and their formulation of the relationship of school to community, and of mental health worker to school, has necessarily been modified. Arrogance has been replaced by a more mature acceptance of responsibility. A community gives a mandate to its school administrators to educate the children of the community, but at the same time it imposes certain limitations on the ways in which the school administration may go about its task. Similarly, the schools give a mandate to their mental health workers to concern themselves with mental health and mental illness in school children, but at the same time the schools impose certain limits on the ways in which the mental health workers may go about this task. But the school administrators cannot be effective educators by leaving all decision-making to their communities. As professionals, they must determine—within the limitations imposed by the community—what they may and what they may not do that will be consistent with current professional consensus about best educational knowledge and practice. Similarly, the mental health workers cannot be effective if they leave all decision-making to the schools. They themselves must determine—within the limits imposed by the schools—what they may and what they may not do that will be consistent with current professional consensus about best knowledge and practice in mental health. As professional mental health practitioners and professional education practitioners—and informed citizens in communities—

develop their interrelationships within this kind of framework, their interaction should become more and more mutually enriching.

It is altogether clear that the role of a professional mental health worker in the school is still in a developmental transition. It is equally clear that any linkage between the community health institution and the community educational institution is still in a developmental transition. The local public health department stands at the focal point of the linkage. It is tied by tradition and by public identification with the total health institution. It must, therefore, often be concerned with human urges for emergency relief from pain and distress, and with community responsibility for the protection from exploitation of the patient, who is wholly dependent in his emergency pain on what seem to him (especially in emotional and mental distress) the almost magical and surely esoteric skills and knowledge of the healer, the mental health professional.

The local health department is not, however, in its own self-concept, a part of clinical medicine. It is not primarily responsible for the care of sick people. Its job is to keep people from getting sick. Accordingly, it is—of all the parts of the community health institution—the part most appropriately oriented for the development of functional linkage with the educational institution. The mental health professional, like other health officers in public health, can more readily modify the traditional clinical role to fit the concerns of the profession and the community. It can discharge a responsibility to the community with minimum conflict with the clinician's prime responsibility for the health of his individual patients. It can deal with large groups of people. It can intervene in both interpersonal processes and intrapersonal processes. It can see and respect the integrity of the varying values and responsibilities of a wide variety of professional practices, for it is, within itself, fiercely multidisciplinary.

In this case history, the roles of the public health, mental health consultant and the roles of the teacher really did effect the linkage. In time, the teacher claimed a right to be free from the expectation that she could conduct psychotherapy in the classroom. She also, however, accepted a duty to create innovations in classroom management. She claimed a right to be relieved of the distress and distraction caused by a deeply disturbed child in her classroom. She also accepted a duty to widen the available range of learning activities in order to provide more freely for the education of a healthy child whose emotional problems were mild enough to be handled in the classroom but troublesome enough to limit the learning he could gain from the standard classroom management.

The mental health "consultant-trainer" claimed a right to be freed from trying to cope with the deeply disturbed child in the school setting, but he also accepted the responsibility to try to arrange for care of the child in the clinic. The consultant claimed a right to be free of specifically clinical responsibilities, but he accepted the responsibility to advise, support, and collaborate in the development of innovations specific to classroom management—in the interest of strengthening the capacity of healthy children to deal with their social and emotional problems.

Both the teacher and the consultant claimed the right to be relieved of dealing with the ill and sorely disturbed; but both accepted the duty to prevent further development of such illness and distress. At the point of focus on prevention—of both academic failure and social-emotional breakdown—the educational institution and the health institution found a viable, developmental linkage.

REFERENCES

Brashear, Ellen L., Eleanor I. Kenney, A. D. Buchmueller, and Margaret C.-L. Gildea. "A Community Program of Mental Health Education Using Group Discussion Methods." *Amer. J. Orthopsychiat.*, **24**, 1954, 554–64.

Buchmueller, A. D., and H. R. Domke. "Preventive Mental Health Services in a Mental Health Setting." *Child.*, 1956, 225–231.

Buchmueller, A. D., and Margaret C.-L. Gildea. "A Group Therapy Project with Parents of Behavior Problem Children in Public Schools." *Amer. J. Psychiat.*, **106**, 1949, 46–53.

Buchmueller, A. D., Frances Porter, and Margaret C.-L. Gildea. "A Group Therapy Project with Parents of Behavior Problem Children in Public Schools: A Comparative Study of Behavior Problems in Two School Districts." *Nerv. Child,* **10**, 1954, 415–422.

Gildea, Margaret C.-L. *Community Mental Health: A School-centered Program and a Group Discussion Program.* Springfield, Ill.: Charles C Thomas, 1959.

Glidewell, J. C., I. N. Mensh, H. R. Domke, Margaret C.-L. Gildea, and A. D. Buchmueller. "Methods for Community Mental Health Research." *Amer. J. Orthopsychiat.* **27**, 1957, 38–54.

Kahn, Jane, A. D. Buchmueller, and Margaret C.-L. Gildea. "Group Therapy with Parents of Behavior Problem Children in Public Schools: Failure of the Method in a Negro School." *Amer. J. Psychiat.* **108**, 1951, 351–358.

Stringer, Lorene A. "The Development of a School Mental Health Service in a Local Health Department." A paper read at the 8th Annual Symposium on School Health, University of Kansas Medical Center, Kansas City, Kansas, October 25, 1962.

Stringer, Lorene A. "The Role of the School and the Community in Mental Health Programs." *J. School Hlth.*, **33**, 1963, 385–390.

Williams, R. M. *The American Society.* New York: Alfred A. Knopf, 1951.

Chapter 17

Consultation Processes as a Method for Improving Teaching

Donald C. Klein

About the Author

What can an adult do when a club of ten-year-old children smears the settlement house walls and floors with gooey clay, when he finds himself pursuing eight-year-old boys at 11:00 at night down the fire escape of a children's home, or when an adolescent gang member hurls a terrified "don't touch me" when he puts a comforting arm around the boy's shoulders? Experiences such as these convinced Don Klein to major in psychology in his final year at Roosevelt University in Chicago, and to go on to a Ph.D. in Clinical Psychology at the University of California at Berkeley.

Before his experiences as a part-time group worker at a settlement house and home for dependent children, Klein had begun undergraduate work at Syracuse University aiming toward a career in radio broadcasting and international relations. By the end of World War II, during which he was factotum at an Armed Forces Radio Service broadcasting station in Karachi (then India), he had quite enough of radio. After the war he explored in rapid sequence possible majors in labor relations, economics, and statistics at Roosevelt College before ending up in psychology through the encouragement of the troubled children he encountered.

The climate at Berkeley favored the emergence of a concern with both the developmental and social psychological aspects of man's adjustment to different environments. Klein made the rounds of a variety of Veterans Administration hospitals and clinics, spent three years in an all-purpose state mental hygiene clinic, and made side excursions to a rehabilitation center for Navy men sentenced to the brig, to adult education programs for parents, and to a citizens group working on the development of a county-wide mental health program.

He returned to his native Massachusetts in 1953 as executive director of the Human Relations Service of Wellesley, Inc., the pioneer community mental health program developed by Dr. Erich Lindemann under the sponsorship of the Harvard School of Public Health. Klein spent ten years as a mental health consultant to the Wellesley public schools. He also studied the reactions of children and their families to school entry and helped launch a check-up program to which parents could bring their children for a prophylactic review of their social and emotional development prior to school.

Since 1953 Klein has been immersed in the public health field. While at Wellesley he was Instructor in Mental Health at Harvard, taught group dynamics, and became interested in the study of epidemiology. At the same time, together with colleagues at the Massachusetts General Hospital's Department of Psychiatry, he was developing pre and postprofessional training in community mental health.

Klein became involved with the National Training Laboratories, a division of the National Education Association, in 1956. NTL represents one of the most potent resources in Klein's development. As a Fellow of NTL, he has been active in efforts to design meaningful approaches to community leadership development which combine sensitivity training (T groups) with sociological and political studies of the community.

Klein has a deep and growing conviction that the road to effective approaches to the promotion of human well-being lies in our understanding of change and our ability to use the knowledge from the behavioral sciences in fostering healthy educational settings and other community environments. In 1962 he moved to Boston University to pursue this conviction as associate professor of psychology and director of the Human Relations Center, a multidisciplinary behavioral sciences consultation, teaching and research center. He works with graduate students in education, psychology, and other disciplines and is carrying out training in group dynamics, consultation and community psychology.

His contribution to this book represents a further attempt to encourage the closest possible collaboration between education, mental health disciplines, and the behavioral sciences in general.

Introduction to the Chapter

The consultation process has become a popular but misty "Camino Real" for the transmission of behavioral science understandings in educational settings. The previous chapters by Glidewell and Stringer, and Lippitt, Fox, and Schmuck have already described the passage of ideological vehicles over this high road of research utilization. Unfortunately, all is not well with this vital artery of communication. Undisciplined, unprepared consultants have ventured forth with bold naivete or professional arrogance only to end up in "wash outs." In addition, the dust of theoretical confusion has sometimes obscured the road signs so that both consultants and consultees lose their way and their goals.

This most valuable method of problem solving and of blending competencies has become diluted as too many professionals have employed the consultant role without accepting its responsibilities. For instance, are we correct in assuming that anyone who holds a Ph.D. or M.D. can become an effective mental health consultant? Does mental health consultation require any specific study of the consultee's mission or the agency framework in which he works? It is odd that some mental health professionals, who would feel it necessary to review the literature before giving a paper, would assume that because they are well versed in interpersonal dynamics they are prepared to serve as consultants in schools, industry, welfare departments, or other settings. This unfortunate denial of the need for consultation competency too often tends to subvert a problem solving relationship into a pseudo-therapeutic, psychologically centered, exploration. This rejection of importance of substance rationalizes away the necessity for disciplined, thoughtful preparation and study.

When all the fantasies and myths that have grown up about mental health consultation have been hammered out against the anvil of reason and feasibility, we will hear less of these "Knight Errants" enthusiastically sharing their "vast experience and loft perspectives" with schools and less of messianic pilgrimages into education to repair the weaknesses, revitalize flagging motivations, and recharge intellectual batteries. We shall also hear fewer statements to the effect that consultation process is an unmixed blessing, that consultants are magical "Jehovahs," or that they might even be diabolical spies for the administration.

As you can see, there is a need for making the essential structure and processes of mental health consultation operational and delineating its nature simply and clearly. As Klein points out, consultation seeks to put knowledge to work when and where it is needed; if successful, it can be the most potent link between educators and behavioral scientists.

Consultation Processes as a Method for Improving Teaching[1]

Consultation represents a challenging opportunity in modern education as a means for effective infusion of new knowledge. Many students, teachers, and administrators need knowledge and resources seldom available in a single school or school system. Special programs for special students; shifting school-community relations; crises evolving out of social forces such as the civil rights movement; increasing complexity of administrative structures; rapid development of educational innovations in mathematics, the sciences, and other fields—all of these developments place demands on educators for great technical and social understanding that are at the outer limits of what is known.

At the same time, fortunately, noneducators in a wide range of disciplines are becoming increasingly ready to involve themselves in education. The extent that schools have been recognized as the critical arena of social (as well as intellectual) development, the attention of those concerned with all aspects of human behavior and organization has tended to focus on the processes of education. The fortunate result of such trends has been a growing interest on the part of both educators and noneducators in some sort of direct collaboration. Consultation is one special form of such collaboration, and an increasingly popular one.

Like their business and medical colleagues, educators are coming to realize the advantages of the consultation relationship, which allows a group to utilize the abilities of a specialist without having to make him a permanent member of that group. The nature of such a relationship creates both an opportunity and a challenge for those involved in educational consultation. The relationship is characterized by great flexibility, by dependence on cooperation and participation, and by presentation of heretofore unrealizable possibilities for the use of skills and knowledge not indigenous to education itself.

[1] With editorial assistance of Mrs. Maureen Steinbrunner.

THE CURRENT SCOPE OF CONSULTATION
TO EDUCATION

There are at least six groups currently involved in consultation to education: university departments or centers for one or more of the behavioral sciences; schools or colleges of education; management consulting firms; governmental education authorities; behavioral specialists and others serving as staff within a school system; and community-based mental health centers.

Each of these groups has its own professional and disciplinary concerns, and each approaches education with specific, and very often different, goals. Some of them are closely identified with the aims and functions of education; others are less so, seeing in the school setting an opportunity to work toward the attainment of independent objectives, whether the general application of the knowledge of the social sciences or a solution to more specific problems. Certain groups are more interested in the objective observation of phenomena; others in bringing about change and innovation in educational practice. Additionally, the attention of any consultant to education may tend to focus specifically on individuals, or it may instead be concerned with groups, systems, organization, planning or other processes, or school-community relations.

We shall try to gain some idea of the general nature and complexity of the consultation relationship and of its demands on the persons involved, by examining the two most common types of behavioral science consultation. They serve to illustrate current trends, and at the same time provide some indication of the distinctions which hold between the methods, objectives, and assumptions of the various groups involved in consulting for education. We shall consider not only the actual operation and immediate goals of each of these groups but also of their disciplinary heritage and the origin of their methodological assumptions.

MENTAL HEALTH CONSULTATION

A growing area of consultation, and one perhaps least directly related to actual classroom instruction, is mental health consultation; more specifically, that which is aimed at promoting mental health among school children, and at creating and preserving that school environment which will encourage it. For the mental health consultants, whether based within the system or acting as representatives of a community organization apart from the school, the school experience represents one of the principal situations in which children may be given necessary emotional supports, protected from the extreme effects of stressful situations, and helped in forming a foundation for sound mental health in their adult years. The primary aim of these consultants is to create for children emotionally supportive environments maintained by the educator's realistic consideration of the children's abilities and emotional needs.

In an orientation derived largely from psychoanalysis, and with techniques modified from those used by child psychiatric treatment teams for work with parents, the interest of the mental health consultant centers on the immediate relationship between teacher and pupil, and on the interpersonal relations of teacher and principal, teacher and parents, parents and pupil, and so forth. The aim is to help school personnel understand and respond more adequately to the psychological processes of the child.[1]

Typically, a mental health consultant is retained by the school and is available to any teacher who may request consultation. The method of consultation with which we are concerned here, and the one most frequently employed, is based on the assumption that a teacher usually turns to the consultant in a state of heightened tension, often an emotional "crisis," or condition of extreme emotional involvement.

Even the experienced teacher, used to working with a wide variety of child personalities and able to respond to most of them without emotional overinvolvement, will find a number of children whose behavior arouses deep feeling. It is a common experience, for example, for a teacher new to teaching to concentrate his or her concern on the loneliness or rejection faced by one or more children who are newcomers to the school. Identification with, and reaction to, the perceived feelings and actions of others, and the consequent reinforcement or aggravation of one's own similar feelings can result in a moment or period of generally heightened emotional tension. The teacher may find usual approaches unsatisfactory or may be reacting to the child in ways which she herself recognizes as ineffective or inappropriate, as certain child behaviors trigger disgust, fright, anger or unusual discouragement. When called in such situations, the consultant seeks to affect the capacity of the teacher to deal more objectively

---

[1] We are not concerned here with another type of consultation more traditional in the schools—that of the school psychologist—because this is not consultation in the present sense. The individual in this role *usually* deals directly with the child as "patient" or client, and does not primarily deal with school personnel in the peer relationship of consultation.

with children who present similar problems in the future. He tries to support the teacher directly and to help her face the complex, intense, and often conflicting demands made on her within school relationships and in the classroom. Through him the teacher may become better able to view the child with an objective, accepting, and unshaken perspective when certain behavior has been particularly upsetting. Sometimes he simply serves to reinforce an approach with which the teacher has been hesitantly experimenting.

Mental health consultants make a fundamental distinction between consultation and psychotherapy, though many teachers participating in mental health consultation tend to wonder whether they are not perhaps being given psychotherapy. They are correct that their perceptions and reactions, both with respect to the pupils and to the consultant himself, are indeed being "analyzed." But this is only a professional extension of the analysis that any individual conducts with regard to another's behavior and feelings and is distinct from the sort of discussion of an individual's personal problems and pathogenic life history in which mental health consultants usually refuse to become involved.

However, mental health consultants are not agreed on the best manner in which to deal with a teacher's emotional involvement in a problem. Some focus directly on the teacher's annoyance, anxiety, or other reaction to a particular child, explicitly pointing up the child's effect on the teacher. Others prefer to avoid any direct confrontation of the teacher's emotions, rather dealing indirectly and implicitly with his or her inner conflicts by discussing their upsetting counterparts in the behavior of the child. The direct approach values, and seeks to promote, psychological insight and emotional openness in the teacher. It assumes that help in accepting one's own personal feelings is an essential aspect of professional development. Those committed to the indirect method, while not denying the desirability of self-awareness, believe that open exploration of an individual's feelings can be threatening and should be done only within the structured atmosphere of psychotherapy. At this juncture, there is no hard evidence in this matter.

The mental health consultant is relatively uninvolved in the curricular aspects of a school system and its administrative structures; he is likely to be unconcerned with the educational activities of the classroom, except insofar as they directly involve the personal relations and personalities of the teacher and pupils. He does not see himself as an expert in the mechanics of education, nor does he concern himself with the dynamics of organization and the workings of the different groups which may be present in a school, except when these impinge on the mental health of one or more children.

GROUP–ORIENTED CONSULTATION

Group-oriented consultants, or applied behavioral scientists, however, are very much interested in both education and the psychology of social organization. They may come from a university-based institute or center for the behavioral sciences, or from a department of sociology or psychology.

Almost all actions and feelings are affected by relationships and attitudes which are part of what is broadly termed "group behavior," a concept including face-to-face groups (the family, the class, an informal playground group); formal aggregates ("teachers," "parents," or "supervisors"); and organized structures and systems (school, school system, community). A group-oriented consultant may be called in for any number of reasons, ranging from a crisis in community—school board relations to a general dissatisfaction with day-to-day relations between the various professional groups within a single school to a concern about the behavior of a classroom of children.

The aim of such a consultant is to improve understanding within and between groups so that the individuals in these groups may function most effectively and productively. A method often used by group-oriented consultants in helping individuals in a school come to understand the dynamics and significance of group behavior, involves the sensitivity training group, or T-group. This is a set of individuals brought together for the specific purpose of learning how their behavior can be modified and reinforced through participation in a group. The T-group exploits the reinforcement and amplification of personal action which is typical of group-related behavior and demonstrates the potentials of such reinforcement. In addition, it is a direct tool for improvement and change, both in substantive problems of group procedures, and in attitude.

In the training group, a generalized process is followed: dissatisfactions are brought out and examined in the open. Then, new approaches to the problem are decided upon in common. The new approaches are trial-practiced by the group, the results of the trials are evaluated by the group, generalized, and applied further. And then the process is begun again on new problems.

The reinforcement of the individual by the presence of and interaction with other members of the group, all involved in the same process of learning about oneself and all sharing in the emotionally satisfying experience of working out common problems together, both eases the process of adjusting to the necessity of changing one's attitudes and behavior and provides the opportunity for actually effecting that change. An added effect of the training group is the opportunity for participants to "internalize" changes in behavior or attitude. "When the primary motivation for improvement (in attitudes and relationships towards working in groups) comes from the strong desires of the person—aided by 'insiders' who are members of the same training group—to improve on ways of working with others, then the changes in his behavior can become increasingly systematic, permanent, integrated, and job-related [1, p. 720]."

Group and organizationally oriented consultation fulfills, or can fulfill, the function of initiating great changes in educational practice in the areas of methods of administration, school-community relations, and cooperation among teachers and, in the end, in teaching itself. If we consider education a process of growth and change, then we can see that the group-oriented consultants, using methods such as sensitivity training, are in fact involved directly in education, in the change and growth of the individual in a school or school system. An awareness of this fact has led to a growing commitment on the part of the group-oriented consultants to become involved in education, to bring it new ways of attaining innovation, change, and growth; to stimulate these in all areas of administration and teaching; and to promulgate the attitude in education that change is possible and even desirable.

A specific example of one individual's reaction to organizational requirements and of the ramifications such reaction can have is found in the situation of one grade-school teacher involved in consultation. She appeared to be unable to allow pupils to be even mildly aggressive in her classroom without becoming angry herself. Boys especially found it difficult to avoid her displeasure and frequently became either apathetic or overtly hostile and destructive in response. A consultant to the school made no real progress on this problem until, after over two years of ineffective individual consultation, it happened that a young, male, informal principal replaced the elderly, female, and somewhat autocratic administrator under whom the teacher had worked for over a decade.

Now there was suddenly a pronounced shift in the teacher's readiness to respond to the consultant's efforts. The problems of authority, the principal's and the teacher's own, in the classroom, had evidently been tied in with the latter's reactions to aggressive behavior. The consultant concluded, on the teacher's sudden change of attitude, that her reaction to aggressiveness in herself and others had been exacerbated by her discomfort at having to submit to the authority of the former principal, against whom she did not dare vent her true feelings. With the new administrator there was less need for suppressing disagreement and also less disagreement actually felt. In turn, she could be more acceptant of the boys' reactions to her own authority, and at the same time, became less likely to arouse their anger against herself.

THE CONSULTATION PROCESS AND ITS RELATIONSHIPS

Throughout this discussion, we have tried to emphasize the idea that, at its best, consultation is collaboration. It has often been pointed out by authors concerned with all kinds of consultation that the consultant and his consultee are both professionals; they enjoy an equal colleagueship, each as a specialist in a particular sphere, each with something to gain from the relationship and from the experience of jointly discerning and solving problems. Both have much to learn. From the point of view of the consultant—whether group-oriented or mental-health oriented—the school and the school system together constitute one of the most fascinating theatres of human existence. Within this theatre is played out the marvelous drama of change and growth in personal behavior and in interpersonal relations, as well as in mental capacity and performance—in short, the drama of education. The educator is both an actor and a director in this drama. Without his assistance, the behavioral scientist can neither observe, nor participate in, the ongoing dynamics of the educational process. Without the guidance of the educator, he can not move successfully within the complexities of the school system, nor can he fully understand what he sees and hears there, without the thoughtful interpretation of the insider. There are even certain phenomena that can never be observed directly by an outsider at all but can only be shared with him by the educator who chooses to do so.

On his part, the behavioral scientist trains the educator in group methods perhaps, or in the psychology of the individual. Group-oriented consultation emphasizes the teaching of teachers about interpersonal processes and group work; mental health consultation concentrates on teaching the teacher about himself and about children. In both cases, consultation is collaboration, in which both educator and consultant have much to gain.

There are large and small examples of the cooperation possible

between educators and consultants. With the introduction of consulting participation by a local mental health agency in the Wellesley,
Massachusetts public schools, a pre-school orientation program, and a
collaborative study of early school adjustment were initiated antici-
pating the "Headstart" program now in operation around the country.
Procedures for a cursory review of the emotional and social development of kindergarten-age children were developed, and finally it became possible, with the cooperation of the Wellesley schools, to experiment with the kind of pre-school check-up program now being
applied in other communities in various parts of the country.

Yet many consultation efforts do less than to produce joint programs; some fail altogether to produce change and improvement in
those systems they were initiated to change and improve. What are
the factors that make collaboration between consultants and school
personnel effective and successful? The single most important consideration, for the consultant and the educator, lies in the establishment
of a good working relationship, a process more complex than may
at first appear.

The Outsider

Obviously, a consultant is not part of the ordinary structure of
a school system and has no specific, institutionalized function within
that system. Like anyone new to a situation, the visitor is apt to
meet with misunderstanding, mistrust, or disapproval along with natural curiosity and speculation, as he arrives to begin his job. Unlike
the first-day teacher, however, or the new principal, the consultant
will continue to be an outsider as long as he continues to be a consultant. Somehow he has to establish good relations with all of the
school personnel, without the benefit of the factor which normally
aids such relations: the emotional ties derived from being part of
a group, the fellowship created by being in a continuing partnership
to perform a specific task, or even the acceptance which usually goes
with the prospect of an inevitable, constant, and long-term interaction.

For these things, the consultant has somehow to substitute other
"sanctions," or specific forms of authorization, support, and encouragement. Achieving and maintaining sanction is one of the consultant's
most crucial problems in getting the job done, because his ability
to get along with and to promote the cooperation of the education
personnel (and therefore his chance of being able to work effectively
with them) depend directly on the establishment of a positive and
productive relationship. Certainly the approval of those in authority
in a school system can contribute to the easier establishment of good

will all along the line. On the other hand, a teacher who has not been part of a decision to hire a consultant may well not want to cooperate, no matter what the wishes of a superior in this regard may be. Trust, understanding, and cooperation can never be assumed; they can only be hoped for, if the visiting behavioral scientist is to be successful in bringing new insights to bear on the old or new problems facing the school.

There are, of course, certain ground rules for consultation which, if formulated early, serve to ease the process of working out sanction. All personnel likely to be involved in the consultation at some point ought to be clear about why the consultant is there, what kind of help he will seek to offer, and to whom. They should know how to go about making contact with him, and they should have a clear understanding of the nature and extent of his responsibility in dealing with what are essentially their problems. Ideally, the original decision to call in a consultant will have been made with the awareness and approval of as many members of the school's staff as possible.

Perhaps equally as critical as the matter of sanction in the non-structured consultation process, is the question of timing. Group-oriented consultation, for example, is usually carried out on an on-and-off basis, often divided into three phases, each of which involves a different frequency and duration of contact. During the first phase, the consultant is usually involved in an appraisal of the problem. He may hold regularly-scheduled meetings during which diverse views of the situation are aired and an attempt is made to understand the factors that may be leading to divergent points of view. The consultant may also confer with individuals or sub-groups in an effort to uncover significant information that may not be apparent to the total group or that cannot be comfortably communicated by one member to another.

During the second phase, the consultant usually needs longer and more concentrated working periods in which to meet with the group. It is during this time that he seeks to create an altered situation, wherein perceptual and mental blocks may be eliminated and new relations and procedures may be established to facilitate communication and collaboration among members of a group or between groups. This might be the time for special workshops or training programs. During the third phase, consultation may be relatively less frequent and concentrated. The consultant's support will probably be helpful at regular intervals, but if he has been successful in introducing new and more effective group procedures, only occasional review and evaluation sessions should be necessary. In actual practice, of course.

this particular three-phase operation may prove entirely inappropriate. Hopefully, both the consultant and the group with which he is working will be flexible enough to recognize when the process of group learning should be speeded up or slowed down.

In mental health consultation, the matter of timing usually reflects different requirements, and is normally handled differently according to these requirements. A regular progression can be seen in the development of mental health consultation relationships that tend to be constant over a period of time. At first, requests for help with problems within the classroom almost invariably involve an element of crisis; teacher and consultant hop from difficulty to difficulty, solving each as best they can for the moment and not feeling much sense of long-term gain. By the end of such a time period, however, collaboration is well-established. The teacher has worked through previously tender or sensitive areas of discussion; he or she now approaches the job of teaching with increased confidence, a greater degree of objectivity, and more willingness to receive help. Typically, the teacher can now approach the consultant early in the school year with a list of pupils who might have special educational or emotional needs. He can seek out the consultant as a collaborator from another discipline, whose knowledge and skills he may borrow when appropriate.

In the early, or crisis state, visits by the consultant ought to be infrequent enough to let crises come to a head, if they are tending to do so, thus allowing both consultant and teacher to recognize the really major problems. On the other hand, if visits are too widely spaced, true crises which emerge between visits may be resolved for good or ill, and never come to the attention of the consultant. As in the matter of sanction, the timing of a consultation relationship must be approached with a great deal of flexibility by all parties concerned.

The Expert

In addition to his status as an outsider, the consultant is also functioning as an expert, a position which often blocks true collaboration between him and the teacher or school administrator. The consultant has generally a more advanced academic degree; he is paid more for his time! Generally, the consultant knows the school better than the teacher knows the consultant and his field. Many mental health people have consulted with schools; few educators have consulted with clinics or other mental health agencies. Group-oriented consultants have often conducted workshops on various topics for educators, but few indeed are education workshops for group-oriented consultants.

And so on. This sort of one-sidedness may be deplored, but it is only a minor obstacle to cooperation compared with others less dependent on attitude and directly related to professional requirements.

In mental health consultation, for example, a difficulty always arises about the consultant's concern for clinical confidentiality. Both he and the educator receive information about pupils and their families or about other staff members of the school, information that must be treated circumspectly. Each of the two is aware about the necessity to maintain confidentiality about certain matters.

The mental health consultant, however, has been trained specifically never to share a confidence with a third party unless permission from the individual concerned has been secured. Although the educator will repeat a confidence to the outside mental health consultant fully trusting that the latter's clinical training ensures that the information will be treated with discretion, the reverse is not true. Rarely will the mental health worker who is interviewing a child, a parent, or another teacher, share privileged information with any other teacher, or with the principal, unless and until special permission has been granted. Thus a teacher or administrator will often feel cut off from sources of information that might help them in their work with children. Whether or not the information would be of value (and there is doubt of the worth of clinical data or insight for the classroom situation), the educator feels that he is being treated as a second-class member of the team.

Presumably, the consultant is always the authority in the situation, a fact which creates an unavoidable and probably necessary element of dependence on the part of the teacher who is asking for help. Dependence however, is not the ideal condition from which to establish collaboration, and the concept of "expertise" can develop into a real obstacle and perhaps, if it is allowed to cause serious or deep resentment on the part of the teacher or administration, may make the consultative relationship totally ineffective.

POINT OF VIEW

In spite of what has been said above, the hardships which the designation of a consultant as "outsider" and as "expert" works on the consultation are neither inevitable nor unavoidable. There is a great deal of flexibility involved in the way we can view a consultation situation—a flexibility that can minimize the difficulties that stem from labeling a consultant an outside expert. In both of the types of consultation described here, mental health consultation and group-oriented consultation, as well as in virtually every other, a common framework of assumptions, expectations, and methods can be found that provides for just such flexibility regarding the nature of the consultation relationship and how we use it.

Basically, consultation occurs when one individual or group (the consultant system) attempts to help another individual or group (the consultee system) with a problem faced in the latter's work situation, possibly involving one or more persons for whom the consultee has responsibility (the client system). It is possible within this basic structure to differentiate at least three types of relationship, any one of which may be in effect in any single consultation. The three types are:

1. Expert consultation. Here the consultant concentrates on arriving at the right answer for a particular problem in a particular situation.

2. Resource consultation. In this case, the consultant directs his efforts towards providing relevant information, so that the consultee can make decisions based on knowledge of the widest possible range of alternatives.

3. Process consultation. This kind of consultation aims at the most thorough change possible. The consultant works with the consultee to bring about changes in the consultee or his behavior that will enable him to solve his problems himself and to handle similar problems more competently in the future.

In practice, the same consultant may perform all three of the above functions in different situations, or occasionally even on one assignment. And more than one of these types may apply to any specific consultation. But in general, one relationship is dominant.

As an *expert* the consultant assumes that solution of the specific problem at hand is the most important consideration. He supposes, since he is presumably filling a gap, that the consultee lacks the special competence needed to arrive at a solution in this problem, and, further, that it is probably not within the professional scope of the consultee to develop competence to deal with future such problems, should they occur.

For example, a consulting psychologist is called upon to help a principal decide whether or not to promote a marginal pupil. The consultant concentrates in this instance upon the child, the specific problem, or "client," of our consultation model. He interviews the child, perhaps administers ability and personality tests, reviews the school record, confers with the teacher, and makes a specific recommendation for or against moving the child ahead a grade. He is not primarily concerned with a consideration of why the educators have not been able to use their own yardsticks for determining placement; neither does he accept responsibility for helping teacher or principal develop the testing or other skills which he believes should be applied to resolve such questions.

As a *resource,* the cansultant also assumes that the consultee lacks competence at the moment to arrive at a solution to a problem. However, any consultant who sees himself as a resource, rather than as an expert, generally operates as if the consultee's lack of competence arises not so much from limitation in training or experience as from a lack of specialized knowledge or information. His job consists usually in providing relevant information about the specific problem, similar situations faced by others, and factors in the situation of which the consultee may have been unaware. He provides his own breadth of experience and skills in observation for use by the consultee. While he may even suggest various alternative solutions or approaches, it is left to the consultee to make final decision about action based upon the consultant's assessment of how best to use the latter's professional skills and experience. Unlike the expert, the resource consultant sees his job as informing as well as problem solving.

For example, a psychologist is called upon to help with the promotion of a child might act more directly with principal and teacher. He reviews with them the results of his own assessment of the child and also the available knowledge about the usual outcome of promotion and nonpromotion in cases of the same kind. He will also suggest various alternatives which have promise of success in such cases. He indicates, however, that the principal and teacher are in the best position to make the final decision because of their own intimate knowledge of the child and other special competence in such matters as curriculum requirements, classroom functions, and progression through the grades.

A *process* consultant places principal emphasis upon fostering the professional development of the consultee himself. He assumes that the consultee has either the requisite knowledge or the ability to gain the information needed in order to assess the problem properly. He further assumes that the consultee has the basic skills necessary for coping with the situation once it has been diagnosed. The real problem is seen as stemming not from noncompetence, but rather from some form of temporary or partial "myopia" on the part of the consultee which makes it difficult for him to use his knowledge and skill appropriately.

Examples of process consultation, of course, can be seen in both the consulting groups described at the beginning of this article, mental health and group-oriented consultants. Not all problems in a school or school system, certainly, will easily lend themselves to process consultation. However, consultation to education can be seen as truly challenging and as truly presenting opportunities for growth and innovation when it is directed toward processes, toward the working out of problems in such a way as to leave the educator (*and* the consultant) richer both in ability and insight.

POSTSCRIPT

As one views the entire spectrum of behavioral science consultation to the schools—mental health, group-oriented, child psychologist, or whatever—it becomes apparent that knowledge and skills concerning human behavior may be used either to bolster and strengthen the status quo, or to introduce productive innovation and change. Mental health consultation aims at change usually though not always in terms of the individual consultee; group-oriented consultation as practiced by Lippitt and others is committed to the objective of innovation and dissemination of new practices for classroom management and school organization. In the latter case, existing ways of establishing classroom groups, of handling teacher-pupil relations and of relating school to community are evaluated in an effort to stimulate more effective environments through the application of behavioral science insights and orientations.

In today's changing society many of our schools are committed to experimentation and innovation. Group-oriented consultation and related fields in organizational process consultation facilitate the process of change and seek to help it occur in an orderly and planful manner. Mental health consultation can become a major supportive force used by individual educators to help them cope with change with a minimum of personal distress and distortion of their professional competence.

Whatever its origin, consultation seeks to put behavioral science to work when and where it is needed. When successful, it is probably the most potent available way to link the manifold concerns of the educator with the growing resources of the behavioral scientist.

REFERENCES

1. Caplan, Gerald. *Concepts of Mental Health and Consultation*. Children's Bureau, U.S. Department of Health, Education and Welfare, 1959, pp. 144.

2. Ferneau, E. F. "Which Consultant?" *Administrator's Notebook,* **2,** No. 8, University of Chicago, 1954.
3. Glidewell, John. The Entry Problem in Consultation, *J. Soc. Issues,* **15,** No. 2, 1959, 51–59.
4. Kevin, David. "Use of the Group Method in Consultation in Social Work Practice." L. Rapoport (Ed.), New York: National Association of Social Workers, 1963, pp. 69–84.
5. Klein, Donald and Elizabeth Lindemann. "Approaches to Pre-School Screening," *J. School Health,* **34,** No. 8, October, 1964.
6. Lippitt, R., Jeanne Watson, and B. Westley. *The Dynamics of Planned Change.* New York: Harcourt, Brace Company, 1958.
7. Miles, Matthew. *Learning to Work in Groups,* New York: Teachers College, Columbia University, 1959.

Additional Readings

Beckhard, R. *The Leader Looks at the Consultative Process.* Washington, D.C.: Leadership Resources, Inc., 1961.
Berlin, I. N. "Mental Health Consultation in Schools as a Means of Communicating Mental Health Principles." *J. Amer. Acad. Child Psychiatry,* **1,** October 1962, 671–679.
Bindman, A. J. "Mental Health Consultation: Theory and Practice." *J. Consult. Psych.,* **23,** 1959, 473–482.
J. Soc. Issues, **15,** 1959, 13–50. (Issue devoted to consultation.)
Rapoport, Lydia (Ed.), *Consultation in Social Work Practice.* New York: National Association of Social Workers, 1963.

Chapter 18

Predicting and Evaluating the Effectiveness of Children in School

Nadine M. Lambert

About the Author

Although she was born in Utah, Nadine M. Lambert was reared in Los Angeles. After graduating from high school, she entered U.C.L.A. where after a brief encounter with an engineering curriculum, she changed her major to psychology, earning her A.B. in 1948. She then became a graduate student at her alma mater with her eye on a Ph.D. in clinical psychology. She left the program for work and marriage after acquiring a General Secondary Teaching Credential with a teaching major in social science and a minor in physical science.

While teaching she attended Los Angeles State College and received an M.A. in Education, her school psychologist certificate, and a General Pupil Personnel Services Credential.

In 1958 Miss Lambert enrolled in the Ph.D. degree program at U.S.C. (under the direction of J. P. Guilford) and in 1965 she received her doctorate in psychology with a major in psychological measurement.

Her work experience, most of which was concurrent with her graduate educational program, has been quite varied: engineering draftsman, kindergarten teacher, elementary guidance consultant, psychometrist and test consultant (ETS). For six years she served as a research consultant for the California State Department of Education.

In 1964 she joined the staff of the University of California at Berkeley as an Assistant Professor of Education. She presently directs the school psychologist training program and teaches courses in measurement and educational psychology. She has directed two cooperative research projects concerned with the problems of identifying children with ineffective school behavior and assessing the variables related to school success.

She is past president of the California Association of School Psychologists and Psychometrists and has authored and co-authored various articles on culture fair tests and techniques for identifying vulnerable children.

Nadine Lambert believes that mental health professionals should not content themselves with a special feeling in their midsections

(I've got it here), but should apply rigorously the searching and abrasive medicament of clean research design to their work so as to develop generalizations about human behavior which can be replicated in practice.

She is married, and has demonstrated her continuing interest in the home study approach to child development by being the mother of two children (a girl fourteen and a boy two-and-one-half).

Introduction to the Chapter

Impatience, often a fault, is rarely a virtue. However, when impatience motivates us to integrate a more holistic view of things, then surely this is one of the rare instances when impatience has become a virtue. Dr. Nadine Lambert has been and still is impatient with the fragmented and negatively focused methods in use to assess and predict the effectiveness of children in schools. How can the data gathering and recommendations we need to help children succeed in school be freed of their present pathological bias? How can we move beyond segmental descriptions of school failure toward more comprehensive assessment of the experiential programs and cognitive-affective capacities available for school success?

In this call for a more positive and holistic approach to school effectiveness, she identifies the deceptions we have engendered by attempting to categorize children or their problems into etiological or disability pigeon holes. She pinpoints the missed cues and the half-truths that are the products of premature labeling of children in terms of the respective frames of reference of the various pupil personnel and medical disciplines involved, each viewing a separate aspect of the child.

Dr. Lambert accepts the challenge implicit in her criticisms. Blending an extensive range of contributions by behavioral scientists with some of her own classroom field testing of standardized instruments, she outlines the pathways to formulating a more practical and comprehensive way of measuring school effectiveness. In the spirit of implementing Hollister's call for the identification of strens, she reviews selected research findings and approaches that will help us assess the strength building experiences and ego capacities pertinent to school functioning. She denotes the "ready ingredients" and the problems that will require solution before this more complete multivariant assessment method can be created. Here is the impatient scientific scholar and classroom tactician combined, searching for a better and more workable integration of "what we know" so that we may some day more thoroughly undergird educational decisions with sound and scientifically researched appraisals of the potentials of students we seek to educate.

Predicting and Evaluating the
Effectiveness of Children in School

Today public schools are increasingly concerned with the rising number of children who will fail in school. School failure occasioned by disorganization in the cognitive and affective domains of functioning is not a new concern. However, it is heightened in contemporary schools by the fact that the school is no longer reserved for those whose parents can afford the costs of an education or for those who readily adapt and succeed. A successful educational experience has been shown to be a necessity for competent adult functioning. The increasing heterogeneity of the public school population places an increasing burden on the classroom teacher.

Since the task of the schools is to accept all children and to find ways in which to provide an optimum educational experience, the variables that affect school functioning must be established and verified and then systematically integrated into a scheme for studying school effectiveness.

The teacher is a principal resource in the identification of the effective and noneffective student. Notwithstanding all of the biases that can affect an adult's perception of a particular child and his behavior, we have relied on teacher perception of problems and referral to school authorities as the principal mode for studying effective school behavior.

LABELS AND LIMITS

Teachers like other people in our society are aware of the transitory nature of behavior. Thus they are likely to wait for a chronic state of school difficulty to set in before making a referral. The school pupil personnel worker's traditional focus has been an attempt to diagnose the cause of the pupil's school difficulties, to classify the child's behavior on the basis of one or more of the categories in the

425

current nosology of school functioning and to make a prognosis for future school effectiveness. The child who is not succeeding in school is first noticed by the teacher and then referred to the school's pupil personnel worker. He confirms the teacher's observations, gathers data from the child and the family, diagnoses the probable causes of the problem, and classifies the symptoms and behavior. Thus the archives of educational and psychological research contain numerous studies identifying the characteristics of the gifted underachiever, the neurologically handicapped, the emotionally disturbed, the school learning problem, the culturally disadvantaged, the autistic child, the delinquent, and the school drop out. The label applied may indicate the area in which the etiology of the difficulty is expected to be found such as in the case of the "emotionally disturbed," the "neurologically handicapped," or the "culturally deprived," or it may emphasize the effects of the disability such as the "drop out," the "delinquent," or the "school learning problem." In any case, whether the emphasis is on cause or effect, the label that is applied often determines the specific variables being studied and emphasized in each group. Consequently, one finds sociological causation to be the independent variable in research for the culturally disadvantaged, interpersonal and intrapersonal variables to be the focus of research investigations concerned with the emotionally disturbed, or neurophysiological variation to be the emphasis in the study of the neurologically handicapped. Nevertheless, all of these groups of children have in common some type of individual handicap in coping with the school situation.

One of the limitations of the present system for studying effectiveness in school is that the focus is on school failure rather than on school success. We know most about children who have caused others difficulty, and our knowledge indicates that the categories in the nosology of school functioning previously indicated are not discrete groups. Cultural disadvantages are frequently found in the emotionally disturbed and neurologically handicapped groups, and emotional and behavioral problems are typical of children from disadvantaged homes and of children suspected of imperfect neurological functioning. Although these terms seem to offer the security of being able to pinpoint probably sources of difficulty, they are deceiving in that once some logical cause of difficulty can be located, other probable sources of problems are ignored, and the educational program is planned around the single etiology chosen.

Even with the excellent diagnostic tools available today, arriving at a definitive diagnosis of a child's problem is usually difficult. It is a relatively simple matter to arrive at a diagnosis of mental retardation when the effects of the retardation are visible, just as a diagnosis of neurological impairment is rather easy to make when there are visible physical handicaps and perceptual motor impairments. Difficulties in determining the diagnosis increase in cases of overlapping etiological factors typical of the borderline mentally retarded group, the mildly neurologically handicapped, or the group of children with moderate to serious learning problems. This fact was demonstrated in a study by Lambert (14a) in which two independent teams of educators, psychologists, pediatricians and neurologists were asked to determine whether the learning and behavior problems of a group of pupils were related to probable organic impairment. There was little agreement on the diagnosis for individual pupils. The results indicated that each team was "looking" for different variables and each was therefore biased concerning the importance it attached to various clinical signs.

An example of the limitations placed on the study of school behavior by this labeling process can be found in a follow-up study by Lambert (14b). This study demonstrated that elementary school pupils identified by their teachers as maladjusted with learning and behavioral problems (and classified as emotionally disturbed by Child Guidance clinics) later became delinquent, dropped out of school, or made poor adaptations to the high school setting. Since the focus was on the cause of the behavior problems, important early predictive information was ignored in their case records. One example of unused information, was that the type of referring symptom at the elementary years for the later delinquent group was different from the types of referring symptoms for those who did not become delinquent or drop out of school. Symptoms of lying, stealing, cheating, and overt acts of hostility toward peers and teachers were found in the to-become delinquent group, and none of these symptoms was found in records of pupils who stayed in school and did not develop delinquent behavior. The teacher and pupil personnel worker had, in fact, identified early in their school lives, children who were having significant problems in adjusting to school. However, by premature labeling of the pupils' problems, important clues to the school problems were ignored, and potentially valuable school interventions were missed that might have affected positively the course of each child's development.

Children who are labeled emotionally disturbed, school drop out, neurologically handicapped, delinquent, or culturally disadvantaged are special cases of ineffective school behavior. Some investigators have demonstrated that it is possible to define a continuum of school behavior from effective to ineffective, and they indicate some of the variables that predict a given child's position on such a continuum. The results of such work suggest that school effectiveness is related to the child's reaction to stress and his ability to cope with normal life crisis situations. A research definition of school effectiveness begins to emerge from such research on school problems. School effectiveness can be studied as a function of the degree to which a child is vulnerable to stresses or partially disabled by the use of a variety of poor adaptive mechanisms resulting from his efforts to manage the developmental demands of growth, family, school, and social environment. The challenge for research specialists is to define the social, biological, cognitive, and affective variables that affect this general vulnerability to stress or the disability arising from poor adaptation. A more satisfactory study of school effectiveness can be made by the commitment of research energies to the study of the general school population than by focus on an easily identified group of pupils such as those referred to the school guidance office or the child guidance clinic. Even though school effectiveness is a fairly nebulous area to study, its ambiguity is consistent with the fact that most problems of children are expressed in many ways rather than in specific outcomes resulting from specific disabilities.

PREDICTING SCHOOL EFFECTIVENESS: RESOURCES AND ADAPTIVE MECHANISMS

What are the supplies, resources, or strength-giving agents that affect the child's ability to cope with school? It is implicit in the teacher's understanding of the child who succeeds and the child who does not succeed in school that the former has better resources to deal with the demands of the classroom. Teachers describe a child in terms of the involvement of the family with the child's education, in terms of the neighborhood in which he lives, and in terms of the child's physical health, intellectual capacity and attention span, motivational characteristics, and whether he is young or old for his age. Teachers' empirical observations that these independent variables have something to do with school functioning have been supported by a number of scientific investigations. However, it is not common practice to supply teachers with such information about children. We have tended to leave teachers to their own devices in gathering pertinent information about individual children. If schools are to succeed in becoming more effective with more children, the pupil personnel worker will need to gather the available information about the resources children possess to cope with the school situation. Then he will be able to provide the teacher with a system for using such information in enhancing the child's chances of success in her classroom. Therefore, when the assumption is made that certain psychological supplies or resources are necessary for optimum coping power in school and that their lack increases the child's vulnerability to school failure, the teacher and pupil personnel worker must collaborate on reducing the effects of inadequate resources in the child's educational program. Such reduction can be accomplished by modifying the stress created in the educational process and by providing the necessary ego enhancing experiences for certain children in their school experiences to obviate the effects of inadequate resources.

Spitz (22) provides a basic reference to an understanding of the psychological supplies necessary for effective functioning. He postulates that the principal variables in the development of the child are the relationship between the infant and his mother and the relationship between the child and his larger environment. Even though Spitz does not deal directly with the organic components of childhood mental illnesses, he indicates the importance of such components. The child's psychic system is not differentiated from his somatic system during the first months of life. His mother must administer his daily schedule in order to ensure his survival and to provide an environment from which he can gradually establish himself as a separate person. In the course of the first six months, a psychological steering organization (his ego) will be separated from his experience. The differentiation of this steering mechanism is a function of the cognitive-affective transactions between the mother and the child. When there are insufficient or inadequate transactions, diffusion rather than differentiation results. Spitz suggests that this comes about when there is the wrong kind of mothering. The mother either acts as a negative agent in the child's development or she may neglect the child (maternal deprivation).

BRAIN AND BEHAVIOR

When a child has a school problem that cannot be explained on the basis of his family environment, socio-cultural status, or intellectual functioning as measured by ability tests, the pupil personnel worker frequently looks for evidence of neurological dysfunction. The focus on possible neurological impairment as a causative factor in school problems does not represent a new emphasis. The early work of Kurt Goldstein (10) on the after effects of brain injuries is typical of the long standing interest of physicians and psychologists in the physical and behavioral correlates of neurological impairment. Lauretta Bender's study of the psychopathology of brain disorders in children is another example of early work in this field (1). Procedures to diagnose neurological impairment were primarily of medical interest until Strauss and Lehtinen (23) suggested specific educational techniques to assist children who had been identified as brain injured. The concomitant increase in pharmaceutical research on medications that influence behavior resulted in increased interest on the part of pediatricians and neurologists in the possibility of mediating some of the more severe behavior problems with medicines.

With the assumption that neurological activity might represent a continuum with the truly brain-impaired at one extreme, the medical scientist began to study children with the behavioral symptoms of neurological impairment who did not have the accepted positive diagnostic findings. Thus Bradley (5), Laufer (17), Oettinger (20), and others studied children with the presumptive diagnosis of "mild neurological handicaps" who had in common hyperactivity, learning disabilities, perceptual-motor handicaps, poor retention, poor concept formation, anxiety, and other patterns of delayed development. Since little or no evidence from the pediatric or neurological examinations in such cases could support a medical diagnosis of brain impairment, the physician looked to the psychologist for supporting evidence from psychological appraisal techniques. Psychological tests, then, became a necessary part of the neurological appraisal of "mild neurological impairment"—an impairment with no visible physical defect, but with evident problems in school learning and behavior.

Much of the research conducted with children presumed to have mild neurological impairment provides support for the correlation of inferred neurological dysfunction and learning and behavior problems.

Even in the case of concrete evidence of the neurological bases of school functioning, one needs to know how the disability affects a particular child. Obviously, as with any handicap, the effects of neurological impairment must be evaluated in terms of what is happening in the rest of the child's life. A handicap may have a psychologically crippling effect on one child and be a motivational boost to another. What we can say now about neurological impairment, even when the diagnosis is indefinite, is that a physical impairment of any type increases the child's vulnerability to school difficulties. The diagnosis is not nearly so important as the educational plans for the child with hyperactive behavior, perceptual motor difficulties, or short attention span. Such plans may be relatively unaffected by whether there is medical support for a neurological impairment or not.

PHYSICAL FACTORS AND SCHOOL FUNCTIONING

There is a lot of appeal in the notion that problems in school functioning can be explained by the biological endowment that the child brings to the school setting. But the behavioral scientist will have to study physical correlates of behavior in representative samples of school children, not just in those who are referred with particular symptoms. We need to know what factors in a child's life can obviate a physical impairment or how schools can assist children with specific difficulties to develop skills in spite of their handicaps. We cannot arrive at this point of understanding school effectiveness unless we sample the childhood population and gather concomitant information about the status of the child's other resources for dealing with the school setting.

Some investigators have attempted to study the interaction between physical characteristics and school behavior. Clarke and Jarman (6) compared the school achievement test scores and physical status of nine- twelve-, and fifteen-year-old boys. They found there was a significant tendency for groups with high scores on a physical fitness index to have higher school achievement test scores. School achievement, personality, and pediatric variables were combined in a study by Michael and Tobias (18). Their analysis indicated 15 factors with little or no overlap between psychological and biological functions, although they offered some type of method variance as an explanation for the lack of congruence. Nevertheless, the pediatric dimensions that were used—heart rate, blood sugar level, bone age, and so forth—may represent variables that can be used in assessing a child's constitutional status. The Wetzel grid (26) is a commonly used tool for comparing height and weight of children with age norms. The physical health of both children and parents have been reported as significant variables affecting functioning in the Midtown Manhattan Study (15). There is need for careful evaluation of the interaction of constitutional factors with other factors affecting school work. Such studies provide an opportunity for fruitful collaboration between the medical and behavioral sciences.

EITHER TOO YOUNG OR TOO OLD

Often teachers suggest that children who are having difficulty in school are developmentally too young or too old for the grade. In one case they take account of the fact that a given child may not be "ready" for work of the grade, whereas in the other case they are referring to the fact that a child may already have been retained in a grade and has resulting embarrassment at being older than other children and still experiences difficulties in school. Most of the concern of educators about the child's developmental status has been focused on the age at which a child will be ready to learn to read, thus ready to attend school for the first time. Initial success in reading and school learning is considered to be dependent on the prior development of certain sensory, verbal, and motor skills that will allow a child to make successful comparisons of likenesses and differences, to have some understanding of quantity, to perceive differences in similar word configurations, and to have a concrete understanding of a word when it is first seen in print. Most first grade teachers can tell, on the basis of observations, which children have acquired these developmental levels and which have not. If a child is not considered to be ready to read in first grade, the usual assumption is that by waiting for further development to take place, he will be ready at a later time.

This assumption that the development of maturity sufficient for school success will depend primarily on unfolding of inherent biological processes can be verified by observation. Many children who are not speaking understandably at the age of five when they can attend kindergarten for the first time are speaking clearly at the age of six. Also many children who have difficulty reading at six can learn easily when they are seven. However, even though this may be true for some children, the concept of readiness as described here does not explain the difficulties that other children will experience.

Ilg and Ames (12) set out to determine the percentage of children from the ages of five to nine who were able to succeed with some standard tasks related to successful first grade performance. They used a variety of developmental tests for appraising the readiness of the children in the sample. Norms for each of the tests were developed for each age level so that investigators who make use of these materials later will have base rates for all of the test variables. One of their findings is rather distressing. On the basis of tests measuring tasks which are common to kindergarten and first grade, less than half of the kindergarten population tested was considered to be ready for first grade. Of those tested 40 per cent were considered to be questionable in readiness status and 14 per cent were definitely considered to be not ready for school at the end of the kindergarten year.

Even the assumption that readiness can be ensured by increasing age of the child was not supported. Ilg and Ames found that the unready children in any grade tended to be older than their peers in spite of the fact that some children who were older on school entrance were considered to have the best chance of success. Such studies of developmental status of children suggest that our former assumptions about maturation being the key factor in readiness to succeed in school work contain only part of the story. The results imply that some children must have learned things along the way before entering school and other children enter school without such learning. Therefore, provisions for "teaching" certain readiness attributes must be made in early childhood education in order to guarantee success in school. Piaget and other environmental interactionist theorists have answers to some of the questions raised by the Ilg and Ames study, but the big answers appear to sit in the laps of the teachers.

A child's background for school functioning such as his maternal and familial environment; social, cultural and economic status; cognitive development; constitutional status; intellectual endowment; and developmental status can be considered predictors of school functioning. Inadequacies in any of these resources predicts some degree of loss in school effectiveness. Inadequacy in any of these resources may be overcome by the adequacy of the other resources; however we know very little about how such deficiencies are best overcome and how specific programs achieve their effects. The task for the behavioral sciences is to study this interaction and to determine how various patterns of resources achieve their effects in school functioning. The task for education is to determine how to help all students develop greater effectiveness in school by classroom procedures. The goal is maximum success for the child and the optimum development of his unique characteristics.

SOCIAL RESOURCES

Even though those variables pertaining to the basic resources for functioning that the child brings to school are interrelated and overlapping, they are treated as rather isolated events when they are studied as individual variables predicting school functioning. The case of the disadvantaged population in our schools is a good example. The criteria used to identify the deprived, poverty-stricken, and economically handicapped are the basic resources of family economics and social environment, defined for ease of application as income, race, or bi-lingual status. It is a rather obvious fact that not all children whose families meet these criteria are disadvantaged in their ability to profit from school. Stories of self-made men who started out as newsboys supporting the family with their earnings are cases in point. Although income and ethnic status are convenient economic and social criteria to use, even though they imply an ethnocentric attitude toward the underprivileged, these criteria do not explain the nature of the disadvantage, nor do they assist in understanding the educational problems of such children. At least one generalization can be made from observations of Head Start programs. Disadvantaged children do not present common behavioral and learning problems, and several sub-groups can be identified on the basis of their need for different structure in the learning environment and differentiation of the modes of presentation of learning activities. For example, the urban Negro child was commonly observed to be hyperactive, characterized by a short attention span, aggressive toward peers, and difficult to control in the classroom. The "rich" environment of the Head Start program presented too many distracting stimuli for him to respond to. In fact the school environment often created so much stimulation that he had considerable difficulty in adjusting to the environment, his peers, and sometimes his teacher. The school itself created stress for these children and as a result made it difficult for them to adapt.

The rural Mexican-American child often differed considerably from the urban Negro. He was quiet and fearful and retreated from contact with strange adults but made a more easy relationship with his peers. For him, the stress of leaving the relative safety of a restricted home environment seemed to explain his difficulty in adapting to the preschool program. Whether or not these are satisfactory explanations of the observed differences between urban Negro and the rural Mexican-American preschool disadvantaged children cannot be determinded at this time. However, one can suggest that the preschool program should be differentiated for these two groups of children.

Educators have found that modifications in the educational program for the hyperactive, acting-out child, can reduce the stress on him in the school setting. Educators have also found that the stress of the new and fearful school setting can be reduced for the withdrawn, frightened child. Other differences in approach between educational programs for the urban Negro and the Mexican-American probably lie in the degree to which the learning experiences should be deductive or inductive. In a highly structured activity the teacher provides the rules and then the children test them in a particular activity. In the free exploration setting, the children gain experience first, and then with the help of the teacher develop the rules to be applied.

The observations of Head Start programs presented above are not meant as another oversimplification of the relationship of a child's basic resources to adapt to school and his success in adapting. The fact of specific racial status does not explain a child's behavior any better than does the status of his family's income. It is evident that one cannot predict a given set of learning and behavior problems on the basis of single selection criteria.

Research aimed at studying the resources critical to school effectiveness should emphasize a multi-variable rather than a single-variable design. One goal of such research is the clarification of the interaction of the identifiable independent variables in the development of effective school learning and behavior. In the absence of such information, the behavioral scientist knows that these independent variables are mediated in a variety of ways. The teacher must learn to use the variety of data pertaining to the child's resources and with the help of the pupil personnel worker to grapple with the possible types of interaction of the independent variables as they relate to individual and groups of children.

EVALUATING SCHOOL EFFECTIVENESS

The school social system in which the child functions provides a large number of dependent variables that are evidence of different manifestations of school effectiveness. As the behavioral scientist continues to clarify the interaction of the independent sources of variation that pertain to resources for adaptation, the school research worker should use care in obtaining multi-variable information about the child's adaptive processes in school.

In the classroom the child judged to be a problem is one who has difficulty learning, who does not observe the teacher's rules for classroom behavior, or who cannot get along with peers. Conversely the child who is judged to be adapting well to school, learns readily, adjusts to classroom rules, and enjoys an easy relationship with his classmates. Since behavior is judged to be adaptive or maladaptive within the context of the social system in which the individual behaves, it is the discomfort of others produced by the behavior of one member of the group that causes him to be judged emotionally disturbed or mentally ill and results in his referral for treatment of the disaffection.

Since teachers vary greatly in teaching style, structuring of the learning environment, procedures for classroom management, and the choice of specific methods of presentation of learning material, children cannot be expected to respond uniformly to a single teacher or to their teachers from one grade level to the next. For a child, adaptation to a particular classroom is in part a function of what the teacher presents to her class as well as how the members of the class interact with these aspects of the classroom environment.

Nevertheless, since the teacher has the longest period of observation of a child in a single setting, she is able to determine more readily than any other professional person in the school, the degree to which a particular child's behavior in her classroom deviates to either a positive or negative extreme on a continuum of school effectiveness. She is able to tell how one child differs from others in terms of specific school behaviors, and she is able to tell how common or uncommon, usual or unusual, a specific piece of behavior is for a particular child. The teacher then has the opportunity to observe the behavior of each member of a class as well as to provide measures of change in effectiveness for a particular pupil over a period of time. Therefore, in spite of differences among teachers, they are best qualified to identify specific behaviors that can be shown to be predictive of a criterion of school effectiveness. They are also in the best position to observe an individual pupil's change as a result of school interventions.

We are a rather long way from understanding all of the predictable variance inherent in a study of school effectiveness as viewed by the teacher. We do have, however, some glimpses into the value of the teacher as a rater of school coping ability and school effectiveness.

Ullman's classic study (25) demonstrated a high correlation between the judgments of teachers and clinicians regarding the mental health status of a school population even though he earlier noted that they did not agree on what specific aspects of behavior were most indicative of poor mental health. In Cooper's (7) study classroom teachers marked on a behavior check list those items which were thought to be indicative of school problems. Using a cut-off score, those children with a sufficient number of marks were referred to a clinic for further examination and were found to have notable adjustment difficulties. These two pieces of research are examples of asking the teacher to cite the presence or absence of behavior symptoms in children in her classroom and then determining the predictive value of these symptoms by validating them against a clinical criterion of mental health or adjustment status.

In California, Bower (2) used a successive category procedure in obtaining teachers' ratings of the behavior children in their classes. Bower's project required the teachers to complete a rating form for every pupil in their classes. The initial validity of this procedure was determined by taking the teacher ratings for those pupils who were known to a child guidance clinic and comparing the ratings for these children to the ratings of the remainder of the pupils in the class. Of the pupils who were known to a child guidance clinic, 87 per cent were rated by their teachers as among the most poorly adjusted children in the classroom. A follow-up study by Lambert (14b) indicated that when those children who had been identified by the school guidance office were compared to the group of children who were rated by their teachers as having problems in school but who were not referred to guidance offices, the two groups had a comparable number of delinquents, drop outs, and school failure. There were some indications that the intelligence test scores for those pupils whom former teachers had referred to the guidance offices were lower than the scores for those pupils judged to be problems but not referred. This follow-up study indicated the limitations of the school referral process and supported the contention that valuable predictive information about school effectiveness is lost when only the "referred for help" category is studied; moreover, the results supported the predictive validity of teacher preceptions of problems and absence of problems when entire classes were rated.

In a later study (4) teachers used a revised rating procedure in over 50 school districts in California in order to locate a group of vulnerable children from the general school population. The teachers in this study rated every child in their classes on eight statements of school behavior by means of a similar successive category procedure (that is, all of the time, some of the time, rarely, never) which assigned a numerical value to each rating. In order to account for differences between teachers in the degree to which they perceived the presence of any of the behaviors in their classrooms, the five pupils with the most negative (highest ratings) in each teacher's class were selected and studied. Clinical psychologists subsequently evaluated each of the children who were selected by the teacher rating. In nine out of ten cases the psychologists confirmed the fact that the children who were rated by the teachers as being most ineffective in school were children with real psychological problems. One anticipated difficulty in the use of the successive category procedure was encountered. Comparisons of teacher ratings of comparable groups of children at the same grade level indicated that some teachers were "harder" or "easier" raters than others. A method for obtaining comparable ratings from teacher to teacher had to be developed. The rating subsequently developed for use by regular classroom teachers belongs to a set of materials for use by teachers in the early identification of children with school adjustment problems (4). It requires the teacher to rate every child in her class on a grid with squares arbitrarily arranged so as to approximate a normal distribution. One grid with names placed according to a teacher's perceptions of the behavior of pupils in her class is used for each of 8 behavior ratings. Every child's name goes into one of the squares on the grid depending on whether they are perceived as being most or least typical of the trait being rated. Those familiar with the Q sort procedure can visualize the grid as the type used for distribution of the Q sort cards. The teacher rates every child in the class with respect to each of 8 behavior ratings. Each of the ratings has been validated by comparing the distribution of the ratings on a given kind of behavior with clinical appraisal of school adjustment status as well as with other criteria of school effectiveness such as grades, achievement test results, and peer ratings of behavior (4). The sum of the eight behavior ratings made by the teacher provides an overall score of the teacher's perceptions of a child's coping ability and school effectiveness. The individual ratings as well as the total rating have been shown to be correlated significantly, individually and collectively with the independent judgments of the presence and absence of school problems made by a clinical team. The former difficulty with halo effect and rater bias appeared to be minimized by this type of rating procedure since children judged to be poorly adjusted on a particular item by one teacher were similar to those judged to be poorly adjusted by another teacher. Only one booklet is required for a teacher's ratings of an entire class, and the procedure takes no longer than rating one child at a time on all behavior traits.

The teacher rating described above provides a useful procedure for assessing children's general coping ability in school. The ratings are made on a continuum so that the entire class is arranged from most to least effective in the behavior being rated; thus children who are judged to be at various points on the teacher-judged school effective-school ineffective continuum can be selected for further study. The rating items represent a teacher's perception of a pupil's behavior in one setting when compared to her perception of his classroom peers. The validity of these items in predicting an independent criterion of clinical judgment indicates that the children teachers judge to be effective and ineffective on the basis of this rating procedure have something in common with what clinicians judge to be effective and ineffective behavior, though moderate rather than high correlations suggest that the teacher's perception and clinicians' perception of children are not identical.

The focus of all of these research investigations using teacher ratings of children's behavior has been to establish the validity of the teacher as a perceiver of a child's school functioning. The validity criteria have been referral to a child guidance clinic, concurrent clinical team judgment of effectiveness of behavior, and follow-up information indicating the persistence of earlier school problems. The result of this work suggests that teachers can provide a good index of the child's ability to cope in the classroom situation and that they are able to make valid judgments of those children who are more or less effective in managing the school setting. For those researchers who would use teacher ratings, the results indicate that rater bias should be anticipated and that teacher referral of specific problem cases should not be viewed as a single index of a pupil's school status.

The selection of teacher rating items obviously has a lot to do with the dimensions of school effectiveness that are uncovered. Future research in this area should be focused on the selection of a maximum number of unique and valid rating items which can be meaningfully used by the teacher in order to provide the investigator with comprehensive data on the teacher's view of children's school coping behavior. A good teacher rating can provide concomitant information on a large number of children as well as a means for evaluating even small changes in the status of a child on a school effectiveness continuum from one year to another.

CHILDREN KNOW EACH OTHER

The investigator will need other assessments of the pupil's effectiveness in the classroom. The children in the class represent the next rather obvious source of information about how effective a child is or how effective particular children are in coping with certain aspects of the school setting. With peer ratings as well as teacher ratings, the investigation of school behavior is limited by the degree to which the dimensions to be evaluated by peers represents a comprehensive view of school effectiveness.

Sociometric devices have been in use for many years in an effort to assess children's perceptions of peers. The usual sociometric procedure requires a child to select one or more classmates for a particular activity—a leader of a team, a seat mate, a companion for a field trip, and so forth. From such information the teacher can make a social map of the class in terms of children most frequently chosen by their peers and those most frequently ignored by their peers in the selection process. Besides having face validity the "favorites" and "isolates" illustrate some aspects of the social structure of the classroom.

One problem with the sociometric procedure described above is that available information is "lost," since each pupil is asked to select only a few members of his class for a single activity. There would appear to be considerable gain in information if each pupil were asked to select pupils for more than one activity and to respond to as many different class members as possible. In other words if every pupil in the class were to "rate" every other pupil in the class on a variety of behaviors, the result would be a large sample of assessment of a single pupil's behavior.

Some progress has been made toward the development of a procedure that requires members of a class to respond to all class members in a sociometric process. Such a peer rating is based on the assumption that children are in a position to provide unique and reliable appraisals of aspects of coping behavior that are typical of an individual child and that are predictive of school effectiveness. An early study on the identification of emotionally disturbed children (2), which also evaluated the teacher rating procedure reported previously, verified this fact. Children in a class where previously identified emotionally disturbed pupils were enrolled were asked to play a game in which each student, as director of a fictitious play, selected a cast for roles in the play. Half of the parts in the play were selected to represent positive behavior typical of children who are adjusting well to school. The other half of the parts were selected to represent behavior typical of children with school problems. The class members perceived the classmates identified as emotionally disturbed significantly more frequently for the negative roles in the play. This finding partially verified the fact that the children can make judgments of behavior which have potential validity in identifying those who might be judged later to be free from or burdened with problems.

This model for a peer rating was used subsequently along with other methods of appraising school effectiveness at all grade levels. The results were consistent with earlier findings. Peer ratings were found to be quite stable (test-retest reliability coefficient from .88 to .91) for all age levels, and children who received a larger percentage of positive nominations from their peers were found later to be relatively free from school problems, whereas children receiving a large percentage of negative nominations were those considered to be least effective in adjusting to the school setting (4). Lambert (13) later encountered a methodological problem in determining the optimum number of items to be used in the peer rating procedure to maintain high reliability.

Another methodological problem remains. In the research described here, the per cent of peer selections was the score used to indicate school effectiveness of a given child as measured by ratings of his classroom peers. The same value for per cent of negative selections obviously is not the same for the child who receives only five peer selections from the entire class and the child who receives 23 peer selections. A variety of procedures have been studied for holding constant the number of selections and then comparing children with varying numbers of negative selections. No satisfactory answer to this problem has been found. Investigators who use this procedure might validate their results by stratifying their sample on the basis of total number of selections and comparing characteristics of pupils with varying numbers of negative peer ratings. In spite of certain methodological problems, the per cent of negative selections is significantly correlated with teacher ratings of school effectiveness and clinical judgment of school adjustment. The low, but significant correlations found in one study of these peer ratings (13) indicates that teacher and clinical judgments have only a small amount of variance in common with peer ratings. Therefore, teacher, clinical, and peer ratings each provide unique assessments of behavior. Further studies need to determine how various behavioral characteristics of pupils influence peer choice as compared to teacher-perceived aspects of children's behavior.

Bower and Lambert have developed peer ratings for primary, elementary, and secondary grades (4). These tests provide data on pupil behavior as viewed by peers. They provide glimpses of the pupil's adaptive behavior in the classroom and cues for further investigation. They do not provide a total picture of the child's many coping capacities or potentials nor do they indicate individual differences in the integration of resources to cope with school environment.

SCHOOL PERFORMANCE AND SELF MEASURES

A child's school grades are rather obvious measures of his ability to cope in school. Although parents and educators commonly assume a rather consistent relationship between scholastic ability and school grades, one can expect significant but low correlations between achievement test scores and grades. The evidence indicates that grade point average reflects a special case of a teacher's evaluation of the ability of the child to deal effectively with the demands of the classroom academic program. In a study of grades assigned to high school students, Hansen (11) demonstrated that promptness, classroom decorum, and a compliant attitude were some of the critical variables predicting teacher's assigned grades. Another study (14b) showed that there was a significant difference between grades assigned to high school students who were judged to be poorly adjusted by their teachers and grades assigned to pupils judged to have few or no problems in school.

In a factor analysis of school-collected data, all of which were selected to reflect some aspect of school problems (14), grades appeared as a specific dimension different from the dimension defined by school ability and achievement tests. The inference from these and the above findings is that single grades as well as the gradepoint average provide a readily available source of information about the child's ability to cope with the learning demands of school.

School achievement as measured by tests has been shown repeatedly to be an important variable in studies of school adjustment. Bower (2) provided data to compare the achievement test scores of pupils diagnosed as emotionally disturbed with those judged to have no school problems at the elementary grades. He showed that as children with problems progress through the grades, their achievement falls further and further behind grade level or expected performance. Stringer (24) developed an academic progress chart that plots achievement test findings against grade level. On the chart significant pupil crises are indicated and compared with expected achievement for the pupil at that grade level. Her comparisons of academic progress for 150 pupils indicated that every time there was a deviation from expected performance, there was either clear evidence of new stress in the child's life situation or the evidence of positive interventions in the learning process by the school or parents. She concludes that a marked change in school performance not only reflects other significant developments in the child's life but also is often one of the first overt symptoms of a new or incipient disturbance. The stability of reading failure has been established by Miller, Margolin, and Yolles (19) in a very large sample of school children. They suggest also that reading performance is a valuable single index of school effectiveness.

The classroom teacher, peers, grades, and achievement test data are four sources of information regarding school effectiveness that can be obtained from the classroom. The child himself can provide certain other information pertaining to the degree to which he is able to cope with and adapt to the school setting. Self-report procedures are often used to assess a pupil's perceptions of his difficulties. Problem check lists are a popular type of self-report inventory. Paper and pencil personality tests are typical examples also. The interrelationship of personality tests for a school population has been studied by Smith (21). She used six group-administered personality and adjustment tests for children. Her conclusions were that none of the tests discriminated well enough for individual predictions. However, she noted that several of the tests had group differences large enough to make them applicable for limited predictions when other test data were combined with this information.

A self-report procedure that appraises the discrepancy between the child's perceived and ideal self has been used extensively by Bower (2,4) and Lambert (13,14). The reliability of the procedures is substantial, but the validity of the instruments in predicting aspects of school effectiveness has been difficult to establish. Independent clinical and teacher judgments of the school adjustment of 7- and 11-year-olds have been compared to self rating scores. Low, but significant correlations (5 per cent level) were obtained between self-ratings and teacher judgment, but the relationship between self-ratings and clinical judgment was significant for boys only. Evidently dissatisfaction with self is more visible for boys than girls in the clinical appraisal process. When children with extremely negative appraisals of self were evaluated, there was some evidence that negative self-appraisal is an important dimension in school functioning. Self-reports provide a source of pupil information that is not being supplied from other sources, but the problem of establishing their validity for predicting school effectiveness still remains.

PSYCHIATRIC EVALUATION

In spite of the methodological problems inherent in standardizing interviews, the psychiatric evaluation is another potentially valid resource for estimating the ability of a child to cope in a given situation. The child's world is administered by the adults in his life as an infant and young child, but he comes more and more to intervene on his own behalf and to manage his own affairs, both in school and in other social relationships, as he grows older. The ability of a child to handle a new situation, to know himself, and to accept his own reality, are all aspects of coping ability. The absence of this ability can be assumed to affect profoundly a child's school functioning. When psychiatrists interviewed children in the school setting, they appeared to be evaluating each child's ability to be an observed person. The child who can talk about his goals, his problems, and his difficulties in school can make himself known to others. He is open to observation. The child who can talk about himself in such a way that a stranger can come to know him in a brief interview is manifesting an ability to cope in a situation where the child has himself as his principal resource.

At this point, we might ask which aspect of school effectiveness is being measured by self-perception. Is self-perception one aspect of how the child perceives his ability to cope in school and other personal situations? Is this indicative of the ability of the child to use his resources to meet the adjustment demands of the school? Is self-perception related to vulnerability to stress, or is it a manifestation of adaptation to stress situations? We need further knowledge about how self perception relates to school effectiveness.

Observable symptoms of individual behavior are a key source of information for classifying mental illness. Degan (8) used a factor analytic procedure to study the presenting symptoms of psychiatric patients with functional psychoses and experimentally verified the logic of the empirically established psychiatric classification procedure. A similar procedure might be employed with observable symptoms in school behavior. The result would be goupings of children's symptoms that might provide a basis for measuring some specific aspects of school effectiveness.

Two related studies are available that describe a school population on the basis of the number of observable symptoms and the signficance of symptoms in relationship to school effectiveness (9). The results of these studies showed a significant relationship between the number, frequency, duration, and severity of symptoms and the school adjustment problems of children.

Somewhat contrary evidence for the usefulness of symptoms in measuring school effectiveness comes from Lapouse and Monk's study (16). There was a general but not significant trend for symptoms to be related to selected adjustment criteria (bedwetting, nightmares, tension). However, the number of fears and worries in children was directly related to socio-economic status, age and sex, all variables which have been shown to be related to criteria of school effectiveness by other studies. The normative information from Lapouse and Monk's work for prevalence of specific fears and worries and selected symptoms does indicate the probability of each occurring in a representative sample of school children. Further investigations of specific systems or symptom dimensions with aspects of school coping behavior might yield results closer to what is reported by Glidewell and Mensh.

CONCLUSION

We have described a frame of reference for studying school effectiveness as an interaction of a variety of individual dimensions in two general domains—basic psychological supplies and resources and effects of the child's coping efforts in the school setting. The use of this frame of reference makes it possible to support the initial assumption that categories such as emotionally disturbed, culturally disadvantaged, slow learning, school drop out, delinquent, or neurologically handicapped can be classified under a general heading of school malfunctioning. Each of these special cases of difficulties in school may represent a unique interaction of specific dimensions in the coping and supply domains. However, additional research and clinical study of school behaviors are needed to determine what interaction exists in each case and how the interaction produces specific effects. Investigators could go far toward clarifying this problem if they gathered data on all of these dimensions of school adjustment instead of making an a priori assumption that only some are important to study and the others have only limited value.

To simplify research problems in the general area of school effectiveness, the behavioral scientist needs continually to refine the measurement in each of the dimensions described previously, to utilize all of the dimensions in a study of school adjustment, and then to determine the relationship between specific variables in each of these domains and a specific type of school success and school difficulty. In addition adolescent and adult problems such as delinquency, drop outs, employment failure, and absenteeism, should be studied as follow-ups of relationships between measures collected in childhood in these coping and supply domains. This is a large order; however by utilizing a comprehensive scheme for evaluating school effectiveness, the result should be better definition of the measurable aspects of each domain and insights into the relationship between individual and groups of coping and supply dimensions in the promotion of effective functioning in school.

With the rising incidence of school failure of various sorts, it is no longer sufficient to diagnose the causes of failure and to describe the differences between ineffective school behavior of one type of another. We must find ways to mediate the resources the child brings to school in such a way that we can increase each child's development toward higher levels of school functioning.

REFERENCES

1. Bender, Lauretta. "The Psychological Treatment of the Brain-damaged Child." *Quart. J. Child Behav.*, **3**, 1951, 123–132.
2. Bower, E. M. *Early Identification of Emotionally Disturbed Children in School.* Springfield, Ill.: Charles C Thomas Co., 1960.

3. Bower, E. M. and Roy Simpson. *Education of Emotionally Handicapped Children*. Sacramento, Calif.: Calif. State Dept. of Education, 1961.

4. Bower, E. M. and Nadine M. Lambert. *A Process for In-School Screening of Children with Emotional Handicaps* (includes Manual for Administration, Technical Report, Behavior Rating of Pupils, A Picture Game, Class Pictures, A Class Play, Thinking About Yourself, Student Survey, and Self Test). Princeton, N.J.: Educational Testing Service, 1961.

5. Bradley, C. "The Behavior of Children Receiving Benzedrine." *Amer. J. Psychiat.*, **94**, 1937, 577–85.

6. Clarke, H. H. and B. O. Jarman. "Scholastic Achievement of Boys 9, 12 and 15 Years of Age as Related to Various Strength and Growth Measures." *Res. Quart. Amer. Assn. Health Educ. Recr.*, **32**, 1961, 155–62.

7. Cooper, S., W. Syan, and B. R. Hutcheson. "Classroom Screening for Emotional Disturbance." *Amer. Psychol.*, **14**, 1959, 340.

8. Degan, J. W. "Dimensions of Functional Psychosis." *Psychom. Monogr.*, No. 6, 1952.

9. Glidwell, J. C. *Parental Attitudes and Child Behavior*. Springfield, Ill.: Charles C Thomas Co., 1961.

10. Goldstein, Kurt. *After-effects of Brain Injuries in War*. New York: Grune and Stratton, 1942.

11. Hansen, P. J. "The Relationship of Certain Biographical Information to the Academic and Behavioral Achievement of High School Boys." Unpublished doctoral dissertation, University of Utah, 1950.

12. Ilg, Frances L. and Louise B. Ames. *School Readiness*. New York: Harper and Row, 1964.

13. Lambert, Nadine M. *The Development and Validation of a Process for Screening Emotionally Handicapped Children*. U.S.O.E. Cooperative Research Project No. 1186. Sacramento, Calif.: Calif. State Dept. of Education, 1963.

14. Lambert, Nadine M. *The Prediction of School Adjustment*. U.S.O.E. Cooperative Research Project No. 1980. Sacramento, Calif.: Calif. State Dept. of Education, 1964.

14a. Lambert, Nadine M. and Grossman H. *Problems in Determining the Etiology of Learning and Behavior Problems*. Sacramento, Calif.: Calif. State Department of Education, 1964.

14b. Lambert, Nadine M. "The High School Dropout in Elementary School." In Schreiber, D. *Guidance and the School Drop Out*. Washington, D.C.: American Personnel and Guidance Assoc., N.E.A., 1964.

15. Langner, T. S. and S. T. Michael. *Life Stress and Mental Health*. New York: The Free Press, 1963.

16. Lapouse, Rema and Mary Monk. "Fears and Worries in a Representative Sample of Children." *Amer. J. Orthopsychiat.*, **29**, 1959, 803–18.

17. Laufer, M. W. and E. Denhoff. "Hyperkinetic Behavior Syndrome in Children." *J. Pediat.*, **50**, 1957, 463–75.

18. Michael, W. B. and M. Tobias. "The Factorial Dimensions of Thirty-Five Selected Achievement, Intellectual, Personality, Psychological, and Maturational Variables." Paper read at Calif. State Psychol. Assoc., Los Angeles, December, 1962.

19. Miller, A. D., J. B. Margolin, and S. F. Yolles. "Epidemiology of Reading Disabilities: Some Methodologic Considerations and Early Findings." *Amer. J. Publ. Hlth.*, **47**, 1957, 1250–1256.

20. Oettinger, L. "The Medical Treatment of Behavior Problems." *Mississippi Valley Med. Journal,* **74,** 1952, 74.
21. Smith, Louis M. "The Concurrent Validity of Six Personality and Adjustment Tests for Children." *Psychol. Monogr.,* **72,** 1958, 30.
22. Spitz, Rene A. *No and Yes.* New York: International Universities Press, 1957.
23. Strauss, A. A. and L. E. Lehtinen. *Psychopathology and Education of the Brain-Injured Child. Vol. I. Fundamentals and Treatment of Brain-Injured Children.* New York: Grune and Stratton, 1951.
24. Stringer, Lorene. "Academic Progress as an Index of Mental Health." *J. Soc. Issues,* **15,** 1959, 16–29.
25. Ullman, C. A. "Teacher, Peers and Tests and Predictors of Adjustment." *J. Educ. Psychol.,* **42,** 1951, 257–276.
26. Wetzel, N. C. "Assessing Physical Condition of Children." *J. Pediat.,* **22,** 1942, 82–86.

Chapter 19

Soviet Methods of Character Education: Some Implications for Research

Urie Bronfenbrenner

About the Author

Urie Bronfenbrenner was born April 29, 1917, Moscow, Russia. He received his A.B. from Cornell in 1938, his Ed.M. from Harvard in 1940, and his Ph.D. from Michigan in 1942.

Bronfenbrenner's military service was as psychologist in U.S. Army Air Forces (1942–43), Office of Strategic Services (1943–44) and Borden General Hospital (1944–46).

He was assistant Chief Clinical Psychologist for Administration and Research, Veterans Administration Central Office, 1946, Assistant Professor of Psychology, University of Michigan, 1946–48, and has been Professor of Psychology and of Child Development and Family Relationships at Cornell University from 1948 to present.

Brofenbrenner is a Fellow, Center for Advanced Study in the Behavioral Sciences, Stanford, California, 1955–56; Fellow, American Psychological Association, and former President of Division of Developmental Psychology. He is a Member of the Society for Research in Child Development; Member of the National Advisory Child Health and Human Development Council, National Institutes of Health; Member, Planning Committee for Project Head Start, Office of Economic Opportunity; Member of the Social Science Advisory Board of the U.S. Arms Control and Disarmament Agency and recipient (with E. C. Devereus, Jr.) of the E. W. Burgess Award for best design for research in the family, 1959–60.

At present Bronfenbrenner is principal investigator on a project financed by the National Science Foundation, Cross-Cultural Studies of Socialization, utilizing data collected from adolescents in the United States, three European nations, and the U.S.S.R.

Introduction to the Chapter

The previous chapters of Part Two have portrayed important patterns of integrating and utilizing behavioral science findings and education, whereas this chapter poses a challenge and depicts a relatively unmet horizon in American education. The traditionally aloof role of the scientist in the area of character and moral education of the young is no longer possible. With the development of the atomic bomb and the laser, with the possibility of the misuse of behavioral understandings through conditioning and "thought control," the scientist is confronted with many moral and social consequences of his role and his research findings.

Bronfenbrenner's incisive comments on Soviet methods in this field confront us with the educational realities of how the Russian schools are utilizing established psychological group methods to create the new Soviet man. As we read, we awaken to the need to ask: What kind of personalities are we building here in the West? What kind of socialization and moral education patterns will help to create the "inner directed" (Riesman), objectively-principled (Bronfenbrenner), autonomous personality guided by Western values and capable of interdependent relationships? Are we leaving the development of capable, effective, sensitive, affectionate personalities with fully developed ego-functioning to chance factors, or are they the result of the planned spontaneity of our culture? Are we intelligently using what we know about psychosocial growth and development to provide the climate out of which will emerge the men and women who will pursue with vigor the values of the kind of life we profess?

Bronfenbrenner's materials will add pertinency to these questions. They will raise again the question of "Is there and should there be character education in American Schools and what kind?" They will again raise the question, "Can character education be avoided in American Schools?" If not, what aspects of character are we developing, and is this character close to the goals we have in mind? What should we do about character education in the U.S.?

One possibility would be to identify and to foster the processes and experiences that will develop both individual potential and socially responsible living. Lippitt and his colleagues in the first chapter in this section of the book have vividly illustrated classroom group interactions, set in motion by the teachers that resulted in wider social sensitivity, group discussion, and reformulation of group goals and behaviors, as well as stimulation of pupils to widen their repertoire of behaviors and understandings. Taking a cue from this and other sources, we could identify and field test a whole range of experiential learning processes for their potential to stimulate effective ego-functioning and social interaction abilities of pupils, to build individual and social intellectual competencies, sensitivities, role flexibility, and team-work skills.

Borrowing from earlier contributions of Thelen, Glidewell, and Biber on the phases of group maturation, we should perhaps train more teachers in the art and science of helping a classroom group move toward the interdependent style of action of a mature group. Such training would enable teachers not only to create a more effective learning environment, but also help pupils move beyond the early stages of submissive dependence upon a teacher to learning healthy ways of channeling the counterdependent protest into constructive channels. Such carefully fostered group interactions also could move on into experiential learnings of the management of conformity pressures, productivity pressures, and peer pressures—vital skills of group membership that the individual must learn if he is to function in a group by conscious choice and avoid involuntary submission to intra-group pressures. Through such group interaction experiences (even while involved in academic subject learning), a pupil can learn a mature style of group interaction, can dilute conformity pressures, and can replace them by the "treasured use of individual talents." This process stands in stark contrast to the more lock step conformity of the Soviet classroom.

Perhaps we can learn from the Soviets, and relearn from our own debating experiences, the values of positive criticism, continuous performance evaluation, and immediate group feedback. Perhaps we can avoid the public intimidation and peer pressure cruelties of the Russian pattern and induce instead competition to improve, to add ideas or insights, and to create more meaningful relationships. Training students in making additive, incisive critiques and in making supplementary presentations with additional ideas or applications seems more productive.

Using the now familiar methods of building group behavior codes, we can not only achieve better pupil behavior but also involve the pupils in the process. Instead of mobilizing group pressures, utilizing the immature cruelties of a juvenile "kangaroo court" and instigating humiliating spread of guilt and punishment to an entire group, we could substitute the positive process of pupil formulated and pupil decided group codes of desirable behaviors as has been well-illustrated in Lippitt's chapter in his paragraphs on the "anti-learning leadership problem."

The objectively principled, self-directed individual can be initiated, encouraged, and enhanced in his development by the use of group methods that will strengthen his ego-development and his capacity to voluntarily collaborate with others. Out of such curriculum development research, we might some day be able to formulate a set of guiding principles of the American approach to character training. The challenge is to develop principles, processes, and procedures consistent with the goals and values of our culture which can be formulated into a curriculum that can be implemented professionally by our teachers and is ethically acceptable to our communities.

Soviet Methods of Character
Education: Some Implications for Research[1]

Every society faces the problem of the moral training of its youth. This is no less true of Communist society than of our own. Indeed, Communist authorities view as the primary objective of education not the learning of subject matter but the development of what they call "socialist morality." It is instructive for us in the West to examine the nature of this "socialist morality" and the manner in which it is inculcated, for to do so brings to light important differences in the ends and means of character education in the two cultures. For research workers in the field of personality development, such an examination is especially valuable, since it lays bare unrecognized assumptions and variations in approach. Accordingly, we shall present a much-condensed account of Soviet methods of character education and examine some of the provocative research questions that emerge from the contrast between the Soviet approach and our own.

THE WORK AND IDEAS OF A. S. MAKARENKO

To examine Soviet methods of character training is to become acquainted with the thinking and technology developed primarily by one man—Anton Semyonovich Makarenko. Makarenko's name is virtually a household word in the Soviet Union. His popularity and influence are roughly comparable to those of Dr. Spock in the United States, but his primary concern is not with the child's physical health but with his moral upbringing. Makarenko's influence extends far beyond his own voluminous writings, since there is scarcely a manual for the guidance of Communist parents, teachers, or youth workers that does not draw heavily on his methods and ideas. His works have been translated into many languages and are apparently widely

[1] Reprinted from: *Relig. Educ.*, 1962, 57 (4, Res. Suppl.), S45-S61. Copyright, 1962, by the Religious Education Association and reproduced by their permission.

read not only in the Soviet Union but throughout the Communist bloc countries, notably East Germany and Communist China. Excellent English translations of a number of his works have been published in Moscow (27,28,29), but they are not readily available in this country.

To turn to the ideas themselves, we may begin with an excerpt from what is possibly the most widely read of Makarenko's works, *A Book for Parents* (29):

"But our [Soviet] family is not an accidental combination of members of society. The family is a natural collective body and, like everything natural, healthy, and normal, it can only blossom forth in socialist society, freed of those very curses from which both mankind as a whole and the individual are freeing themselves.

"The family becomes the natural primary cell of society, the place where the delight of human life is realized, where the triumphant forces of man are refreshed, where children—the chief joy of life—live and grow.

"Our parents are not without authority either, but this authority is only the reflection of societal authority. The duty of a father in our country towards his children is a particular form of his duty towards society. It is as if our society says to parents:

"You have joined together in good will and love, rejoice in your children and expect to go on rejoicing in them. That is your personal affair and concerns your own personal happiness. Within the course of this happy process you have given birth to new human beings. A time will come when these beings will cease to be solely the instruments of your happiness, and will step forth as independent members of society. For society, it is by no means a matter of indifference what kind of people they will become. In delegating to you a certain measure of societal authority the Soviet State demands from you the correct upbringing of its future citizens. Particularly it relies on you to provide certain conditions arising naturally out of your union; namely, your parental love.

"If you wish to give birth to a citizen while dispensing with parental love then be so kind as to warn society that you intend to do such a rotten thing. Human beings who are brought up without parental love are often deformed human beings" (29, p. 29).

Characteristic of Makarenko's thought is the view that the parent's authority over the child is delegated to him by the state and that duty to one's children is merely a particular instance of one's broader duty towards society. A little later in his book for parents, the author makes this point even more emphatically. After telling the story of a boy who ran away from home after some differences with his mother, he concludes by affirming: "I am a great admirer of optimism and I like very much young lads who have so much faith in Soviet State that they are carried away and will not trust even their own mothers (29, p. 37–38)." In other words, when the needs and values of the family conflict with those of society, there is no question about who gets priority. And society receives its concrete manifestation and embodiment in the *collective*, which is an organized group engaged in some socially useful enterprise.

This brings us to Makarenko's basic thesis that optimal personality development can occur only through productive activity in a social collective. The first collective is the family, but this must be supplemented early in life by other collectives specially organized in schools, neighborhoods, and other community settings. The primary function of the collective is to develop socialist morality. This aim is accomplished through an explicit regimen of activity mediated by group criticism, self-criticism, and group-oriented punishments and rewards.

Makarenko's ideas are elaborated at length in his semibiographical, semifictional accounts of life in the collective (27,28). It is in these works that he describes the principles and procedures to be employed for building the collective and using it as an instrument of character education. More relevant to our purposes, however, is the manner in which these methods are applied in school settings, for it is in this form that they have become most systematized and widely used.

SOCIALIZATION IN THE SCHOOL COLLECTIVE

The account which follows is taken from a manual (34) for the training and guidance of "school directors, supervisors, teachers, and Young Pioneer leaders." The manual was written by staff members of the Institute on the Theory and History of Pedagogy at the Academy of Pedagogical Sciences and is typical of several others prepared under the same auspices and widely distributed throughout the USSR.

This particular volume carries the instructive title : *Socialist Competition in the Schools*. The same theme is echoed in the titles of individual chapters: "Competition in the Classroom," "Competition between Classrooms," "Competition between Schools," and so on. It is not difficult to see how Russians arrive at the notion, with which they have made us so familiar, of competition between nations and between social systems. Moreover, in the chapter titles we see already reflected the influence of dialectical materialism: Conflict at one level is resolved through synthesis at the next higher level, always in the service of the Communist collective.

Let us examine the process of collective socialization as it is initiated in the very first grade. Conventiontly enough, the manual starts us off on the first day of school with the teacher standing before the newly assembled class. What should her first words be? Our text tells us: "It is not difficult to see that a direct approach to the class with the command "All sit straight" often doesn't bring the desired effect since a demand in this form does not reach the sensibilities of the pupils and does not activate them."

How does one "reach the sensibilities of the pupils" and "activate them?" According to the manual, here is what the teacher should say: "Let's see which row can sit the straightest." This approach, we are told, has certain important psychological advantages. In response,

"The children not only try to do everything as well as possible themselves, but also take an evaluative attitude toward those who are undermining the achievement of the row. If similar measures arousing the spirit of competition in the children are systematically applied by experienced teachers in the primary classes, then gradually the children themselves begin to monitor the behavior of their comrades and remind those of them who forget about the rules set by the teacher, who forget what needs to be done and what should not be done. The teacher soon has helpers."

The manual then goes on to describe how records are kept for each row from day to day for different types of tasks, so that the young children can develop a concept of group excellence over time and over a variety of activities, including personal cleanliness, condition of notebooks, conduct in passing from one room to the other, quality of recitations in each subject matter, and so on. In these activities considerable emphasis is placed on the externals of behavior in dress, manner, and speech. There must be no spots on shirt or collar, shoes must be shined, pupils must never pass by a teacher without stopping to give greeting, there must be no talking without permission, and the like. Great charts are kept in all the schools showing the performance of each row unit in every type of activity together with their total overall standing. "Who is best?" the charts ask, but the entries are not individuals but social units—rows, and later the "cells" of the Communist youth organization, which reaches down to the primary grades.

At first it is the teacher who sets the standards. But soon, still in the first grade, a new wrinkle is introduced: Responsible monitors are designated in each row for each activity. In the beginning their job is only to keep track of the merits and demerits assigned each row by the teacher. Different children act as monitors for different activities and, if one is to believe what the manual says, the monitors become very involved in the progress of their row. Then, too, group achievement is not without its rewards. From time to time the winning row gets to be photographed "in parade uniforms" (all Soviet children must wear uniforms in school), and this photograph is published in that pervasive Soviet institution, the wall newspaper. The significance of the achievements is still further enhanced, however, by the introduction of competition between *classes* so that the winning class and the winning row are visited by delegates from other classrooms in order to learn how to attain the same standard of excellence.

Now let us look more closely at this teacher-mediated monitoring process. In the beginning, we are told, the teacher attempts to focus the attention of children on the achievements of the group; that is, in our familiar phrase, she accentuates the positive. But gradually, "it becomes necessary to take account of negative facts which interfere with the activity of the class." As an example, we are given the instance of a child who despite warnings continues to enter the classroom a few minutes after the bell has rung. The teacher decides that the time has come to evoke the group process in correcting such behavior. Accordingly, the next time that Serezha is late, the teacher stops him at the door and turns to the class with this question: "Children, is it helpful or not helpful to us to have Serezha come in late?" The answers are quick in coming, "It interferes, one shouldn't be late, he ought to come on time." "Well," says the teacher, "How can we help Serezha with this problem?" There are many suggestions: get together to buy him a watch, exile him from the classroom, send him to the director's office, or even to exile him from school. But apparently these suggestions are either not appropriate or too extreme. The teacher, our text tells us, "helps the children find the right answer." She asks for a volunteer to stop by and pick Serezha up on the way to school. Many children offer to help in this mission.

But tragedy stalks. The next day it turns out that not only Serezha is late, but also the boy who promised to pick him up. Since they are both from the same group, their unit receives two sets of demerits and falls to lowest place. Group members are keenly disappointed. "Serezha especially suffered much and felt himself responsible, but equal blame was felt by his companion who had forgotten to stop in for him."

In this way, both through concrete action and explanation, the teacher seeks to forge a spirit of group unity and responsibility. From time to time, she explains to the children the significance of what they are doing, the fact "that they have to learn to live together as one friendly family, since they will have to be learning together for all of the next ten years, and that for this reason one must learn how to help one's companions and to treat them decently."

By the time the children are in the second grade, the responsibilities expected of them are increased in complexity. For example, instead of simply recording the evaluations made by the teacher, the monitors are taught how to make the evaluations themselves. Since this is rather difficult, especially in judging homework assignments, in the beginning two monitors are assigned to every task. In this way, our text tells us, they can help each other in doing a good job of evaluation.

Here is a third grade classroom.

"Class 3-B is just an ordinary class; it's not especially well disciplined nor is it outstandingly industrious. It has its lazy members and its responsible ones, quiet ones and active ones, daring, shy, and immodest ones.

"The teacher has led this class now for three years, and she has earned the affection, respect, and acceptance as an authority from her pupils. Her word is law for them.

"The bell has rung, but the teacher has not yet arrived. She has delayed deliberately in order to check how the class will conduct itself.

"In the class all is quiet. After the noisy class break, it isn't so easy to mobilize yourself and to quell the restlessness in you! Two monitors at the desk silently observe the class. On their faces is reflected the full importance and seriousness of the job they are performing. But there is no need for them to take any reprimands: the youngsters with pleasure and pride maintain scrupulous discipline; they are proud of the fact that their class conducts itself in a manner that merits the confidence of the teacher. And when the teacher enters and quietly says be seated, all understand that she deliberately refrains from praising them for the quiet and order, since in their class it could not be otherwise.

"During the lesson the teacher gives an exceptional amount of attention to collective competition between "links." (The links are the smallest unit of the Communist youth organization at this age level.) Throughout the entire lesson the youngsters are constantly hearing which link has best prepared its lesson, which link has done the best at numbers, which is the most disciplined, which has turned in the best work.

"The best link not only gets a verbal positive evaluation but receives the right to leave the classroom first during the break and to have its notebooks checked before the others. As a result the links receive the benefit of collective education, common responsibility, and mutual aid."

"What are you fooling around for? You're holding up the whole link," whispers Kolya to his neighbor during the preparation period for the lesson. And during the break he teaches her how better to organize her books and pads in her knapsack.

"Count more carefully," says Olya to her girl friend. "See, on account of you our link gets behind today. You come to me and we'll count together at home."

In the third grade still another innovation is introduced. The monitors are taught not only to evaluate but to state their criticisms publicly:

"Here is a typical picture. It is the beginning of the lesson. In the first row the link leader reports basing his comments on information submitted by the sanitarian and other responsible monitors: 'Today Valadya did the wrong problem. Masha didn't write neatly and forgot to underline the right words in her lesson, Alyoshi had a dirty shirt collar.'

"The other link leaders make similar reports (the Pioneers are sitting by rows).

"The youngsters are not offended by this procedure: they understand that the link leaders are not just tattle-telling but simply fulfilling their duty. It doesn't even occur to the monitors and sanitarians to conceal the shortcomings of their comrades. They feel that they are doing their job well precisely when they notice one or another defect."

Also in the third grade, the teacher introduces still another procedure. She now proposes that the children enter into competition with the monitors, and see whether they can beat the monitor at his own game by criticizing themselves. "The results were spectacular: if the monitor was able to talk only about four or five members of the row, there would be supplementary reports about their own shortcomings from as many as eight or ten pupils."

To what extent is this picture overdrawn? Although I have not direct evidence, the accounts I heard from participants in the process lend credence to the descriptions in the manual. For example, I recall a conversation with three elementary school teachers, all men, whom I had met by chance in a restaurant. They were curious about discipline techniques used in American schools. After I had given several examples, I was interrupted: "But how do you use the collective?" When I replied that we really did not use the classroom group in any systematic way, my three companions were puzzled. "But how do you keep discipline?"

Now it was my turn to ask for examples. "All right," came the answer. "Let us suppose that ten-year-old Vanya is pulling Anya's curls. If he doesn't stop the first time I speak to him, all I need do is mention it again in the group's presence; then I can be reasonably sure that before the class meets again the boy will be talked to by the officers of his Pioneer link. They will remind him that his behavior reflects on the reputation of the link."

"And what if he persists?"

"Then he may have to appear before his link—or even the entire collective—who will explain his misbehavior to him and determine his punishment."

"What punishment?"

"Various measures. He may just be censured, or if his conduct is regarded as serious, he may be expelled from membership. Very often he himself will acknowledge his faults before the group."

Nor does the process of social criticism and control stop with the school. Our manual tells us, for example, that parents submit periodic reports to the school collective on the behavior of the child at home. One may wonder how parents can be depended on to turn in truthful accounts. Part of the answer was supplied to me in a conversation with a Soviet agricultural expert. In response to my questions, he explained that, no matter what a person's job, the collective at his place of work always took an active interest in his family life. Thus a representative would come to the worker's home to observe and talk with his wife and children. And if any undesirable features were noted, these would be reported back to the collective.

I asked for an example.

"Well, suppose the representative were to notice that my wife and

I quarreled in front of the children [my companion shook his head]. That would be bad. They would speak to me about it and remind me of my responsibilities for training my children to be good citizens."

I pointed out how different the situation was in America, where a man's home was considered a private santuary so that, for example, psychologists like myself often had a great deal of difficulty in getting into homes to talk with parents or to observe children.

"Yes," my companion responded. "That's one of the strange things about your system in the West. The family is separated from the rest of society. That's not good. It's bad for the family and bad for society." He paused for a moment, lost in thought. "I suppose," he went on, "if my wife didn't want to let the representative in, she could ask him to leave. But then at work, I should feel ashamed." (He hung his head to emphasize the point.) "Ivanov," they would say, "has an uncultured wife."

But it would be a mistake to conclude that Soviet methods of character education and social control are based primarily on negative criticism. On the contrary, their approach contains as much of the carrot as the stick. But the carrot is given not merely as a reward for individual performance but explicitly for the child's contribution to group achievement. The great charts emblazoned "Who is Best?" which bedeck the halls and walls of every classroom have as entries the names not of individual pupils but of rows and links. It is the winning unit that gets rewarded by a pennant, a special privilege, or by having their picture taken in "parade uniforms." And when praise is given, as it frequently is, to an individual child, the group referent is always there: "Today Peter helped Kate and as a result his unit did not get behind the rest."

Helping other members of one's collective and appreciating their contributions—themes that are much stressed in Soviet character training—become matters of enlightened self-interest, since the grade that each person receives depends on the overall performance of his unit. Thus the good student finds it to his advantage to help the poor one. The same principle is carried over to the group level with champion rows and classes being made responsible for the performance of poorer ones.

Here, then, are the procedures employed in Soviet character education. As a result of Khrushchev's educational reforms, they may be expected to receive even wider application in the years to come, for, in connection with these reforms, several new types of educational institutions are to be developed on a massive scale. The most important of these is the "internat," or boarding school, in which youngsters are to be entered as early as three months of age with parents visiting only on weekends. The internat is described in the theses announcing the reforms as the kind of school which "creates the most favorable conditions for the education and communist upbringing of the rising generation" (17). The number of boarding schools in the USSR is to be increased during the current seven-year plan from a 1958 level of 180,000 to 2,500,000 in 1965 (figures cited in *Pravada*, November 18, 1958), and according to I. A. Kairov, head of the Academy of Pedagogical Sciences, "No one can doubt that, as material conditions are created, the usual general educational school will be supplanted by the boarding school" (25).

If this prophecy is fulfilled, we may expect that in the years to come the great majority of Soviet children (and children in some other countries of the Communist bloc as well) will from the first year of life onward be spending their formative period in collective settings and will be exposed daily to the techniques of collective socialization we have been describing. It is therefore a matter of considerable practical and scientific interest to identify the salient features of these techniques and subject them to research study, in so far as this becomes possible within the framework of our own society.

GUIDING PRINCIPLES OF THE SOVIET APPROACH TO CHARACTER TRAINING

As a first approximation, we may list the following as distinguishing characteristics or guiding principles of communist methods of character education.

1. The peer collective (under adult leadership) rivals and early surpasses the family as the principal agent of socialization.
2. Competition between groups is utilized as the principal mechanism for motivating achievement of behavior norms.
3. The behavior of the individual is evaluated primarily in terms of its relevance to the goals and achievements of the collective.
4. Rewards and punishments are frequently given on a group basis; that is to say, the entire group benefits or suffers as a consequence of the conduct of individual members.
5. As soon as possible, the tasks of evaluating the behavior of individuals and of dispensing rewards and sanctions is delegated to the members of the collective.
6. The principal methods of social control are public recognition and public criticism, with explicit training and practice being given

in these activities. Specifically, each member of the collective is encouraged to observe deviant behavior by his fellows and is given opportunity to report his observations to the group. Reporting on one's peers is esteemed and rewarded as a civic duty.

7. Group criticism becomes the vehicle for training in self-criticism in the presence of one's peers. Such public self-criticism is regarded as a powerful mechanism for maintaining and enhancing commitment to approved standards of behavior, as well as the method of choice for bringing deviants back into line.

There are of course many other important features of the Soviet approach to socialization, but the seven listed above are those which present the greatest contrast to the patterns we employ in the West. It is for this reason that they are selected for special consideration here. We shall now proceed to examine each feature in greater detail with particular attention to the research ideas each may generate.

THE FAMILY VERSUS THE COLLECTIVE

American theory and research on moral development have given almost exclusive emphasis to the family as the principal context and agent of socialization. The Soviet pattern, with its predominant emphasis on the collective, therefore, raises the question of how these two socializing agents may differ in the nature and effect of the techniques they employ. To put the problem in another way: What types of socialization process and character structure emerge under the predominant influence of one or the other agent, or a combination of the two?

Stated in this form, the question seems an obvious and important one. Yet, to the writer's knowledge, research to date has little to offer in reply. True, there have been studies of personality development in several diverse types of children's groups who, for one reason or another, have grown up outside the context of the nuclear family. But for several reasons these studies do not shed much light on the problem at hand. The limitation springs in part from the highly specialized character of the groups investigated: youngsters removed to residential nurserises during war time (12), children rescued from Nazi concentration camps, (20), delinquent gangs (15,16,32,43,47), and kibbutz children (14,19,24,37,41).

Second, by and large these investigations take the form of clinical or case studies focusing on the particular problem at hand; they lack the structured design and comparative frame of reference that enhance the possibility of recognizing important differences, distinguishing characteristics, and functional relationships. The advantages of these strategic devices are evidenced in the researches which employ them. Thus in a comparative ethnographic study, Eisenstadt (18) demonstrated that peer collectives are most likely to develop in a society when there is marked discontinuity between values and role allocations in the family and in the adult world. Exploiting another kind of naturalistic experiment, two investigations (22,39) have studied situations in which parental values conflict with those of the peer group, and have found in each instance that although both sources are influential, the peer group tends to outweigh the parent in the age range studied of 12 to 18. The research bearing most directly on the problem at hand in Boehm's comparative study (7) of conscience development in Swiss and American children. She finds that Americans transfer parent dependence to peer dependence at an earlier age than do the Swiss and that:

"One result of this earlier transferring appears to be that the American child's conscience becomes less egocentric and interiorizes earlier than does that of the Swiss child. There is, however, some indication that the content of conscience differs in these two types of societies. Whereas the American child's conscience is turned, primarily, toward social adjustment, the Swiss child's is geared toward character improvement" (7, pp. 91–92).

The principal shortcoming of all these studies for the issue at hand, however, is their failure to examine and analyze their data from the point of view of the group processes of socialization that may be occurring in the collective setting outside the family. To the extent that socialization is dealt with at all in these investigations, it is treated in conventional fashion with attention accorded primarily to the behavior of a parent or a parent surrogate toward the child. Such a restricted focus is of course understandable, given the traditional emphasis in Western culture, reflected in scientific work, on the centrality of the parent-child relationship in the process of upbringing. It is this circumscribed conception which probably accounts for the fact that Western personality theory and research, highly developed as they are in comparison with their Russian counterparts (10), offer little basis for ready-made hypotheses bearing on processes and effects of socialization in collective settings.

Nevertheless, despite their limitations, the existing researches have considerable potential value. To begin with, many of them, especially the clinical and case studies, contain excellent descriptive data that could be re-examined from our new perspective to discover whether they might not shed some light on phenomena of collective socialization. Second, the more structured investigations suggest research designs that might profitably be employed in future work. The first research paradigm, exemplified by both the Eisenstadt and Boehm studies, makes use of groups with contrasting degrees of exposure to socialization in family versus collective settings. Such contrasts are understandably found most readily in different cultures, but under these circumstances interpretation is complicated by the presence of other factors associated with each culture that might account for the observed differences in character development. Eisenstadt endeavors to circumvent this difficulty by using data from a large number of societies in which other factors besides those under immediate investigation may be expected to vary widely. While highly useful, particularly in the exploratory stages of research, this approach has its serious limitations. Either one must make do with only partially adequate data gathered by other investigators with other objectives in mind, or one must carry out new specially designed cross-cultural studies in a substantial number of different settings.

But there is an alternative strategy which, to the writer's knowledge, has hardly been exploited to date. It involves finding groups exposed to different agents of socialization within the same or closely comparable cultural contexts. Such comparable groups may be difficult to discover, but once identified, they offer rich opportunities for research on differential processes and outcomes of character training in familial versus peer-group settings. The ideal contrast in this regard would be two groups of children from the same social milieu, one group having attended boarding school from an early age, the other raised at home with minimal and relatively late exposure to group influences in school or peer group. Obviously this ideal would be almost impossible to achieve but it can certainly be approximated, especially in such countries as England, Switzerland, or, should the opportunity arise, the Soviet Union, where boarding schools are relatively common; or in Israel, with a focus on the comparison between children raised in the kibbutz, where the young are reared primarily outside the family in collective settings, and the moshav, where adult life is collectively organized but children are brought up in the nuclear family. The last contrast should be particularly instructive, since collective ideology would be present in both settings but the principal agent of socialization would differ.

Another research opportunity found more easily outside the United

States is that provided by families living in relative geographic isolation. An extreme example in a modern Western country occurs in Norway, where some families live in mountainous areas that remain isolated during a large part of the year. A current study of this group by Aubert, Tiller, and their associates at the Oslo Institute for Social Research should shed light on the character development of children raised in a nuclear family under conditions of minimal contact with others outside the home.

The American scene is of course not without its possibilities for research along the same lines, even if over a somewhat more restricted range. Thus we, too, have our boarding schools, and although their enrollment tends to be limited to children who are highly selected on socio-economic, religious, or psychological characteristics, an appropriately matched sample of controls not attending boarding school can usually be found. Indeed, to minimize differences in family values and background one could make use of those private schools which enroll both boarding and day pupils. Similarly, instances of families living in geographic isolation can still be found especially in the receding remnants of the American frontier in mountains, deserts, and north country; moreover, with the occasional influx of skilled technicians to such areas, the possibilities arise of studying families who are living in an isolation which is primarily physical and not cultural as well. Finally, among the run-of-the-mill families in any American community there is likely to be an appreciable range of variation in the amount of socialization children experience outside the nuclear family. Some youngsters participate from an early age in nursery schools, camps, clubs, gangs, and other peer-group settings both with and without adult supervision. Others remain relatively isolated from peers until they enter kindergarten or first grade and, even thereafter extrafamilial associations may be minimal. A study of differences in character development in children exposed to varying degrees of familial versus extrafamilial socialization could be illuminating.

The last proposal highlights a difficulty plaguing all of the research designs outlined above. It is obvious that families in which contact with peers is postponed and minimized are likely to exhibit different value systems and techniques of socialization from those in which children are permitted or encouraged to have early associations outside the home. Such differences will be found also even in the "cleanest" and most closely matched comparisons. Thus day and boarding pupils in the same school will still differ in family background, values, and child-rearing practices. The fact that particular values and techniques may be functionally linked to the setting in which they occur does not remove the necessity of identifying them and taking them into account in the interpretation of results and in the design of subsequent studies.

Comparing groups with differing socialization experience is not the only strategy available for studying the differential influences of the family versus the peer collective. The researches of Rosen and Haire mentioned above suggest still another gambit, that of comparing the relative effects of both types of influence on the same children. The strategy here involves finding instances in which familial and peer-group standards conflict in varying degrees and to observe which influence prevails under what circumstances.

The last strategy focuses even more sharply the question of what dependent variables should be investigated in studies of this kind. Quite naturally one thinks first of the variables that have been emphasized in American studies of moral development; namely, projective measures of conscience and guilt of the type employed by Allinsmith (1,2), Aronfreed (3,4), Hoffman (23), and D. R. Miller and Swanson (31), or the behavioral measures of similar variables growing out of the work of Whiting and Sears and their colleagues at the Harvard Laboratory of Human Development (40,45,46) and implemented most recently in a study of antecedents of resistance to temptation conducted by Burton, Maccoby, and Allinsmith (13).

It would clearly be a matter of considerable theoretical and practical interest whether children experiencing different ratios of exposure to socialization within the family versus within the peer group exhibit differences in types and degrees of self-blame, tendency to blame others, resistance to temptation or in any of the other patterns of moral judgment commonly examined in current research on this topic. The psychoanalytic theories on which most of these instruments are based would lead one to expect stronger internalization and self-blame among children raised primarily within the nuclear family, and this prediction receives at least indirect support from the one study we have found (7) that comes near to dealing with the problem. But much depends on the particular socialization processses employed in one or another collective setting. In the absence of adequate data or theory dealing directly with this issue, we can only resort to speculation on the basis of what knowledge we do have about socialization processes in general. And since this knowledge is based almost entirely on studies of the family, we are forced into the risky expedient of arguing by analogy. Accordingly, in order to try to become aware both of the possibilities and pitfalls of this appproach, we shall begin by assuming isomorphism and then call the assumption into question.

What are the principal generalizations to be drawn from existing studies of factors in the nuclear family affecting the moral development of the child? A growing number of independent researches (8,9,11,23,30,31,40) point to the conclusion that the *internalization of moral standards is a function of the degree and ratio of parental affection and discipline.* Specifically, internalization appears to be maximized *when both affection and discipline are high.* When parents rely primarily on the assertion of power in a relatively nonaffectionate context, the child is likely to be responsive only to external controls (for example, fear of punishment). When both affection and discipline are low or when affection appreciably outweighs discipline, moral standards tend to be weak or ineffective and the child resorts to distortive mechanisms such as denial or displacement (for example, unjustly blaming others). But internalization can also take nonadaptive forms characterized by inflexibility or excessive self-blame. Such rigid or self-deprecatory standards are especially likely to arise when parents are generally affectionate but rely on discipline techniques which "involve ego attack and depreciation of the child" (23, p. 5). In contrast, parents of children whose moral standards are more realistic and responsive to extenuating circumstances tend to "appeal more to approach motives." Hoffman, in the most recent and extensive study of this problem, elaborates on the differences between the two groups of parents as follows:

"The two groups are similar in that their parental discipline relies primarily on the frequent use of inductive techniques within an affectionate context, and the infrequent use of power assertion. What mainly characterizes and differentiates [that adaptive group] is that they report their parents as more frequently using techniques that communicate disappointment in the child for not living up to the parent's expectations and less frequently as using ego attack and love withdrawal techniques. It seems to us that the expression of disappointment, while it indicates that the parent has in a sense hurt the child, also conveys the feeling that the child is capable of living up to an ideal" (23, pp. 37–38).

Pursuing our argument by analogy and shifting the context from the family to the school collective, we may ask whether any of these patterns of socialization apply to the Soviet case and, if so, what kinds of consequences in moral development we might expect. With due regard to the tentative and largely impressionistic character of this initial comparison, it is nevertheless striking to note the correspondence between the techniques recommended in our Soviet manual and Hoffman's description of the pattern of socialization most likely to lead to the internalization of realistic and appropriately flexible moral standards. Both situations involve high levels of discipline and support with the primary emphasis on an appeal to motives of approach rather than of avoidance. (For example, "How can we help Serezha with his problem?".) Also in both instances, there is infrequent use of power assertion. Finally, the many examples of group criticism appearing in the Soviet manual are surely more appropriately described in Hoffman's terminology not as an "ego attack and depreciation of the child" but precisely as statements "that communicate disappointment in the child for not living up to expectations," which "convey the feeling that the child is capable of living up to an ideal."

If the analogy is a valid one, and *if* the Russians actually practice what they preach, we should therefore expect that the pattern of socialization in the peer collective would lead to the development of the same quality of moral standards achieved by an optimal balance of support and control in the American nuclear family. The two "if's," however, can hardly be allowed to stand unquestioned. To consider the purely empirical question first, it seems likely that, as in every society, actual practice in Soviet society falls somewhat short of the ideal, or at least deviates from it. The nature of this deviation must await the results of systematic objective observations in Soviet schoolrooms. And it may be some time before such data are made available by either Soviet or Western behavioral scientists. In the meanwhile, however, there is nothing to prevent American workers from initiating a systematic program of research on group atmospheres in the classroom or other peer-collective settings and observing, through naturalistic or contrived experiments, the differential effects of various ratios of support and control on the development of moral standards and behavior. Indeed, the prototype of such research already exists in the classic experiment of Lewin, Lippitt, and White (26), and it is both regrettable and surprising that this study has not been followed up by others in a systematic program of research on socialization processes in peer-group settings. Perhaps White and Lippitt's (44) recently published reanalysis of their data will help stimulate a renewed interest in this neglected area.

Our second "if" gives rise to even more questions and complexities. It seems hardly likely that generalizations derived from studies of the American family could be applied directly to the analysis of socialization processes in the classroom, and a Soviet classroom at that. To begin with, such an analogy assumes that the teacher and the classroom group have re-enforcement power equivalent to that of the parent. This assumption can be challenged from both directions. On the one hand psychoanalytic theory, and probably common belief as well, discount the possibility that any other social group could approach the family in the strength of its affectional and controlling influences. Yet, a growing body of research stemming from the work of Asch (5) demonstrates that the group is capable of exerting tremendously powerful forces toward conformity, even to the extent of inducing distortions in reality perception. The question of the relative potential of the family and the peer group as agents of socialization therefore remains an open one resolvable only through empirical research.

The issue is complicated further by the fact that, to a greater or lesser degree, the child is usually exposed to some measure of socialization within the family before he enters the collective. In fact the responsiveness of the child to socialization in a group setting may even depend on prior experience in the family. It is noteworthy in this connection that, up until now, most of the children who have been exposed to Soviet methods of character education in school have spent the first seven years of their lives in the bosom of the family. Should the preceding speculation be valid, the Russians may experience some difficulty with their methods once they begin, as they propose, to place children in collectives during the first year of life.

Apart from questions about the relative socializing power of the family and the collective, there are of course important differences in the social structure of the two systems. Yet, while influential theorists like Freud (21) and Parsons and Bales (35) have stressed the analogy between parent and children on the one hand and group leader and group members on the other, little attention has been given to the theoretical implications for the process of socialization of such obvious differences as group size, range of role differentiation, specificity of function, duration through time, and their psychological consequences in degree of ego involvement. At the same time, so far as Soviet society is concerned, we must take note of the two-way theme constantly reiterated in Russian writings on character education that the family must become a collective and the collective must take on the characteristics of a family. As a result, it is conceivable that over time the differences between these two types of social structure in Soviet society will become attenuated and the similarities maximized. This possibility highlights the value of comparative longitudinal studies of the changing character of Western and Communist family and peer-group structures. Such studies would of course have special significance as necessary background for research on character development.

The preceding consideration points directly to the most important difference between American and Soviet socialization practice, whether in the family or out. This is the matter of ideological content and the special procedures that this content inspires.

GROUP INCENTIVES

Principles 2 to 4 emphasize the importance of the collective over the individual as the frame of reference for evaluating behavior and distributing punishments and rewards. As the principles indicate, there are three elements to the pattern: Desired behavior is motivated through competition between groups rather than between individuals; behavior is judged in terms of its implication for the achievement and reputation of the group; and rewards and punishments are given on a group basis so that all members of the group stand to gain or lose from the actions of each individual.

The arousal of motivation through competition between groups is certainly not an unfamiliar phenomenon in American society or in the American schoolroom. But even without the support of systematic evidence, one could confidently assert that this motivating device used to be employed far more frequently three or more decades ago than it is today. This same trend is dramatically reflected in the character of research studies being carried out in the late twenties and thirties as compared with the present time. Thus Murphy, Murphy, and Newcomb in the 1937 revision of their *Experimental Social Psychology* (pp. 476–493) tabulate as many as 25 studies dealing with competition in children's groups, many of them focusing directly on the issue of group versus individual incentive. In contrast, a contemporary survey of group research (42) scarcely mentions the topic. Even though the earlier studies of group incentives focus almost entirely on motor and intellectual tasks rather than attitude formation, the results are instructive. Group competition generally increases output but is less effective as an incentive than self-oriented or individual competition. As Murphy, Murphy, and Newcomb properly caution, however, "Any discussion of . . . studies of the effects of incentives must be seen in relation to the cultural background which has set so much store by individual achievement, and has nourished this movement to find ways of stimulating the greatest achievement in the individual" (33, p. 501).

This caveat carries implications for a potentially fruitful research design in which children with contrasting individualistic versus collectivistic backgrounds would be exposed to both types of competitive situations and their performance observed. Although one's first impulse is to discount such a proposal on the practical ground that it would be virtually impossible to find children with such diverse backgrounds in the same culture, further consideration suggests that good research opportunities do exist. The most obvious example is Israel, where both types of orientation are common even within the same ethnic and socioeconomic subgroups. Furthermore, the contrast can be approximated in our own society, since many private schools differ widely precisely along this continuum. For example, many progressive schools are ultra-individualistic in their philosophy and practice, whereas others would probably be shocked to learn that their emphasis on subgroup solidarity and competition is properly described as collectivistic.

But in view of the dearth of research studies of the phenomenon over the last 25 years, there would be much to learn from research on the effects of group incentives even with children coming from the predominantly individualistic background characteristic of American society. On the independent side, these researches should give attention to such specific variables as the motivating power of intergroup versus interindividual competition, evaluation of individual behavior in terms of its contribution to the status of the group as a whole, and the giving of punishments and rewards on a group basis. On the dependent side, the spectrum of variables should be broadened beyond problem solving to include personality measures such as the indices of moral standards employed in much current research as well as other relevant social attitudes and behaviors. These important additions are more appropriately discussed after we have completed examination of the last three of the distinguishing characteristics of Soviet methods of character education—those having to do with group criticism and self-criticism.

GROUP CRITICISM AND SELF-CRITICISM

The feature of Soviet socialization practices that clashes most sharply with the American pattern is the Russians' widespread resort to the procedure of criticizing others and one's self in public. The practice is common throughout all levels of Soviet society from school farm, and factory to the highest echelons of the party. Thus by being taught these techniques in early childhood, Soviet youth are being prepared in patterns of response that will be expected and even required of them throughout their life span. Since such practices are uncommon in American society, it is not surprising that they have not been subjected to research study in any direct way. As already noted, however, the work of Asch and others (5,6) testifies to the power of an overwhelming majority in forcing the deviant members to conform. Members of the majority do not engage in criticism but simply give responses which conflict with the reality perceptions of the experimental subject. The effect on the subject is to lead him, in an appreciable number of instances, to change his own response in the direction of the majority. In a sense, such alteration represents a confession of his own previous "error." Obviously, the experiments cannot be said to reproduce explicit features of Soviet group criticism and self-criticism, but the fit could be made much closer by instructing confederates to engage in criticism and by asking the subject to admit that his previous responses had not been correct. Such variations would of course make even more salient questions of scientific ethics that invariably arise when experiments of this kind are viewed from the perspective of the Western Judeo-Christian moral tradition. (It is doubtful, incidentally, that such questions would ever be raised in a Communist society.) Still ways can probably be found to conduct experiments on the processes of group criticism and self-criticism without doing serious violence to our own ethical traditions.

The fact remains, however, that such socialization procedures as group criticism and self-criticism have moral implications and hence may be expected to have moral consequences; that is to say, they are likely to influence the moral attitudes, actions, and character structure of the individuals on whom they are employed. Moreover, it is doubtful whether such consequences are fully or even adequately reflected by the measures of conscience and guilt currently employed in research on moral development. Certainly it would be important to know about the nature of conscience and guilt in the "new Soviet men" who have been exposed to a lifetime of experience in group criticism and self-criticism. But in building "socialist morality," Soviet educators are less concerned with such questions as whether the individual tends to blame others or himself than with his sense of commitment to the collective, especially in the face of competing individualistic values and preferences.

Accordingly, perhaps the most important research implication to be drawn from our examination of Soviet methods of character education is the necessity of expanding the spectrum of what we conceive as moral development beyond the characteristically Judeo-Christian concern with personal responsibility and guilt to a consideration of the broader moral issues inherent in the relation of man to man and of the individual to his society.

We have tried to take some beginning steps in this direction in the research on character development being conducted at Cornell by Bronfenbrenner, Devereux, and Suci. Specifically, as a point of departure we have distinguished five hypothetical extreme types of character structure representing the presumed products of five divergent patterns of socialization and moral development in children and adolescents. These five are tentatively designated as self-oriented, adult-oriented, peer-oriented, collective-oriented, and objectively-principled character structures.*

The self-oriented child is motivated primarily by impulses of self-gratification without regard to the desires or expectations of others or to internalized standards. Such an asocial and amoral orientation is presumed to arise when the child's parents are so permissive, indifferent, inconsistent, or indulgent that immediate self-indulgence becomes the practicable and, in the long run, most rewarding course of action for the child. The development of this personality type is further facilitated by participation in peer groups which encourage self-indulgence and exact neither loyalty nor discipline from their members.

The adult-oriented child is one who accepts parental strictures and values as final and immutable. He is completely submissive to parental authority and the moral standards imposed by the parent. This orientation generalizes to adult authority outside the home in school and community. In other words, here is the oversocialized "good child," already a little adult, who causes no trouble but is relatively incapable of initiative and leadership. He is presumed to be the product of intensive socialization within the nuclear family but with minimal experience outside the home.

In contrast, the peer-oriented child is an adaptive conformist who goes along with the group and readily accepts every shift in group opinion or conduct. This is the "outer-directed" character type of Riesman's (38) typology or the future "organization man" described by Whyte (48). His values and preferences reflect the momentary sentiments of his social set. The optical circumstances for the development of this personality type involve a combination of parents who are either permissive or actively encourage conformity to group norms, accompanied by early and extensive participation in peer groups requiring such conformity as the price of acceptance. The norms of such groups, however, are ephemeral in character and imply no consistent standards or goals.

* A similar typology, but unlinked to particular patterns and agents of socialization has recently been proposed by Peck and Havighurst (36).

The prototype of the collective-oriented personality is of course the "new Soviet man"—a person committed to a firm and enduring set of values centering around the achievement of enduring group standards and goals. These group values take precedence over individual desires or obligations of particular interpersonal relationships. Such an orientation presumably springs from a developmental history in which from the very outset the parents place the needs and demands of the collective above those of the child or of particular family members. Affection and discipline are bestowed in the name and interests of the social group and the child spends most of his formative years in collective settings under the guidance of adults and leaders who train him in the skills and values of collective living.

Finally, the behavior of the objectively-principled child is guided by values which, although learned through experience in the family and in peer groups, do not bind him to undeviating conformity to the standards of the one or the other. This is the "inner-directed" personality of Riesman's (38) typology. On one occasion he may act in accordance with the standards of his parents, on another with the mores of the peer group, or in still a third instance he may take a path which deviates from the preferences of both parents and peers. There is, however, a consistency in pattern of response from one situation to the next which reflects the child's own now autonomous standards of conduct. The developmental history posited for this type of character structure assumes a strong, differentiated family organization with high levels of affection and discipline but at the same time considerable opportunity granted to the child to participate in selected but varied peer-group experience both with and without adult supervision. These peer groups, in turn, are also characterized by high levels of affectional involvement and their own particular disciplinary codes. The hypothesis implicit in this developmental sequence is that an autonomous set of moral standards is developed from having to cope with different types of discipline in a variety of basically accepting social contexts, so that the child is forced to compare and come to terms with different codes of behavior imposed by different persons or groups each of whom is supportive and wins his liking and respect. This hypothesis, though highly speculative, derives in part from some of our research results (8,9,11) which suggested that children who are rated by teachers and peers as high in social responsibility and initiative tend to come from families where parental affection and discipline are relatively strong, parental roles are moderately differentiated (for example, one parent tends to exercise authority slightly more than the other), but the child also participates in many group activities outside the home. Unfortunately, in these initial studies very little information was obtained about the child's experiences in peer-group settings.

We are currently in the process of devising instruments for measuring the five types of character structure outlined above as these are manifested both in attitudes and behavior. Several of our instruments have yielded promising results in pilot studies but have also brought to light shortcomings in theory and method. The principal value of the approach in its present stage of development is its capacity to generate fruitful hypotheses and research designs for the investigation of character development as a social process.

Our primary purpose here is not to argue for a particular theoretical orientation or methodology; the sole and central aim is to encourage and assist behavioral scientists and educators to give careful attention to the problems and processes implicit in collective methods of character education such as those employed in the Soviet Union and elsewhere in the Communist bloc. We have tried to show that these problems and processes have considerable social relevance and theoretical importance far beyond their immediate social context. We have also attempted to demonstrate that they can be made amenable to empirical investigation. We hope for a renewal of research interest in the study of extrafamilial groups as socializing agents, for such scientific study should do much to enhance our understanding of the intriguing social processes through which human character is formed.

REFERENCES

1. Allinsmith, W. "Conscience and Conflict: The Moral Force in Personality." *Child Developm.*, **28**, 1957, 469–476.
2. Allinsmith, E. "The Learning of Moral Standards," in D. R. Miller and G. E. Swanson, *Inner Conflict and Defense*. New York: Holt, 1960. Pp. 141–176.
3. Aronfreed, J. "Internal and External Orientation in the Moral Behavior of Children." Paper read at the American Psychological Association, Cincinnati, September 1959.
4. Aronfreed, J. "Moral Behavior and Sex Identity," in D. R. Miller and G. E. Swanson, *Inner Conflict and Defense*. New York: Holt, 1960. Pp. 177–193.
5. Asch, S. E. "Studies of Independence and Conformity: A Minority of One Against a Unanimous Majority." *Psychol. Mongr.*, **70**, (9, Whole No. 416), 1956.
6. Berenda, R. W. *The Influence of the Group on the Judgments of Children*. New York: King's Crown Press, 1950.
7. Boehm, L. "The Development of Independence: A Comparative Study." *Child Develpm.*, **28**, 1957, 85–92.
8. Bronfenbrenner, U. "The Changing American Child," in E. Ginsberg (Ed.), *Values and Ideals of American Youth*. (Also in *Merrill-Palmer Quart.*, **7**, 1961, 73–84.) New York: Columbia Univer. Press, 1961, pp. 71–84.

9. Bronfenbrenner, U. "Some Familial Antecedents of Responsibility and Leadership in Adolescents," in L. Petrullo and B. M. Bass (Eds.), *Leadership and Interpersonal Behavior*. New York: Holt, Rinehart, and Winston, 1961. Pp. 239–272.

10. Bronfenbrenner, U. "Soviet Studies in Personality Development and Socialization," in R. A. Bayer (Ed.), *Some Views of Soviet Psychology*. Washington, D.C.: American Psychological Association, 1962.

11. Bronfenbrenner, U. "Toward a Theoretical Model for the Analysis of Parent-Child Relationships in a Social Context," in J. C. Glidewell (Ed.), *Parental Attitudes and Child Behavior*. Springfield, Ill.: Charles C Thomas, 1961. Pp. 90–109.

12. Burlingham D. and A. Freud. *Infants without Families*. London: George Allen & Unwin, 1944.

13. Burton, R. V., E. E. Maccoby, and W. Allinsmith. "Antecedents of Resistance to Temptation." Washington, D.C.: National Institute of Mental Health, United States Department of Health, Education, and Welfare, undated. (Mimeo)

14. Caplan, G. "Clinical Observations on the Emotional Life of Children in the Communal Settlements in Israel." in M. J. Senn (Ed.), *Transactions of the Seventh Conference on Problems of Infancy and Childhood*. New York: Josiah Macy, Jr., Foundation, 1953.

15. Cohen, A. K. *Delinquent Boys—The Culture of the Gang*. Glencoe, Ill.: Free Press, 1955.

16. Cohen, A. K., and J. F. Short, Jr. Research in Delinquent Subcultures. *J. soc. Issues,* **14**, 1958, 23–37.

17. Communist Party of the Soviet Union. *Ob ukreplenii svyazi skkoli s zhiznyu i o dalneishem razvitii sistemi narodnogo obrazovaniya v strane* [On the strengthening of ties between school and life and the future development of the system of public education in the country.] (Theses of the Central Committee of the Communist Party of the Soviet Union) Moscow: Gospolitizdat, 1958.

18. Eisenstadt, S. N. *From Generation to Generation*. Glencoe, Ill: Free Press, 1956.

19. Faigin, H. "Case Report: Social Behavior of Young Children in the Kibbutz." *J. abnorm, soc. Psychol.,* **56**, 1958, 117–129.

20. Freud, A., and S. Dann. An Experiment in Group Upbringing, in W. E. Martin and C. B. Stendler (Eds.), *Readings in Child Development*. New York: Harcourt Brace, 1954.

21. Freud, S. *Group Psychology and the Analysis of the Ego*. London: Hogarth Press, 1948.

22. Haire, M., and F. Morrison. "School Children's Perceptions of Labor and Management." *J. soc. Psychol.,* **46**, 1957, 179–197.

23. Hoffman, M. L. "Techniques and Processes in Moral Development." Detroit: Merrill-Palmer Institute, 1961. (Mimeo)

24. Irvine, E. E. "Observations on the Aims and Methods of Child-rearing in Communal Settlements in Israel." *Hum. Relat.,* **5**, 1952, 247–275.

25. Kairov, I. A. [Long range plans for the development of pedagogical sciences and coordination of the work of the Academy and Chairs of Pedagogy of Pedagogical Institutes, USSR.] (Translation of an article in *Sovetsk. Pedag.,* **24**, No. 2, 1960, 16–44.) New York: United States Joint Publications Research Service, 1960.

26. Lewin, K., R. Lippitt, and R. K. White. "Patterns of Aggressive Behavior in Experimentally Created 'Social Climates.'" *J. soc. Psychol.*, 10, 1939, 271–299.
27. Makarenko, A. *Pedagogickeskaya poema* [A Pedagogical Poem]. (Available in English under the title *The Road to Life,* translated by Ivy and Tatiana Litvinov. Moscow: Foreign Languages Publishing House, 1951.) Leningrad: Leningradskoye Gazetno-zhurnalnoye i Knizhnoye Izadatelstvo [Leningrad Newspaper-Periodical and Book Publishing House], 1949.
28. Makarenko, A. S. *Learning to Live.* Moscow: Foreign Languages Publishing House, 1953.
29. Makarenko, A. S. *Knigda dyla roditelei* [A Book for Parents]. (Available in English. Moscow: Foreign Languages Publishing House, undated.) Petrozavodok: Gosudarstvennoye Izadatelstvo Karel'skoi ASSR [State Publishing House of the Karelian Autonomous Soviet Socialist Republic], 1960.
30. Miller, D. R., and G. E. Swanson. *The Changing American Child.* New York: John Wiley and Sons, 1958.
31. Miller, D. R., and G. E. Swanson. *Inner Conflict and Defense.* New York: Holt, Rinehart, and Winston, 1960.
32. Miller, W. "Lower Class Culture as a Generating Milieu of Gang Delinquency." *J. soc. Issues,* 21, 1958, 5–19.
33. Murphy, G., L. B. Murphy, and T. M. Newcomb. *Experimental Social Psychology.* (Rev. ed.) New York: Harper and Row, 1937.
34. Novikova, L. E. (Ed.). *Sotsialisticheskoye sorevnovaniye v shkole* [Socialist competition in the school]. Moscow: Uchpedgiz, 1950.
35. Parsons, T., and R. F. Bales. *Family, Socialization and Interaction Process.* Glencoe, Ill: Free Press, 1955.
36. Peck, R. F., and R. J. Havighurst. *The Psychology of Character Development.* New York: John Wiley and Sons, 1960.
37. Rabin, A. I. "Kibbutz Children—Research Findings to Date." *Children,* 5, 1958, 179–184.
38. Riesman, D. (with N. Glazer and R. Denney). *The Lonely Crowd: A Study of the Changing American Character.* New Haven: Yale Univ. Press, 1950.
39. Rosen, B. C. "Conflicting Group Membership: A Study of Parent-Peer Group Cross Pressures." *Amer. sociol. Rev.,* 20, 1955, 155–161.
40. Sears, R. R., E. E. Maccoby, and H. Levin. *Patterns of Child Rearing.* Evanston, Ill: Row, Peterson, 1957.
41. Spiro, M. E. *Children of the Kibbutz.* Cambridge, Mass.: Harvard University Press, 1958.
42. Thibaut, J. W., and H. H. Kelly. *The Social Psychology of Groups.* New York: John Wiley and Sons, 1959.
43. Thrasher, F. M. *The Gang.* Chicago: University of Chicago Press, 1936.
44. White, R. K., and R. O. Lippitt. *Autocracy and Democracy.* New York: Harper, 1960.
45. Whiting, J. W. M. "Fourth Presentation," in J. M. Tanner and B. Inhelder (Eds.), *Discussions on Child Development.* Vol. 2. London: Tavistock Publications, 1954.
46. Whiting, J. W. M. and I. L. Child. *Child Training and Personality.* New Haven: Yale University Press, 1953.
47. Whyte, W. F. *Street Corner Society.* Chicago: University of Chicago Press, 1943.
48. Whyte, W. H. *The Organization Man.* New York: Doubleday, 1956.

Chapter 20

The Pursuit of Meaning: Models for the Study of Inquiry

J. Richard Suchman*

* On leave to the U.S. Office of Education, Department of Health, Education, and Welfare.

About the Author

"Give a child enough rope and he may learn to swing." This statement probably comes closest to Richard Suchman's philosophy of education. Trained neither in philosophy nor education, this psychologist spent eleven years on the faculty of the University of Illinois trying to find ways to make free thinkers out of dependent, conforming learners. This effort emerged as the federally sponsored Illinois Studies in Inquiry Training which devoted its energies to developing and testing ways of inviting and supporting the pursuit of meaning, and training teachers in the art of inquiry-centered education.

Suchman entered Cornell University in 1944 and became so attached to the beauty of Ithaca that he stayed for three degrees and a year of elementary school teaching between his M.A. and doctorate. The PhD in child development led to an appointment at the University of Illinois and a new interest in the learner as a productive thinker and inquirer. Here, too, he began his explorations with the use of computers for creating responsive learning climates rather than programmed teaching. The discrepant event film, the inquiry session, the idea book, the Questest, and the inquiry box are some of the specific techniques and devices that resulted from Suchman's work and are now being incorporated into a growing number of curricula.

In 1964 the educational lieutenants of the "Great Society" invited Suchman to try his hand at building a curriculum research branch in the U.S. Office of Education. This was when the office was in the throes of reorganization, and a year later when things became organized, Suchman was director of the Divisions of Elementary and Secondary Research and Higher Education Research. The research budget skyrocketed and full-time administration left no time or energy for anything else. In the spring of 1966 Suchman left Washington to join Science Research Associates as a Visiting Associate and Author, and to get closer to the real world of children and education.

Introduction to the Chapter

Anyone who has seen Suchman conduct one of his inquiry training sessions with elementary children has a head start in understanding his pursuit of meaning. Some of his ideas hark back to some of Bower's concepts of knowledge and ego-processes. For example, Suchman differentiates "delivered meaning" (I tell you, you listen) from "derived meaning" (meaning derived from activity in which a series of alternatives are wrestled with until understanding takes place). In the inquiry training "games," experiment or demonstration is presented to a group of elementary school children who are then asked to derive the best explanation for the phenomenon. This they can do only by asking questions which can be answered by a yes or no. As they formulate questions and listen to each other, they begin to get close to the meaning of the experiment or demonstration.

Inquiry, according to Suchman, is a child's natural bent. He wants to know but, more importantly, he fights to find out for himself, since he senses perhaps that this skill can strengthen his effectiveness as an information ingesting and utilizing organism. The infant is born and grows up in a world of wonder. As a child he tries to close the gap between what he sees and what he understands. Such gaps can be closed for him by meanings delivered by well-meaning adults; however, in the process the child has lost the opportunity to strengthen his own learning resources. Teaching by telling is an attempt to get meaning to a learner by bypassing real experience. In some cases, it may be the only way of teaching. The risk one takes in such teaching is that symbols may be substituted for the meaning or the meaning level may be so low or distorted that the child has been misinformed.

Certainly no one is suggesting that all knowledge be gained through first- and second-hand inquiry. To some extent, the accuracy of explanations will be based on common experiences that inquiry training can help provide to both teachers and students. It is still sad but true that the greatest instructional fallacy of mother and child, teacher and student, is the notion of telling as learning. Perhaps Suchman can help us lay this myth to rest.

The Pursuit of Meaning: Models for the Study of Inquiry

Let us consider several models for the study of meaningful human learning. These models are rooted in observed classroom behavior rather than experimental laboratory studies. They have been tested repeatedly during their evolution through thousands of observed episodes involving children engaged in inquiry and represent a formulation of the process by which children seek and derive an expansion of meaning through their interactions with the environment.

Human existence involves an interaction between organism and environment in which the organism is continuously and irreversibly changed. Perhaps this is what Dewey meant by the statement, "Living is learning and learning is living."

Inquiry is the controlled use of interaction in the pursuit of meaning. The learner comes to know and understand the nature of his world by increasing his encounters with it. These encounters represent his points of contact with reality. They provide the raw data from which meaning is derived. Inquiry is the generation of new meaning through learner-controlled and interpreted encounters.

It can be argued that free inquiry is the most naturalistic form of learning behavior. Any situation where a person or device intervenes to influence the course of learning is merely a special case of the more fundamental process and can be analyzed as such. We will, therefore, begin with the analysis of the inquiry process and then turn to the analysis of learning under more didactic conditions in order to highlight the ways in which didactic learning constitutes a departure from inquiry.

The reader must understand that this chapter is offered as an hypothesis, notwithstanding the tone of conviction in the language used. If the chapter serves no more than to open some eyes to new variables or to even raise some doubt as to the adequacies of models now implicit in current psychological or educational practices, its intended purpose shall have been served.

484

ASSUMPTIONS

We must begin with a set of basic assumptions about the nature of the human as a perceiving-thinking-acting organism. They are as follows:

1. The human organism is "meaning-hungry." Survival demands that man search for meaning. He must be able to interpret environmental cues to respond to them intelligently. The expansion of meaning also makes life richer and more pleasurable.

2. The human has almost continuous encounters with the environment, many of which are initiated by the individual as a means of making the environment more meaningful.

3. Self-initiated encounters are not random but organized.

4. Action produces new encounters by changing the environment and changing the learner's relationship to the environment.

5. Meaning results when encounters are guided, grouped, and interpreted by conceptual organizers. The human can acquire, generate, and store two kinds of organizers—data and abstract systems.[1] The storage of data is simply the accumulation of pieces of raw experience. Stored data can afford the learner a useful frame of reference for dealing with new items of data as they are taken in. Stored data make possible the establishment of familiarity and provide a basis for recognizing similarities and differences. Abstract systems are inventions that are used to group or order data as a means of deriving more meaning from them (or of attributing it to them).

THE GENERATION OF MEANING

Meaning results from encounters between the learner and his environment. External stimuli are selected, grouped, and internalized through these encounters under the control of internal organizing patterns. For example, a child encounters a fork that is lying on the table in front of him. As he watches it, he selects it out from among the array of other stimuli in his environment. He attends, let us say, to the fork itself and not to the shadow it casts or the spaces that are left between the prongs. Certain organizers available to the learner and used by him are controlling these selections. He has seen many forks in the past and has a vast quantity of stored data pertaining to forks. In addition, he has probably developed an abstract concept "fork" which serves to further organize his perceptions and interpreta-

1. Systems are patterns for selecting, ordering, and interpreting data.

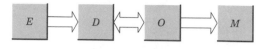

Figure 20.1.

tions of what he is taking in. This may give him expectations as to size, shape, function, and so forth. In any event, the encounter with the fork is meaningful because of the organizing function of what has been stored from previous encounters with forks.

Figure 20.1 is a simple schematic representation of the preceding analysis. E is the encounter with the fork. O is an organizer, perhaps a concept of "fork" growing out of prior experience. The data, D, derived from this encounter depend partly on what is available to be perceived and partly on the organizer that is used. The fork's color, for example, may become an item of data if the attention to color is dictated by an organizer in use. M is the meaning that results from the interaction between E, D, and O.

Figure 20.2 represents a multiple use of an organizer for the selection and interpretation of data. In this case, one organizer in combination with two items of data produces two units of meaning. An example of this might be the comparison of two different types of animals in the study of biology. The study of locomotion patterns might involve a single organizer that, when applied to two different animals, would yield two different meanings. The organizer dictates what variables are attended to and therefore determines what data are obtained from each encounter. Once these data are obtained, the organizer also provides the basis for comparing one set of data with another. For example, in comparing the locomotion of a cat with that of a frog the organizer being used might dictate that we attend to the utilization of the forelegs. In doing so, we note that the cat distributes

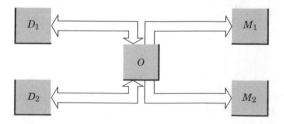

Figure 20.2.

his weight evenly on all four legs, whereas the frog makes very little use of his forelimbs.

Obviously, the greater the number of data items that can be interpreted by a single organizer the greater the power of the organizer. Organizers that add meaning to many different kinds of encounters are seen as powerful and tend to assume influential roles in thought and perception. The concept of "equivalence" or "force" are examples of powerful organizers because they can be used to add meaning to many different events.

Figure 20.3 provides another variation of the generation of meaning. Here a single encounter, E, yields two different meanings, M_1 and M_2, as the result of the application of two different organizers, O_1 and O_2. Different kinds of data result in each case, D_1 and D_2. This is simply a case of looking at the same thing from two different points of view. A glass of water may be regarded as something to drink and as a paperweight. The weatherman perceives a cumulonimbus buildup as evidence of a successful forecast and as the potential terminator of his picnic.

The main point of the preceding analysis is that the key to the generation of meaning is the interaction between organizers and encounters. If we wish to augment meaningful learning in the classroom, we must increase the number of encounters, enlarge the learner's repertoire of available organizers, or create conditions that will bring more of the available organizers into use for the generation of meaning.

Naturally, meaning can be conveyed to people without their using either data or organizers. It is, for example, a simple matter to tell a learner about the conservation of mass without requiring him to derive the concept for himself. As a matter of fact, teachers are quite prone to short-circuit the process of meaning generation by doing a lot of telling. Let us call this delivered meaning as distinct from derived meaning. Delivered meaning involves the verbal conveyance

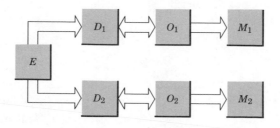

Figure 20.3.

of information to a learner and his acceptance of it. Derived meaning evolves from a series of cognitive operations. The resulting understanding stands out against a background of rejected alternative interpretations. Thus, the meaning that is acquired is seen in the context of the process by which it came into being. Derived meaning is more likely to be recognized as the product of human thinking than is meaning that is delivered verbally as valid and absolute.

THE MEDIATION OF ACCOMMODATION

The models in the foregoing section do not account for the fact that not all of the available organizers are in use at the same time. They are brought into action in a highly selective way and generally only a few of them are operational at any one time. It would be virtually impossible for anyone to perceive the environment at any one time in relation to all the data or abstractions he had available for use. Obviously, there must be some mechanism that regulates the utilization of stored data and stored systems as organizers in the processes of perception and thought.

Furthermore, the human is far more than a perceiving and meaning-generating system. It is also an acting system capable of effecting changes in the environment and changes in the relationship between itself and its environment. The latter change is internal and is brought about by the process of accommodation.

Hunt (1961) shows how accommodation and growth are functions of the match between environmental encounters and existing schemata (organizers). Drawing upon Festinger's (1957) motivation of dissonance (when the matching is off enough to arouse concern) and Inhelder and Piaget's (1955) concept of accommodation (matchmaking through cognitive restructuring), he arrives at the conclusion that the process of finding the match is (1) central to learning, and (2) only vaguely understood.

He makes a crucial distinction between the kind of matching Skinner (1959) engineers to link behavior and perception through conditioning and the much more subtle matching between encounters and existing schemata.

"Because one can see whether a given bit of behavior approximates better or worse the desired form but cannot see the effect that an encounter with a circumstance is having on the central processes that mediate schemata, the art of applying reinforcement is of a lower order than the art of matching circumstances with schemata." (Hunt, 1961)

In other words, shaping a learner's *behavioral responses* to match a set criteria is one process and relating his conceptual structures to his percepts in a meaningful way is quite another. The first process is more forced, crude, and artificial, but can be effected by teachers (and teaching devices) with comparative ease. The second can result only through an accommodative process, over time, and largely through the cognitive efforts of the learner himself. A teacher can reinforce a response, but he cannot accommodate a pupil's conceptual structures. Hunt paints an uncertain picture of the teacher's role in promoting pupil accommodation:

"Anyone who attempts to modify a child's development by manipulating his encounters with environmental circumstances must artfully "cut-and-try" until he finds those situations which will call forth accommodative modifications. Moreover, inasmuch as experience and maturation are continually changing the schemata of the child, maximizing the richness of an environment calls for continual concern with the appropriateness of the match. This means that all too often the process of artful trial and error becomes exhaustive to anyone who attempts to manage a child's encounters to maximize accommodative growth."

Later Hunt cites evidence to support the contention that giving the learner a more autonomous role allows him to utilize his insight into the cause of his own dissonance and thus serves as his own guide in the process of negotiating his own accommodation. The teacher can help by making room for and supporting this process and by resisting the temptation to shape the learner's behavior.

The Illinois Studies in Inquiry Training (Suchman, 1964) has developed strategies and materials to create classroom conditions for stimulating and sustaining self-mediated accommodation by pupils. In order to foster a learner's inquiry development, his attention was focused on dissonance-producing episodes; he was allowed to operate freely as he attempted to assimilate discrepant events; he was given the data for many theoretical formulations; and at each stage of accommodative growth he was given a chance to verbalize his formulations. The Inquiry Training Program leads beyond the focus problem itself to the processes of inquiry, why it exists and how it functions. The door is opened to epistemology—what knowledge is and how it comes into being.

A MODEL FOR COGNITIVE MEDIATION

Figure 20.4 introduces the mediation and action functions in a model that represents the self-regulating, adapting, and acting dimensions of human behavior. Before considering them, let us look at a concrete situation to broaden our understanding of how these functions relate to each other and to the entire system.

Consider the example of a child who has dropped an iron nail into the fish bowl one day and has returned later to find the nail covered with rust. Suppose this child does not know what rust is or how it is formed. He is somewhat surprised at what he sees and dissatisfied with his level of understanding. One could say that a gap had developed between the data taken from encounters and the conceptual organizers available in the storage function. Has this child seen this particular event several times or had he understood the process of oxidation, the events may have been more meaningful to him. In other words, since what he perceives is not matched by what he knows, he is confronted by a discrepant event. If his need for meaning in this instance is great enough, he will try closing the gap in one way or another.

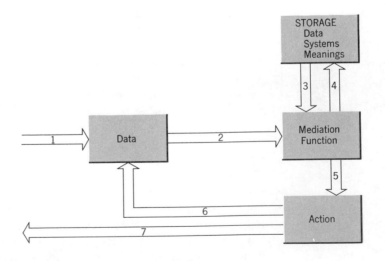

Figure 20.4.

Turning now to Fig. 20.4, we can analyze the behavior of the child within the framework of the model. Data from the encounters with the nail could not be matched with other stored data or with any abstract systems that the learner might have formulated and stored previously. The absence of appropriate organizers precludes the child's assimilation of this event. If he is to find new meaning in his encounters with the nail, he must take action. Perhaps from past experience he has learned that it is helpful to learn the nature of the materials he is dealing with. He might, therefore, try to find out what the nail is made of. This is an attempt to obtain more data, and arrow 6 indicates that the action is directed toward the acquisition of additional data. Learning that the nail is made of iron may yield no more meaning than the child had to start with unless he happens to know or discover that something happens to iron when it is immersed in water for a period of time. Such knowledge constitutes the beginnings of a new system pertaining to the properties of iron. It can be acquired by verbal means or by observing the behavior of iron under conditions described and inferring the properties.

Notice that the arrows 1 through 5 form a kind of loop or cycle: (1) taking in data, (2) checking the data against stored organizers to find meaning, (3) retrieving previously stored organizers for the purpose of finding new meaning in the data, (5) and (6) taking action to generate new data. This loop is what I have come to call the "inquiry cycle" because it represents the characteristic rotational sequence of behaviors followed by people who are engaged in inquiry. If the matching between data and organizers does not yield a meaning level high enough to satisfy the inquirer, he takes further action to generate additional data. These data are again checked against available organizers, and so the cycle continues. In the course of repeated cycles, two things can happen: (1) there can be a buildup of new data that are stored and become available to play an organizing role. Arrow 4 indicates this storage function. (2) Abstract systems can be altered or even generated by incoming data. A repeated re-grouping may occur restructuring systems to create organizers that will generate an acceptable level of meaning. In other words, when a person cannot assimilate a strange or discrepant event, he may achieve assimilation by gathering additional data through analysis, manipulation, or experimentation. The proliferation of data makes more organizers available for possible matchmaking or assimilation. The learner scans his store of organizers for potential data or models that will yield higher levels of meaning from the encounter. In a sense the inquirer is playing both ends against the middle by bringing more data and organizers into play and in so doing increasing the probability of making new matches and finding greater meaning in his encounters.

Arrow 7 leading from the action box simply indicates that some action is directed primarily at modifying the environment rather than generating new data. If the child had simply reached into the fish bowl and retrieved the nail without being concerned with causation, we could say that his motivation was primarily that of producing a change rather than of understanding a process.

MOTIVATION, THE POLARIZER OF INQUIRY

In observing children as they respond to the environment, it becomes quite obvious that events that stimulate the search for meaning for one child may leave another unmoved. As a matter of fact, everyone shifts from moment to moment or day to day with respect to what arouses inquiry and what events are seen as discrepancies. This suggests that the model requires yet another function, one that accounts for the shifting that occurs among the kinds of meanings given top priority by the individual at any given time (see Fig. 20.5).

Let us go back for a moment and review the episode where the child finds the rusty nail in the fish bowl. It is conceivable that his reaction to this might be anger instead of curiosity. He could have put the nail into the bowl for safekeeping and have been very disappointed by the appearance of the coat of rust. His response might

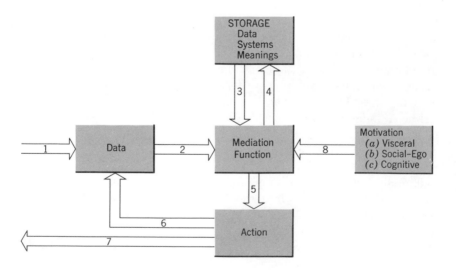

Figure 20.5

well have been one of taking the nail out and scraping the rust off. Having done this he might very well have turned away from the whole situation. In other words, his attention to particular meanings (that is, the consequences versus the causes) is a function of his current motivational state with respect to the encounter.

Thus, motivation provides a kind of pivot point around which all the other functions are mobilized. An example of the effect of motivation is seen in the instance of the soldier being fired upon in wartime. He perceives a tree as a means of survival and runs behind it to save his life. It is unlikely under these conditions that he will wonder whether the tree is an elm or sycamore, although there are other conditions under which he might feel a need to make the distinction.

It becomes important then for us to observe the properties of the mediating center in relation to environmental conditions, particularly those which influence motivation.

MOTIVATIONAL HIERARCHY

There appears to be something of a motivational hierarchy that determines the pivot point around which the entire cognitive system functions. Three motivational systems seem to be in operation simultaneously with a more or less stable priority system governing the order of dominance. The systems are here described in order of the priority they seem to command.

Visceral motivation

At the top rung of the hierarchy is the survival need. The learner seeks and interprets data in light of potential threats to his homeostatic processes. Perception and action are both organized around these biologically determined requirements. Educators know that children who are tired, hungry, or suffering physical pain direct much of their energy to overcoming these pressures and are therefore less able to cope with other kinds of problems. Teachers have long known the importance of reducing visceral stresses on children. As a result, most schools are able to meet the biological needs of the children to the point where these pressures are not so pronounced as to block other motivational systems from dominating the mediating function.

Social-ego motivation

The school child is also striving for social-psychological survival. He has acquired the need for status, for a favorable self-image, and for love and acceptance. These are important to him; unless they are available in sufficient quantity and quality, he may mobilize his mediating functions to achieve and maintain a tolerable degree of social-ego equilibration. Children whose social-ego needs are dominant are more likely to ask questions in order to show what they know than to find out what they do not know. The need to achieve operates on a different basis than the curiosity need. Children differ widely with respect to the strength of social-ego motivation, but unless a child feels he is maintaining a satisfactory level of social-ego satisfaction, he is likely to devote much of his energy to finding such assurance.

Cognitive motivation

When the visceral and social-ego pressures are reduced, learners can more easily turn to searching for new meaning motivated by the intrinsic pleasure found in the products and processes of inquiry. This is inquiry for the sake of acquiring knowledge and the excitement of search and invention. The implementation of ideas becomes subordinated to the formulation and testing of them and to the processing of information and the building and testing of theories. When the other motivational pressures are off, one can play with ideas without having to come up with a solution. Often, cognitive motivation stimulates inquiry that is not even focused on a problem, but is simply directed toward finding more powerful organizers and greater meaning.

One can distinguish at least two subcategories of cognitive motivation. The first of these is the motivation of closure, the desire to assimilate an event, to place it in a meaningful framework. The second kind of cognitive motivation is almost the direct opposite. It is characterized by the desire to open things up, to explore and expand our knowledge and understanding in an area without any specific focus upon a disturbing event or problem. This is truly the motivation of curiosity, the search for new discrepant events rather than the attempt to eliminate one annoying discrepancy.

Probably all levels of motivation in the hierarchy can operate at the same time. Changes may be largely a matter of shifting priorities. A teacher need only reduce visceral and social-ego pressures to shift cognitive motivation into a more dominant role in the inquiry process. The teacher who accepts and supports the ideas of his pupils without judging their intellectual performance in terms of its correctness or quality removes much social-ego pressure. When the fear of failure or disapproval (a social-ego concern) is eliminated, the children can play with ideas and invent and theorize with greater freedom and objectivity. They become less self-centered and more idea-centered. These are the earmarks of cognitive motivation.

TRADITIONAL TEACHING RE-EXAMINED

Patterns of traditional didactic-expository teaching can be analyzed within the framework of this model. The characteristics of the traditional pedagogical approach include a large amount of showing, telling, and explaining. This is a form of planned intervention by the teacher in order to regulate and direct the process of meaning generation. Teaching by telling is an attempt to put data, organizers, and units of meaning into place in the learner's storage system by the use of words and other symbolic systems. One of the consequences of this type of teacher intervention is that the meaning level for the learner may be so low that he retains only the words and not their meaning. An even greater potential danger is that the learner will believe that he has acquired meaning when he has acquired only words.

"Explaining" is an attempt to increase meaning by relating new data or ideas to old and familiar ones. Here the choice of language is exceptionally important. The entire process of directing the formation of new organizers and meaning for a person through the use of language is highly complex, difficult to control, and frequently results in a kind of shooting in the dark. This may be true even when the teacher-pupil ratio is one-to-one, but it gets progressively less controllable as the number of pupils per teacher increases. If a teacher wishes to create a set of desired new meanings for his pupils, he has several channels over which he can exert control. First, he can select the encounters the children have in the classroom. His program is in effect a sequence of planned encounters put together with a certain end result in mind. But the meaning derived from each encounter is a function of the organizers used by each learner in selecting the data to be gathered from the encounter and the interpretation of the data. The use of organizers depends first upon their availability to the learner, and second, upon the learner's predisposition or willingness to use them. The teacher can direct the learner's attention and even suggest what organizers to use, but this manipulation requires great care, since the language used by the teacher must correspond to the learner's terms for the same organizers or else the learner will not be able to conform. And, if the child does not have the desired organizers available at all, nothing will avail.

SOME CORRELARIES OF THE MODEL

By extrapolating from the model, one can infer a set of new definitions for the teaching-learning process. If the model has validity, then teaching cannot be regarded as a simple one-to-one handing out of knowledge. The model puts the learner in the center of the arena, interacting with the elements of his environment at many levels and in many directions. The teacher is just one of these elements with no monopoly of control over the learning process.

Learning is not simply the acquisition and storage of content, but also the restructuring of systems and the grouping of data. The teacher does not really give knowledge or ideas: he attempts to create conditions that will increase the probability that the learner will grow cognitively in a given direction. (The teacher, of course, is concerned with other types of growth as well.)

The most meaningful learning occurs when the learner is trying out his own ideas on data that he has gathered through encounters that he has initiated. The element of learner autonomy is therefore crucial for the maximazation of meaning. The learner is, after all, the best judge of his own conceptual strength and gaps, providing that he has the freedom and resources to try out his own ideas and put them to the test himself. But he can face his own conceptual structures objectively only if he is not concerned by the threat of failure or ridicule and if being "right" is not an essential concern. For this reason the learning climate is particularly important, not only in providing the freedom and resources required for data gathering, but also because of the necessity of protecting cognitive motivation from the interference effects of social-ego pressure. There is a saying in Thailand that "the nothingness of the ego is the way to the truth."

THE ROLE OF THE TEACHER

Inquiry can be thought of as the most natural and fundamental learning mode. The infant is an inquirer long before he becomes anybody's pupil. Intervention and teacher-guided learning represent departures from pure inquiry. There are obvious reasons why education should not prevent the teacher from intervening in the learning process to influence the course of conceptual growth. But the role of the teacher as the programmer of learning must be shifted if the motivational and cognitive advantages of inquiry are to be obtained in the process of education.

Bringing this shift into more practical terms, I would see the following changes in the role of the teacher as conducive to the strengthening of inquiry as a mode of learning.

New classroom goals are needed. The stimulation of independent thinking needs higher priority. The improvement of the self-image through learning as an independent, autonomous inquirer should also be a major goal. Teachers cannot remain in a wholly didactic role and still create conditions that stimulate and sustain search for richer meaning. In order to initiate a shift toward inquiry, teachers must approach knowledge with more open-endedness and tentativeness. They must show greater respect for the ideas of individual children and for derived meaning than on delivered meaning. Finally, there must be a heightened sensitivity to individual differences in conceptual structures, cognitive style, motivational patterns, and the amount and type of stored data. The more the teacher knows about his pupils in these respects, the more effectively he can create the optimal conditions to stimulate and sustain the autonomous search for meaning. These conditions include freedom for the children to search and move about in gathering data and testing ideas. Most important of all is the freedom that is afforded by avoiding any contingencies between cognitive behavior and social reinforcement. Once children find that the social-ego payoff is limited to certain kinds of answers, creative and independent thinking are inhibited.

To be a successful stimulator of inquiry, the teacher must himself be an inquirer, opening up the thinking processes of children, provoking doubt, probing, questioning, and helping the children to derive pleasure in the raising of questions rather than getting answers.

The urge and the capacity to inquire are present in the child almost from birth and continue to exert an influence on his behavior throughout his lifetime. The important question for the educator is whether he is willing and able to create those conditions in the schools that will allow the child to turn his capacity to inquire toward the task of building and extending his own world of meaning.

REFERENCES

Festinger, L. *A Theory of Cognitive Dissonance*. Evanston, Ill.: Row, Peterson, 1957.

Hunt, J. McV. *Intelligence and Experience*. New York: Ronald Press, 1961.

Inhelder, Barbel, and J. Piaget. The Growth of Logical Thinking from Childhood to Adolescence: An Essay on the Construction of Formal Operational Structures. New York: Basic Books, 1958.

Skinner, B. F. "A Case History in Scientific Method," in S. Kock (Ed.), *Psychology: a Study of Science*. Vol. 2, pp. 359–379. *General Systematic Formulations and Special Processes*. New York: McGraw-Hill, 1959.

Suchman, J. R. "The Child and the Inquiry Process," in H. Passow and R. Leeper (Eds.), *Intellectual Development: Another Look*. Washington, D.C.: Association for Supervision and Curriculum Development, 1964.

Chapter 21

A Preventive Approach to Developmental Problems in School Children[1]

M. R. Newton and
Racine D. Brown

[1] This paper reports on a National Institute of Mental Health Project Grant
(MH 947-A1) executed by the South Carolina State Department of Mental
Health in collaboration with the Sumter, South Carolina, School District No.
17.

About the Authors

Robert Newton was drawn to psychology by an extraordinary teacher, Benjamin Gessner at Baker University. In graduate school (Kansas) he became interested in the implications ecological and child development studies had for clinical treatment models under his mentors Roger Barker and Martin Scheerer. He was fortified by such work experiences as psychiatric aide under Karl Menninger and as a psychology intern in a VA training program. While taking time out for the Navy, he served as First Marine Division Psychologist and became intrigued by their greater treatment success in the field (Korea) as an alternative to evacuation to rear hospitals.

After returning to Kansas, a desire to test out ideas led him to become South Carolina's first full-time community consultant. With the title of "community psychologist," he found himself part catalyst and part community "switchboard" to stimulate new programs in a typical county with no formal mental health resources. Parent associations, a tri-county mental health center, school programs, and the state's major mental health research effort described in this chapter, all attest to the success of this program.

Stimulated by the early psychiatric intervention ideas of Lindeman and Caplan, the pragmatism of group dynamics, and the success of able teachers, physicians, and other caretakers on the frontlines of stress in communities, Newton has demonstrated an excitement about positive alternatives to a focus on mental illness in his current research efforts.

Racine D. Brown came to be principal investigator of the Sumter Child Study Project quite by coincidence. With a background of training in community mental health research at Washington University and program evaluation at the St. Louis County Health Department Child Guidance Clinic, he joined the planning staff of the South Carolina Department of Mental Health just at the time the original principal investigator was moving to a new position. The designation of this author as the new principal investigator was a favorable meshing of needs and resources.

Racine Brown began his professional training and career (after several years of marginal success and outstanding misplacement in the sales field) in clinical psychology. Through the influence of Elmore A. Martin he became interested in group and milieu therapies and subsequently in the broader areas of group and community dynamics. The treatment of pathology became increasingly less attractive as the possibility of promoting growth appeared more feasible. This orientation, begun in a state hospital setting, was both strengthened and disciplined through association with John C. Glidewell during three years of training in community mental health research. Six years of association with the National Training Laboratories and with a variety of attempts to apply behavioral science methods and findings to real live problems has provided avenues of development for an interest in creating social systems which promote and sustain the growth of their members.

The legitimacy of the author's role in the Project reported here stems neither from a claim to expertise in child development and child guidance nor from special credentials in education. His contributions are through consultation to the Project staff on research issues and on operational issues having to do with the change process, problem resolution, and the development of a social context which can support change and problem resolution.

The highly significant learnings from the Project acquire much of their meaning through the questions raised about broader concerns with which the author is dealing on other fronts. To cite examples: Is crisis intervention more than a special case of influencing the change process?; what are the parameters of community development necessary to support adequate crisis intervention?; what is the relationship between management style and skill to the success of a project such as this?; how can the growth promotion ideology be incorporated into the conceptualization and operation of community mental health programs generally?; and so on and so on.

Questions such as those above help to define the immense meaning of the work reported for Racine Brown as he pursues his multiple roles of Mental Health Education Unit Coordinator at the South Carolina Department of Mental Health, teacher of graduate psychology students in community mental health, and a variety of consulting relationships of national scope.

Introduction to the Chapter

All of the imaginative ideas and research findings that are extolled in this book will be but as tinkling brass unless they someday find application. The book closes with the story of education and mental health teamwork in a small southern city where "strens," ego-strength building interventions, are being used to help children over the emotional, social, and educational hurdles of school entry. Here, through the frameworks of preschool parent and child interviews, an assortment of special summer activities, and individualized preparation for school entry followed by consultative collaboration with the classroom teacher, a program of prevention and crisis management has become a feasible and well-accepted operation.

Instead of having therapists retreat behind closed doors with referred children already in trouble, all entering school children are seen with their parents, and interventive management is initiated "in situ" within the familiar settings of home and school. Mental health staff and school staff work together to detect incipient problems and to build "bridges of relationships" with all parents to help them enhance the growth and development of their offspring. The staff frequently focuses on reducing tensions in the "human environment" of key individuals in the child's life. Emphasis is placed on helping parents, children, and teachers deal with crises in such a way that the child can acquire new understandings and additional skills or learn new roles. Instead of esoteric therapies, the helping process is defined in terms of day by day modes of operation familiar to the teacher and the parents. Building on the premise that "stress is better managed in the social setting of home and school," the teams have happily developed a creative and rewarding new experience in mental health programming. They call themselves interventionists. I should like to correct that understatement by adding "preventionists." What they do and how they do it is one of the leading frontiers of this book.

A Preventive Approach to Developmental Problems in School Children

Stress and crisis occur so repeatedly in the lives of growing children that we accept them as ordinary. Familiarity with stress and crisis experiences may even blind teachers and parents to the genuine distress and potential for emotional disorder that is very much a part of such experiences for the developing child. Any experienced teacher can supply examples much like the following vignettes drawn from actual case files:[1]

". . . a teacher discovers David, one of her bright, promising first-graders, quite distressed on the playground, apparently because he found the door locked and could not re-enter the classroom. The teacher tries to reassure the child. From this small event, the child's school work quickly deteriorates. He attends school only under excessive pressure from home.

". . . Bobby a bright, rather feminine little boy is urged by his teacher to gradually pursue more masculine behavior as a way of coping with dislike from his peers. She fails and enlists the father's support, only to lose suddenly all rapport with the boy, with a sudden increase in what appear to be trivial absences.

". . . Lemar, a walking index of serious deprivation, primitive, with incomprehensible speech, a suspected mental defective with a great supply of uninhibited energy was declared "hopeless" on a preschool visit as he demonstrated lack of familiarity with indoor plumbing and ate with his fingers. His parents are in desperate straits, fifth grade education, father unemployed, family noted for their suspicious, uncommunicative behavior.

". . . college educated parents enter the classroom for their first parent-teacher conference. Much to their dismay, they hear the teacher's

[1] From Sumter Child Study Project files, disguised only to protect family confidentiality.

perception of their child, Billy, as a behavior problem and retarded well behind the class average. They react with anger and sharp awareness of the teacher's human limitations. The boy continues to make even less progress.

". . . George, a seven-year old boy wets his pants, runs away from school, cries under mild stress, and destroys his desk work and pencils; best efforts to change the situation fail. He begins to be the butt of hazing and rejection from peers, further intensifying this behavior."

What to do? Whose responsibility? Where to turn for help? These are recurrent questions posed by parents, teachers, and school administrators. Increasingly they turn to behavioral science for answers.

Although research on the prevention and alleviation of emotional and mental disorders is notoriously difficult and the translation of research findings into effective action models is often not possible, behavioral scientists are responding to appeals from educators and parents to share in the responsibility to understand and provide action alternatives in the face of stress and crisis. Research is being done; action models are emerging.

MODELS OF INTERVENTION

Various theoretical and action models are employed to cope with the problems posed by disordered behavior in school children. Several of those most frequently encountered will be reviewed.

Inaction

When faced with stress and potential disordered behavior in children, the most obvious model of intervention for the teacher and parent is that of inaction, that is, the approach that "these things take care of themselves." Neglect can indeed motivate some children or families to work out their own solutions to problems. Indifference can provide costly and hard-won self-reliance in some children. In fact, many teachers have found to their acute distress that good intentions, even when strengthened by professional guidance, can sometimes be more harmful than neglect. The tendency to do nothing may be strengthened by the not uncommon admonition from some mental health professionals that stress and crisis are normal and quite to be expected and that most children weather them adequately. Too often, however, neglect and inaction lead to ineffectual acceptance of the problem as is or to antagonism displaced to some convenient scapegoat, for example, "if only parents would . . . ," or "teachers just don't seem to care anymore."

Discipline

Discipline has long served as a way to manage the symptoms of a developmental disorder. The practical educator quickly learns that a child does respond to the setting of limits and the imposition of discipline by authority. Offensive and mysterious, however, is the "incorrigible child" who does not respond, whose disturbance seems to grow on disciplinary measures. The child who wilts and overconforms in the face of punitive efforts is seldom noticed and, significantly, seldom admired. It would be a remarkably naïve person who maintained that a child does not need some controls and external discipline, but discipline applied simply to maintain order abrasively negates a child's potential and strength, typically creating a need for an external, autocratic discipline throughout life. In the heat of frontline classroom maneuvers and the demands of a typical school system, it is the rare teacher who can discipline in tune with the current situation and at the same time choose a reaction that will promote inner discipline and self-control. The fact that this is being done at all by many teachers and principals is exciting enough to call forth a blast from the proverbial bugles.

Treatment

Most of the children referred to in the initial cases might well become clinical cases. Increasingly, disturbed children have been referred for treatment to a special counselor or clinic. Certainly the proliferation of school and community mental health resources makes the treatment approach more feasible than in the past. To be treatable, however, a problem has to be obvious and serious enough to be perceived as warranting referral. Whether the therapist is the capable but overburdened family physician, the school psychologist, a professional in the child guidance clinic or in the emerging community mental health clinic, the majority of cases will never be referred. A case could even be made that many never should be referred. Occasionally the child will settle on a tolerable level of adjustment at the sacrifice of greater potential. Sometimes the child is not referred because of a shortage of resources. Often parents or teachers are reluctant to redefine the child as a clinical case. In any event it is unlikely that our school systems will ever enjoy sufficient mental health manpower resources for the traditional treatment models to be effective on a total population basis.

Education

In the best American tradition we can focus on education as a means of increasing the skills of teacher, parent, or child. This approach would typically involve passing along information about personality development and intervention alternatives. The education model has much to offer and probably will remain a cornerstone in any serious prevention effort. All too frequently agents responsible for a child's growth apply learning to maintain order and find it difficult to apply dynamic concepts designed to promote growth and competency in the child. As one parent commented[2] "too often we read the usual scare article on child care and never see its implications for us, personally; or what's worse, we get so anxious about it, we overreact and forget these articles are too general to blindly apply them to our own unique child."

Crisis or Stress Model of Intervention

A recent trend in the area of mental health has been the extension and exploration of the community services or programs that advance the aims of preventive psychiatry and the public health approach to mental health. These programs are aimed at developing strengths for coping with normal life crises and special stress situations and recommending health and social action to minimize mental health hazards (1).

According to the model of Lindemann, Caplan, and associates, all individuals face stress at certain times in their life cycle. Some are able to handle the stress easily, others do so with difficulty. In still others, the effort is too great and the ensuing crisis may lead to maladaptive behavior or, eventually, emotional breakdown. Each stress for which the individual develops successful coping mechanisms strengthens him to meet future stress. Conversely, stress unsuccessfully handled may weaken the individual and increase his susceptibility to emotional breakdown.

A PREVENTION PROGRAM

The South Carolina Department of Mental Health has long been actively interested in new programs emphasizing early treatment, rehabilitation, alternatives to hospitalization, and promotion of related mental health activities in other agencies. These interests have been

[2] Sumter Child Study Project interview.

both restricted and aroused by insufficient revenues to meet all of the serious mental health needs in the state.

Stimulated by the crisis intervention concepts developed by Lindemann and Caplan, by the work of the Wellesley Project (5,7,9,11), and by the development of early identification programs by Bower and Associates (12,13) the staff of the Mental Health Education Unit of the Division of Community Mental Health Services conceived a proposal for a demonstration project focused on one salient normal life and special crisis situation—school entry. An attempt would be made to identify variables of this "life crisis" and to determine empirically those interventions which facilitate optimal adjustment to the transition from home to school.

It is well-recognized that many behavioral disorders in children originate during the children's early development. The teacher daily confronts a child's crises and growing pains, often in regions beyond the parent's influence, and frequently acts with incredible skill and wisdom in the face of too much to do in too little time with inadequate resources. If mental and emotional disorders are to be prevented, the major agents responsible for a child's development must engage in a dynamic partnership with the child to produce more effective, if not more novel, solutions.

In brief, the proposal was to explore the process of intervention as an alternative to the application of treatment to pathological behavior. The aim is to use and to evaluate creatively inaction, amelioration, consultation, focused education, mobilization of existing strengths, and strategic deployment of treatment at the point of crisis or potential stress.

Initiation of the Program

In 1960 a pilot program was initiated in Sumter County, South Carolina. This is a county with a population of seventy-five thousand with a mixed economy based on agriculture, manufacturing, and a large military facility. It is reasonably representative of the State in terms of population characteristics and cultural mores. An assessment of Sumter County had revealed a high degree of readiness for a mental health program on the part of its leadership, especially in the schools. There had been a long history of keen and active interest in the field of mental health, but there were no mental health professionals in the county.

A mental health consultant with the title of community psychologist was placed in the City of Sumter to initiate mental health resources, for example, the new local three-county mental health center. The primary thrust of the Project at this time emphasized a preventive approach through early intervention in developmental disorders, strengthening of adjustment skills, and attention to ameliorative work in the family, school, and other social institutions affecting the child. These early activities served as a pilot demonstration from which the current project was developed.

The school administration expressed considerable interest in an extended demonstration project focused on problems associated with school entry. Administrators were closely involved in initial planning, offering not only office space but full administrative support and use of facilities. Initial proposals were modified by meetings with the school board, principals, teachers and parent groups. Since there are no public kindergartens in South Carolina, reactions were sought from leaders of private preschool programs. Reactions were also sought from other persons in the community, recognized for their leadership and interest, in order to obtain maximal feedback and the broadest possible community support.

Sumter Child Study Project

The Sumter Child Study Project began operations in February 1963 financed by a grant from the National Institute of Mental Health. A proposal was made to investigate and demonstrate the effectiveness of the model of crisis intervention in preschool and early school years over a five-year period. Three operational goals were established:

1. *A preschool check-up to evaluate children in the spring, prior to school entry in the fall, and predict their ability to cope successfully with school entry and future school stress in the early school years.* The aims of the check-up were to identify techniques that teachers might be able to use and to record as much as possible about the total process. The evaluation consisted of two 45-minute periods. The first was devoted to a structured observation and testing of the child by a psychologist while the parents were being interviewed by a psychiatric social worker. The second period was reserved for team members to summarize impressions individually and to develop collectively a final team summary. Teams later discussed each child's record with a consultant group made up of a regular project staff member, a local pediatrician, and a child psychiatrist.

2. *For staff to make appropriate interventions designed to help the child cope with predicted stresses and increase adaptive skills.* An intervention was defined as an activity intended to develop an

environment favoring the acquisition and reinforcement of skills required in coping with the stress of school entry and early school years. Interventions were determined for each individual child on the basis of findings in the preschool evaluations and subsequent data collected from the school life of the child. Early involvement with school and community leadership made it possible to develop interventions and data collection methods that promised useful data, yet, did not violate the basic values and mores of the community.

3. *To evaluate the effectiveness of these interventions by continual study of the child during the early school years.* This study will continue to collect data from the school and home on the child's development and school programs subsequent to preschool evaluation.

The execution of these procedures will permit extensive studies in the following areas:

1. The effective deployment of available mental health resources at times of greatest need and potential for future individual health, that is, the concept of "emotional first-aid."

2. The development of effective instruments to identify potential emotional problems and their solutions during the developmental process (12,13).

3. The identification of variables related to the ability to adapt to stress and the finding of appropriate interventions to decrease stress and increase coping skills. Such findings would have important implications for clarifying and modifying crisis intervention theory as well as for programming related to mental health (1–6).

4. The identification of the significant variables on which highly skilled mental health professionals make judgments of individual stress and adaptability. If this is possible, these findings may be of great value in training kindergarten and school teachers in early identification of and appropriate intervention with emotional problems in children (6,7).

Operational Structure

Three demonstration schools that sample the socio-economic range of the community were selected. They are roughly matched by three nondemonstration or control schools in size, student background, and resources. Intervention activities are offered only in the three demonstration schools. The 515 children who entered the 18 first grade classrooms in these six Project schools (demonstration plus control) will be followed for four years; the second year's entering first-graders will be followed for three years, and so forth. The fifth year will be reserved for follow-up and review.

Some typical school information is being collected from all elementary schools (parental education and economic background, sibling order, and mobility of family). Much more information is being accumulated from children in the six Project schools to test out the effectiveness of interventions; using, for example, such variables as achievement, adjustment, or absences. The Project has been able to readily obtain meaningful data from the families who have volunteered to participate in the program. As an example, 70 per cent of the eligible parents and children were seen in the preschool check-up.[3] Furthermore, the school system now collects as a regular part of school procedure the information needed by the Project.

Location of Project personnel in the school district administration building has greatly facilitated the maintenance of the relationships essential for continuing research in school and community systems. Although it is too early to include at this time on-going research data from the Project, information on the process of intervention can be presented.

Interventions

In presenting a description of the intervention process and procedures associated with this Project, we are not attempting to relate this work systematically to other crisis intervention theory and research. This task remains for future publications.

An intervention is broadly defined as any activity designed to develop an environment favoring the acquisition and reinforcement of stress-coping skills. Two levels of intervention activity will be presented:

1. Interventions aimed at the entire project sample or at a specific subsample.
2. Specific case intervention program for individual children.

Group Intervention

The preschool check-up, offered in the spring to all incoming first graders scheduled to enter the three demonstration schools in the fall, has proven to be of inestimable value as a stimulus for the development of group-level and single-case intervention resources. Through

[3] A study of "nonvolunteers" so far suggests they do not differ significantly from "volunteers."

the check-up, children were identified at various levels of maturity and competency. A survey was made of their needs to acquire greater coping skills to facilitate school entry. The presence of various subgroups of children having common needs required a new look at the community for possible therapeutic resources. Resources such as medical intervention or social welfare casework were readily identified and available. Many needs, however, could not be met immediately because the resources were either unrecognized or nonexistent.

Four different kinds of group level intervention activities emanating from the preschool check-up are presented below. These activities involve the development of new community and school resources and experiential possibilities.

A group of children identified as immature, weak in adaptive skills, or in some way seriously inexperienced in typical school readiness behavior was enrolled for six weeks during the summer[4] in the school they would attend in the fall.[4] The teacher attempted to carry out "prescriptions" or specific experiences that could promote greater social skill in a child or more competence in handling emotions, or could supply focused enrichment activities. Although attributes such as greater sense of integrity, more maturity, less anxiety, and more self-confidence may be difficult to measure in five- or six-year-olds, observations of change by teachers and parents have assessed this specialized intervention to be quite significant. This program led to the finding, independent of Deutsch and Nimnicht (16), that children were more responsive to gradually introduced enrichment in a less stimulating room than to the usual procedure of a room filled with competing and unfamiliar objects.

In another instance, local children with speech difficulties had only the resources of a traveling state team that was not available until after school was underway, until after the critical entry period when the child most needed optimal confidence and the best communication skills he could muster. To strengthen a child's communication skills prior to the predicted stress period would be not only important in coping with stress but would have important implications for curtailing the speech problem. The team was clearly overwhelmed by the treatment needs of the community and welcomed the opportunity to demonstrate alternatives. The team was able to screen quickly children identified in the preschool checkup as having speech problems (10 to 13%) and to recommend remedial action prior to school entry with a personal program to guide parental efforts over the important summer months. Results were striking in individual cases, and the

[4] This was in 1963 prior to Operation Headstart.

program was instrumental in the decision to hire two full time speech therapists for the school.

In a third example, children identified as weak in social skills and inexperienced in group functioning needed to be provided with a variety of relevant preschool experiences useful in building appropriate coping skills. Parents of these children were guided to use deliberately, not only informal neighborhood play groups, but church programs, regular family outings, and explorations of the world around the child (especially as related to school pathways), positive family separation experiences, and pooled efforts by groups of parents to carry out enriching activities. When a parent was able to relate potential school success to specific need for increased social or cultural experiences, action along these lines was surprisingly effective in families of different social classes and orientations.

In a fourth case, supervised preschool group experiences were most difficult for families most in need, that is, those unable to afford private kindergartens and families with excessive workloads or transportation problems. To meet this need the Project sought help from the City Recreation Department which for many years has operated a successful program for school-age children. The Department, however, had met with less success in deprived areas and had no program for preschool children. Staff exploratory meetings confirmed the mutual goal of fostering healthy development and increasing social skills in children. As a consequence, the Recreation Department decided to establish a new program for preschool children and a new center in a deprived, project demonstration school area. They furnished the necessary operational structure, funds, and experience. The Project supplied an effective communication channel to families of highest need, facilitated motivation to use the program, and provided consultation on an age group new to the department. The programs have continued to be successful and have provided a valuable training opportunity for future youth workers.

Single Case Intervention

Intervention programs for specific children were begun by the Project staff in the preschool check-up. Psychologists often found it possible during the evaluation to help a child clarify his perception of school entry. Social workers found parents responsive to immediate clarification of special concerns about a child's development. Followup reports from parents underscore the value of enhanced parental confidence and skills gained from team emphasis on readiness, normality, and strengths already in use or available for building skills.

Teams were required to list three or more resources or strengths within the child or family that were already promoting school readiness; for example, the observation of at least average intellectual potential or family problem-solving skills. Teams were also required to list three or more suggestions for increasing school readiness; for example, the need for more parental separation experiences or for limited counseling or follow-up studies. Behavior judged suggestive of physical problems was referred for evaluation to family physicians or to the local county health department. All parents were scheduled a follow-up interview for a discussion of findings after the checkup evaluation and less than 2 per cent canceled their appointments. At the end of this interview, the social worker recorded for the parent those resources and readiness suggestions which appeared most meaningful to the parent. Families requiring follow-up interventions were contacted over the summer months.

Three Cases

In order to present some of the sequence and process of interventions with individual children, three cases are presented in brief, descriptive form, using the short condensed manner of presenting data that we used in keeping our notes. The case of David demonstrates the value of prior information in the event of crisis distress; the case of Bobby illustrates the utilization of crisis confrontation to transform debilitating distress into a new level of maturity; and Lemar presents a case that calls for "pulling out all the stops," pointing to the need for developing new resources and revitalizing old ones.

David

Preschool Check-up. Team observed a bright, attractive boy, well-prepared for school entry and with exceptionally good family resources. Could increase initiative and maturity in handling emotions. No major intervention suggestions in follow-up appointment with parents; offer specific suggestions to foster problem-solving skills and more initiative (for example, allow more decision-making from among parent approved choices, less direction and more exposure to various people and social situations).

School Entry. Uneventful, adjustment above average.

One Month Later. Distress signals from teacher and parents to stand-by interventionist; dramatic decrease in adjustment and productivity, attends school only under excessive pressure, tearful, clings to mother and teacher, panics at going out to recess. Teacher puzzled, sees child as overreacting. Parents suspect some hurt at recess, perhaps expectations at school are too high. Family physician considers referral to psychiatrist as situation rapidly deteriorates.

Interventions

Promote fact-finding; focus on the strengths and skills of the key behavior agents (those most affecting the child's behavior) as a means of resolution.

1. Orientation of key behavior agents and interventionist occurred the following day. Distress evidently began when teacher (substitute) found David on the playground quite distressed because he discovered the door to his classroom locked. On the regular teacher's return, she found a "different child," unproductive, distressed, with physical complaints. Similar behavior was noted at home, especially when school was involved. Parents were quite anxious, perplexed and motivated to follow recommendations. In contrast to their expectations, they have observed a steady increase in intensity since distress behavior began five days ago.

A quick summation of the basic conflict situation might be:
Threat (some playground event)—leading to need for security (teacher)—barrier of no familiar adult available (locked door)—lack of coping skills—overwhelmed (setting remains threatening).

Needs. To remain in the situation where the best resources for recovery lie; temporary medication (tranquilizer) may be useful to calm overstimulated emotions; more facts, may be "reliving" earlier, similar experience causing current overreaction to stress; see parents in exploratory interview; reintegration into classroom group; acutely needs what he cannot presently supply (or obtain from key behavior agents): optimism, knowledge his distress is temporary, reassurance, effective model for handling this stress.

2. *Parents.* Established in one initial follow-up contact: The aim is to redefine the situation as a normal response to lack of necessary coping skills with an opportunity now available for developing such skills.

(a) The emotional intensity of current reaction suggests it can be related to an earlier, similar experience. Parent then recalled a traumatic car accident over a year ago in which the child was temporarily trapped (threat) in a wrecked car beginning to burn (need for security); the parents could not immediately reach him (barrier) with much consequent distress behavior (clinging, easily aroused panic and fear). This experience was suppressed as "too horrible to talk about." Parents failed to observe any consequent problems, but speculate he has been more dependent than siblings from the date of the accident.

(b) Concretely relate parent and child on a feeling level to promote closeness and acceptance, for example, help parents to use recall of a specific threat experience of their own; relate subsequent feelings and resolution to child's current situation as a model for the child to use.

(c) Trust teacher to manage recess and classroom situation and drop efforts to manage through notes; work together as a team; require child to follow teacher's lead; recognize skills emerging from situation. Be alert to "false recovery" from this event, with re-emergence of same or worse distress behavior when least expected. Next time agents will be better prepared to offer acceptance and optimism as he gradually becomes less sensitive to stress and more mature in coping skills.

3. *Teacher.* Focus on offering a model for the way the child needs to feel and behave, that is, confident, less anxious, accepting of his reaction as natural, one from which he will recover. This can be facilitated by the teacher sharing a real, concrete stress experience of her own with the child. Some typical specific suggestions:

(a) Concretely retrace with the child the steps for a solution "next time," such as walking with the child the route to adult help when in trouble on the playground.

(b) Pair child to a compatible, "liked" classmate at recess until this breaks up naturally; a younger child effects this easier by "sharing an object," as a ball, rather than putting emphasis on a relationship between the two e.g. ("Look after David at recess").

(c) Expect child to be temporarily vulnerable to new or possible failure experiences for the immediate future. He will need extra reassurance, talking it over, more close contact with teacher whenever possible, less criticism. Such behavior proves the need for closeness, rather than the isolation of being "sick" or different.

Outcome. Immediate reduction of stress behavior followed initial parent and teacher contact, but stress behavior quickly reappeared when the child balked at teacher's first moves back to the playground. Once intervention suggestions by both key agents were underway (within four days), intense behavior ended, child became more productive and comfortable. In two weeks only occasional signals of distress. A check in two months reveals school saw a much more mature, happier child with a significant increase in self-reliance and adaptive behavior. According to measures of teacher perception and school achievement, he is currently one of the outstanding students in third grade.

Bobby

Preschool Checkup. Team observed a rather effeminate boy, skilled with adults, but weak in peer experience; overemphasizing dependence on adults, conformity, exaggerated somatic complaints, and experiences (from pediatrician reports). Parents intelligent, responsible and resourceful, likeable, highly motivated. Father seen as distant, controlling, perfectionistic, demands may be unrealistic; mother warm, impulsive, receives a great deal of management from her mother, apprehensive, may be overprotective. Child judged to be intellectually well-prepared for school entry; immature stress coping skills make him vulnerable, especially in peer and emotional areas. Team predicted: less than average adjustment.

Needs. More experience for social skill with peers, especially in groups; greater self-reliance (less on adults); more mature handling of stress; more stimulation of feeling of a state of well-being and competency.

Interventions

1. *Parents:* follow-up interview to focus on setting up three therapeutic interviews to explore ways of meeting needs. Explore parent roles and attitudes toward child; initiate appropriate action suggestions, for example, more freedom to explore beyond the house, positive parent separation experiences, emphasis on peer experiences and de-emphasis on "grandmothering," more variation in group experiences, such as Vacation Bible School or City Recreation Department.

Outcome. (All interventions routinely checked within two months.) Limited success; self-reliance experiences greatly increased with more freedom from excessive parent control; two telephone calls for reassurance from interventionist when new freedom met with accidents; father attempted to be more supportive and less demanding; mother attempted to communicate less apprehension and more confidence in boy's competence and emerging skills. Basic attitudes and feeling tone of parents remained essentially unchanged; parents note improvement.

2. *School.* (to principal) appears bright; from available choices, place with teacher who can accept some effeminacy, can protect, yet move him out; may be vulverable to stress; likely to do well in classroom for teacher but emotional needs and fears may be overlooked, especially on playground. (To teacher) attractive child; likely to be more successful with classroom learning than in managing fears

and peers; may need help to gradually build up friendships with boys. Needs less protection and mothering than appearance indicates (no label or written communiques, teacher made her own notes during initial conference). Check back with teacher in two months, sooner if requested. School required preschool health physical was clear.

Outcome. School entry reported as satisfactory; parents are pleased with entry and success with teacher.

Three Months Later. Sudden distress signals from teacher and parents. (Information from immediate parent and teacher interview.) Bobby is missing much school with physical complaints, doctor can find no cause; parents anxious, school work deteriorating; ridicule and isolation coming from peers, especially boys; fear of separation from teacher and parents, intolerant of ordinary stress in classroom.

Precipitating Stress. The necessary replacement of teacher (first one moved), with marked change in new teacher expectations and role behavior. Former teacher appears to have repeated mother's relationship of dependency and overprotection. New teacher is young, active, much emphasis on growth and self-reliance, unaccepting of clinging, "immature" behavior.

Conflict. Could be formulated as role conflict: role behavior appropriate at home—accepted by first teacher (barrier) versus new classroom situation (new teacher unaccepting of available role behavior)—inability to change to meet expectations.

Need. Program to develop more coping skills and appropriate role behavior to meet classroom expectations; modify but support teacher efforts; redefinition of stressful situation as learning opportunity; integrate teacher and parent efforts; parents to keep close contact with family physician.

Interventions

1. *To Parents* (in one initial interview and one follow-up): reassurance by clarifying and desensitizing situation; focus on current situation as a learning opportunity.

(a) Need to develop new role behavior; for example, behavior skills that bring satisfaction at home or with first teacher are ineffectual in the "new" classroom (new teacher). Distress behavior is a consequence.

(b) Loss and gain in a significant relationship (loss of old, gain of new teacher) usually produces distress reactions; such distress demonstrates a need for more skill in developing new relationships; child can be made stronger, rather than damaged by shift in teachers.

(c) Although distress reactions are predictable and painful, they are temporary and can be modified, for example, parents' acceptance and relaxation promote similar states in child (especially a dependent child). Distress behavior is more productively viewed as signals for help to develop skill with a situation, rather than signals for avoidance.

(*d*) Support teacher efforts as a team, encourage parents to meet briefly at least twice over next two weeks with teacher. Re-emphasize optimism, eventual recovery, need for extra, temporary, tolerance and support at present.

Outcome. Parents actively followed through on recommendations.

2. *Teacher.* (Developed in initial planning contact; facilitated by three brief follow-up conferences on regular scheduled visits to school by interventionist.)

(*a*) Modification and support of teacher aims: clarification of child's current level of maturity and stress handling skills; need to move more slowly to gain more effective results. Since no agent can resolve the situation alone, time to develop team effort is necessary.

(*b*) Specific intervention actions focused on facilitating peer support, developing freedom from anxiety for growth to be possible, for example, his skill in jumping rope was identified with prize fighters and became a recess activity of the boys, earning him natural esteem; efforts to attempt smaller goals received more teacher recognition; physical complaints were closely observed for relationship to need for temporary reassurance or relaxation.

Outcome. Two months after initial contact: no school absences, classroom improvement clearly observable, more acceptance from peers; school work that of an achieving, bright child. Continued growth needed, but occurring more naturally.

One Year Later. (Based on summer review of school records and recontacts with behavior agents.) Continued growth needed, but productive achievement above average; developing more satisfying experiences with peers. Minimal distress behavior, enjoys new experiences, rare school absences.

Lemar

Preschool Checkup. A walking index of poverty, undernourished, cleaned up for the school visit, speech incomprehensible, suspected mental defective, impulsive, functioning well below norms in all areas. A grim mother determined that her child succeed in school, suspicious of rejection and easily antagonized. Married at sixteen to a man twenty-five years older; after five children is tired and worn at twenty-six. Husband is currently unemployed and in jail; family has moved four times in the last year, is currently living in three rooms, and obtains water from a neighbor. Parents quit school by the fifth grade. Little resources beyond existence and impulsive moments of pleasure; known to welfare sources to be in a chronic state of crisis. Team predicted little chance of school success without major interventions. Most significant strengths are child's energy and mother's determination for school success.

Needs. So excessive in all areas the problem will be to remain focused on school readiness and a realistic school program, rather than to become overwhelmed by family needs.

Interventions

Alerted welfare sources managed to supply immediate food need. The first step was to select a simple, easily attained intervention that responded to urgent needs but did not promise more than could be delivered and was in line with basic aims. Achieving the preschool physical at the local county health department was effective in establishing a working relationship between mother, school, and interventionist, as well as a build-up of body health as a readiness resources.[5]

The following list of interventions focused on key behavior agents using existing or specially developed resources.

1. *Prior to School.*

(*a*) Communication of Project and school efforts toward Lemar's school readiness stimulated renewed welfare interest leading to mother's employment and later, minimal welfare contacts.

(*b*) Speech evaluation by state speech and hearing team helped parents to be more realistic (if not more helpful) about speech handicap, and mobilized school efforts for therapy (school system hired two full time speech therapists).

(*c*) Development of a new city recreation department program for preschool children provided Lemar's first supervised social experiences as well as enrichment and learning opportunities.

(*d*) Development of the new preschool summer program (six weeks) in the school he would enter provided: (1) a gain in school behavior orientation, (2) easily reached goals to build up achievement skills, and (3) maintenance of mother's positive motivation. His IQ was raised 15 points according to brief testing.

[5] This case proved to be an excellent illustration of the value of preventive medical intervention for subsequent local Operation Headstart programs for pre-school children.

2. *During School Entry.*

(*a*) Place Lemar with teacher accepting of seriously deprived children; he may need special tolerance and handling at first; parents' needs are excessive, their negative feelings easily aroused; except need to handle communication distortions.

(*b*) Enrolled in the Junior League "Big Sister" program, aimed at early attack on school dropouts by interest in deprived elementary children (facilitated by the pilot program of current Project). Lemar received human interest and strategic resources, for example, extra dental attention and a birthday cake.

(*c*) School nurse checked on regular visits to his school to build up hygiene and body health; initiated a vitamin program from free physician samples.

(*d*) Interventionist was available at regular intervals to teacher and parent, especially if distress signals occurred.

Outcome. School entry was minimally adequate, but significantly no behavior problems or distress signals occurred from family or school. Difficulties arose with family-school communication but were resolved. Dramatic progress gradually occurred with speech handicap. Repeated first grade; now in second grade, functioning as a slow learner but clearly not mental defective. Is happy and well-motivated, never misses school. Father remains unchanged, mother attends PTA regularly and continues to progress with employment; family remains off welfare rolls.

TENTATIVE FINDINGS AND IMPLICATIONS

The staff learnings from this Project have still to be tested in the crucible of research methodology. Data processing and analysis are only now at a stage where research reports may begin to emerge. The findings reported and implications drawn here are thus quite general and tentative rather than specific and definitive.

A. Professional mental health teams can provide in a brief space of time meaningful data on the strengths and needs of a child.

1. Evidence in the operation of this Project indicates that psychiatric teams can furnish data that greatly facilitate an on-going consultation program with parents and schools. Such information has important, often dramatic, value for emotional first-aid and quick amelioration when trouble first occurs.

2. Initial contact with parents can build positive relationships with them for future use when the need arises. However, the first agent

to evaluate the child, whether teacher or psychiatric team, inevitably must be prepared to deal with some parental anxiety, especially if all is not well.

3. It is possible to offer only preliminary evidence as to a team's ability to predict future school maladjustment. In the check-up, a team had to present a summary prediction rating for each child on a 4 point scale: (1) exceptional, (2) typical, (3) weak, (4) trouble. A comparison of 1's and 2's (typical or better) versus 3's and 4's (potential maladjustment) reveals the following:

(a) Children seen as "typical or better," in the first grade, completed twice as many of the reading requirements as 3's and 4's: only 2.9 per cent failed to complete readiness or pre-primers, whereas 28 per cent of the 3's and 4's failed to get into primer books.

(b) Children seen as "typical or better" had significantly fewer absences.

(c) Of the children rated as 3's and 4's, 66 per cent were promoted to the second grade, while 94 per cent of the "typical or better" children were promoted.

B. Some evidence is emerging on the variables associated with team assessments of children with potential maladjustment. For example, a comparison was made of children selected as "typical or better" in adjustment vs. potentially maladjusted children. Reporting only significant differences, potentially maladjusted children:

1. Expressed more negative or unrecognizable feelings about school, either directly or indirectly through projective material. These children had decidedly more unrealistic concepts about school.

2. Were lower in observed initiative, frequently resorting to inappropriate and ineffectual means.

3. Tended to be overresponsive or underresponsive to adults' wishes; over or under conformity was observed.

4. Were less typical and much lower in observed independent behavior.

5. Wished to be younger than own age or "adult." More children seen as "typical or better" in adjustment wished to be their own age or slightly older. Incidentally, a significant characteristic of potentially maladjusted children has been a child's repeated expression of discontent over his self-image, his age, his looks, or his sex.

6. More children were observed as low in curiosity behavior.

7. In terms of global ratings, rated consistently lower in functional use of body, social development, emotional development, and family resources.

8. Intelligence was not seen as a factor, with one exception: chil-

dren seen as possible mental defective (IQ's estimated to be 75 or below).

C. A school is a dynamic system with its own modes and agents for maintaining equilibrium, both internally (staff) and externally (parents and community). Interventions that appear obvious but fail to take into account the total field of forces in this system create stress that may well produce avoidance or even direct rejection.

1. The principal is the recognized community agent for maintaining the system. Understanding his needs and problems is essential. Maintenance of his position promotes maintenance of other positions and the freedom to move within and influence the system.

2. A significant, positive action in a school system tends to enhance the total field. Tension reduction in one person, for instance, may influence other spheres of functioning. In particular, tension reduction in the case of the principal enhances the total school functioning.

3. Each school has a culture of its own. It is necessary to understand and work within this culture if effective therapeutic interventions are to be feasible. For example, it is vital that principal-teacher modes of dealing with stress or problems be accepted as a point for beginning action. Interventions should be designed to supplement and extend school efforts rather than to supplant or merely evaluate them.

D. Present evidence indicates that parents and schools are unusually receptive to a form of intervention based on confrontation and management of stress.

1. Approximately 70 per cent of the children at spring pre-registration applied for the limited appointments available. It was possible to see 165 children the first year and 152 the second year.

2. There was less than a 2 per cent cancellation of appointments or "no shows."

3. Increasing demand for services has occurred. For example, in the second year of the check-up, principals had a waiting list of volunteers, even before appointments were available and a waiting list for possible cancellations. In the first year of the project, interventions for the preschool checkup children in the first grade averaged 5.5 per child. There was an increase to 8.1 per child in the second year. (Actually, only 25 to 30 per cent of the children provide the foci for a major share of the interventions.)

E. The "crisis model" is an effective concept for making appropriate interventions with children, although, at this point, evidence is largely of the individual case variety. Of special significance for effective interventions has been the use of those factors Lindemann, Caplan, and associates have found common in life stress periods, for example:

1. The need to develop new role behavior; for example, the skill a child may have that allows him to be an adjusted member of the family may be quite inadequate or inappropriate for being an effective member of the classroom.

2. Some loss and some gain in significant relationships: for example, inability to sustain loss of mother or inadequate skills for forming an important new relationship with teacher.

3. Stress reactions are temporary and can be modified; for example, symptomatic behavior, such as regression or tearful distress, is responsive to time and various interventions aimed to develop new skill behavior or a positive relationship with teacher. Parents and teachers have been unusually responsive to this conceptualization as a way of understanding symptomatic behavior and its prevention or amelioration.

F. Three general implications for child development seem important to the authors.

1. *Confrontation of stress and learning to cope with its effects of discomfort or conflict are the building blocks of maturity.* Resources for the stimulation and development of new coping skills and levels of maturity for handling inevitable stress lie in the effective use of stress, rather than in avoidance or protection. Distress symptoms may be evidence of pain, but they are also signals for developing new skills rather than motives for simply regaining comfort. Yet, many treatment maneuvers in effect promote regression, loss of opportunity to develop new coping skills, and discomfort by being isolated as "sick" or "crazy."

2. *Stress is better managed than treated.* An important psychiatric principle has been to treat the distressed person as close to his "home" as possible, largely because this avoids important secondary problems engendered by removal and re-entry from normal living patterns. Extending this principle to the developing child, crisis and stress is not just treated but is managed to promote skill in the child, the mother, or the teacher for coping with future stress in the "home" setting, where the child functions.

A major management technique is to focus on the strengths of the situation and skills of the key behavior agents in order to reduce their anxiety, to enhance their positive influence, and to reduce the tension of the setting as a total field.

Role definition has important stress management implications. Rather than the traditional role redefinition involved in a treatment approach as patient-therapist or client-counselor, the enrichment and strengthening of parent-child and teacher-student roles are the aims.

These are the persons of greatest potential influence with the child, the persons most knowledgeable of specific ways to implement interventions, who can provide the most opportunities for reinforcement of therapeutic insight or resolution. To offer key behavior agents models for handling the stress by relieving their anxiety, but not their responsibility for the child, is to present a more realistic model with which the child can identify. The alternative is to demonstrate their impotency with the problem by referring the child to an "expert."

Conflicting differences in perception between key behavior agents on what is wrong and what to do about it when the child is in stress can also be a basic management tool. These are signals that something important and different is needed, signals that are crucial for stress resolution. Just as ships lost at sea use the triangulation principle of drawing lines from two known signal sources until they bisect, key behavior agents can do likewise. They can draw their lines from the incomplete information they have to the real position of the child in the stressful situation.

Another implication of the value of differences in perception is referred to by the Project staff as the "stereoptic phenomena." Parents are often disturbed that each of them has a different view of their child's behavior and that each of them draws different conclusions as to what is to be done. After much living together parents generally work out some ground rules for handling such differences; then suddenly the teacher emerges, with some different perceptions of her own. Such conflict would seem to lead to behavioral difficulties in the child who may get conflicting messages on how to proceed. Surprisingly, these children actually seem more adaptable and more effective in interpersonal relationships (especially when compared with children with one parent). They seem to have more realistic "in depth" understanding of people. An analogy is grandmother's stereopticon which put two similar but slightly different images of the same situation together and, when viewed in her magic machine, made one picture with exciting depth and realism. The mature child develops important interpersonal skills out of such differences, however stressful they may be.

For prevention and quick success with interventions, it is basic to establish effective contacts prior to the stress crisis. If this cannot be done by the interventionist, for example, a preschool check-up it can be done through a network of prior consultation with key behavior agents who currently influence the child; for example, teacher-parent groups. Community consultation is of vital importance. When intervention is not initiated promptly, crisis intervention as a total approach appears to be less effective and other alternatives may well have more validity.

3. *Spontaneous behavior occurring in natural stress situations may well have more reality and learning significance for the promotion of future skills and resourceful responsibility than conventional treatment or learning models designed to develop insight.* For the child there are more opportunities to learn greater self-direction in stress coping skills. It would seem likely that insights gained in a familiar setting, when motivation for such insights were high, would have broader and more pervasive influence.

There appears to be no one set of techniques that a teacher or parent must use to resolve a child's crisis. Rather there is a relative set of operations, given this child, this situation, the feelings now generated by this situation, that must be performed to be effective. Parents and teachers who learn to operate from this stance in one situation have a "leg-up" for the next encounter.

Concluding Remarks

Educators and behavioral scientists share a common desire to respond to the urgent necessity to do something *now* to meet the needs of growing children and to work toward more effective ways of meeting these needs in the future. The area of adjustment and mental health is one of the most important of these needs but also one of the most perplexing. Desirable or undesirable as the influence of a teacher may be, whether she exercises her influence deliberately or without awareness, the teacher will continue to represent a unique force in the current and future adjustment of children. She stands on the front lines of stress and potential disordered behavior as she daily confronts a child's crises and growing pains. If major behavioral disorders are ever to be prevented, the primary agents responsible for a child's development must be involved in a dynamic partnership that provides a sharing of expertise between parent, teacher, scientist, and of course, the child himself.

Formal mental health resources have dramatically increased in school systems and communities. Guidance programs, school psychologists and social workers, consultants, training programs, and community mental health centers are all beginning to come to the aid of the overburdened educator. Exciting new relationships among professionals are being formed to meet children's needs. Impressive as these resources may be, they are likely to remain critically inadequate for a long time to come. New models are needed for the effective deployment of the resources we have in order to make them available at times of greatest need and potential for future health. In order to make best use of professionals, more effective instruments must be developed to identify not only emotional problems that have already occurred but also potential problems occurring in the crucial developmental process. Solutions for emotional problems will continue to require identification of those variables related to the sources of stress as well as adaptations to stress.

The teacher has no choice! She must be involved in the mental health of children and in the development of their adequacy. She may have doubts about her own adequacy. Being human, she will have mixed feelings about a scientist's evaluation of her efforts or probes into her personality. The reality of the classroom, however, creates quite enough motivation for seeking help or acquiring new skills and insight. It comes as no surprise to discover much ambivalence among teachers who can express themselves candidly. Such a state of affairs is much like a perceptive, delightfully feminine, six-year-old who was asked what she might like to be when she grew up. She replied with all the thoughtfulness of a child taken seriously, "I think I would like to be a teenager, but I haven't decided yet." The wise teacher handles the inevitability of being some sort of practitioner of mental health by remaining open to new ways and new information; then, like Martin Luther, she can do no other but take her stand and do what she is prepared to do.

What will promote the healthy coping skills a child will need now and in the future? Who is maladjusted and is adjustment always desirable? Whose definition of crisis and adjustment are we to use, that of the teacher, parent, scientist, or mental health professional? Where does one begin to resolve some of these problems?

It is the thesis of this program that one begins with a percept of the complex transactional field that represents the child's life space. Interventions may touch the child directly, or they may focus on the network of key people who influence him. It is somewhere within the total resources represented by these key people that the child will likely receive the help that is the best possible for him. It is from these people that his most relevant role definitions emerge. It is the business of this Project, first, to help unlock these resources so that they find their own best answers; and, second, to learn from what we are doing.

REFERENCES

1. Caplan, Gerald (Ed.). *Prevention of Mental Disorder in Children.* New York: Basic Books, 1961.

2. Caplan, Gerald. *An Approach To Community Mental Health*. New York: Grune and Stratton, 1961.
3. Caplan, Gerald. *Principles of Preventive Psychiatry*. New York: Basic Books, 1964.
4. Lindemann, Erich. "Symptomatology and Management of Acute Grief." *Amer. J. Psych.*, **101**, 1944, pp. 141–148.
5. "Tenth Anniversary Report of the Wellesley Human Relations Service, Inc. 1958," mimeographed report.
6. Klein, Donald, and Erich Lindemann. "Preventive Intervention in Individual and Family Crisis Situations," in G. Caplan (Ed.), *Prevention of Mental Disorder in Children*. New York: Basic Books, 1961, pp. 283–306.
7. McGinnis, Manon. "The Wellesley Project Program of Pre-School Emotional Assessment." *J. Psychiatric Social Work*, **23**, 1954, 135–141.
8. Lindemann, Elizabeth B., and Ann Ross. "A Follow-up Study of a Predictive Test of Social Adaptation in Pre-School Children," in G. Caplan (Ed.), *Emotional Problems of Early Childhood*. New York: Basic Books, 1955, pp. 79–83.
9. Klein, Donald C. "Early School Adjustment," in H. Steward (Ed.), *Handbook of Child Development*. Cambridge: Harvard University Press, 1962.
10. Gruber, Sigmund. "The Concept of Task-orientation in the Analysis of Play Behavior or Children Entering Kindergarten," *American J. Orthopsychiatry*, **24**, 1954, 326–335.
11. Klein, Donald C., and Ann Ross. "Kindergarten Entry: A Study of Role Transition," in M. Krugman (Ed.), *Orthopsychiatry and the School*. New York: American Orthopsychiatric Association, 1958, pp. 60–69.
12. Bower, Eli M. *Early Identification of Emotionally Handicapped Children in School*. Springfield, Ill.: Charles C. Thomas, 1960.
13. Bower, Eli M. "Primary Prevention in a School Setting," in G. Caplan (Ed.), *Prevention of Mental Disorder in Children*. New York: Basic Books, 1961, pp. 353–377.
14. Bramlette, Carl A., Jr., M. R. Newton, and Elsye McKeown. "Crisis Intervention in Pre- and Early School Years." Presented Southeastern Psychological Association, Gatlinburg, Tennessee—April 2, 3, 4, 1964.
15. Newton, M. R., Racine Brown, and Jim Crumley. "Crisis Intervention in Pre-School and Early School Years: The Sumter Child Study Project." Presented 42nd Annual American Orthopsychiatric Association Convention, 1965.
16. Deutsch, Martin, Richard Ellis, and Glenn Nimnicht. "For the Disadvantaged Child, An Environment for Learning." Greeley, Colo.: Colorado State College. (Unpublished Manuscript.)

Chapter 22

New Horizons

William G. Hollister
and
Eli M. Bower

New Horizons

Few if any readers of professional books are so dedicated or have sufficient endurance to read final summaries. This is short and, we hope, to the point. As with an oil painting, it is necessary to step back from a book like this in order to see it in its entirety. Such an overview quickly reveals that each author-artist has painted a picture of himself as well as his ideas. Certainly, the composite of this group portraiture should have significant impact on the present attempt by the Nation, the States, and communities to know and practice good education.

From Bower's opening theoretical searching of what must be happening inside the "dark tunnel called the ego," on to Newton and Brown's description of their ways of strengthening the egos, and coping of children entering school, a majority of the authors seem to be striving to define two major themes. First, what is the nature of the various cognitive-affective ego-skills that need to be developed in our children? Second, what do we need to change in our social and humanizing institutions to make these institutions more effective ego-developers? Said another way, "What are the kinds of 'stren experiences' that help to potentiate and/or create mental strengths and how do schools and communities develop programs to do this?"

In the search for ego-potentiating strens, a wide range of strategies has been proposed, from carefully timed interactions to enhance psychological development to measures to prevent the social or group climate from stultifying mental growth. Symbolization has been depicted as the key process in helping the individual toward perceptual differentiation, the categorization of information, and the integration of new conceptions. The awareness and assimilation of value systems, the teaching of conceptual organizers and coping mechanisms, involvement in self-directed change process, free access to our preconcious stream, as well as the use of teaching sequences and socializing experiences in groups have all been described as strength building experiences of promise. Although much remains to be done, this book presents evidence that the psychological concepts available to guide educational practice are becoming more positive in their focus. At last, we are moving beyond "trauma" centered, conflict born, psychopathologically focused explanations of human misbehavior to understandings of human potential based on the constructive interactions between the emerging developmental patterns in children and the environmental "stren" experiences we can provide as educators.

We hope this book heralds the dawn of an era of educational interest and understanding of ego-processes and its significance in learning. It documents our growing awareness that, given a healthy organism, there is almost unlimited potential in the human mind for learning to become human.

For education, this book documents an emerging era of educational curricula in which knowledge is imparted to students in such a way that skills for processing new knowledge are learned.

This book reaffirms the arrival of the long predicted day when education will become mankind's most effective tool for building human beings. Through research and ideas cited here and elsewhere, there is emerging a technology for strengthening or repairing cognitive-affective functions of children. The years of the mental health sciences' long and significant contributions to educational methodology and goals are coming full cycle. Now education is beginning to give back to mental health scientists new tools to fulfill our fondest dreams—the creation of the mentally healthy, actualized, effective, and competent person.

Together the mental health and educational professions will continue to search for new and better ways of enhancing each other's work and of realizing our goals for a healthier, better educated society.

Index